The International Handbook of Creativity

What constitutes a creative person? Is it someone who can perform many tasks innovatively? Is it someone who exhibits creative genius in one area? Is it someone who utilizes her creativity for good and moral causes? Is it someone who uses his creativity to help his company or country succeed? Different cultures have different perspectives on what it means to be creative, yet it is nearly always the American or Western perspective that is represented in the psychological literature. The goal of *The International Handbook of Creativity* is to present a truly international and diverse set of perspectives on the psychology of human creativity. Distinguished scholars from around the world have written chapters for this book about the history and current state of creativity research and theory in their respective parts of the world. The book presents a wide array of international perspectives and research, with much of the work discussed never before available in English.

James C. Kaufman (PhD) is an Assistant Professor of Psychology at the California State University at San Bernardino, where he is also the director of the Learning Research Institute. He received his PhD in Cognitive Psychology from Yale University, where he worked with Robert J. Sternberg. Kaufman also worked as an Associate Research Scientist at Educational Testing Service in the Center for New Constructs before rejoining academia. He received the APA Division 10 Daniel E. Berlyne award and is the author or editor of seven other books.

Robert J. Sternberg (PhD) is the Dean of the School of Arts and Sciences at Tufts University. He was IBM Professor of Psychology and Education and Director of the Center for the Psychology of Abilities, Competencies, and Expertise at Yale University. In 2003 he was President of the American Psychological Association. He is the author of more than 1,000 publications on topics related to cognition and intelligence and has received more than $18 million in grants for his research. He has won numerous awards from professional associations and holds five honorary doctorates.

The International Handbook of Creativity

Edited by

JAMES C. KAUFMAN
California State University at San Bernardino

ROBERT J. STERNBERG
Tufts University

CAMBRIDGE
UNIVERSITY PRESS

CAMBRIDGE UNIVERSITY PRESS
Cambridge, New York, Melbourne, Madrid, Cape Town, Singapore, São Paulo

Cambridge University Press
40 West 20th Street, New York, NY 10011-4211, USA

www.cambridge.org
Information on this title: www.cambridge.org/9780521838429

First published 2006

Printed in the United States of America

A catalog record for this publication is available from the British Library.

Library of Congress Cataloging in Publication data

The international handbook of creativity / edited by James C. Kaufman,
Robert J. Sternberg.
   p.   cm.
Includes bibliographical references and index.
ISBN 0-521-83842-8 (hardcover) – ISBN 0-521-54731-8 (pbk.)
1. Creative ability – Cross-cultural studies.   2. Culture.   I. Kaufman, James C.
II. Sternberg, Robert J.   III. Title.
GN453.I58   2005
153.3′5 – dc22   2005012974

ISBN-13   978-0-521-83842-9 hardback
ISBN-10   0-521-83842-8 hardback

ISBN-13   978-0-521-54731-4 paperback
ISBN-10   0-521-54731-8 paperback

I dedicate my work on this book to David K. Hecht, who has just married a terrific woman, Aviva, and earned his PhD from Yale.

It is so rare to meet someone who you like more with every passing year — someone who knows all the stupid things that you do, and is your friend anyway.

Dave is one of the greatest people I know, and one of the only people for whom I always pick up the telephone.
Thanks, Dave.
– JCK

I would like to dedicate my efforts to Howard Gruber, who recently passed away, and who was one of the great pioneers of all times in the study of creativity. He will be greatly missed.
– RJS

Contents

Acknowledgments   *page* ix

List of Contributors   xi

1   Introduction   1
   Robert J. Sternberg

2   Creativity Research in English-Speaking Countries   10
   John Baer and James C. Kaufman

3   Creativity in Latin America: Views from Psychology,
   Humanities, and the Arts   39
   David D. Preiss and Katherine Strasser

4   History of Creativity in Spain   68
   Cándido Genovard, María Dolores Prieto, María Rosario Bermejo,
   and Carmen Ferrándiz

5   Past, Present, and Future Perspectives on Creativity in
   France and French-Speaking Switzerland   96
   Christophe Mouchiroud and Todd I. Lubart

6   Creativity in Italy   124
   Alessandro Antonietti and Cesare Cornoldi

7   Creativity Research in German-Speaking Countries   167
   Siegfried Preiser

8   Creativity Under the Northern Lights: Perspectives from
   Scandinavia   202
   Gudmund J.W. Smith and Ingegerd Carlsson

9   Creativity in Soviet–Russian Psychology   235
   Olga Stepanossova and Elena L. Grigorenko

10   Creativity Studies in Poland   270
     Edward Nęcka, Magdalena Grohman, and Aleksandra Słabosz

11   Research on Creativity in Israel: A Chronicle of Theoretical
     and Empirical Development   307
     Roberta M. Milgram and Nava L. Livne

12   Creativity in Turkey and Turkish-Speaking Countries   337
     Günseli Oral

13   Development of Creativity Research in Chinese Societies:
     A Comparison of Mainland China, Taiwan, Hong Kong,
     and Singapore   374
     Weihua Niu

14   Creativity – A Sudden Rising Star in Korea   395
     In-Soo Choe

15   Culture and Facets of Creativity: The Indian Experience   421
     Girishwar Misra, Ashok K. Srivastava, and Indiwar Misra

16   African Perspectives on Creativity   456
     *Elias Mpofu, Kathleen Myambo, Andrew A. Mogaji, Teresa-Anne
     Mashego, and Omar H. Khaleefa*

17   Creativity Around the World in 80 Ways ... but with One
     Destination   490
     Dean Keith Simonton

Author Index   497
Subject Index   511

Acknowledgments

We would like to start off by thanking Philip Laughlin of Cambridge University Press – it's a pleasure working with him.

Roja Dilmore-Rios, Michael Lucas, and Robyn Rissman helped enormously by reading, editing, and providing helpful comments on multiple chapters. We are also grateful to Melanie Bromley, Suzanne Grundy, and Cheri Stahl for editorial assistance.

James would like to thank his friends, family, colleagues, and students at California State University at San Bernardino and elsewhere. He is especially grateful to his wife Allison, his parents Alan and Nadeen, his sister Jennie, and John Baer and David Hecht.

Contributors

Alessandro Antonietti, Catholic University of the Sacred Heart, Italy

John Baer, Rider University

María Rosario Bermejo, Universidad de Alicante, Spain

Ingegerd Carlsson, Ali Syd, Sweden

In-Soo Choe, Sungkyunkwan University, Seoul

Cesare Cornoldi, Università di Padova

Carmen Ferrándiz, Universidad de Murcia

Cándido Genovard, Universidad Autónoma de Barcelona

Elena L. Grigorenko, Moscow State University/Center for the
   Psychology of Abilities, Competencies, and Expertise, Yale University

Magdalena Grohman, Jagiellonian University

James C. Kaufman, California State University at San Bernardino

Omar H. Khaleefa, University of Khartoum

Nava L. Livne, University of Utah

Todd I. Lubart, Université René Descartes, Paris

Teresa-Anne Mashego, University of the North

Roberta M. Milgram, Tel Aviv University

Girishwar Misra, University of Delhi

Indiwar Misra, Indian Institute of Technology, Kharagpur

Andrew A. Mogaji, University of Lagos, Nigeria

Christophe Mouchiroud, Université René Descartes, Paris

Elias Mpofu, The Pennsylvania State University

Kathleen Myambo, American University in Cairo

Edward Nęcka, Instytut Psychologii UJ, Krakow

Weihua Niu, Pace University

Günseli Oral, Akdeniz University, Antalya, Turkey

Siegfried Preiser, Institut für Pädagogische Psychologie

David D. Preiss, Center for the Psychology of Abilities, Competencies, and Expertise, Yale University, and Potificia Universidad Católica de Chile, Santiago

María Dolores Prieto, Universidad de Murcia

Dean Keith Simonton, University of California, Davis

Aleksandra Słabosz, MRC Cognition and Brain Sciences Unit, Cambridge, United Kingdom

Gudmund J. W. Smith, Lund University

Ashok K. Srivastava, National Council of Educational Research & Training, New Delhi

Olga Stepanossova, Moscow State University/Center for the Psychology of Abilities, Competencies, and Expertise, Yale University

Robert J. Sternberg, Tufts University

Katherine Strasser, Pontificia Universidad Católica de Chile, Santiago

1

Introduction

Robert J. Sternberg

INTRODUCTION

On June 4, 1989, some Chinese students thought they had a creative idea. The idea was of a democratic government in China. The government of the time found their idea to be neither creative nor amusing. Roughly 1,000 students and other protesters were massacred by government forces that day at Tiananmen Square. A government leader who supported the students, Zhao Ziyang, died in January of 2005, shortly before this introduction was written. He had been under house arrest for years, and his death was given short shrift by the Chinese government.

The idea of democracy would be wholly uncreative in the United States, at least as democracy is traditionally thought of. People in the United States would probably say that the idea is lacking in novelty and hence cannot be creative. In some other country, someone having the idea of democracy might be seen as being very creative indeed and at the forefront of new thought about government. Clearly, different countries, or at least their governments, have different ideas about what constitutes creative thought. What *does* constitute creative thought, and how have people around the world understood and studied creativity?

Preparation of this chapter was supported by a government grant under the Javits Act Program (Grant No. R206R000001) as administered by the Office of Educational Research and Improvement, U.S. Department of Education. Grantees undertaking such projects are encouraged to express their professional judgment freely. This chapter, therefore, does not necessarily represent the positions or the policies of the U.S. government, and no official endorsement should be inferred.

COMMONALITIES IN CREATIVITY RESEARCH

The goal of this book is to explore theories, research, assessment, and programs for the development of creativity in a wide variety of countries around the world. To this end, we have solicited contributions from authors around the world. There seems to be pretty good agreement around the world on certain issues, but not on many of them! If one were to try to draw some generalizations, they might be these:

1. Creativity involves thinking that is aimed at producing ideas or products that are relatively novel and that are, in some respect, compelling.
2. Creativity is neither wholly domain specific nor wholly domain general. It has both domain-specific and domain-general elements. The potential to be creative may have some domain-general elements, but to gain the knowledge one needs to make creative contributions, one must develop knowledge and skills within a particular domain in which one is to make one's creative contribution.
3. Creativity can be measured, at least in some degree.
4. Creativity can be developed, in at least some degree.
5. Creativity is not as highly rewarded in practice as it is supposed to be in theory.

What is perhaps most notable about creativity research around the world is how little of it there is. In every country, there is a dearth of research on creativity relative to other topics, and what research there is proves to be relatively poorly systematized. Why? There are probably several reasons.

First, governments say they want creativity, but their actions belie their words. Many of the world's governments depend on ignorance for their existence. In autocracies, education and especially creative thinkers pose perhaps the greatest threats to their existence. In democracies, one would hope that creativity would be more valued, and it probably is. Nevertheless, many of the governments that are elected got into place only through the ignorance and narrow-mindedness of the people who selected them. The last thing these governments want is critical and creative thinking that would threaten their existence. Indeed, the level of political discourse in many of the world's so-called democracies is only slightly above that of the autocracies, if it is above that level at all.

Second, creativity is hard to study. There is a story of a man who loses a key at night. He looks under a street lamp for the key. A policeman comes along and offers to help him look. After they look for a while, unsuccessfully, the policeman asks the man if he is sure that he lost the key in this particular place. The man looks at him with a puzzled face, and says, "Oh, no, I lost it over there, but the light is much better here." Often, scientists, like the man who lost his key, prefer easier problems to harder ones, even if the easier ones are smaller or less rewarding to study. Creativity as a problem of study is large, unwieldy, and hard to grasp. Many scientists would prefer to study other phenomena that lend themselves more easily to traditional scientific methods of analysis. Moreover, studies of creativity often take a long time to conduct, and there is little incentive in a publish-or-perish world for taking on long-term studies, especially for those who lack tenure.

Third, creativity research is not mainstream. Over the years, certain topics within a field become mainstream and others remain at the margins. In psychology and education, creativity has always been at the margins. Working in an area at the margins has many disadvantages. For one, it is less prestigious to work in such an area. For another, it is therefore harder to get a job. For a third reason, it is harder to get published in top journals, and, for yet another, it is harder to get funding. Thus, many of the best people tend to work in areas where the rewards are greater and certainly more immediate.

Fourth, selection mechanisms in most countries do not favor the generation of creative people to study creativity. How does one get to the point where one can even be an independent researcher studying creativity? Generally, one has to make one's way up an academic ladder that tends most to reward students who do what their mentors want them to. Often, the mentors are more interested in the students' contributions to the mentors' research than to the students' production of their own creative ideas. Furthermore, to get to the point where one actually has mentors, one has to go through an elementary, secondary, and tertiary system of education that often rewards conformity.

Fifth, there are effects of popularization. Creativity, more than some other fields in psychology and education, has been the subject of popularized programs that have not undergone rigorous testing. At least some of the originators would have little incentive for their programs to be rigorously tested. Thus creativity has been linked in many people's minds with commercialization rather than with rigorous science.

Despite these difficulties, creativity has garnered some interest in theory, research, assessment, and development around the world. Let us consider some general points about what has been learned, on the basis of the chapters to follow in this handbook.

CREATIVITY AROUND THE WORLD

What are some of the main ideas about the nature of creativity that have arisen out of work on creativity around the world?

According to Smith and Carlsson, there is no single Scandinavian view regarding how creativity should be understood. Scandinavians, they believe, pay somewhat more attention to potential and somewhat less attention to productivity than do Americans. Creativity is viewed in Scandinavia as an attitude toward life and a way of dealing with the challenges life poses. When too much emphasis is placed on creative products, the tendency is to focus on people who seek the limelight but to ignore those who may be creative in a more reserved and quiet way.

In China, Taiwan, Hong Kong, and Singapore, according to Niu, there has been, historically, a tradition of somewhat devaluing creativity. That has changed, however. The trajectories of thinking about creativity have been slightly different from one place to another. In China, the study of creativity emerged as a sort of by-product of research on intelligence and giftedness. Creativity is seen there as an essential component of giftedness. In Taiwan, creativity is being emphasized and creativity is close to being a regional icon. There is profound valuing of the creative enterprise. A wide variety of methodologies are currently being used to study creativity. There is a push to make the society and its people more creative. In Hong Kong, research has shown some differences between the Chinese and American conceptions of creativity. Westerners emphasize more sense of humor and aesthetic taste, whereas Chinese people tend to emphasize social influences, such as being inspirational to others and contributing to the progress of society. In Singapore, research has been somewhat sparse, but recently there has been a push to teach creativity in the schools.

In English-speaking countries, according to Baer and Kaufman, creativity research is extremely diverse. Historically, J. P. Guilford was extremely influential. He posited that divergent thinking is very important to creativity. For some people, as Baer and Kaufman point out, creativity has become synonymous with divergent thinking, in part as a result of Guilford's work. Also highly influential was E. Paul Torrance, who devised the Torrance Tests of Creative Thinking. These tests measure divergent thinking in both verbal and nonverbal domains. Other influential paradigms in English-speaking countries are of creativity as based on the selection and retention of ideas (using evolutionary theory) and of creativity as influenced by personality, motivational, and environmental factors. A number of programs have been developed for encouraging creative thinking.

In French-speaking countries, according to Mouchiroud and Lubart, the "four Ps" have been particularly influential in research: person, process, product, and press (environment). Research on cognition in French-speaking countries has been very strongly affected by the thinking of Piaget. Piaget, however, had relatively little to say about creativity. Nevertheless, there has been research of various kinds on creativity. Some has emanated from the psychodynamic tradition, and some from the psychometric tradition of Guilford and Torrance from the United States. Interestingly, one of the great French psychologists of all time, Alfred Binet, was very interested in the imagination, but it is more in recent years than in earlier ones that this tradition has become influential.

In German-speaking countries, according to Preiser, an idea is accepted as creative if it is new in a certain situation or if it contains new elements and is viewed as a useful solution to a problem. According to Preiser, person, process, problem, and product constitute the four Ps of creativity research in the German-speaking countries. The main focus of German models is on creative processes, which are instigated by the individual's confronting a problem. In the end, the creative processes should yield a product. Creative processes are viewed as being influenced by many factors, such as general and specific knowledge, expertise, abilities, cognitive styles, motives, personality traits, and interests.

Milgram reviews the thinking about creativity in Israel. Many Israelis are currently interested in the relationship of creativity to real-world problem solving. There have been a variety of approaches to creativity in Israel. One approach studies creativity primarily in the context of gifted education. Another studies the relationship of creativity to self-actualization, in the tradition of Maslow. Still another looks at the relation of creativity to intelligence and personality traits, and another looks at the difference between creativity in understanding art and creativity in producing art. Milgram's own research used a 4 × 4 model. The first dimension of the model contrasts general intellectual ability, on the one hand, and domain-specific intellectual ability, on the other, as well as domain-general creative thinking versus domain-specific creative talent. The second dimension refers to four distinct levels of ability, ranging from nongifted to profoundly gifted.

In Italy, according to Antonietti and Cornoldi, there has been no clear recent indigenous tradition. Rather, much of the theory and research has been stimulated by the thinking of scholars and others outside of Italy. Nevertheless, Italy has a long history of thinking about creativity. One of the more well-known earlier thinkers was Lombroso, whose degenerative theory of genius became internationally known. He claimed that geniuses are different from other people in that they see things in a different manner and are able to see relations between thoughts that others would not see. In the twentieth century, the three major issues for research were reflection about theoretical frameworks for understanding creative processes, measurement of creative abilities, and promotion of creativity in schools. Some recent work showed that relaxation and an increased use of mental imagery could improve creative performance.

Research on creativity in Poland is rooted in the philosophical tradition, according to Nęcka, Grohman, and Słabosz. Creativity was formerly viewed as a divine activity that could not be attained by humans. In more recent work, creativity has been viewed as wholly attainable, and as being applicable to work that is new and valuable. Creativity applies not only to products but also to people's behavior, thinking, and ways of living their lives. Polish researchers have been particularly interested in what is sometimes called "small c creativity," that is, the creativity of people who will never produce any major works or make any truly important discoveries. This is the kind of creativity anyone can show in his or her daily life. Nęcka has proposed a model of levels of creativity: fluid, crystallized, mature, and eminent. Fluid creativity is everyday creativity that anyone can show, even in the absence of any knowledge in particular. Crystallized creativity is the solution of a problem that requires some knowledge to solve. Mature creativity requires a more sophisticated level of domain-specific knowledge or expertise. And eminent creativity is "big C creativity," that which becomes known far and wide.

In Soviet–Russian psychology, according to Stepanossova and Grigorenko, there have been two major trajectories for creativity research. The first can be traced back to Gestalt psychology as reconceptualized through the eyes of Marxist psychology. The other trajectory harks back to the work of Guilford and Torrance, already mentioned. The former line of work looked at productive thinking and insight. The latter work is particularly associated with studies of giftedness. In Soviet psychology, one line of work viewed the creative process as being at the intersection of logic and intuition. Thus, creativity was viewed as constrained intuitive thinking. Some Soviet psychologists, in keeping with the Marxist tradition, were particularly interested in the environmental conditions that could trigger creative thinking. The model of Ponomarev proposed four stages in the process of creative thinking: (a) deliberate, logical search; (b) intuitive search and intuitive solution; (c) verbalization of the intuitive solution; and (d) formalization of the verbalized solution.

In African countries, according to Mpofu, Myambo, Mogaji, Mashego, and Khaleefa, creativity has been viewed as very important for millennia, dating back to the Great Pyramids of Egypt. However, an analysis of African languages revealed only one language, Arabic, that has a word that translates to *creativity*. Muslims have different Arabic words for creativity in secular and religious contexts. In the other languages, words related to creativity include *resourceful, intelligent, wise, talented,* and *artistic*. Definitions of creativity in the African context have been diverse, according to Mpofu, and have tended to emphasize its different aspects: innovative, adaptive personal agency, integrative, incremental, social impact oriented, domain specific, mystical, and imitative.

Oral has reviewed concepts of creativity in Turkey and Turkish-speaking countries. According to the Turkish scholar İnam, fantasy is the power that fuels creative thinking. It can in turn be converted into a thought, action, or product. Creativity has been studied in art, literature, science, and other fields. For example, Dedegil has proposed a five-step model of creativity in modern science: (a) testing an idea for feasibility, utility, required effort, and range of variation; (b) realizing a prototype; (c) testing the results and making connections; (d) creating new ideas from the result; and (e) generating ideas. Oral believes that Islamic authorities and a monarchic regime have posed obstacles to the enhancement of scientific creativity over a period of hundreds of years, but that since the founding of the democratic secular republic by Atatürk in 1920, Turkey has become more Westernized and receptive to creative thinking and productivity.

According to Choe, creativity research in South Korea has been based largely on work that has emanated from the West. Research on implicit theories of creativity in South Korea resulted in certain characteristics that are strongly associated with creativity – having original ideas, being interested in new ideas, and having strong curiosity. Other characteristics were judged as very unlikely to occur in creative people – being selfish, staying alone, and being self-complacent. In general, characteristics found to be important in the West also were found to be important in South Korea. There has been a wide range of kinds of research on creativity in South Korea. They include research relating the construct of creativity to educational methods, programs for developing creativity, environment, and culture, the role of teachers in fostering creativity, and the role of the family in fostering creativity. Several tests of creativity have also been developed for use in South Korea.

In Latin America, according to Preiss and Strasser, creativity is viewed as a multifaceted phenomenon. There has not been a great deal of research on creativity in this region. What research there is often is difficult to locate in databases. In general, Preiss and Strasser point out that there has not been a great deal of scientific research in Latin America, because science does not have great cultural value in the region. Of the studies that have been done, most are aimed at solving practical problems rather than merely at understanding the nature of creativity. There have been some programs for developing creativity, such as Learning for Creating, which was developed by Mena. The program has three core principles: the need to create a teacher–student relationship that allows students to be creative; the need to provide students with the skills, attitudes, and values that allow them to be creative; and the need for meaningful learning.

Genovard, Prieto, Bermejo, and Ferrándiz note that studies of creativity in Spain began at the end of the 1960s at the University of Barcelona. The first research was on the teaching of creativity, and this has remained an important topic for Spanish research. For one of the founders of such research, Huertas, creativity is the production of original behavior or models, rules, or objects that are accepted by society in order to resolve certain situations. The Education Act of 1970 set out principles aimed at encouraging the development of creativity in the classroom, so that, in Spain, the development of creativity actually became mandated in the curriculum. This in turn led to a burgeoning of interest in research in universities. Studies today consider such topics as the qualities of creative individuals, the design of tools to measure creativity, teacher-training programs, and the study of creativity as a characteristic of highly gifted students.

In India, according to Misra, Srivastava, and Misra, creativity is the result of doing something original or novel that is also useful. Creativity has been of interest in India since antiquity. Creation is considered to be a natural desire of human beings that represents their search for an extension of the self. In India, renewability and transformation are important concepts, so the study of creativity is a natural one for researchers in the country. In the Hindi language, two terms are used for creativity. They indicate the desire or purpose to create. The need for creation is located in the humans' needs to adjust to their environment. Interestingly, many Indian myths deal with the topic of creativity and continue to influence thinking about creativity even until the present day.

2

Creativity Research in English-Speaking Countries

John Baer and James C. Kaufman

INTRODUCTION

The Geography of Thought: How Asians and Westerners Think Differently, a new book by Richard Nisbett (2003), convincingly argues that culture influences cognition in powerful (and experimentally verifiable) ways. Nisbett doesn't discuss creativity – it isn't even listed in his fairly extensive index – but his general conclusions are probably as true for creativity as they are for the kinds of cognition he does discuss. He reports numerous studies showing that Western subjects and various groups of Asian subjects respond very differently to a wide range of cognitive tasks. The lesson for psychologists, he tells us in his conclusion, "is that, had the experiments in question been done just with Westerners, they would have come up with conclusions about perceptual and cognitive processes that are not by any means general" (p. 192).

We are pleased that the book of which this chapter is part will help to correct the myopia that can limit the vision of Western creativity researchers. Creativity research in the English-speaking world is such a large field that it is easy to forget that it is just one part of the larger creativity puzzle. The many other pieces of that puzzle can tell us a great deal about the larger picture of which the English-speaking piece is but a part. Creativity research can also teach us much about the English-speaking piece itself by allowing us to understand this research in context.

Our task in this chapter is to summarize creativity research in English-speaking countries, a field large enough to have sometimes assumed it spoke for the whole world of creativity research. It is a daunting assignment. One of us spent several summers long ago teaching in a program for gifted students, and at the end of the summer we presented our students with a take-home exam. This "exam" – it was obviously a joke, although we did receive a number of very interesting responses – was composed of a series of impossible questions such as these:

Describe the history of the papacy from its origins to the present day, concentrating especially but not exclusively on its social, political, economic, religious, and philosophical impact on Europe, Asia, America, and Africa. Be brief, concise and specific.

Define the universe; give three examples.

Being asked to summarize creativity research in English-speaking countries is almost as overwhelming as these questions. It has been impossible to include, or even to mention, more than a small fraction of the important ideas and trends of this large field, and we regret that we must therefore neglect so many important contributions to our field.

We start with a brief history of creativity research in the English-speaking world, touching on some topics that have been of greatest interest to researchers. This review is necessarily more cursory than complete. To help us decide which topics to include, we conducted analyses of all articles published in the *Journal of Creative Behavior* and the *Creativity Research Journal* in the past ten years, 1994–2003, and of those published in the *Journal of Creative Behavior* during its first ten years of publication, 1967–1976. (The *Creativity Research Journal* did not yet exist during those years.) Our review of articles from the *Journal of Creative Behavior* and the *Creativity Research Journal* was fairly exhaustive, but although we went so far as to list and categorize every descriptor from every article over two ten-year periods, we recognize that such categorization is, necessarily, somewhat arbitrary (e.g., should an article about "religiosity" be grouped with articles on motivation, or with those on personality traits, or perhaps with those that examine creativity in the moral domain?). We trust the validity of the general trends that our analyses suggest, but not necessarily the raw numbers, so we have not presented any kind of numerical "hottest topics" scorecard.

After this historical summary, we focus our attention on one area of creativity research in the English-speaking world that we believe will be of particular interest to those interested in international perspectives on creativity research: creativity research that has been published in English on the topics of gender and ethnic group differences in creativity. That review is followed by brief concluding comments.

HISTORY OF CREATIVITY RESEARCH IN THE ENGLISH-SPEAKING WORLD

Creativity Research Before Guilford

The roots of creativity research are deep, extending back, perhaps, to genesis, but we will begin our survey in the nineteenth century. (For an interesting summary of pre-nineteenth-century thinking about creativity, see Albert & Runco, 1999.) Becker (1995) found five themes in her review of nineteenth-century writing about creativity:

1. How should creativity be defined?
2. Who is creative? (The nineteenth century emphasized the role of heredity.)
3. What are the characteristics of creative people? (This included two main kinds of studies, i.e., those about possible connections between creativity and pathology and those that sought cognitive or personality attributes necessary for creativity.)
4. What are the appropriate uses of creativity? (Is creativity simply a gift to be enjoyed by the creator, or should it primarily benefit others? Is it the process that is important, or the product?)
5. Can creativity be increased through effort, societal constraints (or lack thereof), or training?

These questions are not so different from those being asked by creativity researchers today, and some of the answers have a striking resonance as well. Jevons (1877) wrote of "divergence from the ordinary grooves of thought" (p. 576) in a way that reminds us of Guilford's (1956, 1967; Guilford & Hoepfner, 1967) seminal ideas three quarters of a century later. Jevons also anticipated theories of creativity by Campbell (1960) of blind variation and selective retention and by Simonton (1988a, 1988b) of chance configuration, although he dropped these ideas in passing, as it were, because they were not well-developed and carefully researched models like those of Guilford, Campbell, and Simonton a century later.

Despite these early signs of interest, at the turn of the century Ribot (1900) argued that the study of creativity had been "almost wholly neglected" (p. 648), and, although creativity was an occasional subject of psychological interest in the first half of the twentieth century (e.g., Cox, 1926; Duncker, 1945; Freud, 1910/1957; Poincaré, 1913; Rank, 1932/1968; Roe, 1946; Spearman, 1931; Wallas, 1926; Wertheimer, 1945), it was not until Joy Guilford's 1950 presidential address to the American Psychological Association that creativity research finally took off. As Frank Barron (1988) wrote, it is now "traditional in historical reviews of research on creativity to cite J. P. Guilford's 1950 presidential address . . . as a sort of watershed, the beginning of serious empirical work on the topic" (p. 76). Barron should know, having been part of that midcentury explosion of interest. One of Barron's own early articles about creativity, "The Psychology of Imagination" (1958), appeared in *Scientific American* just a few years after Guilford's groundbreaking call for a focus on research in creativity.

Guilford's Contribution

Guilford himself opened one large area of research with his structure of the intellect model, which was well represented in the 1967–1976 sample and was the *most* represented category in the 1994–2003 samples. More than 10 percent of all articles in those ten years included divergent thinking as one of their descriptors. Creativity has come to *mean* divergent thinking (as Guilford's divergent production is now more commonly called) in much research in, assessment of, and theorizing about creativity (Baer, 1993; Torrance & Presbury, 1984).

Divergent production was part of Guilford's attempt to organize all of human cognition along three dimensions: (a) thought processes or operations; (b) contents to which the operations could be applied; and (c) products that might result from performing operations on different content categories. These combined to produce 120 different mental abilities, many of which Guilford and his associates devised tests to measure and to demonstrate by means of factor analysis (Guilford, 1956, 1967; Guilford & Hoepfner, 1971).

Prior to Guilford's extensive factor analytic work, the debate about the number of factors needed to explain intelligence had focused on single-factor theories versus models that posited small numbers of factors. One reason why Guilford found so many more distinct factors was his inclusion of questions to tap divergent thinking. These questions had no single correct answer; two examples are "Imagine all the things that would happen if all national and local laws were suddenly abolished," or "Name as many uses as you can think of for a toothpick."

In defending his 120-factor model, Guilford argued that there is no such thing as general intelligence. People can be very good or very bad at any combination of different components of intelligence. His 120 factors are not entirely independent of one another, however. Thus all of the factors that come about by means of divergent production are linked to one another, and distinct from factors that are produced by one of the other four operations (convergent production, cognition, memory, and evaluation). The divergent-production factors themselves differ in their contents (figural, symbolic, semantic, and behavioral) and their products (units, classes, relations, systems, transformations, and implications).

Although there is a strong empirical flavor to the hypotheses that initially guided Guilford's research (Guilford, 1950, 1967), his model of five operations times four contents times six products led him to develop tests to find some hypothesized skills in the 120-factor matrix that were far from empirically obvious. Inventing tests for these diverse factors was a task requiring considerable imagination, and Appendix B in the 1971 work by Guilford and Hoepfner, "Tests Employed by the Aptitudes Research Project in Its Analysis of Intelligence," contains some of the most unusual tests to be found anywhere in the psychometric literature.

The full structure of intellect model is still used by some psychologists and educators, but simplified versions of the theory in which several factors have been collapsed into one, such as those in which the various divergent-production factors have been grouped either as a single skill or as a set of just a few related skills, have become more common (although there has been some push in the opposite direction; see, e.g., Baer, 1993). Guilford correctly noted that "of all the investigations in any area by the ARP [Aptitudes Research Project], those aimed at creative abilities have been rewarded with the most novel results, have been given the most attention, and have had the most consequences in the form of stimulating thinking and research by others" (Guilford & Hoepfner, 1971, p. 123).

Assessment of Creativity

Assessment is an issue that was in the forefront during both of our surveyed decades. Although the assessment of creativity has taken many forms, Guilford's idea of divergent production remains the most influential. To the extent that Guilford's (1967) original conceptualization has been retained in current creativity theorizing, however, it is generally in the four general categories Guilford posited (fluency, flexibility, originality, and elaboration), and not in the 16 identified (or 24 theorized) divergent-production factors (Kogan, 1983; Torrance, 1990). This is the case of the most influential divergent-thinking theory of creativity, that of E. Paul Torrance. The influence of Torrance's theory derives primarily from the success of his tests of creativity, known as the Torrance Tests of Creative Thinking (TTCT; Torrance, 1966, 1990; see also 1972b, 1984, 1988). According to one comprehensive survey of creativity research (Torrance & Presbury, 1984), the Torrance tests were used in three quarters or approximately 75 percent of all published studies of creativity involving elementary- and secondary-school students, and 40 percent of all creativity studies with college students and adults. The TTCT have dominated the field of creativity research to such an extent that, in one study that was intended as a comprehensive meta-analytic evaluation of the long-term effects of various creativity training programs, only studies that employed the Torrance tests were included (Rose & Lin, 1984).

One important issue of the past half-century is the relationship between intelligence and creativity. Early researchers had assumed a close connection between intelligence and creativity. Cox (1926), using estimates of IQ and rankings of eminence, reported a correlation of .16. However, Simonton (1976) reexamined Cox's data and found no correlation between IQ and eminence. Current research suggests a somewhat complex relationship between IQ and creativity. Sternberg, Kaufman, and Pretz (2002) reviewed this literature and found three general conclusions:

1. Creative people tend to have above-average IQs.
2. Above an IQ level of 120, the correlation between IQ scores and creativity appears to weaken. IQ simply doesn't seem to matter as much to creativity above that level, and some investigators (Simonton, 1994; Sternberg, 1996a) have suggested that having an extremely high IQ may even be a detriment in terms of creative performance.
3. The relationship between creativity and IQ depends very much on what aspects of intelligence and creativity one is measuring.

The assessment of the creativity of actual products has increased considerably in importance in recent years, spurred largely by the pioneering work of Amabile (1982, 1983, 1996), who calls her method the consensual assessment technique. Subjects create some product (such as a poem, a collage, or a story) in response to the experimenter's prompt, and then the creativity of their products is judged by multiple independent expert raters. The experimenter does not tell the experts (poets, artists, etc.) what criteria to use in making their creativity judgments, but coefficient alpha interrater reliability rates tend to be quite good, typically in the .80–.90 range. This technique has been a boon to creativity researchers, but it is not readily amenable for use in most educational contexts because it provides only comparative measurements within the group of products evaluated by a specific group of experts. Baer, Kaufman, and Gentile (2004) have recently shown how the consensual assessment technique can be extended to creative products produced under both diverse and ecologically valid (as opposed to experimentally controlled) conditions. Kaufman, Gentile, and Baer (2005) have shown evidence that gifted novices can produce comparably reliable ratings to experts.

Creativity Training

Becker (1995) noted that one of the chief concerns of nineteenth-century creativity literature was whether creativity might be increased through training, and this continues to be of tremendous interest to creativity researchers. Creativity training was one of the most frequent topics of creativity research in both of the decades we sampled.

Because creativity is highly valued in both school and work settings, there have been many attempts to teach students and workers skills that will improve their creativity. Creativity training has been developed for virtually every imaginable student population, including disadvantaged students (Davis et al., 1972), gifted students (Kay, 1998; Micklus, 1982, 1984, 1986; Renzulli, 1994), disabled students (Taber, 1983, 1985), kindergarten students (Meador, 1994), elementary-school students (Baer, 1993, 1994; Castillo, 1998; Clements, 1991; Eberle & Stanish, 1980), middle-school students (Baer, 1988, 1997b, 1998b), high school students (Fritz, 1993), college students (Daniels, Heath, & Enns, 1985; Glover, 1980; Parnes, 1972; Parnes & Noller, 1973), art students (Rump, 1982), science students (McCormack, 1971, 1974), and engineering students (Maciejczyk-Clapham & Schuster, 1992).

These programs vary as much in their approaches as they do in their intended audiences. One common feature in most of these programs is some kind of training in techniques to promote divergent thinking, which goes back (once again) to the groundbreaking work of Guilford and his colleagues (Guilford, 1956; Christensen, Guilford, & Wilson, 1957; Wilson et al., 1954), although many writers argue that critical or evaluative thinking is also necessary to properly support divergent-thinking skills in the promotion of creative performance (Baer, 1993, 2003; Fasko, 2001; Nickerson, 1999; Treffinger, 1995).

The best-known and most widely researched program of this type is the Creative Problem Solving (CPS) program developed by Parnes and his colleagues (Noller & Parnes, 1972; Noller, Parnes, & Biondi, 1976; Parnes & Noller, 1972). This program consists of six stages of creative problem solving: Mess Finding, Data Finding, Problem Finding, Idea Finding, Solution Finding, and Action Planning. The CPS model is also sometimes called the Osborn–Parnes model, a name that recognizes its indebtedness to Alex Osborn (1953), who invented brainstorming more than half a century ago. The terminologies – including even the names of the six steps of the CPS model – have changed somewhat during the evolution of this model, but the overall framework has remained fairly consistent. Each step involves both divergent thinking, to produce the greatest possible number and variety of responses, followed by evaluative thinking to select from among them the most promising candidate ideas for further exploration or action (Baer, 1997a; Noller & Parnes, 1972; Noller et al., 1976; Parnes & Noller, 1972; Osborn, 1953).

Two meta-analyses of creativity-training research suggest that many such programs are effective. Torrance (1972a) reviewed 142 creativity-training research studies and reported that approximately three quarters of the training programs had been successful. Among the successful programs that he reviewed, those that were based on a multistage model such as the Osborn–Parnes CPS model were the most successful. Rose and Lin (1984), using a smaller and somewhat more carefully selected sample, similarly found that creativity training with CPS and CPS-like programs was effective. These studies all used divergent-thinking test scores as their criterion for success. There have also been studies using success in real-world problem-solving situations to demonstrate the effectiveness of CPS training (Baer, 1988; Bahr et al., 2003; Basadur, Graen, & Green, 1982; Basadur, Graen, & Scandura; 1986; Fontenot, 1993; Hampton, 2004).

Personality, Motivation, Social, and Organizational Psychology

A wide variety of personality traits have been associated with creativity, including independence of judgment, self-confidence, attraction to complexity, aesthetic orientation, tolerance for ambiguity, openness to experience, psychoticism, risk taking, androgyny, perfectionism, persistence, resilience, and self-efficacy (Piirto 2005; Sternberg et al., 2002). Research articles seeking or explaining various personality correlates with creativity were well represented in both decades of our survey of *Journal of Creative Behavior* and *Creativity Research Journal* articles. The wide diversity of personality traits that have been linked to creativity may reflect domain effects (Kaufman & Baer, 2005). Even within a domain, there may be different personality patterns associated with different subfields. Simonton (2005), for example, argued that "scientific psychologists differ from the humanistic psychologists on a host of behavioral, personality, and developmental variables."

Creativity-relevant motivation was not a topic of great research interest three decades ago, at least according to our review of *Journal of Creative Behavior* articles; however, in the past decade, interest in this area has increased significantly, much of it stimulated by the research and theories of Amabile (1983, 1996). The seemingly simple insight that intrinsic motivation would lead to higher levels of creativity than would extrinsic motivation, and the not-so-obvious corollary that increasing extrinsic motivation – by the offering of rewards, or by the expectation that one's work will be evaluated – might actually *decrease* creativity has produced a significant quantity of interesting and increasingly refined research and experimental hypotheses. Amabile built on what is sometimes called "hidden cost of reward" or "overjustification" research (Bem, 1972; deCharms, 1968; Kelly, 1967, 1973; Lepper & Greene, 1975, 1978; Lepper, Greene & Nisbett, 1973), which shows that offering subjects a reward to do a task they already find interesting will often decrease their intrinsic motivation. Recent research has refined the initial hypotheses somewhat. For example, Amabile (1996) noted that "rewards that convey competence information to subjects may not undermine intrinsic motivation" (p. 160) and may, if sufficiently informative, even increase intrinsic motivation. Similarly, evaluations, which generally decrease creativity, may have positive effects if the feedback is "informative, constructive ... and conveys positive recognition of creative work" (p. 152). There also appear to be gender differences in the degree of negative impact on creativity caused by extrinsic constraints, with female subjects showing greater effects than male subjects of both rewards and anticipated evaluation of their work (Baer, 1997b, 1997c, 1998b).

Organizational creativity was a fairly minor topic in the earlier (1967–1976) decade we reviewed, but it has mushroomed in recent years.

There is an inherent tension in organizations between the need for stability and the need for innovation. New businesses and ideas fail more often than they succeed (Aldrich & Kenworthy, 1998; Ford & Sullivan, 2005), making risk taking, well, risky. Of course, every business, and every business environment, also imposes its own special demands and constraints. Basadur (2005) wrote that "different kinds of work favor specific kinds of creativity, which must be synchronized to achieve innovative results for profitability and competitive edge." This has led to a wide variety in the specific topics investigated by those interested in organizational creativity. Basadur (2005) suggested three general kinds of approaches to organizational creativity: identifying creative workers within an organization and matching them to appropriate tasks; using organizational factors likely to nurture or inhibit creativity performance (including structures that encourage intrinsic or extrinsic motivation); and making deliberate efforts to train workers to become more creative. These are all areas in which much research is currently being conducted.

Cognitive Approaches to Creativity

In cognitive approaches to understanding creativity, researchers try to understand the underlying mental representations, processes, and mechanisms that lead to creativity. Hadamard's (1949) early four-stage model (preparation, incubation, illumination, and verification) was quite influential. More recently, Finke, Ward, and Smith (1992; Smith, Ward, & Finke, 1995; Ward, Smith, & Finke, 1999) developed a two-stage model of creative thinking. There is a generative phase and an exploratory phase, and thus the model is called the geneplore model. In the generative phase, a person constructs different kinds of mental representations related to the problem. A variety of processes come into play during the exploratory phase, including association, retrieval, synthesis, transformation, and analogical transfer.

Some researchers (e.g., Gruber, 1981; Gruber & Davis, 1988; Johnson-Laird, 1988) have argued that creativity of the highest level – genius or paradigm-shifting creativity – is quite different than the garden-variety creativity of everyday problem solving. Gruber and Davis (1988) went so far as to argue against "the use of inappropriate populations, such as . . . unselected high school students. Although these are certainly valuable and interesting human beings, usually we can have no guarantee that the sample taken includes a single person who is functioning creatively" (p. 246). Others, such as Baer (1993) and Weisberg (1988,

1999), have argued just the opposite, that studies of normal subjects can elucidate the cognitive mechanisms common to all levels of creativity and that even "great creative achievements also seemed to involve rather ordinary thought processes" (Weisberg, 1988, p. 174). Computer simulations of creativity attempt to demonstrate how human creativity might work by showing well-defined mechanisms that can lead to certain kinds of creative performance (Johnson-Laird, 1988; Langley & Jones, 1988; Langley et al., 1987).

Confluence Models

One relatively new area in creativity theory is that of confluence theories. Confluence theories are multifactor models that posit several separate but interacting components that must come together to yield original and productive outcomes.

Amabile (1983, 1996) described a three-factor model that she termed a "componential framework." The components of her model are (a) task motivation, which is the component she and her colleagues have researched most thoroughly and which has already been discussed; (b) domain-relevant skills, which include knowledge and skills that contribute to creative performance in a given domain but not to creative performance in other domains; and (c) creativity-relevant skills, which are domain-transcending skills that are hypothesized to contribute to creative performance in any and all domains. There has been little controversy regarding the importance of domain-relevant knowledge and skills, but a significant number of research articles in the past decade have challenged the importance and even the existence of creativity-relevant skills (for a summary of the opposing sides to this domain-specificity debate, see Baer, 1998a, and Plucker, 1998).

Gruber and his colleagues (1981; Gruber & Davis, 1988; Gruber & Wallace, 1999; Wallace & Gruber, 1989) posited a very different kind of confluence model, one that emphasizes the unique ways that a creator's ideas, knowledge, goals, and affect grow and interact over time. His work looked in great detail at the development of ideas in a few great creators, such as Charles Darwin. These case studies demonstrate how a very long and complex chain of small creative steps can lead to revolutionary ideas, such as Darwin's theory of evolution through natural selection. Gardner (1988, 1993) and Csikszentmihalyi (1988, 1996) also presented complex models that highlight the interaction among individuals, domains, and society.

Sternberg presented two confluence theories of creativity that describe complex and multilevel interactions among different factors, and also one metatheory of creativity that systematically distinguishes different kinds of creative contributions. His three-facet model of creativity (1988) describes an interaction among intellectual, stylistic, and personality attributes. Sternberg and Lubart (1991, 1995, 1996) expanded on that theory in their investment theory of creativity, in which they argue that the key to being creative is to buy low and sell high in ideas. In this model, a creative person is like a successful Wall Street broker. Sternberg and Lubart posit six interrelated factors as essential to this process: intellectual abilities, knowledge, styles of thinking, personality, motivation, and environment.

More recently, Sternberg and colleagues (Sternberg, 1999; Sternberg, Kaufman, & Pretz, 2001, 2002, 2003, 2004) offered a propulsion model that outlines eight kinds of creative contributions, categorized on the basis of their relationship to the domain. The first four contributions all stay within the framework of an existing paradigm. Perhaps the most basic type of contribution that someone can make is replication. Replication tries to keep things status quo – to reproduce past work. The second type of contribution, redefinition, takes a new look at the domain. A redefinitive contribution doesn't necessarily try to push forward; instead, it tries to present a different perspective. A third contribution, and perhaps the type of contribution that achieves the most immediate success, is called forward incrementation. This type of contribution pushes forward the domain just a little. Maybe the creator makes a slight change in what already exists. These additions usually are not groundbreaking – it takes the domain in the same direction it was heading. The final contribution that stays within the existing definitions of a domain is the advance forward incrementation. This contribution pushes the domain ahead two steps instead of one – and the creator often suffers for it. This type of creative product includes people who were a little before their time.

The final four types of creative contributions represent attempts to reject and replace the current paradigm. Redirection represents an attempt to redirect the domain to head in a new direction. If most of these contribution types represent forward thinking, then reconstruction – redirection looks backward. This contribution is an attempt to move the field back to where it once was (a reconstruction of the past) so that it may move forward from this point – in a different direction. Perhaps the most radical of all of the creative contributions is reinitation. In reiniation, the creator tries to move the field to a new (as yet unreached) starting point, and then progress from there. Finally, the last contribution is integration, in which two diverse domains are merged to create a new idea.

GENDER AND ETHNIC GROUP DIFFERENCES IN CREATIVITY

Gender Differences

The majority of studies have shown no gender differences in creativity, regardless of culture and background (see Baer, 1999, in press; Barron & Harrington, 1981; Kogan, 1974; Saeki, Fan, & Van Dusen, 2001; Wang et al., 1998). The few studies that have found gender differences in other cultures have often been poorly done and are contradictory (see Lubart, 1999). Indeed, one examination of eighty different studies on gender and creativity found that half of them found no differences – and the half that did find differences were split, with two thirds finding higher creativity in women and one third finding men to be more creative (Baer, in press). There is some evidence for a very slight advantage for females in measures of divergent thinking. Rejskind, Rapagna, and Gold (1992), for example, reviewed forty-one studies of elementary-school children and found that, although no differences were found in the majority of studies, four-fifths of those studies that did find differences favored females.

Some studies have examined the question of gender differences in more detail. One repeated result is that in which females outscore males on creativity in the verbal domain, usually as measured by divergent-thinking measures. This finding has been shown in (among others) a sample of 1,445 English-speaking fifth and sixth graders in Montreal (Dudek, Strobel, & Runco, 1993), 160 Indian nine- to eleven-year-old children (Dhillon & Mehra, 1987), 128 high-achieving eighth and ninth graders (DeMoss, Milich, & DeMers, 1993), and 320 sixteen-year-old Jamaican students (Richardson, 1985). It is important to note, however, that many other studies have not found these results, particularly studies using the consensual assessment technique (e.g., Amabile, 1983; Baer, 1993; Kaufman, Baer, & Gentile, 2004). It should also be borne in mind that, because investigations that fail to find statistically significant differences are rather less interesting and therefore less likely to be published, it is possible that the proportion of published studies showing gender differences of any kind is somewhat artificially inflated.

Hargreaves (1977; see also Lewis & Houtz, 1986, for a replication with a younger sample) examined responses to a drawing task and found no differences in creative performance between middle-school-age boys and girls. However, he did find that girls responded more often in the categories of "domestic" and "life," and boys responded more often in "mechanical–scientific" and "sports–games." When the same students were asked to respond as the opposite gender (boys as girls, girls as boys), the results were reversed.

Several studies have found themes of aggression to be more present in male creativity than female creativity. Dudek and Verreault (1989) did a content analysis of school-age children's responses to the TTCT (there were no differences in overall performance), and they found more libidinal primary process in girls and more aggressive primary process in boys. Strough and Diriwaechter (2000) looked at creative story writing in paired middle-school children. All-boy pairs showed lower levels of prosocial ideas than both mixed-gender pairs and all-girl pairs. The all-boy pairs also showed higher levels of overtly aggressive ideas than all-girl pairs.

Finally, as mentioned earlier, females are more susceptible to the situation in which extrinsic motivation has a negative impact on creativity. Baer (1997b) asked eighth-grade subjects (sixty-six girls, sixty-two boys) to write original poems and stories under conditions favoring both intrinsic and extrinsic motivation. In the intrinsic motivation conditions, subjects were told that their poems and stories would not be evaluated; in the extrinsic condition, subjects were led to expect evaluation, and the importance of the evaluation was made highly salient. Experts then judged the poems and stories for creativity. There was a significant Gender × Motivational condition effect. For boys, there was virtually no difference in creativity ratings under intrinsic and extrinsic conditions, but for the girls these differences were quite large. This was confirmed in a follow-up study (Baer, 1998b) using students of the same age, in which the negative impact of both rewards and anticipated evaluation were shown to be largely confined to female subjects. One possible underlying reason could be that boys are less sensitive to interpersonal communications than girls (Gilligan, Lyon, & Hanmer, 1990; Pool, 1994), which would make their levels of intrinsic and extrinsic motivation less susceptible to messages that would affect levels of motivation in girls.

Ethnic Differences

There are several studies that show a lack of racial and ethnic differences in measures of creativity. Torrance (1971, 1973) found that African

American children scored higher than European American children on the Figural tests in fluency, flexibility, and originality; European Americans scored higher on figural elaboration and all Verbal subtests. However, the initial sample compared African American children in Georgia with children of higher socioeconomic status in Minnesota. When a subsequent study used European Americans also from Georgia, the differences were significantly reduced.

Iscoe and Pierce-Jones (1964) compared African American and European American children at five different ages on a measure of intelligence (Wechsler Intelligence Scale for Children) and creativity (Unusual Uses Test). European Americans received higher scores on the intelligence test at all ages, but there were few differences on the creativity measure (European Americans performed better on flexibility at the youngest age; other results were divided or not significant). Price-Williams and Ramirez (1977) found that African American males outperformed European American males on the Unusual Uses Test, but the results were reversed for females.

Other studies showed no significant differences between African Americans and European Americans on the TTCT at the elementary-school level (Glover, 1976b; Knox & Glover, 1978) and the college level (Glover, 1976a), and one study found African Americans to have higher fluency and originality scores on the Figural subtest of the TTCT (Kaltsounis, 1974). In addition, an analysis of poems, stories, and personal narratives written by African Americans and European Americans did not show any significant difference in their creativity ratings by expert judges (Kaufman et al., 2004).

Other studies have shown no racial or ethnic differences in the ability to be trained in creative thinking skills (Moreno & Hogan, 1976) and no differences in the development of divergent-thinking abilities in adolescents from South Africa and the United States (Ripple & Jaquish, 1982). Of thirteen measures of giftedness, measures of creativity showed some of the smallest African American–European American differences (Harty, Adkins, & Sherwood, 1984). Stricker, Rock, and Bennett (2001) found no racial or ethnic differences on measures of aesthetic expression (with questions that tapped into creative abilities, such as artistic accomplishments).

Comparisons of European Americans and Latinos also provide evidence that some measures of creativity show few differences. While three of four TTCT verbal forms showed that European Americans scored significantly higher than Latinos, there were no significant differences on the figural forms (Argulewicz & Kush, 1984). In addition, the Creativity scale of the Scales for Rating the Behavioral Characteristics of Superior Students (SRBCSS) showed no significant differences (Argulewicz, Elliott, & Hall, 1982; Argulewicz & Kush, 1984). Kaufman et al. (2004) found that, although poems written by eighth-grade Latinos were rated as less creative than poems written by eighth-grade European Americans or Asian Americans, there were no differences in the creativity of their stories and personal narratives.

Some studies have indicated that bilingual students may have an advantage in creative abilities (see Garcia, 2003, for a review). Ramirez and Castaneda (1974) proposed that people who are bilingual have more "cognitive flexibility," which allows them to approach problems from multiple perspectives. Price-Williams and Ramirez (1977) found that bilingual Mexican American males outperformed their European American counterparts, with Mexican American females scoring slightly lower than European American females. Carrington (1974) studied Mexican American children and found that "balanced" bilinguals (those who speak each language equally well) outperformed monolinguals on the TTCT; Kessler and Quinn (1987) found similar results in a group of Latino children.

However, low-income Latino elementary students scored below the norms on the TTCT (Mitchell, 1988), and teachers rated European American students as being more creative than Latino students, with highly acculturated Latinos receiving higher marks than less acculturated Latinos (Masten et al., 1999).

Explaining Ethnic Differences

Some researchers have proposed that differences on some IQ or achievement subtests, such as those involved in remembering the details of a story, may show larger African American–European American differences in part because African Americans approach the task differently (Heath, 1983; see Manly et al., 1998). While European Americans approach the task as the test makers intended – by trying to memorize as many appropriate details as possible and sticking to the presented story – African Americans may put more emphasis on telling the story creatively.

This difference in style would be consistent with Shade's (1986) theory of an African American cognitive style. Her research with cognitive style tests found that African Americans were more likely to be spontaneous, flexible, and open minded. In contrast, European Americans were more regulated and structured. Open-mindedness has been found to be highly correlated with creativity, regardless of the measure used – these results have been found with self-reports of creative acts (Griffin & McDermott, 1998), biographical data on creative accomplishments (King, McKee, & Broyles, 1996), studies of creative professions (Domino, 1974), analyses of participants' daydreams (Zhiyan & Singer, 1996), creativity ratings on stories (Wolfradt & Pretz, 2001), and psychometric tests (Furnham, 1999; McCrae, 1987).

Studies using the Myers–Briggs Type Indicator (MBTI; Myers, 1962; Myers & McCaulley, 1992) have shown that African Americans are more likely to favor thinking over feeling (Peeke, Steward, & Ruddock, 1998) and perceiving over judging (Melear & Alcock, 1999). Creative people as measured by the MBTI tend to also fit these patterns (Thorne & Gough, 1991). It is worth noting, however, that African Americans also were more likely to favor sensing over intuition and introversion over extroversion, which are less associated with creativity.

Baldwin (2003) analyzed a list of creative traits and abilities. These abilities included well-researched aspects, such as being open to experience or having high divergent-thinking ability, and more theoretical aspects, such as being antiauthoritarian, having a "zany" sense of humor, and having a low tolerance for boredom (Clark, 1988). Many of these abilities, Baldwin argued, are specifically appropriate and often found in African Americans. Others have seen the unique birth names created by African American parents as an indicator of creativity (Lieberson & Mikelson, 1995).

Less research has been conducted with Latino populations. Some researchers found that European American parents had more favorable perceptions of creativity than Latino parents (Strom & Johnson, 1989; Strom et al., 1992). However, they also found that Latino parents were more likely to engage in play activities with their children and valued play more (Strom & Johnson, 1989). Make-believe play can be a valuable component of a child's developing imagination (Singer & Singer, 1990).

Group Differences and Fairness

Most tests of intelligence and academic achievement show significant differences in scores by ethnicity. A wide variety of measures of intelligence and ability have shown lower scores for African Americans and Latinos (see Loehlin, 1999, for an overview). Standardized tests such as the SAT, ACT, GRE, and AP exams show similar results (Camara & Schmidt, 1999; Morgan & Maneckshana, 1996).

The differences between males and females are not as large for intelligence tests as the differences found between different ethnic groups, although males tend to obtain higher scores on tasks involving mental rotation (Masters & Sanders, 1993) and females tend to obtain higher scores on verbal tests (Hedges & Nowell, 1995). Males tend to outscore females on the SAT, GRE, and GMAT, particularly on the quantitative sections (Coley, 2001).

As we discussed earlier, creativity is related to intelligence, and creativity is part of several new theories of intelligence (e.g., Sternberg, 1985, 1996b). However, as we can see, differences by gender and ethnicity are minimal and mixed on creativity measures. One approach to seeking out more nonbiased assessments is to supplement traditional assessment with additional measures of constructs that may be influencing a score on a traditional test of ability or achievement; creativity certainly seems to be an ideal candidate to be such a supplement (Kaufman, 2005).

CONCLUSION

This chapter is itself a summary (and a necessarily cursory one at that), and therefore, we make no attempt here to summarize our summary. We believe it is fair to conclude, however, that creativity research in the English-speaking world is diverse in both its content and approaches, rich in both its insights and potential, and healthy in both its consensus and controversies. There are two major journals (*Creativity Research Journal* and *Journal of Creative Behavior*) devoted exclusively to creativity research and theory; many other psychological and educational journals include reports of creativity research as a major component of each issue (e.g., *Empirical Studies of the Arts; Imagination, Cognition, and Personality; Metaphor and Symbolic Activity; Gifted Child Quarterly; Roeper Review*). Many journals not primarily devoted to creativity research also frequently include reports of creativity research (e.g., *Review of General Psychology; American Psychologist; Journal of Personality and Social Psychology*). Furthermore, there is a division of the American Psychological Association devoted to creativity (Division 10, Psychology of Aesthetics, Creativity, and the Arts, which also publishes a journal that features creativity research, *Bulletin of Psychology and the Arts*); scores of books about creativity research are published in English each year (such as the one of which this chapter is a part); and creativity research is a major topic at many psychology and education conferences every year.

This chapter has been able only to highlight some major trends in creativity research in the English-speaking world – if one were looking for a complete and thorough diagnostic workup fully describing the current condition of creativity research, what we have been able to describe in this brief chapter would be the equivalent of merely reporting the patient's pulse and blood pressure – and we hasten to point out that the way we organized this chapter inevitably neglected many important themes in creativity research past and present. We nonetheless hope that this overview provides a good general picture of where this research has been and where it is now, showing both the continuity of themes and emphases over time as well as the spectacular growth and vibrant changes in the field in recent decades.

Past behavior is perhaps the best predictor of future behavior, and one might therefore be tempted to use our survey of the field – where it has been and where it is now – as the basis for a forecast of the future of creativity research. Although we invite readers to make their own predictions of such trends, we will resist this temptation. We have no doubt that all the areas discussed herein will continue to be important and that many other areas of research will also see growth, but placing bets on which of these many active research programs will be the ones that would be highlighted in an update to this chapter in, say, twenty-five years, would require far more foresight that we could fairly claim.

We will conclude with one prediction, however: That creativity research in the English-speaking world will become (a) ever more international in its scope; (b) ever more aware of both cultural differences and similarities that influence the development and expression of creativity and our understanding of the cognitive, social, and emotional factors that influence creative performance; and (c) ever more sensitive to the results, insights, and understandings of creativity research being conducted elsewhere around the world. We are pleased that this volume will contribute to that increasingly international future for creativity research.

References

Albert, R. S., & Runco, M. A. (1999). A history of research on creativity. In R. J. Sternberg (Ed.), *Handbook of creativity* (pp. 16–31). New York: Cambridge University Press.

Aldrich, H. E., & Kenworthy, A. (1998). The accidental entrepreneur: Camp-bellian antinomies and organizational foundings. In Joel A. C. Baum and Bill McKelvey (Eds.), *Variations in organization science: In honor of Donald T. Campbell* (pp. 19–33). Newbury Park, CA: Sage.

Amabile, T. M. (1982). Social psychology of creativity: A consensual assessment technique. *Journal of Personality and Social Psychology, 43*, 997–1013.

Amabile, T. M. (1983). *The social psychology of creativity*. New York: Springer-Verlag.

Amabile, T. M. (1996). *Creativity in context: Update to the social psychology of creativity*. Boulder, CO: Westview Press.

Argulewicz, E. N., Elliott, S. N., & Hall, R. (1982). Comparision of behavioral ratings of Anglo-American and Mexican-American gifted children. *Psychology in the schools,19*, 469–472.

Argulewicz, E. N., & Kush, J. C. (1984). Concurrent validity of the SRBCSS Creativity Scale for Anglo-American and Mexican-American gifted students. *Educational and Psychological Research, 4*, 81–89.

Baldwin, A. Y. (2003). Understanding the challenge of creativity among African Americans. *Inquiry, 22*, 13–18.

Baer, J. (1988). Long-term effects of creativity training with middle school students. *Journal of Early Adolescence, 8*, 183–193.

Baer, J. (1993). *Creativity and divergent thinking: A task-specific approach*. Hillsdale, NJ: Erlbaum.

Baer, J. (1994). Divergent thinking is not a general trait: A multi-domain training experiment. *Creativity Research Journal, 7*, 35–46.

Baer, J. (1997a). *Creative teachers, creative students*. Boston: Allyn & Bacon.

Baer, J. (1997b). Gender differences in the effects of anticipated evaluation on creativity. *Creativity Research Journal, 10*, 25–31.

Baer, J. (1997c). The hidden costs of rewards and evaluation: Who gets hurt, and what teachers can do. *Focus on Education, 41*, 24–27.

Baer, J. (1998a). The case for domain specificity in creativity. *Creativity Research Journal, 11*, 173–177.

Baer, J. (1998b). Gender differences in the effects of extrinsic motivation on creativity. *Journal of Creative Behavior, 32*, 18–37.

Baer, J. (1999). Gender differences in creativity. In M. A. Runco, & S. Pritzker (Eds.), *Encyclopedia of creativity* (pp. 753–758). San Diego: Academic Press.

Baer, J. (2003). Evaluative thinking, creativity, and task specificity: Separating wheat from chaff is not the same as finding needles in haystacks. In M. A. Runco (Ed.), *Critical creative processes* (pp. 129–151). Cresskill, NJ: Hampton Press.

Baer, J. (in press). Gender differences in creativity. In M. A. Runco (Ed.), *Creativity research handbook* Vol. 3. Cresskill, NJ: Hampton Press.

Baer, J., Kaufman, J. C., & Gentile, C. A. (2004). Extension of the consensual assessment technique to nonparallel creative products. *Creativity Research Journal, 16*, 113–117.

Bahr, M., Sears, J., Anderson, E., & Walker, K. (2003). *Creative problem solving for general education intervention teams, 2002–2003*. Terre Haute: Indiana State University, Blumberg Center. Available online at www.indstate. edu/soe/blumberg/cpsresearch

Barron, F. (1958). The psychology of imagination. *Scientific American, 199*, 150–166.

Barron, F. (1988). Putting creativity to work. In R. J. Sternberg (Ed.), *The nature of creativity* (pp. 76–98). New York: Cambridge University Press.

Barron, F., & Harrington, D. (1981). Creativity, intelligence, and personality. *Annual Review of Psychology, 32*, 439–476.

Basadur, M. S. (2005). Management: Synchronizing different kinds of creativity. In J. C. Kaufman & J. Baer (Eds.), *Creativity across domains: Faces of the muse.* (pp. 261–280). Mahwah, NJ: Erlbaum.

Basadur, M. S., Graen, C. B., & Green, S. C. (1982). Training in creative problem solving: Effects on ideation and problem finding and solving in an I/O research organization. *Organizational Behavior and Human Performance, 30*, 41–70.

Basadur, M. S., Graen, G. B., & Scandura, T. A. (1986). Training effects on attitudes toward divergent thinking among manufacturing engineers. *Journal of Applied Psychology, 71*, 612–617.

Becker, M. (1995). Nineteenth-century foundations of creativity research. *Creativity Research Journal, 8*, 219–229.

Bem, D. (1972). Self-perception theory. In L. Berkowitz (Ed.), *Advances in experimental social psychology* (Vol. 6, pp. 1–62). New York: Academic Press.

Camara, W. J., & Schmidt, A. E. (1999). *Group differences in standardized testing and social stratification* (College Board Report No. 99-5). New York: College Board.

Campbell, D. T. (1960). Blind variation and selective retention in creative thought as in other knowledge processes. *Psychological Review, 67*, 380–400.

Carrington, D. C. (1974). Creative thinking abilities of Mexican youth. *Journal of Cross-Cultural Psychology, 5*, 492–504.

Castillo, L. C. (1998). The effect of analogy instruction on young children's metaphor comprehension. *Roeper Review, 21*, 27–31.

Christensen, P. R., Guilford, J. P., & Wilson, R. C. (1957). Relations of creative responses to working time and instructions. *Journal of Experimental Psychology, 53*, 82–88.

Clark, B. (1988). *Growing up gifted* (3rd ed.) Columbus, OH: Merrill.

Clements, D. H. (1991). Enhancement of creativity in computer environments. *American Educational Research Journal, 28*, 173–187.

Coley, R. J. (2001). *Differences in the gender gap: Comparisons across racial/ethnic groups in education and work.* Princeton, NJ: Education Testing Service.

Cox, C. M. (1926). *The early mental traits of three hundred geniuses.* Stanford, CA: Stanford University Press.

Csikszentmihalyi, M. (1988). Society, culture, and person: A systems view of creativity. In R. J. Sternberg (Ed.), *The nature of creativity* (pp. 325–339). New York: Cambridge University Press.

Csikszentmihalyi, M. (1996). *Creativity: Flow and the psychology of discovery and invention.* New York: HarperCollins.

Daniels, R. R., Heath, R. G., & Enns, K. S. (1985). Fostering creative behavior among university women. *Roeper Review, 7*, 164–166.

Davis, G. A., Houtman, S. E., Warren, T. F., Roweton, W. E., Mari, S., & Belcher, T. L. (1972). *A program for training creative thinking: Inner city evaluation* (Report

No. 224). Madison, WI: Wisconsin Research and Development Center for Cognitive Learning (ERIC Document Reproduction Service No. ED070809).

deCharms, R. (1968). *Personal causation*. New York: Academic Press.

DeMoss, K., Milich, R., & DeMers, S. (1993). Gender, creativity, depression, and attributional style in adolescents with high academic ability. *Journal of Abnormal Child Psychology, 21*, 455–467.

Dhillon, P. K., & Mehra, D. (1987). *Asian Journal of Psychology and Education, 19*, 1–10.

Domino, G. (1974). Assessment of cinematographic creativity. *Journal of Personality and Social Psychology, 30*, 150–154.

Dudek, S. Z., Strobel, M. G., & Runco, M. A. (1993). Cumulative and proximal influences on the social environment and children's creative potential. *Journal of Genetic Psychology, 154*, 487–499.

Dudek, S. Z., & Verreault, R. (1989). The creative thinking and ego functioning of children. *Creativity Research Journal, 2*, 64–86.

Duncker, F. (1945). On problem solving. *Psychological Monographs, 58*(5), 270.

Eberle, B., & Stanish, B. (1980). *CPS for kids*. Buffalo, NY: D.O.K. Publishers.

Fasko, D. (2001). Education and creativity. *Creativity Research Journal, 13*, 317–328.

Finke, R. A., Ward, T. B., & Smith, S. M. (1992). *Creative cognition: Theory, research, and applications*. Cambridge, MA: MIT Press.

Fontenot, N. A. (1993). Effects of training in creativity and creativity problem finding on business people. *Journal of Social Psychology, 133*, 11–22.

Ford, C. M., & Sullivan, D. M. (2005). Selective retention processes that create tensions between novelty and value in business domains. In J. C. Kaufman & J. Baer (Eds.), *Creativity across domains: Faces of the muse* (pp. 245–260). Mahwah, NJ: Erlbaum.

Freud, S. (1957). Leonardo da Vinci and a memory of his childhood. In J. Strachey (Ed. and Trans.), *The Standard edition of the complete works of Sigmund Freud*, (Vol. XI, pp. 59–137). London: Hogarth Press. (Original work published 1910)

Fritz, R. L. (1993). Problem solving attitude among secondary marketing education students. *Marketing Educators Journal, 19*, 45–59.

Furnham, A. (1999). Personality and creativity. *Perceptual and Motor Skills, 88*, 407–408.

Garcia, J. H. (2003). Nurturing creativity in Chicano populations: Integrating history, culture, family, and self. *Inquiry, 22*, 19–24.

Gardner, H. (1988). Creative lives and creative works: A synthetic scientific approach. In R. J. Sternberg (Ed.), *The nature of creativity* (pp. 298–321). New York: Cambridge University Press.

Gardner, H. (1993). *Creating minds: An anatomy of creativity seen through the lives of Freud, Einstein, Picasso, Stravinsky, Eliot, Graham, & Ghandi*. New York: Basic Books.

Gilligan, C., Lyons, N., & Hanmer, T. (Eds.). (1990). *Making connections: The relational worlds of adolescent girls at Emma Willard School*. Cambridge, MA: Harvard University Press.

Glover, J. A. (1976a). Comparative levels of creative ability in Black and White college students. *Journal of Genetic Psychology, 128*, 95–99.

Glover, J. A. (1976b). Compartive levels of creative ability among elementary school children. *Journal of Genetic Psychology, 129,* 131–135.

Glover, J. A. (1980). A creativity training workshop: Short-term, long-term, and transfer effects. *Journal of Genetic Psychology, 136,* 3–16.

Griffin, M. & McDermott, M. R. (1998). Exploring a tripartite relationship between rebelliousness, openness to experience and creativity. *Social Behavior and Personality, 26,* 347–356.

Gruber, H. E. (1981). *Darwin on man: A psychological study of scientific creativity* (2nd ed.). Chicago: University of Chicago Press.

Gruber, H. E., & Davis, S. N. (1988). Inching our way up Mount Olympus: The evolving-systems approach to creative thinking. In R. J. Sternberg (Ed.), *The nature of creativity* (pp. 243–270). New York: Cambridge University Press.

Gruber, H. E., & Wallace, D. B. (1999). The case study method and evolving systems approach for understanding unique creative people at work. In R. J. Sternberg (Ed.), *Handbook of creativity* (pp. 93–115). New York: Cambridge University Press.

Guilford, J. P. (1950). Creativity. *American Psychologist, 5,* 444–454.

Guilford, J. P. (1956). The structure of intellect. *Psychological Bulletin, 53,* 267–293.

Guilford, J. P. (1967). *The nature of human intelligence.* New York: McGraw-Hill.

Guilford, J. P., & Hoepfner, R. (1971). *The analysis of intelligence.* New York: McGraw-Hill.

Hadamard, J. (1949). *The psychology of invention in the mathematical field.* Princeton, NJ: Princeton University Press.

Hampton, E. M. (2004). *CPS for GEI district trainer and school-based team focus group report.* Terre Houte: Indiana State University, Blumberg Center. Available online at www.indstate.edu/soe/blumberg/cpsresearch.

Hargreaves, D. J. (1977). Sex roles in divergent thinking. *British Journal of Educational Psychology, 47,* 25–32.

Harty, H., Adkins, D. M., & Sherwood, R. D. (1984). Predictability of giftedness identification indices for two recognized approaches to elementary school gifted education. *Journal of Educational Research, 77,* 337–342.

Heath, S. B. (1983). *Ways with words.* Cambridge, U.K.: Cambridge University Press.

Hedges, L. V., & Nowell, A. (1995). Sex differences in mental test scores, variability, and numbers of high-scoring individuals. *Science, 269,* 41–45.

Iscoe, I., & Pierce-Jones, J. (1964). Divergent thinking, age, and intelligence in white and negro children. *Child Development, 35,* 785–797.

Jevons, W. S. (1877). *The principles of science: A treatise on logic and scientific method.* New York: Macmillan.

Johnson-Laird, P. N. (1988). Freedom and constraint in creativity. In R. J. Sternberg (Ed.), *The nature of creativity* (pp. 202–219). New York: Cambridge University Press.

Kaltsounis, B. (1974). Race, socioeconomic status and creativity. *Psychological Report, 35,* 164–166.

Kaufman, J. C. (2005). Non-biased assessment: A supplemental approach. In C. L. Frisby & C. R. Reynolds (Eds)., *Children handbook of multicultural school psychology* (pp. 824–840). New York: Wiley.

Kaufman, J. C., & Baer, J. (Eds.). (2005). *Creativity across domains: Faces of the muse.* Mahwah, NJ: Erlbaum.

Kaufman, J. C., Baer, J., & Gentile, C. A. (2004). Racial and gender differences in creativity as measured by ratings of three writing tasks, *Journal of Creative Behavior, 38*, 56–69.

Kaufman, J. C., Gentile, C. A., & Baer, J. (2005). Do gifted student writers and creative writing experts rate creativity the same way? *Gifted Child Quarterly, 40*, 260–265.

Kay, S. I. (1998). Curriculum and the creative process: Contributions in memory of Harry Passow. *Roeper Review, 21*, 5–13.

Kelly, H. (1967). Attribution theory in social psychology. In D. Levine (Ed.), *Nebraska symposium on motivation* (Vol. 15, pp. 192–238). Lincoln: University of Nebraska Press.

Kelly, H. (1973). The processes of casual attribution. *American Psychologist, 28*, 107–128.

Kessler, C., & Quinn, M. E. (1987). Language minority children's linguistic and cognitive creativity. *Journal of Multilingual and Multicultural Development, 8*, 173–186.

King, L. A., McKee-Walker, L., & Broyles, S. J. (1996). Creativity and the five factor model. *Journal of Research in Personality, 30*, 189–203.

Knox, B. J., & Glover, J. A. (1978). A note on preschool experience effects on achievement, readiness, and creativity. *Journal of Genetic Psychology, 132*, 151–152.

Kogan, N. (1974). Creativity and sex differences. *Journal of Creative Behavior, 8*, 1–14.

Kogan, N. (1983). Stylistic variation in childhood and adolescence: Creativity, metaphor, and cognitive styles. In P. H. Mussen (Ed.), *Handbook of child psychology: Vol. 3. Cognitive development* (4th ed., pp. 628–706). New York: Wiley.

Langley, P., & Jones, R. (1988). Computational models of scientific thought. In R. J. Sternberg (Ed.), *The nature of creativity* (pp. 177–201). New York: Cambridge University Press.

Langley, P., Simon, H. A., Bradshaw, G. L., & Zytkow, J. M. (1987). *Scientific discovery: Computational explorations of the creative process.* Cambridge, MA: MIT Press.

Lepper, M., & Greene, D. (1975). Turning work into play: Effects of adult surveillance and extrinsic rewards on children's intrinsic motivation. *Journal of Personality and Social Psychology, 31*, 479–486.

Lepper, M., & Greene, D. (1978). *The hidden costs of rewards.* Hillsdale, NJ: Erlbaum.

Lepper, M., Greene, D., & Nisbett, R. (1973). Undermining children's intrinsic interest with extrinsic rewards: A test of the "overjustification" hypothesis. *Journal of Personality and Social Psychology, 28*, 129–137.

Lewis, C. D., & Houtz, J. C. (1986). Sex-role stereotyping and young children's divergent thinking. *Psychological Reports, 59*, 1027–1033.

Lieberson, S., & Mikelson, K. S. (1995). Distinctive African American names: An experimental, historical, and linguistic analysis of innovation. *American Sociological Review, 60*, 928–946.

Loehlin, J. C. (1999). Group differences in intelligence. In R. J. Sternberg (Ed.), *Handbook of intelligence* (pp. 176–193). New York: Cambridge University Press.

Lubart, T. I. (1999). Creativity across cultures. In R. J. Sternberg (Ed.), *Handbook of creativity* (pp. 339–350). New York: Cambridge University Press.

Maciejczyk-Clapham, M., & Schuster, D. H. (1992). Can engineering students be trained to think more creatively? *Journal of Creative Behavior, 26,* 165–171.

Manly, J. J., Miller, S. W., Heaton, R. K., Byrd, D., Reilly, J., Velasquez, R. J., Saccuzzo, D. P., Grant, I., & the HIV Neurobehavioral Research Center (HNRC) Group. (1998). The effect of Black acculturation on neuropsychological test performance in normal and HIV positive individuals. *Journal of the International Neuropsychological Society, 4,* 291–302.

Masten, W. G., Plata, M., Wenglar, K., & Thedforf, J. (1999). Acculturation and teacher ratings of Hispanic and Anglo-American students. *Roeper Review, 22,* 64–65.

Masters, M. S., & Sanders, B. (1993). Is the genetic difference in mental rotation disappearing? *Behavioral Genetics, 23,* 337–341.

McCormack, A. J. (1971). Effects of selected teaching methods on creative thinking, self-evaluation, and achievement of studies enrolled in an elementary science education methods course. *Science Teaching, 55,* 301–307.

McCormack, A. J. (1974). Training creative thinking in general education science. *Journal of College Science Teaching, 4,* 10–15.

McCrae, R. R. (1987). Creativity, divergent thinking, and openness to experience. *Journal of Personality and Social Psychology, 52,* 1258–1265.

Meador, K. S. (1994). The effects of synectics training on gifted and non-gifted kindergarten students. *Journal for the Education of the Gifted, 18,* 55–73.

Melear, C. T., & Alcock, M. W. (1999). Learning styles and personality types of Black children: Implications for science education. *Journal of Psychological Type, 48,* 22–33.

Micklus, C. S. (1982). *Problems! Problems! Problems!* Glassboro, NJ: Creative Competitions.

Micklus, C. S. (1984). *Odyssey of the mind.* Glassboro, NJ: Creative Competitions.

Micklus, C. S. (1986). *OM-Aha!* Glassboro, NJ: Creative Competitions.

Mitchell, B. M. (1988). Hemisphericity and creativity: A look at the relationships among elementary-age low-income Hispanic children. *Educational Research Quarterly,* 2–5.

Moreno, J. M., & Hogan, J. D. (1976). The influence of race and social-class level on the training of creative thinking and problem-solving abilities. *Journal of Educational Research, 70,* 91–95.

Morgan, R., & Maneckshana, B. (1996). *The psychometric perspective: Lessons learned from 40 years of constructed response testing in the Advanced Placement Program.* Paper presented at the annual meeting of the National Council of Measurement in Education in New York.

Myers, I. B. (1962). *Manual: The Myers-Briggs Type Indicator.* Princeton, NJ: Educational Testing Service.

Myers, I. B., & McCaulley, M. H. (1992). *Manual: A guide to the development and use of the Myers-Briggs Type Indicator.* Palo Alto, CA: Consulting Psychologists Press.

Nickerson, R. S. (1999). Enhancing creativity. In R. J. Sternberg (Ed.), *Handbook of creativity* (pp. 392–430). Cambridge, England: Cambridge University Press.

Nisbett, R. E. (2003). *The geography of thought*. New York: The Free Press.

Noller, R. B., & Parnes, S. J. (1972). Applied creativity: The creative studies project: The curriculum. *Journal of Creative Behavior, 6,* 275–294.

Noller, R. B., Parnes, S. J., & Biondi, A. M. (1976). *Creative authorbook*. New York: Scribner's.

Osborn, A. F. (1953). *Applied imagination: Principles and procedures for creative thinking*. New York: Scribner's.

Parnes, S. J. (1972). *Creativity: Unlocking human potential*. Buffalo, NY: D.O.K. Publishers.

Parnes, S. J., & Noller, R. B. (1972). Applied creativity: The creative studies project: Part results of the two year program. *Journal of Creative Behavior, 6,* 164–186.

Parnes, S. J., & Noller, R. B. (1973). *Toward supersanity*. Buffalo, NY: D.O.K. Publishers.

Peeke, P. A., Steward, R. J., & Ruddock, J. A. (1998). Urban adolescents' personality and learning styles: Required knowledge to develop effective interventions in schools. *Journal of Multicultural Counseling and Development, 26,* 120–136.

Piirto, J. (2005). The creative process in poets. In J. C. Kaufman & J. Baer (Eds.), *Creativity across domains: Faces of the muse*. (pp. 1–22). Mahwah, NJ: Erlbaum.

Plucker, J. A. (1998). Beware of simple conclusions: The case for the content generality of creativity. *Creativity Research Journal, 11,* 179–182.

Poincaré, H. (1913). *The foundations of science*. Lancaster, PA: Science Press.

Price-Williams, D. R., Ramirez, M., III. (1977). Divergent thinking, cultural differences, and bilingualism. *The Journal of Social Psychology, 103,* 3–11.

Ramirez, M., III, & Castaneda, A. (1974). *Cultural democracy, bicognitive development and education*. New York: Academic Press.

Rank, O. (1968). *Art and artists: Creative urge and personality development*. New York: Knopf. (Original work published 1932)

Renzulli, J. S. (1994). *Schools for talent development: A practical plan for total school improvement*. Mansfield Center, CT: Creative Learning Press.

Rejskind, F. G., Rapagna, S. O., & Gold, D. (1992). Gender differences in children's divergent thinking. *Creativity Research Journal, 5,* 165–174.

Ribot, T. (1900). The nature of the creative imagination. *International Monthly, 1,* 648–675.

Richardson, A. G. (1985). Sex differences in creativity among a sample of Jamaican adolescents. *Perceptual and Motor Skills, 60,* 424–426.

Ripple, R. E., & Jaquish, G. A. (1982). Developmental aspects of ideational fluency, flexibility, and originality: South Africa and the United States. *South African Journal of Psychology, 12,* 95–100.

Roe, A. (1946). Artists and their work. *Journal of Personality, 15,* 1–40.

Rose, L. H., & Lin, H. (1984). A meta-analysis of long-term creativity training programs. *Journal of Creative Behavior, 18,* 11–22.

Rump, E. E. (1982). Relationships between creativity, arts-orientation, and esthetic preference variables. *Journal of Psychology, 110,* 11–20.

Saeki, N., Fan, X., & Van Dusen, L. (2001). A comparative study of creative thinking of American and Japanese college students. *Journal of Creative Behavior, 35,* 24–36.

Shade, B. J. (1986). Is there an Afro-American cognitive style? An exploratory study. *Journal of Black Psychology, 13,* 13–16.

Simonton, D. L. (1976). Biographical determinants of achieved eminence: A multivariate approach to the Cox data. *Journal of Personality and Social Psychology, 33,* 218–226.

Simonton, D. L. (1988a). Creativity, leadership, and chance. In R. J. Sternberg (Ed.), *The nature of creativity* (pp. 386–426). New York: Cambridge University Press.

Simonton, D. L. (1988b). *Scientific genius: A psychology of science.* New York: Cambridge University Press.

Simonton, D. L. (1994). *Greatness: Who makes history, and why.* New York: Guilford.

Simonton, D. L. (2005). Creativity in psychology: On becoming and being a great psychologist. In J. C. Kaufman & J. Baer (Eds.), *Creativity across domains: Faces of the muse.* (pp. 139–152). Mahwah, NJ: Erlbaum.

Singer, D. G., & Singer, J. L. (1990). *The house of make-believe: Children's play and the developing imagination.* Cambridge, MA: Harvard University Press.

Smith, S. M., Ward, T. M., & Finke, R. A. (Eds.). (1995). *The creative cognition approach.* Cambridge, MA: MIT Press.

Spearman, C. (1931). *Creative mind.* New York: Appleton.

Sternberg, R. J. (1985). *Beyond IQ: A triarchic theory of human intelligence.* Cambridge, England: Cambridge University Press.

Sternberg, R. J. (1988). A three-facet model of creativity. In R. J. Sternberg (Ed.), *Handbook of creativity* (pp. 125–147). New York: Cambridge University Press.

Sternberg, R. J. (1996a). IQ counts, but what really counts is successful intelligence. *NASSP Bulletin, 80,* 18–23.

Sternberg, R. J. (1996b). *Successful intelligence.* New York: Simon & Schuster.

Sternberg, R. J. (1999). A propulsion model of types of creative contributions. *Review of General Psychology, 3,* 83–100.

Sternberg, R. J., Kaufman, J. C., & Pretz, J. E. (2001). The propulsion model of creativity applied to the arts and letters. *Journal of Creative Behavior, 35,* 75–101.

Sternberg, R. J., Kaufman, J. C., & Pretz, J. E. (2002). *The creativity conundrum: A propulsion model of kinds of creative contributions.* New York: Psychology Press.

Sternberg, R. J., Kaufman, J. C., & Pretz, J. E. (2003). A propulsion model of creative leadership. *Leadership Quarterly, 14*(4–5), 455–473.

Sternberg, R. J., Kaufman, J. C., & Pretz, J. E. (2004). A propulsion model of creative leadership. *Innovation and Creativity Management, 13,* 145–153.

Sternberg, R. J., & Lubart, T. I. (1991). An investment theory of creativity and its development. *Human Development, 34,* 1–31.

Sternberg, R. J., & Lubart, T. I. (1995). *Defying the crowd.* New York: The Free Press.

Sternberg, R. J., & Lubart, T. I. (1996). Investing in creativity. *American Psychologist, 51,* 677–688.

Stricker, L. J., Rock, D. A., & Bennett, R. E. (2001). Sex and ethnic-group differences on accomplishment measures. *Applied Measurement in Education, 14,* 205–218.

Strom, R., & Johnson, A. (1989). Hispanic and Anglo families of gifted children. *Journal of Instructional Psychology, 16,* 164–172

Strom, R., Johnson, A., Strom, S., & Strom, P. (1992). Parental differences in expectations of gifted children. *Journal of Comparative Family Studies, 23,* 69–77.

Strough, J., & Diriwaechter, R. (2000). Dyad gender differences in preadolescents' creative stories. *Sex Roles, 43,* 43–60.

Taber, T. H. (1983). The effects of creativity training on learning disabled students' creative expression. *Journal of Learning Disabilities, 16,* 264–265.

Taber, T. H. (1985). Effect of instruction for creativity on learning disabled students' creative expression. *Perceptual and Motor Skills, 61,* 895–898.

Thorne, A., & Gough, H. (1991). *Portraits of type: An MBTI research compendium.* Palo Alto, CA: Consulting Psychologists Press.

Torrance, E. P. (1966). *The Torrance Tests of Creative Thinking: Norms – technical manual.* Lexington, MA: Personal Press.

Torrance, E. P. (1971). Are the Torrance Tests of Creative Thinking biased against or in favor of the "disadvantaged" groups? *Gifted Child Quarterly, 15,* 75–80.

Torrance, E. P. (1972a). Can we teach children to think creatively? *Journal of Creative Behavior, 6,* 114–143.

Torrance, E. P. (1972b). Predictive validity of the Torrance Tests of Creative Thinking. *Journal of Creative Behavior, 6,* 236–252.

Torrance, E. P. (1973). Non-test indicators of creative talent among disadvantaged children. *Gifted Child Quarterly, 17,* 3–9.

Torrance, E. P. (1984). The role of creativity in identification of the gifted and talented. *Gifted Child Quarterly, 28,* 153–156.

Torrance, E. P. (1988). Creativity as manifest in testing. In R. J. Sternberg (Ed.), *The nature of creativity* (pp. 43–75). New York: Cambridge University Press.

Torrance, E. P. (1990). *The Torrance Tests of Creative Thinking: Norms – technical manual* (rev. ed.). Bensenville, IL: Scholastic Testing Service.

Torrance, E. P., & Presbury, J. (1984). The criteria of success used in 242 recent experimental studies of creativity. *Creative Child & Adult Quarterly, 9,* 238–243.

Treffinger, D. J. (1995). Creative problem solving: Overview and educational implications. *Educational Psychology Review, 7,* 191–205.

Wallace, D. M., & Gruber, H. E. (Eds.). (1989). *Creative people at work: Twelve cognitive case studies.* New York: Oxford University Press.

Wallas, G. (1926). *Art of thought.* New York: Harcourt Brace.

Wang, H., Zhang, J., Lin., L., & Xu, B. (1998). Study on the creativity attitude development of middle school students. *Acta Psychologica Sinica, 30,* 57–63.

Ward, T. M., Smith, S. M., & Finke, R. A. (1999). Creative cognition. In R. J. Sternberg (Ed.), *Handbook of creativity* (pp. 189–212). New York: Cambridge University Press.

Wertheimer, M. (1945). *Productive thinking.* New York: Harper.

Weisberg, R. W. (1988). Problem solving and creativity. In R. J. Sternberg (Ed.),
  The nature of creativity (pp. 148–176). New York: Cambridge University Press.
Weisberg, R. W. (1999). Creativity and knowledge: A challenge to theories. In R.
  J. Sternberg (Ed.), *Handbook of creativity* (pp. 226–250). New York: Cambridge
  University Press.
Wilson, R. L., Guilford, J. P., Christensen, P. R., & Lewis, D. J. (1954). A factor
  analytic study of divergent thinking abilities. *Psychometrica, 19*, 297–311.
Wolfradt, U., & Pretz, J. E. (2001). Individual differences in creativity: Personality,
  story writing, and hobbies. *European Journal of Personality, 15*, 297–310.
Zhiyan, T., & Singer, J. L. (1996). Daydreaming styles, emotionality, and the big
  five personality dimensions. *Imagination, Cognition, and Personality, 16*, 399–
  414.

3

Creativity in Latin America

Views from Psychology, Humanities, and the Arts

David D. Preiss and Katherine Strasser

INTRODUCTION

The purpose of this chapter is to discuss how creativity is viewed and practiced in Latin America and the Caribbean. Creativity is a multifaceted phenomenon, so several perspectives should be taken into consideration. We have chosen to focus on two. First, we review how psychologists in the region have studied creativity. Most such contributions have regarded creativity from an applied perspective, with an emphasis on its modification. However, this work is not sufficiently informative regarding what is culturally specific about creativity in the region. So, after discussing the scientific work on creativity, we found it necessary to summarize some of the views about creativity held by creative minds in the region, specifically artists and writers. These innovators not only provide a firsthand account of creativity in Latin America and the Caribbean but also put their creative work in a sociocultural perspective; this is an emphasis that we deem very relevant in a region as diverse as this one. It is worth noting that, whereas the work of psychologists has remained within specialized circles, the literary and artistic production of Latin American and Caribbean artists has reached large audiences. Thus, to the extent possible, we intend to make a more or less exhaustive review of the work of the former to provide an account that is instrumental for other researchers in the field. Concerning literary and artistic creators, we approach a few of them with an illustrative purpose and a twofold goal: first, to underscore the cultural differences existing within the region and, second, to inform those readers not familiar with Latin American and Caribbean creative minds.

Before continuing, we think it is worthwhile to clarify certain names. In addition to calling themselves *Latinoamericanos* (Latin Americans), most people in the region that extends from Mexico to Chile through Central and South America call themselves *Americanos* (Americans). *América* is the word used to refer to the whole Western continent (save for the United States and Canada) by people living in the region. Although related to the name of European explorer Amerigo Vespucci, *América* is the more inclusive name of the region. In fact, the region's alternative names (Hispano-America, Indo-América, Afro-América, or the most popular Latin América) all use ethnic prefixes that favorably distinguish one of the multiple ethnicities of the region while at the same time obscuring others (Gissi, 1989, 2002).[1] We would have liked to join our fellow Americanos and use the name *América* to talk about the region. Unfortunately, English use of the word *American* is restricted to designate what comes from the United States, as in the institutional names of the American Psychological Association or the American Educational Research Association, or as in the name of journals such as the *American Psychologist* or the *American Journal of Psychology*. In consequence, adopting the term *América* might have confused Anglo-Saxon readers. Thus, the term we decided to use is what we believe is the second most common name of the region, *Latin America*.[2] By Latin America we refer to the countries located in the American continent between the Rio Grande in Northern Mexico and the Strait of Magellan in Southern Chile. To refer to those countries located in the Caribbean Sea, we use the established geographical name, the Caribbean.[3]

As we experienced during the preparation of this chapter, the lack of agreement regarding the name of the region has serious consequences for research. Articles dealing with these populations are indexed without following a clear norm, so they are not easy to track down, even electronically. Has, on one hand, the time arrived to adopt a common name such as The Americas, or, quite to the contrary, to look for geographical

---

[1] The terms *Latino* or *Hispano* misrepresent immigrants from Latin America to the United States as well.

[2] We could have adopted the less biased term *The Americas*, which is the denomination used in the United States to refer to the region. Not surprisingly, however, this term is not used in the daily life of most people living south of the Rio Grande (the United States–Mexico border) and is not the name adopted by the Organization of American States (the international organization that groups all the countries of the Western Hemisphere).

[3] However, this name is also biased as it refers to the name of its previous inhabitants without making any reference to what is now its most relevant population, which is people of African background.

denominations that are culturally meaningful? On the other hand, the restricted use of the name America to refer to the United States is offensive for most Latin Americans (Gissi, 1989, 2002). Is it time for the scientific community in the United States to review the way it uses the word *America*? Behavioral science has been very successful in cleaning the English language of biased or prejudiced terms, so the time may have come to reconsider how this word is used.

These clarifications made, let us make explicit the outline of our chapter. We start by discussing why it is appropriate to treat Latin America and the Caribbean as a bonded set. We describe cultural and racial hybridization as a unifying element. Afterward, we discuss psychology in the region and present some psychological research done in Latin America about the creative process. (Unfortunately, we are unaware of any psychological research done in the Caribbean.) To enrich Latin American psychological research on creativity with an outsider view, we also review work on creativity done in Latin America by a group of North American psychologists who adopt a cultural approach (Greenfield, Maynard & Childs, 2003). Then, we discuss some conceptions of creativity as expressed by renowned Latin American artists. To make readers outside of Latin America and the Caribbean more sensitive to regional differences, when we mention these contributions, we explain some of the main differences between the cultural areas that comprise Latin America and the Caribbean. We close the chapter by contrasting the paucity of research on the topic with the high productivity the region has shown in the arts and humanities, and venturing an explanation for this disparity.

It is worth mentioning here that we, the authors of this chapter, are Chileans. Consequently, we have been more exposed to Chilean sources than to sources from other Latin American countries. As noted elsewhere (Rosas, Boetto, & Jordán, 1999), dissemination of information in Latin America, particularly in the sciences and social sciences, is scarce and slow. Thus, despite our efforts to seek out research from other countries, our capacity to sample from diverse countries was constrained by lack of adequate databases or access to the material. We tried to compensate for this bias by exploring the artistic and literary works from Latin American countries other than Chile, which are more accessible than the psychological work. Still, some of the bias may remain. We hope that our conclusions will still be informative about the state of the art of creativity in Latin America and the Caribbean in general.

UNITED BY DIVERSITY

Let us start by explaining what makes Latin America and the Caribbean a unit that can be signaled as a more or less cohesive set. Because of a history of colonization by diverse powers and subsequent decolonization and fragmentation, this geographical zone amalgamated people from very different cultural and racial backgrounds. However, different peoples and civilizations cohabitated in the region well before the conquest by Europeans. The most influential of these were the Aztec, Maya, and Inca, who respectively occupied parts of what is today known as Mexico, Central America, and Peru. The Aztec, Maya, and Inca were complex cultures and made independent progress in a number of domains, including architecture, astronomy, and agriculture, to name just a few. Some of their contributions still reach contemporary audiences. Just to illustrate, the Incan Quipus – the complex system of ties the Inca used to count and store information – intrigued famous Russian psychologist Lev Vygotsky (1978), who said that Quipus "demonstrate that even at early stages of historical development humans went beyond the limits of psychological functions given to them by nature and proceed to a new culturally elaborated organization of their behavior" (p. 3).[4] The Aztec, Maya, and Inca do not represent the whole of Amerindian cultures. Before the arrival of the Europeans, there were also other groups occupying large zones: among others, we can name the Caribbean, who lived in the area that now bears their name; the Guarani, whose oral language is today one of the official languages of Paraguay; and the Mapuche, whose belligerence and resistance to Spanish conquest inspired Latin America's first epic poem, *La Araucana* (Ercilla y Zúñiga, 1993). Today, this diversity remains. For instance, Brazil is said to be home to 150 different ethnic groups speaking 340 different languages (Pinheiro, 2004), and the Aymara live in a cultural region spanning three different countries: Bolivia, Peru, and Chile. It is not our intent to provide an exhaustive listing of Amerindian cultures but rather to demonstrate that grouping all of them together under the neutral heading of "indigenous populations" is an overgeneralization.

The diversity of the Amerindian cultures clashed with the diversity of the immigrant cultures. After the arrival of Columbus in 1492, the region

---

[4] Here Vygotsky underestimated the long history and complex organization of the Incan Empire. Indeed, some recent accounts suggest that Quipus may have allowed Incas not only to count but also to store narratives and myths (Urton, 2003), which leave the Inca on the verge of creating a very innovative writing system!

was settled by Spanish, Portuguese, Dutch, French, and British settlers; Spain and Portugal, however, were the most influential powers and therefore their cultural legacy the most germane. The Caribbean islands and Brazil were part of the slave trade route and an infamous door for thousands of African slaves to the Western continent. Brazil was not only the major recipient of slaves in the world but also the last country officially to abolish slavery, in 1888. As a consequence of the slave trade, Brazil has the largest population of people of African descent outside Africa. On one hand, the descendants of these African slaves significantly shaped the ethnic and cultural life not only of Brazil but also of large parts of Latin America such as Colombia and Venezuela, and of the Caribbean. On the other hand, the Southern cone of South America is commonly seen as an area where European influences have been particularly prominent. Indeed, famous Mexican writer Jose Vasconcelos named Buenos Aires, Argentina's capital city, the South American Paris (Miller, 2004), an image that has remained in the Argentinean national imagination (Winn, 1999). There are several reasons why these countries of the Southern cone are relatively more European than other Latin American countries. At the end of the nineteenth century, they experienced a large wave of immigration from Italy, Portugal, Spain, and Germany, among other European countries. Contributing to shape the peculiar features of the Southern cone, racial hybridization was less intense in these countries, allowing the European presence to somewhat supercede the indigenous one. To illustrate, after Argentina declared its independence, the state implemented a process of ethnic cleansing of the native population of Patagonia. Quite different is the case of the Andean countries (Peru, Bolivia, and Ecuador), the countries of Central America, and Mexico, which all host a sizable native population today.

Notwithstanding the racist practices that marked the conquest enterprise and the action of its new independent states, the most relevant shared feature of Latin America and the Caribbean is cultural and racial amalgamation, usually known as *mestizaje* (Gissi, 2002). There was mestizaje in those countries at the Southern cone intensively shaped by late-nineteenth-century European immigrants; in Mexico and in Central America and the Andes, where the indigenous population managed to keep a relevant demographic presence; in those countries where, because of the slave trade, the African population was considerable. As noted by Latin American scholar García-Canclini (2001), "the makeup of all of the Americas requires the notion of *mestizaje*, both biologically – production of phenotypes from genetic crossbreeding – and culturally:

blending of European and native American habits, beliefs and ways of thinking" (p. 7096). Indeed, mestizaje is what makes the Spanish and Portuguese colonization distinctive from the British one: In stark contrast with the latter, in Latin America and the Caribbean, the fall of the native cultures and slave trade coexisted with a large cultural and racial mélange.

A core component of Latin American mestizaje is religious syncretism (Morandé, 1984). The Virgin of Guadalupe in Mexico is commonly quoted as one of its canonical examples. Mexico's national poet, Octavio Paz (1950), noted that she is an indigenous virgin who "appeared" to an indigenous man on a hill that previously was a place of devotion to Tonantzin, the Aztec goddess of fertility. Although the situation of mestizaje in the Caribbean is different than that in the Spanish continental colonies, a hybrid culture and religious syncretism also germinated there. Differences between both areas are worth noting. In addition to the Spanish settlers, the Caribbean was also populated by the British, French, and Dutch. Most of the indigenous Caribbean population disappeared soon after the conquest. Thus mestizaje originated from a different kind of crossbreeding. The Caribbean islands were a place of transit both for the slave trade and for trade in general. Within that context, religious syncretism originated from the hybridization of European and African rituals. When an Asian workforce was brought to the region, Asian religiosity was also imported. Thus, several forms of Christianity can be found in the area, in addition to openly crossbred beliefs such as Haitian Vodoun, Trinidadian Shango, Cuban Santeria, Jamaican Pocomania, and Rastafarianism (Trouillot, 2001).

In short, although the origins of mestizaje are different in Latin America and the Caribbean, both areas have experienced an extensive process of cultural hybridization. From now on, when we employ the term *mestizaje*, we use it in an inclusive manner to reference what we consider the distinctive feature of Latin America and the Caribbean culture.[5]

---

[5] Mestizaje notwithstanding, racial differences persist. European, African, or indigenous influence is more or less extensive in different parts of the hemisphere. Additionally, within each of these zones, new racial borders replicate. Across Latin America and the Caribbean, the populations of African or indigenous descent live in higher poverty than does the population of European descent (Gissi, 1989, 2002; Winn, 1999). Paradoxically, mestizaje might have moderated "racial awareness" to a limit where it did not crystallize as a social issue. Thus, in open contrast with the United States, where clear-cut racial borders not only were the background of a civil war but also fostered the civil rights movement in the 1960s, mestizaje has set an unfavorable scene for an agenda of either racial struggle or affirmative action in Latin America.

Next, we discuss how creativity has been approached by psychologists in the region. If references to culture are made, they refer to cross-cultural research with the developed world, treating most of the continent as an undifferentiated set. Indeed, psychologists of the region have scarcely attended to what is particular to Latin America and the Caribbean. Later, when we discuss the work of Latin American artists and writers, we will put the cultural peculiarities of Latin America back at center stage.

CREATIVITY RESEARCH IN LATIN AMERICA

Research on creativity in Latin America and the Caribbean has been shaped by the same forces that have influenced most psychological research in the region. For this reason, it is convenient to start our review of creativity research in Latin America with some considerations of the main characteristics of psychological science and psychological research in the region. Although, as we have emphasized before, there is considerable heterogeneity in the countries that comprise Latin America and the Caribbean, some of the factors that have contributed to shaping scientific activity in general and the development of psychology in particular are shared among most countries. Several accounts of the development of the discipline in the region agree that psychology in Latin America and the Caribbean has been an active field for almost a century (Ardila, 1982; Salazar, 1995). Although the first psychology departments were not organized until the 1940s in countries such as Chile, Colombia, and Guatemala, and not until the early 1960s in other places (Salazar, 1995), several countries witnessed some research in experimental psychology well before that, which is reflected in the opening of psychology laboratories in Argentina (in 1891 and 1898), Brazil (in 1899), Chile (in 1908), and Mexico (in 1916; see Ardila, 1982; Sánchez Sosa & Valderrama-Iturbe, 2001). In most countries, the opening of a psychology laboratory was followed by an institute of psychology, which then originated a psychology department with training goals (Ardila, 1982). Psychological training in most countries includes approximately five years of professional training in all areas of psychology, including theoretical as well as practical training. This program usually bestows the professional title of "psychologist" or the academic degree of "licentiate in psychology," both allowing the graduate to practice in any area of psychology. At the present time most countries in the region have training programs in psychology; however, few of these countries are consistent generators of psychological research. The disparity between the development of the profession and the discipline has determined some of the unique features of psychological as well as creativity research in the region, especially its bias toward research with clear practical applications, as we will see later.

Among the factors influencing the development of psychology in Latin America, authors have emphasized the lack of infrastructure, as well as social, economic, and political instability, together with the pressures imposed on the discipline by the constant demands for solutions to practical human problems (Salazar, 1995; Sosa & Valderrama-Iturbe, 2001). The peculiarities of the discipline in the region have also been determined in part by the original psychological currents that gave shape to it, among which Ardila (1982) emphasizes three main sources: psychoanalysis, behaviorism, and "French psychology." Psychoanalysis in particular has had an especially strong impact in several countries in the region. A quick look at Latin American psychological journals will reveal that many are psychoanalytic in orientation, and, consequently, many of the publications on creativity are psychoanalytic explanations of the creative process (de Leon de Bernaedi, 1988; Etienne, 1991; Grinberg de Ekboir, 1989; Honigsztejn, 1996; McDougall, 1995; Weissmann, 1992). Most of these articles are exclusively theoretical, so we do not explore them in more detail. Instead, we devote the rest of this section to reviewing empirical research on creativity conducted in Latin America, trying to show how the aforementioned factors – lack of infrastructure, political instability, and particular human problems – have influenced such research.

SCIENTIFIC PRODUCTIVITY IN LATIN AMERICA AND THE CARIBBEAN

Perhaps one of the most evident characteristics of creativity research in Latin America and the Caribbean is its paucity. A search in regional and international databases with the general descriptor *creativity* in English, Portuguese, or Spanish returns a remarkably small number of studies conducted by Latin American researchers in the region, and a similarly small number of studies conducted by foreign researchers in Latin America and the Caribbean. This paucity follows the tendency of publication in psychology and science in general in the region (da Costa, 1995), and it can be attributed to several factors, among which the most cited is lack of adequate infrastructure for scientific research, from lack of adequate office space to the unavailability of scientific publications to oppressive bureaucracies that considerably reduce researchers' productivity (da Costa, 1995; Salazar, 1995). The dearth of research on creativity is, however, very likely overestimated because of the problems associated with dissemination of scientific research in the region, especially in sources that are accessible across countries, such as academic journals or technical books. Some reviews conducted in specific countries report a much greater number of empirical studies on creativity in each of the countries, but many of them are nonpublished sources such as research reports, master's theses, or doctoral dissertations. Vivas, for example, reports at least six doctoral dissertations and twelve master's theses on creativity conducted in Venezuela, which are unfortunately unavailable outside of that country (Vivas, 1999). In the same vein, Fleith (2002) reports a great number of research studies on creativity conducted in Brazil, and although – atypically for the region – many of them are published in international journals, the majority are published in journals available only in Brazil.

Ardila (1982) argued that part of the reason why scientific research is so scarce in Latin America is related to the fact that science is not a cultural value in the region. We disagree with this notion. Although it may seem a logical conclusion when one is considering the disparity in the attention given to humanities and the arts as compared with the sciences, this disparity may be influenced by a host of other factors that are especially influential on scientific development but less so on the arts and humanities. The development of a tradition of relevant empirical research requires investigators to keep up with current research, which is very difficult when they are working at universities whose libraries only hold subscriptions to a few international journals, and with many gaps in the sequence of issues, gaps that often reflect the economic crises of the country. The fact that the slow development of the sciences in Latin America and the Caribbean is more influenced by economic factors than cultural values is reflected in the rate of investment in research and development in Latin American countries, which has hastened during periods of rapid economic expansion, such as the late 1970s and early 1980s, and slowed during periods of economic crisis (Ayala, 1995; Salazar, 1995). This would not be the case if science were not a cultural value in these countries.

CREATIVITY RESEARCH IN THE SCHOOLS

Of the studies conducted in the field of creativity research in Latin America and the Caribbean, most are clearly applied and aimed at solving practical problems rather than understanding the phenomenon of creativity. This follows a pattern for psychology research in general, which reflects in part the pressure created by the actual problems of the countries (Salazar, 1995). Applied psychological research in the region responds to demands from different fields, such as public health and education, with the latter being most prominent. Most applied psychology research in the region, what Sánchez-Sosa and Valderrama-Iturbe (2001) have called "psychotechnics," has been conducted in relation to educational issues, especially during the first half of the twentieth century. Today, educational applications continue to be among the largest areas of application of psychology (Ardila, 1982), and the educational field is one of the most important sources for employment of trained psychologists. Following this pattern, the majority of empirical studies on creativity in Latin America and the Caribbean are concerned with the design and evaluation of programs aimed at elevating creativity in school students. In Chile, for example, Isidora Mena has conducted a research program for several years on the design and evaluation of a program called *Aprender para Crear* (Learning for Creating) aimed at preparing school teachers for instruction that promotes creative thinking in their students (Mena, 2000; Mena & Vizcarra, 2003). The program is based on three core principles. The first one is the need to create a teacher–student relationship that allows the student to be creative. This part of the intervention focuses on helping teachers apply some principles from humanistic psychology, such as unconditional acceptance of students, authenticity, absence of judgment, and interpretation of mistakes as learning opportunities. The second core principle is the need to provide students with skills, attitudes, and values that allow them to be creative in their schoolwork. Teachers were therefore trained to stimulate abilities such as fluency, divergent thinking, and flexibility, as well as tolerance for ambiguity and independent judgment. The third core principle of the program is the need for meaningful learning. In this part of the intervention, teachers were trained on ways to help their students make connections and develop a deep understanding of the new contents. Mena and her colleagues tested their intervention model in several classrooms of students with different socioeconomic backgrounds, using an in-service teacher-training program lasting five months. Teachers in the program were assisted in the design of a Learning for Creating instructional program that they were to execute in their classrooms during the academic year. Results were measured mostly on the basis of depth of student learning, such as the ability to transfer knowledge to new situations, explain it, and use it to solve problems; better results were evident in the experimental group. This research program was also responsible for the construction and validation of several instruments. Barahona (2003) constructed and validated the CPPC (*Cuestionario de Prácticas Pedagógicas para la Creatividad*, or Creativity-Fostering Instructional Practices Questionnaire), which measures schoolteachers' adherence to the three core principles included in the Learning for Creating program, validated using Soh's Index of Creative Fostering Behavior (Soh, 2000, cited in Barahona, 2003). The program also generated another instrument, the TAC (*Test de Apropiación para la Creatividad*, or Appropriation for Creativity Test), also designed to measure instructional practices that foster creativity. This instrument was validated by comparing its scores to students' perceptions regarding the possibility of meaningful learning and creativity in each teacher's classroom.

Examples of applied research whose major goal is to increase creativity in the classroom are available in other countries as well. In Brazil, researchers Eunice Soriano de Alencar and Denise Souza Fleith have been applying and testing creativity development programs in schools for more than twenty years. Alencar (1974, cited in Fleith, Renzulli, & Westberg, 2002), for example, trained fourth- and fifth-grade Brazilian children with a creativity program aimed at increasing figural and verbal fluency, flexibility, and originality, and she observed significant gains after their training. Alencar et al. (1987), working with fifty-four elementary-school teachers, tested a program designed to increase teachers' ability to stimulate creative thinking in their students. These researchers found that this three-month-long teacher-oriented program increased the students' creative abilities as measured by the Torrance Tests for Creative Thinking.

In Mexico, Julio César Peñagos and Rafael Aluni have developed and tested several computer programs aimed at enhancing creative processes in the educational context (Peñagos, 2000). For example, in one of these studies (Aluni, Barrón & Peñagos, 2000), researchers compared the effects of a program based on a computer game and one based on the induction of brain waves on the intelligence and creativity scores of thirty-seven college students, showing that both kinds of programs showed positive effects on creativity but not on intelligence scores. In another study (Aluni, Vergara, & Peñagos, 2000), the effectiveness of a computer game designed to increase creative thinking was tested in forty children ages nine to eleven, showing that some of the games produced significant increases in originality, whereas none of the program components had any effect on elaboration scores. In Venezuela and Colombia, reports of the evaluation of multiple creative thinking programs in students of different ages have been published since the mid-1980s (Vivas, 1999; González, 1999). In Venezuela in the 1980s, David Vivas implemented a creativity and problem-resolution program based on Louis Raths's ideas, called *Operaciones del Pensamiento para Niños de Primer Grado* (Thinking Operations for First Grade Children); the program was tested in six schools, showing positive results (Vivas, 1999).

Another prominent branch of applied creativity research that also deals with the field of education is the adaptation and standardization of foreign tests, as well as the development of original tests. The emphasis on the development and adaptation of instruments follows in part from the needs of research; such instruments are often created by researchers who need to evaluate the effects of their creativity programs. However, the interest in developing measurement instruments appropriate for the educational context also emerges from the professional role of psychologists in the region, one of whose most important perceived functions is that of providing psychological testing for educational purposes (Sánchez Sosa & Valderrama-Iturbe, 2001). Indeed, educational testing for government or for private schools is one of the main sources of employment for psychologists in many countries in Latin America and the Caribbean.

Two examples of instrument development have already been described (Barahona, 2003; García, 2002). Another example is the validation in a Chilean sample of a Spanish translation of the Berlin Intelligence Test (Rosas, 1996), which includes measures of fluency in the verbal, figural, and numeric domains, and which is a popular measure of creativity in that country today. In Brazil, several different instruments have been developed by Alencar and her colleagues. For example, Alencar developed an instrument to detect individuals' characteristics that inhibit the development of their creativity (Alencar, 1999). The instrument (*Inventário de Barreiras à Criatividade Pessoal*) included sixty-six items regarding four kinds of barriers to creativity: inhibition or shyness (e.g., I would be more creative if I weren't afraid to express my thoughts), lack of time or opportunity (e.g., I would be more creative if I had more time to elaborate my ideas), social repression (e.g., I would be more creative if I had the chance to make mistakes without being called "dumb"), and lack of motivation (e.g., I would be more creative if I were able to concentrate more on what I do). Alencar validated this instrument with a sample of 389 college students, showing good reliability and construct validity, and she has subsequently used the scale in several studies (Alencar, 2002; Alencar & Fleith, 2003). She has also constructed an instrument to detect characteristics of the educational context that stimulate or inhibit the development of creativity (Alencar, 1995, cited in Alencar, 1999), which she has subsequently used in several studies of creative environments in schools, colleges, and graduate programs in Brazil. In one of these studies, conducted with college students, Alencar compared the creativity environment in high- versus low-prestige universities in Brazil, finding that students in high-prestige institutions rated their educational environment as much more creativity- fostering than those attending low-prestige ones, providing hints to help explain the success of some educational institutions and the low performance of others, in terms of whether or not they provide an environment that stimulates creativity (Alencar, 1998).

These examples emphasize the applied nature of most of the creativity research conducted in Latin America. It is important to note that forces that push educational research in general and creativity research in particular toward the solution of practical problems arise from the reality of the countries in the region as well as from their governments. Researchers feel pressured to respond to the obvious needs of developing countries – poverty, education, and health – and this pressure is increased by the allocation of resources on the part of governments to studies with an evident practical benefit. A case in point is the Venezuelan Ministry for the Development of Intelligence: Created in the early 1980s in the midst of the economic boom in Venezuela, this organization invested large sums of money to pursue the goal of infusing Venezuelan education with new ideas about thinking and intelligence, including ideas about the relevance and development of creativity. To this end, the ministry imported educational programs based on the works of psychologists such as De Bono, Sternberg, and Feuerstein (Vivas, 1999) and implemented them in schools across the country. The program *Aprender a Pensar* (Learning to Think), based on De Bono's ideas, was implemented in fourth, fifth and sixth grades in all public schools. Also nationally implemented were the *Proyecto Inteligencia* (Intelligence Project) from Stanford University and Feuerstein's instrumental enrichment program. The large amount of economic resources allocated to the Ministry of Intelligence were thus mainly invested in satisfying the needs of these specific programs – mostly teacher education and elaboration of materials – but not to any significant extent on basic research in creativity. Thus, in the region, even when economic resources are plentiful, it is not basic science that is most likely to benefit, but research applied to the current needs of countries as perceived by the government in charge. Furthermore, the fact that this program was promptly discontinued with the next government helps us understand the way in which political instability contributes to the difficulties in establishing continued lines of research, either basic or applied.

Similar examples, although less extreme, of how psychological research has been shaped by political forces can be found in other countries. For example, many publications on the development of creativity programs for school children in Chile were prompted during the late 1990s by the inclusion, on the part of the Ministry of Education, of creativity and critical thinking as minimum objectives in the national curriculum. Many studies designed and conducted in this context were devoted to finding ways to help schools fulfill these objectives (Solar, Segure, & Domínguez, 1998). In Mexico, the *Ley General de Educación* (General Law of Education) also mentions creativity development as an educational goal, prompting a number of creativity-development experiences in schools, presumably directed at increasing creativity in a specific context at a specific time (Peñagos, 2000), and not at increasing our understanding of the phenomenon. Similarly, Mitjáns (1999) reports that, in Cuba, research on creativity training and development originated in the 1970s when the Ministry of Education explicitly introduced creativity-related objectives into the school and college curricula.

Not only empirical studies but also narrative reviews on creativity conducted in the region are characterized by their applied nature. Most of them focus on models of intervention or guidelines for working on creativity at the school level. For example, in Mexico, Miguel Ángel Casillas (1999) writes a review with the explicit purpose of "stating the challenges faced when developing creativity in the classroom" (p. 7); in the same country, Peñagos (2000) focuses his review on the relevance of creativity for the economic development of countries, especially Latin American countries. However, exceptions do exist: Upon request by the Chilean Ministry of Education, Ricardo López (1993) published a review to inform some aspects of the 1990s educational reform, which nevertheless remained theoretical in its focus, dealing with problems associated with different views on creativity. Another outstanding exception to the norm of narrative reviews dedicated to specific problems is Fleith's (2002) narrative review of the history of creativity research in Brazil, but this is probably attributable to the fact that it was destined for publication as a book chapter in the United States, and on a Web page on cross-cultural views of creativity.

CREATIVITY BEYOND THE SCHOOL

Although applied studies do have potential for contributing to basic scientific knowledge about creativity – when researchers use findings from applied studies to develop new hypotheses about the phenomenon under study, or to generalize previous findings to new populations or contexts – this is seldom the case in the kind of applied studies conducted in Latin America. A review of the purposes and potential applications of the empirical studies on creativity conducted in the region suggests that each study fulfills mostly practical purposes related to national educational goals, or seeks to solve specific problems faced by the participants in the study. For example, some studies may be prompted by educational institutions that contact researchers to help them face some institutional need (see Rivera, n.d.).

However, the potential of the region's applied research to contribute to the comprehension of the creativity phenomenon might be increasing. In the past decade some of these applied studies have allowed researchers to make some potentially valuable contributions to theory as well. Fleith (2002) claims that, beginning in 1990, creativity research in Brazil shifted from a focus on enhancing student creativity toward identifying determinants of creativity in the educational setting, as well as toward the development of instruments to measure creativity and the climate in which to foster it. Alencar and her colleagues, for instance, have conducted several studies aimed at identifying environmental as well as personal determinants of creativity. In a study focused on the workplace, Alencar and Bruno-Faria (1997) interviewed twenty-five workers from different organizations about the characteristics of their work environment that promoted and inhibited creativity. They identified stimulating factors such as colleagues' support and organizational structure, as well as inhibiting factors such as some aspects of organizational culture, boss characteristics, and personal relations. In this study, Alencar and Bruno-Faria also attempted to generalize findings from previous research to the Brazilian population: They emphasized the similarity of their results to results observed in other cultural contexts. Alencar has also studied contextual determinants of creativity in educational contexts. For example, in a study with graduate students, she measured their perceptions of whether their programs fostered creativity or not

(Alencar, 2002). In addition to environmental factors, Alencar has also pursued the study of personal barriers to creativity, investigating the experiences and characteristics that are viewed by schoolteachers and also by college students as the greatest obstacles for their creative thinking and comparing them with those personal barriers found in other cultural contexts (Alencar, 2002a; Alencar & Fleith, 2003). Alencar and Fleith found that their subjects perceived lack of time or opportunity as the most important barrier to their creativity, with shyness and inhibition as the second most important factor, and social repression as the least important barrier. The authors also compared these findings with those observed in other cultural contexts. Their results, according to the authors, are very similar to those found for college students in other countries (Alencar, Martínez, Gravié & Fleith, 2001, cited in Alencar & Fleith, 2003).

Also in Brazil, Solange Wechsler has made some important contributions to the understanding and measurement of creative processes. One noteworthy study is a qualitative investigation into the role of mentors on the development of creativity (Wechsler, 2000). Wechsler interviewed twenty Brazilian writers and poets aged twenty-five to forty-five and asked whether they had had a mentor who they thought significantly contributed to their creative achievements. The most striking result of this study was that interviewees reported unanimously that their mothers had been the most important influence on their creative achievements, and they viewed them as their mentors. This finding contrasts with some American studies that show that most mentors are masculine figures (Halcomb, 1980, cited in Wechsler, 2000). Another difference between this Brazilian sample and American ones is the absence of the teacher as an influential figure in the development of these writers' creativity: Only one poet in the study mentioned a teacher as an important influence, while college professors are frequently cited as mentors by American subjects (Torrance, 1995, cited in Wechsler, 2000). Wechsler has also made important contributions to the measurement of creativity in Brazil (Wechsler, 2003). Focusing on real-life creative achievements, she evaluated the validity of using the Torrance Tests of Creative Thinking to predict social recognition of creative achievements through awards. She found that both the Figural and Verbal tests were able to predict these real-life creative indicators. Another example, also from Brazil, of basic research in creativity is provided by a study conducted by Figueiredo & Sisto (1997), in which they compared the evolution of verbal creativity in 200 Brazilian and 200 American children ages four to thirteen years. The children were asked to produce an original story, expand on it, and, finally, create a title for it. The children's productions were later analyzed for story grammar elements, as well as for the number of ideas produced. The authors observed a similar progression of these features in both samples.

The tendency to go from the strictly applied to more theoretical approaches can also be seen, although to a lesser degree, in other countries of the region. In Argentina, for example, Armesto (2001) investigated the relationship between creativity and self-esteem. In this study, conducted with college students from Mar del Plata, Armesto found that students with higher scores on a self-concept measure also tended to score higher on a creativity measure, specifically, the *Prueba de Producción de Respuestas Originales* (Original Responses Production Test), a test based on some of Guilford's items measuring fluency, flexibility, originality, and elaboration. The test had been previously adapted for Argentineans by the author and her colleagues (Vivas, Urquijo, & Armesto, 1995, cited in Armesto, 2001). In other countries, however, there is little or no research that escapes the field of the strictly applied, especially if one takes into consideration only those studies conducted by Latin American researchers, although scholars from outside the region sometimes seek to replicate their studies in Latin American countries. Basadur, Pringle, and Kirkland (2002), for example, conducted a study in which they evaluated a program for increasing creativity in managers from Peru and Chile. The program tested in this study had already been proven successful in the United states and Japan, and the researchers – none of whom were from Latin America or the Caribbean – were interested in replicating their previous findings in a different cultural setting, given some cultural differences that were expected to affect attitudes toward creative thinking. Indeed, the researchers chose Peru and Chile because managers in these countries had been shown in previous research to exhibit greater collectivism and uncertainty avoidance than their North American and Japanese counterparts (Hofstede, 1983, cited in Basadur et al., 2002), and these cultural values were assumed to influence managers' attitudes toward creative activity. The program had two main goals: increasing preference for active divergence and decreasing the tendency for premature critical evaluation of ideas. In spite of the differences in cultural values already mentioned, the results of the program in Peru and Chile were similar to those in the United States and Japan. The changes in premature critical evaluation were greater than those observed in active divergence. Researchers interpreted this finding as showing that the same basic concepts for training of creative thinking hold for these four cultures, and that the conditions for increasing creative thinking in Peruvian and Chilean managers are similar to those that have been successful in Japan and North America.

All of these studies, although they have evident practical implications, escape the realm of the exclusively applied, either because they seek to generalize findings from other cultural contexts to Latin American samples or because they seek to identify the factors that are relevant in the development of the creative process.

CREATIVITY FROM A LATIN AMERICAN PERSPECTIVE

Is it possible to talk about a uniquely Latin American perspective on either psychology or creativity? Salazar (1995) emphasized that, although Latin American psychology has many shared values with Western psychology, there is also evidence for claiming the emergence of a "Latin American psychology" permeated by the cultural identity of the region. In Salazar's view, this is mostly reflected in the areas of psychology that respond to specific needs and characteristics of the region, such as community psychology, national identity, and cross-cultural research. Cross-cultural psychology has been an active area of research in Latin America and the Caribbean since the early 1950s (Ardila, 1982), likely because the peculiar social and economic conditions in Latin America and the Caribbean have prompted an interest in the region for the study of psychological processes in context (Sánchez Sosa & Valderrama-Iturbe, 2001). We have seen this tendency in creativity research in the region as well. Research of this kind usually starts with a researcher from the United States or Europe contacting a researcher from the region with an interest in comparing some psychological process across cultures. Especially salient in this area are cross-cultural studies on cognitive development, some of which can be considered part of creativity research. One case in point is the research program conducted by Patricia Greenfield (2003) with the Zinacanteco of south-central Mexico. In a series of studies with the Zinacantec Maya in Chiapas, Mexico, Greenfield and her collaborators showed that as the population's main activity evolved from agriculture to commerce, the patterns of weaving evolved from a conservative style toward a more innovative, abstract style, which in turn related to changes in the forms of weaving apprenticeship. As mothers became more involved in commerce, girls learned to weave more independently than in previous times, which opened the door to a trial-and-error style of apprenticeship. In turn, this was related to more skill in representing culturally novel patterns.

As Greenfield and her associates illustrate, psychological research that is informed by culture can be done in the region with promising results. Unfortunately, as we have attempted to clarify, references to culture as a constitutive factor of creative practices are marginal. Quite different is the situation of writers and artists, to whom we turn next.

CREATIVITY IN THE ARTS AND HUMANITIES IN LATIN AMERICA AND THE CARIBBEAN

With a didactic purpose in mind, we proceed to distinguish creative practices as they are affected by European, African, or indigenous influences. However, the reader must be aware that, although these distinctions are informative to understand the general characteristics of the region, creative practices in the region are always nurtured by these multiple cultural sources. As noted herein, what makes Latin America and the Caribbean distinct is the cohabitation of multiple cultures and races that are constantly open to reciprocal influence.

Brazil is a paradigmatic case of this cohabitation and of the kind of creative practices it generates. For instance, novelist Jorge Amado is commonly quoted as providing one of the richest portraits of Brazilian *mestiçagem*[6] and of the city of Salvador, Bahia, as the nucleus of Brazilian identity (Miller, 2004). Similarly illustrative is the *Anthropophagite Manifesto* by Brazilian poet Oswald de Andrade (1928/2004), which, as Frank (2004) noted, proclaims that Brazilian Modernism will cannibalize European art and political forms the same way native peoples cannibalized European explorers. Brazilian mestizaje also finds expression in music. Polemic and multifaceted Rio de Janeiro's Carnival is just one of the most famous. Brazilian contributions include the dissemination of bossa nova in jazz, the Samba Carioca, and a long list of compositions by popular Bahian musicians such as Caetano Veloso and Maria Betania. It is worth noting here that most Brazilian arts have been largely shaped by the country's African heritage, yet African influence on creative productions has not been limited to Brazil. In neighboring Argentina, the African presence was influential enough to plant the seeds of the dance that is today known as the tango. Indeed, not only did tango originate from African dance meetings at poor black clubs in the Rio de la Plata region,

---

[6] Here we use the Portuguese word for mestizaje.

but early composers of tango music, such as Rosendo Mendizabal, were black (Miller, 2004). The Caribbean has multiple examples of creative productions rooted in the African experience. Haiti's 1791 slave revolt, for instance, made Haiti the first country in the Western hemisphere both to abolish slavery and to establish a republic ruled by and for people of African descent. This revolt was later beautifully narrated and fictionalized in Alejo Carpentier's novella *El Reino de Este Mundo* (*The Kingdom of This World*). The Caribbean has also produced a number of rhythms that are deeply informed by African influences, such as rumba in Cuba and cumbia in Colombia.

Creativity contributions in Argentina and most of the Southern cone are strongly connected to an imaginary European referent. Sometimes this connection is more than imaginary. Jorge Luis Borges, Argentina's national writer, was personally influenced by Anglo-Saxon literature and has been particularly influential in the Anglo-Saxon world. Harold Bloom writes, "In Borges we have the anomaly of a Hispanic writer who first read *Don Quixote* in English translation, and whose literary culture, though universal, remained English and North American in its deeper sensibility" (1994, p. 432). Brussels-born yet quintessentially Argentinean narrator Julio Cortazar places half of one of his most famous stories, *Rayuela* (*Hopscotch*), in Paris. Yet *Hopscotch* is written not in standard Spanish but in everyday Argentinean jargon. In neighboring Chile, at the beginning of the twentieth century, Modernist poet Vicente Huidobro predated his peers in Spain in developing an avant-garde tradition in poetry written in Spanish. He also wrote in French while living in Europe. Home to famous surrealist painter Roberto Matta and famed pianist Claudio Arrau, Chile treats them as national artists even though most of their significant work was done in Europe. Psychoanalysis not only dominates Argentinean psychology but also permeates Buenos Aires' everyday life and jargon. Still some other European psychologies have also found followers in Argentina. For instance, Argentinean Emilia Ferreiro, whose work on preschool literacy has had a large impact in and out of Latin America (Ferreiro & Teberovsky, 1979), did his doctoral work under the supervision of Jean Piaget.

European cosmopolitism has found detractors, however. Painter Pedro Figari declared this in 1924: "We have lost our day. Cosmopolitanism has erased what is ours, replacing it with exotic civilizations, and we, blinded by the brilliance of the ancient and glorious culture of the Old World, have come to forget our own tradition" (Figari, 1924/2004, p. 17). In spite of Figari's warning, European influences seemed to have prevailed during a significant part of the twentieth century. A large survey study of Chilean writers published in 1970 found that most Chilean writers placed as their favorite readings works by European authors, with the French in first place (Godoy, 1970). After Latin American literature experienced what was called its boom (Donoso, 1972), the situation might have changed. Still, Godoy's large survey has not been replicated and we are unsure how most Chilean writers would respond if asked about their literary preferences. After all, the language they use is a European one, yet we believe contemporary writers are more aware of their cultural peculiarities. When receiving his Nobel Prize, Mexican writer Octavio Paz talked about this issue, stating clearly how European languages have been creatively transformed by the work of Latin American artists: "The European languages were rooted out from their native soil and their own tradition, and then planted in an unknown and unnamed world: they took root in the new lands and, as they grew within the societies of America, they were transformed"(Paz, 1990, Nobel Lecture, para. 2).

Thus, balancing the cultural pendulum, the core of Latin American creativity has addressed *mestizo* issues. Although its writers endorsed European models, Chile's two Nobel Prize winners in literature, Pablo Neruda and Gabriela Mistral, were not only mestizo but intensively cultivated their mestizo roots. Neruda is an illustrative case, as he evolved from a neutral cosmopolitan attitude toward a specifically Latin American cosmopolitan attitude. Thus, when receiving the Nobel Prize, he asserted: "In the midst of the arena of America's struggles I saw that my human task was none other than to join the extensive forces of the organized masses of the people, to join with life and soul with suffering and hope, because it is only from this great popular stream that the necessary changes can arise for the authors and for the nations." (Neruda, 1971, Nobel Lecture, para. 21). Gabriela Mistral also developed a mestizo literature. Unlike Neruda, she did not have periods marked by different influences. Like Neruda, she was self-affirmative of her mestizo and native roots. For instance, she denounced the translations that Paul Valéry made of her works to French, because he lacked the cultural background to understand her poems properly. In an address to Latin Americans, she asked Latin American teachers not to get drunk with Europe but to teach their students their own cultural roots (Gissi, 2002). When receiving the Nobel Prize she expressed this: "At this moment, by an undeserved stroke of fortune, I am the direct voice of the poets of my race and the indirect voice for the noble Spanish and Portuguese tongues"

(Mistral, 1945, Banquet Speech, para. 3). Mestizo self-affirmation is not only authorial but also part of popular practices. In Northern Chile, a process of mestizaje has proceeded slowly enough to allow the native population to keep a relevant cultural presence and to celebrate mestizo festivities, such as *La Fiesta de la Tirana*. Next to Chile, in Oruro, Bolivia, the population yearly celebrates a famous mestizo carnival, *El Carnaval de Oruro*.

The Central Andes have produced exemplary samples of mestizo art. The work of painters of the Colonial period in what is now Ecuador, Bolivia, and Peru is deeply mestizo and mixes Christian symbols with indigenous ones. A particular epicenter of creativity was in Cusco, where mestizo painting blossomed. One of the most representative painters of the Cusco school is Diego Quispe (1611–1681), whose works can be seen today in numerous Colonial museums in Peru and Bolivia. A mestizo tradition of painting is alive and well in this area, and so today we can mention famous Ecuadorian painter Oswaldo Guayasamin as an illustrious case of mestizo art. Through his paintings, as well as his explicit declarations, he affirmed the common cultural roots of Latin America:

We, who have had a cultural unity for 8000 years from the Rio Bravo to Patagonia, remain divided. We speak the same language, we have the same religion from top to bottom, our aspirations as a continent, our poverty – that whole identity is cut in pieces. For me the first step is to try to reduce the importance of borders and hope that someday they may disappear. (Murphy, 1992/2004, pp. 62–63)

Guayasamin's work is strongly related to the world of Mexican muralists Orozco, Rivera, and Siqueiros, whose influence he recognized. All of these painters asserted their Latin American condition very firmly and closely connected it to everyday politics, as illustrated by the famous dealings of Diego Rivera with magnate Nelson Rockefeller: The former could not finish a mural requested by the latter for the Rockefeller Center in New York because he would not agree to remove an image of Lenin from his work. A counterproposal of Rivera to Rockefeller is illustrative of his political commitments:

I should like, as far as possible, to find an acceptable solution to the problem you raise, and suggest that I could change the sector which shows society people playing bridge and dancing and put in place, in perfect balance with the Lenin portion, a figure, of some great American historical leader, such as Lincoln, who symbolizes the unification of the country and the abolition of slavery. (*New York Times*, 1933/2004, p. 39)

Like Neruda, Rivera, or Guayasamin, most Latin American authors who asserted their mestizo condition have also asserted a politically committed view of their craft. Other Nobel Prize winners come to mind as an example. When receiving the Nobel Prize, Guatemalan writer Miguel Ángel Asturias reviewed all the Latin American literature of his time that dealt with poverty. After doing so, he made this assertion:

We, the Latin American novelists of today, working within the tradition of engagement with our peoples which has enabled our great literature to develop – our poetry of substance – also have to reclaim lands for our dispossessed, mines for our exploited workers, to raise demands in favor of the masses who perish in the plantations, who are scorched by the sun in the banana fields, who turn into human bagasse in the sugar refineries. It is for this reason that – for me – the authentic Latin American novel is the call for all these things, it is the cry that echoes down the centuries and is pronounced in thousands of pages (Asturias, 1962, Nobel Lecture, para. 31).

In summary, poverty is a topic that has marked the nature of a large part of the reflection and contributions of Latin America's premier artists and the way they understand their work. However, the consideration of poverty has not been limited to the arts. In Brazil, still characterized by urban *favelas* and peasants without access to land, poverty has set the tone for social science research, as illustrated by the work on street mathematics developed by Terezinha Nunes (Nunes, Schliemann, & Carraher, 1993) and the pedagogical school of Paulo Freire (Freire, 2000). Poverty is also a main topic of study for Chilean psychologists (Gissi, 1990), and it was one of the main topics addressed by famous Salvadorian psychologist Ignacio Martín-Baró, whose political psychology papers have been highly influential across Latin America (Martín-Baró, Aron, & Corne, 1994). Some of the researchers on poverty emphasize initiatives people take to deal with a pressing context, as in the cases of Nunes and Freire. Others address the paired issues – how the culture of poverty has shaped behavior in a way that is functional to reproducing it (Gissi, 1990). Both lines of work, without addressing creativity directly, deal with issues that are relevant to its study. On one hand, strategies such as those applied by street kids to survive are indeed creative strategies; on the other hand, what psychologists consider typical attributes of a culture of poverty are indeed factors that very much limit people's potential for creativity, such as fatalism, hopelessness, and feelings of inferiority, among others.

CONCLUSIONS

From the previous review, it appears that the Latin American region has made a number of creative contributions to humanity's cultural stores. These contributions bear the mark of the many cultural influences that have shaped Latin America itself, including the indigenous ones and those brought to the region either by colonization, slavery, or immigration. The region's ability to capitalize on these influences to produce original contributions to music, art, and literature seems to have been boosted when Latin American artists have dared to be self-affirmative of their unique background, including not only their mestizo and native roots, but also the particular way in which European influences have crystallized in the region. Unfortunately, as Ardila (1982) pointed out, creative production has not seen an equal growth in the field of the sciences. This dearth is especially true of the social sciences, including psychology, and may be attributable to scientists' exaggerated reliance on foreign scientific models and values, as opposed to artists' and humanists' search for their unique cultural identity, and their ability to integrate it into their creative work. Perhaps Latin American psychology – as well as other sciences – would do well in trying to follow the model set by the arts and humanities in the region, searching for those aspects that would characterize a Latin American psychological science, instead of investing all of its efforts in trying to replicate the models imposed by the countries currently leading the field. As we mentioned earlier, some of Latin America's potential contributions to psychology come from its unique problems: Research on poverty, education, health, and even political issues that are unique to Latin America and the Caribbean can generate interesting lines of research that would be much more difficult to illuminate through studies conducted in other parts of the world. Therefore, the large proportion of the region's psychological and creativity research that is applied to specific problems already constitutes a small step in the direction of giving shape to a uniquely Latin American psychological science with its own valuable contributions to creativity research. However, psychologists in the region need to take this applied research a step further, to a level where it may contribute not only to the solution of practical problems but also to the understanding of the phenomenon of creativity at a theoretical level. This has been already done with other psychological topics in Latin America, as the influential works of Terezinha Nunes on street mathematics and Emilia Ferreiro on preschool literacy illustrate. In the field of creativity, we can observe a trend in this direction in some of the studies from Brazil, especially those that seek to compare some aspects of the creative processes between Brazilians and other cultural groups. We observed this tendency in studies by Wechsler of mentors in Brazilian writers, by Alencar of personal and environmental barriers to creativity, and by Figueiredo and Sistos of the evolution of verbal creativity in children. Some of these studies have already shed light on differences and similarities between the creative process in Latin America and in other countries, especially the United States, showing for example that although some of the conditions that foster and inhibit creativity are the same, their relative importance may not be equivalent.

Another group of studies that contribute to advancing Latin American psychology toward its own identity are those that capitalize on the cultural peculiarities of the region to promote a better understanding of psychological processes in context. However, these studies are scarce or have been conducted mostly by researchers from outside Latin America and the Caribbean, which again may show that scientists in the region are too concerned with either solving specific problems in applied psychology, or, when it comes to basic science, do not yet see the value of their unique cultural perspective. The time may have come for researchers in psychology to acknowledge the value of their own cultural roots, and to integrate them into their science, just as many of Latin America's most renowned men and women in the arts and humanities have done before them.

References

Alencar, E. M. L. S. (1998). Developing creative abilities at the university level. *European Journal for High Ability, 6*, 82–90.

Alencar, E. M. L. S. (1999). Barreiras à criatividade pessoal: Desenvolvimento de um instrumento de medida [Barriers to personal creativity: Development of a measurement instrument]. *Psicologia Escolar e Educacional, 3*, 123–132.

Alencar, E. M. L. S. (2002a). Obstacles to personal creativity among university students. *Gifted Education International, 15*, 133–140.

Alencar, E. M. L. S. (2002b). O estímulo à criatividade em programas de pós-graduação segundo seus estudantes [Incentives to creativity in postgraduate programs according to their students]. *Psicologia: Reflexão e Crítica, 15*, 63–70.

Alencar, E. M. L. S., & Bruno-Faria, M. F. (1997). Characteristics of an organizational environment which stimulate and inhibit creativity. *Journal of Creative Behavior, 31*, 271–281.

Alencar, E. M. L. S., & Fleith, D. S. (2003). Barreiras à criatividade pessoal entre professores de distintos níveis de ensino [Barriers to personal creativity among school teachers]. *Psicologia: Reflexão e Crítica, 16*, 63–69.

Alencar, E. M. L. S., Fleith, D. S., Shimabukuro, L., & Nobre, M. A. (1987). Efeitos de um programa de treinamento de criatividade para professores do ensino de primeiro grau nas habilidades de pensamento criativo do aluno [Effects of a creativity training program for first-grade teachers on their students' creative thinking]. *Interamerican Journal of Psychology, 21*, 56–71.

Aluni, R., Vergara, P., & Peñagos, J. C. (2000). *Programa ThinkFast, como medio para mejorar la ejecución en la prueba de creatividad de Torrance* [ThinkFast program as a medium for improving performance in the Torrance creativity test]. Retrieved October 28, 2004, from http://homepage.mac.com/penagoscorzo/creatividad_2000/creatividad.html

Aluni, R., Barrón, W., & Peñagos, J. C. (2000). *Influencia de la inducción de ritmos electroencefalográficos y videos instructivos en la ejecución de una prueba de creatividad* [Effects of electric brain rhythm induction and instructional videos on creativity performance]. Retrieved October 28, 2004, from http://homepage.mac.com/penagoscorzo/creatividad_2000/creatividad.html

Ardila, R. (1982). Psychology in Latin America today. *Annual Review of Psychology, 33*, 103–122.

Armesto, M. C. (2001). Creatividad y autoconcepto: Un estudios con estudiantes de psicología [Creativity and self-concept: A study with psychology students]. *Revista Interamericana de Psicología, 35*, 79–95.

Asturias, M. A. (1962). *The Latin American novel. Testimony of an epoch*. Retrieved November 11, 2004, from http://nobelprize.org/literature/laureates/1967/asturias-lecture.html

Ayala, F. J. (1995). Science in Latin America. *Science, 267*, 826–827.

Barahona, E. (2004). Estudio de validez del Cuestionario de Prácticas Pedagógicas para la Creatividad [Validity of the Questionnaire of Teaching Practices for Creativity]. *Psykhe, 13*, 157–174.

Basadur, M., Pringle, P., & Kirkland, D. (2002). Crossing cultures: Training effects on the divergent thinking attitudes of Spanish-speaking South American managers. *Creativity Research Journal, 14*, 395–408.

Bloom, H. (1994). *The Western canon: The books and school of the ages*. New York: Harcourt Brace.

Casillas, M. A. (1999). Aspectos importantes de la creatividad para trabajar en el aula [Important aspects of creativity to develop in the classroom]. *Revista Educar, 10*, 7–14.

da Costa, L. N. (1995). Future of science in Latin America. *Science, 267*, 827–828.

de Andrade, O. (2004). Anthropophagite manifesto. In P. Frank (Ed.), *Readings in Latin American modern art* (pp. 24–27). New Haven, CT: Yale University Press. (Original work published 1928)

de Leon de Bernaedi, B. (1988). Interpretation, analytic approach, and creativity. *Revista Uruguaya de Psicoanalisis, 68*, 57–68.

Donoso, J. (1972). *Historia personal del "boom"* [The boom in Spanish American literature: A personal history]. Barcelona: Anagrama.

Ercilla y Zúñiga, A. D. (1993). *La Araucana* [The Araucana]. Madrid: Cátedra.

Etienne, S. M. (1991). At the edge of the abyss: Creativity and psychosis. *Revista de Psicoanalisis, 48,* 1093–1108.

Ferreiro, E., & Teberovsky, A. (1979). *Los sistemas de escritura en el desarrollo del niño* [Writing systems in child development]. Coyoacán, Mexico: Siglo XXI Editores.

Figari, P. (2004). Regional autonomy. In P. Frank (Ed.), *Readings in Latin American modern art* (pp. 17–18). New Haven, CT: Yale University Press. (Original work published 1924)

Figueiredo, E. L., & Sisto, F. F. (1997, November 12–14). *Opening of schemes and the expression of knowledge structures in the construction of novelty: A developmental study of Brazilian and American children.* Paper presented at the annual meeting of the Mid-South Educational Association, Memphis, TN.

Fleith, D. S. (2002). Creativity in the Brazilian culture. In W. J. Lonner, D. L. Dinnel, S. A. Hayes, & D. N. Sattler (Eds.), *Online Readings in Psychology and Culture* (Unit 5, Chapter 3). Retrieved October 15, 2004, from http://www.ac.wwu.edu/~culture/index-cc.htm

Fleith, D. S., Renzulli, J. S., & Westberg, K. L. (2002). Effects of a creativity training program on divergent thinking abilities and self-concept in monolingual and bilingual classrooms. *Creativity Research Journal, 14,* 373–386.

Frank, P. (Ed.). (2004). *Readings in Latin American modern art.* New Haven, CT: Yale University Press.

Freire, P. (2000). *Pedagogy of the oppressed* (30th anniv. ed.). New York: Continuum.

García, M. C. (2002). Estudio de validez del Test de Apropiación para la Creatividad (T.A.C.), dentro del Contexto de una Enseñanza Orientada al Logro de un Aprendizaje en Profundidad para Crear [Validity of the Appropriation for Creativity Test, within the context of the Learning for Creating teaching model]. *Psykhe, 11,* 69–85.

García-Canclini, N. (2001). Hybridity. In N. J. Smelser & P. B. Baltes (Eds.), *International encyclopedia for the social & behavioral sciences* (pp. 7095–7098). Oxford, U.K.: Pergamon Press.

Gissi, J. (1989). *Identidad latinoamericana: Psicología y sociedad* [Latin American identity: Psychology and society]. Santiago: Psicoamérica Ediciones.

Gissi, J. (1990). *Psicoantropología de la pobreza, Oscar Lewis y la realidad chilena* [Psychoanthropology of poverty: Oscar Lewis and the Chilean reality]. Santiago: Psicoamérica Ediciones.

Gissi, J. (2002). *Psicología e identidad Latinoamericana. Sociopsicoanálisis de cinco premios nobel de literatura* [Psychology and Latin American identity: Sociopsychoanalysis of five literature Nobel prizes]. Santiago: Ediciones Universidad Católica de Chile.

Godoy, H. (1970). *El oficio de las letras* [The work of writing]. Santiago: Editorial Universitaria.

González, C. A. (1999). Creatividad en el escenario educativo Colombiano. Pedagogía y currículum [Creativity in the Colombian educational context: Pedagogy and curriculum]. *Educar: Revista de Educación, 10,* 60–65.

Greenfield, P., Maynard, A., & Childs, C. (2003). Historical change, cultural learning, and cognitive representation in Zinacantec Maya children. *Cognitive Development 18,* 455–487.

Grinberg de Ekboir, J. (1989). Creativity and re-elaboration. *Revista de Psicoanalisis, 46*, 255–267.

Honigsztejn, H. (1996). Creativity and power. *Revista de Psicoanalisis, 5*, 77–95.

Lopez, R. (1993) Encuentres y desencuentres en el universo conceptual de la crebtivided [Understandings and misunderstandings in the conceptual universe of creativity] *Psykhe, 2*, 115–122.

Martín-Baró, I., Aron, A., & Corne, S. (1994). *Writings for a liberation psychology.* Cambridge, MA: Harvard University Press.

McDougall, J. (1995). Creativity and its inhibitions. *Revista Chilena de Psicoanalisis, 12*, 29–37.

Mena, I. (2000). Aprender para crear [Learning for creating]. *Psykhe, 9*, 143–153.

Mena, I., & Vizcarra, R. (2003). Evaluación de los Aprendizajes para incentivar la creatividad [Learning assessment that stimulates creativity]. *Boletín de Investigación Educativa de la Facultad de Educación de la P. Universidad Católica de Chile, 18*, 273–283.

Miller, M. G. (2004). *Rise and fall of the cosmic race: The cult of mestizaje in Latin America.* Austin: University of Texas Press.

Mistral, G. (1945). *Banquet speech.* Retrieved November 11, 2004, from http://nobelprize.org/literature/laureates/1945/mistral-speech.html

Mitjáns, A. (1999). Los estudios sobre la creatividad en Cuba: Actualidad y perspectivas [Creativity studies in Cuba: Current status and perspectives]. *Revista Educar, 10*, 53–59.

Morandé, P. (1984). *Cultura y modernización en América Latina* [Culture and modernization in Latin America]. Santiago: Instituto de Sociología, Pontificia Universidad Católica de Chile.

Murphy, F. (2004). An interview with Oswaldo Guayasamin. In P. Frank (Ed.), *Readings in Latin American modern art* (pp. 61–63). New Haven, CT: Yale University Press. (Original work published 1992)

Neruda, P. (1971). *Towards the splendid city.* Retrieved November 11, 2004, from: http://nobelprize.org/literature/laureates/1971/neruda-lecturé.html

Nunes, T., Schliemann, A. D., & Carraher, D. W. (1993). *Street mathematics and school mathematics.* Cambridge, U.K.: Cambridge University Press.

Paz, O. (1950). *El laberinto de la soledad* [The Labyrinth of solitude]. DF, City, Mexico: Cuadernos Americanos.

Paz, O. (1990). *In search of the present.* Retrieved November 11, 2004 from: http://nobelprize.org/literature/lourentes/1990/piz–lecture-e.html

Peñagos, J. C. (2000). *Creatividad. Capital humano para el desarrollo social* [Creativity: Human capital for social development]. Retrieved October 28, 2004, from http://homepage.mac.com/penagoscorzo/creatividad_2000/creatividad.html

Pinheiro, P. S. (2004). *Indians.* Retrieved October 21, 2004, from http://www.mre.gov.br/cdbrasil/itamaraty/web/ingles/polsoc/dirhum/grvulner/indios/index.htm

Rivera, M. (n.d.). *Sistematización del Proyecto de Mejoramiento Educativo: La investigación en el aula y actividades que desarrollen el pensamiento divergente como metodologías para lograr aprendizajes significativos* [Systematization of an Educational Improvement Program: Classroom research and other activities that develop divergent thinking as methods for achieving meaningful learning]. Retrieved November 8, 2004, from http://www.preal.cl/GTEE/pdf/comp1o2.pdf

Rosas, R. (1996). Replicación del Modelo de Estructura de Inteligencia de Berlín [Replication of the Berlin Model of the Structure of Intelligence]. *Psykhe, 5,* 39–56.

Rosas, R., Boetto, C., & Jordán, V. (1999). *Introducción a la psicología de la inteligencia* [Introduction to the psychology of intelligence]. Santiago: Ediciones Universidad Católica de Chile.

Salazar, J. M. (1995). Factors influencing the development of psychology in Latin America. *International Journal of Psychology, 30,* 707–716.

Sánchez Sosa, J. J., & Valderrama-Iturbe, P. (2001). Psychology in Latin America: Historical reflections and perspectives. *International Journal of Psychology, 36,* 384–394.

Solar, M. I., Segure, T., & Domínguez, L. (1998). Los estilos comunicativos y sus efectos en la creatividad de los alumnos: Un aporte a los objetivos fundamentales transversales de la educación básica [Communicative styles and their effects on student creativity]. *Pensamiento Educativo, 22,* 259–273.

Trouillot, N. (2001). Caribbean: Sociocultural aspects. In N. J. Smelser & P. B. Baltes (Eds.), *International encyclopedia for the social & behavioral sciences* (pp. 1484–1488). Oxford, U.K.: Pergamon Press.

Urton, G. (2003). *Quipu: Contar anudando en el imperio Inka* [Quipu: Knotting account in the Inka empire]. Santiago: Museo Chileno de Arte Precolombino & Harvard University.

Vivas, D. (1999). La creatividad en Venezuela [Creativity in Venezuela]. *Revista Educar, 10,* 66–70.

Vygotsky, L. (1978). *Mind in Society.* Cambridge, MA: Harvard University Press.

Wechsler, S. M. (2000). Talent development in Brazil: As viewed by adult writers and poets. *Roeper Review, 22,* 86–88.

Wechsler, S. M. (2003). Assessing Brazilian creativity with Torrance Tests. In M. S. Stein (Org.), *Creativity global correspondents.* (pp. 8–14). New York: Winslow Press.

Weissmann, J. (1992). History and creativity in Freud. *Revista de Psicoanalisis, 2,* 337–344.

Winn, P. (1999). *Americas: The changing face of Latin America and the Caribbean* (updated ed.). Berkeley: University of California Press. (Original work published 1995)

4

History of Creativity in Spain

Cándido Genovard, María Dolores Prieto,
María Rosario Bermejo, and Carmen Ferrándiz

Studies of creativity focusing on education originated in the United States, with the first experimental works dating from the 1950s. Pioneers in the field include Guilford (1950), Osborn (1953), Taylor (1956), Torrance (1962), and Getzels and Jackson (1962). We should also mention the publication in 1883 of Galton's *Inquiries into Human Faculty*, which had already offered ideas on measuring creativity (Taylor & Barron, 1963) and which gave rise to a great deal of research into creativity and imagination during subsequent decades.

During the 1930s, American psychologists and psychometrics experts prepared a series of tests aimed at measuring originality and its relationship with intelligence. Results, however, showed very little correlation. Subsequent research focused on the creative personality. It was not until 1950, however, that scientific research on creativity gained prominence with Guilford's work on the subject and his 1950 presidential address to the American Psychological Association. Guilford defined creativity as the mental abilities implicit in the creative effort. In his famous model on the structure of intelligence, he defined divergent thought as the capacity to generate information from a given idea or other piece of information, in which the emphasis lies in the variety of responses resulting from the original idea, the product of innovation, originality, an unusual synthesis, or perspective. Divergent thinking includes the factors of fluidity, flexibility, originality, and elaboration. Around 1951, Osborn established the Creative Education Foundation, and two years later he published work on applied imagination and a review of creativity. Taylor's (1956) studies and seminars on creativity and its applications were aimed at teaching children to think creatively. His creativity project for schools has continued to operate as a teacher training school of creativity.

Torrance (1962) made great advances in the area of creativity, pursuing three main objectives: (a) analyze different definitions of creativity in order to come up with a more complete classification; (b) design instruments to measure it; and (c) create certain tactics to favor its development. He saw creativity as a process of artistic production and a process of reorganizing the knowledge, skills, and abilities that humans possess (Torrance, 1988). In order to measure this process, he designed the Torrance Test of Creative Thinking (TTCT; Torrance, 1974), one of the most frequently used tests of creativity. The aim of the TTCT is to evaluate individuals in terms of their fluidity, flexibility, originality, and elaboration. Finally, he also designed certain strategies that would encourage creative thinking, strategies that are particularly useful for teachers and involve providing children with materials and other resources that encourage imagination, opening up the mind, and developing different points of view.

Creativity studies in Spain began, for the most part, at the end of the 1960s at the University of Barcelona, under the direction of Nicanor Ancochea and Fernández Huerta. Ancochea oversaw the first study of creativity, a graduate thesis by Martínez Beltrán (1976) on the teaching of creativity. The study offered various definitions of creativity and analyzed the creative process and act, establishing a series of strategies designed to favor creative elements in the school environment. Fernández Huerta (1968) published several academic programs for the development of creativity. For him, creativity is the production of original behavior or models, rules, or objects that are accepted by society in order to resolve certain situations. When a product resolves an important situation, it is called an invention. Work on creativity has continued uninterrupted at the University of Barcelona ever since.

Research into intelligence by Yela and García Hoz at the University of Madrid (1954–1977) demonstrates the difficulties involved in using a scientific and methodological base to study creativity. These authors carried out work in several areas, including the creation by children of arithmetic problems, the development of an ability to interpret fables, mental factors and mechanical skills, intelligence and musical age, the language of color in school, creativity and academic achievement, children's art, and dramatic expression in an educational context.

The 1970s were a productive period for the field of creativity. The Education Act (1970) gave a great boost to study of the subject by setting provisions for creativity in the law, and specifically describing and recommending the use of educational methods and programs aimed at favoring originality, inventiveness, initiative and, in short, creativity. Thus, creativity along with individual responsibility, singularity, communication, and openness became the principles that formed personalized teaching. This period saw the translation of foreign research and articles and books dealing with creativity. Around 1973, Novaes published *Psicología de la Aptitud Creadora* (*The Psychology of Creative Ability*). Poveda (1973) also published a book on *Creatividad y teatro* (*Creativity and Theater*), while Ricardo Marín (1974) wrote *La creatividad en la educación* (*Creativity in Education*). Spanish journals, too, were filled with articles on creativity.

Creativity became a hot subject of study in educational institutions, and this climate formed the backdrop for the First International Symposium on Creativity (1976), presided over by Ricardo Marín. The first European journal on creativity, *Innovación Creadora* (*Creative Innovation*), was published by the Polytechnic University of Valencia. The journal contained accounts of work on creativity by Spanish researchers and by some of the leading figures in the United States. In 1978, the University of Valencia founded its *Instituto de Creatividad e Innovaciones Educativas* (Institute of Creativity and Educational Innovations).

The period between 1980 and 1990 saw a vast increase in the amount of work, research, and publications on creativity. Genovard chaired the First International Congress on the Highly Gifted, at which creativity was a central theme, and was responsible for several works focusing on the study of creativity and its relationship with talent and the highly gifted. De la Torre (1984) published his work *Creatividad Plural* (*Plural Creativity*), in which he brilliantly summarized the various theories, evaluation models, and interventions relating to creativity. Later, in 1989, he published a monograph listing a complete bibliography of works published in the United States, France, and Spain.

Since 1990, research work, postgraduate courses, and teacher training have all been consolidated at Spanish universities. Following this brief preamble, we define the points examined in this work relative to the history of creativity in Spain. First, we analyze the different studies and themes researched at several Spanish universities and institutions (Barcelona, Valencia, Madrid, Santiago de Compostela, and Murcia). Second, we present ideas and models proposed by various experts in the field of creativity. Third, we examine the data that have resulted from research into creativity. Fourth, we list the techniques and instruments used to assess creativity. Finally, we set out certain conclusions.

THE HISTORICAL PERSPECTIVE

Before the 1960s, there were scarcely any publications on creativity in Spain, with the exception of a few translations of French texts. The most productive period for research on creativity was between 1976 and 1980. When the General Education Act was implemented in 1970, it referred directly to the importance of creativity throughout the educational cycle, from preschool through secondary education. It established that a principal element in education would be the use of methods designed to develop spontaneity, creativity, responsibility, initiative, and a critical mind (Marín, 1976).

The First Publications on Creativity

The first publications on creativity appeared in Barcelona, with contributions from a variety of authors. Ruyra (1938) published a book on *l'Educació de la Inventiva (Teaching Inventiveness)*, Fontcuberta (1963) focused on a study of creative personality, and Rof Carballo (1964) tackled the issue of medicine and creative activity. Huerta (1968) took several approaches to creativity based on American models. For Huerta, creativity was linked with mental maturity and the quality of the result. According to him, creative thinking was characterized by the following elements: openness to new experiences, intellectual curiosity, sensitivity to problems, mental fluidity, flexibility, originality, and ambivalence or tolerance of the ambiguous, the equivocal, and the humoristic. Huerta's work on the teaching of creativity was continued by Martínez Beltrán (1976); Beltrán worked on measuring creativity, which is discussed in the section of this chapter dealing with evaluation. Martorell (1968), inspired by Guilford, looked for possible relationships between convergent and divergent factors. He concluded that (a) the subjects who obtain the best results in divergent thinking tests are not those who excel in convergent-type tests, and vice versa; and (b) students who show convergent thinking receive higher marks from teachers, obtaining better academic grades than divergent thinkers. These results, in Martorell's opinion, should make one reflect on the teachers themselves.

However, it is De la Torre at the University of Barcelona who has arguably made the most contributions to the field of creativity in Spain. These contributions include the following.

De la Torre systematizes and conceptualizes the issue of creativity, placing it in an integrated and pluralist context. He writes that the vast body of work on creativity since the beginning of the twentieth century represents a strenuous and commendable effort, given the complexity of a subject in which the differences are much greater than the similarities. He sets out four main topics in the study of creativity: the characteristics of the creative individual, the processes implicit in creative procedures, the medium or method of encouragement, and the product or result of the creative process (De la Torre, 1982, 1984, 1989, 1996).

He defines the concept. De la Torre argues that the meaning of the term *creativity* has gradually changed over the years, moving from the analytical and factorial toward the more holistic and comprehensive. As a result, the differences in the way creativity manifests itself should be sought in the interaction between the personal aptitudes of the individual and a socially organized and culturally enriched medium. For him, creativity is the capacity and willingness to generate new ideas and communicate them. Emotional tension is a key concept in the creative process.

De la Torre offers a didactic view of creativity. To this end, he has designed various strategies and tactics for use in teaching in a classroom environment. According to De la Torre, creativity should be regarded as part of the school curriculum and as an educational objective.

He assesses creativity. Assessment is a continuous process and the aim of any academic curriculum. De la Torre has developed various tests to evaluate creativity, which we discuss in the section dealing with methods of evaluation.

In 1980, Genovard began work on various projects dealing with the importance of creativity as a differentiating characteristic in the highly gifted and talented (Castelló, 1993; Castelló & Batlle, 1998; Genovard, 1985; 1990; Genovard & Castelló, 1990). His current work is focused on a study of the psychobiographical profiles of different talents, in which creativity is configured as a significant aspect of exceptional output (Genovard, 1999, 2000, 2001).

Creativity and Education

It was at the University of Valencia where Marín (1974), a pioneer in the field of creativity in Spain, began a series of scientific studies of creativity focusing on education. In 1972, he published *Principios de la Educación Contemporánea* (*Principles of Contemporary Education*), the first chapter of which dealt with creativity. In 1976, he planned and chaired the First International Congress on Creativity. Among its various conclusions, the congress pointed to the need to create a journal of creativity. This journal, *Innovación Creadora (Creative Innovation)*, was the first of its kind in Europe, and it provided a vehicle for the dissemination of different kinds of scientific work being done in Spain. For Marín, creativity was any form of spontaneous behavior that included a personal emphasis that was not merely repetitive – everything that could simply be classified as original (Marín, 1980; 1995a). His studies focused on the definition of creativity, the establishment of indicators of creativity, and the design of tests to measure it (Marín, 1989).

Marín wanted to establish indicators for creativity, and by trawling through the history of creativity he attempted to establish criteria (which had not always found unanimous agreement among psychologists specializing in the field) that could be used to distinguish and understand what creativity was and what it wasn't. He therefore studied the criteria most used by creativity experts such as Guilford, Lowenfeld, and Torrance, concluding, as they did, that the indices of creativity could be defined follows.

1. There is originality, which appears in very small proportions in a given community.
2. There is productivity or fluency, referring to an abundance of resulting products.
3. There is flexibility, which involves creative fertility appearing as a constant, with the mind able to see various points of view, perceiving innumerable possibilities, and being able to select the most valuable path from among a great many divergent possibilities.
4. There is elaboration, a characteristic that requires great mental discipline and great dedication.
5. There is sensitivity in the detection of difficulties, imperfections, faults, and deficiencies.
6. There is the rethinking of a situation or problem.
7. There is the analysis of an object, or the breaking down of a whole into its constituent parts, discovering new meanings and relationships between the individual elements of a single item.
8. There is synthesis, consisting of bringing several elements together in order to create a new whole.
9. There is organization, which demonstrates that the creative mind understands the distance between its original idea and the final

product, meaning that it is always open to subsequent improvements, following the path of constant superior modifications (this is the concept of synthesis expressed by Bloom, who says that it consists of the combining of elements or parts in order to form a complete whole).

10. There is communication, the capacity to shape new products that are easily disseminated in the context in which they are created.
11. There is a degree of inventiveness, which consists of introducing a truly new product that contributes something that is actually of interest.

Regarding diagnosis, Marín states that to identify creative people (to distinguish them from those who do not offer anything new) and define their typical characteristics and behavior, it is necessary to consider the novelty and value of the creative product; the qualities he ascribes to the creative individual are a multiplicity of responses, an indication of novelty, and ingeniousness in response and flexibility.

Like Torrance, Marín (1989) established a set of creative "commandments" aimed at teaching creativity. These can be summarized as follows. First, create something personal, new, and valuable, however modest it may be. Second, don't waste time judging others. Third, avoid stifling pretexts. Fourth, try to be yourself. Fifth, help to encourage a climate of creativity around you. Sixth, recognize and stimulate the expression of the qualities that each individual prefers, and everyone will feel as though they are creating. Seventh, the world is full of possibilities that have not yet been realized. Eighth, enrich yourself by enriching what is around you. Ninth, the authenticity of life is achieved in moments of creation, never through passivity, complaint, or destruction. Tenth, renew yourself every day and break your routines.

Creativity as a Particular Way of Structuring Cognitive Functions

Although the early work completed at Madrid's Complutense University (between 1954 and 1977) concentrated on intelligence and certain aspects of creativity, it was around 1979 that Sampascual presented his doctoral thesis on creativity and the experimental approaches of the time. He later published the results in two different works. In one, while not denying the validity and usefulness of differentialist studies (which conclude that creativity is a gift), he argued that creativity is a particular structuring of the psychological functions required to act in an open system, and which can be modified by training the different functions. This training would only affect the functions in question and not the output of other psychological functions. According to this experimental approach, the same psychological functions and processes exist in all individuals; although they may act in different ways, the same processes that act on the production of convergent thinking also act on divergent thinking. The difference lies in the results achieved by one type of thinking or another. What distinguishes the creative thinker from the noncreative thinker when tackling the solution to a problem is merely the difference between their products: an original, valuable and nonconventional solution (Sampascual, 1982a).

To prove his hypothesis regarding the perception of creativity, Sampascual (1982b) carried out an experimental study in which he created two small samples (forty-four subjects between the ages of ten and twelve) comprising individuals with both higher and lower IQs. The instruments used were two IQ tests (Thurstone's Primary Mental Abilities (PMA) and Raven's Progressive Matrices Test), Benton's Visual Retention Test, the TTCT, and the first part of Guildford's series. From the data obtained, Sampascual concluded that (a) it is possible to view creativity not as a gift but as a special structuring of psychological functions; (b) it is possible to give specialized and specific training by properly exercising the different psychological functions instead of using nonspecific training in tasks that are called creative and refer to a specific skill; (c) this training has a precise effect on creativity and not on the output from other intellectual functions, such as general intelligence, or specific abilities, such as spatial skills, reasoning, verbal fluency, perception as a skill, and reproductive memory, as can be confirmed from the experimental study; and (d) this functional analysis allows the determination of the specific functions in which those diagnosed as creative should be trained, as well as the establishment, in a specialized and specific way, of work that should be carried out by different subjects in order to gain improved results regarding creativity.

Around 1980, Menchén began training at the Creative Education Foundation in Buffalo (California). In addition, his intellectual contact with various experts, including Torrance, Gowan and Parnes, led him to pursue several research projects. One of his main contributions to the field of creativity is his IOE (imagination, originality, expression) model, which involves developing intelligence with both convergent and divergent thinking (Menchén, 1984, 2002). This model is aimed at encouraging awareness of certain abilities and skills that belong to the hidden curriculum. The model seeks to encourage creativity as a way of improving quality of life: To achieve this, it works on the stimulation of association, intuition, fantasy, independence, curiosity, spontaneity, sensitivity, perception, and observation (Menchén, 1982, 1984). The IOE model led Menchén to develop a curriculum aimed at introducing creativity into the classroom by using different academic disciplines (math, languages, social sciences, natural sciences, etc.). Menchén's idea, like those of Williams and Torrance, consisted of offering the teacher a series of tools that could be introduced as part of the curriculum, and thus encourage divergent thinking (Menchén, 1991, 2002).

Creativity and Teacher Training

At the University of Santiago de Compostela, the study of creativity has mainly been led by De Prado, who has spent more than twenty years studying the subject of teacher training in creativity. He is a multifaceted author who is particularly skilled in the arts, communication, organization, and improvisation, with a broad range of interests. His contribution to the subject of creativity can be summarized under the following headings.

The first is creativity as an innovative strategy in teacher training. De Prado uses different models in order to train teachers to develop creativity in an academic context. The second is the stimulation of creativity through the development of techniques such as imaginative relaxation (IR) and brainstorming. The third is the use of creativity as a strategy for educational orientation. De Prado has incorporated several counseling models aimed at advising students in their career choices. The fourth is the search for an overall form of applied creativity. Special mention should be made of the program designed to stimulate creativity, his model for creativity in highly gifted children, and his teacher training program, all of which ensure training that is both practical and effective (De Prado, 1987, 1991a).

In Galicia, Cajide is carrying out research on student creativity and sociogeographic environment. This work has been described in the journal *Innovación Creadora* (Cajide 1981), and it is aimed at establishing whether children from urban environments show higher levels of creativity than those living in rural areas. A sample of 100 students was examined, 50 boys and 50 girls, all aged fourteen, and three creativity tests were applied: (a) the Creative Self-Assessment Inventory

(*Inventario de Autoevaluación Creativa*, or *IAC*), aimed at assessing perseverance, independence, curiosity, and flexibility; (b) the Creative Assessment Scale (*Escala de Evaluación de Creatividad*, or *EEC*), in which the teacher assesses the same four qualities; and (c) a series of inventive tasks that require original and nonconventional solutions (Cajide, 1995). Factors such as perseverance, independence, curiosity, and flexibility were studied in children from the city, small towns, and villages (rural areas). Results showed that the differences between children in urban environments and those who live in a village (rural) environment are significant in favoring urban children. Differences between the sexes can be explained more on the basis of where children live than on the basis of sex itself. No differences were observed between boys and girls living in the same place, whereas differences were observed when children live in different environments. Cajide concluded that creativity is not a phenomenon that can be explained solely by intelligence, as some have suggested, but that it depends on individuals and the surroundings in which they live. As a result, students who show a high level of intelligence combined with both effort and perseverance, but who lack material resources, may find many potential paths closed to them.

Creativity as a Differentiating Characteristic in Exceptional Behavior

At the University of Murcia, Alonso (1983, 2000) and Corbalán (1990a, 1990b) have attempted an overall theoretical approach to creativity from the angle of cognitive differential psychology, as opposed to the classical view of creativity as behavior that corresponds more to the final stages of information processing. From this point of view, they suggest an interpretation of creativity as a cognitive style, that is, an individual way of taking a cognitive approach to identifying and solving the problems inherent in one's environment. Empirical research confirms these suppositions, and individual differences are found that can be attributed to creativity in processes relating to attentiveness, memory, representation, cognitive images and metaphors; in ways of using cognitive diagrams; and in certain indicators relating to functional distribution and levels of attentiveness to the process. As a fundamental differentiator of the cognitive approach, creativity suggests the raising of questions, an elementary method of generating cognitive ideas from preexisting ones (Martínez Zaragoza, 2001).

Around 1990, Prieto began a series of studies of creativity and the highly gifted. The objectives can be summed up as follows. The first was to study the way highly gifted individuals deal with the insight processes suggested by Sternberg (selective encoding, selective comparison, and selective combination). For Prieto, the mechanisms that define insight are superior in highly gifted individuals in comparison with their colleagues. Bermejo (1995) arrived at similar conclusions when he found significant differences in the three processes that favored students with high skill levels. We analyze the data from this research at a later stage.

Prieto's second objective was to analyze the different components from which creativity is formed (fluidity, flexibility, originality, and elaboration) and the characteristics that relate to high levels of giftedness and creative talent. To measure these components, he used the TTCT. He used the Group Inventory for Finding Creative Talent (GIFT) Creativity Questionnaire to assess creative talent. We analyze the data from these studies in the section dealing with recent research (Bermejo et al., 2003; López, 2001; Prieto, López, & Ferrándiz, 2003).

DEFINITIONS AND MODELS OF CREATIVITY

Our aim in this section is to discuss various definitions and models designed to understand and encourage creativity.

Creativity as a Process of Transformation

Aznar (1974) believes that creativity is the ability to come up with new solutions without following a logical process, because the most important characteristic of creativity is the capacity to resolve problems by skirting them, or distancing oneself from the problem for a moment to tackle it from a different angle. According to Aznar, the creative process follows these steps: Abandon the problem, look for stimuli, and link these stimuli with the problem. To favor these processes, he designed various models. One, known as the *proceso rodeo creativo* (creative skirting process), consists of understanding that the most important characteristic of human thinking is the capacity to resolve problems by distancing oneself from the problem temporarily – to tackle it from a different angle.

The second model was a random words test, a technique inspired by the enforced associations of Whiting (1958); the test consists of provoking a hiatus from the problem by using a list of words that is evoked, jumbled, or suggested at random. This activity should lead to a stimulus word that relates to the problem.

The third model is a variation of brainstorming known as angles of attack or points of view, and it consists of analyzing the problem from very different perspectives. If nothing results, it is useful to change the approach again, "breaking up" the problem into its constituent parts: concept, individual elements, functions, context, end users, and so on. Aznar proposed five forms of attack – more, less, invert, delete, and modify the relationship.

Creativity as Innovation

Marín (1980) defines creativity as an innovative process that requires coming up with something that didn't exist before, breaking the routine, being unexpected. It is original, a novel contribution, something that is previously unknown or that arises in a way that is unexpected and unforeseeable. The product that results from this innovation is valuable and serves to help society progress. He suggests various techniques to facilitate this in the classroom.

One technique is known as the *art of relating*. The art of relating consists of a group of strategies that allow for the strengthening of the originality of ideas by seeking similarity, contrast, and proximity between different things in remote environments. Unexpected or unusual relationships, such as humor and irony, are examples of Marín's creative relationship types (1980). It is a question of locating and discovering the links between things that, at first glance, appear disparate or hidden. Relationships that are logical and usual, the result of convergent thinking, are of no interest. Only the creative, the unusual, and the unfamiliar are of interest, and they must be pluralistic as well as innovative. This capacity for relation is what Sternberg (1985) calls insight components (selective encoding, combination, and comparison), manifested in different and superior ways in highly gifted students (Bermejo, 1995).

Another technique is known as the *art of questioning*. As indicated by Socrates, Aristotle, and Plato, the use of the creative power of questioning broadens the mind and takes one beyond individual pieces of information. By asking questions, individuals can combine disparate ideas that escape those around them. This dialectical method allows an individual to make integrated syntheses, aware that to synthesize is to escape from mutilated visions of reality in order to reach higher goals (Marín, 1991c).

Creative synthesis is yet another technique. Bringing together fragmented elements offers innovative combinations. Giving a title to a particular text is a good example of creative stimulation by synthesis. Developing a capacity for synthesis is the same as strengthening one's ability to combine disparate materials or pieces of information in order to reach a superior whole. Scientists, poets, and painters all offer us personal syntheses of the way they interpret, perceive, or discover reality (Marín, 1991b).

Creativity in Human Processes that Include Person, Process, and Product

De la Torre (1991a, 1991b) believes that creativity is the capacity and willingness to generate and communicate new ideas. The creative process includes different phases: (a) sensitivity to the problem; (b) acclimatization, the creation of an environment of trust and spontaneity in order to express oneself; (c) stimulation, using resources and strategies to succeed in creating new and personal ideas; (d) assessment, the evaluation and recognition of contributions made; and (e) orientation, correcting what doesn't work and returning to the use of patterns in order to come up with ideas that are original, suitable, and varied. He defines creativity as an intrinsically human phenomenon, based on four fundamental keystones: person, process, promotion, and product (De la Torre, 1984, 1989). He suggests various models for encouraging creativity.

One technique involves the use of ideograms. An ideogram is an analytical synthesis technique that structures and transforms verbal codes into ideographic ones. It requires a graphic representation of the relevant ideas in a text or work, and it is highly useful as a study technique that at the same time encourages creative skills. Practice strengthens a student's aptitude for analytic synthesis, structuring, and creative transformation. It promotes invention and original expression and can be applied at all academic levels and in any communicative environment (De la Torre, 1982).

Another technique uses a series of "whys." One of De Bono's techniques (1974), it consists of raising questions that allow us to review certain assumptions that we simply accept. It compels us to reassess our opinions and accepted hypotheses. The best example of the series of "whys" is found in children, who tirelessly ask "why" about everything that catches their attention. One criterion to bear in mind when responding to questions is to avoid answering "because," which precludes other alternatives (De la Torre, 1982).

The design technique consists of drawing a diagram of a project or task, either in school or another environment. In today's world, every product goes through a design stage. The clothes we wear, the objects we use – all of them have been subjected to a process of design and selection, which includes the rejection of other proposals. The design process allows us to outline the possible forms and functions inherent in an idea. The resolution of a problem or the creation of a composition must pass through a design stage or a solution-development plan. With the use of this technique, drafts (so commonly used in writing) will have improved communicative quality (De la Torre, 1987). This technique for improving a design is used in the Harvard intelligence project.

The sociocognitive model involves explaining the phenomenon of creativity through the interaction of individuals with their social and human environments. According to this model, differences in creative potential are due to certain preexisting conditions (interaction between personal and motivational skills and the surrounding human environment) and accompanying factors such as situation and creative processes. These interactions offer results that are more or less creative, depending on command of the communication system used, the degree of transformation achieved, and the extent to which the result corresponds with social values. This model therefore takes into account three levels of analysis: background (person, environment), accompanying factors (situation, process), and consequences (creative product, degree of transformation; see De la Torre, 1991a).

The tree structure technique is the preferred method for teaching written composition, and it is aimed at teaching students to plan their expression in accordance with certain rules and structures. It is not really an inventive technique, but rather a communicative one; that is, it is concerned with the way in which results are presented so that they can acquire greater status. Once the theme (trunk) has been chosen, the main sections or blocks of ideas (branches) are identified. The ideas, metaphors, or images (offshoots) that will help give shape to the draft are then noted. Thus a tree has been created. Before a draft is prepared, it is a good idea to leave it to rest a while, put down roots, during which time new ideas can arise (De la Torre, 1991b).

Creativity as an Educational Objective

Various authors have designed models aimed at favoring creativity in an educational context. We have already discussed some techniques used by De Prado, who is an expert in the training of teachers as mediators in the creativity process through the use of the curriculum. He designed his Creative Stimulation program for teachers interested in updating their teaching skills and who show a preference for two creative techniques: imaginative relaxation, or IR, and brainstorming.

IR is a technique that brings in fantasy as a learning strategy and a way of experiencing what has been learned. Although it can be applied to all areas of the curriculum, it is of most interest in the social and natural sciences. De Prado attributes a number of effects to the technique, including relaxation, the integrated harmonization of words and images, experiencing the meaning of knowledge, and identification with the phenomena being represented. IR follows several steps: (a) adjustment; (b) relaxation of the muscles; (c) preparation for narration; (d) narration; (e) the return to reality; and (f) didactic applications. IR gives meaning to learning and stimulates creativity (De Prado, 1991b).

Brainstorming is a technique used by Osborn (1953) to facilitate and stimulate creativity. De Prado (1982) uses brainstorming to (a) stimulate and develop the different aspects of creativity (fluency, or the ability to generate multiple ideas; flexibility, or a broad view of category and analysis; and originality, or the ability to produce unique, rare, and unusual ideas); (b) generate new ideas and alternatives to complete a working project; and (c) create a working climate of trust, happiness, and productivity, which favors free expression, group cohesion, and efficiency. De Prado states (1991c) that brainstorming helps facilitate participation among members of a working team, promotes mental flexibility and a wealth and variety of innovative ideas, teaches attitudes of tolerance and respect for all ideas, and encourages the development of vocabulary in the classroom.

INSTRUMENTS FOR MEASURING CREATIVITY

Our purpose in this section is to discuss the different measuring instruments designed and used in Spain to assess creativity.

Martínez Beltrán Creativity Tests

Martínez Beltrán designed two tests to assess divergent thinking. The first consists of several secondary tests: (a) possible uses, which consists of proposing improvements to a particular object; (b) impossible situations, in which five impossible situations are suggested and the participant must generate impossible things that could result from these situations (such as, for example, traveling through the telephone); (c) circle tests, consisting of creating figures by using thirty-two circles; (d) "what are things for?," in which students are invited to create the greatest possible number of responses; and (e) incomplete story tests, in which different endings must be created. These tests are used with high school students (Martínez Beltrán, 1976).

The second set of tests, known as GIFT, which stands for Group Inventory for Finding Creative Talent, consists of thirty-two items grouped into three categories: interest, independence, and imagination. The final score is calculated by adding together the scores from all three. The interest factor measures a student's liking for art, writing, and learning new subjects and hobbies. The independence factor refers to a preference for working alone or without the help of others, and a lack of fear at tackling new tasks. The imagination factor indicates curiosity, sense of humor, and a tendency to generate new ideas (Martínez Beltrán & Rimm, 1985).

Test of Academic Creativity

The test of academic creativity can take one of two forms, I or II, and is used to evaluate the four factors that indicate creativity (fluidity, flexibility, originality, and elaboration) from age six to adulthood. Form I consists of three secondary tests:

1. In the causality–consequence test, children are shown a picture of a family scene and have seven minutes to list the different "whys" and "what fors."
2. In the transformation test, children are shown a photograph of a city district and have to propose improvements by changing, removing, and adding various things.
3. In the invention test, two vignettes are presented, one showing three children and the other showing a child turning toward a married couple. Students are asked to explain what has happened, why, and what will happen next.

Form II also consists of three secondary tests: (a) completing abstract lines to form an object; (b) constructing a drawing from a rectangle; and (c) inventing, in which children describe two inventions that they have come up with and explain what they are for (Fernández Pozar, 1976).

Remote Association Tests

Rivas (1978) designed two cognitive tests aimed at evaluating certain creativity indicators. The *Tests de Asociaciones Raras* (Rare Association Test), inspired by Mednick's Remote Associate Test, is aimed at assessing originality. Students are given eighteen pairs of words and asked to look for a third word that will link them and give meaning to all three as a group. He also designed the *Test de Viñetas* (Vignettes Test) to measure ideational fluency, spontaneous flexibility, and originality. Students are shown two vignettes (such as one might find in a comic book) showing opposing situations, and they must look for a common title that could be used for both.

Verbal and Graphic Tests

Inspired by Torrance's tests and creativity theories, Marín (1995b) designed two tests (one verbal and the other perceptive or graphic) to assess various creativity levels.

The verbal test takes ten minutes. As a stimulus, someone appears and half opens a door, looking at something with interest. Students are asked to voice all the questions that they can think of about what is happening. Levels of productivity, flexibility, and originality are measured on the basis of certain established criteria.

The perceptive or graphic test comprises two models (I and II) that, according to Marín, allow productive ability to be measured more effectively. There are some differences between the two models. In models I, the same figure is repeated in each row (five times), meaning partial use of the Torrance criterion that consists of encouraging the student to offer different responses to the same stimulus, but only using five figures. In model II, all the figures are different. They appear in frames and the majority of the stimuli are unconnected lines. Six criteria are normally used to measure creativity; in order of importance, these are originality, mental flexibility, productivity or fluency, ability to synthesize, elaboration, and sense of humor. Originality is assessed by using a judging system in which there is always an odd number of judges. Flexibility is measured on the basis of the number of different categories offered by the student. Productivity involves assessing the number of responses. In order to evaluate the ability to synthesize, Marín suggests that the integration of different figures into other superior ones should be taken into account. Elaboration is assessed on the basis of the details that students include in their creations, while humor is judged by weighing up the elements that are new, unexpected, relieve tension, and make one laugh.

Test Your Own Creativity

De la Torre (1991a) designed a test called Test Your Own Creativity, which involves completing figures, and it can be applied either collectively or individually, from preschool through high school. Although several different evaluation criteria are used, the first and most important in the use of this test is control of tension at the end. Originality, elaboration, fantasy, connectivity, range, extent, wealth of output, graphic ability, aesthetics, and creative style are also measured. It can be presented as a play activity or as game involving artistic and creative expression, and it comprises twelve open figures that must be completed and that encourage closure (according to one of the Gestalt principles). It is based on the Gestalt theory from which one obtains the factor known as control of tension when figures are closed, though it allows expressive potential and creative communication to be measured at the same time.

RECENT RESEARCH INTO CREATIVITY

This section contains an analysis of the work carried out in relation to creativity over the past ten years in Spain.

Creativity and the Highly Gifted

Since 1990, the team researching "high skill levels" under Prieto has concentrated its efforts on the study of creativity in the highly gifted. One line of research relates to a study of insight processes (selective encoding, comparison, and combination) as a characteristic inherent in the highly gifted, while another focuses on the study of creativity as a differentiating characteristic of precocious, highly gifted, or talented students.

Insight and the Highly Gifted
Bermejo (1997) attempts to study the use of insight processes in highly gifted students and to establish the differences between these students and those with average skill levels. This research entails the use of insight tasks developed by Sternberg and Davidson (1983), consisting of a set of trial tasks aimed at evaluating selective encoding, comparison, and

combination processes. These tasks are characterized by the fact that they involve situations that are different from academic tasks, requiring the implementation of insight processes in order to obtain a solution. Some problems involve selective encoding, others require selective combination processes, and still others require selective comparison. However, the common denominator in these tasks is that they require high levels of insight in order to reach the most ingenious and least conventional solution. The results of this research indicate differences between highly gifted individuals and those with average skill levels. The highly gifted display a greater ability to implement cognitive insight mechanisms, thus allowing them to identify new relationships and find new solutions to problems by using selective encoding, comparison, and combination processes, which are supposedly involved in insight tasks (Sternberg, Bermejo, & Castejón, 1997; Sternberg & Davidson, 1983). In short, this research will allow us to develop procedures to improve both insight and thinking in general.

Creativity as a Differentiating Characteristic Among Students with Advanced Intellectual Abilities

According to some researchers, creativity would seem to be one of the characteristics that differentiates precocious or highly gifted students (Renzulli, 1986; Sternberg & Lubart, 1995). Research has been carried out in order to verify whether creativity combined with intelligence really does allow us to differentiate highly gifted students from those with average abilities. A sample of 232 students aged five to nine was constructed. Highly able pupils were identified by means of an IQ test, a teacher's checklist, a parents' checklist, and peer nomination. The instruments used to measure creativity were the GIFT, already described, and the TTCT, used to measure four divergent thinking abilities: fluidity, flexibility, originality, and elaboration. The TTCT involves two secondary tests: one is figurative, aimed at measuring creativity through drawings, and the other is verbal, measuring creativity through words. In this study, only the secondary test, Thinking Creatively with Pictures, was used. This test comprises three games: "Let's invent a drawing," "Let's finish a drawing," and "Parallel lines" (Torrance, 1974).

The results of analyses of differences in creativity (measured by using the GIFT method) indicate that highly able students tend to be more creative, showing a greater interest in learning, inventing, collecting objects, and creating new things. They also have a wide range of hobbies.

The results of the TCCT reveal the existence of statistically significant differences in all creativity variables, except that of elaboration.
In other words, highly gifted children were found to be superior in
the areas relating to fluency, meaning that they gave more responses to
each stimulus than those of average ability. Their responses were also
more original and unusual, which shows their superiority with respect
to originality. As far as flexibility is concerned, highly gifted students
again showed significant differences, playing with different ideas, models, categories, and meanings when they were presented with the same
stimuli. They were also able to change their strategy in order to complete
a particular task. In regard to elaboration, however, no differences were
observed between highly gifted students and those of average ability.
Perhaps, as Guilford (1950) established, elaboration would seem to be
less related to creativity and more associated with conceptual organization and semantic relationships. In short, we could say that the TTCT
is an appropriate measure of creativity in students at early learning
stages.

Personality and the Creative Process: A Study Carried Out Among Artists

De la Torre (1998) engaged in research aimed at studying creative personality and the creative process in different occupations: artists and
painters, inventors, designers, comic-book creators, and actors. He was
interested in studying differences in personality and the creative process, based on the views of the people who took part in the study. Three
instruments were used: (a) Cattell's 16PF (Personality Factor) questionnaire, to evaluate personality traits; (b) a Likert-type questionnaire on
extrinsic attributes and a questionnaire on intrinsic attributes or self-
qualification, in which participants were asked to reflect on the frequency and intensity of the characteristics attributed to creative people;
and (c) the Creative Process Questionnaire developed by De la Torre,
which consists of eighteen items aimed at evaluating cognitive, emotional, and tension factors. The aim of this questionnaire was to evaluate aspects of the creative process: imagination, intuition, originality,
sensitivity, independence, level of initiative, intelligence, ingeniousness,
preparation, pluralism of ideas, wit, perseverance, and unconventionality. The sample was formed from 100 creators (45 artists and painters, 20
inventors with patented products, 18 designers, 12 comic-book artists,
and 5 actors). Results are as follows.

Profile of the Creative Person

According to data from the 16PF, artists are characterized by their greater sensitivity and imagination, showing a certain self-sufficiency; inventors stand out as a result of both their intelligence and their suspicious nature, being less trusting and less easy to fool; designers are dominant and imaginative, standing out slightly in regard to simplicity and self-sufficiency; actors are dominant with a low level of ego; and entrepreneurs are imaginative but show low levels of integration.

Extrinsic Features

According to data from the questionnaire in relation to extrinsic features, the individuals studied value the following features most in themselves: sensitivity to problems, the abstraction of ideas, imagination, intellectual curiosity, intuition, openness to experience, adaptability to new things, independent thinking, sense of humor, ease of association, the ability to dream, idealism, persistence, and independence.

The Creative Process

The data from the Creative Process Questionnaire indicates that this process occurs as follows. First comes the idea; the participants involved in the study said that, before they settle on an idea, several ideas bounce around, "a thousand ideas dance in their heads," "an idea attacks them," they have premonitions, they are agitated, there is a certain nervousness, and they lose concentration. Then, creative individuals say that a new idea presents itself. They pay close attention to it, though they remain in a nervous state. Finally comes satisfaction, a state of relief, a desire to communicate the idea, relaxed imagination, peace, and tranquility. They feel optimistic and think about the results that the idea might bring.

De la Torre concluded that creativity is in itself a single entity, though its manifestations are many. The personality differences observed among different professional activities (artists, inventors, designers, comic-book artists, and actors) are diverse, though this does not break up creativity as a single concept. As far as the creative process is concerned, there are three points in all the professions: the cognitive, emotional, and tension aspects of any creative act. The author also observes characteristics inherent in creative people, which are as follows: dominance, sensitivity, imagination, self-sufficiency, reservation, adaptation, simplicity, security, and nonchalance about social rules. During the creative process, sentiment, tension, and cognition all interact. Education relating to creativity is a balance between knowledge, affectivity, and action. As a result, teaching a student to think, feel, and make decisions provides the foundation for creativity. Three stages can be identified in the creative process in any professional field – before invention, accompanying invention, and after invention – and these underlie the three elements of cognition, emotion or affection, and tension. Counterintuitively, the earlier stage is of greater importance to the creator than the stage at which invention occurs, and it is, of course, more important than the subsequent stage. De la Torre has stated that he has confirmed that a creator is audacious enough to ignore the similar in order to do something different.

CONCLUSIONS

The study of creativity in Spain began toward the end of the 1960s, and it began to gain importance following the Education Act of 1970, which set out educational principles aimed at encouraging creativity in the classroom (from nursery school through high school). The act stated that the methodology of teaching would be based on the principles of individuality, sociability, activity, and creativity. This meant that the curriculum would include various techniques that would encourage creative thinking, such as debating, brainstorming, the art of inquiry, creative synthesis, and the like.

Spanish universities encouraged research into creativity. Following directives from the United Nations Educational, Scientific and Cultural Organization, universities began a series of projects focusing on promoting creativity and preserving the originality and creative ingenuity of individuals (Faure et al., 1972). The University of Valencia held the First Symposium on Creativity (1976), and teacher training courses began to be developed soon after. The first Spanish journal offering a forum for discussion and debate about work being done in relation to creativity, *Innovación Creadora*, appeared in 1976. Several tests and models aimed at encouraging creativity in the classroom began to appear around this time.

The 1980s were marked by growing interest in discovering and defining the skills and mechanisms implicit in the creative process. It was suggested that the notion of creativity should be established as a form of work that required unusual solutions for particular problems. Work during this decade concentrated on the study of the qualities that define a creative person (cognitive, emotional, and social aspects), the process that leads to an ingenious solution or a brilliant idea, and the product or result of this process, which must be workable.

The Organic Law for the General Organization of the Educational System (*Ley Orgánica de la Ordenación General del Sistema Educativo* or *LOGSE*, 1990) stated that the planning of educational activities would take into account the development of creative abilities and the critical mind. The theme of creativity was taken up once again, and educational science institutes and teacher training colleges became responsible for advancing the creative movement in Spain. Teacher training courses aimed at introducing teachers to the management of educational techniques have been given at many universities, most notably in Barcelona, Valencia, and Santiago de Compostela.

There are currently several studies underway in Spain, including work directed toward studying the qualities of creative individuals, the design of measuring tools, teacher training programs, and the study of creativity as a differentiating characteristic in highly gifted students.

References

Alonso, M. (1983). *Autonomía afectiva y creatividad* [Affective autonomy and creativity]. Madrid: Universidad Complutense.
Alonso, M. (2000). *¿Qué es la creatividad?* [What is creativity?] Madrid: Biblioteca Nueva.
Aznar, G. (1974). *La creatividad en la empresa* [Creativity and business]. Barcelona: Oikos-Tau.
Bermejo, M. R. (1995). *El insight en la solución de problemas: Cómo funciona en las superdotados* [Insight and solving problems: How they function in gifted children]. Doctoral dissertation, University of Murcia, Spain.
Bermejo, M. R. (1997). El insight como variable diferenciadora en el estudio de la superdotación [Insight as a variable in the study of giftedness]. In M. D. Prieto (Coord.), *Evaluación y atención a la diversidad del superdotado* [Assessment and attention to diversity of the gifted] (pp. 79–95). Malaga: Aljibe.
Bermejo, M. R., Gonzalez, E., Ballester, P. et al. (2003). Evaluación de la creatividad [Assessment of creativity]. In M. D. Prieto, O. López, & C. Ferrándiz (Eds.), *La creatividad en el contexto escolar. Estrategias para favorecerla* [Creativity in the school context. Strategies to develop it]. (pp. 45–65). Madrid: Pirámide.
Cajide, J. (1981). Creatividad escolar y medio socio-gráfico: Investigación sobre la población en Galicia [School creativity and socio-graphic: research on Galicia population]. *Innovación Creadora, 12*(13), 9–18.
Cajide, J. (1995). Cuestionarios. Escalas. Listas de valoración [Questionnaires. Scales. Checklists]. In R. Marín (Ed.), *La creatividad: Diagnóstico, evaluación e investigación* [Creativity: Diagnostic, assessment and research] (pp. 135–168). Madrid: UNED.

Castelló, A. (1993). Creatividad. In L. Pérez Sánchez (Dir.). *Diez palabras clave en superdotados* [The key words in giftedness] (pp. 113–136). Navarra: Verbo Divino.

Castelló, A., & Batlle, C. (1998). Aspectos teóricos e instrumentales en la identificación del alumno superdotado y talentoso. Propuesta de un protocolo [Theoretical and instrumental aspects in the identification of gifted and talent children. A Protocol proposal]. *FAISCA, 6,* 26–66.

Corbalán, J. (1990a). *Creatividad y procesos cognitivos* [Creativity and cognitive processes]. Unpublished doctoral dissertation, University of Murcia, Spain.

Corbalán, J. (1990b). Creatividad como estilo cognitivo [Creativity as cognitive style]. *Investigaciones Psicológicas, 11,* 99–120.

De Bono, E. (1974). *El pensamiento lateral* [Lateral thinking]. Barcelona: Programa Ed.

Fernández Huerta, J. (1968). Originalidad y creatividad docente y discente: ¿Cómo desarrollar la originalidad y la inventiva del alumno durante la escolaridad? [Teacher and student originality and creativity: How to develop the student originality and inventiveness during the school period?]. In *Enciclopedia Tiempo y Educación* (vol. 2, pp. 329–343). Madrid: Compañía Bibliográfica Española.

Fernández Pozar, F. (1976). Test de creatividad escolar [Test of school creativity]. *Innovación Creadora, 1,* 40–51.

Fontcuberta, X. (1963). *La personalidad creadora* [The Creative personality]. Barcelona: Elicen.

Galton, F. (1883). *Inquiries into human faculty.* London: Macmillan.

Galton, F. (1869). *Hereditary genius.* New York: Macmillan.

Gardner, H. (1988). Creativity: An interdisciplinary perspective. *Creativity Research Journal, 1,* 8–26.

Gardner, H. (1993). *Creating minds: An anatomy of creativity.* New York: Basic Books.

Genovard, C. (1985). Lo paradójico, lo metafórico y lo excepcional [The paradoxical, the metaphorical and the exceptional]. In J. Mayor (Ed.), *Actividad humana y procesos cognitivos* [Human activity and cognitive processes] (pp. 274–277). Madrid: Alhambra.

Genovard, C. (1990). *Estudio preliminar sobre la identificación del alumno superdotado* [Preliminary study about the identification of gifted students]. Madrid: Fundación Juan March, Serie Universitaria.

Genovard, C. (1999, March 9–11). *La estructura creativa del viaje y sus uso por el talento literario.* [The creative structure of journey and its uses for literary talent]. Conference offered during the course "Respuestas Educativas para los Alumnos Superdotados y Talentosos en el Ámbito Escolar, Familiar y Social," [Educative answer for gifted and talent students in the social, familiar and school context]. Murcia, Spain.

Genovard, C. (2000, March 14–17). *Talento y diversidad musical. Los ejemplos de Satie, Callas y Nuréiev.* [Talent and musical diversity. The examples of Satie, Callas and Nuréiev]. Conference offered during the course "Estrategias de Aprendizaje y Mejora Cognitive," [Learning strategies and cognitive development]. Murcia, Spain.

Genovard, C. (2001, March 12–16). *Conflicto personal y el talento creativo: La mujer en la obra de Hemingway* [Personal conflict and creative talent: the woman in the work of Hemingway]. Conference offered during the course "Intervención Psicopedagógica: Habilidades Sociales y Solución de Conflictos," [Psychopedagogical intervention: Social skills and conflict solving]. Murcia, Spain.

Genovard, C. & Castelló, A. (1990). *El límite superior. Aspectos psicopedagógicos de la excepcionalidad intelectual* [The highest limit. Psychopedagogical aspects of intellectual exceptionality]. Madrid: Pirámide.

Getzels, J. W., & Jackson, P. W. (1962). *Creativity and intelligence: exploration with gifted students.* New York: Wiley.

Guilford, J. P. (1950). Creativity. *American Psychologist, 5,* 444–454.

López, O. (2001). *Evaluación y desarrollo de la creatividad* [Assessment and development of creativity]. Murcia, Span: Universidad de Murcia, Servicio de Publicaciones.

Marín, R. (1972). *Principios de la educación contemporánea* [Principles of contemporary education]. Madrid: Rialp.

Marín, R. (1974). *La creatividad en la educación* [Creativity in education]. Buenos Aires: Kapelusz.

Marín, R. (1975). *Técnicas del pensamiento creativo* [Techniques of creative thinking]. Valencia, ICE: U. Politec.

Marín, R. (1976). La creatividad en la ley general de educación [Creativity in general educational law]. *Innovación Creadora, 1,* 5–56.

Marín, R. (1980). *La creatividad* [Creativity]. Barcelona: CEAC.

Marín, R. (1989). *La formación para la creatividad* [Teacher training for creativity]. Madrid: UNED.

Marín, R. (1991a). Técnicas generales de estimulación creativa [General techniques to foster creativity]. In R. Marín & S. De la Torre (Coords.), *Manual de la Creatividad: Aplicaciones educativas* [Handbook of creativity: educative applications] (pp. 235–326). Barcelona: Vicens Vives.

Marín, R. (1991b). Síntesis creativa [Creative synthesis]. In R. Marín & S. De la Torre (Coords.), *Manual de la Creatividad: Aplicaciones educativas* [Handbook of creativity: educative applications] (pp. 274–277). Barcelona: Vicens Vives.

Marín, R. (1991c). El arte de preguntar [The art of inquiry]. In R. Marín & S. De la Torre (Coords.) *Manual de la Creatividad: Aplicaciones educativas* [Handbook of creativity: educative applications] (pp. 278–282). Barcelona: Vicens Vives.

Marín, R. (1995a). Qué es la creatividad. Historia, definición e indicadores [What is creativity. History, definition and indicators]. In R. Marín & S. De la Torre (Eds.), *Creatividad: Diagnóstico, evaluación e investigación* [Creativity: diagnostic, assessment and research] (pp. 15–53). Madrid: UNED.

Marín, R. (1995b). Tests de creatividad de autores españoles [Creativity tests of Spanish authors]. In R. Marín (Ed.), *La creatividad: Diagnóstico, evaluación e investigación* [Creativity: diagnostic, assessment and research] (pp. 97–132). Madrid: UNED.

Marín, R. (1998). Creatividad su actualidad y su futuro [Current creativity and its future]. In R. De la Calle (Coord.), *En torno a la creatividad. Homenaje al profesor*

Ricardo Marín Ibáñez [Around creativity. Honoring Professor Ricardo Marín Ibáñez] (pp. 15–28). Valencia: Polytechnic University of Valencia.

Martínez Beltrán, J. M. (1976). *Pedagogía de la creatividad* [Pedagogy of creativity]. Madrid: Luis Vives.

Martínez Beltrán, J. M., & Rimm, S. (1985) *Cuestionario de creatividad* [Questionnaire of creativity]. Madrid: San Pío X.

Martínez Zaragoza, F. (2001). *Creatividad, impulsividad, atención y arousal: Del rasgo al proceso* [Creativity, impulsivity, attention and arousal]. Unpublished doctoral dissertation, University of Murcia, Spain.

Martorell Pons, A. (1968). *La creatividad. Un nuevo aspecto de la inteligencia: El pensamiento divergente* [Creativity. A new intelligence aspect: divergent thinking]. Unpublished master's thesis, University of Barcelona, Spain.

Menchén, F. (1982). Estimulación de la creatividad en el aula [Fostering creativity in the classroom]. *Innovación Creadora, 14–15*, 211–223.

Menchén, F. (1984). *La creatividad en E.G.B.* [Creativity in Basic General Education] Madrid: Escuela Española.

Menchén, F. (1991). Un modelo para implantar la creatividad en la clase [A model to implement creativity in the classroom]. In R. Marín & S. De la Torre (Coords.), *Manual de la Creatividad: Aplicaciones educativas* [Handbook of creativity: educative applications]. (pp. 329–355). Barcelona: Vicens Vives.

Menchén, F. (2002). *Descubrir la creatividad* [Discover creativity]. Madrid: Pirámide.

Novaes, H. M. (1973). *Psicología de la aptitud creadora* [The psychology of creative ability]. Buenos Aires: Kapelusz.

Osborn, A. F. (1953), *Applied imagination: Principles and procedures of creative thinking*. New York: Scribner's.

Poveda, D. (1973). *Creatividad y teatro* [Creativity and theater]. Madrid: Narcea.

Prado, D. (1982). *El Torbellino de ideas. Hacia una enseñanza más participativa* [Brainstorming. To much more participative teaching]. Madrid: Cincel.

Prado, D. (1987). *Modelos creativos para el cambio docente* [Creative models for teaching change]. Santiago: CEC.

Prado, D. (1991a). Programa de estimulación creativa en Galicia [Program of creative stimulation in Galicia]. In R. Marín & S. De la Torre (Coords.), *Manual de la Creatividad*: Aplicaciones educativas [Handbook of creativity: educative applications] (pp. 216–225). Barcelona: Vicens Vives.

Prado, D. (1991b). El relax imaginativo [Imaginative relaxation]. In R. Marín & S. De la Torre, (Coords.), *Manual de la Creatividad: Aplicaciones educativas* [Handbook of creativity: educative applications] (pp. 306–320). Barcelona: Vicens Vives.

Prado, D. (1991c). El brainstorming. In R. Marín & S. De la Torre (Coords.), *Manual de la Creatividad: Aplicaciones educativas* [Handbook of creativity: educative applications] (pp. 321–326). Barcelona: Vicens Vives.

Prieto, M. D., O. López, & C. Ferrándiz. (2003). *La creatividad en el contexto escolar. Estrategias para favorecerla* [Creativity in the school context. Strategies to develop it]. Madrid: Pirámide.

Renzulli, J. (1986). *Systems & models for developing programs for the gifted & talented*. Mansfield Center, CT: Creative Learning Press.

Rivas, F. (1978). Estudio psicométrico y dimensional de dos tests cognitivos de creatividad [Psychometric and dimensional study of two creative-cognitive test]. *Innovación Creadora, 7,* 40–56.

Roff Carballo, J. (1964). *Medicina y actividad creadora* [Medicine and creative activity]. Madrid: Revista Occidente.

Ruyra, J. (1938). *L' educació'de la inventiva* [Inventive education] Barcelona: Rosa dels Vents.

Sampascual, G. (1979). *El entrenamiento de la creatividad (un enfoque experimental)* [Creativity training: an experimental focus]. Unpublished doctoral dissertation, Madrid Complutense University, Spain.

Sampascual, G. (1982a). La creatividad: Un enfoque experimentalista, [Creativity: an experimental focus]. *Revista de Psicología General y Aplicada, 37*(3), 437–458.

Sampascual, G. (1982b). El entrenamiento de la creatividad según un enfoque experimentalista [Creativity training: an experimental focus]. *Revista de Psicología General y Aplicada, 37*(4), 609–631.

Sternberg, R. (1985). Implicit theories of intelligence, creativity, and wisdom. *Journal of Personality and Social Psychology, 49,* 607–627.

Sternberg, R. J., Bermejo, M. R., & Castejón, J. L. (1997). Factores intelectuales y personales en la cognición creativa definida por el insight. *Boletín de Psicología, 57,* 41–58.

Sternberg, R. J., & Davidson, J. E. (1983). Insight in the gifted. *Educational Psychologist, 18,* 51–57.

Sternberg, R. J., & Lubart, T. I. (1995). *Defying the crowd: Cultivating creativity in a culture of conformity.* New York: The Free Press.

Taylor, C. W. (1956). *Research conference on the identification of creative scientific talent.* Salt Lake City, Utah: University Utah Press.

Taylor, C. W. & Barron, F. (1963). *Scientific creativity: Its recognition and development.* New York: Wiley.

Torrance, E. P. (1962). *Guiding creative talent.* Englewood Cliffs, NJ: Prentice-Hall.

Torrance, E. P. (1974). *The Torrance Tests of Creative Thinking.* Bensenville, IL: Scholastic Testing Service.

Torrance, E. P. (1988). The nature of creativity as manifest in its testing. In R. J. Sternberg (Ed.), *The nature of creativity* (pp. 43–75). Cambridge, England: Cambridge University Press.

Torre, S., De la. (1981). *Creatividad: ¿Qué es, cómo medirla, cómo potenciarla?* [Creativity: What is, how to measure and how to develop it?] Barcelona: Sertesa.

Torre, S., De la. (1982). Vías integradoras de acercamiento a la creatividad [Integration routes of approximation to the Creativity]. *Innovación Creadora, 14–15,* 91–114.

Torre, S., de la. (1984). *Creatividad plural. Sendas para indagar sus múltiples perspectivas* [Plural creativity. Paths to investigate its multiple perspectivas]. Barcelona: PPU.

Torre, S., De la. (1987). *Educar en la creatividad. Recursos para el medio escolar* [Teaching in creativity. Resources for school context]. Madrid: Narcea.

Torre, S., De la. (1989). *Aproximación bibliográfica a la creatividad* [Biography of creativity]. Barcelona: PPU.

Torre, S., De la. (1991a). *Evaluación de la creatividad* [Assessment of creativity]. Madrid: Escuela Española.

Torre, S., De la. (1991b). Técnica de la arborificación en la composición escrita [Tree tactic in written composition]. In R. Marín & S. De la Torre (Coords.), *Manual de la Creatividad: Aplicaciones educativas* [Handbook of creativity: educative applications] (pp. 392–399). Barcelona: Vicens Vives.

Torre, S., De la. (1996). *Para investigar la creatividad. Thesaurus y bibliografía española* [To research creativity. Thesaurus and Spanish bibliographical]. Barcelona: PPU.

Torre, S., De la. (1998). Persona y proceso creativo [Person and creative process]. In R. de la Calle (Coord.), *En torno a la creatividad. Homenaje al profesor Ricardo Marín Ibáñez* [Around creativity. Honoring Professor Ricardo Marín Ibáñez] (pp. 29–47). Valencia: Universidad Politécnica de Valencia.

Whiting, Ch. S. (1958). *Creative thinking.* New York: Reinhold.

5

Past, Present, and Future Perspectives on Creativity in France and French-Speaking Switzerland

Christophe Mouchiroud and Todd Lubart

A summary of past and present research on creativity in France and *Romande* (French-speaking) Switzerland is proposed in this chapter. This task is difficult, however, because of the cultural diversity of France and Romande Switzerland. Historically, this region has long been a European crossroad for ideas and scientific knowledge. In the field of psychology, only a quick glance at its development reveals the depth and breadth of other cultures' influence, such as the nineteenth-century British empiricist and German experimental approaches, as well as positions of major psychologists such as Freud or James on the nature of the mind. We thus seek to isolate the specific contributions of researchers in France and Romande Switzerland in the understanding of creativity.

We primarily organize our review in a chronological fashion. In the first part, we discuss the writings of early thinkers and researchers, followed by theories exposed at the turn of the nineteenth-century, together with an examination of early empirical contributions. Then, between the two world wars, it seems that studying creativity became less of an issue for psychologists in France and Romande Switzerland, as the field concentrated on more graspable constructs. In the meantime, however, local experiments in the field of education led to the development of various tools and teaching methods that promoted creativity in children. After the Second World War, interest in creativity gained some momentum in France and Romande Switzerland as in many other geographical areas. This was partially due to the diffusion of a series of empirical studies, creativity techniques, and therapies using creativity as medium, many of them inspired by U.S.-based contributions. This second fruitful period for interest in creativity still continues, except for empirical research, which paused for about two decades, as the very few initiators did not find many adherents. It was only recently that this scientific field grew again, when it adopted a differential approach, integrating cognitive, conative, and environmental components in a psychological model for creativity, and when it made links to adjacent disciplines. Finally, in the last section, we draw some perspectives for the future of creativity in this area.

A HISTORY OF RESEARCH ON CREATIVITY

As in other geographical areas, the term *creativity* is a rather novel word, appearing in French (*créativité*) only after World War II; we thus have to turn to other related terms if we wish to depict the development of research on creativity. In the literature, three terms are encountered frequently that closely match the concept: *invention, discovery,* and *imagination.*

Early Speculations

The creativity puzzle can be considered one of the foremost questions raised by scientists. In the eighteenth century, driven by an empiricist perspective, the quite ambitious goal of Diderot and d'Alembert in their *Encyclopaedia* was to classify and expose for the largest possible audience the "whole of human knowledge."[1] This massive piece of work was organized in three sections: Memory, Reason, and Imagination. However, a closer inspection of the taxonomy of Diderot and d'Alembert shows that they positioned the fields of philosophy and psychology within the second section, Reason, whereas they devoted the third section, Imagination, to the Arts such as poetry, music, and painting. The focus of this third section of the encyclopaedia was more on categorizing and describing artistic creativity rather than attempting to explain the origins of human creativity. A new theory, exposed at the beginning of the nineteenth century and popular for decades, offered a rather straightforward account of the origins of mental activities, such as imagination.

---

[1] This encyclopedia included 72,000 articles, written by more than 140 authors; 25,000 copies were sold between 1751 and 1782.

The Rise of Phrenology

Following in part the perspective of Genevan naturalist Charles Bonnet,[2] who recommended studying the brain because it had so much importance on the operations of the soul (Braunstein & Pewzner, 1999), the Austrian physician and anatomist Francis Gall settled in Paris[3] and published between 1810 and 1825 a series of volumes that exposed a materialist theory that was later termed *phrenology* (etymologically, the "science of intelligence"). A first and central aspect of Gall's theory was a belief in the innate nature of human faculties. A second was that faculties could be isolated in specific parts of the brain. Third, Gall declared that there was a direct link between the psychological development of a faculty and the physiological development of the corresponding brain area. Last, as the skull bones were believed to be faithful imprints of the brain, Gall asserted that it was possible to establish a precise topography of each brain area and thus to probe a person's skills and deficiencies through a simple palpation of the skull's shape. This thesis was further "validated" by Gall, as he and his disciples probed the heads of several plaster and bronze busts or sculptures of famous historical figures as well as of living – from gifted to feeble-minded – individuals. Consequently, talents in domains such as music, linguistics or mathematics could be revealed by use of this method.

It is easy today to understand why this method for assessing creative abilities could not lead to much success. However, phrenology was more than a temporary blunder (or wrong turn). Unfortunately for creativity research, it contributed to the refutation of a certain kind of data, namely introspective data, which could have been gathered early on in order to bring additional knowledge to the understanding of the creative process. As we will see next, Comte and his positive philosophy were largely responsible for the dismissal of introspection.

Positivism Versus Introspection

Introspection as a source of psychological knowledge goes back to the founding of most religions and philosophies (see, e.g., Augustine, in Lyons, 1986), and it was still being used as a technique of investigation in nineteenth-century experimental psychology, as exposed in the famous work of German psychologist Wundt. In fact, introspection was considered to be an important branch of psychology since Wolff (1738)

---

[2] Incidentally, Bonnet also coined the word *psychology* in French.
[3] Eventually, Gall became a French citizen.

defined this field.[4] This approach was severely criticized by Comte, who contended that introspecting one's consciousness could lead only to illusory data. Using Cicero's argument that "the eye cannot see itself" (Nicolas, 2002), he pointed to the impossibility for the thinker to divide consciousness in two parts, one that thinks and the other that simultaneously observes the thinking happening. Even though this criticism was addressed by psychologists such as Mill or James, who retorted that introspection did not involve a split in consciousness because thoughts were actually accessed after they had been produced (introspection as retrospection; see Lyons, 1986), Comte's definitive refusal was a serious blow to the introspective method (and thus to psychology) in France, at least until the end of the nineteenth century. According to his philosophical system, introspective psychology should be eradicated and replaced by phrenology, a field devoted to the study of the mind in a static perspective. In addition, science should focus on "social physics" (later called "sociology" by Comte), dedicated to the study of the mind in a dynamic (i.e., interactive) perspective. Sociology was perceived as the central field in sciences because Comte considered individuals first as social beings.

According to Braunstein and Pewzner (1999), the scientific impact of Comte's positivist philosophy in the field of psychology was such that it could partly explain both the delay observed in France regarding the development of experimental psychology as well as the strong orientation toward psychopathology. For our concern, it should not be surprising that many researchers turned their backs on the study of creativity and other related phenomena for decades. It was not until the introduction of British associationist theories that the question of creativity was brought back to the field of psychology.

English Associationism
The associationist approach developed by A. Bain, J.-S. Mill, and H. Spencer had a considerable influence in France, and it allowed the question of creativity to be raised again, after it had been solved quite abruptly in France by Gall's phrenology.

First, associationists were empiricists in that they rejected innate explanations on the origins of abilities proposed by Gall. As a result, external causes could be invoked and sought to explain the origins of

---

[4] This definition of psychology later circulated in the encyclopedia by Diderot and d'Alembert.

creative behavior. Second, as noted earlier, associationist philosophers such as Mill were favorable to the study of inner thoughts, and introspection was considered one fruitful way to isolate the laws that governed the "train of ideas." Among the authors that first exposed the associationist perspective of psychology, Flournoy (Flournoy, 1894/1919) and Claparède (Claparède, 1903) in Switzerland, and Taine (Taine, 1870) and Ribot (Ribot, 1875) in France can be noted.

In France, Ribot contributed significantly to the construction of psychology as a scientific discipline that was independent from philosophy (Braunstein & Pewzner, 1999; Nicolas, 2002). Ribot not only exposed the field to foreign research such as British associationist or German experimental studies, but he also developed his own psychopathological approach to the study of the mind. He contributed to the field of creativity research in the later part of his career, and in 1900 he authored *Essay on Creative Imagination*, a book we present in the following section.

Studies on Creativity at the Turn of the Nineteenth Century

Ribot and several other researchers exposed novel views on the study of ideas in the beginnings of psychology in France and Romande Switzerland. The scientific literature began to develop notably in the beginning of the twentieth century, with Binet and Toulouse in France as well as with Flournoy and Claparède in Switzerland. We turn first to theoretical proposals based on more subjective data. We then concentrate mainly on the theories of the creative process developed by Ribot and Bergson, as well as the introspective reports by mathematicians Poincaré and Hadamard.

Theoretical Proposals

Following Taine's proposal that psychologists and physiologists were best suited to analyze and critique the arts (Carroy, 2000; Huteau, 2003), Sully (1876) called for the development of a science of aesthetics. In a similar vein, dozens of papers were published in the *Revue Philosophique (Philosopical Review)*,[5] drawing psychological portraits of famous (yet often dead) artists, scientists, philosophers, and statesmen, such as Proust, Pascal, Beaudelaire, Saint Simon, or Napoleon (see, e.g., Joly, 1882). The inventive process was also examined. Two works were

---

[5] This journal was founded and directed by Ribot.

published on this issue that led to opposite conclusions. According to Souriau (1881), invention was simply due to chance.[6] The inventive process, he said, was similar to the tip-of-the-tongue phenomenon. Accordingly, it is often when we are occupied with a different matter that the idea – similar to a name, date, or event that we were previously looking for – appears to consciousness. This creativity-as-chance perspective was clearly rejected by Paulhan (1904), who conceived invention as a result of logical thinking. Paulhan stated that the inventive process was unnecessarily complicated by considering the unconscious to be "an essential principle and a kind of cause" (p. 96).[7]

RIBOT'S ESSAY ON CREATIVE IMAGINATION. Ribot's (1900) approach to creative ideas was more complex. Although at first he held associationist positions, his late work was characterized by a growing interest in the role of affect and subconsciousness in psychological processes. Consequently, the implication of both primary and secondary processes was fully acknowledged in his conception of creative imagination. After concluding in a previous volume (Ribot, 1897) – based on 103 interviews of male participants professionally involved in intellectual activities (such as artists, painters, historians, and physicians) – that there was not one single way to produce mental images, Ribot proposed in his essay to investigate the concept of creativity along several dimensions.

A CREATIVITY CONTINUUM. First, creative behaviors should be examined from one end to the other of the small-c to big-C creativity continuum, an idea later expressed by Guilford (Guilford, 1950). Ribot's interest for creativity expressed in everyday life is clear in the following passage[8]:

Every person creates a lot or a little. One can, out of ignorance, invent what has already been invented a thousand times; if it is not a creation for the species, it remains so for the individual. It has been wrongly said that an invention is "a novel and important idea": only novelty is essential, it is the psychological

---

[6] Incidentally, Souriau (1881, pp. 6–7) authored a phrase that later would be often cited in the field of creativity techniques: "pour inventer, il faut penser à côté [to invent, one must think "aside"]."

[7] The actual wording was as follows: "Un principe essentiel et une sorte de cause."

[8] The actual wording was as follows: "Tout homme normal crée peu ou beaucoup.Il peut, dans son ignorance, inventer ce qui l'a été mille fois; si ce n'est plus 'une création pour l'espèce, elle reste telle pour l'individu. On a dit à tort que l'invention est 'une idée nouvelle et importante': la nouveauté seule est essentielle, c'est la marque psychologique... on restreint donc indûment l'invention en ne l'attribuant qu'aux grands inventeurs."

mark...thus invention has been mistakenly restricted to famous inventors. (pp. 129–130)

HOW TO INVESTIGATE CREATIVE IMAGINATION? According to Ribot, the study of creative ideas should be pursued along three paths: intellectual, emotional, and subconscious. Concerning the intellectual dimension, Ribot, along with Claparède (1903), remarked that previous studies have overly emphasized associative processes to the detriment of dissociative processes such as the ability to sort out sensory information, an ability later named *selective encoding*. Conversely, a key associative feature is the ability to form analogies, defined by Ribot as "an imperfect form of similarity." Analogies are produced by two means: first, through personification, as when we assume that objects and beings around us have desires, passions, and motivations similar to ours (invention *ex analogia hominis*); second, through transformation and metamorphosis, from one object to another, with links based on both partial similarities as well as through relations established by means of emotions, whose influence on the creative process is also discussed.

Indeed, Ribot fully acknowledged the importance of affect in the creative process, together with the interplay between intellect and affect. More specifically, he recognized that both positive and negative emotions could influence creative performance. He also developed the idea of emotions as mediators for creative associations, a proposition recently modeled by Lubart and Getz (1997).

The third factor worth investigating is the role of the unconscious. Ribot saw the unconscious as being responsible for the occurrence of mediated associations, themselves sources of creative behaviors. In his view, this unconscious work mainly concerns the part of the process later called the illumination phase (Wallas, 1926). The "reality" of this unconscious work could be demonstrated, according to Ribot, because among other aspects it could be altered experimentally with psychotropic drugs. The role of chance is also discussed, but only with relation to conscious work; in the same vein as the French scientist Pasteur, Ribot wrote that "Luck happens only to those who deserve it."[9]

RIBOT'S TYPOLOGY OF FORMS OF CREATIVE IMAGINATION. An additional value of Ribot's (1990) essay is his attempt to list the various forms of creative behaviors. He first noted that genius appears at

---

[9] The actual wording was as follows: "Le hasard heureux n'arrive qu'à ceux qui le méritent."

different ages, depending on the domain. Musicians are generally more precocious (twelve to thirteen years old) than poets (sixteen years) or scientists (twenty years). Ribot interpreted this variation in terms of the "psychological conditions" necessary for the development of each form of imagination. For example, he argued, the acquisition of musical sounds occurs before speech develops.

The two first forms of imagination in Ribot's typology were artistic: Plastic imagination, based on images and thus on perceptions and sensations more than affects, is opposed to diffuse ("diffluente") imagination, a form that uses images between perceptions and concepts – called *emotional abstracts*. Examples of this form of imagination are impressionists' painting or symbolists' music. Next, Ribot argued for the existence of numerical imagination, supported by the symbolic uses of numerals such as found in religions and myths. He also discussed a fourth type, mystical imagination. Here perceptions and sensations are considered useless and reasoning fallacious, which led Ribot to consider this type as a pure form of diffuse imagination. He presented scientific imagination next. It includes different subtypes, such as geometry, chemistry, or physics, yet all proceed from three basic activities: to observe, to hypothesize, and to verify. Ribot underlined the need for more studies on each of the subtypes.

Sixth, we find practical or mechanical imagination, a form that is conceived as depending in large part on flexibility. Ribot cited an anonymous engineer who proposed four steps in this creative domain, a sequential model that closely matched that of Wallas (1926): problem finding, incubation, birth of the solution, and finalization. Ribot insisted that the last step was not the least but rather the most difficult part, because one needs an unusual degree of perseverance in adjusting every detail of the solution.[10] The seventh form is commercial imagination. Assimilated to a form of war, this type is characterized by intuition and the ability to draw precise hypotheses on the fluctuation of market values. Contrary to previous types, Ribot argued, commercial imagination leads to a protean form of invention, as the initial plan must be

---

[10] Ribot cited French writer Georges Sand, who witnessed the creativity of composer Frederick Chopin: "the creation was spontaneous, miraculous...it came complete, sudden,...passed the crisis, then started the most upsetting work I ever witnessed" ["La creation était spontanée, miraculeuse... qu'elle venait complète, soudaine,... la crise passée, alors commençait le travail le plus navrant auquel j'ai assisté"] (p. 134).

constantly readjusted. The eighth and final type is utopian imagination, which specifically concerns the social and moral domains. According to Ribot, this form of imagination follows from the fact that moral judgment is not innate but socially constructed. Simply stated, morality stems from the inventions of moralists. Examples illustrate this form, as the individuals who in some ancient cultures were forerunners in opposing human sacrifice, or in the personal story of prophets and philosophers like Buddha, who took years of solitary reflection to devise a novel philosophical system and who devoted the rest of their lives to both its practice and transmission.

Ribot was a precursor in acknowledging both the creative nature of every human activity, the interplay between cognition and affect in the creative process, as well as a first approach to the question of the domain specificity of creative behaviors.

BERGSON AND CREATIVITY. Even though Bergson's writings are more often considered as a philosophical work, he offered further psychological reflections on the creativity concept. Between 1901 and 1912, he presented a series of conferences for psychological and philosophical institutions that were later compiled in a volume (Bergson, 1919). As we will see, Bergson's views both echoed and added to Ribot's contribution.

A BROAD DEFINITION OF CREATIVITY. First, Bergson shared with Ribot the idea that creative behaviors were not the prerogative of famous individuals. In fact, Bergson considered invention as the primary marker of humanity, the one that best differentiated humans from other species. Human life was conceived as a life of invention, as a "a creative evolution." Bergson wrote the following[11]:

Human life finds its essential meaning in a creation that can, contrary to those of artists or scientists, be pursued at every moment in every man: the creation of the self by the self, the growth of personality through an effort that draws a lot from a little, something from nothing, and adds continually to the wealth of the world. (p. 24)

In addition to this broad definition of creativity, Bergson was singular in his emphasis on the creative process rather than on the creative product,

---

[11] His words were as follows: "La vie humaine a sa raison d'être dans une création qui peut, à la différence de celle de l'artiste et du savant, se poursuivre à tout moment chez tous les hommes: la création de soi par soi, l'agrandissement de la personnalité par un effort qui tire beaucoup de peu, quelque chose de rien, et ajoute sans cesse à ce qu'il y avait de richesse dans le monde."

far from the usual Western view on creativity (Lubart, 1999). Consider the following passage[12]:

It is the materialization of the poem into words, of the artistic conception into a statue or a painting that demands an effort. The effort is laborious, but it is also precious, even more than the final work, for because of it one has drawn from oneself more than there was, one rises above oneself. (p. 22)

CONSIDERATIONS ON DREAM AND EMOTION. Regarding the unconscious and affective aspects of creativity, in which Bergson (1919), raised the issue of dreams as sources of creativity, which had been a subject of debate since Freud (1895/1986) gave dreams a singular role in his creative process as well as in the creative process in general (dreams were seen as expressions of desires). Clearly, Bergson opposed this idea. True, many artists and scientists have recounted how ideas or solutions were "given" to them through dreams, yet Bergson remained doubtful on the reliability of these recollections. The solution, he argued, could well become conscious during the awakening phase, with the process of remembrance of the dream actually being an active process of imagination. Concerning the British novelist Stevenson's *Chapter on dreams* (Stevenson in Norquay, 1999), in which the author declared that his most original tales were composed or sketched in dreams, Bergson noticed that Stevenson himself admitted in the same volume that, during certain periods of his life, he was barely able to tell whether he was awake or asleep.

Affect is also considered in Bergson's approach to creativity, with a strong emphasis on joy, considered as "a tool given by nature to inform us that our destination has been reached" (p. 23). Designated as the best indicator for creative accomplishment,[13] joy is neither pleasure – for "pleasure is only a trick imagined by nature to get conservation of life from beings" – nor longing for praise – because searching for honors, he argued, is linked to a negative feeling of worthlessness.

MORAL CREATIVITY AS AN ULTIMATE GOAL. Even though Bergson did not methodically list creative domains as Ribot did, he did present various types of creativity. In addition to artistic and scientific creativity, Bergson also considered commercial and industrial creativity, but he

---

[12] Bergson said this: "C'est la réalisation matérielle du poème en mots, de la conception artistique en statue ou tableau, qui demande un effort. L'effort est pénible, mais il est aussi précieux, plus précieux encore que l'oeuvre où il aboutit, parce que, grâce à lui, on a tiré de soi plus qu'il n'y avait, on s'est haussé au-dessus de soi-même."

[13] Later J. Bruner will speak about surprise, which may also be related to joy.

gave the highest rank to moral creativity: " Especially creative is the one whose action, itself intense, is capable of intensifying as well the actions of others, and to ignite, generously, other's generosity" (p. 25).[14]

Even though Bergson opposed positivism on major grounds,[15] this consideration for social life brings him fairly close to some of Comte's writings.

AWAY FROM ASSOCIATIONISM. Bergson and other thinkers in the beginning of the twentieth century were less than satisfied with associationism, which could not fully explain the origins of ideas. For instance, Piéron (1903) criticized the sequential aspect of thoughts he believed was implied in associationist theory. He asked this question[16]:

How can one explain all the cross-roads, the different switches, so to speak, in the conception of a chain of associations? One must complexify and complexify again, bend, soften, multiply the links. Soon we are forced to give up the mechanistic metaphor. (p. 145)

Bergson's idea of the creative process as a dynamic schema was one attempt to go beyond associationism (Sartre, 1948). In problem solving or Gestalt terms, his dynamic schema was conceptualized as the procedure or the architecture that would transport the thinker forward from the initial problem state to the solution state. Invention consists in "converting the schema into an image"(p. 167). However, Bergson saw a contradiction in this view, which focuses mainly on what Ribot (1900) named directed, or unit-to-details invention, as opposed to undirected, details-to-unit invention,[17] a form that occurs when the solution precedes the problem, as it does at times in the scientific domain, for example. Bergson illustrates this second type of discovery with the example of Kepler's finding Mars' elliptical motion and using it later to solve the question of the solar system's planetary motions. Bergson

---

[14] Bergson said this: "Mais créateur par excellence est celui dont l'action, intense elle-même, est capable d'intensifier aussi l'action des autres hommes, et d'allumer, généreuse, des foyers de générosité."

[15] Bergson refuted psycho-physiological parallelism endorsed by Comte and most nineteenth century-French and Swiss psychologists as a sophism: "To accept the *parallelist* postulate, one has to endorse both idealism and realism, two mutually exclusive philosophical standpoints "(Bergson, 1919, p. 191).

[16] Piéron asked this: "Comment expliquer tous ces carrefours, ces aiguillages différents, peut-on dire, dans la conception de l'enchaînement associatif ? Il faut compliquer et compliquer encore, tordre, assouplir, multiplier les chaînes. Bientôt on est forcé de renoncer à pousser plus loin cet effort d'interprétation mécaniste."

[17] Claparède speaks of "end to means" versus "means to an end" invention (Centre International de Synthèse, 1938)

tries to take this type into account, as he formulated a schema evolving in time, modified by the images that had been attracted to it, until sometimes nothing of the initial schema was left in the final image. This dialectical activity may not seem completely satisfying, as in his view the schema was always anterior to the image. Possibly Bergson shared with Claparède (Centre International de Synthèse, 1938) and Hadamard (Hadamard, 1945) the idea that every invention was somehow directed. The example of Kepler could be thus considered as an end-to-means or unit-to-details discovery, with the ellipsis merely being the means to solve Kepler's underlying problem (the planets' motions).

MATHEMATICIANS' METAPHORS OF THE CREATIVE PROCESS: POINCARÉ AND HADAMARD. Before we turn to nomothetic approaches to creativity, we discuss the writings of two mathematicians who introspected about their creative process – Poincaré (Poincaré, 1908, 1921) and Hadamard (Centre International de Synthèse, 1938; Hadamard, 1945).

In his autoanalysis of the creative process, Henri Poincaré used a metaphor borrowed from molecular chemistry. Accordingly, mathematical invention consists of building "useful combinations of mathematical beings" (Poincaré, 1921, p. 51). He explained how these combinations could occur. First, mathematical entities could be represented as Epicure's atoms (*atomes crochus d'Epicure*). When the mind is at rest, these atoms are immobile, as if they were hooked on the walls of a room. No combination seems possible during this period. "On the contrary," Poincare, wrote, "during a period of unconscious work, some of them are detached from the wall and put into motion. They criss-cross the room in which they are locked in, . . . as do gas molecules according to the kinetic theory of gas. Then, their mutual collisions can produce novel combinations" (p. 63). This seemingly random nature of associations in Poincaré's view on the creative process can be related to what will be later considered to be a Darwinian process (Campbell, 1960; Simonton, 1999).

To the question of how novel combinations are selected and brought to consciousness, Poincaré invoked the idea of a "delicate sieve" (1921, p. 62), through which useful combinations will be separated from useless ones. As for verbal creativity, the sieve should be particularly sensitive to the aesthetic beauty and harmony of the mathematical combinations, for only best combinations are able "to move the aesthetic sensitivity of the geometrician" (p. 62). In this process, the "filtered" idea is brought to consciousness and will lead to an invention if it passes the conscious phase of verification. As we see, this molecular metaphor emphasizes the role of unconscious or preconscious processes in the incubation and illumination phases, yet Poincaré also insisted on the conscious preparation phase. To stay within the chemical metaphor, it could be said that the atoms first had to be brought together in the room before unconscious work could put them into motion.

Regarding the sequence of mental activities that leads to mathematical creation, Poincaré's (1908) description of his discovery of Fuschian functions later inspired Wallas' (1926) model of the creative process. The process began with two weeks of conscious work (preparation), during which the mathematician tried to prove that this type of function could not exist. Then, after a sleepless evening caused by drinking coffee, a first step toward a solution was reached. This work was later left aside for a while (incubation), as Poincaré had to take a trip to Normandy. There, as he got onto a bus for further travel, an idea came suddenly to his mind (illumination). Back in Paris he studied the implications of his idea (verification), which took him one move closer to the solution. After two additional sequences also characterized by the four steps of the creative process, Poincaré finalized his mathematical invention.

Later, Hadamard (Centre International de Synthèse, 1938; Hadamard, 1945) also wrote on mathematical invention. Along with Poincaré, he noticed the implication of nonconscious aspects in the creative process, based on his as well as other mathematicians' introspective reports.[18] Breadth of attention, he believed, determined the success of scientific creativity. One of his metaphors for the process was borrowed from hunting: To increase the possibility of "hitting" a fruitful solution among many possible combinations, attention had to be directed or aimed with the right amount of dispersion, as a good cartridge that should spray shots neither too widely – thus giving too much scope to chance – nor too focused – as an excess of logic would surely lead to a conventional solution and miss the truly original solution (Centre International de Synthèse, 1938, p. 93).

Hadamard and Poincaré's accounts differed on some grounds. Regarding the structure of the mathematician's creative profile, Poincaré considered logic and intuition as stable interindividual differences. In contrast, Hadamard believed in the intraindividual interplay of both

---

[18] In line with Galton and James, Hadamard supposed that the mind was able to capture the occurrence of the creative process after the production of a solution (1945, p. 32; see James' concept of retrospection).

factors in creative mathematicians, and he called for further study of this form of variability in mathematical creativity. He formulated three hypotheses on the advantages of intuition (1945, pp. 106–107): first, it allows for a deeper search into the unconscious; second, spreading activation may be greater when one uses intuition as compared with logic; and third, an intuitive mathematician may benefit from auxiliary forms of representations, different from verbal or numerical symbols.

Empirical Approaches to Creativity

Here we survey the first attempts to approach creativity by using empirical methodologies. Early work explored creativity through both systematic case studies, as in Toulouse's thorough examination of writer Emile Zola, in Binet's exploration of the imaginative skills of his two daughters (Binet, 1903), or in Flournoy and Claparède's data based on a standardized questionnaire. Meanwhile, Toulouse and Binet proposed the first measures of imagination-related abilities (Huteau, 2003).

TOULOUSE AND ZOLA'S "CONFESSIONS." In 1896, Toulouse published his psychiatric report of the novelist Emile Zola. Zola was very popular and controversial, and this type of exploratory investigation was novel (Carroy, 2000). Moreover, Zola was involved in the Dreyfus Affair and had to face additional critics because of his political opinions. For this reason, and because of his positivist's confidence in science, he decided to display his goodwill and honesty by complying with an incredibly long (and tedious!) series of measures. Toulouse wished nevertheless to test the hypothesis of a relationship between madness and genius. This relationship had already been extensively discussed and debated (Lombroso, 1889; Moreau de Tours, 1859), but Toulouse wished to explore in more detail what he defined as a dynamic interaction between *nephropathical temperament* and intellectual activities. Nephropathical temperament was described by exaggerated emotionality and a disequilibrium between mental abilities, abilities that were unevenly developed (Huteau, 2003).

To explore this notion, Toulouse administered not only a series of psychological measures but also clinical observations and physiological assessments, including familial history, personal history, anthropometrical[19] measures, and medical measures (circulatory, respiratory, digestive, nutritional, urinary, and dental analyses). In the psychological domain, most assessments focused on elementary processes (i.e., sensory thresholds, reaction time, and memory), and little was devoted to

[19] Francis Galton collaborated on this part of the analysis (Carroy, 2000)

imagination. As a psychiatrist and in line with his working hypothesis, Toulouse may have been more interested in the creative personality than the creative abilities of Zola. For example, Toulouse asked Zola to react to stimuli made of inkblots,[20] or to words with strong emotional content (Carroy, 2000).

The results of this comprehensive checkup were interpreted by Toulouse as partially supporting his hypothesis. Zola was portrayed as a so-called nevropath, having frequent obsessions, impulses, and morbid ideas,[21] but Toulouse was restrained in his conclusions, stating that this emotional unbalance could not in itself explain Zola's exceptional abilities (Toulouse, 1896, p. 279, as cited in Huteau, 2003). Even though several other renowned individuals were solicited (such as Auguste Rodin, Pierre Loti, and Henri Bergson), Toulouse did not pursue this type of investigation. Only in 1910 did Toulouse publish a second study, this one concerning Henri Poincaré, but Toulouse left aside the question of the link between pathology and madness. One of the outcomes of these case studies was to promote the psychological assessments of mental capacities (Huteau, 2003).

FLOURNOY AND CLAPARÈDE'S QUESTIONNAIRE FOR CREATIVE PERSONALITY IN MATHEMATICS. In order to gather additional data on mathematical creativity, Flournoy and Claparède (1902/1912)[22] devised a questionnaire evaluating various factors relevant to the creative process, such as family antecedents and cognitive, affective, and environmental variables. This thirty-item questionnaire was completed anonymously by approximately eighty mathematicians.[23] Responses were not always quantified, but some results can be cited concerning each phase of the creative process. First, half of the sample favored an elementary as opposed to global approach to problems, that is, a focus on parts of the general problem at hand (27 percent said they used a mixed approach). Second, mathematicians were fully aware of the benefits of a period of incubation. More than 90 percent felt that interruptions were necessary

---

[20] This type of task was developed further by Swiss psychiatrist Hermann Rorschach.

[21] Toulouse noted a form of arithmomania (an impulse to count objects without any reason).

[22] A former student of Wundt, Flournoy founded experimental psychology in Romande, Switzerland. His nephew Claparède later took charge of his laboratory. Both psychologists created the School for Educational Sciences, which became the Jean-Jacques Rousseau Institute.

[23] Henri Poincaré was not included in this sample, yet the publication of this study drove him to reflect on his own creative process, which led to the publication of his introspection (Hadamard, 1945).

in the process, and 97 percent declared leisure time as profitable. Among their distractions, physical activities ranked first (79 percent), followed by music (49 percent) and literature (39 percent). Next, the solution seemed in large part to appear swiftly (75 percent reported sudden solutions to problems) and rarely by means of dreams (only three mathematicians reported having found a solution through a dream). Finally, the verification phase was seen as temporally separated from the emergence of the solution, as 60 percent deferred writing up their results.

CREATIVITY IN THE MENTAL TESTS OF BINET AND TOULOUSE. In the realm of the new field of mental testing, Binet (Binet, 1911; Binet & Simon, 1905, 1908) and Toulouse (Toulouse & Piéron, 1911; Toulouse, Vaschide, & Piéron, 1904) each developed aptitude scales. In 1895 (Binet & Henri, 1895), Binet and Henri proposed that higher processes such as memory, judgment, comprehension, and imagination should be the focus of individual psychology, rather than traditional measures of perceptions or sensations, popularized by Galton. Using tasks of variable complexity, Binet was able to rank children's performances with reference to the age at which each task could be solved on average (Lautrey & De Ribaupierre, 2004). This led to the concept of *mental age*. In the realm of imagination-related skills, a task corresponding to the age of ten consisted of inventing a phrase that included three given words (*Paris, fortune*, and *river*). A divergent-thinking task, for age eleven, was to name as many words as possible (the criterion for success was sixty words in three minutes). At age twelve, children had to find rhymes for the word *obedience* (the criterion was to find at least three words).

Toulouse was also interested in assessing creative abilities. His scale included divergent-thinking tasks, such as responses to stimuli such as words or illustrations (Huteau, 2003).

In spite of its novelty and value for pedagogy, and contrary to a widespread belief, Binet's *Metric Scale* had little impact on the identification of children with deficiencies in early-twentieth-century France (Huteau, in press). One has to wait until the end of World War II to see the issue of creativity assessment raised again. As we see next, however, the creativity concept did gain momentum in the field of pedagogy, exemplified in Célestin Freinet's contribution.

Freinet: Developing Creativity in Education

The work of school teacher Célestin Freinet began between the two world wars (Clandfield & Sivell, 1990). As humanity had just faced one of its most brutal conflicts in history, many thinkers underlined the accountability of education to avoid further decline into barbarism. This issue was debated within psychology and education, two fields that were tightly interconnected during this period.[24] Novel methods of education that involved fostering children's creativity were developed. Experimental schools were organized, such as those by Dewey in the United States, Makarenko in the former USSR, Montessori in Italy, Claparède and Ferrière in Switzerland, Decroly in Belgium, and Freinet in France; this organizing was sometimes referred to as "the new school movement" (Maury, 1988). Proponents of this movement had in common approaches such as active learning through inductive reasoning, and a stronger focus on the environment outside school and the life of pupils, as well as learning autonomously through group activities.

Freinet's approach also had certain specificities, however. Like that of other contemporary researchers in education, Freinet's approach revolved around the central question of how to arouse the desire for learning in children. Freinet's response focused on a pragmatic approach. Unlike other contemporary educators, Freinet did not base his novel educational practices on psychology – even though his proposals can be examined within a psychological frame. Freinet mistrusted psychology because he felt that theories based on psychological findings presented the risk of creating fixed and thus inflexible educational practices. His approach was tool based, and it was later referred to as *pedagogical materialism*. One central device was the printing press in classrooms, which Freinet believed was needed as early as the kindergarten level. The potential role of the printing press as an educational tool was foreseen by Rousseau (Emile, cited in Maury, 1988), and Freinet was a precursor in implementing this technique in classrooms. Students used it on a daily basis by printing small essays written collectively on topics brought from the immediate surroundings of the children, such as recent or present, natural, and social events. The implication of real-life events and the possibility for the child to communicate to a large audience, Freinet believed, was the best way to incite children to develop a thirst for composing text, reading, communicating, and ultimately learning.

This method was and still is under criticism, in part because it rejects standard manual-based forms of teaching, which were unable according to Freinet to fit the individuality of each student. For creativity, through active production-based learning, we can see how Freinet's students were given the opportunity to develop creative skills (Meirieu, 2001). In addition, creativity was considered as integral to knowledge acquisition.

[24] See, for instance, the implication of Piaget in education (Xypas, 1997).

Accordingly, creating one's own knowledge must be accessed through inductive reasoning and proceed by means of trial-and-error and experiments.

Furthermore, creativity was considered at the social and moral level in Freinet's pedagogy. Because democracy is represented as a system of perpetual social invention, the best way to prepare children to become actors within this social system is, again, to experience it firsthand. Group activities were practiced within the school, such as collective decision making, together with open criticism, cooperative work, and classroom management (see Clandfield & Sivell, 1990). Thus, citizenship must be acquired through collective constructions of social rules within the class. This view on the social development of children as experienced through creativity echoed, for instance, some of Piaget's early contributions (Piaget, 1932). The Swiss psychologist saw the child's social development as transiting from an "heteronymous position," characterized by a belief that social norms are eternal, immutable, and imposed by external authorities, toward an "autonomous position," according to which the individual and the group define their own rules. This transition, Piaget believed, was facilitated by social play activities, as in the perpetual drive he saw children display for collectively defining and creating new rules for their games.[25] Freinet's view seems quite close, especially if one takes into account his conception of play activities, which should not be distinguished from learning activities (i.e., the concept of work-play).

Freinet's contribution has since found many adherents, and his influence has been and still is significant throughout the world (Clandfield & Sivell, 1990). In France and Romande, Switzerland, some of his proposals have been integrated in official texts and the national educational programs used in school systems (Maury, 1988)

Creativity After World War II: A Guilfordian Aftershock?

Research on the understanding and the development of creativity came back to the foreground after the Second World War, which was due in part to Guilford's (1950) call to psychologists and educators. Creativity techniques such as those exposed by Osborn (1953), Gordon

---

[25] An example was given of a group of eight boys, aged ten to eleven. On their way to play snowballs, they spent more than fifteen minutes on voting for a president of the group, deciding on the rules for this vote, forming two camps, and defining throwing distances, together with the penalties applied in case of deviant behaviors (Piaget, 1932, p. 31).

(1956), and De Bono (1992) were gradually introduced in some organizations, but no experimental research was conducted to assess the validity of these approaches. In this section, we concentrate on empirical work accomplished primarily by Rieben, Piaget, and their collaborators, together with a brief description of the growth of art therapy during this period.

Empirical Findings

In France, some studies were conducted to further validate findings collected in the United States (see Beaudot, 1971). For example, Carlier (1973) examined the nature of flexibility in numerous creative thinking tasks. In the realm of social psychology, Faucheux and Moscovici (1958, 1960) included the dimension of divergent versus convergent thinking in experiments on adult group communication. Their results showed that the cognitive structure of the task (divergent or convergent) could in itself affect a group's communication structure. Intragroup variability was observed. Convergent-thinking tasks lead preferentially to a centralized organization of the group, with evidence for the presence of leaders and followers, contrary to divergent tasks, which were mostly solved by means of an uncentralized network of communications.

In the field of developmental psychology, Rieben's study (1982) in Switzerland aimed at evaluating the relationship between creative potential and cognitive development within Piaget's framework, in addition to the now-classical exploration of the nature of the link between measures of intelligence and creative potential. Rieben examined two groups of children (six to eight years old). She measured general intelligence by using Weschler's scale for children, whereas Piagetian assessments included probabilities quantification and class inclusion tasks, allowing for an estimation of each child's position along the developmental stages postulated by Piaget. Rieben measured creativity by using tests by Torrance (1976) and Wallach and Kogan (1965).

The results observed by Rieben concerning the link between creativity and intelligence are comparable with those obtained by Wallach and Kogan. The variance shared by the two types of abilities appears stronger in Rieben's younger sample, and the link weakens on average for children between six and eight years of age, with the range of correlation coefficients dropping from $.23 < r < .43$ at age six to $-.09 < r < .36$ at age eight. This result can be interpreted in terms of a gradual differentiation of aptitudes when children are between six and eight years old, in line with the weak relationship reported by Wallach and Kogan for children at age eleven. A relation between creativity and operational thinking was also established, as Rieben observed that children who had reached the stage of concrete operations displayed better performances in creativity tasks. However, after this stage was reached, following intrastage differences did not translate into differences in divergent-thinking performances.

Piaget and Creativity

As part of our review on creativity research in France and Romande, Switzerland, the question of creativity in Piaget's work must be discussed. As we described in the section on education, Piaget considered in his early works that children's socialization proceeded in large part from the practice of creative social behaviors. Nevertheless, the bulk of his research was mainly concerned with secondary and logical processes. As Rieben put it (Rieben, 1982), a superficial answer to this issue could be to state that Piaget either never discussed the phenomenon of creativity, or was always concerned with it, if we admit that the development of creative thinking can be assimilated with the child's invention of more and more advanced cognitive structures (p. 103).[26] A more cautious examination of Piaget's contribution to developmental psychology led Rieben to conclude that only the first and especially the very last part of his career dealt with creative thinking. As early as 1924, in the same vein as his predecessor Claparède, Piaget acknowledged two forms of intelligence, one for inventing solutions and the other to verify them. About fifty years later, after originating and exploring the field of genetic epistemology, Piaget (1976, 1981) returned to imaginative skills with experiments in his laboratory with divergent-thinking type of tasks (such as building structures based on rods and connections). Rieben deplored that Piaget's approach to the development of imaginative skills left the creativity puzzle unsolved. First, Piaget seemed only interested in quantitative aspects of the evolution of children's responses. Second, his focus remained on reasoning skills. Last, there lacked a dynamic component in his view on the articulation between divergent and logical thinking. Piaget conceived the attainment of concrete and formal operations as necessary but not sufficient conditions for the emergence of creativity, yet at the same time he hypothesized

---

[26] Rieben, however, refers to Lautrey's analysis (Lautrey, 1981), which underlined the limitation of Piaget's theory of equilibration, which was that it was unable to account for the creation of accommodative schemes.

a direct link between invention and divergent thinking, a position that was not validated by experimental data (Rieben, 1978).

The Psychodynamic Approach to Creativity

Quite distinct from Guilford's pragmatic approach to the components of creativity, work on creativity from a psychodynamic perspective developed considerably from the 1950s in France and Romande, Switzerland. This line of investigation, which continues to be active today, explores the underling motives, psychic conflicts and personal issues, and fantasies and dreams that are considered the basis of creativity (Anargyros-Klinger, Reiss-Schimmel, & Wainrab, 1998). In particular, there are numerous case studies of creative people and creative products in art, literature, or scientific fields drawing on psychoanalytic concepts. The psychoanalytic process is viewed by some authors as a creative act because one's self-concept is constructed or revised through the therapeutic process. The link between psychopathology and creativity has been particularly studied. Didier Anzieu (1981; Anzieu et al., 1974), one of the main authors in the French psychoanalytic literature on creativity, extensively examined the creative process. In his view, there is an initial phase, characterized by psychic anguish, then a regressive movement, and then inspiration. This is followed by a preconscious organization and an initial perception, perhaps a dream or a hallucination. The idea is next transcribed into a familiar expressive code (linguistic, mathematical, visual, etc.), which is then elaborated into a composition. Finally, the production is exposed to the exterior world and the creator must overcome the separation anxiety associated with this last phase.

Concerning the development of creativity-based therapeutic approaches, we find instances in which institutions organize theater plays, journals, or concerts for and with patients from the early nineteenth century. However, the idea of artistic creativity as a therapeutic approach faced some initial resistance. According to Sudres (2003), French psychotherapy and psychiatry, in which the psychodynamic approach has long been dominant, was slow to integrate foreign (notably American and British) concepts and methods. Art therapy did, however, gain interest among practitioners in the second part of the twentieth century. For example, *art brut* (naive art) produced spontaneously by mentally ill individuals was gathered by Dubuffet and largely appreciated by both public and critics, bringing back to the foreground the complex nature of the link between creativity and psychopathology. Following the seminal work of therapists such as Volmat (Sudres, 2003) and Anzieu

(1981; Anzieu & Mathieu, 1974), art therapy was integrated into some university programs, which promoted its development.

CREATIVITY TODAY AND TOMMORROW

In addition to the aforementioned psychodynamic approach to creativity, which remains an active line of work, it is important to note recent initiatives in France in the fields of differential psychology and industrial–organizational psychology, which are also likely to be pursued in the future.

Multivariate–Differential Approach

After early attempts by Binet and Toulouse to use an empirical approach to study individual differences in imaginative skills, psychologists interested in individual differences began again to examine the phenomenon of creativity during the past decade. In particular, a multivariate approach has been used to investigate creative behaviors, aiming at better understanding the emergence of creativity, conceived as being produced by nonlinear interactions between cognitive, conative, affective, and environmental factors (Lubart et al., 2003).

Within this framework, several lines of work have been undertaken to explore creativity. For example, in the cognitive sphere, individual differences on cognitive flexibility and their relation to creative performance have been studied (Georgsdottir & Lubart, 2003). Concerning conative variables, cognitive styles, such as the preference for intuitive thinking, and personality traits, such as tolerance of ambiguity, have been examined (Raidl & Lubart, 2000–2001; Zenasni, Besançon & Lubart, 2004). For the affective component, empirical and theoretical examinations of the influence of emotional states, traits, and abilities on the creative process have been conducted (Lubart & Getz, 1997; Zenasni & Lubart, 2002). Finally, research on the impact of family and school environments, including alternative pedagogies such as Freinet's methods, on creativity has been conducted (Besançon & Lubart, 2004). Developmental issues have also been investigated. Some recent work examined the links between cognitive development and creative thinking in schoolchildren, the dimensionality (specificity–generality) of creativity with attention to interindividual and intraindividual differences in different forms of creativity (e.g., social creativity; Mouchiroud & Lubart, 2002), and the development of creatively-gifted children (Besançon & Lubart, 2004; Guignard & Lubart, 2004). Work conducted within the multivariate approach also seeks to advance issues of creativity measurement, evaluating the psychometric properties of classic divergent-thinking tests (Mouchiroud & Lubart, 2001), production-based tasks (such as story writing and drawing tasks), as well as developing measures of creative potential based on direct measures of cognitive, personality, and emotional factors underlying creativity.

Industrial–Organizational Psychology

Since the mid-1960s, there has been an active interest in creativity in the workplace. A number of books have been published concerning creativity techniques (Aznar, 1971; Moles & Caude, 1970), and several major industrial companies created creative groups in their organizations or called on creativity consultants to foster the creativity of employees through seminars or participation in projects. Recently, a French association for the development of creativity was created, mainly composed of creativity consultants. In the late 1990s, a few higher educational institutions began to foster teaching and research on creativity in business. Notably, the Parisian School of Management (ESCP-EAP) and the National Center for Continuing Education in the Workplace (CNAM) developed courses on creativity and innovation management. The French Ministry of Education funded a special university summer school in 2002 on creativity in the workplace. This seminar, organized at the University of Paris 5, was the first officially sponsored event in France on the topic of creativity (see Lubart, & De Weerd-Nederhof 2004 for a selection of papers).

Applied research on creativity in industrial settings has also been conducted. For example, work based on case studies of creative businesses led to the development of an idea management system with massive employee participation in innovative thinking (Getz & Robinson, 2003). In another line of work, experimental research on industrial designers concerning the processes of conception and evaluation of new designs has drawn on a cognitive ergonomic approach (Bonnardel & Marmèche, 2004). This work has led to proposals for computer-based systems to foster creativity in industrial design tasks.

CONCLUSION

The overview of work on creativity in France and Romande, Switzerland, presented in this is chapter, shows that there is a rich history of specific contributions to the field from this region. Drawing on the popular "four Ps" approach to the study of creativity, we can see that historical and more recent contributions have been made concerning the creative person, process, product, and press (environment). The future of creativity research in this area of the world is promising, because there is growing interest in both theoretical and applied work on the topic, organized around three main sectors: (a) a multivariate approach to understanding individual differences of creativity and the creative process; (b) an industrial, organizational approach to creativity in the workplace; and (c) a clinical, psychodynamic approach to creativity and psychopathology.

References

Anargyros-Klinger, A., Reiss-Schimmel, & Wainrib, S. (1998). *Créations, psychanalyse* [Creations, psychoanalysis]. Paris: Presses Universitaires de France.

Anzieu, D. (1981). *Le corps de l'oeuvre* [The body of the work]. Paris: Gallimard.

Anzieu, D., Mathieu, M., Besdine, M., Jaques, E., & Guillaumin, J. (Eds.). (1974). *Psychanalyse du génie créateur* [Psychoanalysis of the creative genius]. Paris: Dunod.

Aznar, G. (1971). *Pratique de la créativité dans les entreprises* [Creativity practices in business]. Paris: Editions de l'Organisation.

Beaudot, A. (1971). *Recherches sur la créativité* [Research on creativity]. Caen, France: Université de Caen.

Bergson, H. (1919). *L'Energie spirituelle* [Spiritual energy] (132 ed.). Paris: Presses Universitaires de France.

Besançon, M., & Lubart, T. I. (2004, September 11–13). *Creative giftedness: Developmental and educational issues.* Paper presented at the European Council for High Ability, Pamplona, Spain.

Binet, A. (1903). *Etude expérimentale de l'intelligence.*[Experimental study of Intelligence]. Paris: Alcan.

Binet, A. (1911). Nouvelles recherches sur la mesure du niveau intellectuel chez les enfants des écoles [New research on the measurement of intellectual level in school children]. *L'Année Psychologique, 17*, 145–201.

Binet, A., & Henri, V. (1895). La psychologie individuelle [Individual psychology]. *L'Année Psychologique, 2*, 415–465.

Binet, A., & Simon, T. (1905). Méthodes nouvelles pour le diagnostic du niveau intellectuel des anormaux [New methods for the diagnosis of intellectual level in mentally deficient children]. *L'Année Psychologique, 11*, 191–244.

Binet, A., & Simon, T. (1908). Le développement de l'intelligence chez les enfants. [The development of intelligence in children]. *L'Année Psychologique, 14*, 1–94.

Bonnardel, N., & Marmèche, E. (2004). Evocation processes by novice and expert designers: Towards stimulating analogical thinking. *Creativity and Innovation Management, 13*(3), 176–186.

Braunstein, J.-F., & Pewzner, E. (1999). *Histoire de la psychologie* [History of psychology]. Paris: Colin.

Campbell, D. T. (1960). Blind variation and selective retention in creative thought as in other knowledge processes. *Psychological Review, 67*, 380–400.

Carlier, M. (1973). *Etude différentielle d'une modalité de la créativité: La flexibilité.*[Differential study of one modality of creativity: flexibility]. Paris: Editions du C.N.R.S.

Carroy, J. (2000). "Mon cerveau est comme dans un crâne de verre": Emile Zola sujet d'Edouard Toulouse [My brain is like a glass skull: Emile Zola as Edouard Toulouse' subject]. *Revue d'histoire du XIXème siècle, 20/21.*

Centre International de Synthèse (Ed.). (1938). *Neuvième semaine internationale de synthèse. L'invention* [Ninth international week of synthesis. Invention]. Paris: Alcan.

Clandfield, D., & Sivell, J. (Eds.). (1990). *Co-operative learning and social change: Selected writings of Celestin Freinet.* Toronto: Ontario Institute for Studies in Education.

Claparède, E. (1903). *L'association des idées* [The association of ideas]. Paris: Douin.

De Bono, E. (1992). *Serious creativity: Using the power of lateral thinking to create new ideas.* New York: HarperCollins.

Faucheux, C., & Moscovici, S. (1958). Etudes sur la créativité des groupes: Tâche, situation individuelle et groupe [Studies on group creativity: Task, individual situation, and group]. *Bulletin de Psychologie, 152*(9).

Faucheux, C., & Moscovici, S. (1960). Etudes sur la créativité des groupes: Tâche, structure des communications et réussite [Studies on group creativity: Task, structure of communications, success]. *Bulletin du CERP, 9*(1).

Flournoy, T. (1919). *Métaphysique et psychologie* [Metaphysics and psychology] (2nd ed.). Genève: Kundig. (Original work published 1894)

Flournoy, T., & Claparède, E. (1912). *Enquête de "L'enseignement Mathématique" sur la méthode de travail des mathématiciens.*[Survey for the review "Mathematics Teaching" on the working method of mathematician]. Paris: Gauthier-Villars Fehr. (Original work pusblished 1902)

Freud, S. (1986). Esquisse d'une psychologie scientifique [Outline of a scientific psychology]. In M. Bonaparte, A. Freud, & E. Kris (Eds.), *La naissance de la psychanalyse.* Paris: Presses Universitaires de France. (Original work pusblished 1895)

Georgsdottir, A. S., & Lubart, T. I. (2003). La flexibilité cognitive et la créativité: Une approche développementale, différentielle et expérimentale [Cognitive flexibility and creativity: A developmental, differential and experimental approach]. *Psychologie Française, 48*(3), 29–40.

Getz, I., & Robinson, A. G. (2003). *Vos idées changent tout* [Your ideas change everything]. Paris: Editions d'Organisation.

Gordon, W. J. (1956). Operational approach to creativity. *Harvard Business Review, 34*, 41–51.

Guignard, J.-H., & Lubart, T. I. (2004, July 11–15). *Empirical study of links between convergent thinking, divergent thinking and childhood giftedness.* Paper presented at the Eighteenth Biennial of the International Society for the Study of Behavioural Development, Ghent, Belgium.

Guilford, J. P. (1950). Creativity. *American Psychologist, 5*, 444–454.

Hadamard, J. (1945). *An essay on the psychology of invention in the mathematical field*. Princeton, NJ: Princeton University Press. (Published in France in 1975)

Huteau, M. (2003). *Psychologie, psychiatry et société sous la troisième république: Edouard Toulouse's Biocracie (1865–1947)* [Psychology, psychiatry and society in France's third republic: The Biocracy of Edouard Toulouse]. Paris: L'Harmattan.

Huteau, M. (in press). La réception de l'Echelle métrique de l'intelligence en France [The acceptance of the metric scale in France]. In *Le centenaire de l'échelle métrique de Binet*. Paris: L'Harmattan.

Joly, H. (1882). Psychologie des grands hommes [Psychology of great men]. *Revue Philosophique de la France et de l'Étranger, 13*, 361–376.

Lautrey, J. (1981). L'équilibration suffit-elle à guider la coordination des actions [Does equilibration suffice to guide the coordination of actions]? *Psychologie Française, 26*, 359–372.

Lautrey, J., & De Ribaupierre, A. (2004). Psychology of human intelligence in France and French-speaking Switzerland. In R. J. Sternberg (Ed.), *International handbook of intelligence*. Cambridge, U.K.: Cambridge University Press. 104–134

Lombroso, C. (1889). *L'homme de génie* [Man of genius]. Paris: Alcan.

Lubart, T. I., & De Weerd-Nederhof, P. C. (2004). Special Issue-Creativity in the Workplace. *Creativity and Innovation Management,13*, 143–144.

Lubart, T. I. (1999). Creativity across cultures. In R. J. Sternberg (Ed.), *Handbook of creativity* (pp. 339–350). Cambridge, U.K.: Cambridge University Press.

Lubart, T. I., & Getz, I. (1997). Emotion, metaphor, and the creative process. *Creativity Research Journal, 10*, 285–301.

Lubart, T. I., Mouchiroud, C., Tordjman, S., & Zenasni, F. (2003). *La psychologie de la créativité* [Psychology of creativity]. Paris: Armand Colin.

Lyons, W. (1986). *The disappearance of introspection*. Cambridge, MA: MIT Press.

Maury, L. (1988). *Freinet et la pédagogie* [Freinet and pedagogy]. Paris: Presses Universitaires de France.

Meirieu, P. (Ed.). (2001). *Célestin Freinet. Comment susciter le désir d'apprendre* [Celestin Freinet: How to arouse the desire for learning]? Paris: PEMF.

Moreau de Tours, J. J. (1859). *La psychology morbide dans ses rapports avec la philosophie de l'histoire, ou de l'influence des névropathies sur le dynamisme intellectuel* [Morbid psychology in its relationship with the philosophy of history, or on the influence of neuropathologies on intellectual dynamism]. Paris: Masson.

Moles, A., & Caude, R. (1970). *Créativité et méthodes d'innovation* [Creativity and methods of innovation]. Paris: Fayard-Mame.

Mouchiroud, C., & Lubart, T. I. (2001). Children's original thinking: An empirical examination of alternative measures. *Journal of Genetic Psychology, 162*(4),382–401

Mouchiroud, C., & Lubart, T. I. (2002). Social creativity: A cross-sectional study of 6- to 11-year-old children. *International Journal of Behavioral Development, 26*(1), 60–69.

Nicolas, S. (2002). *Histoire de la psychology française. Naissance d'une nouvelle science.* [History of French psychology. Birth of a new science]. Paris: In Press Editions.

Norquay, G. (Ed.) (1999). *R. L. Stevenson on fiction.* Edinburgh: Edinburgh University Press.

Osborn, A. F. (1953). *Applied imagination.* New York: Scribner's.

Paulhan, F. (1901). *Psychologie de l'invention* [Psychology of Invention]. Paris:Alcan

Piaget. (1932). *Le jugement moral chez l'enfant* [Children's moral judgment]. Paris: Presses Universitaires de France.

Piaget, J. (1976). Le possible, l'impossible et le nécessaire (Les recherches en cours ou projetées au Centre International d'Epistémologie Génétique) [The possible, the impossible and the necessary (Research in process or planned at the International Center for Genetic Epistemology)]. *Achives de Psychologie, 172,* 281–299.

Piaget, J. (1981). *Le possible et le nécessaire chez l'enfant. I. L'évolution des possibles chez l'enfant.* [The possible and the necessary in the child. I. The evolution of the possibles in the child]. Paris: Presses Universitaires de France.

Piéron, H. (1903). L'association médiate [Mediate association]. *Revue Philosophique de la France et de l'Étranger, 56,* 142–149.

Poincaré, H. (1908). *Science et méthode* [Science and method]. Paris: Flammarion.

Poincaré, H. (1921). *The foundations of science.* New York: Science Press.

Raidl, M.-H., & Lubart, T. I. (2000–2001). An empirical study of intuition and creativity. *Imagination, Cognition and Personality, 20*(3), 217–230.

Ribot, T. (1875). *La psychologie anglaise contemporaine* [Contemporary English Psychology]. Paris: Germer Baillère.

Ribot, T. (1897). *L'évolution des idées générales* [The evolution of general ideas]. Paris: Alcan.

Ribot, T. (1900). Essai sur l'imagination créatrice [Essay on creative imagination]. Paris: Alcan.

Rieben, L. (1978). *L'examen des fonctions cognitives chez l'enfant: Intelligence, créativité et opérativité* [Examination of cognitive functions in the child: Intelligence, creativity and operativity]. Neuchâtel, Switzerland: Delachaux et Niestlé.

Rieben, L. (1982). Processus secondaires et créativité: Partie émergée de l'iceberg [Secondary processes and creativity: The emerging part of the iceberg]? In N. Nicolaïdis & E. Schmid-Kitsikis (Eds.), *Créativité et/ou symptôme* (pp. 97–111). Paris: Clancier-Guenand.

Sartre, J. P. (1948). *L'imaginaire. Psychologie phénoménologique de l'imagination* [The imaginary. Phenomenological psychology of imagination] (11th ed.). Paris: Gallimard.

Simonton, D. K. (1999). Creativity as blind variation and selective retention: Is the creative process Darwinian? *Psychological Inquiry, 10*(4), 309–328.

Souriau, P. (1881). *Théorie de l'invention* [Theory of invention]. Paris: Hachette.

Sudres, J.-L. (2003). Créativité, expression et art-thérapie: Trajectoires ... [Creativity, expression and art therapy: Trajectories...]. In P. Moron, J.-L. Sudres, & G. Roux (Eds.), *Créativité et art-thérapie en psychiatrie.* Paris: Masson.

Sully, J. (1876). L'art et la psychologie [Art and Psychology]. *Revue Philosophique de la France et de l'Étranger, 2,* 321–334.

Taine, H. (1870). *De l'intelligence* [On intelligence]. Paris: Hachette.

Torrance, E. P. (1976). *Tests de pensée créative* [Tests of Creative Thinking]. Paris: Les Editions du Centre de Psychologie Appliquée.

Toulouse, E. (1896). *Enquête médico-psychologique sur les rapports de la supériorité intellectuelle avec la névropathie. I. Introduction générale. Emile Zola* [Medico-psychological study of the relationships between giftedness and neuropathology. General introduction, Emile Zola]. Paris: Société d'Éditions Scientifiques.

Toulouse, H. (1910). *Enquête médico-psychologique sur la supériorité intellectuelle. II. Henri Poincaré* [Medico-psychological study of giftedness. II. Henri Poincaré]. Paris: Flammarion.

Toulouse, E., & Piéron, H. (1911). *Technique de psychologie expérimentale de Toulouse, Vaschide et Piéron.*[Toulouse, Uaschide and Piéron's technique of experimental psychology] Paris: Douin.

Toulouse, E., Vaschide, N., & Piéron, H. (1904). *Technique de psychologie expérimentale* [Technique of experimental psychology]. Paris: Douin.

Wallach, M., & Kogan, N. (1965). *Modes of thinking in young children.* New York: Holt, Rinehart & Winston.

Wallas, G. (1926). *The art of thought.* New York: Harcourt Brace.

Wolff, C. (1738). *Psychologia empirica.* Olms; Hildesheim

Xypas, C. (1997). *Piaget et l'éducation* [Piaget and Education]. Paris: Presses Universitaires de France.

Zenasni, F., & Lubart, T. I. (2002). Effects of mood states on creativity. *Current Psychology Letters,* 2(8), 33–50.

Zenasni, F., Besançon, M., & Lubart, T. I. (2004). A developmental study of tolerance of ambiguity and its links with creativity. Manuscript submitted for publication.

6

Creativity in Italy

Alessandro Antonietti and Cesare Cornoldi

INTRODUCTION

According to an oft-quoted statement by Ebbinghaus, psychology has a long past and a recent history. Even though psychological topics have been explored by historians, philosophers, theologians, religious and spiritual guides, poets, and novelists from the early stages of Western culture, the scientific investigation of such topics began only in the nineteenth century. A similar comment could be made about the psychological study of creativity in Italy, as well as, presumably, in other countries (see Albert & Runco, 1999). Italian research on creativity has a recent history but a long past. Indeed, even though studies explicitly analyzing, assessing, and promoting *creativity* only appeared in Italy in the 1960s, issues associated with creativity were pondered earlier, under different labels within more general theoretical topics.

Human creativity represents one of the most important and intriguing aspects of psychological functioning, but it is still in search of a clear and unequivocal definition. If we assume, in general terms, that creativity concerns the possibility that human beings produce, either in a physical–material or in a cultural sense, something that did not exist before and that is appreciated by other people because of its practical, intellectual, or aesthetic value, then we realize that the problem of explaining how humans can succeed in this endeavor was already being addressed by many scholastic thinkers in Italy in the Middle Ages. For instance, in many parts of his monumental corpus of philosophical–theological writings, Thomas Aquinas (1221–1274) discussed the process through which people rearrange previous sensations and notions in order to conceive fantastic entities or new ideas. During the Renaissance period, many Italian humanists addressed issues linked to the creative power of the human mind, stressing alleged correspondences between the forces underpinning cosmological processes and what occurs in the individual mind. For example, in a literary–philosophical work titled *Il Candelaio* [The chandler] written in 1582, Giordano Bruno (1548–1600) proposed the theory that man can achieve the complete fulfillment of his potential in fields such as artistic creation or altruistic social action because he is an instrument of an unlimited cosmic force that conditions him and that, in turn, is conditioned by the infinite ways in which he can develop his potential. However, it was only later that speculation about the generative power of the human mind became more circumscribed and focused. In 1745 the historian Ludovico Antonio Muratori (1672–1750), interested in analyzing the source of poetic inspiration, wrote the essay *Della Forza della Fantasia Umana* [About the Strength of Human Fantasy], in which he tried to assess and explain the role played, respectively, by bodily sensations and by intellect in determining the influence exerted by cultural products on the human mind.

Concepts that can be more easily connected to what we currently call *creativity* were developed during the second part of the nineteenth century. Our review of the Italian contribution to the investigation of creativity begins with this period. In the initial part of this chapter, we try to give an account of ideas about the psychological origins of the creative act and the psychological profile of eminent creative persons that were presented in essays concerning topics such as *genius*, *originality in thinking*, and *imagination* or *fantasy*, which were written up to the middle of the past century.

The renewal of interest in creativity – accompanied by an approach more tuned to the methodological criteria of scientific inquiry – that started to occur in Anglo-Saxon psychology in the 1950s and 1960s, then reverberated in Italy in the 1970s. It was at that time that important readings and books about creativity were translated into Italian, empirical inquiries about the thinking processes and the personality of divergent people began to be carried out, and the first attempts to apply principles and techniques aimed at enhancing creative skills in educational settings were made. Italian studies of creativity focused mainly on three issues: reflection about theoretical frameworks relevant to conceiving the creative process and basic experiments conducted according to such frameworks; measurement of creative abilities; and ideation and the application of methods to promote creativity. Therefore, in the

subsequent parts of the present chapter, we consider these issues separately. We describe how international approaches to creativity have been
assimilated in Italy and how, more recently, some theoretical and experimental work having implications for creativity has been developed by
one of us in the context of a long study on individual differences in visuospatial cognition. Then, we provide the reader with a presentation of
the literature and of the studies carried out by the other of us in the areas
of assessment and training in creativity. In the last part of the chapter
we offer some conclusions.

It seems to us that three levels can be identified in the Italian contribution to the study of creativity. The first level consists of the translation
of relevant works, in the standardization of widely used tools, and in
the popularization of ideas developed by foreign authors, as well as the
compilation of readings and manuals. The second level concerns the
replication of some important investigations or their extension through
new empirical studies, as well as the adaptation or modification of existing psychometric and didactic instruments. At the third level we can
identify original contributions, consisting either of attempts to synthesize different points of view within a new conceptual framework or to
bring ideas, often drawn from fields that are parallel to creativity (for
instance, problem solving), into the mainstream research about creativity. In each part of the chapter, we present content according to these
three distinct levels.

HISTORICAL ANTECEDENTS

In the second half of the nineteenth century and in the first decades
of the twentieth century, some issues involving the analysis of what
occurs in the human mind when it generates original products
were considered by Italian philosophers and psychologists who were
interested in exploring the origins of genius. In that period, Italian culture was dominated by two main but opposite philosophical
perspectives: Positivism and Idealism. Consequently, reflections about
human genius (Bovio, 1900) were inspired by one of these two theoretical
viewpoints.

A strong positivist position was held by Cesare Lombroso (1855,
1877, 1892, 1897), the well-known founder of criminal anthropology,
whose degenerative theory of genius gave rise to debate in Italy (see
De Sanctis, 1898) and reached international notoriety. Lombroso maintained that geniuses were originals; that is, they differed from other

people in that they saw things in a different manner, associated ideas usually considered separate, detected hidden relations between disparate thoughts (incidentally, demonstrating that the conception of creativity as ability to find remote associations was suggested earlier than Mednick, 1962), and, as a result, could generate new material or cultural products. According to Lombroso (1877, p. 34), genius differs from talent since the former allows people to reach new insights in a sudden and unconscious way, whereas the latter leads people to be aware of the process followed to reach a new idea. Lombroso assumed that the genius must be different from ordinary people: The genius was atypical. More precisely, he or she was affected by physical or psychological deficits, or both. Thus, genius is close to insanity, since a series of features are shared both by creative persons and by insane persons. By analyzing biographical data of eminent scientists, mathematicians, inventors, novelists, poets, painters, sculptors, philosophers, historians, economists, politicians, army leaders, and so on, Lombroso provided a list of these deficits. They included biological characteristics (low stature, thinness, anomalous shape of the skull, and barrenness), mental disorders (compulsive ideation, mania, hallucinations, delirium, amnesia, paresthesia, anesthesia, stutter, and epilepsy) and deviant behaviors (alcoholism, vagabondage, and suicide), special psychological features (hypersensitivity, left-handedness, intellectual precocity, somnambulism, vivid dreams, and odd calligraphy), personality traits (melancholia, being sulky or afraid, ambiguity, and tendency to share prejudices and stereotypes), social tendencies (being misunderstood, being refused by the contemporary environment, having difficulty in accepting other people's ideas, and having the tendency to remain unmarried and without issue), and moral traits (perversity and arrogance). What made the difference between the genius and the insane person was that the former, but not the latter, had the ability to reflect, to criticize, and to inhibit the ideational products; that is, the unusual combinations of previously unrelated ideas that were generated.

From Lombroso's point of view, all the so-called anomalies that characterize the genius are rooted in the brain (he spoke of *lacunae in the brain*). What are the causes of these anomalies? They emerge because of a degenerative process that, through hereditary mechanisms, tends to hand such anomalies down from one generation to the next and to increase them. At the origin of this degenerative process, Lombroso identifies three main kinds of alleged factors: biological factors (race crossing and influences of climatic variations on races), pathological factors (illnesses and trauma), and environmental factors (for instance, poverty and other curious factors, such as the presence of democratic forms of government), which, in Lombroso's opinion, played a minor role.

Lombroso acknowledged the sources of his theory: Some suggestions that he developed can be found in works by ancient philosophers such as Aristotle (see Ciani, 1983) or in more recent thinkers such as Diderot and in previous empirical observations. (For instance, in 1566, Tommaso Garzoni reported cases of genius affected by madness in an essay titled *L'hospitale de' Pazzi Incurabili* or The Hospital of the Incurable Madmen.) Lombroso also shared ideas drawn from contemporary authors: Jacoby, Moreau, and Richet (who argued that *no genius lacks some element of madness*). Moreover, his work can be placed in a field that was cultivated by other Italian scholars who described geniuses affected by mental disorders. Andrea Verga in 1850 wrote an essay about the lipemania of the poet Torquato Tasso, whose psychopathological profile – characterized by paranoia and epilepsy – was also later sketched by Luigi Roncoroni (1896, quoted in De Sanctis, 1898). Augusto Tebaldi (1895), a hypnotist from Padova, identified alleged neuropathic and epileptoid traits in Napoleon. Giovanni Mingazzini (1895) attributed the originality of Lord Byron's writings to the alcohol and opium intoxication affecting the poet. Mariano Luigi Patrizi (1896), a physiologist from Sassari, reported possible links between the pessimism of the poet Giacomo Leopardi – analyzed also by Sergi (1899) – and his neuropsychopathy. Gioachino Brognoligo (1899) commented on *Il Medico Olandese* [The Dutch Physician] by Carlo Goldoni and stressed that the neurotic protagonist of that theater work reflected psychopathological characteristics of the author of the comedy. Giuseppe Vetrani (1899) corresponded the religious originality and hallucinations of the Dominican reformer Gerolamo Savonarola with the abnormal shape of his skull. Francesco Del Greco, by continuing the investigation of the relationships between genius and madness (Del Greco, 1896, 1927), investigated the originality shown by famous mystics (Del Greco, n.d.). In an essay preceded by a long introduction written by Lombroso, Antonio Renda (1900) identified parallels between the psychological development of August Comte, which led him toward neurosis, and the maturation of his philosophical system. (It has to be mentioned that Lombroso's investigation of genius–madness relationships began with an essay, published in 1855, about the madness of the mathematician Gerolamo Cardano). The field continued to be cultivated in subsequent decades – for instance, by

De Stefanis (1932) and Banissoni (1940), who described the life of famous inventors in psychological terms.

Lombroso's merit was to have synthesized a wide amount of disparate data and to have acquired new data by himself – for instance, he noted that suicides of people involved in intellectual jobs were particularly frequent: He computed in Italy a ratio of 619:1,000,000 suicides in persons devoting themselves to literary studies and 355:1,000,000 in teachers, compared with a ratio of 33:1,000,000 in porters or of 53:1,0000,000 in clergymen (Lombroso, 1877) – and to have included them within a coherent, while questionable, framework. Lombroso's ideas were very influential. They were substantially accepted by many contemporary Italian scholars such as Giuseppe Sergi, Enrico Morselli – who, while he criticized some points of Lombroso's theory (see De Sanctis, 1898, pp. 9–10), applied a similar approach to studying the dreams of geniuses – and Luigi Ventura, according to whom genius is produced by progressive, divergent variations that occur during evolution. Lombroso's work was often invoked to support an innatist view of the human being, sometimes not free from discriminatory intent, beside the original intentions of Lombroso himself. For instance, Sergi – who thought that intuition played a central role in genius, namely, a kind of intellectual vision characterized by acuteness and quickness (Sergi, 1904) – maintained that women could never be geniuses, not for sociocultural reasons, but because of structural biological reasons (they could not achieve the complete development reached by men), even though they could generate sons who were geniuses (Sergi, 1894).

Another perspective inspired by Positivism, but in an opposite direction to that followed by Lombroso, was provided by Antonio Padovan (1907, 1909), who considered the problem of how genius develops. The author distinguished *genius* from *ingenious*: The former yields novel and original products; the latter concerns the capacity to construe artifacts that mimic nature (Padovan, 1909, p. 50). Padovan claimed that genius is grounded on the material dimension of the human being ("Genius is evolutionary, natural, and physiological"; 1909, p. 81), more precisely on "a brain physiologically perfect and exuberant of exquisite nervous substance" (1909, p. 2). Lombroso identified the natural basis of genius in a pathological nervous system; at the opposite side, Padovan argued that genius is present in "neurologically superior" men (Padovan, 1909, p. 45). Because of this close relationship with the neurological substrate, the origins of genius were searched for in the biological evolution of men. The author assumed that the root of genius had to be found in animal intelligence, rather similar to that of primitive man. Animal intelligence consists not only of instinct (even though instinct is prevalent in animals since it is sufficient to ensure the survival), but also of intellectual-like acts: Animals can anticipate future events, perform detour-reaching behaviors, and so on, thus showing themselves to be able to go beyond their present conditions. This ability was more developed in primitive men: the lack of somatic resources to face the environmental challenges – above all the reduced acuity of the sensory systems – and the need to transmit to children effective ways to overcome the survival problems encountered induced primitives to devise new tools. This induced, in turn, an increased development of the brain. (In this respect, Padovan anticipated ideas subsequently developed by Soviet historical–cultural psychology).

Genius, according to Padovan, is prevalently a synthetic ability, whereas animal intelligence is analytical: animals "specialize" in managing efficiently only one kind of environmental information; by contrast, the originality of human thinking is characterized by the capacity to integrate different sensorial sources of information to process holistic representations, thereby allowing individuals to discover new solutions to fit survival needs. On these grounds, Padovan predicted that, in the future, genius should become more rare because of the increasing specialization of the skills required by the environment.

On the Idealistic side we find Leone Vivante (1925), who wrote *Note sopra la originalità del pensiero* (Remarks about the originality of thinking; This was also published in an English version since the author was to present the ideas expressed in that essay at the Congress of Psychology held in Oxford in July 1923). Vivante addressed this question: How is it possible that thinking may be original if it is conditioned by matter? By assuming a framework suggested by Actualism (a version of Idealism developed by Giovanni Gentile), Vivante maintained that thinking, strictly speaking, cannot be predetermined by any external factor, since the mind is free to determine the direction of its thoughts by itself. Thinking develops by following a path that it draws by itself. Thinking is driven by a sort of intrinsic necessity. External stimuli do not cause thinking but provide opportunities for thinking to occur. A reciprocal, circular relationship binds together the act of thinking and the external conditions: Intentions to think do not preexist stimuli and stimuli do not preexist the intended act of thinking (Vivante, 1925, p. 12). Within a synthetic activity, thinking and its contents become concurrently real. This can justify how the human mind can generate novel ideas by assuming given materials: Preexisting elements are restructured by means of the act of thinking so as to reach new meaning.

Besides genius and originality, Italian scholars in the latter half of the nineteenth century and the early twentieth century proposed notions and carried out analyses of imagination and fantasy. In fact, in the nineteenth century, imagination was thought of as a function that allows individuals to conceive – in a representational format intermediate between the sensory trace and the abstract, conceptual meaning – new situations so as to open the possibility that original ideas, discoveries, inventions, and novel artistic products emerge. As Amelia Augusta Bindoni (1899, p. 19) wrote, "Imagination is the material of the inventive genius." Rosa Heller-Heinzelmann (1933) considered imagination the ground of the arts, in which a creative process parallel to that of nature is displayed, even though the arts overcome nature thanks to the multiplicity of the variations and to the freedom of transformation that they allow. This aspect of imagination was often labeled in the nineteenth and early twentieth century as *fantasy*. However, the distinction between imagination and fantasy was largely debated.

Some authors discussed this question with reference only to abstract concepts (Bellu, 1909; Biuso, 1903), but others – more tuned into the first attempts to analyze psychological phenomena scientifically – based their arguments on concrete examples and empirical cases and considered the positions of contemporary French and German psychologists. Among these, Cipriano Giacchetti (1912) included memory, imagination, and fantasy in the category of *secondary psychic facts*, namely, mental representations that draw their contents from *primary facts* (sensations, perceptions, desires). Memory consists of remembering past experiences, whereas both imagination and fantasy have to do with the creation of something new, and for this reason they play a fundamental role in artistic production. The distinction between imagination and fantasy lies in the fact that imagination is a spontaneous and mechanical function (images rise in the mind out of the individual's control), whereas fantasy is always addressed toward a goal, is under conscious control, and is strictly linked to thinking. A more precise distinction was made by Giacchetti (1912) between *passive fantasy*, a form of fantasy free from the constraints imposed by reality, with the primary role of relaxation and enjoyment and of allowing people satisfaction of unexpressed and unrealizable desires, and *active fantasy*, where the ideational flow is oriented to the generation of useful thoughts. Other authors, such as Carlo Ravizza (1844), attributed a creative dimension only to fantasy, by considering imagination as a function whose aim is to reproduce previous sensations (referred both to external objects and to internal states) and by denying that imagination can yield new products. According to Ravizza (1844, p. 18), fantasy collects and combines sensations; imagination reproduces in the mind the products of fantasy. An intermediate position was held by Luigi Ambrosi (1892), who distinguished a kind of imagination involved in the reproduction of previous experiences and another that can generate, by combining previous elements, new entities (see also Ambrosi, 1898). In addition, Giovanni Antonio Colozza (1899) distinguished a reproductive from a constructive form of imagination. The constructive imagination, involved in scientific discovery and in the solution of ill-defined problems, allows people to formulate new hypotheses on the basis of the overall consideration of the elements of a given situation and of the relations among them, and it allows them to evaluate and criticize the generated hypotheses. The constructive imagination is characterized not only by cognitive qualities but also by emotional and motivational qualities: It is accompanied by an increase in arousal and curiosity.

In the debate about the distinction between imagination and fantasy, we can identify a silent opposition – which also occurs in more recent perspectives – between an associationistic perspective and an antiassociationistic perspective. The first perspective was shared by authors such as Ambrosi (1892) and Renda (1900), who thought that in genius-level thinking, ideas are linked through irrational connections grounded in kinesthetic impulses, emotions, and aesthetic perception. The second perspective was shared by Colozza (1899), who anticipated some holistic tenets peculiar to French functionalistic psychology (e.g., Claparède) and Gestaltist description of productive thinking, and by Del Greco (1898), who identified five phases in genius ideation: subconscious processing; increase of the *tonalità psichica* [psychic tonality], emergence of the creative idea (a sort of insight); tiredness; and semi-inspiration.

THEORETICAL PERSPECTIVES AND BASIC EMPIRICAL RESEARCH ABOUT CREATIVITY IN ITALY

A clear turning point in the study of creativity, which led to the abandonment of speculative discussions about imagination and fantasy (which by then had become futile) and of biographical reconstructions (which failed to provide new insights about the mechanisms of genius ideation), occurred after the popularization in Italy of American perspectives on psychology after Guilford's (1950) "manifesto." A good basis to update the Italian public was provided by the translation of the proceedings of the interdisciplinary symposium held at Michigan State University at the end of the 1950s (Anderson, 1959/1972) and of Parnes and Harding's (1962/1972) reading, anticipated and followed by translations of some synthetic presentations of new studies of creativity (Cropley, 1967/1969; Beaudot, 1973/1977; Lytton, 1971/1977). Later, original work on creative thinking and the creative personality was conducted by Italian psychologists (Pagnin & Vergine, 1974 and 1977). The first book written by an Italian scholar, an exhaustive overview of the subject, appeared in 1980 (Rubini, 1980b). Updated literature reviews about creativity were published in subsequent decades (Trombetta, 1989; Antonietti & Cesa-Bianchi, 2003). Some of the most recent theories about creativity, concerned above all with the cognitive aspects, were directly presented to Italian readers through the translations of relevant books (Weisberg, 1986/1988; Johnson-Laird, 1988/1990; Gardner, 1991/1993, 1993/1995; Singer & Singer, 1990/1995; Sternberg & Spear-Swerling, 1997). Psychoanalytic perspectives on creativity were described not only in general readings and manuals mentioned earlier (Anderson, 1959/1972; Pagnin & Vergine, 1977; Rubini 1980a, 1980b, 1980c), but also in an overview by Vanni (1976), in collections of papers (Rossi, 1977; Galli, 1999), and in translated books originally authored by Arieti (1976/1979), Chasseguet-Smirgel (1971/1973), Neumann (1955/1975), and Spira (1986). The same was true for the study of the creative personality (Jaspers, 1922/1977; Barron, 1968/1971) and for the perspectives inspired by humanistic psychology (Maslow, 1962/1971; Rogers, 1969/1973).

Thanks to such literature, empirical inquiry about creativity flourished in Italy. At the Catholic University of the Sacred Heart in Milan, Gabriele Calvi (1962; Calvi et al., 1965) tried to overcome what he perceived to be the limits of the factorialistic perspective on divergent thinking by proposing new constructs aimed at explaining the deep cognitive elaboration involved in generating creative responses, of the semantic, and not merely formally assessed (through measurement of fluidity parameters), values of such responses, and of the relationships between the intellectual aspects of creativity and emotional commitment. Albino Claudio Bosio (1979) and other collaborators investigated perceptual, linguistic, and cognitive factors of creativity, also with reference to attitudes and to psychopathology. In Pavia, Ornella Andreani

Dentici (Andreani & Orio, 1972), inspired by the famous investigation by Getzels and Jackson (1962), studied a large sample of gifted preadolescents by means of cognitive tasks, projective tests, and interviews to assess relationships between creative aptitudes and intellectual, motivational, affective, personality, and social characteristics. In Padova, Vittorio Rubini (1978, 1980a, 1980b, 1984; Rubini & Cornoldi, 1985; see also Cristante, 1982) promoted the investigation of divergent aspects of thinking and of personality in different contexts. In Rome, Paolo Bonaiuto (Bonaiuto, Giannini, & Biasi, 1999) was interested in highlighting possible links between creativity, personality, and aesthetic sensibility. An overall consideration of Italian research on creativity leads us to identify some topics that were privileged: creativity in children (Petter, 1998), preadolescents (Brissoni, 1971), and elderly people (Cesa-Bianchi, 2002); relationships between creativity and psychopathology (Calvi, 1970); creativity and media (Quadrio, 1973); creativity and altered states of consciousness (Biasutti, 1988); and relationships between student creativity and teacher behavior (Olmetti Peja, 1988; Antonietti & Cerioli, 1991).

It must be mentioned that, in Italy, aside from the heavy influence of Anglo-Saxon psychology on interpretations of creativity, the Gestaltist tradition has also been influential: While not directly concerned with creativity, studies about productive thinking supported the explanation of a holistic point of view in which the qualitative transformation that occurs when a new insight is reached is taken into account. In particular, Gaetano Kanizsa (1975) discovered the role that structural factors play in hindering people from reorganizing the cognitive field in unusual ways. The restructuring process, in problem solving as well as in everyday discourse, was also investigated by Giuseppe Mosconi (Mosconi 1990; Mosconi & D'Urso, 1974), who elaborated an original theoretical model aimed at explaining gaps in communication. Such gaps, which induce people to interpret messages in a deceptive way and to look at situations from a misleading point of view, occur because of the discrepancy between the meaning intended by the speaker or writer and that received by the listener or reader. This discrepancy depends on linguistic ambiguities and biases generated by the tendency to decode messages according to their usual, instead of alternative and uncommon, meanings.

In reviewing recent Italian contributions to work on creativity and related basic mechanisms, we must mention a line of research developed at the University of Padova that is based on the identification of the role of working memory (WM) in cognitive activities, including creative production. In fact, WM necessarily supports the processes that lead to creative production by maintaining and processing used information. This line of research has been developed by use of an individual differences approach (e.g., Vecchi, Monticelli, & Cornoldi, 1995) and with reference to a specific continuity model of WM.

On the basis of the available evidence, one of us (C. Cornoldi; see Cornoldi & Vecchi, 2003) developed a modified model of WM that postulated the articulation of the WM system according to continua, distinguishing between parts of the system devoted to different types of processing and to different content. The model aimed to overcome the difficulties of models based either on the assumption of a single comprehensive system that does not explain the material-specific effects reported in WM literature, or on the fractionation of a number of independent components that, in contrast, do not explain the relationships between components.

Difficulties with a single unitary view of WM emerge on the basis of an impressive amount of experimental evidence. For example, studies using a selective interference paradigm (e.g. Brooks, 1968) have repeatedly shown that a secondary concurrent WM task can produce different degrees of interference on a primary WM task, according not only to the similarity of the material but also to the sharing of specific WM resources (Baddeley, 1986, for a review). The study of individual differences has been critical for the differentiation of cognitive abilities, including components of both WM (e.g. Miyake & Shah, 1999) and creative processes. A critical distinction concerns the separation between verbal and visuospatial processes, which appears to be important both in the case of WM (Baddeley, 1986) and creativity (Guilford, 1967; Torrance, 1974/1992). According to Cornoldi and Vecchi (2003), this separation reflects the extreme opposite poles of a horizontal continuum that concerns the different types of content that can be processed by WM. In fact, it has been shown that dissociations of many components are possible within the broad area of visuospatial processes, but the distance between these components can be conceived as lower than the distance between them and the verbal ones.

Evidence concerning the differentiation between visuospatial and verbal processes both in memory and in creativity also comes from the psychology laboratory in Padova. In an early study, Rubini and Cornoldi (1985) administered a series of memory, intelligence, and creativity tests to a group of forty-eight children who were all nine years old. Tasks were taken from Italian instruments in wide use at that time; in the case of creativity, Rubini and Cornoldi (1985) used the *Espressioni* test (Calvi, 1962), which we describe in detail later. Despite the fact that the separation between a verbal and a visuospatial component was more evident for memory and intelligence tasks (with the creativity tasks mainly loading on a single factor), the pattern of correlations suggested specific relationships between creativity and WM. For example, a combined score on forward and backward digit recall significantly correlated with tasks requiring the production of the highest number of three-word sentences beginning with a given letter or to giving the highest number of suitable titles and original titles for a passage. In contrats, only a visuospatial WM score (obtained by combining the scores on the forward and the backward Corsi task) significantly correlated with the ability to propose the highest number of symbols representing three atmospheric events (fog, snow, and storm).

Unlike Baddeley (1986), Cornoldi and Vecchi (2003) assumed that highly controlled WM processes (involving a second continuous dimension: the control vertical dimension) can maintain some modality-specific features. Examples of highly controlled tasks are represented by many creative tasks, which involve active manipulation of material maintained in WM. It is assumed that these tasks reflect controlled operations and then are disturbed by highly controlled concurrent operations, but, unlike Baddeley's group approach, they cannot be referred to as a single central control system because they appear in many respects to have different and specific functional properties.

Figure 6.1 presents the two fundamental dimensions based on continuum relations: the horizontal continuum, related to the different types of material (e.g., verbal, visual, spatial, and haptic); and the vertical continuum, related to the degree of control required by the process. Each process is then defined on the basis of these two dimensions, and the degree of independence between tasks is represented as a distance between positions in the model. The conical structure suggests that higher degrees of distance between modalities are present in passive, peripheral processes, in contrast with high-level active tasks. At a peripheral level, it is also possible to hypothesize completely independent subsystems that are related to the early processing of perceptual inputs. As the system is unitary, it is assumed that different parts of the system share a single pool of resources, but – as the system is also articulated – it is assumed that each point of the system has specific local resources. Furthermore, common rules may govern different parts of

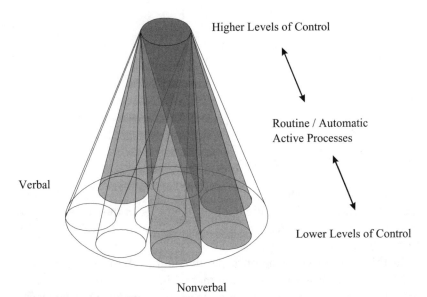

Higher Levels of Control

Routine / Automatic
Active Processes

Verbal

Lower Levels of Control

Nonverbal

FIGURE 6.1. Schematic representation of the continuity model of WM (Cornoldi & Vecchi, 2003)

the system, as in the case of interaction with long-term memory and in the inhibitory control of interfering information.

In the continuity model (e.g. Cornoldi & Vecchi, 2003), it is possible to distinguish between specific resources conceded to each position of the system and the global amount of resources available to the overall WM system. Each task is related to a specific amount of cognitive resources; that is, it is associated with the corresponding position in the system. As a logical consequence of a continuum model, the resources still available for a second task will be related to the distance between the two tasks. Two cognitive tasks could be performed together with more or less difficulty, also depending on their position on the vertical continuum: Two passive tasks require a low amount of resources and the global amount is likely to be within the limits of the WM system. This should not be true in the case of active tasks.

This resource view can be used for examining the individual difference issue. In fact, individual differences can be due either to a low degree of local resources at one or more points of the WM system (as happens in people with specific failures) or to a lower degree of overall resources. This latter circumstance is present in people with more general cognitive impairments, such as in mentally retarded individuals

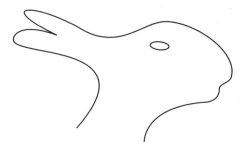

FIGURE 6.2. The duck–rabbit image.

who show impairments with most WM tasks, but also meet increasing difficulties in correspondence with increases in the degree of control (and then of resources request) implied by the task (Lanfranchi, Cornoldi, & Vianello, 2001).

In this section we focus on tasks that imply the use of visuospatial WM. Examples in this field are mental imagery tasks, which have often been associated with core aspects of creativity. In fact, some basic imagery tasks can be considered good examples of original or uncommon types of responses. For example, as it has been frequently shown (Cornoldi et al., 1996), people are generally unable to reverse the image of the duck–rabbit. If they have seen a duck, as in the example in Figure 6.2, and they have to maintain in WM the corresponding image, they are generally unable to see with their mind's eye that the pattern also represents a rabbit. Only a few individuals are able to make this reversal, and this minor group could be considered as particularly creative. In fact, it has been found that conditions that favor this type of reversal (like the block of interpretative convergent processes) are also active in creative production. In particular, Brandimonte and her coauthors (see Cornoldi et al., 1996) blocked the verbal processes that were assumed to support interpretative processes, finding that this manipulation was able to significantly increase the number of people who were able to reverse the image.

Another well-known imagery task associated with creativity is the mental synthesis task (see Finke, 1990; Finke & Slayton, 1988) a task that, if individuals are appropriately trained, can increase their levels of creativity (Antonietti & Martini, 2000; Lupi & Antonietti, 2000). The debate concerning the role of WM in the creative mental synthesis task was presented and commented on by Pearson, De Beni, and Cornoldi (2001). It appears that different interpretations of the role of visuospatial WM in the task are possible.

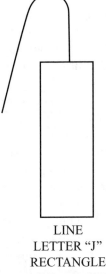

LINE
LETTER "J"
RECTANGLE

FIGURE 6.3. An example of synthesized forms resulting from the combination of simple images (from Finke, 1990).

The mental synthesis task requires that people mentally manipulate simple pictorial elements in order to find a pattern that could combine them (see Figure 6.3, where a short line, the shape of the letter J, and a rectangle were arranged to create a firecracker).

In a study on mental synthesis Cornoldi and Vecchi (2003) found that a condition inducing relaxation and increased use of mental imagery highly improved performance, reducing the size of individual differences. This suggests that the control for nonspecific processes (obtained by focusing on mental imagery) and intrusive information (obtained by inducing a relaxed condition) may enhance the creative process. (Similar results were obtained by inducing a hypnagogic state that enhanced the creative solution of problems based on mental manipulations of images; see Barolo et al., 1991). These aspects have been shown to be critical keys for an efficient use of WM.

In fact, a large body of evidence examines the relationship between success in WM tasks and the ability to control irrelevant information. Basic WM tasks are differentiated from traditional short-term memory tasks by the fact that, in the first phase, people must process the whole presented material, but then they must focus only on a part of it, the other part having become irrelevant. For example, in one active visuospatial

WM task (Cornoldi & Vecchi, 2003), people are presented with a series of positions on matrices, pressing a button when certain positions are presented. In a second phase they have to remember only some of these positions, such as the last one of each series. It has been shown that subjects who fail in the task are specifically affected by the other positions, and intrusive errors caused by other positions may increase if their activation has been also increased (Cornoldi & Vecchi, 2003). There are good reasons for assuming that a similar mechanism could be active in creative tasks if success in the tasks also depends on the ability to exclude typical associations or responses that have already been given. This control mechanism represents, in the continuity model, a high point along the vertical control continuum. It is assumed that it shares some resources and functioning rules with the verbal counterpart, but it is still specific. The consequent prediction is that people who are good at controlling intrusive information in WM and creative tasks within the visuospatial domain would be only to some extent similarly good within the verbal domain.

The control view of WM and creativity can be also partially supported by neuropsychological evidence, as the previously described processes seem to rely, at least in part, on the activity of prefrontal lobes. In fact, Italian cognitive neuropsychology has deeply studied the role of different brain areas in a series of cognitive processes, which may also have implications for the study of creativity.

Coming back to the WM approach illustrated here (Cornoldi & Vecchi, 2003), we find that the differentiation between different visuospatial components could offer some insight within creative tasks that are based on the manipulation of visuospatial information. As we have already anticipated, we assume that creative tasks should, in general, involve active tasks more than passive tasks. Furthermore, we assume that they could be distinguished according to the specific type of content. Different proposals have been advanced for distinguishing visuospatial contents. For example, many authors (e.g. Baddeley, 1986) suggest that visual and spatial components should be separated. Kosslyn (1994) proposed the distinction between coordinate and categorical spatial relationships: A relationship is categorical when it is based on a whole-or-nothing base (inside vs. outside, above vs. below); a relationship is coordinate when it involves more subtle topological properties (e.g., the specific degree of distance from a border). Kosslyn (1994) found both psychological and neurological evidence supporting such distinction. It is intuitive that categorical relationships are closer to the verbal pole than coordinate ones. However, there are no good reasons for excluding the possibility that both types of components, and thus also the categorical ones, could be used in the creative act. Furthermore, Pazzaglia and Cornoldi (1999) introduced the distinction between spatial sequential and spatial simultaneous processes. The distinction can be used for differentiating typical visuospatial WM tasks. For example, the standard forward Corsi spatial span measures the sequential component of visuospatial WM, whereas tests of memory for positions in a matrix typically measure the simultaneous one (Cornoldi & Vecchi, 2003). Using a dual-task manipulation, Pazzaglia and Cornoldi (1999) found that these components are also involved in understanding and memorizing spatial texts; the spatial sequential process is mainly involved when the information is sequential (e.g., in a route description), whereas the simultaneous one is mainly involved when the description is based on bird's-eye view.

We agree with the suggestion (e.g. Guilford, 1967; Sternberg, 1988) that creative productions could involve all the different types of content and that they can also be distinguished according to it. In fact, we think that each task can be analyzed with reference to this distinction in order to better understand its nature and to individuate the specific WM resources that could be involved in the task.

Some mental imagery tasks, such as the duck–rabbit task, seem mainly to involve the visual component of active WM, as happens when the mind has to recognize a single pattern. Vecchi and his coauthors (e.g. Richardson & Vecchi, 2001) have devised a visual puzzle task that has good psychometric properties and can be used for examining the role of active visual processes in WM. The task (see Figure 6.4) requires subjects to examine a series of figure parts and decide how they must be combined in order to obtain the overall figure. Unlike in the traditional puzzles, people cannot try to combine the borders of the different parts and must necessarily rely on their ability to perceive the overall figure. This task has been shown to predict other cognitive functions and could be considered in relationship with other more creative tasks.

Despite the fact that the puzzle task and other similar tasks mainly involve visual components of WM, spatial components may also be involved. This is particularly evident when not only the displacement (or change of size) of parts is required but also other more spatial manipulations, such as mental rotation in particular. It is interesting to notice how mental rotation tasks, which typically have been considered as good measures of spatial intelligence (e.g., Thurstone, 1938;

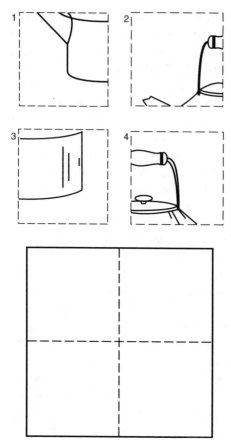

FIGURE 6.4. Visual puzzle task.

Thurstone & Thurstone, 1947), could be also related to creative tasks. For instance, Barolo, Masini, and Antonietti (1990) found that the mental rotation of three-dimensional objects was associated with the intuitive solution of geometrical problems. Actually, Frigotto and Cornoldi (2001; see Cornoldi & Vecchi, 2003) found a high correlation between the scores in a mental rotation task and the scores in the mental creative synthesis task. This is not surprising, as one of the most successful operations for the creation of new original syntheses of visuospatial elements is based on their appropriate rotation.

Within the taxonomy derived from the continuity model (Cornoldi & Vecchi, 2003), mental rotation should also involve visual and spatial sequential components, but it could be substantially considered as a simultaneous spatial task as the memory of an ordered sequence is not particularly critical. Therefore, one could ask how creative processes should involve sequential memory in the field of visuospatial WM. In other fields, for example music, the specific sequence is obviously critical, but what about the visuospatial domain? A counterpart of music could be the cinema, as creative film production is based on the sequence of images and a change of their order could affect the quality of the artistic production. Other visuospatial creative tasks may also partly rely on sequential spatial information, if memory of preceding operations is critical either for using it or for excluding it.

THE ASSESSMENT OF CREATIVITY IN ITALY

Currently the translations of two foreign standardized creativity tests are available in Italy. One of the most frequently employed psychometric tools to assess creativity, the Torrance Test of Creative Thinking (TTCT; see Torrance, 1974/1992), has been published in an Italian version (however, only Form A of the test is included), accompanied by norms drawn from an Italian sample constitued by 485 individuals ranging in age from seven to fourteen years (standardization occurred in 1984). As a relatively long time is needed for the administration of the TTCT, some researchers and educators prefer to use the Italian translation of the Creativity Assessment Packet by Williams (1993/1994), whose administration is simpler than that of the TTCT. However, no Italian norms are available for this test.

In the past, to measure creativity in kindergarten children, researchers adapted the tasks originally devised by Wallach and Kogan (1965) – employed by Banissoni and Ercolani (1973) and by Giannattasio, Nencini, and Romagnoli (1988) – to be used with Italian preschoolers (D'Alessio & Mannetti, 1976). The application of the Italian version of the Wallach–Kogan test allowed both the assessment of some psychometric properties of the instrument and the investigation of the role of factors such as gender, age, social status, intellectual level, school achievement, child's position within the family, and educational style on creativity.

Before these attempts to make foreign tests available, an original Italian instrument was usually employed to assess creativity in children, preadolescents, adolescents, and adults: the *Espressioni*, or Expressions, test devised by Calvi (1962). The test was constructed from the usual tasks designed to measure the factors of divergent thinking, even if the factorial framework was not shared by the author of the instrument, who tried to integrate the conceptualization of the cognitive dimensions of creativity with notions drawn from the psychodynamic tradition (such as the distinction between primary and secondary processes). The preliminary version of the test, consisting of sixteen tasks, was successively substituted by the final version including six tasks: three verbal and three graphical. The first task requires participants to draw as many figures as possible by using three lines. The second task requires participants to write as many sentences as possible that are composed of three words with the same given initial. In the third task, respondents have to invent symbols to denote a given concept. In the fourth task, individuals have to look for possible titles relevant to a given story. The fifth task is a figure completion task. The final task requires respondents to figure out a stage decoration for a plot. According to Calvi, the first and second tasks involve unlimited ideational productivity; the third and fourth tasks activate an ideational flow oriented toward a synthetic outcome; and the fifth and sixth tasks require the achievement of the maximum outcome with the minimum effort and the discovery of conceptual implications. Scoring is based on both quantitative and qualitative indices. The test was often used in Italy during the 1960s and 1970s (Calvi et al., 1965; Fattori, 1968; Bosio, 1979).

Another original Italian test was constructed more recently by Antonietti and Cerioli (the test materials, as well as the description of the process from preliminary versions to final version, are reported in Cerioli & Antonietti, 1992b). The instrument, called *Test di Creatività Infantile* (TCI; Test of Child Creativity), is intended for children ranging in age from four to ten years. It is based on the assumption that creative thinking involves a set of processes that includes (a) the free production of ideas generated by a starting stimulus; (b) the search for correspondences, similarities, and shared elements among disparate elements; and (c) the shift in view from which a given situation may be interpreted. The tasks included in the battery activate both the verbal and the visual code. The TCI consists of six tasks: listing as many objects as possible that have a given feature, finding all possible uses of an object, giving several interpretations of a drawing, inventing a story about a given picture, imagining the consequences of an event, and solving unusual practical problems. For each task, fluidity, flexibility, originality, and elaboration scores are recorded. The TCI is available in two parallel forms, which is useful for test–retest studies. The psychometric properties of the TCI have been assessed (Cerioli & Antonietti, 1992b); the original norms valid for Italian children (Cerioli & Antonietti, 1992b) have recently been updated (Gilberti, Corsano, & Antonietti, 2004).

In addition, the TCI has been used repeatedly: The validity of the test has been examined both in experimental studies, where it allowed detection of the effects of creativity training (Cerioli & Antonietti, 1993), and in correlational studies, showing no relationships between the TCI and intelligence and analytical–sequential processing (Benedan, Verga, & Antonietti, 1998).

All the aforementioned instruments are aimed at measuring "general creativity" without making reference to the features of the domain where creativity should emerge. By contrast, in everyday life, as well as in educational settings, individuals are asked to be creative in specific contexts. Consistent with this idea, in recent years contextualized measures of creativity have been devised (e.g., Diakidoy & Spanoudis, 2002). A collaboration between the Department of Psychology of the Catholic University of Milan and MUBA (the Museo del Bambino, or Children's Museum), an Italian association affiliated with the international Hands On network, provided the opportunity to devise a particular contextualized test of creativity (Antonietti & Roveda, 2004). MUBA was interested in verifying whether children participating in its educational activities increased their creativity. The activities were included in an exhibition about color whose purpose was to promote divergent thinking by means of activities focused on a feature of color. In the case of the MUBA exhibition, creativity was defined as a set of abilities involved in detecting hidden colors, in realizing misleading effects induced by color, and so on. Therefore, all these abilities concerned attitudes and mental operations focused on a specific dimension (color). In this particular context, a general measure of creativity didn't seem to be relevant or able to catch the hypothesized influence of the exhibition on creativity. Thus, a creativity test based on the specific topic of color was designed. The first step was to devise a relevant theoretical model. Researchers agreed on the assumption that creativity, even in a narrow context such as the one provided by the exhibition, is a multidimensional construct. How many dimensions constitute creativity? The authors reflected about the elements of creativity that were involved in the educational activities in the exhibition and tried to reduce the long list to a lower number by grouping similar aspects into a restricted range of categories. In the end, three main sets of processes were identified as underlying the different aspects of creativity activated by the exhibition.

The first process was *widening*. It concerns the tendency to keep an open mind, to be aware of the great number of elements that can be identified in a given situation, to recognize possible, not obvious, meanings, to discover hidden aspects, and to overcome apparent constraints. The second process was *connecting*. It refers to the capacity to establish reciprocal relationships among different elements, to draw analogies between remote things, to combine ideas in odd ways, and to synthesize the multiplicity of disparate elements into an overall structure. The third process was *restructuring*. It consists of changing perspective, of assuming a different point of view, of seeing things by inverting relationships between their elements, of asking original questions, and of imagining what should happen if alternative conditions occurred.

The second step was to devise a set of possible tasks relevant to measuring the level of expertise reached by the children in each process. Some constraints had to be taken into account:

1. The tasks should be suitable for children whose age corresponded to the target of the exhibition, without being either too hard for the younger ones or too simple for the older ones.
2. All tasks should be focused on color.
3. Each task, even if involving other aspects of creativity, should predominantly measure only one of the three processes described by the theoretical model.
4. The tasks should be administered without preliminary experience, with no special training needed for testers and no special environmental features requested for administration.
5. The instructions should be easily understood.
6. The tasks had to be completed in a short time.
7. The tasks should be motivating.

Furthermore, the tasks had to be easily modifiable for a computerized version for online, self-administered use.

The third step consisted of the administration of the chosen tasks to a pilot sample of children to verify their adequacy. The creativity test consisted of three tasks, each aimed at measuring a creative process included in the theoretical model. The tasks were printed in a booklet that was given to each child. The pupils had to complete each task by following the instructions and the time schedule given by the experimenter.

Widening abilities were assessed by showing children two pictures and by asking them to identify all the nuances of a given color that they could find in the pictures. Pictures were printed onto a sheet; at the bottom of each picture a palette of different colors was reported. The instructions for this task were as follows: "Look at the picture below. Under the picture you will find a series of colors. Check the colors you can see in the picture." Children were given ten minutes to complete the task. The score was determined by assigning each selected color a value from 1 to 3 according to the originality of the response, assessed on the basis of the frequency distribution of the children's correct choices. Value 1 was attributed to colors chosen by several children, Value 2 to colors chosen by an average percentage of children, and Value 3 to colors chosen by few children. Total scores for the task were computed by summing the values corresponding to the chosen colors.

Connecting capacities were measured by presenting the children with the name of a color surrounded by the written names of eight objects. Pupils were asked to choose three objects they associated with that color. The instructions were as follows: "Look at the color written in the center of the circle below. What does that color make you think about? Tick three things you think about." The task included two trials, each concerning a different color. Scores were computed by summing the values of each object selected by the child. The values varied from to 1 to 3 as in the previous task.

Restructuring skills were assessed by describing a strange situation (for instance, "What might happen if men looked at the world through yellow glasses?") and by asking the pupils to select three consequences within a set of eight alternatives (for example, "Cloudy days should appear sunny days," "People should fail to distinguish ripe from unripe fruits"). The instructions were: "Read the question reported below. Tick the three answers that you'd give." Two trials, using different situations, were included in the task. Scores were determined by using the same procedure as in the first task. A total creativity score was computed by summing the scores obtained by the pupils in each task.

The distribution of the total creativity scores for the sample show that the distribution of the total scores for the sample approximated the normal curve. Furthermore, an experimental design in which tasks were administered to 343 children attending fourth grade in an Italian primary school confirmed the validity of the test. Both the control and the treatment groups were administered the creativity test twice, with an interval of about ten days between the first ("pre") and the second ("post") administration. Classes that had planned to visit the exhibition about color were included in the treatment group. Classes that would not visit the exhibition were included in the control group. In treatment and control classes, no educational activities concerning color were carried out by teachers either during the weeks before the first administration of the test or during the period between the first and the second administration of the test. A significant Group × Phase interaction effect on the total creativity scores emerged. The treatment children increased their creativity scores from pretest to posttest to a larger extent than did the control pupils.

TRAINING CREATIVITY IN ITALY

In Italy, interest in creativity has always been closely related to educational aims. It is worth noting that the first translations of international readings and manuals about creativity were promoted by two publishers (Editrice La Scuola and La Nuova Italia) specializing in educational and school books. Thus, research on creativity and the construction of psychometric instruments has kept up with researchers' attempts to increase the creativity of children and adults through instructional activities (Mencarelli, 1976; Larocca, 1983; Bocci, 1999).

On the one hand, suggestions provided by approaches based on progressive and active pedagogies and, more specifically, by learning through discovery were applied to enhance pupils' creativity at school (Becchi, 1963, 1969a, 1969b; Metelli Di Lallo, 1973; Trombetta, 1969, 1973). The main purposes of such attempts were to arrange school settings to induce students to be active, to express personal ideas, to look for new and not obvious solutions to problems and unusual situations, and so on. Usually no specific materials were devised for these aims; educators were generally invited to modify traditional ways of managing school activities. On the other hand, some sets of exercises useful for stimulating divergent forms of thinking were created and, sometimes, tested (Pedrabissi & Stramba-Badiale, 1985). At least two Italian authors who reached an international audience should be mentioned: Neither are pedagogues or psychologists, but the activities they devised and their reflections about features of the creative process are very close to pedagogical and psychological intuitions. Gianni Rodari (1973), a writer of novels, poems, and rhymes for children, adopted an innovative approach to these genres by devising different, unusual ways to induce readers to figure out possible ends, different solutions, and alternative linguistic expressions for the situations described. Bruno Munari (1977), a designer, invented several funny games, curious experiments, and practical trials to stimulate children's creativity, mostly through the manipulation of concrete materials, graphical signs, and visual patterns. Other original collections of tasks were devised to enhance children's creativity (Antonietti, 1999; Antonietti & Armellin, 1999; Rossetto, 1980).

However, they did not provide a general educational framework that allowed teachers to stimulate creativity in systematic ways.

Cerioli and Antonietti (1992a) devised a well-structured training aimed at enhancing children's creativity. The training reflected an awareness that, in recent years, many objections have been raised to attempts to promote creativity as a general ability without making reference to specific domains. The authors of the program criticized some features of the traditional training methods for creativity. Schematically, five main questionable assumptions seem to be shared by many of these methods:

1. Creativity consists of a unique mental mechanism; thus, people can be trained in such a single mechanism. For instance, a single creative technique like brainstorming – one of the best known creativity techniques, focused on the free, abundant production of bizarre ideas in order to promote innovation – could be used as a general tool for developing creative ideas and skills.
2. Trainees are like a *tabula rasa*; that is, before being instructed, they know virtually nothing about how to be creative; they have no ideas or opinions about creative strategies and are not able to control them. All this has to be "imprinted" into their allegedly empty minds.
3. Even though trainees are instructed with nonecologically valid materials (such as puzzles, riddles, and so on), the programs can succeed in prompting the subsequent spontaneous transfer of creative strategies to everyday problems.
4. The development of creative thinking can be induced by simply asking trainees to perform a specific mental operation a given number of times. In other words, getting some practice in executing an operation should be sufficient to allow people to learn it.
5. Creativity is only a matter of cognitive processes; therefore, trainees must be taught only to activate particular kinds of cognitive operations, without any reference to the complex interaction of these operations with other cognitive processes, emotion, motivation, and the context.

Given these assumptions, it is not surprising that the traditional programs designed to stimulate creativity failed to reach their goals. In fact, ordinary situations in which creative thinking is needed are usually complex situations that involve multiple mental operations. Furthermore, in everyday life, explicit hints to employ the relevant strategy are seldom

TABLE 6.1. *Differences Between Traditional Creativity Training and the Children's Creativity Enhancement Training Program (PSCI)*

Traditional Trainings	PSCI
Children are trained in a single dimension, since creativity consists of a unique mental mechanism	Children develop an integrated structure of various mental mechanisms, each playing a role in a particular phase of the creative process
Children are *tabulae rasae*: they, before being instructed, know nothing about how to be creative	Children's spontaneous beliefs and tendencies toward creativity are considered
Even though children are instructed with non-ecologically valid materials, they can transfer the learned creative strategies to everyday problems	Children are trained by means of materials that mimic real-life situations and are prompted to catch correspondences between the training tasks and such situations
Creativity can be enhanced by asking children to perform a specific mental operation a given number of times	Children are trained not only to apply creative strategies but also to select them and to control their application
Creativity is only a matter of cognitive processes; thus, children are taught only to activate particular kinds of thinking operations	A creative attitude is encouraged: children are invited to take the risks and the discomforts that creativity involves, to overcome the tendency to avoid familiar responses and to look for novelty

given, so that individuals need to be able to identify the specific features of the situation at hand and choose the appropriate way to deal with it. Finally, individuals must not only *know* how to think creatively, but also must *want*, that is be inclined or motivated, to process situations creatively.

With this perspective, in order to produce in trainees a stable aptitude to think and behave creatively in extratraining contexts, it seems (also see Table 6.1) that instructional devices should do the following.

1. Develop an integrated structure of various mental mechanisms, each playing a role in a particular kind of situation or in a particular phase of the creative process.
2. Use materials that mimic real-life situations, or at least help trainees to recognize the relationship between the training tasks and such situations.

3. Consider individuals' spontaneous beliefs and tendencies toward creative thinking and start teaching from their naïve creative competencies, with the hope of changing spontaneous beliefs, tendencies, and strategies by means of an internal restructuring process.
4. Show a metacognitive sensibility; that is, train students not only to execute creative strategies but also to control their execution (e.g., to select the strategy to be applied and to monitor its application).
5. Encourage a creative attitude; for example, encourage students to accept the risks and discomforts that creativity involves, to avoid the tendency to stick to familiar responses, and to look for novelty.

These remarks stressed the need for a different approach to promote creativity, one that was more in tune with some recent perspectives in the psychology of thinking. More precisely, various components had to be identified as occurred in various domains such as intelligence or cognitive style more attention to common reasoning and to complex real-life situations was required; and the role of metacognition in the acquisition of new competencies had to be highlighted.

Various attempts to integrate cognitive, emotional, and personality aspects of thinking have been made. A constructivist point of view – aimed at substituting the spontaneous beliefs and tendencies of an individual with new and evolved strategies by means of an internal restructuring process – is shared by many contemporary learning theories. Hence, Cerioli and Antonietti presumed that these directions should be followed to enhance creativity (see Sternberg, 1988).

The training, *Programma di Sviluppo della Creatività Infantile* (PSCI; Children's Creativity Enhancement Training), was specifically addressed to children four to ten years of age and tried to take into consideration the suggestions already mentioned. The PSCI consists of a book that tells a story, divided into twenty episodes. In the story, two children have to discover why a volcano, which in the past produced magic bubbles, is now inactive. Three pets, who play the role of tutors, accompany the children in their journey in search of the secret of the volcano (Table 6.2). Each tutor represents an aspect of creative thinking – the fluid production of unusual ideas, the ability to find analogies and to look for similarities between different things, and the capacity to restructure situations, that is, to consider them differently by changing the point of view. During the journey within the volcano, the children meet some characters that personify psychological features that hinder

TABLE 6.2. *Schematic Description of the Features of the Three Tutors (pets) of the PSCI*

Name of the pet/tutor: Fluò
Aspect of creativity: The fluid production of
    unusual ideas

Name of the pet/tutor: Comecomé
Aspect of creativity: The ability to find analogies
    and to look for similarities between different
    things

Name of the pet/tutor: Piedaria
Aspect of creativity: The capacity to restructure
    situations, that is, to consider them differently
    by changing the point of view

creativity. In each episode the children have to overcome the negative and noncreative aspects of the situations they encounter and to adopt a productive and innovative perspective.

The PSCI story involves interplay among three different levels (Table 6.3)

- Reality (RE) is the world where the teacher and his or her pupils live and the storytelling occurs;
- Fantasy 1 (F1) is the everyday world where the protagonists of the story live; and
- Fantasy 2 (F2) is the imaginary world within the volcano.

TABLE 6.3. *Levels of the PSCI*

From RE to F2	From F2 to RE
The teacher, by telling pupils the story and by asking them to do things related to the story (RE), introduce them into Sarò and Sarà's adventures (F1). In Sarò and Sarà's life (F1) the three pets–tutors appear: they invite the two children to follow them within the volcano (F2) to discover its secret.	Within the volcano (F2) Sarò and Sarà encounter several characters, who induce the two children to make links to their home and family (F1); these episodes lead the teacher to involve pupils in training activities (RE).

The standard procedure to use the program is as follows. The teacher reads each episode of the story in two to three sessions that last about an hour each. The teacher stops reading the story at some crucial points and asks the students to help the protagonists of the story face the problem they have encountered. For instance, students are asked to propose ideas according to the strategies suggested by the tutors, to interpret ambiguous stimuli, to combine various elements to yield a new product, to imagine things from a different point of view, to modify a given pattern, and to find everyday situations similar to those of the story. The activities that students have to carry out involve verbal (written and oral) expression, music, drawing, drama, and the manipulation of various materials. The implementation of the whole program requires three weekly sessions for four months. (Shortened versions of the training, however, have been tested with good results.) The program requires no structural change in the organization of the school setting where it is implemented; moreover, teachers, who can be easily instructed in its use, are not required to have particular competencies.

An example of some teacher–pupil interactions devised in the story might help foster an understanding of which kind of activities are included in the training. In one of the first episodes, the protagonists are in front of the mysterious door to the volcano. The problem is how the door can be opened. The teacher interrupts the story and takes students in front of a poster simulating the volcano's door. Here students are asked to give their first responses. Children usually find trivial solutions (to push or to pull the door, to turn the key, and so on). Because such responses do not work, the teacher goes on with the story. The first tutor (Fluò) appears and hints at producing as many bizarre ideas as possible. Students' responses are written on the blackboard and are discussed. Also in this case the solution of the problem is unlikely to occur. Hence, the second pet (ComeComé) is introduced in the story; Come-Comé suggests thinking of similarities with everyday-life situations: For instance, opening a door is like uncorking a bottle. Students are stimulated to find further analogies and to test the solutions they inspired by simulating them on the poster. Finally, children are requested to anticipate the strategy associated with the third pet (Piedaria; considering situations from a different point of view) and to apply it to the door problem. The story helps them in doing so and leads them to discover the solution that allows them to go into the volcano. Through this procedure, pupils are induced to go beyond the obvious responses, are engaged in suggesting more original ideas, and are prompted to become aware of some mental strategies they can adopt in facing novel problems.

Some features of the program show how it is in agreement with the issues discussed previously. First, it induces children to learn a set of reasoning strategies that can result in a creative way of thinking. Further, it makes children aware of the strategies they employ, of their relevance, of their benefits and costs. In other words, the program stimulates a metacognitive attitude. It also tries to encourage autonomy in the management of thinking strategies, because the hints given by the tutors become less and less frequent during the course of the story, so that in the last episodes students have to choose by themselves how to face the problems they encounter. Moreover, even though the story is a fantastic adventure, the critical situations in which students are trained to be creative are real situations or have obvious counterparts in real life. Finally, the application of a given thinking technique is linked to the development of a corresponding attitude, such as to be open to the experience, to recognize the emotional states, to look for novelty, or to accept contradictions.

Since 1992, several attempts have been made to validate the program in Italian kindergarten and elementary schools, and positive results have always been recorded. The main findings were obtained in two experimental studies.

The first study involved 275 children attending kindergarten schools in Basilicata (a region of Southern Italy). A larger increase of creativity scores – measured by means of the previously mentioned TCI – was found in the training conditions than in the control condition. The PSCI was more effective when implemented by ad hoc instructed teachers – trained to control their feelings, attitudes, and communicative patterns – than it was when it was impemented by naïve teachers (Figure 6.5). Such an effect occurred mainly in four-year-olds rather than in five-year-olds.

The second study involved 833 children attending kindergarten (ages four and five) and Grade 1 and 2 of primary schools (ages six and seven) in Lombardia (a region of Northern Italy). By consideration of scores in the first administration of the TCI children were classified as low, medium, or high in starting creativity. In general, training conditions succeeded in enhancing children's creativity, especially for children in primary school, where there was a clear superiority of the

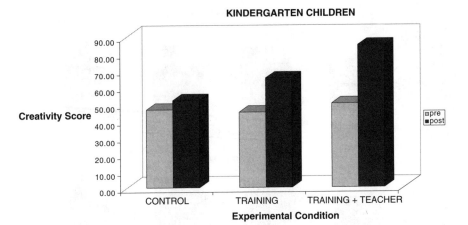

CONTROL = no activities concerning creativity
TRAINING = implementation of the training described above (three weekly sessions of one hour, for four months) by naive teachers
TRAINING + TEACHER = implementation of the training by teachers previously instructed about the psychological aspects of creativity

FIGURE 6.5. Results of the first study aimed at assessing the validity of the PSCI.

program over simple and isolated tasks similar to those included in traditional creativity exercises (Figure 6.6). Creativity scores on the pretests and posttests were analyzed separately according to children's initial level of creativity. Highly creative pupils increased their scores only

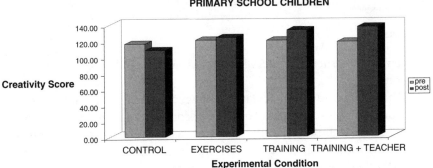

CONTROL = no activities concerning creativity
EXERCISES = traditional creativity tasks, not integrated into a whole training structure
TRAINING = implementation of the training described above (three weekly sessions of one hour for four months) by naive teachers
TRAINING + TEACHER = implementation of the training by teachers previously instructed about the psychological aspects of creativity

FIGURE 6.6. Results of the second study aimed at assessing the validity of the PSCI.

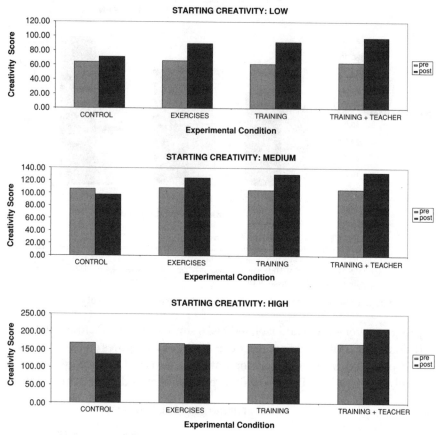

FIGURE 6.7.

when a well-structured intervention was carried out by expert teachers (Figure 6.7).

There was evidence that classes engaged in the PSCI obtained a significant test–retest increase of creativity scores as compared with control classes in which no creativity training was activated and with classes in which traditional creativity activities were used (Antonietti, 1997). Besides these quantitative results, a generally enthusiastic reaction by children and modifications in their behavior (higher motivation, activation, attention, and so forth) in other school tasks were reported by their teachers. (A complete account of these experimental studies is presented in Antonietti & Cerioli, 1996.)

Investigations carried out with the PSCI showed that children can learn to be creative. Such learning is possible, however, only if teachers employ instructional methods that are consistent with the complex nature of creativity stressed by recent research and that involve learning procedures that are not simply based on repetitive activities. In conclusion, applications of the PSCI showed the following.

1. Children should know various creative strategies and the conditions under which each of them is adequate.
2. Children engaged in a creative task should be aware of the mental operation that they are activating in order to monitor its application.
3. Children should recognize the attitudes and emotions that accompany the implementation of a creative strategy and should be inclined to adopt such attitudes and emotions.

The message that can be drawn is that a particular learning environment is needed. Creativity requires a global involvement of pupils, who should be taught to manage by themselves the mental mechanisms that promote creativity. The experience in training children with the PSCI allows some general suggestions to be made that can be valid for every attempt to encourage creativity (see Table 6.4).

Finally, we must mention what has been done in Italy about the enhancement of adult creativity in job settings, even though reflection about this aspect of creativity came relatively late in Italy (Amietta, 1991; Cocco, 1998; De Masi, 2003 Melucci, 1994; Rosati, 1997; Vicari, 1998). The brainstorming technique devised by Osborn (1986) is well known and was widely applied long ago. In addition, the translation of books by De Bono (1969, 1991, 1992), Demory (1990), and Jaoui (1992, 1993) provided alternative models for teaching creativity. Finally, further methods have been devised autonomously by some Italian trainers (Zingales, 1974; Amadori & Piepoli, 1992; Bertone, 1993).

An overall consideration of what Italian scholars have published about creativity induces us to admit that no revolutionary theories have been proposed and no radically innovative studies have been conducted in our country. The picture that emerges is that of a set of research trends triggered by hints coming from abroad, then assimilated according to specific local traditions, and finally resulting in new contributions. Some contributions were successful enough to be considered by the international community, which, in turn, assimilated and developed them; other contributions, made known only in Italy, failed to reach a broader, foreign public and so, even if stimulating, had no impact on the literature about creativity. Further steps in the recent history of the research on creativity in Italy that can live up to its long past are hoped for.

TABLE 6.4. *General Educational Recommendations Derived from the Italian Experiences in Creativity Promotion*

1. It is important to induce children to realize when creativity is needed and when not, for example by stressing that creativity is relevant when there is not a unique correct answer, past experience cannot be useful, rules to be applied are not available. In school activities, both convergent and divergent tasks are usually presented. Such tasks, however, require different approaches; students should recognize the kind of task to be carried out in order to adopt the pertinent approach. This appears to be the first step so that children develop spontaneously, when it is necessary, a creative attitude.

2. Children must know various creative strategies and the conditions under which each of them is adequate. It is not sufficient to give instructions about how to carry out a mental operation and to get practice in performing it. The description of a strategy must be followed by examples of its range of application. Prototypical instances of application could serve as models to be transposed by analogy to other cases. This facilitates the transfer from the original setting in which a strategy is learned to different novel situations.

3. When a creative problem is given, students should learn to ask to themselves, before starting to do something: "Which kind of situation is this?" "Which are the strategies that I could adopt?"; "Which is the most relevant strategy to be used?". These reflections enable students to select the most appropriate way to face the task at hand.

4. Children engaged in a creative task should be aware of the mental operation they are activating in order to monitor its application. For instance, children may be asked: "What are you trying to do now?"; "Why are you doing so?"; "Are the available resources (time, materials, additional aids, and so forth) enough to allow you to do so?"; "Are you reaching the goal?"; "Do you think that it is better to go ahead or to switch the strategy?".

5. Teachers should help children to recognize which are the attitudes and emotions that precede and/or follow the implementation of a creative strategy and render children inclined toward such attitudes and emotions. In other words, students, when encountering a situation requiring creativity, should be already oriented toward the activation of the creative thinking and allow it to work productively. For instance, children should learn that when they are engaged in a creative task they have to deal with many ideas and that these ideas are sometimes confused, conflicting, ambiguous, crazy; so, a quick and precise response cannot be given; rather, students have to accept a period of uncertainty, of "mental fog," of anxiety, and so on. Children should be persuaded that such troubles are necessary to reach a creative result and are, at the end, rewarding.

References

Albert, R. S., & Runco, M. A. (1999). A history of research on creativity. In Sternberg, R. J. (Ed.), *Handbook of creativity*. Cambridge, U.K.: Cambridge University Press.

Amadori, A., & Piepoli, N. (1992). *Come essere creativi* [How to be creative]. Milan: Sperling & Kupfer.

Ambrosi, L. (1892). *Saggio sull'immaginazione* [An essay on imagination]. Rome: Loescher.

Ambrosi, L. (1898). *La psicologia dell'immaginazione della storia della filosofia* [Psychology of imagination in the history of philosophy]. Rome: Società Editrice Dante Alighieri.

Amietta, P. L. (1991). *La creatività come necessità* [Creativity as necessity]. Milan: ETAS.

Anderson, H. H. (Ed.). (1972). *La creatività e le sue prospettive*. Brescia: La Scuola. (Original work published 1959 as *Creativity and its cultivation*. New York: Harper).

Andreani, O., & Orio, S. (1972). *Le radici psicologiche del talento* [The psychological bases of talent]. Bologna, Italy: Il Mulino.

Antonietti, A. (1997). Unlocking creativity. *Educational Leadership, 54*(6), 73–75.

Antonietti, A. (1999). *Creatività in classe 2* [Creativity in the classroom 2]. Brescia, Italy: La Scuola.

Antonietti, A., & Armellin, M. N. (1999). *Creatività in classe 1* [Creativity in the classroom 1]. Brescia, Italy: La Scuola.

Antonietti, A., & Cerioli, L. (1991). Sviluppo del pensiero creativo e interazione educativa [Enhancement of creative thinking and teacher–student interaction]. In G. Gilli & A. Marchetti (Eds.), *Prospettive sociogenetiche e sviluppo cognitivo* (pp. 131–148). Milan: Raffaello Cortina.

Antonietti, A., & Cesa-Bianchi, M. (2003). *Creatività nella vita e nella scuola* [Creativity in everyday life and at school]. Milan: Mondadori.

Antonietti, A., & Cerioli, L. (Eds.). (1996). *Creativi a scuola* [To be creative at school]. Milan: Franco Angeli.

Antonietti, A., & Martini, E. (2000). Suggesting strategies improves the creative visual synthesis. *Perceptual and Motor Skills, 90*, 364–366.

Antonietti, A., & Roveda, A. (2004). Assessing creativity in children's museum [www.unicatt.it/psicologia/labpsicognitiva/]

Arieti, S. (1979). *Creatività: La sintesi magica*. Rome: Il Pensiero Scientifico. (Original work published 1976 as *Creativity: The magic synthesis*. New York: Basic Books).

Baddeley, A. D. (1986). *Working memory*. Oxford, England: Oxford University Press.

Banissoni, F. (1940). *La psicologia dell'inventore* [The psychology of inventors]. Rome: n.p.

Banissoni, M., & Ercolani, A. P. (1973). Dogmatismo educativo dei genitori e "creatività" dei figli [Parents' educational dogmatism and children's creativity]. *Psicologia Sociale e dello Sviluppo, 3*, 27–47.

Barolo, E., Antonietti, A., Cecchini, I., & Stramba-Badiale, P. (1991). Problem-solving e elaborazioni iconiche in stato ipnagogico-simile [Problem-solving and visual processing in a hypnagogic-like state]. *Ikon, 23,* 199–212.

Barolo, E., Masini, R., & Antonietti, A. (1990). Mental rotation of solid objects and problem-solving in sighted and blind subjects. *Journal of Mental Imagery, 14,* 65–74.

Barron, F. (1971). *Creatività e libertà della persona.* Rome: Astrolabio. (Original work published 1968 as *Creativity and personal freedom.* Princeton, NJ: Van Nostrand).

Beaudot, A. (Ed.). (1977). *La creatività* [Creativity]. Torino: Loescher. (Original work published 1973 as *La créativité.* Paris: Bordas).

Becchi, E. (1963). *Appunti per un'educazione alla creatività* [Notes for educating creativity]. Milan: A. Nicola & C.

Becchi, E. (1969a). Creatività artistica nella scuola [Artistic creativity in the school]. *Scuola e Città, 1,* 4–10.

Becchi, E. (1969b). Per una didattica dell'indagine [For a teaching based on inquiry]. *Scuola e Città, 4,* 172–179.

Bellu, R. (1909). *L'immaginazione* [Imagination]. Cagliari, Italy: Serreni.

Benedan, S., Verga, T., & Antonietti, A. (1998). Immagine mentale, pensiero astratto e creatività in bambini di 5–7 anni [Mental imagery, abstract thinking, and creativity in 5- to 7-year-old children]. *Età Evolutiva, 61,* 3–14.

Bertone, V. (1993). *Creatività aziendale* [Creativity in the world of work]. Milan: Franco Angeli.

Biasutti, M. (1988). Bibliografia ragionata sul rapporto creatività-stati alterati della coscienza: Alcune interpretazioni [An annotated bibliography about the relationships between creativity and altered states of consciousness: Some interpretations]. *Attualità in Psicologia, 3*(2), 33–38.

Bindoni, A. A. (1899). *L'imaginazione* [Imagination]. Treviso, Italy: Zoppelli.

Biuso, C. (1903). *La fantasia* [Fantasy]. Catania, Italy: Giannotta.

Bocci, F. (1999). La creatività, cinquant'anni dopo Guilford [Creativity: fifty years after Guilford]. *Scuola e Città, 50,* 449–458.

Bonaiuto, P., Giannini, A. M., & Biasi, V. (Eds.). (1999). Personalità, esperienza estetica e creatività [Personality, aesthetic experience, and creativity] [special issue]. *Rassegna di Psicologia, 16*(3).

Bosio, A. C. (Ed.). (1979). *Sulla creatività* [On creativity]. Milan: Vita e Pensiero.

Bovio, G. (1900). *Il genio. Un capitolo di psicologia* [Genius. A topic of psychology]. Milan: Treves.

Brissoni, A. (1971). *Saggi sull'inventività preadolescente come conoscenza* [Essays on preadolescents' inventive forms of knowing]. Florence, Italy: Giunti-Marzocco.

Brognoligo, G. (1899, March 15). Nevrastenia in Goldoni [Goldoni's neurastenia]. *Biblioteca della Scuola Italiana,* Issue 12.

Brooks, L. R. (1968). Spatial and verbal components in the act of recall. *Canadian Journal of Psychology, 22,* 349–368.

Calvi, G. (1962). *Il problema psicologico della creatività* [The psychological problem of creativity]. Milan: Ceschina.

Calvi, G. (1970). La natura e limiti della creatività nevrotica [The nature and the limits of the neurotic creativity]. *Contributi dell'Istituto di Psicologia dell'Università Cattolica di Milan, 30*, 685–702.

Calvi, G., et al. (1965). *Ricerche sulla creatività* [Inquiries on creativity]. *Contributi dell'Istituto di Psicologia dell'Università Cattolica di Milan, 27*, 00–00.

Cerioli, L., & Antonietti, A. (1992a). *Programma di sviluppo della creatività infantile* [Child creativity enhancement training]. Teramo: Giunti e Lisciani (2nd rev. and enlarged edition published 2001 as *Diventare ciò che si è. Un laboratorio per sperimentare la creatività e l'autonomia a scuola* [To become what someone already is. A laboratory to experience creativity and autonomy at school]. Milan: Franco Angeli).

Cerioli, L., & Antonietti, A. (Eds.). (1992b). *Sviluppare la creatività infantile a scuola. Un contributo sperimentale* [Stimulating children's creativity in the schools. An experimental study]. Potenza, Italy: IRRSAE Basilicata.

Cerioli, L., & Antonietti, A. (1993). Lo sviluppo del pensiero creativo: Training dei bambini e formazione degli insegnanti [The enhancement of creative thinking: Children's stimulation and teachers' training]. *Età Evolutiva, 45*, 22–34.

Cesa-Bianchi, M. (2002). Comunicazione, creatività, invecchiamento [Communication, creativity, and aging]. *Ricerche di Psicologia, 25*(3), 175–188.

Chasseguet-Smirgel, J. (1973). *Per una psicoanalisi della creatività e dell'arte.* Rimini: Guaraldi. (Original work published 1971 as *Pour une psychoanalyse de l'art et de la créativité.* Paris: Payot).

Ciani, M. G. (1983). *Psicosi e creatività nella scienza antica* [Psychosis and creativity in ancient science]. Venezia: Marsilio.

Cocco, G. C. (1988). *Creatività, ricerca e innovazione* [Creativity, research, and innovation]. Milan: Franco Angeli.

Colozza, G. A. (1899). *L'immaginazione nella scienza. Appunti di psicologia e di pedagogia* [Imagination in science. Psychological and pedagogical notes]. Torino, Italy: Paravia.

Cornoldi, C., Logie, R., Brandimonte, M. A., Kauffman, G., & Reisberg, D. (1996). *Stretching the imagination.* New York: Oxford University Press.

Cornoldi, C., & Vecchi, T. (2003). *Visuo-spatial working memory and individual differences.* Hove, England: Psychology Press.

Cristante, F. (1982). Gli effetti del pensiero divergente e convergente sulla abilità creativa [Effects of divergent and convergent thinking on creative aptitudes]. *Archivio di Psicologia, Neurologia e Psichiatria, 47*, 202–211.

Cropley, A. J. (1969). *La creatività.* Florence, Italy: La Nuova Italia. (Original work published 1967 as *Creativity.* London: Longmans, Green).

D'Alessio, M., & Mannetti, L. (1976). *Sul pensiero creativo: Ipotesi e contributi di ricerca* [On creative thinking]. Rome: Bulzoni.

De Bono, E. (1969). *Il pensiero laterale.* Milan: Rizzoli. (Original work published 1967 as *The use of lateral thinking.* London: Cape).

De Bono, E. (1991). *Sei cappelli per pensare.* Milan: Rizzoli. (Original work published 1985 as *Six thinking hats.* City: New York: Little, Brown & Co.).

De Bono, E. (1992). *Strategie per imparare a pensare.* Torino, Italy: Omega. (Original work published 1986 as *CoRT.* London: Pergamon Press).

Del Greco, F. (1896). *Dei rapporti tra genio e follia* [About the relationships between genius and madness]. n.p.

Del Greco, F. (1927). *Di alcuni schizofrenici pseudo-geniali* [About some schizophrenic geniuses]. Genova, Italy: Marsano.

Del Greco, F. (n.d.). *La psicologia del genio e i grandi mistici* [Psychology of genius and famous mystics]. Bologna, Italy: Stabilimento Poligrafico Emiliano.

Del Greco, F. (1898). *Pazzi e delinquenti nelle opere d'arte* [Madmen and criminals in works of art]. Ferrara, Italy: Eridano.

De Masi, D. (2003). *La fantasia e la concretezza: Creatività individuale e di gruppo* [Fantasy and concreteness: Individual and group creativity]. Milan: Rizzoli.

Demory, B. (1990). *Sette tecniche per la creatività.* [Seven techniques for creativity] Milan: Editoriale Itaca.

De Sanctis, S. (1898). *La teoria degenerativa del genio in Italia* [The degenerative theory of genius in Italy]. Rome: Capaccini.

De Stefanis, P. (1932). *Novità inventive nell'epoca degli inventori* [Innovative inventions in the age of inventors]. San Casciano in Val di Pesa, Italy: Società Editrice Toscana.

Diakidoy, I.-A. N., & Spanoudis, G. (2002). Domain specificity in creativity testing. *Journal of Creative Behavior, 36*, 41–61.

Fattori, M. (1968). *Creatività ed educazione* [Creativity and education]. Bari, Italy: Laterza.

Finke, R. (1990). *Creative imagery. Discoveries and inventions in visualization.* Hillsdale, NJ: Erlbaum.

Finke, R. A., & Slayton, K. (1988). Explorations of creative visual synthesis in mental imagery. *Memory and Cognition, 16*, 252–257.

Frigotto, D. S., & Cornoldi, C. (2001, April 1–3). The effects of a "relaxation visualization condition" on a creative mental synthesis task. Abstract of the Eighth European Workshop on Imagery and Cognition, Saint-Malo, France.

Galli, P. F. (1999). *Preconscio e creatività* [Preconscious processes and creativity]. Torino, Italy: Einaudi.

Gardner, H. (1993). *Aprire le menti. La creatività e i dilemmi dell'educazione.* Milan: Feltrinelli. (Original work published 1991 as *To open minds.* New York: Basic Books).

Gardner, H. (1995). *Intelligenze creative.* Milan: Feltrinelli. (Original work published 1993 as *Creating mind.* New York: Basic Books).

Garzoni, T. (1566). *L'hospitale de' pazzi incurabili* [The hospital of incurable madmen]. Venice: Giacomo Antonio Somascho.

Getzels, J. W., & Jackson, P. W. (1962). *Creativity and intelligence.* New York: Wiley.

Giacchetti, C. (1912). *La fantasia* [Fantasy]. Torino, Italy: Bocca.

Giannattasio, E., Nencini, R., & Romagnoli, A. (1988). Il test di creatività di Wallach e Kogan. Presentazione e risultati [The creativity test by Wallach and Kogan. A presentation and some results]. *Archivio di Psicologia, Neurologia e Psichiatria, 49*, 47–72.

Gilberti, N., Corsano, P., & Antonietti, A. (2004). La rilevazione del pensiero creativo nei bambini in età prescolastica: Un'analisi del Test di Creatività Infantile (TCI) [The assessment of creative thinking in preschool children:

An analysis of the Children Creativity Test]. *Psicologia dell'Educazione e della Formazione, 6,* 357–372.

Guilford, J. P. (1950). Creativity. *American Psychologist, 5,* 444–454.

Guilford, J. P. (1967). *The nature of human intelligence.* New York: McGraw-Hill.

Heller-Heinzelmann, R. (1933). *L'immaginazione e la vita estetica* [Imagination and aesthetic life]. Florence, Italy: Bemporad.

Jaoui, H. (1992). *La creatività: Istruzioni per l'uso* [Creativity: instructions to use it]. Milan: Franco Angeli. (Original work published 1990 as *La créativité: mode d'emploi.* Paris: ESF).

Jaoui, H. (1993). *Creatività per tutti.* Milan: Franco Angeli. (Original work published 1991 as *Créatif au quotidien.* Paris: Hommes et Perspectives).

Jaspers, K. (1977). *Strindberg e Van Gogh.* Florence, Italy: Colportage. (Reprinted in *Genio e follia. Malattia mentale e creatività artistica.* Milan: Rusconi, Milan 1990. Original work published 1922 as *Strindberg und Van Gogh. Versuch einer pathographischen Analyse unter ergleichender Heranziehung von Swedenborg und Hölderlin.* Bern: Bircher).

Johnson-Laird, P. N. (1990). *La mente e il computer.* Bologna, Italy: Il Mulino. (Original work published 1988 as *The computer and the mind.* London: Collins).

Kanizsa, G. (1975). Praegnanz as an obstacle to problem-solving. *Italian Journal of Psychology, 2,* 417–425.

Kosslyn, S. M. (1994). *Image and brain.* Cambridge, MA: MIT Press.

Lanfranchi, S., Cornoldi, C., & Vianello, R. (2001, August 31–September 2). *Working memory deficits in individuals with and without mental retardation.* Paper presented at the Third European Conference of Psychological Theory and Research on Mental Retardation, Geneva, Switzerland.

Larocca, F. (1983) *Oltne la creatività: l'educatione* [*Beyond creativity: Eduction*]. Brescia, Italy: La Scuola.

Lombroso, C. (1855). *Sulla pazzia di Cardano* [On Cardano's madness]. Milan: Chiusi.

Lombroso, C. (1877). *Genio e follia* [Genius and madness]. Rome: La Stella.

Lombroso, C. (1892). *L'uomo di genio* [The genius]. Torino, Italy: Bocca.

Lombroso, C. (1897). *Genio e degenerazione* [Genius and degeneration]. Palermo, Italy: Sandron.

Lupi, G., & Antonietti, A. (2000). Sviluppo della creatività infantile attraverso la sintesi di immagini mentali [Enhancing children's creativity through visual mental synthesis]. *Psicologia dell'Educazione e della Formazione, 2,* 353–370.

Lytton, H. (1977). *Creatività e educazione.* Rome: Bulzoni. (Original work published 1971 as *Creativity and education.* London: Routledge & Kegan Paul).

Maslow, A. H. (1971). *Verso una psicologia dell'essere.* Rome: Astrolabio. (Original work published 1962 as *Toward a psychology of being.* New York: Van Nostrand).

Mednick, S. A. (1962). The associative basis of creativity. *Psychological Review, 69,* 220–232.

Melucci, A. (1994). *Creatività: Miti, discorsi, processi* [Creativity: Myths, discourses, processes]. Milan: Feltrinelli.

Mencarelli, M. (1976). *Creatività* [Creativity]. Brescia, Italy: La Scuola.

Metelli Di Lallo, C. (1973). Educazione scientifica e creatività [Scientific education and creativity]. *Scuola e Città, 1–2,* 9–15 and *3,* 75–83.

Mingazzini, G. (1895). *Il cervello in relazione con i fenomeni psichici* [The brain and its relationships to psychic phenomena]. Torino, Italy: Bocca.

Miyake, A., & Shah, P. (Eds.). (1999). *Models of working memory.* Cambridge, U.K.: Cambridge University Press.

Mosconi, G. (1990). *Discorso e pensiero* [Discourse and thinking]. Bologna, Italy: Il Mulino.

Mosconi, G., & D'Urso, V. (1974). *Il farsi e il disfarsi del problema* [The construction and deconstruction of problems]. Florence, Italy: Giunti.

Munari, B. (1977). *Fantasia* [Fantasy]. Bari, Italy: Laterza.

Neumann, E. (1975). *L'uomo creativo e la trasformazione* [The creative man and the transformation]. Padova, Italy: Marsilio. (Original work published 1955 as *Die schöpferische Mensch und die Wandlung.* Zürich: Rhein Verlag).

Olmetti Peja, D. (1988). Creatività e comportamento insegnante [Creativity and teachers' behavior]. *Psicologia e Scuola, 9*(41), 17–28.

Osborn, A. F. (1986). *L'arte della creativity.* Milan: Franco Angeli. (Original work published 1957 as *Applied imagination: Principles and procedures of creative thinking.* New York: Scribner's).

Padovan, A. (1907). *Che cos'è il genio?* [What is genius?]. Milan: Hoepli (2nd enlarged ed.).

Padovan, A. (1909). *Le origini del genio* [The origins of genius]. Milan: Hoepli.

Pagnin, A., & Vergine, S. (Eds.). (1974). *Il pensiero creativo* [Creative thinking]. Florence, Italy: La Nuova Italia.

Pagnin, A., & Vergine, S. (Eds.). (1977). *La personalità creativa* [The creative personality]. Florence, Italy: La Nuova Italia.

Parnes, S. J., & Harding, H. F. (Eds.). (1972). *Educare al pensiero creativo.* Brescia, Italy: La Scuola. (Original work published 1962 as *A source book for creative thinking.* New York: Scribner's).

Patrizi, M. L. (1896). *Saggio psico-antropologico su Giacomo Leopardi* [A psycho-anthropological essay on Giacomo Leopardi]. Torino, Italy: Bocca.

Pazzaglia, F., & Cornoldi, C. (1999). The role of distinct components of visuo-spatial working memory in the processing of texts. *Memory, 7,* 19–41.

Pearson, D., De Beni, R., & Cornoldi, C. (2001). The generation, maintenance, and transformation of visuo-spatial mental images. In M. Denis, R. H. Logie, C. Cornoldi, M. De Vega, & J. Engelkamp (Eds.), *Imagery, language and visuo-spatial thinking* (pp. 1–27). Hove, England: Psychology Press.

Pedrabissi, L., & Stramba-Badiale, P. (1985). Diventare creativi è possibile? [Is it possible to become creative?]. *Studi di Psicologia dell'Educazione, 4*(1), 66–72.

Petter, G. (1998). *Fantasia e razionalità nell'età evolutiva* [Fantasy and rationality in the development]. Florence, Italy: La Nuova Italia.

Quadrio, A. (1973). *Rapporti tra la TV e lo sviluppo della creatività nei ragazzi* [Relationships between TV and creativity development in children]. Torino, Italy: ERI.

Ravizza, C. (1844). *Sulla memoria e sull'immaginazione* [On memory and imagination]. Milan: Chiusi.

Renda, A. (1900). *L'ideazione geniale* [Genius' ideation]. Torino, Italy: Bocca.

Richardson, J. T. E., & Vecchi, T. (2001). A jigsaw-puzzle imagery task for assessing active visuospatial processes in old and young people. *Behavior Research Methods, Instruments & Computers, 33*, 217–219.

Rodari, G. (1973). *Grammatica della fantasia* [The grammar of fantasy]. Torino, Italy: Einaudi.

Rogers, C. (1973). *Libertà nell'apprendimento*. Florence, Italy: Giunti. (Original work published 1969 as *Freedom to learn*. Columbus: OH: Merrill).

Rosati, L. (Ed.). (1997). *Creatività e risorse umane* [Creativity and human resources]. Brescia, Italy: La Scuola.

Rossetto, A. (1980). *Guida alla pratica della creatività* [A guide to the practice of creativity]. Milan: Fabbri.

Rossi, S. (Ed.). (1977). *Saggi sulla creatività* [Essays on creativity]. Rome: Il Pensiero Scientifico.

Rubini, V. (1978). Rapporti tra fattori di pensiero convergente e divergente nella rilevazione testistica [Relationships between convergent and divergent thinking factors in testing]. *Formazione e Cambiamento, 3*, 35–56.

Rubini, V. (1980a). Analisi trasversale della componenti divergenti dei processi cognitivi [A cross-sectional analysis of the divergent components of cognitive processes]. *Orientamenti Pedagogici, 6*, 990–1009.

Rubini, V. (1980b). *La creatività* [Creativity]. Florence, Italy: Giunti-Barbèra.

Rubini, V. (1980c). Le componenti divergenti dei processi cognitivi [The divergent components of cognitive processes]. *Orientamenti Pedagogici, 3*, 635–643.

Rubini, V. (1984). Caratteri cognitivi e di personalità del soggetto creativo [Cognitive and personality characteristics of creative individuals]. *Studi di Psicologia dell'Educazione, 3*(1), 47–67.

Rubini, V., & Cornoldi, C. (1985). Verbalizers and visualizers in child thinking and memory. *Journal of Mental Imagery, 9*(3), 77–90.

Sergi, G. (1894). *Se vi sono donne di genio* [Are there geniuses among women]? Torino, Italy: Bruno.

Sergi, G. (1899). *Leopardi al lume della scienza* [Leopardi considered in a scientific perspective]. Milan: Sandron.

Sergi, G. (1904). *Problemi di scienza contamporanea* [Issues of contemporary science]. Milan: Sandron.

Singer, D. G., & Singer, J. L. (1995). *Nel regno del possibile*. Florence, Italy: Giunti. (Original work published 1990 as *The house of make-believe*. Cambridge, MA: Harvard University Press)

Spira, M. (1986). *Creatività e libertà psichica*. Rome: Borla.

Sternberg, R. J. (Ed.). (1988). *The nature of creativity*. New York: Cambridge University Press.

Sternberg, R. J. (1995). Investigating in creativity: Many happy returns. *Educational Leadership, 53*(4), 80–84.

Sternberg, R. J., & Dess, N. K. (Eds.). (2001). Creativity of the new millenium [Special section]. *American Psychologist, 56*(4).

Sternberg, R. J., & Spear-Swerling, L. (1997). *Le tre intelligenze*. Trento, Italy: Erickson. (Original work published 1997 as *Teaching for thinking*. Washington, DC: American Psychological Association)

Tebaldi, A. (1895). *Napoleone: Una pagina storico-psicologica del genio* [Napoleon: A historical–psychological essay on genius]. Padova, Italy: Draghi.

Thurstone, L. L. (1938). *Primary mental abilities. Psychometric monographs, 1.* Chicago: University of Chicago Press.

Thurstone, L. L., & Thurstone, T. G. (1947). *Primary mental abilities.* New York: Psychological Corporation.

Torrance, E. P. (1992). *Test di pensiero creativo.* Florence, Italy: OS. (Original work published 1974 as *Torrance Test of Creative Thinking.* Lexington, MA: Personell Press).

Trombetta, C. (1969). Appunti per una pedagogia della creatività [Notes for a pedagogy of creativity]. *Pedagogia e Vita, 30,* 575–586.

Trombetta, C. (1973). Creatività ed educazione [Creativity and education]. *Scuola di Base, 5–6,* 26–35.

Trombetta, C. (1989). *La creatività. Un'utopia contemporanea* [Creativity: A contemporary utopy]. Milan: Bompiani.

Vanni, F. (1976). *Psicoanalisi della creatività artistica e scientifica* [Psychoanalysis of artistic and scientific creativity]. Milan: Cortina.

Vecchi, T., Monticelli, M. L., & Cornoldi, C. (1995). Visuo-spatial working memory: Structures and variables affecting a capacity measure. *Neuropsychologia, 33,* 1549–1564.

Vetrani, G. (1899). *Genio e pazzia in Savonarola* [Genius and madness in Savonarola]. Bologna, Italy: n.p.

Vicari, S. (1998). *La creatività dell'impresa* [Creativity in enterprises]. Milan: ETAS.

Vivante, L. (1925). *Note sopra la originalità del pensiero* [Remarks about the originality of thinking]. Rome: Maglione e Strini. (English translation by Prof. Brodrick-Bullock with a Foreword by H. Wildon Carr, *Intelligence in expression. With an essay: Originality of thought and its physiological conditions,* London: C. W. Daniel).

Wallach, N. A., & Kogan, N. (1965). *Modes of thinking in young children.* New York: Holt, Rinehart & Winston.

Weisberg, R. W. (1988). *Guida alla creatività.* Milan: Meb. (Original work published 1986 as *Creativity: Genius and other myths.* New York: Freeman).

Williams, F. (1994). *Test TDC: test della creatività e del pensiero divergente.* Trento, Italy: Erickson. (Original work published 1993 as *Creativity assessment packet.* Austin, TX: PRO-ED).

Zingales, M. (1974). *L'organizzazione della creatività* [The organization of creativity]. Bologna, Italy: Cappelli.

7

Creativity Research in German-Speaking Countries

Siegfried Preiser

Who or what is creative? Is it a person with especially brilliant ideas? An inventor, scientist, or artist? Is it a certain way of thinking? Is it imagination, inspiration, intuition, or systematic problem solving? Is it the environment, in which problems are worked on? Is it the perceived problem itself, the starting point, which enables creative problem solving? Or is it the result, as a product of problem-solving processes? All of these have been used in defining creativity.

Person, process, press, problem, and product are integrated in basic models of creativity (see Mooney, 1958; Preiser & Buchholz, 2004; Urban, 2003a) in the United States as well as in German-speaking countries. The models' focus lies on creative cognitive processes, which are initiated by a problem. These can be subdivided into different phases. In the end they should lead to a creative product. The creative processes are influenced by general and specific knowledge; by expertise, abilities, cognitive styles, and strategies; and by creativity-relevant personality traits, motives, interests, and task commitments (cf. the componential model of creativity by Urban, 2003a). Supporting or hindering environmental conditions and creativity techniques are also important. Only the result shows if an idea can be seen as successful and creative, explaining why the definitions of creativity revolve around the final result. The central criteria, which have been adopted from the United States, are novelty, suitability or usefulness, and social acceptance. What is accepted as useful or original depends on the historical situation as well as the social context. This is valid not only for artistic products but also for political projects and scientific theories. Therefore, creativity is seen as a social construct (see Westmeyer, 1998). As a consequence, definitions like the following have been formulated:

An idea is accepted as creative in a social system, if it is new in a certain situation or contains new elements and if it is seen as a useful contribution to the solution of a problem. (Preiser, 1976/1986, p. 5)

CULTURAL AND SOCIAL BACKGROUND

The modern cultural history in German-speaking countries has often been declared and idealized as a continually creative prime of thought and culture. Martin Luther's Reformation, Immanuel Kant's philosophy of enlightenment, the establishment of psychology as a science through Wilhelm Wundt, and Sigmund Freud's perspective change to the unconsciousness are milestones that are named. World-famous German, Austrian, and Swiss poets and thinkers represent the openness of the intellectual landscape over many centuries: Heinrich Schütz and Johann Sebastian Bach, Josef Haydn, Wolfgang Amadeus Mozart and Ludwig van Beethoven, Johannes Brahms, Richard Wagner, Richard Strauss and Arnold Schönberg, Johann Wolfgang von Goethe and Friedrich Schiller, and Alexander von Humboldt and Albert Einstein. In the Germanic cultural history, trends of fixations on outstanding heroes are evident, such as Siegfried of the Nibelung legend; thus it is tempting to explain cultural progress as the work of a few brilliant people. Artists and authors, like Goethe, have contributed to pushing the mystic gift of ingenuity to the forefront (see Schmidt, 1985). The myth of ingenuity is content with explaining creative brilliance with intuition and even irrationality. In contrast, modern problem-solving and creativity research have "democratized" creativity: Gestalt psychology assumes that every being has the ability to generate new ideas by processes of self-regulation. Personality psychology postulates interindividual varying abilities instead of the ingenuity of a few outstanding people.

Some scientists have attempted to view ingenuity and insanity as equivalent processes under reference of psychologically disturbed artists and poets, but also of creative achievements of psychotic patients. Sigmund Freud interpreted creativity as quasi-neurotic processing of inner conflicts. The psychiatrist Lange-Eichbaum (1927) entitled his book *Genie, Irrsinn und Ruhm (Genius, Insanity and Fame)*. He postulated that ingenuity and mental illness often merged. Despite impressive examples from intellectual history, these assumptions are not empirically verified (e.g., Csikszenmihalyi, 1996). Only for authors, among several creative professions that were analyzed, does Ludwig (1995) report a modest connection between creativity and mental illness (especially alcoholism and depression). He argues that the direction of causal influences is not clear; the writing profession and the circumstances of greatness and reputation could be the cause of mental problems. Nevertheless, newer editions of *Genie, Irrsinn und Ruhm* (Lange-Eichbaum & Kurth, 2000) testify to the unbroken public interest in this myth.

The question as to the extent to which German cultural history has positively influenced creativity is judged differently in public and scientific discussions: Some refer with pride to the intellectual achievements of the past; others deplore with regret or shame the destruction of cultural creativity by the Nazis. Still others try to discriminate which historical and political developments should be seen as creativity stimulating and which as hindering.

Important creativity impulses went along with the change from the Middle Ages to modern history. Complete alterations in the view of the world and of science took place. The Reformation by Luther in Germany, and by Calvin and Zwingli in Switzerland, played a prominent role in this changing process. The Reformation movement underlined intellectual freedom and personal responsibility for one's self and caused an internal liberation from institutions, dogmas, and spiritual authorities. One of Luther's core statements was of salvation "solely out of mercy," which means without man's earlier quid pro quo. This theological message reduced the religious pressure imposed on each individual by the church and enabled an intrinsic religiousness.

One striking fact shows the role that institutionalized Protestantism played in German cultural and intellectual life: In the time between 1650 and 1950, the *General German Biography* shows that more than half of the famous personalities listed were ministers' children or grandchildren (Greiffenhagen, 1982). The Protestant rectories had apparently taken over the inheritance of the Catholic monasteries of the Middle Ages as the intellectual impulse givers. The deep respect the German reformers Luther and Melanchthon had toward school and other forms of intellectual education was probably responsible for this development (see Luther, 1530).

The Age of Enlightenment brought a continuation of the intellectual liberation. The spirit of the Reformation spread to many dynasties and royal houses. "Enlightened Absolutism" was characterized by tolerance, intellectual freedom, reforms toward civil rights but also – as protection against arbitrariness and injustice – obligatory administrative rules, which later stiffened in Prussia into bureaucratic principles. The demands for democracy and the unsuccessful civil revolutions in 1848 finally contributed to the Restoration, the return of authoritarian rule; with the foundation of the German empire in 1871 came strong centralism and a consolidation of bureaucracy. Even so, new views of society developed with the help of Karl Marx and the Socialist Worker movement. The depth psychology theories by Freud, Adler, and Jung led to a change in the psychological view of humankind. Albert Einstein initiated a revolution of the scientific view of the world.

Since the end of the nineteenth century, several models of reform education have been established in Germany, such as the Art Education movement, the Outward Bound movement, and the Waldorf School (see Serve, 1996; Stocker, 1988). Despite some differences, these approaches have many common interests: The teaching concepts are not restricted to verbal and abstract learning. They promote learning by discovery, learning with all senses, and learning by doing. Such schools teach in an interdisciplinary way in order to stimulate complex thinking and operating. Fundamental educational aims are the gaining of personal autonomy and the developing of a sense of social responsibility. Education of the fine arts is considered as important as scientific subjects. Poets, musicians, artists, or theater producers are invited into schools to supervise cultural projects.

World War I and the following Weimarer Republic, a politically unstable epoch, entailed the overcoming of stiffness, but also the dissolution of intellectual and political arrangements. This period facilitated unrestricted creative production in arts as well as in science. On the other side, the extensive lack of religious and cultural orientation may lead to intellectual overtaxing and may prevent existing personal freedom from being creatively used. The loss of orientation makes any new authority seem tempting. Between 1933 and 1945, German National Socialism led, through forced ideological conformity and through voluntary and involuntary emigration, to the destruction of cultural variety. At the same time, scientific and cultural ideas from Germany were carried into and continued in other countries.

Many reasons explain why a creative new beginning of cultural life was difficult after 1945: the partly uncritical reception of foreign influence from the Western countries, a new authoritarianism of the Federal Republic of Germany (FRG) under Chancellor Adenauer, the totalitarianism of the Stalin-shaped German Democratic Republic (GDR), and the concentration on the East–West conflict. At the same time, the historic experience with nationalism and racism led to a rejection of elitist thinking and, therefore, a broad support of creativity for individuals on all educational levels, including the mentally ill and mentally handicapped.

SCIENTIFIC BACKGROUND: THE TRADITION
OF GESTALT PSYCHOLOGY

Modern creativity research in German-speaking countries looks, at first sight, like a pure science import from the United States. A peek at the bibliographies of relevant publications shows mainly U.S.-American titles. At second glance, however, a long research tradition that is connected with the terms *problem solving* and *productive thinking* becomes apparent. Freud's view about the quasi-neurotic conflict structure of creative processes has already been mentioned, along with the psychiatric thesis about the connection between creative ingenuity and mental illness. Since the beginning of the twentieth century, cognitive psychology in Germany has been concerned with productive and creative problem solutions. Gestalt psychologists in particular investigated processes while solving new problems (e.g., Duncker, 1935/1963; Köhler, 1917; Wertheimer, 1925).[1]

Gestalt psychology developed as an antithesis to elementarism and associationism, which reduced all intellectual functions to mental or psychophysical elements and their associative connections. Gestalt psychology proved that perception and thought are not constructed of isolated elements, but of ordered relations and systems. In contrast to associationism – and later, in an adversary role to the behaviorist perspective, as well – the Gestaltists stressed that universal Gestalt principles, like the law of Prägnanz (good figure, precision, and conciseness), come into effect during each experience.

Many psychologists were politically integrated into the National Socialist system, not only for opportunistic reasons. Some were also absorbed into the ideology, allowing their theories to be deformed.

---

[1] The development of Gestalt psychology and its long-term effects are well documented (e.g., Ash, 1998), but many colleagues in Germany have lost awareness of this scientific tradition. I am grateful for these references from personal contacts with the Lewin disciples Anitra Karsten and Ralph K. White and the Wertheimer disciples Wolfgang Metzger and Edwin Rausch, as well as with my colleague Dieter Schmidt.

Others kept their scientific and personal integrity even inside of Germany. Some had to save themselves by emigrating. Leading representatives of Gestalt psychology like Köhler, Lewin, and Wertheimer left Germany for political reasons, carrying their research approaches into the United States, which were still dominated by behaviorism. From there the theories were later reimported into German-speaking countries.

Gestalt psychology's approaches and postulates proved to be very important for creativity research: Wertheimer proceeded with his studies on problem solving in the United States. They were published after his death with the title *Productive Thinking* (Wertheimer, 1945) and were translated into German by his earlier disciple, Wolfgang Metzger, in 1957. According to Wertheimer, the main processes during problem solving are the change of focus and cognitive restructuring of the problem area. The constructivist theory of the Swiss biologist and psychologist Jean Piaget had close relations to Gestalt psychology. The adaptation processes that occur while one is thinking and learning, which Piaget called assimilation and accommodation, can also be seen as cognitive restructuring. Inquiries by Duncker about the interfering and blind-making influence of *Einstellung* (habitual ways of thinking) were later taken up and systematically continued by Wertheimer disciple Luchins (1942). The investigations by Maier (1930) on problem solving also refer explicitly to Gestalt psychology.

Characteristic of Gestalt psychology is the system approach: It is not the elements of a person–environment relationship that are crucial, but their connections and structural arrangement. There are no isolated cause–effect relationships, but complex multicausal interactions. In Guilford's theory of creativity, many aspects of Gestalt psychology can be discovered: units and classes, as well as relations, systems, and transformations, are the products of mental operations. Guilford (1950, 1959) integrated the concept of "reorganization respective redefinition," Gestalt psychology's main principle of problem solving, into his formulation of creative abilities. Interdependent person–environment relationships are also the focus of Lewin's theory, which was continued by Barker in his ecological psychology. The assumption that behavior is a function of the interaction between person and environment was at that time not self-evident, neither for the trait-oriented European psychology nor for American behaviorism. In creativity research, however, the interaction between person and environment has always been seen as significant for creative processes.

The principle of self-regulation of complex cognitive and social systems was also influential: Cognitive elements organize themselves – without deliberate or conscious control of the thinking person – according to Gestalt principles like conciseness or consistency. Leon Festinger, a disciple of Lewin, developed his theory of cognitive dissonance from these assumptions. Similar approaches can be found in the balance theory of Fritz Heider, likewise an U.S.-emigrated Gestalt psychologist. Cognitive self-regulation was included in newer theories about the creative process and the production of ideas.

After the end of National Socialism, several German psychologists were interested in problem-solving processes – even before the inception of modern American creativity research. The assumptions made by the Gestalt psychologist Metzger (1962, 1979) were pioneering and pointed the way ahead. His use of terms like *passion, being deeply stirred by the problem*, and *delicacy* sound somewhat antique and even nonscientific today. However, Metzger astonishingly derived numerous personality traits and requirements out of a theoretical analysis that have turned out to be relevant in modern theoretical and empirical analyses. In today's terminology, Metzger's propagated personal requirements are formulated as such: drive for knowledge and insight, scientific curiosity, personal freedom, mental independence and nonconformism, enthusiasm for the topic, persistence and patience, openness and immunity to prejudice, problem sensitivity, selectiveness of the information processing, and complexity.

THE CREATIVITY BOOM

Applied American creativity research – especially creativity techniques such as brainstorming and synectics – had been practiced in Germany since the 1960s, particularly in advertising, but also in the fields of invention and construction. At the end of the 1960s, a few years after the American creativity boom, a strong interest in creativity arose in Germany. Creativity became a vogue expression. A range of scientific publications mainly traced the development in the United States. Prominent milestones were research reviews by Ulmann (1968) and Landau (1969), as well as omnibus volumes, published by Mühle and Schell (1970) and Ulmann (1973). Several empirical research projects and a compact review, which summarized the state of affairs, followed (Preiser, 1976/1986). At the same time, numerous guidebooks and tutorials concerning creativity practice were published.

In the socialist GDR, a somewhat more moderate creativity boom arose as well. Polemic attacks on the economic, political, and military abuse of creativity in the capitalistic system were obligatory in GDR publications. Otherwise, Western creativity research was systematically absorbed, especially as applied to the solution of technical problems (Mehlhorn & Mehlhorn, 1976; 1977; Wallner, 1989).

In the 1970s, the stimulation of creativity was raised to a pedagogical ideal that appeared in kindergarten and school curricula – but more as a diffuse term than as a concrete learning target. The foundation of an art competition by a Bavarian bank alliance in 1970 fit into this atmosphere. This contest, named *Jugend kreativ* (Creative Youth), first spread to the other German states and then to other European countries. Today, with 1 million participants from Germany and another 500,000 from other European countries, it is the biggest contest for young people in the world. Meanwhile, many local, regional, and national contests for German and other European schoolchildren have been established, such as *Jugend forscht* (Youth Researches), in which pupils can send in their own scientific research projects and results.

Creativity is deep seated as an ideal in public awareness and has settled into everyday speech – if sometimes used tritely. *Creative* as a keyword is found on more than 1,000,000 German Web pages. As a comparison, the keyword *creative* can be found by Google on 20,000,000 pages worldwide. However, the creativity boom of the 1970s in research, education, and further education has waned. In scientific databases, the keyword *creativity* still appears quite often, but frequently just as an accompanying label.

THE MAIN FOCUS POINTS OF CREATIVITY RESEARCH AND PRACTICE IN GERMAN-SPEAKING COUNTRIES

After 100 years of problem-solving research and after 50 years of systematic creativity research, many aspects of creative processes are clarified and documented in reviews and handbooks (e.g., Runco, 1997; Sternberg, 1999; Ward, Smith, & Vaid, 1997). Even so, the object of research is still regarded as indistinct from the scientific standpoint: It seems impossible to find a definition that can be operationalized. Creativity turns out to be a social construction and not a clearly definable scientific construct. The line between creative processes and other complex problem-solving processes, like imagination, intuition, and artistic productivity, stays blurry. In everyday life, however, there is wide unity over what is to be accepted as creative – this is the result of shared social constructions, explaining why the optimization of creativity practice and stimulation as a task of applied creativity research is still an important scientific field.

Creativity can occasionally be found in German-speaking countries as a topic in scientific journals and congress programs. However, the topic is most publicly visible in other disciplines. First are pedagogics, starting with kindergarten or preschool education over school pedagogics and university didactics up to professional training programs; next, the applied fields of economy and administration, especially the areas of research, development, marketing, and organizational development.

What is specific about the focus on creativity in Germany and the German-speaking neighbor countries? This question is not easy to answer, given the uninhibited reception of U.S.-American theories. At a second glance, though, several focus points can be identified. For none of the following topics is there a German-speaking monopoly, at best an accentuation of special requests. The main focus points can be captioned as follows:

- complex problem-solving processes;
- personality development;
- economic and scientific application;
- the social context;
- creativity in the education system;
- the learning and working environment; and
- creativity diagnostics.

Complex Problem-Solving Processes – The Integration of Convergent and Divergent Thinking, Analysis, and Intuition

It is not well known that, next to his experimental psychology, Wilhelm Wundt formulated an extensive cultural psychology (*Völkerpsychologie*), which was based predominantly on descriptive and interpretive methods and – unlike his experimental psychology – left room for complex processes. Since the beginning of Gestalt psychology, complex topics were supposed to be made approachable by an exact research methodology. Characteristic of Gestalt psychology's approaches is the assumption that systematic problem analysis and cognitive self-organization interact: After a situation, problem, and goal clarification within problem solving, a reorganization according to the law of Prägnanz into a "good Gestalt" takes place, which implies the sudden restructuring of the problem area in the form of an idea.

Shortly after World War II, the Swiss astronomer Zwicky, who worked in the United States, developed methods for analyzing problems and raised them into the status of a scientific religion under the title *Morphological View of the World* (Zwicky, 1957; 1989). The "morphological box" became especially well known: For an exactly defined problem, all parameters that could influence the solution are considered; qualitative values of the parameters are now combined to build a multidimensional matrix; and finally, all possible combinations on the basis of certain criteria are verified concerning their realization. An established example of a three-dimensional morphological box is the structure of intellect model of Guilford, with the parameters of mental operations, contents, and products. Characteristic of the morphological approach is the combination of divergent thinking (the search for relevant parameters) and convergent thinking (the systematic combination of all parameters and their values).

In Germany, Süllwold (1954) investigated insight with the help of classic brainteasers and differentiated between a phase without insight, in which thought processes occur without restructuring, and a phase of sudden insight, in which the necessity arises to restructure the problem area. Facaoaru (1985) examined the influence of problem-solving abilities and cognitive styles on creative performance in the technical-scientific field on planning and research engineers. Next to convergent, divergent–associative, and divergent–analytical abilities, she also postulated divergent–convergent abilities as an in-between field and designed tests for this new construct. The divergent–convergent ability means the capability first to develop many alternatives and then to discover the only fitting or optimal solution. For instance, the Test of Spatial Setting requires drawing as many geometric figures as possible into a given frame following certain rules. To produce an optimal solution, different options must be developed divergently and the most effective solution must be chosen and realized convergently. The divergent–convergent ability was clearly distinguishable from the other abilities in a factor analysis and correlated with external criteria for technical-scientific problem-solving ability.

Dörner and his research group analyzed complex planning, problem-solving, and decision-making processes, such as within the fictitious administration and political–economical governance of a city or a less-developed country (e.g., Dörner et al., 1983; Dörner & Wearing, 1995).

Complex problems are characterized by a great number of networked variables that are to be controlled by the problem solver, by dynamic systems with unknown, even nonlinear relations, by spontaneous or non predictable changes in the variables, and by complex, sometimes contradictory targets (cf. Funke, 2003). Intellectual or creative abilities alone do not allow a prediction of complex problem-solving performance; motivational factors and socioemotional abilities seem comparably important. For the context of creativity, it seems fundamental that the readiness and possibility to deliberately change between convergent and divergent thinking benefits complex problem solving.

The integration of rationally controlled intuition and expertise in a computer-assisted construction process was also the concern of psychologists and engineer scientists in the GDR (Heinrich, 1989; Mehlhorn & Mehlhorn, 1986). Wallner (1990), a Marxist scientist, inspected unpublished reports by Einstein in the Center for the Collected Papers of Albert Einstein in the United States about his insight processes to complement the reported memories of Wertheimer (1945). Apparently, the interaction of systematic–analytical thought processes and consciously controlled imagination was characteristic of Einstein's way of thinking. During the development of the relativity theory, Einstein evidently used precise figurative images: For instance, he visualized a man falling together with several other objects from the roof of a house, and concluded that for this man neither a gravitational field nor a movement, relative to his likewise falling tools, would exist during the fall.

Personality Development: The Therapeutic Context

Creative processes are considered in different therapy forms; admittedly, some forms have been reimported from the United States back into Germany. What these approaches have in common is that they support the free development of the personality and of personal resources. In particular, the ability to creatively solve personal problems and social conflicts is fostered.

Jacob L. Moreno (1946/1959/1969), an Austrian, published training and therapy forms for psychodrama and sociodrama after his emigration to the United States. Here, a problem is transformed into a concrete conflict situation; group members take over the position of the persons involved in the conflict in role play; subsequently, the acted-out situation and the acting behavior are collectively discussed and alternatives are compiled. The couple Laura and Fritz Perls, natives of Germany, developed body- and movement-oriented Gestalt therapy in loose association with Gestalt psychology. Psychodrama and Gestalt therapy attempt to rearrange deadlocked perception and behavior patterns (cf. Petzold, 1973; Petzold & Orth, 1991).

Outside of psychological psychotherapy research and practice, different forms of music and art therapy have been established in Germany with their own study. In these therapy forms the processing of personal problems and conflicts is aimed at through free improvisation or artistic designing. Some of these therapy forms are not accredited by the public health system but are used in privately financed therapy. Many elements of these therapy forms can be found in courses on personality development, which are offered mostly for managers in in-company training courses as well as in open seminars.

Economic and Scientific Application: Creativity Methods in Organizations

Development
With the first modern publications in German language, creativity was transferred into practice at the same time. The Team for Psychological Management, founded by Preiser, and trainer Bernd Rohrbach, have been most likely the first to regularly host creativity courses in Germany since the end of the 1960s. In the beginning of the 1970s a creativity team from the Batelle Institute, an application-oriented research institution, was established (see the paragraph on creativity as a social movement). The first creativity techniques were developed and propagated in the marketing field, so it is not surprising that economists are especially inclined to use systematic creative idea-finding processes. In the German economic and social science database, WISO-net, one can find eighty to ninety publications annually for the years between 1994 and 2003 that explicitly pick out creativity as a central economic theme. The publications are primarily concerned with the following objectives: (a) advertising and marketing, (b) idea and innovation management, system of employees' suggestions for improvement, (c) corporate policy and leadership, (d) evaluation, selection, and promotion of creative potential, and (e) creativity techniques.

In the field of technical innovations, creativity techniques have also been systematically used (in the FRG, e.g., DABEI, 1987; and Heister, 1991; in the GDR, e.g., Mehlhorn & Mehlhorn, 1976; 1986; and Wallner, 1989).

Techniques

In the scope of the application of creative idea-finding methods to concrete operative or social questions, different creativity techniques have been designed or adapted in the German-speaking countries since the 1970s. Some of these techniques are introduced in the following paragraphs.

METAPLAN CARD TECHNIQUES. The Metaplan method works with written communication and visualization. This so-called moderation method was developed by a German consulting team. It is based on some specific rules of communication and a set of materials (oval, cloud-shaped, and rectangular cards, felt-tipped pens, and pinboards). The characteristic course of action is that the participants independently write their ideas on small cards in large letters. The cards are then jointly arranged on the pinboard by the group. Consequently, the ideas are transformed into precise work assignments. A moderator or facilitator organizes the communication process in the group. The advantage of this method is that no one in the group dominates and that all suggestions are treated equally. The methods originally developed under the name Metaplan are widely spread in Germany. There is hardly a university or larger company that does not work with these instruments. Today, these methods are present worldwide; the Metaplan Association works in many countries and has branches in France and the United States (cp. www.metaplan.com). In the meantime, the methods have been modified and advanced by several teams (e.g., Klebert, Schrader, & Straub, 1991).

MODIFIED BRAINSTORMING. Brainstorming was taken up very early in Germany and its use is still widespread – despite the empirically justified criticism of its efficiency (e.g., Stroebe & Diehl, 1994; Stroebe & Nijstad, 2004). Mainly, modifications and alternatives have been sought to benefit from the postulated advantages of brainstorming and at the same time to overcome its limits. One variant that I am fond of using implies three simple modifications of classic brainstorming: First, the participants are explicitly called on to think in different directions and not to be confined to the suggestions of the others. Second, for a few minutes before starting the group brainstorming, the participants have the opportunity to note their own ideas on Metaplan cards, in order to generate a broader spectrum of ideas. Third, the ideas are then placed on the Metaplan pinboard; the participants can let themselves be encouraged by these ideas, or can continue to work independently without being disturbed. In some studies, modified brainstorming has been proven to be more effective than conventional instructions and classic brainstorming.

BRAINWRITING 635. Rohrbach (1969) introduced Brainwriting 635, which is a written version of brainstorming: Six members of a team formulate three ideas each for a given topic on a piece of paper; after five minutes, respectively, they hand the paper to the person next to them and receive a paper from the other side; now the task is to elaborate and advance the given ideas. After thirty minutes, each group member has a piece of paper with eighteen ideas each. The advantage of this variant is that the participants do not disturb each other and that ideas are systematically developed.

BRAINWALKING. Preiser (1982) combined the postulated advantages of brainstorming (among other things, spontaneity, free association, reciprocal encouragement, and higher originality by means of evaluation-free phases) with the advantages of brainwriting (among other things, systematic cogitation, elaboration, and the advancement of ideas) in the brainwalking method: Many versions of a topic or many different problems are written on large sheets of paper and hung in different parts of a room. The participants now go from poster to poster and write down their ideas; they can note new ideas or pick up the suggestions and advance them as a mindmap. The walking around and the change between different mindmaps should activate the organism, promote a change in perspective, and contribute to the overcoming of cognitive inhibitions and fixations. The method contributes to physical and mental regeneration, reduction of performance pressure by cutting back the stress, broadening the horizon through a larger distance to the problem, selective deletion of the working memory, activation of remote associations, and random connections with ongoing perception and thought contents.

THE SCENARIO-TECHNIQUE. This technique was developed in the 1970s by the Batelle Institute. Starting with a description of the current environment, experts estimate future trends. By means of brainwriting, discussions, and standardized evaluation techniques, they develop three different scenarios and rate them comparatively: an optimistic scenario, a pessimistic scenario, and a scenario projected from the previous development. Experts then derive goals and strategies for future action from these scenarios.

LARGE GROUP METHODS: The Future Conference method (according to Weisbord) and the Open Space method (according to Owen), which were developed in the United States, were taken up in German-speaking countries and mainly applied in large organizations (e.g., Witthaus &

Wittwer, 2000). A similar form of method is the information market, established by Metaplan: Booths with different topics are set up in a hall and are each attended by one to three moderators. The participants can work on their own preferred topic, but they can also go from booth to booth.

THE FUTURE WORKSHOP. The workshop was developed in the 1960s by the futurologist Robert Jungk, in order to let social development be designed not only by experts but also by the affected citizens. Future workshops were first used in civil protest movements, although the method has also been integrated into processes of organizational development. The future workshop begins with a phase of criticism, in which a critical survey is taken of the present situation. A phase of utopia follows, in which the visions of an optimal future are developed. Subsequently, during the phase of realization, the central aspects of the visions are identified and a course of action for the practical realization is designed (Jungk & Müllert, 1989).

The Social Context

A lot of attention has been paid to the social aspect of creativity. Ernst Bornemann, the longstanding chairman of a German association for political psychology, was never tired of propagating the concept of a heightened civil involvement in social problems. Analogous to industrial concepts, the government could install an information system, by which citizens could send in their suggestions for improvements in society. It is not a coincidence that a new creativity technique, the aforementioned brainwalking, was first applied at a symposium for political psychology under a social topic – the promotion of responsibility (Preiser, 1982). The research by Dörner and his group is also about how to manage complex political and social tasks and not how to solve trivial everyday tasks like "What can you do with a brick?" Metaplan and moderation methods, information markets, open space methods, and future workshops are deployed in companies as well as in political organizations, in order to benefit from the creative potential of the employees or citizens (cf. Apel et al., 1998; see www.wegweiser-buergergesellschaft.de/politische_teilhabe/). The social environment also plays a central role in the analysis and improvement of the creative atmosphere in companies and schools.

In the reform era around 1970, independent painting courses were established in many German cities to create new forms of art education. The *Kreativitätsschule Wuppertal* (School of Creativity) became especially

famous. The principal, Gunter Wollschläger (1972), attempted to integrate multi-media-based artistic creations (including painting, handicrafts, clay sculpture, and acting in role and stage plays) with social
learning. Spontaneous, self-initiated behavior and learning, playing,
and working in groups, as well as the use of artistic media, were meant to
promote spontaneity, expressiveness, imagination, and social creativity.
According to Wollschläger, the process of creativity stimulation takes
place in the following steps:

1. Sensitization: The personal freedom to play with all available
   artistic media should encourage spontaneous behavior and sen-
   sitize the senses.
2. Group reflection: Spontaneous experiences are worked through
   and multimedially processed in groups with the supervision of
   an educator.
3. Synthesis: On the basis of these experiences, constructive and realistic solutions for social problems should be derived.

Thus, playing and artistic activities both serve as a medium to promote political and social creativity. Some creativity schools still work
on the basis of combining esthetic and artistic education with social
learning and political socialization, thus enabling creativity education
in a social context (cf. Landesarbeitsgemeinschaft Kreativitätspädagogik
NRW, 1989; for current information, see www.bjke.de, www.lkd-nrw.de,
www.jeux.de, www.krea-online.de).

Creativity in the Education System

Development
Since the 1970s and into the twenty-first century, there has been a public demand to reinforce creativity and innovative spirit in society, the
economy, and the education system. For example, an omnibus volume
by Mühle and Schell (1970), entitled *Creativity and School*, deals with
the relations between school performance, intelligence, and creativity.
It discusses creativity-stimulating education and contains training and
teaching models. Serve (1996), from an educational standpoint, declares
creativity stimulation as a fundamental mission of school education. The
following paragraphs deal with the realization of psychological postulates for creativity education.

Nursery schools (for children aged three to six) implemented creativity education most successfully among all educational institutions:

Personal freedom, learning by playing, and the cultivation of imagination and artistic education have always been important elements of nursery school. As a result, activities like playing, storytelling, improvising with musical instruments, painting, and handicrafts are now subsumed under a new generic term: *creativity stimulation*. However, seen from the outside, the code of practice of kindergarten work hasn't changed much. In some nursery schools today, so-called creative designing still consists of coloring in ready-made Santa Clauses or gluing ears on cutout Easter Bunnies. Nevertheless, one can state that the positive term *creativity* released further impulses for imaginative designing, painting, and thinking in preschool education.

Creativity stimulation has also been strongly demanded in the schooling of teachers and in curriculum development. However, changes in daily school practice have developed slowly. The reasons for this may be that adaptations usually are a longer lasting process, that the general framework of teaching barely changed, and that experienced teachers have been unable or unwilling to alter their teaching style from one day to the next.

A look at university catalogs of lectures from the 1970s shows that only a few lectures dealt with creativity, at best with thinking and problem solving. Training courses on how to stimulate students' creativity or how to teach in a creativity-stimulating way were rarely offered. Creative working methods were integrated into research and classes in technical colleges and universities of applied sciences more often than in psychological institutes. The education of creativity has played an inferior role until today: In university catalogs, training courses for the promotion of creativity can rarely be found. Still, some examples of innovative teaching concepts exist: In introductory courses for freshmen, some creativity techniques are negotiated to communicate successful study and work techniques. They are taught at technical universities in connection with constructive tasks, integrated in computer-aided design processes, or even applied together with other study and work techniques in introductory courses. One new didactic approach at universities deals with replacing students' conventional oral presentations with creative methods: For instance, communicating scientific topics by use of posters, which allow imaginative and inspiring visualizations. Scientific matters can also be illustrated through scenic stage presentations with original and creative ideas, for example in the form of podium discussions, talk shows, or plays like a simulated parent–teacher conference (Preiser, 2003a).

Creativity methods have been taught and practiced most intensively in professional training courses. Pioneers of applied creativity methods have held hundreds of training courses in different organizations. On one hand, specific creativity techniques have been taught and used on the participating group's concrete practical problems; on the other hand, training tasks have been given in order to stimulate creative abilities. What is this training like today? Publicly offered courses for executives are regularly introduced in the magazine *Manager Seminare*. In the years from 1997 to 2004, about thirty creativity training courses a year were announced, which is about 1 percent of all courses. Fifty different providers share this open vocational market. Company offers for advanced training and independent trainers' field reports show that creativity plays a relatively small role in professional training – especially compared with the boom of the 1970s.

In terms of promoting the gifted, since the 1980s, different research groups concerned with gifted students have been established in Germany (cf. Urban, 2003b; for relevant internet addresses, see www. hochbegabungs-links.de). Some researchers such as Heller (2001) or Urban (www.erz.uni-hannover.de/~urban) focus on creativity as well as on intelligence. Regional counseling centers for families with gifted children, which offer intelligence and personality diagnostics, have also been established. The counselors compile recommendations for further school education, but also for extracurricular activities. Intellectually and creatively gifted children have the possibility of being taught in special classes or schools. Within the scope of research on gifted children, diagnostic methods have been developed, such as the Test for Creative Thinking (Urban & Jellen, 1995) or the Munich Gifted Test System (Heller & Perleth, 1999), which measures, among other things, intelligence, creativity, musicality, and social competence.

Despite the broad discussion of creativity in school and educational practice, this topic has a shadowy existence in scientific educational psychology. In introductory books for teachers, as well as in concise dictionaries, contributions on creativity can be found (e.g., Cropley, 2001; Preiser, 2003b). In contrast, the keyword *creativity* can be found neither in a current educational psychology textbook (Krapp & Weidenmann, 2001) nor in the volume *Psychology of Instructions and School* of the comprehensive *Encyclopedia of Psychology* (Weinert, 1997). However, the large practical significance of creativity stimulation is shown in the following paragraphs.

Creativity Stimulation in Education Practice

PROMOTION OF CREATIVITY IN CHILDREN'S PLAY. Some features of playing are equivalent to conditions of creative processes. Playing stimulates intrinsic motivation and creative imagination. Since the 1970s, various descriptions of games have been published that are supposed to promote creativity. These collections of games exist for different ages. Wohlgemuth (1995, 1998), for instance, published writing games as teaching material in order to stimulate students' creativity. However, systematic and controlled evaluations of such "play projects" rarely exist.

CREATIVITY TRAINING. In several publications, classic creativity techniques are propagated to be applied at school (e.g., Bugdahl, 1995). Furthermore, there have been attempts to introduce a systematic creativity training course as a school subject. The most important argument for this course has been that only a separate training not included in traditional subjects could guarantee enough freedom to create innovative learning and working forms. Results across all German-speaking countries show that creativity training may help to increase creative abilities. Despite the multitude of positive evaluation reports from the United States, Hany (2001) regards these findings skeptically, emphasizing that similar positive results could also be achieved simply by a change in the instruction.

TEACHER EDUCATION AND TRAINING. The goal of academic teacher training has been to change the behavior and attitude of teachers (Cropley, 1991; Heinelt, 1974). Teachers should bring about a friendly and stimulating atmosphere of encouragement and promote the students' self-assessment. Teaching methods have been changed insofar as intellectual freedom has been admitted, more open-ended questions have been asked, and complex tasks have been introduced. Autonomous information processing promotes learning success, boosts transfer abilities, and helps develop problem-solving strategies. Rudolf Wohlgemuth leads the Creativity at School project with high personal dedication. He distributes exercises and teaching materials (Wohlgemuth, 1995, 1998), offers advanced training for teachers, and supervises processes of organizational development at schools. His webpage, www.wohlgemuth-media.de, deals with literature concerning creativity research as well as creative writing, and it gives suggestions and information about creativity blocks, creativity techniques, and arranging a positive learning atmosphere.

TEACHING APPROPRIATE PROBLEM-SOLVING STRATEGIES. Wertheimer's (1945) observations in school classrooms demonstrated deficiencies in the support of critical thinking in conventional instruction: Students learn to use mathematical rules without deeper understanding. This is why they have trouble applying these rules to new problems. By using examples of math and logic problems, Wertheimer demonstrated how to make insightful learning processes and thus how to make productive problem solving possible through the right kind of problem formulation. Fiedler and Windheuser (1974) showed that, by learning from a model, people could be brought to systematically use different phases of the problem-solving process and so optimize their problem-solving behavior. Modern psychological teaching concepts explicitly demand that the development of learning and problem-solving strategies be one of every teacher's general goals.

CREATIVE WRITING. Apparently, creative writing already played an important role in the medieval Latin schools that were supported by Carl the Great (768–814). The term *creative writing* summarizes various tasks: Writing essays or short stories; writing to given pictures, a piece of music, or a fantasy journey; "automatic writing" as a form of free association; creative text interpretations; and so on. Creative writing found its place in German schools throughout different epochs. In the 1970s, divergent thinking, playful and surreal alienation, controlled violation of correct language use, and nonsense texts dominated. In the 1980s, personal experiences were to be expressed in words. Nowadays, more complex projects such as the collective writing of a play or a detective story are typical. Ideas and instructions concerning creative writing in German lessons can be found in books (e.g., Merkelbach, 1993) and in regular contributions to pedagogical journals.

AN INTEGRATIVE CONCEPT. Jutta Wermke (1989) developed a comprehensive integrative concept to stimulate students' creativity in German lessons for Grades 5 to 9. She tested four units including twelve lessons each for Grade 5 and evaluated her program successfully. Wermke postulates four general objectives, each of which leads to a personal developmental goal:

1. Generate freedom of action for the subject.
2. Explore everyday life and find new perspectives.
3. Invent dream worlds.
4. Question stereotypical communication and overcome its restrictions.

TABLE 7.1. *Relations of General and Personal goals, Tasks, and Required Results in Creativity Training*

Four General Objectives for Creativity Stimulation	Personal Developmental Goals (Examples)	Tasks and Activities (Examples)	Features of the Required Results from the Students (Examples)
generating freedom of action for the subject	humor and tolerant nonconformism	playing with words, writing games, transforming texts into pantomime, and inventing clowneries	expressive behavior; ambiguity
exploring everyday life and finding new perspectives	curiosity, patience, and tolerance of ambiguity	inventing onomatopoeias; converting scenes into sounds and noise	dealing playfully with texts
inventing dream worlds	activity, calmness, and lateral thinking	writing and producing radio plays, drama scenes, and science fiction	using free association; spinning a yarn
questioning stereotypical communication and overcoming its restrictions	responsible autonomy and ability to take criticism	creating alienations and parodies of comics, thrillers, advertisements, and propaganda	producing variations; trying alternatives

Table 7.1 demonstrates how general goals are transformed into personal developmental goals, then into concrete tasks and activities, and finally into features of the results required of the students.

EXTRACURRICULAR PROJECTS. More and more of the principles of reform schools are integrated into public schools. Many schools organize so-called project weeks that go on for a limited time. The students individually choose a project that they are interested in. The topics are not limited to school subjects or curricula. Projects make miniature models of self-organized, discovery-oriented learning possible. In some schools, multi-media-based projects are realized, such as movies, theater plays, or musicals. The students write their own texts for musicals or stage plays, compose their own musical pieces, songs, and medleys, and design scenery and costumes. Plays are staged, rehearsed, and finally performed publicly. Other projects include running a school radio, designing Web presentations, and creating a school magazine, book, or exhibition that deals with historical, political, or cultural topics. The students also write articles for a newspaper, which are regularly published on a special page (for additional examples, see Preiser, in press-b).

CREATIVITY SCHOOLS. Creativity schools with artistic and social learning goals have already been mentioned. Hans-Georg and Gerlinde Mehlhorn have established a comprehensive concept: the BIP Creativity Center in Leipzig (see www.uni-leipzig.de/kreativ). This center aims to foster the all-around development of talent, intelligence, and personality. The educational subjects comprise painting, dance, theater, music, creative language use, computer science, and chess. The courses are offered twice a week in the afternoon. Since 1997, the BIP Center has founded a creativity nursery school, a creativity high school, and seven elementary schools that take up the concepts of reform schools, complement traditional school subjects with diverse learning and acting opportunities, and can be attended instead of public school.

The Learning and Working Environment

Next to personality factors, abilities, cognitive styles, and problem-solving strategies, the environment plays an important role in creativity stimulation. Situational factors such as the formulation of the problem, the adoption of rules and creativity techniques, or the working atmosphere can affect the production of creative insight. Success and acceptance of creative ideas depend on the reception and evaluation of experts in the field. The environmental conditions of various systems may discourage, inhibit, and suppress or nurture, stimulate, inspire, and cultivate creative processes. Environmental frames influence children's development of creativity, actual creative processes, and finally the acceptance and appreciation of creative products (cf. Urban, 2003a).

The Organization as a Condition for Innovation

Inspired by U.S.-American and European studies on the working environment, Meissner (1989) investigated internal ecological factors as predictors for individual creative performance in two large high-tech companies. Of a total of 131 interviewees, the number of innovative ideas as the criterion was predicted with a multiple correlation of .52 by five operational factors: importance of the task, openness of the communication, frequency of official meetings, permeability of information, and (with negative weight) professional support by the superior. The fact of particular interest seems to be that intrinsically motivated employees are promoted in their creative production by different factors than less-motivated employees.

A research group of the Frankfurt University developed questionnaires in order to measure the quality of the learning and working environment in various organizations, such as kindergartens, schools, businesses, and administrations: these are known as KIK (*Kreativitäts- und Innovationsfreundliches Klima*, or Creative and Innovative Climate; see Preiser, in press-a). On one hand, these questionnaires are used for research; on the other hand, they provide information about what could be improved in the learning and working environment. Four main aspects concerning the creative atmosphere were derived from classic and modern research results: (a) activation of curiosity, thinking, and action through stimulating learning and working environments; (b) goal-oriented and intrinsic motivating settings; (c) an open and trusting atmosphere; and (d) fostering personal freedom and nonconformity.

Other research groups gained similar results concerning the relevance of leadership and atmosphere for innovative processes: Perceived press for change, expected changeability of the work processes, and professional stimulation by the expertise of the superior proved to enhance innovations (Gebert, 2002; Krause, 2004).

KIK

The aforementioned questionnaires contain, among others, the following topics:

1. Activation means, for example, creating stimulating and diversely outfitted, but not ornate, classrooms and offices, and making miscellaneous information material available.
2. Goal-oriented motivation implies triggering interest and promoting self-assessment.
3. An open and trusting atmosphere is achieved by guaranteeing confidentiality and discretion and by openly discussing conflicts without offending others.

4. Personal freedom and nonconformity can be reached by creating decision leeway and mental scope, allowing playful testing, and welcoming different opinions as an expansion of views.

The KIK version for the working atmosphere in organizations was studied by factor and item analysis in several large samples (Giesler, 2003). Some results support the validity of the questionnaire. Among other things, employees' suggestions for improvements were included as a validity criterion.

In several studies by our research group in Frankfurt, the relationship between aspects of the learning environment and the children's performance in drawing and verbal creativity were analyzed. In twenty kindergarten groups, a significant statistical relation between the creative atmosphere estimated by the educators and the average scores, which were measured with a creative drawing test and by the originality in the children's paintings and handicrafts, was demonstrated. Empirical studies in German and Chinese elementary schools including almost 1,000 students allow the following conclusions: The creative atmosphere in institutions such as schools and kindergartens goes along with the creativity and originality of children's ideas and handicrafts. The teachers' own verbal creative skills and a positive attitude toward creativity have a promoting effect on the originality of the students' drawing and verbal performance (Preiser, in press-a).

In addition, personality traits that favor creativity such as self-confidence, independence, and self-assuredness positively correlate with the school atmosphere and the teachers' personality traits. The results indicate that a positive learning environment affects children's creativity in a significant way, but they also emphasize that efficient education is especially promising in early childhood. The effects of creativity-enhancing teaching conditions depend on the time the teacher has taught in the particular class. At least two years of teaching in the given class were necessary in order to prove consistent effects (Böger-Huang, 1996; Preiser, in press-a). So, we must provide continuous guidance and be patient if we want to promote creativity at school.

Creativity Diagnostics

Only a few specific creativity tests exist on the German test market. Problems developed in the United States are adapted, especially those developed by Guilford (1967) and Torrance (1966a, 1966b, 1981). The

Verbal Creativity Test (Schoppe, 1975) was the first German standardized creativity test. It is directly derived from Guilford's structure-of-intellect model and measures word fluency, thought fluency, semantic spontaneous flexibility, associational fluency, expressional fluency, and verbal originality. The Creativity Test by Mainberger (1977) is oriented by Guilford's concept as well. Both semantic and figural problems are evaluated concerning divergent thinking.

The Creativity Test for Preschool and School-Age Children (KVS) (Krampen, Freilinger, & Wilmes, 1996) is a nonverbal test in which the children are to perform motor activities: types of locomotion, action alternatives, and drawings. The evaluation is carried out under the dimensions of idea fluency and idea flexibility. The concept of diagnostics refers to Guilford's structure-of-intellect model (1967), to the Berlin intelligence structure model (Jäger, 1984; Jäger, Süss, & Beauducel, 1997), and to the investment theory of creativity (Sternberg & Lubart, 1991).

At a closer glance, European traditions can be found in the tests developed in the United States.

Shape Interpretation Problems
The Rorschach test (1921) and its variants are projective tests, in which standardized inkblots are to be interpreted by test persons. It is apparent that an imaginative perception should be reflected in the given answer. Indeed, the originality of the given answers is a basic evaluation principle. A stringent theory of the method was never developed; there is no standardization and no comprehensive verification of validity. In spite of this, shape interpretation problems for simple line drawings can also be found in modern creativity tests (e.g., Wallach & Kogan, 1965; Mainberger, 1977).

Drawing Production
Simple figurative fragments, which are to be added to or completed, are used in American as well as in German creativity tests, for instance as "decorations" in Guilford's (1967) test or "picture completion" in Torrance's (1966a) test. This type of problem evidently reaches back to the Wartegg Drawing Test, first published in 1939: In eight rectangles, small picture elements such as dots or lines are given, which are to be completed through drawing. Next to characterological principles that are considered antiquated today, this test measures the originality of the drawn end product (Wartegg, 1957). This type of problem was recently converted by Urban and Jellen (1995) into a relatively simple

test for creative drawing (Test for Creative Thinking – Drawing Production), which is astonishingly applicable from preschool to adulthood as
a screening method or as an evaluation criterion for creativity training.
The test consists of a piece of paper with figural fragments printed on
it. These fragments can be completed into any drawing. The evaluation
results from fourteen criteria, such as continuing given elements, adding
new elements, producing graphic and thematic connections, and using
humor. In contrast to previous methods, which primarily measure fluency and (at best) flexibility, this test should measure the quality and
originality of the end product as well.

Prospective Imagination

An example for the independent development of similar scientific ideas
in Germany and the United States is the task to think oneself into a
utopian assumption and to deduce possible consequences. According
to Süllwold (1999), this type of problem contains an aspect of "prospective fantasy," which is the inductive ability to imagine future events
and then to draw conclusions concerning future developments from
given circumstances. Such problems with "grotesque premises" were
first recommended for the exploration of originality by Chassell (1916)
and Giese (1925) and then used by Süllwold (1954). Utopian situations
can be found under the title "consequences" (Guilford, 1959) or "Just
suppose" (Torrance, 1966b). Jäger (1967) integrated this type of task into
his intelligence model as an aspect of "imagination and productivity."
Schoppe (1975) used utopic assumptions to measure divergent thinking, as well. Süllwold (1999) eventually constructed a Test of Utopian
Assumptions with unusual, but not completely unrealistic, future scenarios. For instance, the test persons are briefly informed about the dam-
age of forests through harmful substances and the destruction of trees
to make land for residential areas and roads. Then they are asked this
question: "What would happen if the ratio of forest area to total land
area in Germany went back from 30 percent to 1 percent, so that forests
were hardly existent?"

CREATIVITY AS A SOCIAL MOVEMENT

Experiences with creative problem-solving strategies can lead to unlimited enthusiasm. However, many assumptions concerning creativity
turned out to be myths; creative problem-solving processes are looked

at more rationally today. The focus broadened from the genius to the process, the environment, and the person–environment interaction. In spite of this progression, the fascination of creativity as an individual, educational, and social challenge has remained unshaken. In German-speaking countries, several initiatives and groups of people have dedicated their lives to the promotion of creativity. Management trainer and attorney Gerhard Huhn (1990) argues in his juridical dissertation that the one-sided cognitive orientation of school curricula violates the right of personal development. Taking the functional distinction between the two brain hemispheres into account, he went one step further and filed a lawsuit against the German school system in the Federal Constitution Court, because traditional teaching methods supposedly neglect the right hemisphere. (However, eventually he had to take back this action as the situation seemed without prospects.) The single-man Creativity at School project by Wohlgemuth has already been mentioned, as well as the quasi-religious morphological approach of Zwicky. Two further initiatives are introduced here.

Creando – The International Foundation for Creativity and Leadership

In Switzerland, Gottlieb Guntern and Greta Guntern-Gallati established Creando – International Foundation for Creativity and Leadership, a nonprofit organization, in 1979 (see www.creando.org; www.gottlieb.guntern.org). Creando organizes the international symposium for creativity and leadership annually, during which highly respected, internationally known personalities, who are honored for their creativity, lecture on their experiences with creativity and their mobilization of personal resources. Nobel Prize winners and other leading performers are speakers, such as authors, musicians, dancers, scientists, and managers. Creando pursues and initiates research and publications about creativity and leadership (e.g. Guntern, 1993). On the one hand, Guntern takes up classic theses of creativity practice that partially sound like antiquated myths of creativity because of their simplistic formulation, such as, "So-called soft issues are often the hardest facts in life" or "When information flows in the right direction, a creative stream emerges" (Guntern, 1994). On the other hand, he discusses the relevance of altered states of consciousness, as they exist, for example, under the influence of drugs or under the rites of shamanism, and refers to modern neurophysiological approaches.

The Association for Creativity

In the early 1970s, a team of consultants at the Batelle Institut, a noted research, development, and testing institution, launched the first comprehensive research project in Europe, known as Methods and Organization of Idea Generation (cf. Gesellschaft für Kreativität, 2005). The aims of the study were (a) compiling all methods of idea generation worldwide; (b) analyzing the methods for their underlying principles of idea generation; (c) testing the basic principles of idea generation for use on everyday problems; (d) finding the snags in real-life application and developing method improvements; and (e) assisting the clients with the implementation of the methods.

In 1993, the Fourth European Conference on Creativity and Innovation was organized by members of this team in Darmstadt, Germany (Geschka, Moger, & Rickards, 1994). During this event, the European Association on Creativity and Innovation and the German Circle of Darmstadt – Initiative for Creativity were founded. The Circle's major goal was to create more awareness of the importance of creativity.

In 1998, the Circle published a charter, including twelve essential statements about creativity, its nature, peculiarities and needs "including these:"

4. Fear and lack of freedom in a work environment can heavily obstruct creativity.

9. Creative thinking and behavior give motivation and lead towards successful outcomes. They bring more meaning and fulfillment to one's life.

11. Creativity is the source of all innovations; it generates high standards of life and secures the wealth of individuals and of society.

Taking notice of and applying this charter is not only an approach to overcome contemporary problems such as unemployment, environmental pollution, social cuts, and violence, but also a contribution toward a higher degree of contentment of humankind. For this purpose, the Association for Creativity has devoted itself to encouraging the enhancement of creativity in all societal areas (see www.kreativ-sein.de/docs/thesenengl; revised: Geschka et al. 2005).

The Circle established the Day of Creativity, to promote creative problem solving in education and work life. September 5 was chosen for this event, because on this date Guilford gave a speech on creativity of worldwide recognition. Fifty years later, the Circle celebrated the Day of Creativity with a special emphasis on creativity in school projects at the Expo 2000 World Exhibition in Hannover, Germany. In 2002, the Circle changed its name to *Gesellschaft für Kreativität* (Association for Creativity). The association took the responsibility to organize the Eighth European Conference on Creativity and Innovation in 2003, with the focus topic of cross-cultural innovation. During this conference, the national Day of Creativity was extended to an European Day of Creativity.

CONCLUSION

Whoever propagates creativity as a social task, writes advisory books, or conveys creativity training must be filled with enthusiasm about creativity. He or she will be convinced of the possibilities, which the promotion of creativity provides, and will not focus on its limitations and risks. Regarding existing deficiencies – concerning, for example, the efficiency of brainstorming in groups – he or she will search for improvements in techniques and methods. However, scientific and practical creativity is narrowed down if single methods (such as brainstorming, the morphological box, or Metaplan) are regarded uncritically as a universal remedy or if single research approaches (such as the functional differences of the two brain hemispheres) become the only focus. In the most extreme case, the fascination with creative ideas and creativity-stimulating methods can lead to excessive fantasies about omnipotence. Again and again we encounter the vision to improve or to control the world through a morphological picture of the world with specific ways of thinking (Zwicky), through the activation of the right brain hemisphere (Huhn), through education (Wohlgemuth), through economic, cultural, or scientific innovations (Creando), or, last but not least, through a general improvement of society (Association for Creativity). We can only hope that all these approaches show persistence for their important social task and that they remain – according to the results of scientific research – on the ground of reality, rationality, and feasibility.

References

Apel, H., Dernbach, D., Ködelpeter, Th., & Weinbrenner, P. (Eds.). (1998). *Wege zur Zukunftsfähigkeit – ein Methodenhandbuch* [Ways to future prospects – a methodological manual]. Bonn: Stiftung MITARBEIT.

Ash, M. G. (1998), *Gestalt psychology in German culture, 1890–1967: Holism and the quest for objectivity*. Cambridge, U.K.: Cambridge University Press.

Böger-Huang, X. (1996). *Von Konfuzius zu Picasso: Kreativitätserziehung in der Grundschule in China* [From Konfutse to Picasso: Creativity education in elementary school in China]. Unpublished doctoral dissertation, University Frankfurt/M.

Bugdahl, V. (1995). *Kreatives problemlösen im unterricht* [Creative problem solving in class]. Frankfurt/M: Cornelsen Scriptor.

Chassell, L. M. (1916). Test for originality. *Journal of Educational Psychology, 7,* 317–329.

Cropley, A. J. (1991). *Unterricht ohne Schablone: Wege zur Kreativität* [Class without a template: A means to creativity] (2nd ed.). München: Ehrenwirt.

Cropley, A. J. (2001). Kreativität und kreativitätsförderung [Creativity and creativity promotion]. In D. H. Rost (Ed.), *Handwörterbuch Pädagogische Psychologie* (2nd rev. ed., pp. 366–373). Weinheim: Beltz.

Csikszenmihalyi, M. (1996). *Creativity: Flow and the psychology of discovery and invention.* New York: HarperCollins.

DABEI-Deutsche Aktionsgemeinschaft Bildung – Erfindung – Innovation (Ed.). (1987). *DABEI-handbuch für erfinder und unternehmer* [Manual for inventors and entrepreneurs]. Düsseldorf: VDI-Verlag.

Dörner, D., Kreuzig, H. W., Reither, F. & Stäudel, T. (Eds.). (1983). *Lohhausen: Vom umgang mit unbestimmtheit und komplexität* [Lohhausen: Problem solving in uncertain and complex problems]. Bern: Huber.

Dörner, D., & Wearing, A. J. (1995). Complex problem solving: Toward a theory. In P. A. Frensch & A. Fink (Eds.), *Complex problem solving: The European perspective* (pp. 65–99). Hillsdale, NJ: Erlbaum.

Duncker, K. (1963). *Zur Psychologie des produktiven Denkens* [Psychology on productive thinking]. Berlin: Springer. (Original work published 1935)

Facaoaru, C. (1985). *Kreativität in wissenschaft und technik: Operationalisierung von problemlösefähigkeiten und kognitiven stilen* [Creativity in science and technology: Operationalization of problem-solving ability and cognitive styles]. Bern: Huber.

Fiedler, P. A. & Windheuser, H. J. (1974). Modifikation Kreativen Verhaltens durch Lernen am Modell [Modification of creative behavior by modeling]. *Zeitschrift für Entwicklungs psychologia und Pädagogische Psychologie, 4,* 262–280

Funke, J. (2003). *Problemlösendes denken* [Problem-solving thinking]. Stuttgart: Kohlhammer.

Gebert, D. (2002). *Führung und innovation* [Leadership and innovation]. Stuttgart: Kohlhammer.

Geschka, H., König, D., Mehlhorn, J., Schaude, G., & Schlicksupp, H. (2005). History of the German Association for Creativity. In B. Jöstingmeier & H.-J. Boeddrich (Eds), *Cross-Cultural Innovation: Results of the 8th European Conference on Creativity and Innovation* (pp. 527–536). Wiesbaden: Deutscher Universitäts-Verlag.

Geschka, H., Moger, S., & Rickards, T. (Eds.). (1994). *Creativity and innovation. The power of synergy. Proceedings of the Fourth European Conference on Creativity and Innovation.* Darmstadt, Germany: Geschka.

Giese, F. (1925). *Handbuch psychotechnischer Eignungsprüfungen* [Manual of psychotechnological aptitude tests]. Halle, Germany: Marhold.

Giesler, M. (2003). *Kreativität und organisationales klima: Entwicklung und validierung eines fragebogens zur erfassung von kreativitäts-und innovationsklima in betrieben* [Creativity and organizational climate: Development and validation of a questionnaire for the assessment of creativity and innovation climate in organizations]. Münster: Waxmann.

Greiffenhagen, M. (1982). Anders als andere? Zur sozialisation von pfarrerskindern [Different from others? Socialization of ministers' children]. In M. Greiffenhagen (Ed.), *Pfarrerskinder: Autobiographisches zu einem protestantischen thema* (pp. 14–34). Stuttgart: Kreuz Verlag.

Guilford, J. P. (1950). Creativity. *American Psychologist, 5*, 444–454.

Guilford, J. P. (1959). *Personality.* New York: McGraw-Hill.

Guilford, J. P. (1967). *The nature of human intelligence.* New York: McGraw-Hill.

Guntern, G. (Ed.). (1993). *Irritation und kreativität: Hemmende und fördernde faktoren im kreativen prozess* [Irritation and creativity: Hindering and promoting factors of creative processes]. Zürich: Scalo.

Guntern, G. (1994). *Sieben goldene regeln der kreativitätsförderung* [Seven golden rules of creativity promotion]. Zürich: Scalo.

Hany, E. A. (2001). Förderung der kreativität [Promotion of creativity]. In K. J. Klauer (Ed.), *Handbuch kognitives training* (2nd ed., pp. 262–291). Göttingen, Germany: Hogrefe.

Heinelt, G. (1974). *Kreative lehrer – kreative schüler* [Creative teachers – Creative students]. Freiburg: Herder.

Heinrich, W. (1989). Einführung in das lösen komplexer probleme im konstruktionsprozess [Introduction to the solving of complex problems in constructive processes]. *Maschinenbautechnik, 38*, 100–227.

Heister, M. W. M. (Ed.). (1991). *Techno-ökonomische kreativität: Möglichkeiten und massnahmen ihrer besonderen förderung* [Technological-economical creativity: Chances and treatments of their special promotion]. Bonn: Köllen (DABEI).

Heller, K. A. (Ed.). (2001). *Hochbegabung im kindes- und jugendalter* [Giftedness in childhood and adolescence] (2nd ed.). Göttingen, Germany: Hogrefe.

Heller, K. A., & Perleth, Ch. (Eds.). (1999). *Münchner Hochbegabungs-Testsystem (MHBT)* [Munich Gifted Test system]. Göttingen, Germany: Hogrefe.

Huhn, G. (1990). *Kreativität und schule: Risiken derzeitiger lehrpläne für die freie entfaltung der kinder. Verfassungswidrigkeit staatlicher regelungen von bildungszielen und unterrichtsinhalten vor dem hindergrund neuerer erkenntnisse der gehirnforschung* [Creativity and school: Risks of contemporary curricula for the personal development of students]. Berlin: VWB/Synchron Verlag.

Jäger, A. O. (1967). *Dimensionen der Intelligenz* [Dimensions of intelligence]. Göttingen, Germany: Hogrefe.

Jäger, A. O. (1984). Intelligenz-strukturforschung: Konkurrierende modelle, neue entwicklungen, perspektiven [Structural research on intelligence. Divergent models, new developments, perspectives]. *Psychologische Rundschau, 35,* 21–35.

Jäger, A. O., Süss, H. M., & Beauducel, A. (1997). *Berliner Intelligenzstruktur-Test (BIS-Test). Form 4* [Berlin Intelligence Structure Test – Version 4]. Göttingen, Germany: Hogrefe.

Jungk, R., & Müllert, N. R. (1995). *Zukunftswerkstätten: Mit fantasie gegen routine und resignation* [Future workshops: With imagination against routine and resignation] (5th ed.). München: Heyne.

Klebert, K., Schrader, E., & Straub, W. G. (1991). *Moderations methode: Gestaltung der meinungs- und willensbildung in gruppen, die miteinander lernen und leben, arbeiten und spielen* [Moderation methods: Formation of opinions and volition in groups, who live, learn, work and play together] (5th ed.). Hamburg: Windmühle.

Köhler, W. (1917). *Intelligenzprüfung an menschenaffen* [Intelligence tests on anthropoid apes]. Berlin: Preussische Akademie der Wissenschaft.

Krampen, G., unter Mitarbeit von Freilinger, J., & Wilmes, L. (1996). *KVS-P: Kreativitätstest für vorschul- und schulkinder – Version für die psychologische anwendungspraxis* [Creativity test for preschool and school-age children – Educational psychology form]. Göttingen, Germany: Hogrefe.

Krapp, A., & Weidenmann, B. (Eds.). (2001). *Pädagogische psychologie: Ein lehrbuch* [Educational psychology: A textbook] (4th, rev. ed.). Weinheim: Beltz.

Krause, D. E. (2004). *Macht und vertrauen in innovationsprozessen: Ein empirischer beitrag zu einer theorie der führung* [Power and trust in innovative processes: An empirical contribution to a theory on leadership]. Wiesbaden: Gabler.

Landau, E. (1969). *Psychologie der kreativität* [Psychology of creativity]. München: Reinhardt.

Landesarbeitsgemeinschaft Kreativitätspädagogik NRW e.V. (Ed.). (1989). *20 jahre kreativitätspädagogik* [20 years of creativity pedagogics]. Köln: Landesarbeitsgemeinschaft Kreativitätspädagogik.

Lange-Eichbaum, W. (1927). *Genie, irrsinn und ruhm* [Genius, insanity and fame]. München: Reinhardt.

Lange-Eichbaum, W., & Kurth, W. (2000). *Genie, irrsinn und ruhm* [Genius, insanity and fame]. (7th, rev. ed). Frechen: Komet.

Luchins, A. (1942). Mechanisation in problem solving: The effect of Einstellung. *Psychological Monographs, 54*, No. 6.

Ludwig, A. M. (1995). *The price of greatness: Resolving the creativity and madness controversy.* New York: Guilford.

Luther, M. (1530). *Eine Predigt, dass man kinder zur schule halten solle* [A preach on having children attend school]. Wittenberg, Germany: Nickel Schirlentz.

Maier, N. R. F. (1930). Reasoning in humans: I. On direction. *Journal of Comparative Psychology, 10*, 115–143.

Mainberger, U. (1977). *Test zum divergenten denken (kreativität) TDK 4–6* [Creativity test for 4th to 6th graders – divergent thinking]. Weinheim: Beltz.

Mehlhorn, H.-G., & Mehlhorn, G. (1976). *Ideenschule: Übungen zum schöpferischen denken* [School of ideas: Exercises on inventive thinking]. Leipzig: Urania.

Mehlhorn, H.-G., & Mehlhorn, G. (1977). *Zur kritik der bürgerlichen kreativitätsforschung* [Criticism of bourgeois creativity research]. Berlin: Verlag der Wissenschaften.

Mehlhorn, H.-G., & Mehlhorn, G. (1986). Intuitive komponenten im schöpferischen prozess [Intuitive components in inventive processes]. *Maschinenbautechnik, 35*, 259–263.

Meissner, W. (1989). *Innovation und organisation. Die initiierung von innovationsprozessen in organisationen* [Innovation and organization. The introduction of innovative processes in organizations]. Stuttgart: Verlag für Angewandte Psychologie.

Merkelbach, V. (Ed.), (1993). *Kreatives schreiben* [Creative writing]. Braunschweig: Westermann.

Metzger, W. (1962). *Schöpferische freiheit* [Inventive freedom] (2nd rev. ed.). Frankfurt/M: Kramer.

Metzger, W. (1979). Gestalttheoretische ansätze zur frage der kreativität [Gestalt-oriented approaches concerning creativity]. Reprinted in W. Metzger (1986), *Gestaltpsychologie: Ausgewählte werke aus den jahren 1950 bis 1982*. Frankfurt/M: Kramer.

Mooney, R. L. (1958). A conceptual model for integrating four approaches to the identification of creative talent. In C. W. Taylor (Ed.), *The second (1957) University of Utah research conference on the identification of creative scientific talent* (pp. 170–180). Salt Lake City: University of Utah Press.

Moreno, J. L. (1946/1959/1969). *Psychodrama Vols. I–III*. New York: Beacon House.

Mühle, G., & Schell, Ch. (1970). *Kreativität und schule* [Creativity and school]. München: Piper.

Petzold, H. (Hrsg.). (1973). Kreativität und konflikte [Creativity and conflicts]. Paderborn: Junfermann.

Petzold, H., & Orth, I. (Eds.). (1991). *Die neuen kreativitätstheorien* [New creativity theories] Vol. I. Paderborn: Junfermann.

Preiser, S. (1986). *Kreativitätsforschung* [Creativity research] (2nd ed.). Darmstadt, Germany: Wissenschaftliche Buchgesellschaft (Original work published 1976).

Preiser, S. (Ed.). (1982). *Kognitive und emotionale aspekte politischen engagements* [Cognitive and emotional aspects of political engagement]. Weinheim: Beltz.

Preiser, S. (2003a). Poster und szenische präsentationen statt referate – eine kooperative, interaktive und kreative präsentationsform [Posters and scenic presentations instead of oral presentations: A cooperative, interactive, and creative form of presentation]. In G. Krampen & H. Zayer (Eds.), *Psychologiedidaktik und evaluation IV* (pp. 269–275). Bonn: Deutscher Psychologen Verlag.

Preiser (2003b). *Pädagogische psychologie: Psychologische grundlagen von erziehung und unterricht* [Educational psychology: Psychological basis of education and instruction]. Weinheim: Juventa.

Preiser, S. (in press-a). Kreativitätsförderung: Lernklima und erziehungsbedingungen in der grundschule [Creativity stimulation: Learning atmosphere and educational conditions at elementary schools]. In M. K. Schweer (Ed.), *Das kindesalter*. Frankfurt/M: Lang.

Preiser, S. (in press-b). Creativity in the German education system. In K. Yumino (Ed.), *Creativity education in the world*. Kyoto, Japan: Nakanishiya.

Preiser, S. & Buchholz, N. (2004). *Kreativität. Ein trainingsprogramm in 7 stufen für alltag und beruf* [Creativity: A training program in 7 steps for everyday life and work] (2nd ed.). Heidelberg: Asanger.

Rohrbach, B. (1969). Kreativ nach regeln – Methode 635, eine neue technik zum lösen von problemen [Creativity following rules – Method 635, a new technique on problem solving]. *Absatzwirtschaft, 12*, 73–76.

Rorschach, H. (1921). *Rorschach-test*. Bern: Huber.

Runco, M. A. (Ed.). (1997). *Creativity research handbook, Vol. I*. Cresskill, NJ: Hampton Press.

Schmidt, J. (1985). *Die geschichte des genie-Gedankens in der deutschen literatur, philosophie und politik 1750–1945* [The history of the idea of ingenuity in

German literature, philosophy, and politics 1750–1945]. Darmstadt, Germany: Wissenschaftliche Buchgesellschaft.

Schoppe, K.-J. (1975). *Verbaler kreativitätstest* [Verbal creativity test]. Göttingen, Germany: Hogrefe.

Serve, J. (1996). *Förderung der kreativitätsentfaltung als implizite bildungsaufgabe der schule* [Promotion of creativity development as an implicit educational goal in schools] (3rd ed.). München: PimS.

Sternberg, R. J. (1999). *Handbook of creativity*. Cambridge, England: Cambridge University Press.

Sternberg, R. J., & Lubart, T. (1991). An investment theory of creativity and its development. *Human Development, 34*, 1–31.

Stocker, Th. (1988). *Die kreativität und das schöpferische: Leitbegriffe zweier pädagogischer reformperioden* [Creativity and inventiveness: Concepts of two pedagogic reform periods]. Frankfurt/M: Brandes & Aspel.

Stroebe, W., & Diehl, M. (1994). Why groups are less effective than their members: On productivity losses in idea-generating groups. In W. Stroebe & M. Hewstone (Eds.), *European Review of Social Psychology* (vol. 5, pp. 271–303). London: Wiley.

Stroebe, W., & Nijstad, B. A. (2004). Warum brainstorming in gruppen kreativität vermindert: Eine kognitive theorie der leistungsverluste beim brainstorming [Why brainstorming in groups impairs creativity: A cognitive theory of productivity losses in brainstorming groups]. *Psychologische Rundschau, 55*, 2–10.

Süllwold, F. (1954). Experimentelle untersuchungen über die rolle des einfalls im denkprozess [An experimental investigation concerning the part played by sudden insight in thinking]. *Zeitschrift für Experimentelle und Angewandte Psychologie, 2*, 175–207.

Süllwold, F. (1999). Die prospektive phantasie als persönlichkeitsvariable und diagnostische kategorie [Prospective fantasy as a personality variable and diagnostic category]. *Zeitschrift für Differentielle und Diagnostische Psychologie, 20*, 133–141.

Torrance, E. P. (1966a). *Thinking creatively with pictures*. Lexington, MA: Personell Press.

Torrance, E. P. (1966b). *Thinking creatively with words*. Princeton, NJ: Personell Press.

Torrance, E. P. (1981). *Thinking creatively in action and movement*. Bensenville, IL: Scholastic Testing Service.

Ulmann, G. (1968). *Kreativität: Neue amerikanische ansätze zur erweiterung des intelligenzkonzeptes* [Creativity: New American attempts to extend the concept of intelligence]. Weinheim: Beltz.

Ulmann, G. (Ed.). (1973). *Kreativitätsforschung* [Creativity research]. Köln: Kiepenheuer und Witsch.

Urban, K. K. (2003a). Towards a componential model of creativity. In D. Ambrose, L. M. Cohen, & A. J. Tannenbaum (Eds.), *Creative intelligence: Toward theoretic integration* (pp. 81–112). Cresskill, NJ: Hampton Press.

Urban, K. K. (2003b). *Hochbegabung: Eine bibliographie deutschsprachiger literatur* [Giftedness: A bibliography of German literature] (3rd ed.). Rodenberg: Klausur-Verlag.

Urban, K. K., & Jellen, H. G. (1995). *TSD-Z: Test zum schöpferischen denken–zeichnerisch* [Test for creative thinking–drawing production (TCT-DP)]. Frankfurt/M: Swets.

Wallach, M. A., & Kogan, N. (1965). Modes of thinking in young children: A study of the creativity–intelligence distinction. New York: Holt, Rinehart & Winston.

Wallner, M. (1989). Angewandte kreativitätsforschung in den USA: Entwicklung und ergebnisse [Applied creativity research in the USA: Developments and results]. *Der Neuerer, 38,* 162–166.

Wallner, M. (1990). *Kreativitätsforschung in den USA. Eine erkenntnistheoretische studie zu entwicklung und ergebnissen wissenschaftlicher untersuchungen der kreativität* [Creativity research in the USA: An epistemic study on developments and results of scientific research on creativity]. Unpublished doctoral dissertation B, Karl-Marx-Universität Leipzig.

Ward, T. B., Smith, S. M., & Vaid, J. (Eds.). (1997). *Creative thought: An investigation of conceptual structures and processes.* Washington, DC: American Psychological Association.

Wartegg, E. (1957). *Wartegg-Zeichentest (WZT)* [The Wartegg Drawing Test]. Göttingen, Germany: Hogrefe.

Weinert, F. E. (Ed.). (1997). Psychologie des unterrichts und der schule [Psychology in class and school]. *Enzyklopädie der Psychologie, Pädagogische Psychologie, Vol. 3.* Göttingen, Germany: Hogrefe.

Wermke, J. (1989). *"Hab a talent, sei a genie!": Kreativität als paradoxe aufgabe* ["Have a Talent, Be a Genius!": Creativity as a paradox problem]. (vol. 1/2). Weinheim: Deutscher Studien Verlag.

Wertheimer, M. (1925). *Drei abhandlungen zur Gestalttheorie* [Three dissertations on Gestalt theory]. Erlangen: Enke.

Wertheimer, M. (1945). *Productive thinking.* New York: Harper. (Published in Germany 1957 as *Produktives denken.* Frankfurt/M: Kramer)

Westmeyer, H. (1998). The social construction and psychological assessment of creativity. *High Ability Studies, 9,* 11–21.

Witthaus, U., & Wittwer, W. (Eds.). (2000). *Open Space: Eine methode zur selbststeuerung von lernprozessen in grossgruppen* [Open space. A method for the self-regulation of learning processes in large groups]. Bielefeld: Bertelsmann.

Wohlgemuth, R. B. (1995). *Schreibspiele, Kreatives Schreiben* [Writing games, creative writing] (Vol. 1/2). Bad Zwischenahn: Wohlgemuth Media.

Wohlgemuth, R. B. (1998). *Schreibspiele, Kreatives Schreiben,* Vol. 2 [Writing games, creative writing]. Bad Zwischenahn: Wohlgemuth Media.

Wollschläger, G. (1972). *Kreativität und gesellschaft* [Creativity and society]. Frankfurt/M: Fischer.

Zwicky, F. (1957). *Morphological astronomy.* Berlin: Springer.

Zwicky, F. (1989). *Entdecken, erfinden, forschen im morphologischen weltbild* [Discovery, invention, research in the morphological view of the world] (2nd ed.). Glarus, Switzerland: Baeschlin.

8

Creativity under the Northern Lights

Perspectives from Scandinavia

Gudmund J. W. Smith and Ingegerd Carlsson

This chapter is meant to cover the Scandinavian region of Europe. It includes research mainly from the discipline of psychology, but with excursions to the fields of education and philosophy. Besides theoretical and empirical results from Denmark, Norway, and Finland, it reviews data from both applied and laboratory settings in Sweden. The time span covered stretches back approximately three decades. At the start, only a handful of pioneers can be spotted, but the number of creativity researchers has increased rapidly over the years.

While pondering on the catch in our net, we have come to the conclusion that there is no typically or coherent Scandinavian opinion about how creativity should be understood. Still, Scandinavian work does not unconditionally reflect mainline North American approaches to the matter. If most American researchers would probably agree with Mumford's (2003) emphasis on productivity when evaluating creative behavior, Scandinavian researchers would be more inclined to pay attention to Runco (2003), who gives more weight to potentials. Here creativity is rather understood as an attitude toward life, a way to come to grips with the problems of existence. We believe that an exclusive focus on tangible creative products may lose sight of many creative individuals who do not give priority to being in the limelight.

Thus, there has been more focus on different conditions that are positive or negative for creativity, whether they are prerequisites in the individual or conditions seen from other angles in a system's perspective (cf. Csikszentmihalyi, 1999). Some of these angles would be the creative climate or what kind of mood is conducive for creativity. We come back to these and several other research domains later. We start with an outline of how Scandinavians define their "elephant" – that is, creativity under the Northern lights.

ASPECTS OF THE CREATIVITY CONSTRUCT

Creative Cognition

Novelty and adaptability are the crucial criteria in Christensen's (2002) definition of creativity. Novelty in creativity is a novelty in kind; that is, there is a structure in the creation that stretches beyond the particular product. Usefulness or adaptability implies potential for adaptive spread. However, in the creative process, search is also a crucial concept, used, for example, by Perkins (1981) and Boden (1991). Christensen followed these researchers closely to begin with, but finally considered them as too narrow, too constructivist – that is, not enough adapted to reality. In order to overcome the problems and limitations of prevailing information-processing theories, he preferred an ecological approach to creativity and proposed a creative cycle, partly on the basis of Neisser's (1976) theorizing. The cycle is a construct that is more closely related to creative action in the real world (cf. West, 1990).

Creative cognition should, according to Christensen, not be viewed as an "inner" process, in the head of the creator, but as an active process linking the subject to objective possibilities and impossibilities, through actualization and simulation. Christensen pointed at problems inherent in a one-sided information-processing approach to creativity, such as the overemphasis of rationality.

Kaufmann (2002) argued that the theoretical clarification of the creativity concept is lagging behind the construction of instruments for diagnosing individual creativity. One core problem is the collision between intelligence and creativity, partly because successful novelty is one of the essential hallmarks of both. Instead of accepting previous attempts at distinguishing between intelligence and creativity, Kaufmann preferred a distinction between novelty on the stimulus side and novelty on the response side, that is, task novelty versus solution novelty. Intelligence is mainly associated with task novelty and solution familiarity, whereas creativity includes two subcategories: the often-neglected proactive creativity in a task familiarity–solution novelty category and reactive creativity belonging to a task novelty–solution novelty category. The issue of the success trap is also relevant here, such as when early success blocks continued creative efforts.

The Complexity of Creativity

The tenor of creativity was the theme of a workshop that convened in Venice and was published in a book edited by Andersson and Sahlin (1997). In her contribution to the book, Brinck (1997) maintained that the basic task of creativity research should be to track what lies behind all the things labeled *creative*. In order to be called creative, they should involve efforts on the part of the individual. These creative acts could be characterized as a specific kind of problem solving, not bound by any well-defined goal or terminated when a correct answer is in sight, but instead searching for new directions. In order to attain this, the subject matter has to be reorganized or recategorized to gain more freedom of action and thought. Metaphors are often used as transfers of features across domains.

In another contribution, Sahlin (1997) held that so-called computational psychology, that is, the study of computation processes whereby mental representations are formed and transformed, will never disclose the enigma of creativity because it underrates the value aspects. Creativity has to do with the dynamics of our expectations that form our map of the world, and these dynamics should be the main object of creativity research. Like Brinck, Sahlin saw the shift from one space to another as a sign of profound creativity. What characterizes such a shift is the creation of new expectations.

In Venice, Smith (1997) criticized the major cognitive theories of creativity because they often miss the emotional basis of perceptual processing. One reason appears to be computational functionalism, which is tying cognition to the computer metaphor; another reason is the static model of perceiving and thinking that pervades much of the contemporary cognitive theorizing. For the serious student of creativity, meaning must precede conscious articulation in the process of reality construction. Smith reformulated the definition of creative functioning in terms of a process model of personality. The reformulation made possible a more specific definition of creative functioning in connection with a test instrument developed to describe how the perceiver tackles a new situation, more or less creatively (see a later section in this chapter).

CREATIVITY IN A SYSTEM'S PERSPECTIVE

The Creative Climate

A fair amount of empirical research as well as speculation has dealt with the role of environmental factors in the generation of creativity. When adopting a system's view, let us first describe the creative organizational climate, which has long since been one of the main interests for Ekvall (1983, 1997). Ekvall has defined the climate of a group or organization as a composite of behavior, attitudes, and feelings that characterize the life in the organization. This composite is close to the observable reality, in certain contrast to organizational culture, which consists of deep-rooted, partly preconscious basic assumptions. The climate is shaped in the daily meetings between members in the organization, and when they are confronted with the structure and processes in the organization or group. We return in a later section to empirical studies made by Ekvall and associates. (A review of climate and cultural organizational research can be found in Dackert, 2001.)

The Creative Environment

In his book on the philosophy of creativity, Sahlin (2001) has tried to circumvent the unreliability of the traditional historiography of science by referring to his own experience of supposedly more or less creative environments. Naturally, his experience is limited and should be treated as such. Nevertheless, his selection of factors that likely aid creative thought and action is of undoubted interest to all researchers in the field of creativity who have attempted to take hold of this evasive topic.

Upon entering the doorway to a creative place, Sahlin first remembers the welcoming warmth, whereas the uncreative atmosphere has an unmistakable smell of death. Creative environments are thus distinguished by openness and generosity. People working in such environments also give evidence of a sense of community, of belonging to a group, even if the participants have very different cultural backgrounds. Without trust and tolerance, the openness to alien and groundbreaking thoughts, necessary to creative work, will be in jeopardy. Closely associated with this feeling of trust is a sense of equality, not implying total equalization but a shared commitment to the goal of research. Sahlin discerned another striking difference between a creative and an uncreative environment: the intellectual acuity and curiosity about life encountered in the former. This presupposes a freedom of spirit that does not feel obliged to dwell on the formal details of its activity. The goal has an overpowering importance.

It may seem evident that a research group cannot function creatively unless its members have solid scientific qualifications. However, it is important not only that group members display awareness of what they know but also of what they do not know. By the same token, cultural diversity (in the field of science) serves to promote creativity whereas uniformity only promotes productivity.

It would seem to follow that these prerequisites can easily be threatened in a case in which the environment expands over a certain size, say ten to fifteen people. Still, small islands of creativity may exist in large organizations. What could be particularly important for a creative environment to persist is preserved personal contact between members of the research group, implying a sense of security and intellectual fellowship.

In a similar vein, Agrell and Gustafson (1994) proposed analyses at the individual, group, and organizational levels. There are facilitating and inhibiting characteristics and processes at each level. Freedom of action is facilitating, as is a participatory and collaborative leadership style. A bureaucratic structure is often described as an obstacle to creativity. According to Ekvall (1996), such a structure has complicated and time-consuming paths of decision making, strong formal control and reliance on rules and principles, a "top run" organization, and mainly formal communication channels.

Prize-Winning Environments

When preparing the exhibition to celebrate the centennial of the first Nobel Prizes in 1901, the organizers specifically focused on creative environments, that is, places from which an unusual number of Nobel laureates had hailed. It is probably true, as Sahlin (2001) has observed, that renowned researchers are not always the most creative of people and, moreover, that we can only speculate about which factors in these environments were conducive to the generation of pioneering ideas. Nevertheless, let us just select a sample of fertile environments and the assumptions accompanying their selection (Larsson, 2002).

Budapest was celebrated for several Nobel laureates, among them Albert Szent-György and Leo Szilard. The effective environmental factors were often traced to the gymnasiums of the Hungarian capital. Before World War II, they seem to have been characterized by a certain elitism combined with a spirit of competition. Students were encouraged to formulate their own rules of investigative labor. Under the pressure of mounting anti-Semitism, science offered a way of escape.

Copenhagen was the center of untiring education orchestrated by the nuclear physicist Niels Bohr. Among many visitors, some of the most renowned were Werner Heisenberg, Erwin Schrödinger, and Wolfgang Pauli. All of them gave evidence of the special atmosphere in the circle surrounding Bohr, an atmosphere of informality and ease even if sometimes intellectually taxing. When Bohr detected talent in young researchers, he was also ready to find support for them.

Cold Spring Harbor on Long Island was a meeting place for molecular biologists, Max Delbrück and Barbara McClintock among them. For many workers in the field, summer at Cold Spring Harbor was the peak of the year. The spirit was open, an intellectual oasis.

The institute for immunology at Basel has also been singled out as a fertile hotbed for biological research. Every visitor was invited to participate in the intellectual life of the place. Divisions of authority were carefully avoided. According to Niels Jerne, the intellectual hub of the institute, without chance meetings and exchange of ideas, science could not develop. However, applicants for a place at the institute were carefully selected so as to keep second-raters outside the gates.

The Pasteur Institute in Paris is another center of cutting-edge research. It has been described by one of its most prominent members, Francois Jacob, as a place full of gaiety, curiosity, and imagination. Its openness also implied that everything, from whoever it emanated, could be constantly questioned.

THE CREATIVE DISPOSITION DEFINED BY THE PERCEPTUAL PROCESS

In their research, Smith and Carlsson (1990) were influenced by psychoanalytic thinking when they constructed a heuristic model of creative functioning. Hartmann (1939), for instance, considered adaptive regression to be an important prerequisite for the generation of novel ideas. Kris (1952) created the well-known concept of "regression in the service of the ego," later to be paraphrased as "cognitive regression" by Suler (1980). Despite the reactualization of more primitive modes of thinking, the individual retains or has easy access to his or her habitual, more rational functional level.

On the basis of a series of empirical studies, Smith and Carlsson (1990) got solid support for their theoretical model, which implies that the creative individual keeps open channels of communication with her or his own subjective roots. They contended further that the creative disposition is not primarily a matter of talent or productivity, but has to do with the way that the person perceives and constructs the reality. In this construcion of reality, which to a large extent takes place outside conscious awareness, the creative individual is inclined to assign at least equal weight to his or her own way of seeing things, but is at the same time not oblivious to reality as others comprehend it. This method of functioning implies cognitive flexibility and less strict borders between cognition and emotion. The cognitive regression gives an opportunity for subjective imagery to surface into consciousness (in perceptual terms, to be reconstructed; Carlsson, 1992).

In this theoretical perspective, as Carlsson (2002) suggested, the creative disposition may also be a risk factor – the flexible functioning and close connection to one's feelings might lead to overstraining and ensuing depressive or other kinds of reactions. Thus, adaptive regression, more or less controlled, may, when put under stress, eventually turn into a less well-controlled state of mind and slip out of the hands of the ego (cf. Martindale et al., 1996).

EMPIRICAL STUDIES

Creativity and Organizational Climate

Climate is seen as an attribute of the organization that both influences and is influenced by organizational processes. Ekvall (1983, 1993) constructed the Creative Climate Questionnaire (CCQ), which consists of fifty items covering ten dimensions: freedom, ideas, support, trust or openness, dynamism or liveliness, playfulness or sense of humor, debates, conflicts, risk taking, and idea time. The instrument is intended to reveal how members of the organization actually perceive it. It has proved to possess high reliability and stability over time. It also mirrors the difference between innovative and stagnant organizations. It should be mentioned that Ekvall makes an important distinction between the dimensions of debates and conflicts. They both concern opposition and tension, but personal tensions and conflicts are seen as negative, whereas opposing ideas in the organization (debates) are seen as positive and stimulating for creativity.

Another work by Ekvall (1983) recognized two styles or levels of creative functioning: adaptive and innovative. The adaptor tries to make better what is already in existence while the innovator seeks solutions from new angles. These styles may also be seen as levels of creativity, with the innovative styles representing the higher or more radical level.

Considering the renowned four Ps of creativity (product, person, process, and place), Ekvall asked how the last of these relates to creative style. He studied four divisions in a chemical company and compared two of them: one where innovative activities were of the adaptive type and another division that was more radically oriented toward novelty. According to the results of a questionnaire about behavior and practices, the divisions were clearly different. The adaptive type was more characterized by order and structure, and the innovative type by risk taking. A similar research design was later applied in a mechanical industry, using the CCQ and producing analogous data. Ekvall concluded that the two styles (or levels) of creativity have parallels in organizational constructs; in other words, the two different levels of creativity are differentially facilitated by organizational conditions.

Using the same instruments as in his other studies, Ekvall (1993) followed a high-tech product development by measuring climate on eleven occasions. The study demonstrated that a project, ill adapted to the rules of conventional management books and appearing to be a failure upon conclusion, turned out a success in the long run, evidently because of freedom from strangling control.

In another study, 242 participants remembered different workplaces (Ekvall, 2000). The philosophies and practices steering the place of business had a significant influence on the climate. Most positive were the use of project groups and new methods of problem solving.

The CCQ has been translated and investigated in North American research (Isaksen & Lauer, 1999; Isaksen, Lauer & Ekvall, 2000–2001) as the Situational Outlook Questionnaire (SOQ). This research established preliminary reliability and construct validity measures of the SOQ by using a sample of 1,111 participants. Further research was suggested, focusing on the relationship of the climate with personality. The CCQ has also been applied in various studies in Sweden, which are not reviewed here.

Team Climate

A slightly different organizational aspect, which has been adapted to Nordic conditions, is team climate (West, 1990). Team climate could be said to be linking climate and innovation in work teams. The Team Climate Inventory (TCI; Anderson & West, 1998) uses thirty-eight items that group into four factors – vision, participative safety, support for innovation, and task orientation. The inventory was translated into Swedish by Agrell and Gustafson (1994). They analyzed a Swedish sample ($N = 124$) consisting of seventeen work teams in several different types of private enterprises. They showed the translated version to have high reliability, acceptable validity (against an independent judge), and a confirmation of the original factor structure. Finnish versions of the TCI have been constructed by Kivimäki et al. (1997), who suggested that, in high-complexity jobs, interaction frequency should be considered as a fifth factor. The Swedish version of the TCI has been applied by Dackert (2001), after the merging of two organizations within the Swedish Social Insurance Service. One of the findings described in her doctoral thesis was that, in the newly merged units, levels of participative safety and support for innovation were lower compared with results from the sample in Agrell and Gustafson (1994), implying that the conditions for innovation processes to occur were less than satisfactory (as reported in Dackert, Brenner, & Johansson, 2002).

Creative Leadership

Closely related to climate is the leadership in the organization. The importance of leadership style for stress and climate was shown by Ekvall, Frankenhaeuser, and Parr (1995). In Sweden, this research was initiated by Ekvall and Arvonen (1991, 1994). In a doctoral thesis, Arvonen (2002) described and integrated a model of leadership that included a change dimension in leadership behavior. The relevance of this dimension as a supplement to the two-factor model (production- and employee-oriented leadership) was suggested in the context of so-called post-bureaucratic organizations. A total of 6,434 subordinates in thirteen countries rated their immediate managers' behavior. Exploratory and confirmatory factor analyses consistently verified the three leadership dimensions, both in Nordic countries and the United States, and also across different company samples. The model indicated significant relevance in terms of the psychological and organizational outcomes, such as cost and change effectiveness (Arvonen & Pettersson, 2002).

Using different combinations of the three dimensions, Arvonen (1995) discerned seven leadership profiles and combined them with 781 employees' assessments of their own mental health. The creative leader profile was associated with co-workers' stress to a greater extent than the other profiles. However, the respondent's position of employment moderated the effect. Arvonen also found other situational contingencies. Managers who are change oriented were located at the top level in organizations, and production-oriented managers were located at the lower level. Employee-oriented managers were found at both levels, suggesting that employee-oriented leadership is important in most situations. The conclusion from these studies is that successful managers may have to combine all three behaviors. For future research, Arvonen suggested that, to know more about how managers handle the three dimensions in their daily work, observational and reflexive studies are needed, which might result in the development of longitudinal studies and analyses of interactions between person and situation.

Dackert, Lööv, and Mårtensson (2004) investigated Arvonen's leadership questionnaire as well as the TCI referred to earlier. Their results indicated a positive relation between a leadership style that combines employee and change orientation and team climate for innovation as a whole. However, innovative team processes such as participation and clarity of objectives were more associated with team membership than leadership in the investigated setting.

Mood and Creativity

Kaufmann (2003) summarized a new line of research dealing with the functional significance of mood on creativity, with mood understood as the background state of the overt manifestation of affect. Many investigators have shown that positive mood facilitates creative functioning; the reason was assumed to be that this mood state promotes a heuristic style of problem solving. According to Kaufmann, the theoretical formulations underpinning these explanations are often problematic and even internally inconsistent. There is also contradictory evidence suggesting that a positive mood may impair problem solving; at the least, it calls into question the assumption of a simple causal link between mood and creativity. Kaufmann and Vosburg (1997) used Russel's Adjective Check List to measure mood immediately prior to task performance, and they found evidence of a negative influence of a positive mood. Kaufmann and Vosburg (2002) also noted an interaction between mood and early versus late production, with positive mood facilitating early production, in particular, and neutral and negative moods leading to more efficient production later in the time series.

Kaufmann (2003) attempted to formulate a more general theory about the relation between mood and creativity. Such a theory must account for the fact that both mood and creativity are complex concepts. Mood not only represents a frame of mind but also indicates a state in the internal environment, such as degree of self-confidence. Mood, first of all, defines the problem as an opportunity – positive mood – or as a threat – negative mood. In regard to solution strategies, a negative mood is more likely to favor unconventional methods because the task is perceived as difficult. It must be kept in mind, however, that feedback may influence the choice of strategy considerably, and mood may not be the most important determinant of creative problem solving. Task requirements are likely to effecively moderate the influence of mood.

CREATIVITY AS REFLECTED IN THE PERCEPTUAL PROCESS

Percept–Genetic Process Theory

The theoretical perspective on creativity put forward in a monograph summarizing some fifteen years of empirical creativity research (Smith & Carlsson, 1990) was founded in the percept–genetic (PG) theory of perception (Kragh & Smith, 1970; Smith, 2001). To put the empirical results in their proper context, this section starts with a short description of the theoretical assumptions. In the PG theory, perception is conceived as a brief construction process, and its end product, the percept, as being influenced by underlying, emotion-tinged layers of the psyche. Instead of speculating about how outside stimulation affects the viewer's conception of reality, PG theory rests on the presumption that the surrounding world is created from within, founded in subjective experience, and continually constrained by feedback from the outside world. This idea was put succinctly by Brown: "That is, the feeling, meaning and recognition of an object are not attached to things out there in the world after they are perceived, but are phases ingredient in the process through which the perception occurs" (Smith, 2001, p. v; see also Brown, 1991).

Since the perceptual process leading to a stable percept is very brief, proceeding beyond awareness, it is difficult to scrutinize under regular circumstances. Even if isolated portions of these processes may pop up as associations, often after the process has been completed, the viewer is hardly able to reconstruct what came before the ultimate percept. In order to learn more about the perceptual construction, the original founders of PG research developed a reconstructive methodology (for descriptions, see Smith, 2001). In this methodology, presentations of a stimulus picture were fragmented, starting with subthreshold values, which were subsequently prolonged (or intensified). It should be stressed that meaningful stimulus pictures, new to the person and sufficiently complex, must be used in such experimentation.

Thus, to circumvent the problem of time, the researchers in the PG tradition often used a tachistoscope to accomplish a protraction of the visual perceptual process; the stimulus picture was presented in several extremely short exposures, one after the other, and very gradually prolonged. In this way it became possible to trace subjective and personal associations to the picture in a (quasi-) experimental setting. As the stimulation is gradually strengthened, for example, through longer presentations, the subjective characteristics are flaked off, replaced by a seemingly independent outside perceptual world, less private and idiosyncratic and more adapted to a consensual comprehension of what is "out there."

In brief, the process assumed to shape the viewer's perception of outside reality is reconstructed by means of series of tachistoscopic presentations of the stimulus motif, starting from exposures just below the threshold of recognition and ending when the motif has been correctly described. In PG experimentation, pictures have been used that strike at different psychological areas, such as themes of attachment, separation, aggression, and the like (described in Smith, 2001). However, it is also possible to use a quite neutral picture, such as is the case in the test of creative functioning, described by Smith and Carlsson (2001, and in the paragraphs that follow here).

The Creative Functioning Test

The Creative Functioning Test (CFT) is thus rooted in PG process theory. In order to give the reader a better grip on this unusual methodology, it may be convenient to start with a straightforward description before the more theoretical formulation. Let us therefore map the testing procedure, which consists of two interconnected halves: the increasing, upward series, and the reversed, or downward, series.

In the upward series, a picture motif is presented on a TV with a fast screen converted into a tachistoscope, starting with extremely brief exposure times, about 0.01 s, that are very gradually prolonged. The stimulus is a photo of a black-and-white drawing of two common objects (a bottle and a bowl), done by a professional artist. The picture consists mainly of shadings with diffuse contours, which makes it fairly easy to see other things in it. The viewer is asked, after each presentation, to report what he or she had seen and is not told until afterward that it was only one picture. The quality and number of interpretations of the short flashes on the screen in this first part vary from person to person, and they have been shown to correlate moderately with independent creativity criteria. The upward exposure series is supposed to reflect the viewer's general ideational fluency. At some point in the exposure series, the participant will be able to correctly perceive and describe the stimulus picture.

In the reversed series, from the point of correct recognition, the testing continues without interruption into the second part. Thus, after the viewer has been adapted to the proper meaning of the stimulus, exposure times are gradually shortened, and the support of a "correct" description of the stimulus thus eroded step by step. The testing terminates when the viewer can no longer discern anything on the TV screen.

In this reversed series, the inclination of a participant to shift her or his cognitive set is put to a test. The possible variation of reactions in different individuals is quite impressive. Certain people do not refrain from the logical–analytical way of thinking, even when the picture cues on the screen get very vague. They may say: "I know that it is a bottle and a bowl even if I can't really see it any more." At the other extreme, someone may state: "Now I saw a completely different picture – it looked like a landscape with a man standing there." These two attitudes are considered end poles on a continuum, on which many people get placed somewhere in between (i.e., they acknowledge both facts and fantasy). In the CFT manual, the categorization of this continuum is made on a scale with six steps. These can often be compressed into three main categories: a high, a medium, and a low level of creative functioning (Smith & Carlsson, 2001).

It was postulated that the correct apprehension of a PG stimulus would have a compelling influence on the viewer's report, even if the basis for such an interpretation was gradually undermined by a successive abbreviation of exposure times. This assumption proved to be reasonable when the CFT was applied in a series of investigations of adults, youngsters, and children and compared with other signs of creativity (more on that later). The more persistently a viewer maintained that the picture exposed on the screen was still the same as that seen at the longest exposure value, the more incapable he or she would be of deviating from the tracks of consensual thinking, that is, the less creative. Those viewers who eventually chose to give idiosyncratic interpretations, often the same reports as given in the series of increasing exposures that always preceded the inverted series, were consequently labeled *creative*.

In more overarching terms, a creative person's generative quality is, according to the PG model, favored by an open communication between different levels of experience. Hence, less reality-adapted types of experience and psychological functioning therefore become accessible for reconstruction and "recycling." Herein lies the opportunity to start all over again and to give up ingrained opinions. A theoretical formulation in psychodynamic terms would be that the creative man or woman liberates himself or herself to a certain degree from secondary thought processes and activates a more primary-process stamped way of thinking (cf. Suler, 1980). Furthermore, from the rather distant cognitivistic perspective, a formulation in terms of a relative lack of cognitive inhibition appears quite feasible (Eysenck, 1995, as also proposed by Carlsson, Wendt, & Risberg, 2000).

The validity and reliability of the CFT have been tested in an extensive series of investigations against different external criteria, such as the scientific work of researchers, paintings of professional artists, products of architecture students in advanced classes, college teachers, and several others (Ekvall & Ryhammar, 1999; Schoon, 1992; Smith & Carlsson, 1990). In all investigations there have been at least two independent judges of the test protocols. For basic and more detailed psychometric data, the reader is referred to the original monograph (Smith & Carlsson, 1990) and to the manual (Smith & Carlsson, 2001).

Two additional studies further elucidated the characteristics of the CFT. In one of them the participant took the first part of the CFT. Thereafter the experimenter administered a pill (in reality a placebo). Half of the individuals in the group were told that the effect of the pill would be increased attention and concentration; the other half that the effect would be mild relaxation and increased sensitivity to one's own mental life. The two groups clearly differed with respect to their results in the reversed PG, with people in the relaxation condition retrieving more subjective themes. A relaxed attitude obviously facilitates open communication between the final phase and the phases preceding it (see Smith & Carlsson, 1990).

In another sample, the reversed PG was preceded by the presentation of a subliminal stimulus: a threatening face for half of the participants and a neutral pattern for the remaining participants. Each participant was also judged with respect to various creative attributes. It was obvious that the threat group more easily attained optimal results with respect to degree of creativity. Subjects judged as having weak creative inclinations were excluded as being impervious to subliminal influence. The subliminal threat evidently had a beneficial effect in subjects susceptible to that kind of stimulation (see Smith & Carlsson, 1990).

To highlight the association between creativity, on the one hand, and self-image, on the other, a special experimental technique was employed (Smith, Carlsson, & Andersson, 1989). It made use of an electronic tachistoscope where two pictures could be flashed on a TV screen, one after the other. The second of these stimuli was a face to which the participant was adapted beforehand; the first stimulus was a verbal message (e.g., I GOOD or I BAD).

The scoring dimensions suitable in the present context were occurrences of regressions in the viewer's age estimations over, altogether, ten presentations of the double stimuli. If reports of only adults were contrasted with intermittent reports of a child or a youngster and if creativity, as defined by the CFT, was partitioned into high creativity, medium creativity, and low creativity, then a positive correlation between age regression and creativity appeared.

One conclusion based on this result would be that creative people keep open channels of communication with their own subjective roots. In other words, their identity, as projected on the flash of a face on the screen, did not necessarily remain within the confines of adulthood but might as well adopt a young, even childish, individuality.

Gender Perspectives on Creativity

Carlsson and Smith (1987) investigated 171 youngsters aged ten to seventeen with the CFT. The youngsters also took a PG test of defense mechanisms, called the Meta-Contrast Technique (MCT; Smith, Johnson, & Almgren, 1989), a test constructed to study the (defensive) handling of threatening and anxiety-arousing stimuli. The MCT protocols were scored in three main categories: isolation, repression, and sensitive-projective reports. There was no gender difference in creativity.

In contrast, in the MCT, significant differences were found between the genders. Boys had more signs of isolation; girls more of sensitivity projection. When creativity was compared with results on the MCT, we found that the defensive structures differed with degree of creativity. Highly creative children significantly more often had a combination of all three defensive categories. Children low in creativity were more characterized by a single category, either isolation or sensitivity, or by a combination of the two. Repression turned out to be the "creative" category par excellence. It was concluded that reality-oriented logic (related to isolation), an intuitive sensitivity to apparently insignificant nuances, and a symbolic reshaping of inner conflicts, when they operate in concert, all contribute positively to the creation of an original product.

Jönsson and Carlsson (2000) also investigated gender in relation to creativity. They tested 163 adults with the CFT; participants also filled out the Bem Sex Role Inventory (BSRI; Bem, 1974). It was shown that participants with a balanced score on the BSRI (either high on both masculinity or femininity, or low points on both) got higher scores on the CFT than the rest (female- or male-typed people).

Similarly, Norlander, Erixon, and Archer (2000) investigated the BSRI and creativity and found the androgynous group to score highest on creativity.

Recently, Carlsson, Hoff, and Jönsson (2005) approached the creativity construct from a gender perspective. They pointed at the importance of investigating in what ways society constructs and frames, both what counts as creative and, especially, who will be regarded as a creative individual.

A New Questionnaire

A self-descriptive creativity test was compared with results in the CFT (Smith & Fäldt, 1999). Thirty-nine university students took the test in the original study; twenty-two students were included in a cross-validation group. The results of the two tests did not correlate directly. However, highly creative participants, as defined by the CFT, preferred to apply the high-creative descriptive items both to characterize their ideal self and its opposite, leaving many of the low-creative items unused.

CREATIVITY IN ACADEMIA

Ryhammar's (1996) doctoral thesis on creativity in a university setting was written in Swedish, but two studies based on the original material (Andersson & Ryhammar, 1998; Ryhammar & Smith, 1999) provide the English-speaking reader not only with a comprehensible picture of the thesis but also with the continued processing of the material.

The background population in Ryhammar's study consisted of teachers at a new university in Sweden. A proportionally stratified sample included 149 teachers (102 men, 47 women).

Three groups of instruments were used: (a) questionnaires derived from research by Ekvall (1993, 1996, and others, also described elsewhere); (b) the CFT; and (c) two PG personality tests, the modified Defense Mechanism Technique (DMTm) and the Spiral Aftereffect Technique (SAT), both methods previously presented by Andersson (Andersson, 1972; 1995; Andersson & Bengtsson, 1985).

Among the questionnaire items related to how the teachers experienced the organization and functioning of their workplace, those concerning openness and diversity were of particular interest in the sphere of creativity as defined here by the CFT. The use of CFT data, however, differed in some respects from how they were understood in the original monograph (Smith & Carlsson, 1990). The increasing series, originally supposed to reflect ideational fluency, was here regarded as an additional indication of creativity, in case the viewer delivered at least four, mutually independent interpretations.

The DMTm is an elaboration of the Defence Mechanism Test as originally constructed by Kragh (1985). It differs from Kragh's test in the choice of thematic stimuli, but above all in its reliance, not on classical Freudian pychoanalysis, but on the variations introduced by Klein (1935), Kohut (1971), and Gedo and Goldberg (1973). An important distinction in this context is made between affect defense and identity defense. The reliability of the DMTm has proved to be solid. Amnér (1997), for instance, reported an agreement of more than 90 percent between the scorings of two independent judges.

The SAT belongs to the serial category of process-oriented instruments. The subject is confronted, in ten consecutive trials lasting 45 s each, with an inwardly rotating spiral. The aftereffect is defined by how long the participant reports that a stationary circle, fixated on by him or her after each induction period, appears to expand or draw closer. What is of particular interest here is the final level of duration and whether the series of measurements is even, increasing, or decreasing.

In a factor analysis encompassing both organizational variables and the CFT data, openness–diversity formed a factor of its own together with creativity scorings in one or both of the CFT geneses. Thus creative people regarded the university as a place of openness and diversity.

In adding the other personality tests to the factor solution, many interesting associations were detected. Affect anxiety and the accompanying defense of repression belonged to the same dimension of creative functioning, whereas various forms of identity defense (denial, non-recognition, etc.) were negatively correlated with it. In the SAT, participants with either brief or long aftereffects were singled out as more creative, that is, people in whom the distinction between subjective and objective determinants of the aftereffect was less well established than in people with moderate durations, often combined with little change over the ten measurements.

It could be added that, in creative people studied by the MCT, advanced signs of repression were particularly indicative of their defensive strategies. These signs implied an almost metaphorical reinterpretation of the threat. In a way, their test protocols were poetic.

Ekvall and Ryhammar (1999) continued the Ryhammar study at Örebro University. Besides the expected results, supporting the influence of climate on creativity, there were some unexpected correlations. One of the positive factors was work load, which has a stimulating effect on creativity. In the academic situation, up to a point, work load is more of a trigger than a strain. Maybe the fact that it was a new, expanding workplace contributed to the positive experience of work load.

Recently, four empirical studies in a doctoral thesis investigated environmental factors on scientific productivity (Widenberg, 2003). In all, approximately 100 research units were studied, mainly technological and interdisciplinary consortia. Correlations between the psychosocial research environment and scientific productivity were generally modest but still noticeable, particularly as far as the quality of research output was concerned. Among important positive determinants were scientific competence, task commitment, and self-confidence among members of the staff. Leadership clarity and openness to change were other decisive factors. Scope for independent thinking was another working condition worthy of attention. The participants also stressed the value of scientific exchange and debate, not only within the confines of the research group but in a broad international context. The book, written in Swedish, also contains suggestions for continued work within this important area.

CREATIVITY IN A DEVELOPMENTAL PERSPECTIVE

From Preschoolers to Sixteen-Year-Olds

In a project devoted to developmental aspects of creativity, Smith and Carlsson (1990) investigated 275 children aged four to sixteen years. Whole preschool classes participated, and the cohort consisted of eleven different age and maturity groups, with group sizes between twenty-one and thirty-three. Maturity was assessed, to differentiate in the youngest age groups, with the Piagetian three-mountain test of degree of egocentricity. The main instrument was the CFT, but the children were also interviewed on creativity-related themes. The contents in the interview naturally varied from the young to the older groups. Furthermore, all children produced a clay figure (the younger groups) and a drawing for the interviewer. Their products were subsequently judged by two professional artists on two criteria: originality and expressiveness. In addition, the children's defensive structure and anxiety level were assessed with the MCT.

The main result in the preschool years was that a first "high tide" in creativity, as measured by the CFT, took place in the age group of mature six-year-olds. Those slightly less mature were characterized in the testing by an expansive subjective world, while the four-year-olds had difficulties in reconstructing the CFT stimulus picture. Accordingly, the correlations were low between the CFT and the independent judges in the youngest groups, but high in the group of mature six-year-olds.

Next, the investigation turned to those that were in their first school year and compared them with a group of school children aged ten to eleven years. In Sweden, at that time, school started at seven years of age. This young group was divided with the Piagetian test into two subgroups. It was discovered that the subgroup of immature first graders was the least creative among these three groups. One might even speak of a "low tide" at that period, possibly caused by a combination of demands in the new environment and developmental factors. In contrast, the ten- to eleven-year-olds were the most creative. They showed more maturity in their defensive structure, and a positive correlation was found between medium anxiety and creativity. Interestingly enough, the artist judges preferred the children with medium anxiety. This was discussed as support for the (psychodynamic) thought that too much anxiety or total lack of worries are both detrimental to a creative hold.

The final group in the developmental project was distributed about equally on each of the years from twelve to sixteen. Here it was possible to make a split on the basis of MCT defense and anxiety, into three groups: Prepuberty, high puberty, and the oldest, adolescent group. The youngest ones, aged twelve to thirteen-and-a-half, showed compulsive tendencies and little anxiety. Thus, they had little creativity in the CFT but were not quite as devoid of positive signs as the seven-year-olds. In high puberty the anxiety levels rose, and the youngsters were unwilling to confide in the interviewer. There were no correlations to be found between tests and interviewing, but the balance seemed to be on its way to be restored in the adolescents, especially for the girls.

In sum, shifts were found between high and low tides in creativity, probably as a result of a combination of inner and outer factors. Among the environmental factors, parents with an academic background appeared to promote a positive result on the CFT. Perhaps these children were more inclined than others to question adopted interpretations of reality.

Creativity in Middle Childhood

Hoff (2003a, 2003b), in a series of studies included in a dissertation, explored creativity in middle childhood (ten-year-olds). She developed some new instruments especially suitable for this age group, but she also used the CFT and the Unusual Uses Test (Guilford, 1967).

In one study, Hoff and Carlsson (2002) investigated self-descriptions of these children. Using a self-image inventory (How I think I am; Ouvinen-Birgerstam, 1999), the researchers studied whether there were any self-image differences between more creative and less creative children with regard to school abilities, mental well-being, physical self-image, relationships with friends, and relationships with parents. However, Hoff and Carlsson did not find *one* particularly creative self-image profile for these children. Among the highly creative children, there were both those who described themselves as well adapted with many friends and high psychological well-being and those who described themselves as lonely and with psychological problems, such as anxiety and sleeping problems. There were more highly creative children found in both the extreme ends of self-images.

Hoff (2003a) demonstrated that children with imaginary companions were significantly more creative than those who did not have such companions. Among the children with imaginary companions, those who had developed more elaborated companions, who had more than one companion, who played with them at several different places and also in company with actual friends, scored higher on the creativity measurements.

Hoff further explored creativity by using qualitative methods, first by interviewing children about their sources of inspiration for solving a creative task (Hoff, 2000). The more creative children utilized more personal and subjective influences than their less creative peers. Second, interviews about childrens' imaginary companions were performed (Hoff, 2003b). Imaginary companions were assumed to be a naturally existing creative phenomenon. The ability to invent an inner device to help children take care of problems that their outer environment had failed to tackle requires creativity. Some functions that imaginary companions were found to perform included providing company, motivation, self-regulation, possibilities for self-enhancement, personality expansion and, as with all kinds of play, purely life-quality enhancement.

In another study, the ability of teachers to rate creativity was explored and compared with their ability to rate other characteristics in their pupils (Hoff & Carlsson, to be published). Teachers' ratings were compared with creativity measurements, a self-image inventory, and pupils' self-ratings in different school subjects. There was a substantial degree of agreement between the teacher ratings and the pupils' self-image descriptions and also between the teachers' gradings in Swedish, math, and art, and the children's self-ratings in those subjects, whereas there was little relation between the creativity measures and the teacher ratings. The teachers also rated their pupils' characteristics in order to make a comparison possible with implicit theories about most typical and least typical self-features of creative people. The pupils rated high in creativity by the teachers were also reported to have the most typical characteristics of creative persons, such as independence, impulsiveness or emotionality, richness of ideas, and nonconformism. However, teachers also rated those children as particularly creative whom they assessed to have the least typical traits of creative persons, such as being responsible, logical, following rules and instructions well, and being acceptant toward other children. In line with some other research (Westby & Davidson, 1995), the authors concluded that teachers seem to have a confused picture of what is a favorite pupil and what is a creative pupil.

Learning to Assess Your Creative Process

In connection with these developmental studies, it seems appropriate to describe an effort to build a platform aiming to teach schoolchildren to evaluate their creative process. According to Lindström (2001), a stronger emphasis on the process aspect in creative work is needed among teachers and pupils. He formulated four assumptions about what is demanded of schools if they are to be supportive of creativity. First, pupils need tasks that stretch over a longer time and concern central themes within a field of knowledge. Second, teachers should emphasize the process as well as the product and encourage students to do experiments, investigate, and try anew. Third, to be able to learn from good examples, it is important that the teaching situation connects the production stage with perception and reflection. Fourth, it is essential to train one's ability to self-evaluation, outgoing from clear and open criteria. Inspired by the American program Arts PROPEL (Gardner, 1989), Lindström constructed a Swedish manual for assessing creative skills in the visual arts. The assessment is based on a portfolio containing both finished works and sketches and a videotaped interview. Among performance criteria, three refer to the final product (visibility of intention, design of the product, and ability to select materials and techniques), and four refer to the creative process (investigative work, discovery of new problems, persistence in the pursuit, and imagination and risk taking).

Creativity in Elderly People

Using the CFT, Smith and van der Meer (1990) could demonstrate that creativity can still be evident in old age and, among other things, serve as a key factor in adaptation to aging.

A controlled study by Wikström, Ekvall, and Sandström (1994) demonstrated that, through exposure to genuine works of art, elderly women can be stimulated to respond in a less constricted and more imaginative manner to several creativity tests. The question remains, however, whether the stimulation is due only to the works of art or to the change in the everyday routines caused by the presence of the experimenters.

CREATIVITY AND PSYCHOSOMATICS

A central handicap in a psychosomatic patient (Smith & van der Meer, 1994) appears to be the faulty communication between preconsciousness and consciousness along the microprocesses shaping his or her perspective on reality. This was particularly illustrated by the CFT in groups of patients suffering from ulcerative colitis and Crohn's disease.

Smith, Lilja, and Salford (2002) studied the relation between creativity as defined by the CFT and prognosis in fifty-nine premenopausal women suffering from breast cancer. For most of these patients, high creativity was related to a favorable prognosis. As shown in a previous study (Lilja et al., 1998), the unfavorable prognosis was also related to intolerance of aggressive impulses. These relations were reversed, however, in a small group of patients with comedo carcinoma; this is discussed more in subsequent paragraphs.

Creativity and Aggression

If aggression is not simply considered as an urge to destruct but, more broadly, as self-assertion or territorial defense, then an assoca- tion between acknowledgment of aggressive impulses on the one hand and creativity on the other would not be unthinkable. In order to test such an assumption, a special test design was utilized (Smith & Carls- son, 1990). The apparatus constructed for the CFT (see earlier text) was provided with a picture showing an "aggressor" and a "victim" stand- ing face to face. Immediately before this picture appeared on the TV screen, the word *I* (Swedish *jag*) was flashed subliminally on the posi- tions of either of these figures. These projections were supposed to affect the viewer's impression of or attitude toward the contrasting roles they represent.

The picture was a black-and-white drawing depicting an aggressor and a victim, both male, stand half-facing each other, with the aggressor to the left. The victim is holding his arms stretched downward in an open gesture; the aggressor's arms are bent at the elbows and his fists clenched. The mouths of both figures are half-open as if they are talking; that of the aggressor is twisted in a snarl.

Starting with an exposure time of 0.01 s, the picture was flashed PG fashion until it had been correctly recognized. Thereafter, the exposure time was cut back to 0.057 s (enough for guaranteeing correct recogni- tion). The word stimulus was presented at 0.014 s and thus kept sub- liminal. The entire identification test (IT) included four series of five presentations each: (a) the picture stimulus alone, (b and c) the picture stimulus preceded by the word stimulus projected on either the aggres- sor or the victim, the order randomized, and (d) the picture stimulus alone again.

The protocols were divided into three main categories: (a) Clear aggression or gradually increasing aggression reported when *I* was pro- jected on the aggressor, (b) no aggression in any series, and (c) evasive or no reports of aggression in the aggression series, but at least some indication of aggression when *I* was presented behind the victim. The validity of the method had been established in previous research and the reliability of interrater scorings was almost perfect (cf. Smith & Carlsson, 1990).

The first group consisted of twenty-eight participants who were sixteen years old. As predicted, results indicated clear identification with the aggressor in the IT, contrasted with evasion and no aggression correlated with their results in the CFT, the latter divided by the best possible median.

The next group was thirty-three participants aged ten to twelve years. The results on the IT were less straightforward, because these youngsters were generally more reluctant to identify with the aggressor in the test picture. The group was, therefore, divided into those who were less anxious or defensive when *I* was projected on the aggressor (Group A) and those who did not differ in their responses to aggressor or victim (Group B), and those who encountered more problems in their victim series (group C). The contrast between Groups A and C with respect to creativity scores was highly significant.

Among the older children, creativity was obviously associated with self-assertion. Among the younger children, self-assertion was less openly recognized. Instead, they clearly avoided the role of a passive victim. The less creative participants showed less resistance to the surrendering role while shying away from the active aggressor.

The association between aggression and creativity had been observed in previous studies of adults. The equivalent of aggression here was self-confidence as estimated in an interview. High self-confidence was typical of both high- and low-creative people. Outgoing from the assumption that only highly creative people have full access to early stages of their PGs, our tentative conclusion was that the self-confidence of highly creative people rested on full command of their creative processes, whereas the self-confidence of uncreative people originated in obliviousness (Smith, Carlsson, & Andersson, 1989).

Early observations (e.g., Thomas & Greenstreet, 1972) had demonstrated a probable connection between suppression of aggression and cancer. That was one of the main reasons why the CFT was included in studies of women with breast cancer (reported in detail by Lilja et al., 1998, 2003). The other main instrument was the IT as just described. The most obvious indicator of resistance against identification with the aggressor was reversal of the roles of victim and aggressor. Four biological prognostic variables were tried: tumor size, S-phase (i.e., growth rate of cancer cells), lymph node metastases, and comedo carcinoma (which denotes if the border between tumor and surrounding tissue is indistinct and the tumor therefore more aggressive).

There were 59 participating patients, all premenopausal, in one of the test groups, and 129 patients in a combined group, 35 of them postmenopausal. Reversal of roles in the IT showed a particularly strong correlation with the presence of lymph node metastases and was thus a negative prognostic sign.

The CFT was scored at three levels: high (H), medium (M), and low (L). As expected, it was associated with a positive prognosis in the premenopausal group as far as lymph node metastases and S-phase fraction were concerned. Cross-tabulations disclosed similarly positive prognoses with respect to S-phase in the new group and tumor size in the combined group.

However, the association between creativity and cancer prognosis was reversed regarding comedo carcinoma. Both high and medium creativity were danger signals in this cancer group. It was typical of them that aggression was reported as gradually increasing over the phases in the IT. Although creative people are generally able to handle aggression, these patients seemed to lose control when repeatedly confronted with an aggressive theme. Without a natural command of aggressive impulses, creativity does not retain its positive meaning as a mediator, transferring aggression to constructive ends. Instead, it represents danger. In these cases, low creativity is the safe alternative – to put the lid on (Smith et al., 2002).

CREATIVITY IN NEUROPSYCHOLOGICAL SETTINGS

As described in Carlsson et al. (1991), PG methodology is well suited to application in neuropsychological research, since one of its main attributes is the instantaneous presentation of complex and meaningful stimuli, thus (at least aiming at) matching the brain's own speed and range when it handles stimulation. This idea was taken advantage of by Carlsson, as summarized in her doctoral dissertation (1992). In three of the dissertation studies, hemispheric functioning was studied by way of a visual half-field technique. This technique was applied when the participants were tested with the aforementioned Defense Mechanisms Test, the MCT. Different kinds of defenses were found to prevail in each hemisphere. Moreover, when these results were related to the CFT, as tested in the ordinary way, it was found that in low-creative people the hemispheric differences were very pronounced. In contrast, highly creative persons in both hemispheric groups showed a similar, bilateral defensive response, with medium-creative persons in an intermediate position. The results supported the view held by Lezac (1995) that "the bilateral integration of cerebral function is most clearly exhibited by creative artists who typically enjoy intact brains" (p. 69).

Later, Carlsson and colleagues (2000) continued to study creativity in a neuropsychological setting. This study had a complex design and yielded several results. Among the more prominent can be mentioned that highly creative people showed bilateral, or right-sided, activation in prefrontal areas when doing a test of creative fluency, while the low-creative group showed decreases. The high-creative group also had higher levels of cerebral blood flow during rest than did the low-creative group. Furthermore, they had higher trait anxiety and performed significantly worse on a test of logical ability (Raven's Matrices) and on perceptual speed than did the low-creative group. The groups did not differ on verbal and spatial tests.

Another part of the output from this research design focused on a comparison between creativity and defense mechanisms, with the added angle of anxiety levels (Carlsson, 2002). It was shown that the high-creative group had a greater number of different defensive categories than did the low-creative group. The number of defense categories was positively correlated with number of different themes in the CFT. On two different tests of anxiety, the creative individuals scored higher than the low-creative group. Carlsson put forward the concept of creative defensive style: "This would include the concomitant appearance of both mature and immature defenses, in certain analogy with the way that creative men and women move relatively freely along the primary–secondary process continuum" (p. 347).

Norlander (2000–2001) has also addressed the neuropsychological area. He tied it to Guilford's (1967) demand for more research on the incubation phase in the creative process. More light on this phase may be cast with new neuroimaging techniques.

Further, Norlander and colleagues have investigated the effect of both moderate alcoholic intake on the creative process as well as deep relaxation accomplished by rest in a flotation tank. After having reviewed the effects of alcoholic beverages, they hypothesized that modest alcohol consumption inhibits aspects of creativity based mainly on the secondary process (preparation, certain parts of illumination, and verification), and it disinhibits those based mainly on the primary process (incubation, certain parts of illumination, verification, and restitution; Norlander, 1999). As regards the deep relaxation accomplished in a flotation tank, results indicate that it has a positive effect on creativity but the opposite effect on logical thinking (Norlander, Bergman, & Archer, 1998; Norlander, Kjellgren, & Archer, 2002–2003).

CONCLUDING REMARKS

Creativity research in the Nordic countries has, over a relatively brief period, reached a substantial volume as well as degree of diversity. Topics range from the influence of environmental factors on ideational productivity and originality to the interplay between crucial subjective determinants of creative functioning. The research methods used are likewise multifarious, including questionnaires, interviewing, and laboratory techniques. Since the definitions of creativity depend on the choice of topic and research method, they are apt to vary between authors and projects. However, it is still obvious that the Scandinavian perspective has its own hallmark, above all less concern with the eventual utility of the endeavors of creative individuals and more with the basic characteristics of the processes involved, be they socially acceptable, interesting, useful, or not.

As far as theories are concerned, two opposites can be discerned – Christensen versus PG. Even though both focus on the creative process, they utilize different perspectives, which in many ways complement one another, thus acknowledging the complexity of the "elephant." At the same time, a comment could be made upon certain constraints in Christensen's writing, leading to a dismissal of unconscious or preconscious influences on the creative cognitive process. Perhaps the gap between inner and outer could also be bridged by adopting a PG process approach to personality, where these opposites are part of the same perceptual construction process.

Among unexpected conclusions, one rests on the finding that a positive mood does not necessarily promote creative solutions. In laboratory studies, executed by means of a process-oriented (PG) technique, the role of anxiety and defense against anxiety has been highlighted, in reference not only to psychodynamic theory but to brain functioning as well. Anxiety seems to be a necessary companion of creative efforts. Contrary to popular belief, creative functioning is not relegated to the right brain hemisphere, but to both hemispheres in cooperation. Another related theme has concerned psychosomatic illnesses, their roots in inhibited aggression, and consequent negative influences on creativity. Experimental evidence corroborated the inclination of creative individuals to identify with an aggressor rather than his victim.

Environmental influences have been studied systematically in industrial and other organizational settings. The positive role of openness, trust, and tolerance tallies with the impressions of the organizers of the centennial Nobel exhibition about which background factors are most likely to further creative excellence. At the same time, it is emphasized that creativity at the laureate level is not the only kind of creativity worth studying.

References

Agrell, A., & Gustafson, R. (1994). The team climate inventory (TCI) and group innovation: A psychometric test on a Swedish sample of work groups. *Journal of Organizational and Occupational Psychology, 67*, 143–151.

Amnér, G. (1997). *Fear of flying in civil airline passengers*. Lund, Sweden: Lund University, Department of Psychology.

Andersson, A. L. (1972). Personality as reflected in adaptive regulation of visual aftereffect perception: A review of concepts and empirical findings. In A. L. Andersson, A. Nilsson, E. Ruuth, & G. Smith (Eds.), *Visual aftereffects and the individual as an adaptive system*. (pp. 159–171). Lund, Sweden: Gleerup.

Andersson, A. L. (1995). *Defense Mechanism Test, modified*. Lund, Sweden: Lund University, Department of Psychology.

Andersson, A. L., & Bengtsson, M. (1985). Percept–genetic defenses against anxiety and a threatened sense of self as seen in terms of the Spiral Aftereffect Technique. *Scandinavian Journal of Psychology, 26*, 123–139.

Andersson, A. L., & Ryhammar, L. (1998). Psychoanalytic models of the mind, creative functioning, and percept–genetic reconstruction. *Psychoanalysis and Contemporary Thought, 21*, 359–382.

Andersson, Å. E., & Sahlin, N.-E. (1997). *The complexity of creativity*. New York: Kluwer.

Anderson, N., & West, M. A. (1998). Measuring climate for work group innovation: Development and validation of the team climate inventory. *Journal of Organizational Behavior, 19*, 235–258.

Arvonen, J. (1995). *Leadership behavior and coworker health. A study in process industry*. Reports from Department of Psychology, 801. Sweden: Stockholm University.

Arvonen, J. (2002). *Change, production and employees – An integrated model of leadership*. Sweden: Stockholm University, Department of Psychology.

Arvonen, J., & Pettersson, P. (2002). Leadership behaviours as predictors of cost and change effectiveness. *Scandinavian Journal of Management, 18*, 101–112.

Bem, S. (1974). The measurement of psychological androgyny. *Journal of Consulting and Clinical Psychology, 42*(2), 155–162.

Boden, M. A. (1991). *The creative mind. Myths and mechanisms*. London: Basic Books.

Brinck, I. (1997). The gist of creativity. In Å. E. Andersson & N.-E. Sahlin (Eds.), *The complexity of creativity* (pp. 5–16). Dordrecht: Klüwer.

Brown, J. W. (1991). _Self and process: Brain states and the conscious present._ New York: Springer-Verlag.

Carlsson, I. (1992). _The creative personality. Hemispheric variation and sex differences in defence mechanisms related to creativity._ Lund, Sweden: Lund University, Department of Psychology.

Carlsson, I. (2002). Anxiety and flexibility of defense related to creative functioning. _Creativity Research Journal, 14,_ 341–349.

Carlsson, I., Hoff, E. V., & Jönsson, P. (2005). Creativity and gender identity. In F. Columbus (Ed.), _The psychology of gender identity_ (pp. 81–93). Hauppauge, NY: Nova Science.

Carlsson, I., Lilja, Å., Smith, G. J. W., & Johanson, A. (1991). Application of a percept genetic methodology to neuropsychology. In R. E. Hanlon (Ed.), _Cognitive microgenesis. A neuropsychological perspective_ (pp. 212–239). New York: Springer-Verlag.

Carlsson, I., & Smith, G. J. W. (1987). Sex differences in defense mechanisms compared with creativity in a group of youngsters. _Psychological Research Bulletin, 26_ No. 1.

Carlsson, I., Wendt, P., & Risberg, J. (2000). On the neurobiology of creativity. Differences in frontal activity between highly and low creative subjects. _Neuropsychologia, 38,_ 873–885.

Christensen, B. T. (2002). The creative process and reality. An analysis of search and cognition in the creative process and a call for an ecological cognitive framework for creativity research. _Psykologisk studieskriftserie, University of Aarhus. 3._

Csikszentmihalyi, M. (1999). Indications of a systems perspective for the study of creativity. In R. Sternberg (Ed.), _Handbook of creativity_ (pp. 313–335). Cambridge, U.K.: Cambridge University Press.

Dackert, I. (2001). _Integration and creative experiences after a merger of two organizations within the Social Insurance Service._ Lund, Sweden: Lund University, Department of Psychology.

Dackert, I., Brenner, S-O., & Johansson, C. R. (2002). Team climate inventory with an merged organization. _Psychological Reports, 91,_ 651–656.

Dackert, I., Lööv, L-Å., & Mårtensson, M. (2004). Leadership and climate for innovation in teams. _Economic and Industrial Democracy, 25_(2), 301–318.

Ekvall, G. (1983). _Climate, structure and innovativeness of organizations: A theoretical framework and an experiment_ (Report 1). Stockholm: FA-rådet – The Swedish Council for Management and Work Life Issues.

Ekvall, G. (1993). Creativity in project work: A longitudinal study of a product development. _Creativity and Innovation Management, 2,_ 17–26.

Ekvall, G. (1996). Organizational climate for creativity and innovation. _European Journal of Work and Organizational Psychology, 5,_ 105–123.

Ekvall, G. (1997). Organizational conditions and levels of creativity. _Creativity and Innovation Management, 6,_ 195–205.

Ekvall, G. (2000). Management and organizational philosophies and practices as stimulants or blocks to creative behavior: A study of engineers. _Creativity and Innovation Management, 9,_ 94–99.

Ekvall, G., & Arvonen, J., 1991. Change-centered leadership: An extension of the two-dimensional model. _Scandinavian Journal of Management, 7,_ 17–26.

Ekvall, G., & Arvonen, J. (1994). Leadership profiles, situation and effectiveness. *Creativity and Innovation Management, 3,* 139–161.

Ekvall, G., Frankenhaeuser, M., & Parr, D. (1995). *Change oriented leadership, stress and organizational climate.* Stockholm: FA Institute.

Ekvall, G., & Ryhammar, L. (1999). The creative climate: Its determinants and effects at a Swedish university. *Creativity Research Journal, 12,* 303–310.

Eysenck, H. (1995). *Genius: The natural history of creativity.* Cambridge, U.K.: Cambridge University Press.

Gardner, H. (1989). Zero-based arts education: An introduction to Arts PROPEL. *Studies in Art Education, 30*(2), 71–83.

Gedo, J. E., & Goldberg, A. (1973). *Models of the mind. A psychoanalytic theory.* Chicago: University of Chicago Press.

Guilford, J. P. (1967). *The nature of human intelligence.* New York: McGraw-Hill.

Hartmann, H. (1939). *Ego psychology and the problem of adaptation.* New York: International Universities Press.

Hoff, E. (2000). En målares gåta – en berättelse som utgångspunkt för att studera kreativitet hos 10-åringar. (A painter's mystery – a story as starting-point to study creativity in 10-year-old children). *Nordisk Psykologi, 52*(1), 37–77.

Hoff, E. V. (2003a). *Imaginary companions, creativity, and self-image in middle childhood.* Part of an unpublished doctoral dissertation, Lund University, Sweden.

Hoff, E. V. (2003b). *A friend inside me: The forms and functions of imaginary companions.* Part of an unpublished doctoral dissertation, Lund University, Sweden.

Hoff, E. V., & Carlsson, I. (2002). Shining lights or lone wolves? Creativity and self-image in primary school children. *Journal of Creative Behavior, 36,* 17–40.

Hoff, E. V., & Carlsson, I. (to be published). Teachers are not always right – Links between ratings and pupils' creativity scores, self-images and self-ratings in school subjects. Manuscript submitted for publication.

Isaksen, S. G., & Lauer, K. J. (1999). Situational outlook questionnaire: A measure of the climate for creativity and change. *Psychological Reports, 85,* 665–674.

Isaksen, S. G., Lauer, K. J., & Ekvall, G. (2000–2001). Perceptions of the best and worst climates for creativity: Preliminary validation evidence for the situational outlook questionnaire. *Creativity Research Journal, 13,* 171–184.

Jönsson, P., & Carlsson, I. (2000). Androgyny and creativity: A study of the relationship between a balanced sex-role and creative functioning. *Scandinavian Journal of Psychology, 41*(4), 269–274.

Kaufmann, G. (2002). What to measure? A new look at the concept of creativity. *Scandinavian Journal of Educational Research, 47,* 235–251.

Kaufmann, G. (2003). Expanding the mood–creativity equation. *Creativity Research Journal, 15,* 131–135.

Kaufmann, G. (2003). The effect of mood on creativity in the innovative process. In L. V. Shavinina (Ed.), *International handbook of innovation* (pp. 191–203). Amsterdam: Elsevier.

Kaufman, G., & Vosburg, S. K. (1997). "Paradoxical" mood effects on creative problem solving. *Cognition and Emotion, 11,* 151–170.

Kaufmann, G., & Vosburg, S. K. (2002). The effects of mood on early and late idea production. *Creativity Research Journal, 14,* 317–330.

Kivimäki, M., Kuk, G., Elovainio, M., Thomson, L., Kalliomaki-Levanto, T., & Heikkila, A. (1997). The team climate inventory (TCI) – four or five factors? Testing the structure of TCI in samples of low and high complexity jobs. *Journal of Occupational and Organizational Psychology, 70,* 375–389.

Klein, M. (1935). A contribution to the psychogenesis of manic-depressive states. *International Journal of Psychoanalysis, 16,* 145–174.

Kohut, H. (1971). *The analysis of the self.* New York: International Universities Press.

Kragh, U. (1985). DMT, The defence mechanism test. Stockholm: Persona.

Kragh, U., & Smith, G. (Eds.). (1970). *Percept–genetic analysis.* Lund, Sweden: Gleerup.

Kris, E. (1952). *Psychoanalytic explorations in art.* New York: International Universities Press.

Larsson, U. (2002). *Cultures of creativity. The centennial exhibition of the Nobel price.* Canton, MA: Science History.

Lezac, M. D. (1995). *Neuropsychological assessment* (3rd ed). New York: Oxford University Press.

Lilja, Å., Smith, G. J. W., Malmström, P., Salford, L., & Idvall, I. (1998). Psychological profile related to malignant tumors of different histopathology. *Psychooncology, 7,* 376–386.

Lilja, Å., Smith, G., Malmström, P., Salford, Leif, G., Idvall, I., & Horstman, V. (2003). Psychological profile in patients with Stages I and II breast cancer: Associations of psychological profile with tumor biological prognosticators. *Psychological Reports, 92,* 1187–1198.

Lindström, L. (2001, September). *Criteria for assessing students' creative skills in the visual arts. A teachers manual.* Paper presented at the "A Must or a Muse. Arts and Culture in Education: Policy and Practice in Europe" conference, Rotterdam, Netherlands.

Martindale, C., Anderson, K., Moore, K., & West, A. N. (1996). Creativity, oversensitivity, and rate of habituation. *Personality and Individual Differences, 20,* 423–427.

Mumford, M. D. (2003). Where have we been, where are we going? Taking stock in creativity research. *Creativity Research Journal, 15,* 107–120.

Neisser, U. (1976). *Cognition and reality.* New York: Freeman.

Norlander, T. (1999). Inebriation and inspiration? A review of the research on alcohol and creativity. *Journal of Creative Behavior, 33*(1), 23–44.

Norlander, T. (2000–2001). Conceptual convergence in creativity. Incubation and brain disease state. *Creativity Research Journal, 13,* 329–333.

Norlander, T., Bergman, H., & Archer, T. (1998). Effects of flotation rest on creative problem solving and originality. *Journal of Environmental Psychology, 18,* 399–408.

Norlander, T., Erixon, A., & Archer, T. (2000). Psychological androgyny and creativity: Dynamics of gender-role and personality trait. *Social Behavior and Personality, 28*(5), 423–436.

Norlander, T., Kjellgren, A., & Archer, T. (2002–2003). Effects of flotation- versus chamber-restricted environmental stimulation technique (rest) on creativity and realism under stress and non-stress conditions. *Imagination, Cognition and Personality, 22*(4), 341–357.

Ouvinen-Birgerstam, P. (1999). *Jag tycker jag är* [How I think I am]. Stockholm: Psykologiförlaget. (Original work published 1985).

Perkins, D. N. (1981). *The mind's best work.* Cambridge, MA: Harvard University Press.

Runco, M. A. (2003). Commentary on personal and potentially ambiguous creativity. You can't understand a butterfly unless you also watch the caterpillar. *Creativity Research Journal, 15,* 137–141.

Ryhammar, L. (1996). *Kreativ funktion, perceptgenetisk rekonstruktion och organisatoriska förutsättningar för kreativ verksamhet: En studie av högskolelärare* [Creative functioning, perceptgenetic reconstruction and organizational conditions for creative activity. A study of university teachers]. Lund, Sweden: Lund University Press.

Ryhammar, A. L., & Smith, G. J. W. (1999). Creative and other personality functions as defined by percept–genetic techniques and their relations to organizational conditions. *Creativity Research Journal, 12,* 277–286.

Sahlin, N.-E. (1997). Value-change and creativity. In Å. E. Andersson & N.-E. Sahlin (Eds.), *The complexity of creativity* (pp. 59–66). Dordrecht: Klüwer.

Sahlin, N.-E. (2001). *Kreativitetens filosofi* [The philosophy of creativity]. Nora: Nya Doxa.

Schoon, I. (1992). *Creative achievement in architecture: A psychological study.* Leiden, Netherlands: DSWO Press.

Smith, G. J. W. (1997). The internal breeding-ground of creativity. In Å. E. Andersson & N.-E. Sahlin (Eds.), *The complexity of creativity* (pp. 23–33). Dordrecht: Klüwer.

Smith, G. J. W. (2001). *A process approach to personality.* New York: Plenum Press.

Smith, G. J. W., & Carlsson, I. (1990). The creative process: A functional model based on empirical studies from early childhood up to middle age. *Psychological Issues, Monograph 57.* New York: International Universities Press.

Smith, G. J. W., & Carlsson, I. (2001). *CFT, the creative functioning test.* Lund, Sweden: Lund University, Department of Psychology.

Smith, G. J. W., Carlsson, I., & Andersson, G. (1989). Creativity and the subliminal manipulation of projected self-images. *Creativity Research Journal, 2,* 1–16.

Smith, G. J. W., & Fäldt, E. (1999). Self-description and projection: Comparison of two methods to estimate creativity. *Creativity Research Journal, 12,* 297–301.

Smith, G. J. W., Johnson, G., & Almgren, P.-E. (1989). *MCT – the Meta-Contrast Technique.* Stockholm: Psykologiförlaget.

Smith, G. J. W., Lilja, Å., & Salford, L. (2002). Creativity and breast cancer. *Creativity Research Journal, 14,* 157–162.

Smith, G. J. W., & van der Meer, G. (1990). Creativity in old age. *Creativity Research Journal, 3,* 249–264.

Smith, G. J. W., & van der Meer, G. (1994). Creativity through psychosomatics. *Creativity Research Journal, 7,* 159–170.

Suler, J. R. (1980). Primary process thinking and creativity. *Psychological Bulletin, 88,* 144–165.

Thomas, C. B., & Greenstreet, R. L. (1972). Psychological characteristics in youth as predictors of five disease states: Suicide, mental illness, hypertension, coronary heart disease and tumor. *Johns Hopkins Medical Journal, 132,* 16–43.

West, M. A. (1990). The social psychology of innovation in groups. In M. A. West & J. L. Farr (Eds.), *Innovation and creativity at work. Psychological and organizational strategies* (pp. 309–333). Chichester, U.K.: Wiley.

Westby, L., & Davidson, L. (1995). Creativity: Asset or burden in the classroom? *Creativity Research Journal, 8*, 1–10.

Widenberg, L. (2003). *Psykosocial forskningsmiljö och vetenskaplig produktivitet* [Psychosocial research background and scientific productivity]. Göteborg, Sweden: University of Göteborg, Department of Psychology.

Wikström, B. M., Ekvall, G., & Sandström, S. (1994). Stimulating the creativity of elderly institutionalized women through works of art. *Creativity Research Journal, 7*, 171–182.

9

Creativity in Soviet–Russian Psychology

Olga Stepanossova and Elena L. Grigorenko

INTRODUCTION

In this chapter we present an overview of creativity in Soviet–Russian psychology. We are using the term *Soviet–Russian psychology* to indicate that the content of this chapter is based primarily on studies and conceptions developed in the context of Soviet psychology prior to December 1991, when the Soviet Union was disassembled, as well as on studies and theories that have appeared more recently in Russia. This chapter shows an existing mosaic of approaches to creativity in Soviet–Russian psychology. We present original conceptual and methodological solutions to questions on the nature of creativity and ways to study, and we discuss similarities and common characteristics of these solutions with Western psychological tradition.

With all its richness and diversity, the field of Soviet–Russian psychology of creativity can be understood as reflecting two major trajectories. The first trajectory can be traced back to conceptualizations

Preparation of this essay was supported by Grant REC-9979843 from the National Science Foundation and by Grant R206R00001 under the Javits Act Program as administered by the Institute for Educational Sciences, U.S. Department of Education. Grantees undertaking such projects are encouraged to express their professional judgment freely. Therefore, this article does not necessarily represent the position or policies of the National Science Foundation, the Institute for Educational Sciences, or the U.S. Department of Education, and no official endorsement should be inferred.

We express our gratitude to Ms. Robyn Rissman for her editorial assistance. For correspondence, please write to Dr. Elena L. Grigorenko, Yale University, PACE Center, 340 Edwards Street, PO Box 208358, New Haven, CT 06520-8358 (or e-mail elena.grigorenko@yale.edu).

of insight and creative process in Gestalt psychology (Duncker, 1945; Wertheimer, 1959). Soviet–Russian psychologists, attempting to understand this work, reinterpreted and reconceptualized creative process by implementing general principals of Marxist psychology developed, by that time, in the area of the psychology of thinking (see Grigorenko, Ruzgis, & Sternberg, 1997). The intention was to demystify insight by finding its concrete psychological mechanisms and the objective environmental conditions that lead to its occurrence, and, further, to explain creative processes from deterministic positions.

The second trajectory can be traced to the acquaintance of Soviet–Russian psychological thought with Guilford's view of creativity and with the Guilford and Torrance tests of creativity. This trajectory resulted in a change of approach to creativity research, with some psychologists accepting Guilford's (1950) and Torrance's (1962) theories and methodology, others rethinking and building on these views, and still others criticizing and rejecting them. No matter what the content of a specific theory, the focus of this approach was not on the psychological mechanisms of insight and creative process but, rather, on internal and external determinants of creative products. In the following section, we present various approaches that exist within each trajectory.

FIRST TRAJECTORY: IN SEARCH OF PSYCHOLOGICAL MECHANISMS AND OBJECTIVE ENVIRONMENTAL CONDITIONS OF INSIGHT AND CREATIVE PROCESS

Early Studies of Creativity and Initial Conceptualization of Creative Thinking

The psychology of creativity in the Soviet Union began with experimental studies of *productive thinking* (thinking that arises in novel solutions or represents new ways of solving problems) and *insight* or *guess* (defined as a sudden realization of a principle of solving a problem – a concept that Soviet psychologists were allowed to use in a time where any references to Western thought and vocabulary were prohibited; Petukhov, 1999). In using the term *guess*, Soviet psychologists wanted to distance themselves from the concept of understanding insight as an undetermined, spontaneous, unpredictable phenomenon; they attempted to explain insight from deterministic positions. In related methodological paradigms aimed at studying creativity as productive thinking, participants are typically presented with a problem for which they do not have immediate, internalized ways of problem solving; correspondingly, they have to discover the principle of solving the task for themselves (Obukhova & Churbanova, 1994). However, these "novel" solutions are well known to (and studied by!) the experimenters, who designed the tasks to create a situation that forces participants to seek an unknown, but existing and definite, solution. These tasks were developed on the basis of Duncker's insight problems (Duncker, 1945). Since the inception of the field in Russia, creativity has been interpreted as productive thinking that produces novel results in relation to the previous experience, thoughts, and ideas of an individual, and not necessarily in relation to the history of human thought in general. As Aleksei Leontiev (1998) put it, novelty belongs not to the novel final product, but to independent thinking, the independent transformation of the world by means of personal activity.

This understanding is very different from the second developmental trajectory of Soviet–Russian creativity research, which has its roots in the theories of Guilford and Torrance, with their emphasis on originality and the uniqueness of a creative product in comparison with other products of its type. Consequently, since the creative product was predetermined in many cases, many Soviet–Russian psychologists were interested, on the one hand, in studying the general process of creative thought and its mechanisms, and, on the other, in studying environmental conditions that enhance or prevent experiment participants from discovering principles of solving novel problems. In subsequent sections, we consider major conceptions and experimental work that describe both the process of creative thought and environmental conditions that influence creativity. Even though the creative process also was one of the key topics of creativity research in Western psychological tradition, it is important to note that, in this tradition, it is often assumed that creative process leads to the production of results that excel in their novelty and usefulness (Lubart, 2001).

Rubinstein's Approach

Sergei Rubinstein and his students and colleagues were interested in understanding the origin of guess and insight (Brushlinsky, 1997). Rubinstein and his colleagues described insight as a continuous process that transforms past knowledge into actual, present knowledge. This theoretical account conflicts with an understanding of insight as an instantaneous, sudden awareness of the solution or part of the solution to a problem (see Duncker, 1945; Wertheimer, 1959). According to

Rubinstein, even though it seems like insight occurs suddenly and unexpectedly, the mind is constantly involved in analyzing different qualities of a problem and in synthesizing them in a novel and creative way. Therefore, the mechanism of analysis through synthesis was theorized as a main mechanism of creative thinking. Andrei Brushlinsky (1997) further developed and elaborated Rubinstein's ideas. He theorized that thinking is a continuous process of forecasting, which allows a person to imagine how to solve a problem before the problem is actually solved (Brushlinsky, 1996). According to Brushlinsky, any type of human thinking is creative to some extent because it produces results that have never existed before in that person's mind. Therefore, to understand creativity, one should study thinking. The criterion of creative process, according to Brushlinsky, is that the thinking process leads to a solution that is novel for an individual, regardless of whether this product is novel for others. Consequently, for Brushlinsky, novelty and originality of a creative product play a less important role in distinguishing creative from noncreative processes. Brushlinsky also agreed with Rubinstein that the mechanism underlying creativity is a continuous process of analysis through synthesis. For Brushlinsky, this mechanism means that, as thinking progresses, an object of cognition is represented in one's mind in a number of different ways: A person discovers different qualities of the object (analysis), which in turn leads to the understanding of different relations between this object and other objects (synthesis). All these different representations of the object, then, can lead to novel solutions and new ideas.

Leontiev's Views of Creativity

Aleksei Leontiev's (1978a, 1978b) approach to creativity was also based on the assumption that studies of guess or insight are central to the understanding of creative thinking. Leontiev and his colleagues studied external environmental conditions that trigger or inhibit a guess, but not the process of insight in itself (Leontiev, Ponomarev, & Gippenreiter, 1981). The central goal behind their research program was to identify objective determinants of the creative process. In a typical experiment, subjects were presented with the same creative problem (how to make four triangles by using six matches)[1] and with a prompt designed to

---

[1] The article by Leontiev et al. states that the task was obtained from Yulia B. Gippenreiter, but there is no information on whether it was developed by her or adapted from someone else's work.

facilitate creative thinking (how to place a number of boxes within a provided area). Experimental conditions were formed on the basis of the type of prompt presented, the time of prompt presentation, and the frequency of exposure to a prompt. For example, one study found that multiple presentations of a prompt hinder occurrence of insight (Leontiev et al., 1981). Other studies tested the efficiency of prompts that differ in the level of complexity for eliciting a guess, and they measured the best possible moment during the creative process for the presentation of a prompt. Leontiev's approach to creativity was further developed by Yakov Ponomarev. In subsequent sections, we consider his views on creativity in more detail.

Galperin's Views on Creativity

Another significant approach to studying insight is associated with Petr Galperin (1969, 1989) and his colleagues, who addressed the question of internal determinants of insight. Specifically, they addressed the role of systematic thinking (consistent, organized, sequential analysis of every condition present in the problem) on creative process (Galperin & Kotik, 1982; Obukhova & Churbanova, 1994). Galperin used the same type of tasks as Leontiev and Rubinstein, that is, tasks that required finding a novel way of solving a problem. Studies conducted with middle-school children demonstrated that participants with structured and organized thinking styles have advantages in solving these types of tasks ahead of participants with unstructured, chaotic thinking styles (Galperin & Kotik, 1982). In Galperin's view, students with structured thinking styles are capable of systematic analysis (consistent consideration) of all qualities of objects and the relationships between them that are present in the task. Consequently, sooner or later they come across qualities essential for solving creative tasks. Students with unstructured thinking styles are prone to thinking chaotically: They often consider and analyze incidental qualities and relationships that may or may not lead to the discovery of the correct principle for solving a novel problem; therefore, they often have false guesses and solve novel problems incorrectly.

In sum, the psychology of creativity in Russia began with studies of productive thinking and insight. Creative thinking, in the initial conceptualizations of Soviet psychologists, can be characterized as attributing novelty to the production of ideas heretofore missing from an individual's experience and not necessarily to the production of ideas that are novel in comparison with the ideas of others. Specifically, the field was compelled to demystify creativity and to find objective mechanisms of creative process (Rubinstein), environmental conditions that facilitate creative process (Leontiev), and internal determinants of insight (Galperin).

Objective Sociohistorical Determination of the Creative Process

In this section we examine a theoretical approach that reflects the search of Soviet–Russian psychologists for objective social determinants of creative process. Mikhail Yaroshevsky (1985), on the basis of analyses of the history of psychological science, developed a conception of sociohistorical determination of creative scientific thinking. Specifically, Yaroshevsky was interested in the role the scientific community plays in the development of creative ideas of individual scientists as well as in the objective factors that effect change in scientific theories, models, and paradigms. Therefore, the focus is not on what the scientist contributes to the field but rather on how the field helps the scientist to generate new ideas. According to his theory, with a change of paradigms in any system of knowledge, the greatest shift is observed in the categorical constructs used rather than in the logical basis of knowledge (Grigorenko & Kornilova, 1997). This phenomenon is not accidental: According to Yaroshevsky, a research program used by a scientist – whether new or old – is represented in his or her mind by means of a cognitive–motivational categorical grid. Important structural elements of this categorical grid are schematized images. Schematized images serve as heuristics that help to develop a new research program and to organize the semantic space of a scientific thought. When creative scientists develop new research programs, they develop new ways of thinking about their areas of study and new schematized images and methods with which to pursue and categorize their research. Redefining the field requires personal input from individual scientists, but it also necessitates objective tendencies in the development of scientific knowledge. In this sense, the individual creativity of scientists is heavily influenced by shared, historically developing categorical networks.

In addition, Yaroshevsky theorized that scientific creativity is always a dialogical activity. In other words, creative thought inevitably reflects multiple viewpoints, both incorporating and rejecting various thoughts and ideas. According to Yaroshevsky, a circle of opponents serves as a second type of social determination of creative scientific thought. This view builds on Mikhail Bakhtin's (1984) ideas and is similar to Vladimir

Bibler's (1983) theory, which also emphasized the dialogical determination of creative theoretical thought. According to Bibler, when ideas existing in a given sociohistorical context are internalized, they are transformed into a dynamic and dialogical stream of thought in an individual who exists in this context. It is the dialogue of these different ideas – a dialogue between different parts of the self – that leads to the creation of new knowledge, ideas, and works of art.

In sum, Yaroshevsky, on the basis of historical analysis of the development of psychology, proposed two types of objective social determinants of creative scientific process. He theorized that creative scientific process is, on one hand, influenced by shared, historically developing categorical networks, and, on the other, by a circle of opponents to a specific idea. This approach seems to depart from the early theories just described. However, it has the same intention to demystify creativity and focus on the objective external determinants of the creative process, while undermining the uniqueness and originality of creative products.

The Role of Unconscious and Intuitive Processing in Creativity

Creative Process as an Interrelation Between Logic and Intuition

Even though Leontiev, Rubinstein, and other researchers studied productive thinking and insight, Yakov Ponomarev (1960, 1987) was the first Soviet psychologist to develop a comprehensive conception of creativity. Ponomarev's approach combined an investigation of environmental conditions that trigger creative solutions with the theoretical accounts and studies of creative process. He was particularly interested in understanding the psychological mechanisms of creative process that he found in the interaction between intuition and logic. Ponomarev was the first among Soviet psychologists to point out that creativity involves more than deliberate and logical problem solving – it involves intuition. He suggested that there is a continuum of structural levels of organization of intelligence, with a total of five different levels. These levels are transformed, reorganized stages of childhood intellectual development. One side of this continuum, or the lowest structural level of the organization of intelligence, is represented by pure intuition and the other side, or the highest structural level of organization of intelligence, by pure logical thinking. Both intuition and logic are present at the remaining structural levels, with higher levels of organization of intelligence being more logical than lower levels.

Ponomarev developed a four-stage conception of the process of creative thinking: (1) deliberate, logical search; (2) intuitive search and intuitive solution; (3) verbalization of intuitive solution; and (4) formalization of verbalized solution (Ponomarev, 1987). These stages, at first glance, resemble the classic four-stage model of creative process that was first formalized by Wallas (1926). However, as we shall demonstrate, the similarities are somewhat superficial, because Ponomarev did not merely describe stages of creative process; he was looking for concrete mechanisms that underlie each stage. According to Ponomarev, when people encounter an intellectual problem, they first try to find a solution by means of the highest structural level of organization of intelligence. Therefore, the first stage of creative problem solving involves implementing existing knowledge and logical thinking. In the case of non-creative problems (for which methods of problem solving are readily available), the solution can typically be found by relying on analytical skills. However, in the case of a novel problem, people experience failure. People feel that logic and prior knowledge don't work, which forces them to use intuition as a means of solving a creative problem.

It is interesting to note that Ponomarev developed his understanding of human cognition as having two extreme modes of functioning – an intuitive or tacit, automatic, unconscious system and a logical or analytical, deliberate, conscious system. This conceptualization is often encountered in the writings of modern Western cognitive psychologists (e.g., Epstein, Pacini, Denes-Raj, & Heier, 1996; Hammond, 2000; Hogarth, 2001). However, unlike many of these psychologists, who theorize that intuition is a primary, immediate response to the problem that occurs prior to analytical and logical considerations (e.g., Hogarth, 2001; Kahneman & Tversky, 1982), Ponomarev understood intuition as an optional way of solving the problem and not as an immediate, uncontrollable response. Only after logical approaches fail can intuition be used in creative problem solving.

When logical thinking does not lead to a successful solution and a person sustains his or her motivation to solve a problem, the person engages in actions that are progressively less conscious, that is, that are less and less controlled metacognitively; this leads to the second stage of creative problem solving – intuitive search and intuitive solution. Most of Ponomarev's studies were designed to achieve a better understanding of this stage of creative problem solving. One of the central notions in his theory of intuitive search and intuitive solution is the notion of indirect product. In Ponomarev's view, actions often result in two types of products: direct and indirect. A direct product of actions corresponds with the goal of actions; it is conscious and can be consciously used in further actions. In contrast, an indirect product occurs independently of the goal of actions; it is unconscious, and it can be used only unconsciously in the future. An indirect product is based on the qualities of the objects and phenomena that are involved in one's actions, but that are not essential for achieving the goal.

For example, in one of Ponomarev's (1960) studies, participants were given four stimuli: one long and two short strips of cardboard with an arc-like line painted on each of them, and a panel with four pins. Participants were instructed to attach the strips of cardboard to the panel by using the prefixed pins so that the ends of the painted lines would touch each other and form a figure. Participants usually solved the problem quite quickly. Often the arcs were used as implicit hints of what the object was – if the arcs were brought together, they formed an ellipse and the strips formed a triangle. Ponomarev argued that because many participants in solving this problem appeared to be focused on bringing the arcs together, the corresponding figure – the ellipse – appeared to be the goal of the participants' actions and, therefore, it was the direct product of their problem solving. However, the object that was formed as a by-product of putting the arcs together – the triangle – was unintentional and could not be viewed as a goal of action. Therefore, the triangle was considered to be an indirect product of problem solving. Accordingly, on request after solving the problem, every participant was able to reproduce the direct product (the ellipse); however, most were unable to reproduce the indirect product (the triangle).

In a similar study (as cited in Ushakov, 1997), Ponomarev showed how an indirect product could be implemented in a completely different activity without being consciously reflected on or understood. In this study, participants in the experimental condition were presented with two problems: First, they had to put strips on the panel as described earlier; second, they had to find a way through a labyrinth. The first task was organized in such a way that the final position of strips (or the indirect product of actions) was the same as the optimal way through the labyrinth. Participants in the control condition had to solve only the labyrinth problem. Study results demonstrated that participants in the experimental condition made significantly fewer errors than did participants in the control condition. However, when participants in the experimental condition were asked to explain the reasons behind their choice of way through the labyrinth, the number of errors increased.

How are indirect products related to intuitive search and intuitive solution of creative problems? Ponomarev proposed that unconscious experience consisting of indirect products often contains the key to solving a novel problem. Indirect products may appear as hints that will lead to an intuitive solution. When an intuitive solution is reached, a person has a conscious representation of a solution and a conscious feeling that the problem is solved, or what is often referred to as an insight. However, the way of solving a novel problem is still unconscious, and there is no conscious representation of an indirect product that leads to an intuitive solution. It is important to note that, even when unconscious experience contains the necessary indirect products, intuitive solution is not guaranteed. In addition, much of Ponomarev's experimental work was dedicated to finding environmental conditions under which an intuitive solution is probable. For example, he demonstrated that an indirect product was ineffective and did not lead to an intuitive solution if it was formed before the person attempted to solve a novel problem (Ponomarev, 1960). An indirect product was much more effective if it was formed during a person's attempts to solve a novel task. Furthermore, an indirect product reached its maximum efficiency if it was formed after all logical means were exhausted, but an interest in solving the creative problem was still sustained. Ponomarev's understanding of the role of indirect products in intuitive solution is similar to some modern conceptions of intuition, in which intuition is theorized to result from implicit learning (Reber, Walkenfeld, & Hernstadt, 1991; Shirley & Lagan-Fox, 1996). What makes Ponomarev's approach unique is, first, that he applied the notion of indirect product to creativity and, second, that he emphasized that indirect product does not necessarily lead to intuitive solution – that the gap between them can only be overcome under a limited set of circumstances (such as timing of indirect product formation).

The third step of creative problem solving is to verbalize an intuitive solution. Once an intuitive solution has been found, the problem solver must return to the highest structural level of the organization of intelligence: She has to use logic. As Ponomarev puts it, by using an intuitive solution, the problem solver has to "climb the ladder" of structural levels of organization of intelligence. The simplest way of "climbing" occurs in communication – in a dialogue – when, for instance, an experimenter requires a participant to explain his problem-solving strategies step by step. The last stage of creative problem solving is the formalization of a verbalized solution. Intuitive solutions could be expressed and thus formalized if they were used in a context different from that in which they were first acquired (Ponomarev, 1960). This stage involves the logical level of organization of intelligence. Ponomarev studied the last two stages to a lesser extent.

To summarize, Ponomarev was the first Soviet psychologist to offer a comprehensive theoretical understanding of the creative process and environmental conditions that enhance the creative process, as well as a methodology to study creativity. He theorized that the mechanism of creative problem solving lies in the interaction between intuition and logic. Ponomarev paid special attention to and emphasized the role of unconscious processing in creativity, thus providing other Soviets or Russians with an opportunity to study unconscious processing and intuition on a scientific basis.

Ponomarev's innovative ideas were further developed by Dmitrii Ushakov. Ushakov attempted to combine Ponomarev's approach to creativity with traditions of Western psychology. In one of his studies (Ushakov, 1999), he examined the role of intelligence (understood as psychometric general intelligence), persistence, and motivation in solving novel problems (analogous to those used by Ponomarev). He found that these factors contribute to success in solving a novel task in different stages of creative problem solving. Specifically, Ushakov demonstrated that intelligence is important in the first (logical) stages of creative problem solving, whereas persistence and motivation are important at the end of creative problem solving (intuitive stages). Ushakov explained that persistence and motivation affect intuitive search because they help to mitigate feelings of failure and fatigue (as cited in Kholodnaya, 2002). Additionally, Ushakov was interested in the role of metaphors in creative problem solving. He theorized that metaphors could help with indirect product formation, because they allow creative thinking to structure complex and complicated objects and, therefore, can trigger intuitive solutions (Ushakov, 1988). In his study with seven- and eight-year-old children, Ushakov found out that introducing metaphors during creative problem solving increased the likelihood of finding the solution. Thus, metaphors act as hints that lead to intuitive solutions for novel problems.

Nonverbal and Emotional Regulation of the Creative Process of Chess Players

The role of unconscious regulation of creative thought was further studied and analyzed by Oleg Tikhomirov and his colleagues (Tikhomirov,

1975; Tikhomirov et al., 1999). Tikhomirov developed a different theoretical approach to creativity as well as a different method to study the creative process. Specifically, Tikhomirov studied nonverbal and emotional regulation of the creative process while analyzing different external and internal indicators of thinking in chess players. Even though the approach was different, once again, the emphasis was on the process of creative thinking – the process of finding an unknown method of solving a problem – and not on the production of novel results. Tikhomirov analyzed the role of nonspecific emotional activation in enhancing and inhibiting creativity, the role of intellectual emotions (emotions appearing during the thinking process that guide problem solving and evaluate its success) in creativity, and the role of emotional solutions in creative problem solving (Tikhomirov et al., 1999). It is interesting to note that Tikhomirov and his students and colleagues used chess as a means of studying creative thinking (Krogius, 1981; Tikhomirov, 1975). In the Western psychological tradition, chess and chess players were studied in the context of expertise and in relation to the role of intuition in expert thinking (Frantz, 2003; De Groot, 1993; Simon, 1989). As Tikhomirov and others suggested, a chess player is not just an expert at recalling, sorting out, and evaluating a number of moves and positions; a chess player creates new moves and combines different elements of chess in a novel and original way (Krogius, 1981; Tikhomirov, 1975; Ushakov, 1999).

In a typical Tikhomirov study, three types of indicators of the creative process were registered while chess players had to solve a chess problem (Tikhomirov, 1975). First, either eye movements of chess players with normal eyesight or tactile activity of blind chess players were registered to assess the size of a search field, nonverbal search strategies, and moves that chess players considered before solving a novel problem. Second, skin conductance was registered to measure level and dynamic of emotional activation. Third, chess players were asked to give verbal reports of their thinking process. Results of Tikhomirov et al.'s (1999 research demonstrated that nonspecific, positive emotional activation enhanced creativity, whereas nonspecific, negative emotional activation inhibited creative activity. The situation was different for intellectual emotions. Both positive and negative intellectual emotions, according to Tikhomirov, serve as a means of organizing the problem and help to connect in a meaningful way significant elements of a situation; therefore, both negative and positive intellectual emotions enhance creative thinking. Tikhomirov's studies also demonstrated that sudden insight (which was often revealed in the verbal reports of chess players) is actually preceded by complex thought activity, a large part of which is unconscious. Consequently, insight, in Tikhomirov's view, cannot be understood as an instantaneous phenomenon (analogous to Rubinstein and Brushlinsky's positions, discussed earlier). For example, it was shown in several studies that a verbalized creative solution was preceded by an emotional nonverbal solution. An emotional solution, in turn, resulted from an active nonverbal inspection of elements of the problem (which was evident from the analysis of eye movements or tactile activity of chess players) that led to emotional fixation of important relations, significant elements, and possible developments of the situation that are present in the problem. If an emotional solution wasn't formed and then verbalized, a creative solution was not reached (Tikhomirov et al., 1999).

In sum, Tikhomirov studied the nonverbal and emotional regulation of creative process in chess players. He used different objective indicators of problem-solving strategy and emotional activation to achieve a better understanding of the nonverbal activity that precedes creative solutions. His studies demonstrated that the conscious realization of a creative solution is preceded by an emotional solution, which in turn is preceded by complex nonverbal inspection of elements, relations, and opportunities present in the problem situation.

The Role of Intuitive Abilities in Creativity

Interest in the intuitive aspect of creativity can occasionally be found in more recent works of Russian psychologists. However, even though notions are the same and authors may refer to Ponomarev, Tikhomirov, and others' theories as the roots of their research, there has been a shift in how creativity and intuition are understood and studied. With the popularity of the tests by Guilford (1950), Torrance (1962), and Mednick (typically referred to as Remote Associates Tests, or RATs; see Mednick & Mednick, 1967) in Soviet–Russian psychology, there came an understanding of creativity as an ability to produce a number of novel, original, and useful results. The focus shifted from identifying mechanisms of creative process to studying certain abilities that are involved in creativity. This shift in research is not oriented toward capturing the creative process; rather, the main interest lies in discovering relationships of creative productivity with external (e.g., type of instruction) and internal (e.g., level of intuitive anticipation) factors; therefore, it belongs to the second line of Soviet–Russian creativity research identified at the beginning of this chapter. For example, Tatyana Ryabova and Vladimir Mendelevich (2002) studied the relationship between intuition and creativity; however, they used very different theoretical frameworks for understanding both concepts. They understood intuition as an ability to anticipate or to foresee one's behavior and the course of events in an unfavorable and frustrating situation. They defined creativity as an ability to produce novel, original, and useful results. Ryabova and Mendelevich were interested in exploring the relationships between creativity and anticipation in mentally healthy individuals and in schizophrenic patients. Creativity was measured with the Torrance and Guilford tests, whereas intuition was measured with a self-report measure originally developed by Mendelevich that allows the capture of communicative anticipation, spatial anticipation, and temporal anticipation (the instrument consists of eighty-one items: fifty-five items evaluate communicative anticipation, fourteen evaluate spatial anticipation, and twelve evaluate temporal anticipation). The results of this study demonstrated that schizophrenic patients had significantly higher originality of creative thinking, whereas mentally healthy participants were more competent in intuitive communicative anticipation. As for the relationships between intuition and creativity, study results demonstrated that intuitive anticipation and flexibility of creative thinking appear to have a common root, which was evident in both mentally healthy and schizophrenic patients. In contrast, originality and ability to form accurate intuitive anticipations appeared to be independent of one another.

To summarize, from the very beginning of Soviet–Russian research on the concept of creativity, unconscious processing was theorized to play a major role in creative problem solving. Studies that originated from two different research paradigms (Ponomarev and Tikhomirov) analyzed specific psychological mechanisms that underlie the creative process. Both paradigms demonstrated that conscious, deliberate, logical search for a creative solution constituted only part of the creative thinking process. Such nonverbal and unconscious elements of creative thinking as indirect products, emotions, and emotional solutions play important roles in guiding people toward finding solutions to creative problems. More recent developments in the field of intuitive components of creativity (Ryabova and Mendelevich) demonstrate a shift of interest to intuitive abilities as an internal determinant of creative productivity. In conclusion, from its inception, Soviet–Russian psychology of creativity emerged in the context of studies of productive thinking and insight. It was oriented toward the discovery of psychological mechanisms of insight (guess), as well as toward the identification of objective social and environmental determinants of creative process. Several mechanisms were proposed, such as analysis through synthesis (Rubinstein, Brushlinsky), organized systematic thinking (Galperin), interaction of logic and intuition (Ponomarev, Ushakov), active nonverbal search, and unconscious emotional regulation (Tikhomirov). This research resulted in interesting and valuable findings and improved understanding of the role of unconscious, nonverbal processing in the creative process. Creative product and creative productivity were not of much interest to these psychologists. This focus appeared as a result of the common assumption that novelty of discovered ideas and solutions should be assessed in relation to one's previous knowledge and not in relation to the uniqueness and originality of these ideas in a broader sociocultural context. In a typical Russian study, participants were presented with a problem that had one known (to the experimenter) solution. Participants did not know the solution and did not have readily available methods of problem solving. This research approach changed completely once Soviet–Russian psychologists became acquainted with Guilford's (1950, 1967) conceptions of creativity. In subsequent sections, we consider the new developmental trajectory in creativity research that was fueled by this famous figure in Western psychological tradition.

SECOND TRAJECTORY: IN SEARCH OF INTERNAL AND EXTERNAL DETERMINANTS OF CREATIVE PRODUCTION

One of the major changes that came with Guilford's popularity in the Soviet Union and later in Russia was the type of tasks used for studying creativity and the type of research questions asked. Novel problems no longer had one known solution; they implied variability in answers and methods of solving them. Interest also shifted from the search for mechanisms of creative process to the search for internal (e.g., intelligence and motivation) and external (e.g., environmental conditions) determinants of creative productivity. However, many Soviet–Russian psychologists not only implemented this new research program, but also reexamined and even rejected it and created novel theoretical conceptions of creativity. In reviewing this line of research, we pay the most attention to novel and original ideas, theories, and experimental work.

The most commonly used tests of creativity within the second line of Soviet–Russian creativity research are the Torrance tests of nonverbal creative thinking. The Torrance Tests of Creative Thinking were first translated and validated in Russia by the Center of Creative Giftedness of the Scientific Research Institute for General and Pedagogical Psychology (Shumakova, Shcheblanova, & Shcherbo, 1991). These tests were validated on children ages six to eighteen and are widely used in psychological research in Russia. The Laboratory of Abilities of the Institute of Psychology of the Russian Academy of Sciences translated and validated the RAT (Druzhinin, 1999). The Russian version of the RAT has both child and adult forms. The Guilford tests have never been dealt with in a centralized, systematic manner: Each study used its own translation and adaptation of the test.

The Role of Motivational Determinants in Creative Production

The concepts of motivational determination and regulation of creative production have been well studied. Different determinants, such as motivation, values, and personality characteristics, were proposed in an attempt to understand what makes the creative process unique and also how creative and noncreative production differ. This approach focuses on the question of what types of people exhibit the highest level of creative production and what kinds of motivation result in the highest level of creative performance. For example, Margarita Kanevskaya and Lyubov Firsova (1990) theorized that success in creativity is related to the central values and interests of a person. In their study, they demonstrated that children are more likely to achieve success in literary creativity when the content of creative activity is related to values and interests that have meaning and significance to them.

Yuliya Babaeva (1997) demonstrated the influence of external motivation on creativity (as measured by the Torrance test). Contrary to the findings of Amabile and colleagues (Amabile, Goldfarb, & Brackfield, 1990), Babaeva found that children, on average, are more eagerly engaged in the creative process in the presence of observers who can appreciate their work and who constitute external motivation of children's efforts, and less eagerly engaged in the absence of such observers. In Babaeva's study, fear of creativity was another important factor that determined the level of creative production exhibited by children.

Children who feared creativity, who didn't want to take risks, and who preferred known ways of solving problems were less creative than children who didn't fear being creative. Moreover, when children were able to overcome their fear of being creative, their scores on tests of creativity improved.

Elena Shcheblanova was interested in personality characteristics that affect the quality of performance in gifted children (with both intellectual and creative giftedness). Her study of gifted high school students demonstrated (Shcheblanova, 1999) that there were no significant differences among children with high and low school achievement on tests of intellectual abilities (as measured by Kognitive Fahigkeits Tests; see Heller, Gaedike, & Weinlader, 1985), creative abilities (as measured by the Torrance test), and speed of cognitive processing. However, students differed significantly on a number of personality characteristics. The group of gifted students that performed poorly in school had high fear of failure, low self-esteem, high anxiety, and an external type of attribution.

Diana Bogoyavlenskaya (1983, 1995, 1999, 2002) developed a comprehensive conception of the role of motivation in creativity. Her theoretical account rejects Guilford's theory; the only common elements are the emphasis on creative productivity, the search for internal factors that are involved in creativity, and the use of problems that allow for more than one correct answer. Creativity, according to Bogoyavlenskaya, has two important characteristics. First of all, creativity is a productive thinking activity – oriented toward the production of novel results. Second, it is a spontaneous activity in the sense that it is not stimulated by external requirements, reward, or predetermined problems. According to Bogoyavlenskaya, creativity is not some special ability; rather, any activity can be characterized as either creative or noncreative. The key to distinguishing between creative and noncreative types of activity lies in a person's motivation. Creativity is determined by free choice; it involves the development and transformation of activity. It comes from internal motivation and from passion for an activity in itself, and not from some type of external motivation. When people work only to get a reward or when they work because they have high achievement motivation, they can do high-quality work; however, the results of this work will correspond with requirements – they won't go beyond that which is required. Activity in itself does not motivate these people; therefore, there is no room for creativity, no opportunity for going beyond what is given or predetermined by someone else.

In a sense, Bogoyavlenskaya's view on creativity motivation is very similar to Mihaly Csikszentmihalyi's (1990) notion of flow. Both approaches emphasize the absence of the expectation of a reward as a feature of creative activity as well as acknowledge that the motivation of a truly creative person comes from the creative activity in itself.

Bogoyavlenskaya proposes that there are three types or hierarchical levels of productive thinking activity. Only one of them, the highest level, can be called creativity in a strict sense.

The first is the stimuli-productive level. This type of activity may appear productive, but it is only an illusion, according to Bogoyavlenskaya. One's productive activity is determined by external stimuli: People solve predetermined tasks of creating novel products only because they are asked to do so. An individual at the stimuli-productive level cannot go beyond what is required; she or he cannot exhibit creativity. Achievements on this level of productive activity, according to Bogoyavlenskaya, reflect a person's level of intelligence.

The second is the heuristic level. This type of activity has some characteristics of true creativity. With this level of productive activity, when people have a reliable, tested method of solving a problem, they start analyzing the content and structure of their activity and the similarities and differences between tasks, which leads them to the discovery of new, original, and witty ways of problem solving. Each finding is experienced as a discovery. People at this level can go beyond the requirements of the predetermined task. They are internally motivated by the novel problem; however, they can be described as pragmatists because they are looking for novel means to solve current tasks. Therefore, external motivation doesn't fully disappear.

The third is the creative level. On this level, people also discover new methods of problem solving. However, they are not merely using their findings to facilitate task completion. Discovery becomes a new, independent problem that a person pursues in an attempt to justify his or her findings. No one requires the person to justify the discovery. Furthermore, by doing so, the person is wasting time that could have been used to fulfill requirements and solve an original task. According to Bogoyavlenskaya, creativity in a strict sense starts when activity is no longer merely a solution to an objectively defined problem. To be considered creative, people must define their own problems and be internally motivated to solve them.

Bogoyavlenskaya developed a method to study creativity as intellectual activity and demonstrated that theoretical differences between the levels of productive activity, indeed, exist. Her method – "creative field" – consists of a set of typical tasks that could be divided into two different levels of activity: The first level is explicitly given to participants as a requirement to solve a series of predetermined problems. The second level – finding rules and principles that underlie the set of tasks – is hidden from participants and is not required for them to be successful on predetermined tasks. To ensure that participants didn't have any prior knowledge of rules and principles underlying the experimental task, Bogoyavlenskaya used cylindrical chess as an experimental material. In cylindrical chess, a standard chessboard is used, but this board is rolled in a pipe. Because the chess field is cylindrical, the rules and heuristics that can be used in standard chess cannot be applied directly to this game. People who participate in these experiments must learn how to play cylindrical chess. The typical experiment with a creative field consisted of two stages (Bogoyavlenskaya, 1983). First, participants were trained to work with cylindrical chess; they learned the rules and moves that figures could make on a cylindrical chessboard. Second, participants were presented with twelve different chess tasks in a predetermined order. The situation was unregulated in that it was left up to the participants themselves if they would merely solve the problems or if they would exhibit creativity and go beyond of what was required of them.

Bogoyavlenskaya was interested in studying, on one hand, the relations between the creative field as a means of assessing creativity and real creative production, and, on the other, the relation of the creative field to other tests of creativity. One of her studies was conducted with high school music majors (Bogoyavlenskaya, 1983). She found that sixteen participants were on the stimulus-productive level, whereas twenty-one were on the heuristic level. None of the students were on the creative level. She also assessed the musical success of the students (by a combination of grades and teachers' reports). Results demonstrated that students with the highest level of intellectual or productive activity (heurists) were the most successful in their musical careers. In a different study (Bogoyavlenskaya, 2002), the relation between scores on creative field and quality of artistic production was investigated. She found that works of artists who achieved the heuristic level of intellectual or productive activity were considered to be more creative and original (as measured by expert ratings). As for the relation with other tests of creativity, Bogoyavlenskaya's (1995) studies demonstrated that, in different samples of both children and adults, there were no significant correlations between creativity scores as measured by creative field and by the Torrance and Guilford tests.

One of the interesting implications of Bogoyavlenskaya's conception is that achievement motivation actually interferes with and even disrupts creative activity. One study was designed to test this hypothesis by comparing predominant motivation and level of creativity. Results demonstrated that participants who were mainly motivated by achievement motivation or by motivation to avoid failure mostly showed the stimulus-productive level of creativity, whereas participants who were predominantly creativity motivated mostly exhibited the heuristic level of creativity (Bogoyavlenskaya, 1983). Bogoyavlenskaya explains that truly creative thinking requires risk and willingness to explore uncertainty. It requires people to put aside the goal of achieving quick and effective results and to set their own goals and define their own problems.

However, the traditional Soviet–Russian educational system is oriented toward results. Children are expected to achieve predetermined results quickly and are encouraged and praised when they do so. Independent problem finding and independent research are not encouraged. Therefore, a very small proportion of children develop internal creative motivation and achieve a creative level of productive activity. For example, Bogoyavlenskaya (1983) found that, among middle school children, only 7 percent reached a creative level of productive activity. This situation should be improved by the use of an educational intervention that aims to encourage creative process, independent problem finding, independent research, and reflection (Bogoyavlenskaya, 2002).

In sum, a number of Soviet–Russian psychologists looked at motivational determinants of creative production. Diana Bogoyavlenskaya developed a comprehensive conception of the role of motivation in creativity, especially the role of intrinsic (internal) motivation. She theorized that creativity begins when people stop solving predetermined problems and go beyond what is required of them. She also designed a method that allowed researchers to study whether participants exhibit spontaneous creativity while solving predetermined noncreative problems. Her studies demonstrated that spontaneous, productive, undetermined activity is, on the one hand, related to real-life creative achievements, and, on the other, unrelated to traditional measures of creative production (Torrance and Guilford's tests).

The Role of Cognitive and Intellectual Determinants
in Creative Production

In this section we consider conceptions of creativity that deal with the problem of intellectual determination and regulation of creative production. Specifically, we briefly review the work of Marina Kholodnaya and Vladimir Druzhinin.

THE ONTOLOGICAL APPROACH TO CREATIVITY. Marina Kholodnaya (2001, 2002) developed an ontological approach to studying intellectual giftedness and creativity by conceiving of intelligence as a special form of organization of individual mental experience. She proposed that intelligence consists of four different structures that organize individual mental experience: (1) cognitive (mental structures that process current information); (2) metacognitive (mental structures that allow voluntary and involuntary regulation of one's intellectual activity); (3) intentional (mental structures that underlie an individual's preferences and beliefs); and (4) intellectual abilities (mental structures that characterize productive, creative, and other individual and original characteristics of intellectual activity). Thus, Kholodnaya understands creative abilities as part of intellectual abilities, as divergent abilities that determine the type of creative production exhibited by an individual (which is very similar to Guilford's views on creativity). Kholodnaya proposed the following characteristics of intellectual activity as criteria of creativity: (a) fluency (production of a number of ideas that occur during a given time interval); (b) originality (production of infrequent ideas that differ from stereotypical responses); (c) susceptibility (sensitivity to unusual details, contradictions, uncertainty, and readiness to switch from one idea to another flexibly and quickly); and (d) use of metaphors (readiness to work with fiction, in unreal context, and a tendency to use symbolic means to express one's thoughts).

One of Kholodnaya's studies (2001) empirically tested relationships between components of mental experience and convergent and divergent abilities. Results demonstrated that creativity as a production of novel ideas is related, on the one hand, to characteristics of the organization of concepts, and, on the other, to the level of development of involuntary intellectual control. Therefore, as Kholodnaya interpreted the results, creativity cannot be understood as a spontaneous process; on the contrary, it is a regulated process. Creative ideas are filtered through the structures of a person's conceptual and metacognitive experience. This study also suggested that the indicator of originality (as measured by the Torrance test) is not homogeneous, but rather that there are two different types of creativity: "productive creativity" and "paradox creativity." Paradox creativity occurs when participants who have some cognitive deficits (low levels of categorical and spatial transformations) suggest original ideas as hypercompensation for these deficits. Productive creativity, in contrast, is not related to cognitive deficits but to the development of conceptual and metacognitive experience (as just discussed).

DRUZHININ'S COGNITIVE RESOURCE MODEL. Vladimir Druzhinin (1997, 1999) developed a so-called cognitive resource model that allows for an explanation of individual differences in creative productivity. Level of cognitive resource is understood as a quantitative characteristic of the cognitive system and as a capacity of interrelated cognitive elements (such as iconic and short-term memory, attention, reaction time, and size of cognitive space) that are responsible for the creation of multifaceted representations of reality during problem solving (Goryunova & Druzhinin, 2001). According to Druzhinin, creative productivity is determined by the presence of a "spare" cognitive resource that can be used, for example, to find additional information, test conditions of a creative problem, and expand a search field. Druzhinin demonstrated some empirical support for his model: In one of his studies, the scope of iconic and short-term memory as well as reaction time were measured in conjunction with verbal protocols of solving creative puzzle problems. Results demonstrated that participants with higher creative productivity (as measured by success in solving puzzle problems) had a larger scope of iconic memory and smaller reaction time than did participants with lower creative productivity (Goryunova & Druzhinin, 2001).

Thus, Kholodnaya and Druzhinin's approaches to creativity provide examples of the search for intellectual and cognitive determinants of creative production. Kholodnaya developed an ontological approach to studying creativity, which she understood as a part of intellectual abilities (part of mental structures that organize experience). Her research demonstrated the relationships that exist between different cognitive and metacognitive mental structures and level of creative production. Druzhinin proposed (and demonstrated some empirical support) that creative productivity is determined by the presence of a spare cognitive resource or by the presence of spare capacity of the cognitive system that is responsible for creating representations of reality.

The Role of a Combination of Intellectual and Motivational Determinants in Creative Production

Soviet–Russian psychologists theorize that a combination of intelligence and motivational regulation determines the characteristics of creative production. Specifically, Viktoriya Yurkevich proposed a developmental conception of creativity. She built on a well-known Vygotskian idea that each psychological function has two forms – natural and cultural (Vygotsky, 1962). Lev Vygotsky developed a hypothesis about the socially mediated nature of higher or cultural mental functions. He proposed that higher or cultural mental functions differ from natural mental functions in their structure, nature, and control mechanisms. Yurkevich (1997) expanded Vygotsky's general idea, developing it in the domain of creativity and proposing that there are two different stages of the development of creativity. Yurkevich understands creativity in adults – developed or cultural creativity – as the production of novel results and the active overcoming of stereotypes of thinking and behavior. Young children have a different type of creative process. They have not yet acquired a repertoire of stereotypes; therefore, there is nothing in their experience that they should overcome. According to Yurkevich, young children have naïve or natural creativity, which is characterized by the naturally occurring behavior of a child in a context lacking stereotypes. All children have naïve creativity that is developed to a greater or lesser extent. When children draw blue grass and yellow sky, they do so because they want to express the world they are living in, not because they are trying to find a way to overcome the common knowledge that the grass is green and the sky is blue. As children age, their repertoire of stereotypes and social conventions expands, which leads to dramatic changes in creativity. Children begin to acquire cultural creativity that is similar to creativity in adults. To exhibit creativity, children now have to actively overcome stereotypes. Cultural creativity results from the development of both cognition and personality. To be culturally creative, children must demonstrate an effort or motivation to overcome or even destroy cultural stereotypes.

Yurkevich uses the distinction between naïve and cultural creativity to explain the decline in creative abilities in early childhood. She proposes that this decline is a necessary step in the transition from naïve to cultural creativity that results from intellectual development and the acquisition of stereotypes and models of thinking and behavior. One of Yurkevich's (1997) studies demonstrated that significantly fewer children with highly developed creativity were found in a group of seven- to eight-year-old intellectually gifted children than in a group of nongifted children. Furthermore, more children from a nongifted group had higher motivation to engage in creative activities. A different study was conducted with elementary-school children who took lessons designed to improve creative imagination (Yurkevich, 1996). Results of this study demonstrated that intellectually gifted children had, on average, dramatically less developed creative abilities (as measured by the Torrance test) at the beginning of the first grade than did children with moderate levels of intelligence. However, at the end of third grade, intellectually gifted children improved in their creative abilities and had higher levels of creativity than did their counterparts with moderate levels of intelligence. Yurkevich explains these results by applying her theory of naïve and cultural creativity. Intellectually gifted children acquire social norms and stereotypes at a faster rate than do their less gifted peers; therefore, they begin to lose naïve creativity at a younger age (at the time of first assessment). The situation is reversed at the second assessment: Children with moderate levels of intelligence lose naïve creativity as they gain social knowledge and stereotypes, although they have not yet begun to acquire cultural creativity. In contrast, intellectually gifted children who develop faster begin to acquire an ability to overcome stereotype, or cultural creativity.

In the study just described, not every intellectually gifted child demonstrated shifts in creative abilities by the end of third grade. Yurkevich theorized that intellectually gifted children who differ in their creative abilities also have different types of predominant cognition motivation. To test this hypothesis, she studied children who not only had high intelligence scores but also were extremely successful – who won different international or national contests in chemistry (Yurkevich, 1996). In addition to completing the Torrance test, the children had the choice to participate in a series of creative and intellectual tasks. Results demonstrated that creative children were more likely to invest in one problem that really interested them, whereas noncreative children were more likely to solve a number of different problems. This trend was evident even in creative types of tasks. In addition, noncreative children requested the answers to the problems they solved more often than did creative children. Therefore, creative children appear to be motivated by the process of cognition in itself, whereas noncreative children are more oriented toward achieving a significant number of results of cognition. These findings support the hypothesis that creative and noncreative intellectually gifted children have different types of predominant cognition motivation.

To summarize, Yurkevich proposed a developmental conception of creativity that emphasized the role of intelligence and motivation in levels of creative production of children. She proposed that creative production could result from either of the two stages of development of creativity – naïve and cultural creativity – and explained the difference between them in terms of intellectual development, acquisition of cultural stereotypes, and motivational development.

External Determination of Creative Process

Within the second developmental trajectory of creativity research, Soviet–Russian psychologists analyzed immediate environments of individuals and studied factors that could enhance the creative process instead of environmental conditions that led to the occurrence of insight (as was the case in the first research trajectory). This line of research is oriented to educational practice and is conducted with the goal of finding ways of fostering creativity in educational settings. Aleksei Matyushkin and his colleagues were interested in studying types of instructional practices and curricula that stimulate the development of creativity in children of all ages, from kindergarten through high school. Matyushkin (1989, 1990, 1993) developed a conception of creative giftedness. He understood giftedness as the level of creative potential of a child that could be realized in any area of human practice. Every child has a different level of creative potential; however, gifted children have the highest level of creative potential. Therefore, research on types of instruction that benefit the development of gifted children constitutes an ideal model for understanding which conditions foster creative development. Matyushkin elaborated the idea of giftedness as the highest level of creative potential and proposed that giftedness and creativity have essentially the same psychological structure. The central component that constitutes creative giftedness is the need for cognition, which can manifest itself in a variety of forms such as curiosity, openness to novelty, and exploration. Other components include creative activities that result in the discovery of novel ideas, finding original solutions;

ability to define and solve problems; ability to anticipate and forecast; and ability to create ideal models and standards (from aesthetical, intellectual, and ethical points of view).

Natalya Shumakova (1996) developed a comprehensive program of interdisciplinary instruction called Gifted Child, which is based on Matyushkin's conception of creative giftedness as well as on Treffinger's (1980) model of creative learning for the gifted and talented. This program is designed to promote creative potential in children from kindergarten to ninth grade. The program fosters curiosity of gifted children, and helps them develop abstract thinking, generalization, independent thinking, and a holistic understanding of the world. For each grade, the curriculum is structured around global philosophical themes such as "Geneses," "Change," and "Influence"; such thematic structure allows children to connect the content of different school subjects. Grade-level curricula include interdisciplinary lessons that introduce philosophical themes and provide generalization as well lessons in typical school subjects. Each subject course aims to solidify the general objective by providing the unique perspective of its field. Additionally, the curriculum implements discovery learning and encourages students to do independent research. It is also oriented toward enhancing students' creative skills, such as originality, flexibility, elaboration and fluency, creative problem solving, and ability to define creative problems.

Shumakova's (1996) study with fifth through ninth graders demonstrated that the Gifted Child program had a significantly more positive impact on gifted and highly gifted children, who experienced higher satisfaction with the program and higher interest in learning than did nongifted children. Gifted children appreciated the opportunity to learn independently, whereas nongifted children enjoyed independent research and learning less.

In a different study, Elena Shcheblanova (2000) looked at the effect of Gifted Child versus traditional instruction on the development of gifted elementary/school children (Grades 1–3). Teacher ratings in combination with tests of intellectual abilities (as measured by Kognitive Fahigkeits Tests – German tests of intellectual abilities) and creative abilities (as measured by the Torrance test) were used to select gifted children for the experimental condition and to identify gifted children in the control condition. Results demonstrated that 30 percent of gifted students taught within the traditional settings showed decline in their intellectual and creative abilities. None of the students in the Gifted Child program showed decline in their abilities; on the contrary, most children showed gains, especially in their creative abilities. Therefore, the study indicated that the interdisciplinary instruction of Gifted Child matches children's intellectual and creative abilities, their curiosity, and their independent learning styles and makes it possible to develop their creative potential.

Vladimir Druzhinin focused on a narrower set of environmental factors that foster creativity. He was interested in studying specific influences of characteristics of immediate environment on creative production: ambiguity, possibility of implementing a number of different approaches, and presence of exemplars of creative behavior. Druzhinin theorized that creative productivity could be enhanced in ambiguous environments, environments that have a number of potential outcomes and potential approaches, and environments that contain a number of exemplars of creative behavior and creative outcomes. This hypothesis was tested on a group of three- to five-year-old children, using an active–forming experiment (Druzhinin & Khazratova, 1994). Children in the experimental condition experienced little formal regulation of cognitive behavior (high ambiguity), richness of available materials and information (high chance of implementing a number of different approaches), and the presence of exemplars of creative behavior. Children in the control condition, in turn, experienced a more regulated environment, had fewer available materials, and were not stimulated by the presence of exemplars of creative behavior. Children in the experimental and control conditions were matched on initial level of creative abilities. Creativity was tested twice (pretest and posttest) and measured on the basis of invented uses of game objects and on invented game events. Results of this study demonstrated that intervention was successful: The experimental group had significantly higher levels of creative productivity and creativity motivation on the posttest than did the control group.

Druzhinin also studied the effect of instruction on the creative production of children with different levels of creative abilities. He hypothesized that external conditions can affect creativity only to a limited extent. Favorable environmental conditions cannot affect creative productivity if a person doesn't have creative abilities. In one study (Druzhinin, 1999), the RAT (Mednick & Mednick, 1967) was administered to two different groups of participants: those with and those without time limits on the completion of the test. Results demonstrated that both highly creative and noncreative individuals did better without time constraints; however, experimental manipulation had a significantly

greater effect on highly creative individuals than on noncreative people. A different study (Druzhinin, 1999) revealed that instruction to
give creative (e.g., original) answers affected less creative children to
a greater extent than more creative children: Their level of creativity
(as measured by the Mednick test) improved much more. Druzhinin
explains that in this study, instruction affected levels of motivation in
less creative children, whereas more creative children already have high
internal creativity motivation; therefore, external manipulation did not
have much influence. These results suggest that, indeed, effectiveness
of environmental factors in fostering creative production is limited by
one's creative abilities and internal creativity motivation.

Galina Ozhiganova (2001) also studied environmental influences on
creativity in elementary-school children. She was particularly interested
in examining two environmental factors: exemplars of creative behavior
presented by teachers, and requirements to exhibit creative behavior. She
used the Torrance and Mednick tests at both the beginning and the end
of her study. She also designed several educational interventions that
allowed teachers to (a) demonstrate to children exemplars of creative
behavior; (b) create an unregulated environment where children were
allowed to choose a creative task and where there were no time limits;
and (c) create a regulated environment where children were required to
exhibit creativity as a part of their school activities. Results of this study
revealed that the children exhibited creativity more frequently when
their teacher demonstrated exemplars of creative behavior. In this situation, the children reacted positively and emotionally to creative exemplars and were more likely to engage in creative activities themselves.
However, Ozhiganova observed delayed reactions to the presence of
creative exemplars: Most children observed up to ten different creative
exemplars before engaging in their own creative activities. In addition,
the children were more likely to exhibit creativity in an unregulated
environment than in a regulated one. This result was also confirmed
when an index of creative productivity (as measured by the children's
real creative achievements in the experimental situation) was compared
with their scores on the Torrance and Mednick tests. No correlations
were found between these two types of assessment. Even more striking, there was no improvement in creative scores as measured by the
Torrance test of creativity, whereas the level of creativity exhibited in an
unregulated environment improved dramatically. Ozhiganova (2001)
suggested that the regulated environment of commonly used creativity tests (such as the Torrance and Mednick tests) inhibits children's

creativity and is an inadequate assessment tool of children's creative potential.

Tatyana Tikhomirova (as cited in Kholodnaya, 2002) studied the influence of family, extended family, and kindergarten environment on the development of creativity (understood as creative production). Results of this study demonstrated that extended family environment (as measured by amount of communication with grandmothers and grandfathers) and attendance of kindergarten had a positive impact on the children's creative development. This effect is theorized to be due to the differences in parenting styles as compared with styles of grandmothers and grandfathers and styles of kindergarten teachers. Immediate families usually emphasize requirements to fulfill one's everyday duties and stimulate exercises and studies; other environments (such as extended family and kindergarten) emphasize emotional self-expression of a child and praise for her or his creative achievements.

In sum, a number of Soviet–Russian psychologists were interested in studying external (environmental) factors that could enhance and foster creative production with the application of these factors to educational settings. This line of research demonstrated that an interdisciplinary instructional curriculum enhances the development of children's creative potential by promoting curiosity, creative activities, independent learning, and a holistic understanding of the world (Matyushkin, Shumakova, and Shcheblanova). In addition, specific environmental factors that can enhance levels of creative production were identified: the presence of creative exemplars and little formal regulation (Druzhinin, Khazratova, and Ozhiganova), emphasis on emotional self-expression (Tikhomirova), richness of available materials (Druzhinin and Khazratova), and absence of requirements to exhibit creativity (Ozhiganova).

The second line of Soviet–Russian psychological research of creativity developed with studies and theories of creative production as well as studies of internal (motivation, cognition and intelligence) and external (environmental characteristics) determinants of creative productivity. Novel problems no longer had one known solution; they implied variability in answers and methods of solving them. This research program widened as Guilford's and Torrance's conceptions of creativity became more and more popular. However, this approach was nowhere near being homogeneous, with a number of Soviet–Russian psychologists reexamining and reconsidering Guilford's views on creativity. Bogoyavlenskaya developed an understanding of creativity as spontaneous productive activity, with the main role in determination of creative productivity belonging to intrinsic motivation. Yurkevich proposed a developmental conception of creativity according to which creative production could result from either of two stages of development of creativity – naïve and cultural creativity – and explained the difference between them in terms of intellectual development, acquisition of cultural stereotypes, and motivational development. Other authors (e.g., Druzhinin, Ozhiganiva, and Kholodnaya) proposed and tested interesting and original hypotheses about different intellectual and environmental determinants of creative production that were not investigated by Guilford and theorists of creative production. Still others (Matyushkin, Shumakova, and Shcheblanova) developed original programs for enhancing giftedness as the highest level of creative potential.

CONCLUSION

In this chapter we aimed to provide a comprehensive account of how Soviet–Russian psychology has addressed the notion of creativity. In addition, we tried to note common assumptions that underlie theories and empirical studies as well as to emphasize the common core that Soviet–Russian psychology shares with Western psychological views on creativity. We presented Soviet–Russian creativity research as consisting of two major developmental trajectories. The first trajectory emerged in the study and conceptualizations of insight and creative process in Gestalt psychology and in the attempt to find concrete psychological mechanisms of insight and objective social and environmental conditions that lead to its occurrence. The second trajectory emerged after the acquaintance of Soviet–Russian psychological thought with the views of Guilford and Torrance on creativity and in an attempt to build on these views to achieve a better understanding of internal and external determinants of creative production. We noted that there are two main differences between the outlined developmental trajectories. First, novelty of a creative idea is assessed either in terms of previous experience and knowledge of an individual or terms of uniqueness, usefulness, and originality of this idea in a broader sociocultural context. Second, problems used either have one correct solution (participant's answer is known beforehand) or have multiple possible solutions (participant's answer could vary and is unexpected). The evolution of the Soviet–Russian psychology of creativity resulted in a number of original theories, methodological solutions, and empirical studies that were at one time unknown to Western readers as a result of the breakdown in communication between the Soviet Union and the West. However, ideas, conceptions, and research methods discussed throughout this chapter have real creative potential and could be usefully incorporated in Western psychological views on creativity in the future.

References

Amabile, T. M., Goldfarb, P., & Brackfield, S. C. (1990). Social influences on creativity: Evaluation, coaction, and surveillance. *Creativity Research Journal, 3*, 6–21.

Babaeva, Y. D. (1997). Dinamicheskaya teoriya odarennosti [The dynamic theory of giftedness]. In D. B. Bogoyavlenskaya (Ed.), *Osnovnye sovremennye kontseptsii tvorchestva i odarennosti* (pp. 275–294). Moscow: Molodaya Gvardiya.

Bakhtin, M. (1984). *Problems of Dostoevsky's poetics*. Minneapolis: University of Minnesota Press.

Bibler, V. S. (1983). Thinking as creation: Introduction to the logic of mental dialogue. *Soviet Psychology, 22*, 33–54.

Bogoyavlenskaya, D. B. (1983). *Intellectual'naya aktivnost' kak problema tvorchestva* [Intellectual activity as a problem of creativity]. Rostov-na-Donu, Russia: Rostovskii Gosudarstvennyi Universitet.

Bogoyavlenskaya, D. B. (1995). O predmete i metode issledovaniya tvorcheskikh sposobnostei [About the subject and method of studying creative abilities]. *Psikhologicheskii Zhurnal, 16*, 49–58.

Bogoyavlenskaya, D. B. (1999). Sub'yekt deyatel'nosti v problematike tvorchestva ["Activity subject" in creativity context]. *Voprosy Psikhologii, 2*, 35–41.

Bogoyavlenskaya, D. B. (2002). *Psikhologiya tvorcheskikh sposobnostey* [The psychology of creative abilities]. Moscow: Akademiya.

Brushlinsky, A. V. (1996). *Sub'yekt: Myshleniye, ucheniye, voobrazheniye* [Individual: Thinking, learning, imagination]. Voronezh, Russia: Institut Prakticheskoy Psikhologii.

Brushlinsky, A. V. (1997). O sub'yekte myshleniya i tvorchestva [About the subject of thinking and creativity]. In D. B. Bogoyavlenskaya (Ed.), *Osnovnye sovremennye kontseptsii tvorchestva i odarennosti* (pp. 39–56). Moscow: Molodaya Gvardiya.

Csikszentmihalyi, M. (1990). *Flow: The psychology of optimal experience*. New York: Harper & Row.

Druzhinin, V. N. (1997). Struktura psikhometricheskogo intellekta i prognoz individual'nykh dostizhenii [The structure of psychometric intelligence and prediction of individual achievements]. In D. B. Bogoyavlenskaya (Ed.), *Osnovnye sovremennye kontseptsii tvorchestva i odarennosti* (pp. 161–185). Moscow: Molodaya Gvardiya.

Druzhinin, V. N. (1999). Psikhologiya obschikh sposobnostei [Psychology of general abilities]. Saint Petersburg, Russia: Piter.

Druzhinin, V. N., & Khazratova, N. V. (1994). Eksperimental'noe issledovanie formiruyuschego vliyaniya mikrosredy na kreativnost' [An experimental study of the formative influence of microenvironments on creativity]. *Psikhologicheskii Zhurnal, 15*, 83–93.

Duncker, K. (1945). On problem solving. *Psychological Monographs, 58*, 1–113.

Epstein, S., Pacini, R., Denes-Raj, V., & Heier, H. (1996). Individual differences in intuitive – experiential and analytical – rational thinking styles. *Journal of Personality and Social Psychology, 71*, 390–405.

Frantz, R. (2003). Herbert Simon. Artificial intelligence as a framework for understanding intuition. *Journal of Economic Psychology, 24*, 265–277.

Galperin, P. Y. (1969). Stages in the development of mental acts. In M. Cole, & I. Maltzman (Eds.), *A handbook of contemporary Soviet psychology* (pp. 34–61). New York: Basic Books.

Galperin, P. Y. (1989). Mental actions as a basis for the formation of thoughts and images. *Soviet Psychology, 27*, 45–64.

Galperin, P. Y., & Kotik, N. R. (1982). K psikhologii tvorcheskogo myshleniya [On the psychology of creative thinking]. *Voprosy Psikhologii, 5*, 80–84.

Goryunova, N. B., & Druzhinin, V. N. (2001). Operatsional'nye deskriptory kognitivnogo resursa i productivnost' resheniya testovykh zadach i zadach-golovolomok [Operational descriptors of the cognitive resource and productivity of test tasks and puzzle solving]. *Psikhologicheskii Zhurnal, 22*, 13–22.

Grigorenko, E. L., & Kornilova, T. V. (1997). The resolution of the nature–nurture controversy by Russian psychology: Culturally biased or culturally specific? In R. J. Sternberg & E. L. Grigorenko (Eds.), *Intelligence, heredity, and environment* (pp. 393–439). New York: Cambridge University Press.

Grigorenko, E. L., Ruzgis, P., & Sternberg, R. J. (Eds.). (1997). *Psychology of Russia: Past, present, future.* Commack, NY: Nova Science.

Guilford, J. P. (1950). Creativity. *American Psychologist, 5*, 444–454.

Guilford, J. P. (1967). *The nature of human intelligence.* New York: McGraw-Hill.

De Groot, A. D. (1993). Intuition as a dispositional concept. In G. L. Van Heck, P. Bonaiuto, I. J. Deary, & W. Nowack (Eds.), *Personality psychology in Europe* (Vol. 4, pp. 7–50). Tilburg, Netherlands: Tilburg University Press.

Hammond, K. R. (2000). *Judgments under stress.* New York: Oxford University Press.

Heller, K. A., Gaedike, A. K., & Weinlader, H. (1985). *Kognitiven Fahigkeitstest (KFT4–13+)* [Test of Cognitive Capabilities (KFT4–13+)]. Weinheim, Germany: Beltz.

Hogarth, R. M. (2001). *Educating intuition.* Chicago: University of Chicago Press.

Kahneman, D., & Tversky, A. (1982). On the study of statistical intuitions. *Cognition, 11*, 123–141.

Kanevskaya, M. E., & Firsova, L. A. (1990). Svyaz' uspeshnosti khudozhestvennogo tvorchestva s napravlennost'yu lichnosti u detei [Correlation between successfulness of artistic creativity and personality trends in children]. *Voprosy Psikhologii, 3*, 69–75.

Kholodnaya, M. A. (2001). *Psikhologiya intellekta: Paradoksy issledovaniya* [Psychology of intelligence: Research paradoxes]. Saint Petersburg, Russia: Piter.

Kholodnaya, M. A. (2002). Osnovnye napravleniya izucheniya psykhologii sposobnostei v institute psikhologii RAN [Major approaches to studying psychological abilities elaborated in the Institute of Psychology, RAS]. *Psikhologicheskii Zhurnal, 23*, 13–22.

Krogius, N. V. (1981). *Psikhologiya shakhmatnogo tvorchestva* [Psychology of chess creativity]. Moscow: Fizkultura Sport.

Leontiev, A. A. (1998). "Nauchite cheloveka fantazii..." (tvorchestvo i razvivayuschee obrazovanie) ["Teach a fantasy..." (Creativity and developing education)]. *Voprosy Psikhologii, 5*, 82–85.

Leontiev, A. N. (1978a). *Activity, consciousness, and personality.* Englewood Cliffs, NJ: Prentice-Hall.

Leontiev, A. N. (1978b). Thinking. In *Great Soviet Encyclopedia* (3rd ed., trans., pp. 708–709). New York: Macmillan Educational Corporation.

Leontiev, A. N., Ponomarev, Y. A., & Gippenreiter, Y. B. (1981). Opyt eksperimental'nogo issledovaniya myshleniya [An experience of an experimental study of thinking]. In Y. D. Gippenreiter & V. V. Petukhov (Eds.), *Khrestomatiya po obschey psikhologii: Psikhologiya myshleniya* (pp. 269–280). Moscow: Moskovskii Gosudarstvennyi Universitet.

Lubart, T. I. (2001). Models of the creative process: Past, present and future. *Creativity Research Journal, 13*, 295–308.

Matyushkin, A. M. (1989). Kontseptsiya tvorcheskoi odarennosti [The conception of creative giftedness]. *Voprosy Psykhologii, 6*, 29–33.

Matyushkin, A. M. (1990). A Soviet perspective on giftedness and creativity. *European Journal for High Ability, 1*, 72–75.

Matyushkin, A. M. (1993). *Zagadki odarennosti: Problemy prakticheskoi diagnostiki* [The puzzles of giftedness: The issues of practical diagnostics.] Moscow: Shkola-Press.

Mednick, S. A., & Mednick, M. T. (1967). *Examiner's manual: Remote Associates Test.* Boston: Houghton Mifflin.

Obukhova, L. F., & Churbanova, S. M. (1994). *Razvitiye divergentnogo myshleniya v detskom vozraste* [Development of divergent thinking in childhood]. Moscow: Moscovskii Gosudarstvennyi Universitet.

Ozhiganova, G. V. (2001). Diagnostika i formirovanie kreativnosti u detey v protsesse uchebnoi deyatel'nosti [Diagnostics and forming of creativity in children in the process of school learning]. *Psikhologicheskii Zhurnal, 22*, 75–85.

Petukhov, V. V. (1999). Problema osmyslennogo deistviya (po resheniyu tvorcheskikh zadach) [The problem of intelligent action (in creative problem solving)]. In A. E. Voiskunsky, A. N. Zhdan, & O. K. Tikhomirov, *Traditsii i perspektivy deyatel'nostnogo podkhoda v psikhologii: Shkola Leontieva* (pp. 235–262). Moscow: Smysl.

Ponomarev, I. A. (1960). *Psikhologiya tvorcheskogo myshleniya* [The psychology of creative thinking]. Moscow: Academiya Pedagogicheskikh Nauk RSFSR.

Ponomarev, I. A. (1987). Osnovnye zven'ya psikhologicheskogo mekhanizma tvorchestva [The major components of psychological mechanism of creativity]. In M. I. Panov (Ed.), *Intuitsiya, logika, tvorchestvo* (pp. 5–23). Moscow: Nauka.

Reber, A. S., Walkenfeld, F. F., & Hernstadt, R. (1991). Implicit and explicit learning: Individual differences and IQ. *Journal of Experimental Psychology: Learning, Memory and Cognition, 1,* 888–896.

Ryabova, T. V., & Mendelevich, V. D. (2002). Tvorcheskoe myshlenie i antitsipatsiya u bol'nyh shizofreniey i psikhicheski zdorovikh [Creative thinking and anticipation in schizophrenic patients and mentally healthy people]. *Voprosy Psikhologii, 1,* 69–75.

Simon, H. A. (1989). Making management decisions: The role of intuition and emotion. In W. H. Agor (Ed.), *Intuition in organizations: Leading and managing productively* (pp. 23–39). Newbury Park, CA: Sage.

Shirley D. A., & Lagan-Fox J. (1996). Intuition: A review of the literature. *Psychological Reports, 79,* 563–584.

Shcheblanova, E. I. (1999). Osobennosti kognitivnogo i motivatsionnolichnostnogo razvitiya odarennykh starsheklassnikov [Characteristics of cognitive and motivational-personality development of gifted high school students]. *Voprosy Psikhologii, 6,* 36–47.

Shcheblanova, E. I. (2000). The dynamics of cognitive and noncognitive personality indicators of giftedness in younger schoolchildren. *Russian Education and Society, 42,* 5–27.

Shumakova, N. B. (1996). Mezhdistsiplinarnyi podkhod k obucheniyu odarennykh detei. [Interdisciplinary approach to the teaching of gifted children]. *Voprosy Psikhologii, 3,* 34–43.

Shumakova, N. B., Shcheblanova, G. I., & Shcherbo, N. P. (1991). Issledovanie odarennosti s ispol'zovaniem testov P. Torrensa [The usage of P. Torrance's Tests in study of giftedness]. *Voprosy Psikhologii, 1,* 27–32.

Tikhomirov, O. K. (1975). *Psikhologicheskie issledovaniya tvorcheskoy deyatel'nosti* [Psychological studies of creative activity]. Moscow: Nauka.

Tikhomirov, O. K., Babayeva, Y. D., Berezanskaya, N. B., Vasilyev, I. A., & Voyskunsky, A. E. (1999). Razvitie deyatel'nostnogo podkhoda v psikhologii myshleniya [Development of the activity approach to the psychology of thinking]. In A. E. Voiskunsky, A. N. Zhdan, & O. K. Tikhomirov, *Traditsii i perspektivy deyatel'nostnogo podkhoda v psikhologii: Shkola Leontieva* (pp. 191–234). Moscow: Smysl.

Torrance, E. P. (1962). *Guiding creative talent.* Englewood Cliffs, NJ: Prentice-Hall.

Treffinger, D. J. (1980). *Encouraging creative learning for the gifted and talented. A handbook of methods and techniques.* Ventura, CA: Ventura County Superintendent of Schools Office.

Ushakov, D. V. (1988). Rol' metafory v tvorcheskom myshlenii [The role of metaphor in creative thinking]. *Vestnik Vysshey Shkoly, 1,* 24–28.

Ushakov, D. V. (1997). Odarennost', tvorchestvo, intuitsiya [Giftedness, creativity, intuition]. In D. B. Bogoyavlenskaya (Ed.), *Osnovnye sovremennye kontseptsii tvorchestva i odarennosti* (pp. 78–89). Moscow: Molodaya Gvardiya.

Ushakov, D. V. (1999). Myshleniye i intellekt [Thinking and intelligence]. In V. N. Druzhinin (Ed.), *Sovremennaya psikhologiya: Spravochnoye rukovodstvo* (pp. 241–266). Moscow: Infra-M.

Vygotsky, L. S. (1962). *Thought and language.* Cambridge, MA: MIT Press.

Wallas, G. (1926). *The art of thought*. New York: McGraw-Hill.

Wertheimer, M. (1959). *Productive thinking*. New York: Harper & Row.

Yaroshevsky, M. G. (1985). Psikhologiya tvorchestva i tvorchestvo v psikhologii [Psychology of creativity and creative work in psychology]. *Voprosy Psikhologii, 6*, 14–26.

Yurkevich, V. S. (1996). *Odarennyi rebenok: Illyuzii i real'nost'* [A gifted child: Illusions and reality]. Moscow: Prosveshchenie.

Yurkevich, V. S. (1997). O "naivnoi" i "kul'turnoi" kreativnosti [About naïve and cultural creativity]. In D. B. Bogoyavlenskaya (Ed.), *Osnovnye sovremennye kontseptsii tvorchestva i odarennosti* (pp. 127–142). Moscow: Molodaya Gvardiya.

10

Creativity Studies in Poland

Edward Nęcka, Magdalena Grohman,
and Aleksandra Słabosz

HISTORY

Creativity studies in Poland are deeply rooted in philosophical inquiries. One particularly influential work was authored by Władysław Tatarkiewicz (1976). In his brilliant analysis, the author detailed the historical and cultural development of *creativity*. Creativity was originally conceived as a divine activity, inaccessible for humans, who at most could aspire to skills, mastery, and craftsmanship. During the age of romanticism, creativity developed into the notion of inspired activity that cannot be understood or accounted for in terms of natural forces and mechanisms. Only in the twentieth century did creativity obtain its more naturalistic meaning as a human activity that results in a new, original work. Interestingly, Tatarkiewicz did not confine his criteria of creativity to sheer novelty, even if matched with other criteria, such as value or social impact. His definition of creativity clearly emphasizes the importance of human effort and energy used for the creation of pieces of art and other artifacts. Mental energy and effort employed in the process of creation appear to be as essential as novelty or originality of the output. In this way, Tatarkiewicz anticipated the modern psychological conceptions of "potential creativity" (Runco & Charles, 1997).

An important predecessor of modern creativity studies in psychology and education was Stefan Szuman (1927). He analyzed the phenomenon of play, particularly children's drawings, as a naturally creative activity. As a connoisseur of mature artistic creativity and a friend of Stanislaw Ignacy Witkiewicz, a famous writer and painter, Szuman had no doubt that children's drawings should be regarded as being creative in nature.

He also initiated studies on the reception of art by children. In this way, Szuman's work should be regarded as a precursor of many modern approaches to creativity.

Contemporary researchers, mostly psychologists and educators, remained under the influence of Guilford's (1950, 1967) work. This work was assimilated by Andrzej Strzałecki (1969) and Zbigniew Pietrasiński (1969). Although their books did not include original studies and research findings, the comprehensive and state-of-the-art character of these publications made them rather influential and important for future creativity studies in Poland, which began in the 1970s.

DEFINITIONS AND CRITERIA

The philosopher Andrzej Góralski (1978) proposed a widely accepted definition of creativity in Poland: He suggested calling a piece of work creative if it is "new and valuable." A creative product does not have to materialize itself in any way because, the author argued, creative qualities may be attributed not only to pieces of art, designs, or new devices but also to people's behaviors, thoughts, or even ways of life. The conjunction of novelty and value as criteria of creativity makes Góralski's definition very close to the classic stance held by Morris I. Stein (1953), according to which creativity is a process resulting in the creation of a product that is judged useful or tenable by a group of people during some period of time. However, Stein's definition makes an impression of being more relativistic than Góralski's. The latter does not take into account the possibility that a product may gain or lose creative qualities depending on the ever-changing needs or preferences held by its potential recipients. Historic and cultural relativity of the criteria of creativity, so strongly emphasized by Stein, are not worthy of consideration, according to Góralski, who seemed to believe that, if something is new and valuable, it will remain so always and everywhere.

A comparable idea may be found in the work of Władysław Stróżewski (1983), another philosopher interested in the nature of creativity. Stróżewski believed that human creativity consists of recognition and affirmation of values that exist as absolute entities, independent of human cognition and appreciation. God, as a source of all genuine values, is the only real Creator, whereas human beings are "called and chosen" just to discover what is good or bad, beautiful or ugly, valuable or worthless. In other words, human creative acts involve striving to get to the closest possible proximity with real, absolute values, rather than attempting to create their own values. According to Stróżewski, creators usually find themselves duty bound; that is, they feel they have to comply with some necessary requirements that a piece of work imposes on them. Of course, creative acts are not regarded as deterministic in nature. Creators can neglect the implicit necessities imposed by a piece of art; however, very frequently they voluntarily agree with them. Stróżewski believes that genuine creativity always involves this element of appreciation of necessities.[1] It also involves the element of dialectic synthesis of oppositions. For instance, creative acts comprise such oppositions as freedom and necessity, or novelty and conservatism. Stróżewski (1983) listed thirty-two such oppositions that have to be dialectically approached and overcome during the creative activity.

Generally speaking, philosophers are rather absolutist in their efforts to define creativity and to establish its criteria, whereas psychologists and educators are much more relativistic in their approach. Psychologists and educators are also more inclined to appreciate forms of creativity that are not developed or mature enough. For instance, a distinction between eminent creativity and everyday creativity is clearly understood in the field, although there are countless debates and frequent misunderstandings concerning the problem of what kind of behavior is entitled to be classified as creative. Is preparation of a good meal an act of creation if the meal is really good and the social or emotional consequences of its preparation are significant? Does a similar rule apply to other disputed areas, such as telling jokes or organizing physical exercises? Specialists in the field tend to answer positively, whereas laypersons are usually unconvinced. This situation probably does not differ too much from what can be observed in other countries. However, the problem is even more troublesome in Poland because of the linguistic connotations. The word *creativity* (*twórczość* in Polish) is commonly associated with high-level artistic or scientific endeavors but not with everyday or lower-level creativity. It also refers to the life contribution made by an artist, a writer, and the like (e.g., Stanisław Lem's creativity consists of many books). Ambiguity of the key word used in the area, as well as its specific connotations, make it rather difficult for people to agree on the definition and criteria of creativity. It is therefore more and more frequent in the psychological literature to use the

---

[1] Stróżewski cites Beethoven's phrase *"Muss es sein? Es muss sein* [Must it be this way? It must be this way]," as an example of the composer's realization that the necessity has to be respected.

term *kreatywność* as referring to everyday creativity, and particularly to creativity understood as a personal trait, whereas the traditional term *twórczość* is reserved for eminent creativity resulting in distinguished achievements.[2]

Creativity of the person "who will never produce anything original or useful" (Nicholls, 1972) is a phenomenon particularly popular among Polish researchers. Tomasz Kocowski (1991) introduced the phrase "potentially creative activity," defined as a kind of behavior that would result in interesting (i.e., new and valuable) achievements if continued for a sufficiently long period of time. Kocowski was particularly interested in those cases in which the individuals did not have any socially acclaimed accomplishments in spite of invested time and effort – a phenomenon quite common among distinguished artists or scientists who have to take great risk without any guarantee of success. From this perspective, the activity of a creator who has not achieved anything acceptable or "tenable" (Stein, 1953) does not differ psychologically from the activity of a creator who was lucky enough to get the solution, Kocowski argued. Although the idea of potential creativity was born to account for eminent creativity without results (at least temporarily), it proved useful to account for other phenomena, too. Kocowski himself was deeply interested in creative thinking groups, both in real life (e.g., task groups in scientific research) and in the laboratory (e.g., brainstorming, creativity training groups). Such "organisms" are apt to achieve highly valued solutions with no apparent authors who might be responsible for the process of idea generation and development. For instance, members of a brainstorming group act in a freewheeling mode, amusing themselves rather than trying to invent something of high value, but the result may be strikingly novel and, after implementation, extremely valuable. For Tomasz Kocowski, acts of behavior presented by particular participants are not creative as such, but they contribute to the synergistic effect of group creativity. Therefore, such acts of behavior should be called *potentially creative* acts. The idea of potentially creative activity appears particularly useful in education. Children's creativity usually lacks maturity, which typically results from field-specific knowledge, acquired skills, and immense self-devotion. Does it mean that children lack creativity at all? Such a conclusion would be harmful

---

[2] Polish, like other Slavic languages, has two words that refer to creativity: *Twórczość* (cf.: *tvorčestvo* in Russian) is a Slavic word, whereas *kreatywność* has a Latin root(similar to *creativity* in English or *créativité* in French).

for any attempts to support children's productions and to teach creative thinking skills, for instance, in the classroom (cf. Runco & Charles, 1997).

However, the notion of potential creativity had to be redefined in terms of specific mental operations that take part in "creativity without masterpieces." Nicholls's idea of the person who will never think of anything original and useful seems rather fatalistic, whereas Kocowski's initial idea that potential creativity would change into real creativity provided it is continued for a sufficient period of time seems one sided. For the essence of this phenomenon to be captured, potential creativity has been described as a set of mental operations, typically found in "genuine" creativity (Nęcka, 2001). These operations include, for instance, the use of analogy, making remote associations, redefining a problem at hand, or posing questions. These are behaviors typical of children and participants of creative thinking groups but also of mature creators who have outstanding achievements. If such an activity appears, it can be called creative even though it does not necessarily lead to new and valuable products.

The problems with different types of creativity and different criteria of creative achievements have recently been conceptualized by Nęcka (2001) in his model of levels of creativity (Figure 10.1). This model is based on the assumption that there are two criteria that might be used to differentiate among levels of creativity. The first criterion is the probability of appearance of a creative act; the second criterion refers to the time needed to accomplish a creative act. Drawing on such assumptions, we can talk about four levels of creativity. First, there is a phenomenon of *fluid creativity*, which is typical of every human individual, does not need any former preparation, and usually lasts about a few minutes. Second, we have a phenomenon of *crystallized creativity*,[3] which consists of solution of a problem. This kind of creativity requires at least some amount of knowledge and acquired skills and it lasts a bit longer than the act of fluid creativity. The longevity of the acts of crystallized creativity depends on the complexity of the problem solved, which means that it may vary a lot. This kind of creativity is still quite common because solutions given to the problem at hand need not be very original, novel, or valuable in any

---

[3] Compare this phenomenon with Horn's and Cattell's concepts of fluid and crystallized intelligence, in which fluid intelligence is related to very basic biological and cognitive processes; it is also defined as a skill that is independent from our experience. Crystallized intelligence, in contrast, refers to the ability of acquiring information and knowledge characteristic of a given society or culture (Horn & Cattell, 1966).

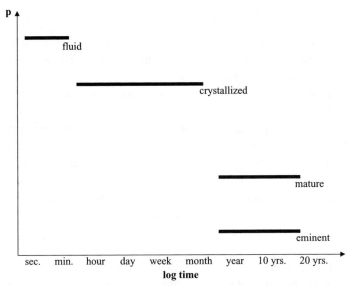

FIGURE 10.1. Four types of creativity: their probability and relative duration (Nęcka, 2001).

sense of the words. If they are, we are already talking about the third level of analysis, namely, *mature creativity*. Mature creativity usually requires thorough field-specific knowledge or even expertise, which means that it develops with personal experience and does not happen very frequently. The act of mature creation also takes time, a few months or even years. Fourth, there is the phenomenon of *eminent creativity*, which psychologically does not seem to differ from mature creativity but has its own criteria of product acceptance and recognition. Eminent creativity results in achievements that introduce fundamental changes within the chosen area. Such fundamental contributions usually require some time to be recognized and judged properly, and their frequency is obviously very low.

TRADITIONS AND SCHOOLS OF THOUGHT

In this part of our chapter, we concentrate on four theories of creativity that we believe have considerably influenced Polish studies in the field. These theories originate from the systemic approach to the phenomenon of creativity, both macroscopic (Kozielecki and Kocowski) and microscopic (Trzebiński and Nęcka).

Macroscopic Theories of Creativity

Psychologist Józef Kozielecki (1966, 1969) initiated research on creativity in Poland. In the 1980s, he came up with the so-called transgression theory, which he further develops in his recent works (e.g., Kozielecki, 1997). The author defined *transgression* as the intentional and deliberate overcoming of physical, social, or symbolic boundaries that shape our everyday functioning. There are two ways in which transgression occurs: expansion and creativity. The former does not bring about anything new or valuable, although it permits the extension of one's personal, societal, economic, or political influence. Imperial wars and colonization are examples of this kind of transgression. The latter amounts to the creation of something new and valuable. Transgressive actions, creative or not, are contrasted with adaptation, that is, struggling to preserve the status quo.

Acts of transgression are rooted in a person's motivational system, particularly in his or her hubristic attitude. This kind of motivation involves continual attempts by an individual to endorse or increase his or her personal value. In this way, the term has little in common with the connotations of the word *hubris*, understood as an "arrogant pride." Instead, hubristic motivation should be understood as one of the most distinguished and noble motivations. Actions or productions generated on the basis of hubristic motivation may differ in their scope and significance. Personal transgression (Type P) results in changes that are important for an individual, whereas historic transgression (Type H) causes changes that are important from the broad social or historical perspective. Thus, only Type H transgressions are important for high-level creativity, providing that they are lasting and broad in scope. The distinction between Type P and Type H transgressions is echoed in Margaret Boden's (1994) distinction between P-creativity (personal) and H-creativity (historical). According to Boden, creative achievements that are historically important are just a subset of creative achievements that are important for an individual. Ideas that are P-creative sometimes become H-creative. Such a transformation depends, however, on social and political factors, as well as good luck. Thus, it is possible to study P-creativity in order to acquire knowledge about H-creativity, because both are psychologically alike.

Tomasz Kocowski's (1991) approach is also inspired by the system theory perspective. The author proposed a holistic conception of the human mind, based on philosophical anthropology and the theory of evolution. According to this theory, every human individual is an "anthropo-system" that operates on three levels of organization: biosystemic, sociosystemic, and psychosystemic. Such anthropo-systems accomplish ten functions that are vital for human survival and development. Creativity is linked with three of these functions, namely, the function of self-organization (i.e., development), the function of self-preservation, and the function of self-reproduction. These functions are fulfilled not only by creative but also by less innovative acts of behavior. However, creativity is an evolutionary supreme, socially valuable, and distinctively human way of accomplishment of three basic functions of every anthropo-system. In this way, Kocowski pointed out both naturalistic and sociocultural roots of creativity. At a purely psychological level of analysis, Kocowski defined creativity as a two-phase process of generation of diverse ideas and selection of the ones that are best fitted to the problem at hand. Although the first phase is constituted by numerous components, it is the transfer of knowledge and experience between different domains that is regarded as one of the most important tools for the generation of diverse ideas.

Microscopic Theories of Creativity

The microscopic theories of creativity are not as broad in scope, and they are limited to the structure of the creative process, its psychological mechanisms, and factors influencing its progression. In his theory of creative interaction, Nęcka (1987/1995, 2003) assumes that the creative process is nothing but refining so-called tentative structures, defined as preliminary answers to the goal's requirements. Sometimes the goal of creative activity, be it solving a problem or anything else, causes the emergence of first attempts to achieve that goal. These attempts, whether ideas, sketches, associations, or analogies, either diminish the gap between the real situation and the ideal one, or contribute to redefinition, change, and even abandonment of the initial goal. In this way, tentative structures are able to influence the goal from the very beginning of the creative process. Sometimes, it is a tentative structure that originates the creative process. An unexpected idea, remote association, or sudden comprehension of something may cause a goal of creation to emerge. By virtue of this, the goal may become, at least to some extent, consciously realized by the creator. According to the author, creative ideas need not be produced in response to the problem or previously established goal. In fact, they may appear independent of any goal, thus contributing to its emergence and refinement.

The creative process is therefore conceptualized as a continual and mutual interaction between the goal of creative activity and the tentative structures that are supposed to meet the criteria set by the goal. The result of such interaction is usually unexpected and very different from the original goals. That is so because the tentative structures are real "partners" of such interaction; that is, they can modify the goal to a very large extent and even contribute to its conclusion. The modified goal causes the emergence of new tentative structures, which can contribute to its evolution, and so on. In this sense, the interaction is cyclic and, in fact, may never come to an end, providing that a person involved in creative process strives for perfection. Thus, the creative process appears to be a continual attempt to reduce the gap between the goal and the tentative structures. In some cases, however, based on individual criteria of an "acceptable outcome," the gap is reduced to such a degree that a creator decides to present his or her work to a larger audience.

The creative process, conceptualized as an interaction between the goal and the tentative structures, is guided by specific strategies. They are responsible for the transformation of cognitive structures, or noticing the similarities between those structures. Nine such strategies have been identified. For instance, according to the "alertness strategy," the main features of a future idea should be identified first. Then the creator should be alert and should look for the appearance of relevant cues in the environment. In other words, the strategy in this case would be to "look for potentially relevant and helpful information." Usually the strategies are employed habitually by the creator. Some of them, however, can be used deliberately, particularly if they originate from certain heuristics in creative problem solving (Nęcka, 1994). For example, the "creative distancing strategy," which amounts to a temporary abandonment of the problem at hand in order to find a remote analogy, has been discovered and described by the authors of synectics (Gordon, 1961; Prince, 1970). Besides the strategies, Nęcka also points to mental operations, such as inductive and deductive reasoning, association building, transformations, and the like. Their role is to reduce the discrepancy between the goal and the tentative structures. There are also "feeding mechanisms," which are responsible for supplying information and energy. Information feeding is performed by selective attention and altered states of consciousness, whereas energetic feeding is possible by means of emotions and intrinsic motivation.

The concept of creative interaction is consistent with works of Weisberg (1986, 1999) and Perkins (1981), in the sense that ordinary cognitive operations, already mentioned, lead to unexpected and creative results. It gives, however, a more precise description of inherent logic and components of creative process. Similar to other contemporary theories of creative process (e.g., the Geneplore model; see Finke, Ward & Smith, 1992), the theory of creative interaction seems to be useful when one is describing various forms of creativity, independent of their quality and domain in which they appear. It also permits a description of individual styles of creating (e.g., one prefers to define the goal before creating, and the others like it to be unspecified). Altogether, the theory may lead to future research in the field of individual differences in creativity, and it still awaits its empirical verification.

Nęcka's theory of creative interaction, on one hand, defines the creative process in more general terms. Trzebiński's theory of conceptual structure and its relation to creative thinking, on the other hand, represent a more specific approach to creative process and its cognitive determinants (Trzebiński, 1981, 1978). In his theory, Trzebiński attempts to show that creative thinking may benefit from certain characteristics of conceptual structures. According to Trzebiński, the content of a concept is determined by its so-called conceptual core and by a possible degree of transformation of this core. The conceptual core encompasses representations of typical characteristics of a given category's exemplar (in this sense, the term *conceptual core* is similar to the concept of *prototype* as proposed by Rosch, 1973). The process of object identification is understood as an adjustment of the core to a given exemplar, and it is operationalized in terms of object classification to a given category. The less typical the object is, the greater the transformation that is required. For instance, a concept of *pleasant danger* may require numerous transformations, since danger is usually associated with something that is rather unpleasant. Thus, the transformation of the conceptual core – *unpleasant danger* into *pleasant danger* – requires a certain flexibility, which is defined as the range of possible transformations.

The main assumption of the theory is that the flexibility of conceptual cores determines the level of creativity. In a series of ingenious experiments, Trzebiński showed that creative individuals are highly flexible in conceptual core transformations. They tend to modify the meaning of a concept, and broaden the range of it. The author also showed that experimentally induced modification influences creative thinking. For example, in one experimental condition, the concept of *freedom* was modified by the adjectives *sad, shallow, dumb,* so that identifying what freedom was in this situation involved many transformations. Subjects in the control condition were to describe what freedom was, and none of the concept modifiers were presented to them. It was observed that participants in the experimental condition outperformed subjects in the control group in creative thinking tests (Trzebiński, 1981). Similar to Ward's structured imagination theory (Ward, 1994), Trzebiński's concept of flexible conceptual cores suggests that creative process may depend on the structure and function of conceptual categories.

The theories just described, macroscopic as well as microscopic, treat creativity and creative process in general terms. In the next section we present approaches to creativity that have a somewhat narrower range (e.g., Tokarz's theory of autonomic motivation or Kolańczyk's theory of creative intuition). The approaches are still being developed by their authors, and thus we present them in the section dedicated to contemporary creativity research and its application.

CURRENT RESEARCH

Up-to-date reviews of Polish research on creativity have been comprehensively presented in the annual reports titled "Creativity Global Correspondents," edited by Morris I. Stein (see Tokarz & Groborz, 2001; Tokarz & Słabosz, 2002). These reports show the ever-increasing interest in creativity and a rising number of publications. There are three centers of such research in the country: the Jagiellonian University in Krakow, the Cardinal Stefan Wyszyński University in Warsaw, and the Marie Curie–Skłodowska University in Lublin. There are also two centers in which applied creativity studies are conducted: the Academy of Special Pedagogy in Warsaw and the University of Łódź. The current review differs from those provided by so-called global correspondents in the sense that it is problem oriented rather than people oriented. Therefore, our goal in this section is to introduce current research on creativity in Poland in relation to the problems, techniques, and paradigms that are visible in mainstream psychological research. Our attempt is also to present topics that are particularly popular in Poland as well as those that, in our opinion, are underrepresented. The current review is thought to be an appropriate supplement to the reports published by global correspondents.

According to Mumford, Baughman, and Sager (2003), four research areas contribute to real progress in our understanding of the creative act.

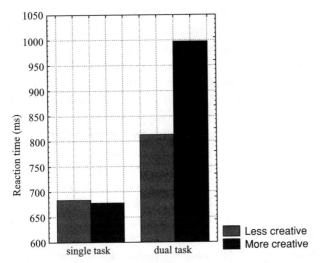

FIGURE 10.2. Results obtained by less creative and more creative participants in the single- and dual-task conditions of an attention test (Nęcka, 1999).

These areas include (a) creative thinking and creative thought; (b) the role of motivation, affects, and dispositions in creativity; (c) situational influences on creative processes and their outcomes; and (d) development of creativity. In the paragraphs that follow, we present a review of Polish research related to these areas.

Cognitive Aspects of Creativity

Linking creativity to human cognitive functioning has a very long tradition in Poland. The majority of studies in this area have investigated attentional mechanisms related to creativity. The studies presented herein have been inspired by Mendelsohn's (1976; Mendelsohn & Griswold, 1964) hypothesis that creativity benefits from broadened states of attention. In a series of experiments, Nęcka (1999) demonstrated that psychometrically creative people, compared with less creative ones, showed decreased efficiency of selective attention, particularly visible in a divided-attention condition (Figure 10.2). It is worth mentioning that the experimental procedure required participants to respond to single letters that were not relevant to any higher-order mental activity. Participants were shown a target letter in the middle of the screen and a handful (three, four, or five) of probe letters that constantly appeared and disappeared on the screen. Their task was to press a button if one of the probe letters matched the target (e.g., *E* and *E*, or *E* and *e*, depending on the task's difficulty). Simultaneously, the participants were supposed to control the location of a small horizontal bar, which tended to drop down below the tolerable boundary if neglected. So, the procedure was designed within the dual-task paradigm, but neither of these tasks required any creativity; still, creative persons tended to perform worse than less creative persons. It seems that if the stimuli had been meaningful and connected with some creativity task, then the deficiency of selective attention characteristic of creative people probably would have not been observable. However, the abstract nature of the stimuli that had to be selected on the basis of arbitrary rules made creative people vulnerable to "leaks" in the filter of selective attention. Nęcka, like other researchers in this area (Green & Williams, 1999; Kasof, 1997; Mendelsohn, 1976; Mendelsohn & Griswold, 1964, 1966; Mendelsohn & Lindholm, 1972; Rawlings, 1985; Słabosz, 2000; Stavridou & Furnham, 1996), pointed to some positive outcomes of such leaks. It is reasonable to suggest that they may increase the likelihood of seemingly irrelevant or apparently useless information to be included in creative processes, thus facilitating creation of unpredictable ideas (cf. Mednick, 1962; also see Martindale, 1989, 1995). From this point of view, what looks like deficiency of cognitive functioning may in fact be beneficial to such creative behavior as the generation of novel ideas.

A hypothesis that creativity benefits from a weakened filter of selective attention also has been confirmed by studies in which a negative priming effect was observed (Słabosz, 2000). In these studies, a person has to respond to a stimulus that was to be ignored in the previous trial. People usually respond with increased reaction time in such conditions, and the difference between reaction time in the priming and control conditions serves as an index of the strength of cognitive inhibition. Greater values of the difference are interpreted as a result of strong inhibition of reaction in the preceding trial. If the difference is smaller, it is interpreted as an index of weakened inhibition: A formerly inhibited response can be executed in the next trial without huge temporal costs. In the study by Słabosz (2000), psychometrically creative people, compared with less creative ones, obtained lower indices of strength of inhibition. This result is interpreted in terms of the attentional mechanism of screening out irrelevant information in order to concentrate only on the relevant aspects of stimulation. If a person is less able to actively inhibit irrelevant information, or less inclined to do so, he or she will show lowered negative priming effects. That is exactly what has been found in the case of more creative persons.

In the study by Słabosz and Nęcka (2005), creative and less creative persons were supposed to select objects defined by one, two, three, or four defining features. These objects were hidden among five, ten, or fifteen distracters. It was hypothesized that the increase of reaction time with the number of features and distracters would indicate the serial mode of information processing, whereas lack of such a relationship would represent a parallel mode of processing. It appeared that creativity was connected with a parallel rather than serial analysis of the visual field. It seems that states of broad attention may be responsible for that result. It is worth noticing, though, that more creative persons were particularly able to scan their visual field in the parallel mode.

The results of these studies pertain to Martindale's (1989, 1999) stance, according to which creativity requires the simultaneous activation of numerous nodes of the semantic network so that unusual and atypical connections between various cognitive representations are possible. Such a global activation requires lowered cortical arousal. According to the author, the states of low arousal incite primary thinking processes and are characteristic of broadened attention. Low cortical arousal, and hence broadened attention, may result in a flat association gradient. Research by Gruszka and Nęcka (2002) shows that the intensity of the activation process and a multitude of connections and associations in the semantic network may have a decisive influence on a person's ability to make remote associations, which is characteristic for creative individuals.

Polish studies on the relationship between creativity and attention have been significantly stimulated by the theory developed by Alina Kolańczyk (1989, 1991a, 1991b, 1998). Kolańczyk proposed to make a distinction between "intensive" and "extensive" states of attention. In the intensive state of attention, on one hand, a relatively small amount of information is selected so that it can be analyzed at the deep level of processing (i.e., semantic). In the extensive state of attention, on the other hand, a relatively large amount of information enters consciousness, but it is analyzed at a shallow level of processing (i.e., sensory or perceptual). Thus, two states of attention may be described in the zoom-lens metaphor: A panoramic picture does not allow concentration on details, whereas detailed processing does not allow taking into account a large scene. According to Kolańczyk, the creative process is characterized by a specific sequence of both attentional and motivational states. At the beginning, a person is stimulated by task motivation, that is, by his or her willingness to accomplish the goal of creative activity, providing that the goal has been formulated prior to the activity. This kind of motivation has been called "telic,"[4] since it is goal oriented. Kolańczyk proposes that this kind of motivation usually intensifies attention, which means that a person is able to concentrate on a very limited amount of information relevant to the problem at hand. Thus, an intense state of attention may be an impediment to idea generation, because a thorough semantic analysis of information relevant to the task may cause blocks in the creative process. So, a person has to pause in the creative activity because his or her attempts usually do not bring about any acceptable solution.

During the incubation period that follows, a person has an opportunity to switch to an alternative type of motivation. This type has been called "paratelic," which means that there is no specific goal that dominated the activity. Rather, a person temporarily forgets about the problem and engages himself or herself in activities that are entirely different from the formerly executed creative process. Such an alteration in motivational states causes cognitive adjustment as well. Specifically, attention switches from an intensive to an extensive mode of functioning. Thanks to such a switch, the system of attention is now able to process plenty of information, including peripheral stimulation that may be crucial for finding acceptable solutions to a formerly abandoned problem. Extensive attention, instigated by paratelic motivation, also helps to activate the broad spectrum of information encoded in long-term memory. Thus, both peripheral external stimulation and seemingly unimportant memory data provide a chance to go back to the problem and look at it from a different perspective. This is what is supposed to happen in the act of insight. According to Kolańczyk, the processes of intuition that take place during the incubation break, and that lead to insightful redefinition of the problem, are rooted in the mechanisms of telic versus paratelic motivation and, accordingly, in the mechanisms of intensive versus extensive states of attention.

The idea that states of attention are systematically changing during the creative process has been recently addressed by Magdalena Groborz (2004; Grohman, in press). Groborz's main assumption is that different states of selective attention underlie two phases of creative process, generation and exploration (cf. Finke, et al., 1992). Each phase of creative processing has different goals and requires a different set of representations to be activated. According to the proposed model of dynamic selective attention in creative processes, the generation phase

---

[4] The term comes from the Greek root *telos*, meaning goal.

requires weaker selection mechanisms, which may allow various potentially enriching pieces of information to enter consciousness. This in turn may result in new ideas (see also Martindale, 1989). The goal of the exploration phase is to interpret and evaluate the new combinations and close down the process, so to speak. If so, then this phase would require stronger selection mechanisms, so that hardly any distracting information would influence the process of exploring and interpreting. The results of three experiments seem to confirm the predictions of the dynamic selective attention model. During the generation phase, the attention may indeed be broader and selection mechanisms weaker: New ideas (graphic objects composed of three geometric shapes and alphanumeric signs; cf. Finke & Slayton, 1989) were the most creative when some incidental information was presented while subjects were generating ideas. As for the exploration phase, creativity of interpretation did not depend on presented information, which may be due to intensified attention and stronger selection mechanism.

The aforementioned results may imply that the creative process requires interplay of both bottom-up and top-down processes, whereas the bottom-up processes are responsible for activation of representations and the top-down processes for efficient selection of information to be processed. Nęcka, Gruszka, and Orzechowski (1996) found that intellectually gifted children responded faster than children in a control group in the incongruent condition of the Navon (1977) task. This finding was interpreted in terms of increased efficiency of selection mechanisms (cognitive control) shown by the gifted children. However, no similar effect was found concerning the Stroop task, which makes the relation of attentional mechanisms to intellectual giftedness and creativity disputable. Cognitive control also seems to be a good predictor of evaluation skills, especially in the case of persons with a tendency for the global information processing style (Groborz & Nęcka, 2003).

The role of unconscious information processes is highlighted in models of intuition, incubation, and insight. The results of studies carried out in Poland on the relationship between creativity and implicit learning, as measured with the Artificial Grammar Learning Task, suggest that interindividual variation in creative thinking does not depend on implicit processes (Balas, Słabosz, Żyła, & Groborz, 2001). It seems, then, that implicit processes are phylogenetically older; thus, their interindividual variability is severely limited. This assumption is consistent with Reber's evolutionary hypothesis (Reber, 1992). In contrast, Nęcka and Kałwa (2001) showed that when, using the incidental learning task (designed according to the theory of levels of information processing by Craik and Lockhart), creative individuals outperformed their less creative counterparts in efficiency of incidental learning, especially when the learning process took place on a shallow (i.e., perceptual rather than semantic) level of processing. The results seem to be compatible with the notion of highly efficient perceptual information processing in creative people (Smith, 1990; Smith & van der Meer, 1994).

Creative ideas can be generated in different ways (cf. Finke et al., 1992). For instance, one can use metaphors, analogies, transformations, or associations to come up with novel ideas. In a study carried out by Balas (2001), metaphorical premises led to more creative solutions to given problems. In addition, individuals who were especially sensitive to such cues (the premises) were also more intuitive in their thinking. Intuitive thinking was positively correlated with the level of solution creativity. Metaphor seems to broaden conceptual categories and increase tolerance for new information (Nęcka & Kubiak, 1989; Thagard, 1997).

It seems that the range of Polish research on cognitive determinants of creativity is consistent with the research in other countries. Moreover, the research on elemental mechanisms of creativity and different types of mental operations is more prevalent than in the other domains of psychology (personality, affect, etc.). Attempts to study more complex interactions between the course of creative process, types of tasks (divergent and convergent), and cognitive endowment are less frequent.

Motivation, Affect, and Dispositions

Current Polish research in this area concentrates on the role of autonomic motivation in creativity, on profiles of creativity dispositions typical of different vocational groups, and on giftedness and factors that constitute it. The first of these areas has been thoroughly explored theoretically and empirically by Aleksandra Tokarz (1985, 1996, 1998). In her 1985 book, she described a research project in which three types of motivation were induced. Autonomic cognitive motivation, closely related to the concept of intrinsic motivation (Amabile, 1996), was triggered by lack of time pressure and the freedom to choose any of possible directions of activity, particularly freedom to choose the type of task to deal with. Four tasks were presented to the participants: one requiring technological inventions, another one based on the necessity to forecast future developments of science, the third one requiring interpretation

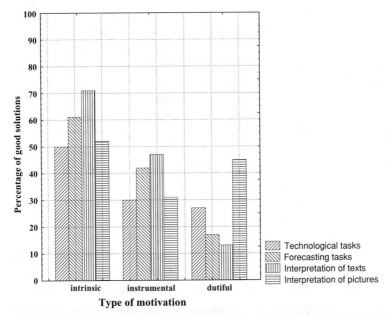

FIGURE 10.3. The influence of type of motivation (intrinsic, instrumental, or dutiful) and type of task on the percentage of good solutions (Tokarz, 1985).

of a text, and the fourth one requiring interpretation of a picture. In addition, a characteristic instruction was presented that was supposed to activate the "pure curiosity" of the participants for the task and the process of its solution. In the instrumental cognitive motivation, in contrast, the instruction encouraged participants to get interested in the task because it would supposedly serve their future educational needs. So, new information was searched for, gathered, and analyzed, not because it was interesting as such but because of its instrumental value. Finally, in the dutiful condition, participants were asked just to do their best in order to comply with the experimenter's expectations. It appeared that the autonomic cognitive motivation (intrinsic motivation) caused the highest percentage of good solutions, although an influence of the type of task was also visible (Figure 10.3).

The results of these explorations are reflected in Tokarz's model of autonomic cognitive motivation. According to the model, autonomic cognitive motivation plays a fundamental role in the polymotivational system of creative activity. It is distinct from both instrumental and dutiful motivations. Outcomes of the author's more current studies (Tokarz, 1996, 1998) introduced some modification to the model. These studies were performed on a sample consisting of young researchers, assistant professors, and postdoctoral students. In order to describe the motivational structure in this sample, Tokarz used the Inventory of a Scientist's Work (Kocowski & Tokarz, 1991). This inventory enabled her to describe frequency, as well as valuative and motivational factors typical of scientific work. Obtained results suggest that emotional and motivational processes, which are essential for creativity, are quite diverse from what had been anticipated on the basis of previous research.

In the studied sample, the motivation that seemed to play an important role during early phases of idea generation was hubristic motivation. This type of motivation is linked to the drive to confirm one's self-esteem. Moreover, results of the research on the relationship between motivational system and the temperament of young researchers led to the conclusion that efficient and productive scientific work also requires a stable nervous system. Specifically, it turned out that the higher-level factor "self-actualization" comprises two lower-level factors: internal motivation and conscientiousness. The latter was negatively correlated with the temperamental trait of reactivity, measured by Strelau's Temperament Inventory (Beauvale & Tokarz, 1996; Strelau, Angleitner, & Ruch, 1990). This trait reflects an inclination to overreact to external stimuli and to exaggerate the significance of stressful situations. According to Beauvale and Tokarz (1998), efficient young scientists score low on this dimension of temperament.

Another line of research on predispositions for scientific work is represented by Andrzej Strzałecki, who conceptualized creativity as a certain style of behavior (Strzałecki, 1989). Using his own questionnaire, Strzałecki analyzed creative potential of designers (Strzałecki, 1989) and also undergraduate students who chose academic careers (Strzałecki, 1998). His main assumption was that those students would be more creative than the ones that chose a different kind of career. A factor analysis of the questionnaire revealed five factors of style of creative behavior, which were positively correlated with the level of creativity as measured with divergent thinking tests: Life Approval, Self-Actualization, Flexibility of Cognitive Processes, Ego Strength, and Nonconformism. Contrary to expectations, students who declared an academic career scored lower on the first three factors. These results have been explained in terms of the poor conditions of the Polish higher education system. It is possible that an academic career in Poland is not the most desirable type of occupation for truly creative young people.

The validity of Strzałecki's model was also confirmed in a study carried out on a sample of entrepreneurs (Strzałecki, 2001; Strzałecki & Kot, 2000, Strzałecki & Kusal, 2002). The results showed that successful entrepreneurs differ from their less successful counterparts in relation to strength of ego, self-realization, and internal locus of control. These variables were the strongest predictors of the entrepreneurs' level of achievements in comparison other variables used in the study, such as motivation, anxiety level, and divergent thinking. The results of this research are interpreted according to the threshold hypothesis. It states that being an efficient entrepreneur depends first of all on lowered reactivity, which helps to combat stress, and, to a lesser extent, on other dimensions of temperament (e.g., emotionality). Only if the reactivity threshold is not surpassed do cognitive factors that determine creativity level turn out to be of greater significance. In other words, creativity is important for an entrepreneur if and only if he or she is emotionally stable enough to cope with stress. The study seems interesting because it focuses on a group that is often neglected in the research of creativity and personality (cf. Mumford et al., 2003).

The variable of self-actualization, identified in the studies of Tokarz and Strzałecki, seems to play an important role not only in eminent and mature creators but also in younger ones. The role of this variable is especially salient in the case of gifted eighteen-year-olds, as shown in studies done by Pufal-Struzik (1999). In addition, observed Pufal-Struzik observed that development of a tendency toward self-realization might be inhibited by external factors such as family and school, and internal ones, such as low levels of self-knowledge. For gifted students with a developed tendency for self-realization, high levels of self-acceptance and a need for cognitive stimulation were characteristic. In the case of these individuals, the need for novelty, adventure, and risk correlated positively with flexibility of thinking and tolerance of ambiguity (Pufal-Struzik, 1996). Higher levels of self-acceptance and internal locus of control predicted a higher level of divergent thinking in thirteen- and fourteen-year-olds (Pufal-Struzik, 1998).

It seems that the domain of affect and its relation to creativity is the least explored in Polish literature and research, with the exception of curiosity (Tokarz, 1989a, 1989b). In one of the very few studies in this domain, it was shown that affect is crucial for creativity. For instance, Czarnocki and Siekierzyński (2000) showed that experimentally induced positive mood influenced the number (not quality) of solutions in a task that required categorizing different stimuli. The effect of positive mood was the most salient in case of nonverbal stimuli and least so in the case of numeric ones.

Situational Influences

There is a scarcity of studies in Poland on situational factors that may determine creativity, even though the significance of such factors is discussed in some theoretical approaches (cf. Kozielecki, 1997).

Research by Tokarz (Tokarz, Beauvale, Żyła, & Rudowicz, 2004; Tokarz & Słabosz, 2001a, 2001b; Tokarz, Żyła, Beauvale, & Rudowicz, in press; Tokarz, Żyła, Ganczarek, Kudyba, & Latocha, in press) represents an attempt to identify cultural differences in how creativity is perceived among various populations in Poland. One of the studies concerned naïve theories of creativity that could be characteristic for Polish elementary-school and high school teachers (Tokarz & Słabosz, 2001a, 2001b). In this study, a modified version of Fryer's Ideal Pupil Check List was used (Fryer, 1996). By means of the scale, the authors investigated the teachers' opinions about characteristics of creative, noncreative, ideal, and conduct-challenging students. The results suggest that teachers had difficulty in adequately identifying creative students' characteristics; they tended to mix ideal students' trait with those of a creative one. Moreover, they showed a tendency to ignore the personality characteristics typical for creative personality syndrome. Furthermore, noncreative students were mostly characterized as challenging ones.

Tokarz continues this line of research and expands it to the populations of students and experts who represent the area of psychology of creativity (Tokarz et al., 2004; Tokarz et al., in press). The results are compatible with those of studies done by Rudowicz in Hong Kong (Hui & Rudowicz, 1997; Rudowicz & Hui, 1997, 1998; Rudowicz & Yue, 2002; Yue & Rudowicz, 2002), and they seem to converge into a coherent picture of differences between Western and Eastern cultures. As expected, representatives of Eastern culture perceive creativity through its product and social usefulness. Typical for Western cultures, Polish people understand creativity as self-expression, with stress on artistic attributes (cf. Lubart, 1999). It is important to mention the methodological issues that concern this kind of research. One of the qualitative methods of defining the concept of creativity used by Rudowicz, Tokarz, and their coworkers is the analysis of traits of eminently creative people, both contemporary and historical figures.

Developmental Studies

An integrated approach to the development of creativity was implemented by Dorota Kubicka (2000, 2003). Kubicka adopted a method called Scenotest (von Staabs, 1964, 1991), which is based on children's symbolic play. The test set consists of 115 elements, including pictures of people, animals, plants, vehicles, and various devices, and also building blocks. These elements are provided in separate containers, according to their category membership. They are colorful and bendable. A child is supposed to make a scene out of them, using a 40 cm × 54 cm stage. Thanks to magnets, the elements can be positioned in vertical and horizontal positions. This method was originally employed for the clinical analysis of children's personality disorders through the assumed mechanism of projection. In Kubicka's studies, it served to assess children's strategies of creative activity, as Kubicka asked her participants to compose the elements "in the way nobody has done so far." There were 176 children, aged three to eight years, who succeeded in composing one scene, and 72 of them agreed to compose a second one after a break.

The author found that younger children preferred simple constructions that represented their everyday experience, whereas older participants were able to create complex thematic scenes. Older participants could represent imaginary situations or illustrations of stories and fairy tales. Some of the thematic compositions were scored as creative on the basis of a number of criteria, such as active rather than passive composition, active role playing, humor, unusual topics, or unusual manipulation with elements of the Scenotest. The author observed a significant increase of the number of creative compositions during the second attempt (from 23 percent to 43 percent). At the same time, the number of simple representations dropped down from 62 percent to 46 percent. It should be taken into account, though, that second compositions were assembled only by the minority of willing participants, so it is quite probable that this subsample consisted of children who were generally more creative. Another interesting finding refers to the effect of age. The percentage of creative works linearly increased between the ages of three and eight, but this relationship was observed only in the case of the second compositions. As far as the first compositions are regarded, the increase of the percentage of creative results was much less salient, although the increase of the percentage of thematic scenes was clearly observable. It seems as if creative solutions, which were just a special subcategory of thematic solutions, could find their way only after some less creative solutions were assembled and presented. Regardless, Kubicka's results suggest that the relationship between age and creativity does not comply with the simplistic stance, according to which older children are obviously more creative.

Another interesting developmental project was undertaken in the decade between 1985 and 1995. It was supervised by Wiesława Limont (1991a, 1991b, 1994), who sought to find possibilities for stimulating creativity in elementary school. More than 300 students aged seven to fifteen took part in this program. Besides other techniques, the program included some elements of Gordon's (1961) synectics. For twenty-four weeks, students in the experimental group participated in the core activity, which was attending classes of artistic expression. At the same time, students from the control group attended regular classes in the standardized educational program. After twenty-four weeks, the level of divergent thinking skills was measured. Results indicated that students from the experimental group outperformed their peers in the control condition.

Limont's more current research focused on mechanisms of creative imagination (Limont, 1996) and metaphorical thinking. Limont designed a special six-month program for seven- to fourteen-year-olds that aimed at stimulating and developing creative imagination. The program included exercises in music and artistic expression, and metaphorical thinking. At the same time, another group of age-matched students were in a more traditional program that focused on verbal expression. According to the results of the study, the former program influenced the development of creative imagination to a greater extent than did the traditional one. Limont claimed that imagery has strong emotional components, and the processes underlying it are metaphorical in nature; their basis includes visual and spatial representations.

STIMULATING AND DEVELOPING CREATIVE ABILITIES

Creativity stimulation programs have been being developed since the 1970s, when Andrzej Góralski and his team of coworkers from the Academy of Special Pedagogy started to organize summer camps for young scholars and teachers. The participants studied theoretical and applied issues in philosophy, psychology, and pedagogy of creativity. They also had a chance to exercise some practical techniques of creative problem solving. Góralski's approach was rational rather than intuitive. He borrowed and developed the ideas of George Polya, a mathematician who was interested in teaching creative thinking. Góralski was also under the influence of philosophers who developed heuristic thinking, such as Socrates and Descartes. He has published extensively in the field of applied creativity and is the author of a book, *Creative Task Solving* (Góralski, 1989), in which all major heuristic systems are described and systematized. Góralski is also an editor of a series titled *Task, Method, Solution: Creative Thinking Techniques*. This seven-volume series contains both original works and review papers. It is the most comprehensive attempt to cover the field of applied creativity in the Polish literature.

Apart from publicizing his own ideas, Andrzej Góralski is to be recognized for his popularization of foreign authors, mainly French and Russian. For instance, he propagated a technique developed by Michel Fustier (1976, 1977) called functional analysis. According to this technique, a problem at hand should be defined in terms of functions that a future solution or invention should have. Such redefinition of a problem helps generate inventions that will function in an optimal way. Another author introduced by Góralski is Genrik Altshuller (1974), a Russian inventor whose ideas became quite popular in Poland, thanks to Góralski. Altshuller has developed several creative thinking techniques. One such technique is called the small-people technique. It helps to model a problem in terms of intelligent and self-sufficient dwarfs, whose goal is to solve the problem. This technique is based on the principle of the self-solving task, which allows one to get rid of the overwhelming responsibility for novel and good solutions. Another of Altshuller's techniques is principal antinomy. The main purpose of this technique is to look for paradoxes and contradictions in a task's description. The author believes that most technological problems are difficult because there is a need to overcome basic contradiction, like the conflict between the endurance of a machine and its overall costs. For instance, it is quite easy to design something that is long lasting but expensive, or cheap but short lived. The real challenge for an inventor, though, is to design something that is enduring enough and not very expensive. Overcoming basic contradictions is the core of invention, according to Altshuller (cf. Prince, 1970). He offers a number of heuristics to achieve this goal, such as the principle of replacement of "hard" metallic constructions with their "softer" hydraulic or pneumatic substitutes, or the principle of automatic regeneration of worn parts of a machine without discontinuation of its functioning (Altshuller, 1974; Góralski, 1989).

In the 1980s, cooperation between scholars from the Jagiellonian University and the Wrocław Technical University enabled further development of a creativity stimulation approach. The *spiritus movens* of this project was Tomasz Kocowski, affiliated with both institutions. He succeeded in organizing a series of summer schools of creativity, which ran from 1979 to 1988. Summer school students were Technical University scholars, who formed creative thinking groups, and psychologists from the Jagiellonian University, who worked as group facilitators. The idea was to disseminate the knowledge on applied creativity among technical scholars, scientists, and inventors. Another goal was to gather experience in the field of practical methods of creative problem solving, particularly if exercised in group settings. The methodology was based mostly on synectics (Gordon, 1961; Prince, 1970), although a number of other techniques were also employed. The influence of Kaufmann, Fustier, and Drevet (1970), the French authors who developed a system called "inventics," was also very important.

The group sessions usually started with basic creative thinking exercises, such as the use of analogy or metaphor, deferment of judgment principle, and group thinking principle (listening, cooperation, and productive criticism). Then, the participants worked on real-life problems, mostly technological ones. These problems were provided by participants themselves and were connected with their own scientific work. So, every participant served as an expert at least once during the summer school; otherwise, he or she served as a regular participant. This procedure proved its overall effectiveness as a method of enhancement of creative potential of experts and professionals (Nęcka & Brocławik, 1984).

The summer schools were like a firing ground for development of methodology of the practical use of creative thinking techniques. During the 1980s, there was no demand for creative ideas in the bureaucratic, state-regulated economy. Although the present situation is still far from perfect, the experience gathered during these summer schools has become extremely useful, especially in the aftermath of the outbreak of a market economy in Poland in 1989. Private companies are more and more interested in organizing creative thinking workshops for their employees. Applied creativity is also quite popular in education, as various colleges and other educational institutions include creativity in their curricula. A more thorough review of educational opportunities is presented in Tokarz and Słabosz (2002).

The experience gathered during the Wrocław–Kraków cooperation has led to many publications. Perhaps the most popular and influential one is the handbook, *Creativity Training*, by Edward Nęcka. This handbook has already been through four editions (1989, 1992, 1995, 1998), and the fifth and revised edition will be published in 2005. The book consists of five chapters that describe the following aspects of creativity training: interpersonal processes, motivations, abilities, obstacles, and group issues. There are about 150 exercises that address particular goals of the training, such as, how to defer judgment, how to make an analogical transfer, how to develop intrinsic motivation in the task, and the like. In another book, *TRoP . . . Creative Problem Solving* (Nęcka, 1994), the author describes his own system of getting creative solutions to formerly defined problems. The system consists of two phases, the first one devoted to various manipulations of a problem and the second one to looking for solutions. Each phase consists of three stages. Thus, the first phase involves the following stages: realization of the existence of a problem, problem understanding, and problem definition. The second phase consists of building up a vicarious problem, solution of the vicarious problem, and application of this solution to the real problem's requirements. Construction of the vicarious problem is assumed to be a heuristic method that allows overcoming fixation, overconfidence to already existing solutions, and other frequently met obstacles in creative thinking. In this way, the TRoP system is basically rooted in synectics, which is the system of getting new ideas through the use of analogy.

One of the most comprehensive attempts to stimulate creative thinking at schools is Krzysztof Szmidt's Creativity Classes Program. The program has been in progress since 1994 and consists of two subprograms: Order and Adventure: Creativity Lessons (Szmidt, 1995/1996/1997; also see Szmidt, 1998) and Elements. Creativity Lessons in Early Elementary Education (Szmidt & Bonar, 1998). The latter includes textbooks for teachers that cover issues on basic elements, such as water, fire, earth, and air.

The main assumptions underlying the program are that it is possible to (a) develop creative abilities; (b) develop creative attitudes that comprise cognitive, emotional and motivational, and behavioral dispositions; and (c) introduce ways of teaching creativity that enhance the development of creative abilities and attitudes (Szmidt, 2003). In his handbooks, Szmidt proposes that creative attitude should be developed through tasks that aim at the three groups of dispositions just mentioned. In addition, the tasks should be divergent, diverse, real life, and prompt the use of heuristics. In order to teach creativity, Szmidt says, one cannot neglect basic principles that facilitate creating. Most of them are compatible with rules for group creativity, but Szmidt adds to that a rule that teachers should also be creative. Altogether, Szmidt's educational program seems to be consistent with modern approaches to creativity and creative abilities development (cf. Renzulli, 1986). Diverse, motivating, and challenging tasks make the program especially appealing and interesting to educators and students.

Another program to stimulate creative thinking that proved to be efficient is targeted at children aged four to ten (Ligęza, 2000a, 2000b). The program is based on Renzulli's (1986) model of creative abilities and on Nęcka's concept of mental operations that are involved in creative process (Nęcka, 1987/1995). The main observation of Ligęza's study and the program for stimulation is that, by employing the techniques of creative thinking, even children as young as four years old can learn to use not only inductive but also deductive thinking. Another of Ligęza's studies (Ligęza, 2001) showed that the creative thinking of children aged four to ten can be stimulated with group creative thinking. However, it is crucial, the author holds, that children do some parts of the task individually rather than in groups. Work in groups may in fact result in a decrease in creative thinking abilities.

It is also worth noting that there are quite a few studies on the effectiveness of given creative thinking techniques in the Polish literature. For instance, Sołowiej (2000) has done research on brainstorming, and Nęcka and Kubiak (1989) showed that metaphorical thinking training enhances levels of creative thinking and decreases individual levels of dogmatism.

CURRENT TECHNIQUES OF ASSESSMENT OF CREATIVITY

It seems that the worldwide research on creativity conducted during the past two decades has given researchers sufficient grounds for designing new diagnostic tools (Mumford et al., 2003). Nevertheless, in Polish psychology of creativity, the progress in research has resulted in just a few new measurement tools. Two questionnaires have been the most popular recently: Strzałecki's Style of Creative Behavior (SCB) and Popek's Creative Behavior Questionnaire (CBQ). Both scales are based on the authors' conceptions of creativity. Strzałecki's SCB (1985) is meant to diagnose personality-based predispositions toward creativity, which is understood as a behavior style. In the older version of SCB, there were ninety-eight questions that formed the basis for ten factors. These factors are as follows: Strength of Ego, Flexibility and Complexity of Cognitive Structures and Processes, Nonconformism, Spontaneity, Tolerance for Ambiguity, Internal Locus of Control, Autonomic Cognitive Motivation,

Aesthetic Attitude, Originality and Freedom for Personality Expression, and Tendency to Self-Realization. According to Strzałecki, all of these factors correlate positively with creativity. Recent studies led to a revision of the SCB. The latest version has been reoriented to a more general population, and it has helped to extract profiles of different vocational groups, based on five factors: Appreciation of Life, Strength of Ego, Self-Actualization, Flexibility of Cognitive Processes, and Internal Locus of Control. SCB is one of the few questionnaires that diagnoses levels of creativity.

The other tool – Popek's CBQ (2000) – helps to diagnose predispositions toward creativity in the areas of cognition and personality. In his research, Popek focuses mostly on artistic talents and personality correlates of creativity (Popek, 2001, 1998, 1988). The CBQ is based on a theory that creativity results from the interaction of intellectual abilities, talents (or special abilities), creative abilities (cf. Renzulli, 1986), motivation, emotions, and environment. The questionnaire is composed of four scales: Conformity, Nonconformity, Algorithmic Behavior, and Heuristic Behavior. The first two scales refer mostly to personality predispositions, whereas the Algorithmic and Heuristic Behavior scales measure cognitive abilities. Creative behavior is diagnosed by means of adding scores from Nonconformity and Heuristic Behavior scales; reproductive behavior is described in terms of Conformity and Algorithmic scales. Creative behavior is determined by the domination of heuristic and non-conformist behavior. The heuristic, algorithmic, nonconformist and conformist traits of behavior are understood dynamically, not as discreet entities. The questionnaire consists of fifteen pairs of statements per scale, such as activity–passivity; dependence–independence; and logical memory–rote memory. The CBQ can be used in the general population for individuals older than twelve years of age.

In many experimental research projects and for individual diagnosis, there is an adaptation of the Test for Creative Thinking–Drawing Production by Urban and Jellen (Matczak, Jaworowska, & Stańczak, 2000). Tasks similar to those of Guilford that measure divergent thinking are also quite popular among both scientist–psychologists and practitioner–psychologists (Trzebiński, 1978, 1981). Less popular is the consensual assessment technique, or other tools that use trained raters (see Grohman, Wodniecka, & Kłusak, in press).

Apart from individual testing, there are also attempts to measure institutional creativity. It is well recognized that the climate for creativity in a company is not synonymous with the individual creativity of the employees and the managers (Amabile, 1996). Therefore, institutional creativity requires a special kind of approach and specialized measurement tools. Very recent developments in this area (Kwaśniewska & Nęcka, 2004; Nęcka & Kwaśniewska, 2005) permitted researchers to construct valid tools to assess climate for creativity within Polish companies. These tools are used not only for research but also for practical issues, such as consulting and training.

CONCLUDING REMARKS

To sum up, Polish creativity studies seem to cover all major topics and problems addressed in the field. However, there are some topics that we believe are particularly well developed. First, there are interesting studies on cognitive processes in creativity, particularly the basic mechanisms of attention and cognitive control. Studies on memory and creativity also fall into this category. Second, basic laboratory studies are frequently accompanied by the individual differences approach. Even though a basic problem is addressed, various authors attempt to look for differences between people scoring high and low on some criterion task, such as divergent thinking tests. This kind of approach seems quite promising because the basic cognitive mechanisms and correlates of creativity may differ, depending on the participant's level of creativity. Third, many Polish studies are heading for discovery of educational applications. The works of Krzysztof Szmidt and his coworkers are of particular importance, because of their in-depth scrutiny and ambitious scope. If this line of research is continued, the country's educational system should evolve more and more into the realm of creativity stimulation and instruction. This goal requires close cooperation among psychologists, educational scholars, teachers, and school system representatives.

References

Altshuller, G. S. (1974). *Algorytm wynalazku* [The algorithm of invention]. Warszawa: Wydawnictwa Naukowo-Techniczne. (translated from Russian by A. Góralski)

Amabile, T. (1996). *Creativity in context*. Boulder, CO: Westview Press.

Balas, R. (2001). Intuicyjny styl poznawczy i metafory jako funkcja twórczości. [Intuitive cognitive style and metaphors' function in creativity]. *Przegląd Psychologiczny, 44,* 175–187.

Balas, R., Słabosz, A., Żyła, K., & Groborz, M. (2001, November 9–11). *Konserwatyzm ewolucji, czyli o rónicach indywidualnych w uczeniu mimowolnym*

[Conservatism of evolution. On individual differences in implicit learning]. Paper presented at the meeting of the Autonomic Psychology Club, Kazimierz Dolny, Poland.

Beauvale, A., & Tokarz, A. (1996). Temperamental factors and the structure of motivation for scientific activity. *High Ability Studies, 7,* 119–127.

Boden, M. A. (1994). What is creativity? In M. A. Boden (Ed.), *Dimensions of creativity* (pp. 75–117). Cambridge, MA: MIT Press.

Czarnocki, M., & Siekierzyński, W. (2000). Wpływ stanu emocjonalnego na efektywność myślenia twórczego [The influence of emotions on creative thinking]. *Psychologia Wychowawcza, 43,* 128–134.

Finke, R. A., & Slayton, K. (1988). Explorations of creative visual synthesis in mental imagery. *Memory and Cognition, 16,* 252–257.

Finke, R. A., Ward, T. B., & Smith, S. M. (1992). *Creative cognition: Theory, research, and applications.* Cambridge, MA: MIT Press.

Fryer, M. (1996). *Creative teaching and learning.* London: Paul Chapman.

Fustier, M. (1976). *Pratique de la créativité.* Paris: Entreprise Moderne d'Edition.

Fustier, M. (1977). *La résolution de problèmes.* Paris: Entreprise Moderne d'Edition.

Góralski, A. (1978). Czymze jest twórczość [What is creativity, then]? In A. Góralski (Ed.), *Zadanie, metoda, rozwiązanie: Techniki twórczego myślenia* [Problem, method, solution: Creative thinking techniques] (Vol. 2, pp. 9–14). Warszawa, Poland: Wydawnictwa Naukowo-Techniczne.

Góralski, A. (1989). *Twórcze rozwiązywanie zadan* [Creative task solving]. Warszawa, Poland: Państwowe Wydawnictwo Naukowe.

Gordon, W. J. J. (1961). *Synectics: The development of creative capacity.* New York: Harper & Row.

Green, M. J., & Williams, L. M. (1999). Schizotypy and creativity as effects of reduced cognitive inhibition. *Personality and Individual Differences, 27,* 263–276.

Groborz, M. (2004). *Procesy generatywne i eksploratywne w procesie twórczym a dynamika mechanizmów uwagi selektywnej* [Generative and explorative processes in creative process and dynamics of selective attention]. Unpublished doctoral dissertation, Jagiellonian University, Kraków.

Groborz, M., & Nęcka, E. (2003). Cognitive control and creativity: Explorations of generation and evaluation of ideas. *Creativity Research Journal, 15,* 183–197.

Grohman (Groborz), M. (2004). Wpływ informacji dodatkowych na proces twórczy: Generowanie i interpretacja prostych form graficznych [The influence of incidental cues on generating and interpreting simple graphic forms]. In S. Popek, R. E. Bernacka, C. W. Domański, B. Gawda, D. Turska (Eds.). Twórczość w teorii i praktyce [Creativity in theory and practice] (pp. 113–124). Lublin, Poland: Wydawnictwo UMCS.

Grohman (Groborz), M., Wodniecka, Z., & Kłusak, M. (in press). Divergent thinking and evaluation skills: Do they always go together? *Journal of Creative Behavior.*

Gruszka, A., & Nęcka, E. (2002). Priming and acceptance of close and remote associations by creative and less creative people. *Creativity Research Journal, 14,* 193–205.

Guilford, J. P. (1950). Creativity. *American Psychologist, 4,* 444–454.

Guilford, J. P. (1967). The nature of human intelligence. New York: McGraw-Hill.

Horn, J., & Cattell, R. B. (1966). Refinement and test of the theory of fluid and crystallized general intelligences. Journal of Educational Psychology, 57, 253–270.

Hui, A., & Rudowicz, E. (1997). Creative personality versus Chinese personality: How distinctive are these two personality factors? An International Journal of Psychology in the Orient, 40, 277–285.

Kasof, J. (1997). Creativity and breath of attention. Creativity Research Journal, 10, 303–315.

Kaufmann, A., Fustier, M., Drevet, A. (1971). L'Inventique: nouvelles méthodes de créativité [Inventics: New methods of creativity]. Paris, France: Entreprise moderne d'edition. Polish edition: Inwentyka: Metody poszukiwania twórczych rozwiązań [Inventics: Methods of search for creative solutions]. Warszawa: Wydawnictwa Naukowo-techniczne.

Kocowski, T. (1991). Aktywność twórcza człowieka. Filogeneza. Funkcja. Uwarunkowania [Human creative activity. Phylogenies. Function. Determinants]. In T. Kocowski (Ed.), Szkice z teorii twórczości i motywacji [Essays on theory of creativity and motivation] (pp. 9–35). Poznań, Poland: SAWW.

Kocowski, T., & Tokarz, A. (1991). Prokreatywne i antykreatywne mechanizmy motywacji aktywności twórczej. [Creative and anticreative mechanisms of creative activity motivation]. In A. Tokarz (Ed.), Stymulatory i inhibitory aktywności twórczej [Stimulators and inhibitors of creative activity] (pp. 79–94). Poznań, Poland: SAWW.

Kolańczyk, A. (1989). How to study creative intuition? Polish Psychological Bulletin, 20, 57–68.

Kolańczyk, A. (1991a). Intuicyjność procesów przetwarzania informacji. [Intuition and information processing]. Gdańsk, Poland: Uniwersytet Gdański.

Kolańczyk, A. (1991b). Rola uwagi w procesie intuicji twórczej [The role of attention in the process of creative intuition]. In A. Tokarz (Ed.), Stymulatory i inhibitory aktywności twórczej [Stimulators and inhibitors of creative activity] (pp. 33–49). Poznań, Poland: SAWW.

Kolańczyk, A. (1998). Czuję– myślę– jestem. wiadomość i procesy psychiczne w ujęciu poznawczym [I feel – I think – I am. Consciousness and cognitive processes]. Gdańsk, Poland: Gdańskie Wydawnictwo Psychologiczne.

Kozielecki, J. (1966). Zagadnienia psychologii myślenia [Problems in the psychology of thinking]. Warszawa, Poland: Państwowe Wydawnictwo Naukowe.

Kozielecki, J. (1969). Rozwiązywanie problemów [Problem solving]. Warszawa, Poland: Państwowe Zakłady Wydawnictw Szkolnych.

Kozielecki, J. (1997). Transgresja i kultura [Transgression and culture]. Warszawa, Poland: Wydawnictwo Akademickie "Żak."

Kubicka, D. (2000). Kontrowersje wokół pomiaru twórczości u dzieci [Controversies over measurement of creativity in children]. Psychologia Wychowawcza, 2–3, 208–220.

Kubicka, D. (2003). Twórcze działanie dziecka w sytuacji zabawowo-zadaniowej [Child's creative activity in the playful-task situation]. Kraków Poland: Wydawnictwo Uniwersytetu Jagiellońskiego.

Kwaśniewska, J., & Nęcka, E. (2004). Perception of the climate for creativity in the workplace: The role of the level in the organization and gender. *Creativity and Innovation Management, 13*, 187–196.

Ligęza, W. (2000a). Twórczość dziecka w wieku 4–10 lat a komunikacja interpresonalna [Creativity in four to ten years olds, and interpersonal communication]. In R. Derbis (Ed.), *Jakość rozwoju a jakość zycia* [Quality of development and quality of life]. Częstochowa, Poland: Wyższa Szkoła Pedagogiczna.

Ligęza, W. (2000b). Stymulowanie twórczego rozwoju dzieci w wieku przedszkolnym i szkolnym poprzez pracęw małych grupach twórczego myślenia. [Stimulating the creative development in preschool and primary grade children by means of work in small creative groups]. In B. Kaja (Ed.), *Wspomaganie rozwoju. Psychostymulacja i psychokorekcja* [Enhancing development. Psychostimulation and psychocorrection] (Vol. 2, pp. 150–155). Bydgoszcz, Poland: Wydawnictwo WSP.

Ligęza, W. (2001). Co wiedządzieci o twórczości i tworzeniu [What do children know about creativity and creating]? *Psychologia Rozwojowa, 6*, 47–55.

Limont, W. (1991a). Stymulowanie rozwoju zdolności twórczych dzieci poprzez aktywizowanie kierowanej ekspresji plastycznej. Część I [Stimulated development of children's creative abilities by activating plastic expression under guidance: Part I]. *Psychologia Wychowawcza, 34*, 235–244.

Limont, W. (1991b). Stymulowanie rozwoju zdolności twórczych dzieci poprzez aktywizowanie kierowanej ekspresji plastycznej. Część II [Stimulated development of children's creative abilities by activating plastic expression under guidance: Part II.]. *Psychologia Wychowawcza, 44*, 325–334.

Limont, W. (1994). *Synektyka a zdolności twórcze* [Synectics and creative abilities]. Toruń, Poland: Wydawnictwo Uniwersytetu im. Mikołaja Kopernika.

Limont, W. (1996). *Analiza wybranych mechanizmów wyobrani twórczej* [Analysis of certain mechanisms of creative imagination]. Toruń, Poland: Wydawnictwo Uniwersytetu im. Mikołaja Kopernika.

Lubart, T. I. (1999). Creativity across cultures. In R. J. Sternberg (Ed.), *Handbook of creativity* (pp. 339–350). Cambridge, U.K.: Cambridge University Press.

Martindale, C. (1989). Personality, situation, and creativity. In J. A. Glover, R. R. Ronning, & C. R. Reynolds (Eds.), *Handbook of creativity* (pp. 211–232). New York: Plenum Press.

Martindale, C. (1995). Creativity and connectionism. In S. M. Smith, T. B. Ward, & R. A. Finke (Eds.), *The creative cognition approach* (pp. 249–268). Cambridge, MA: MIT Press.

Martindale, C. (1999). Biological bases of creativity. In R. J. Sternberg (Ed.), *Handbook of creativity* (pp. 137–152). Cambridge, U.K.: Cambridge University Press.

Matczak, A., Jaworowska, A., & Stańczak, J. (2000). *Podręcznik do rysunkowego testu twórczego myślenia TCT-DP K. K Urbana i H. G. Jellena* [Manual for Urban and Jellen's TCT-DP. Polish edition]. Warszawa: Poland: Pracowania Testów Polskiego Towarzystwa Psychologicznego.

Mednick, S. A. (1962). The associative basis of the creative process. *Psychological Review, 44*, 220–232.

Mendelsohn, G. A., & Griswold, B. B. (1964). Differential use of incidental stimuli in problem solving as a function of creativity. *Journal of Abnormal and Social Psychology, 44,* 431–436.

Mendelsohn, G. A., & Griswold, B. B. (1966). Assessed creative potential, vocabulary level, and sex as predictors of the use of incidental cues in verbal problem solving. *Journal of Personality and Social Psychology, 44,* 423–431.

Mendelsohn, G. A., & Lindholm, E. P. (1972). Individual differences and the role of attention in the use of cues in verbal problem solving. *Journal of Personality, 44,* 226–240.

Mendelsohn, G. A. (1976). Associative and attentional processes in creative performance. *Journal of Personality, 44,* 341–369.

Mumford, M. D., Baughman, W. A., & Sager, C. E. (2003). Picking the right material: Cognitive processing skills and their role in creative thought. In M. Runco (Ed.), *Critical creative processes* (pp. 19–68). Cresskill, NJ: Hampton Press.

Navon, D. (1977). Forest before trees: The precedence of global features in visual perception. *Cognitive Psychology, 44,* 353–383.

Nęcka, E. (1995). *Proces twórczy i jego ograniczenia* [Creative process and its constraints] (2nd ed.). Kraków, Poland: Impuls Publishers. (Original work published 1987).

Nęcka, E. (2005). *Trening twórczości* [Creativity training]. Gdańsk, Poland: Gdańskie Wydawnictwo Psychologiczne. (Original work published 1989; 2nd, 3rd, and 4th eds. published 1992, 1995, and 1998, respectively)

Nęcka, E. (1994). *TRoP . . . Twórcze Rozwiązywanie Problemów* [TroP: Creative problem solving]. Kraków, Poland: Impuls Publishers.

Nęcka, E. (1999). Creativity and attention. *Polish Psychological Bulletin, 44,* 85–97.

Nęcka, E. (2001). *Psychologia twórczosci* [Psychology of creativity]. Gdańsk, Poland: Gdańskie Wydawnictwo Psychologiczne.

Nęcka, E. (2003). Creative interaction: A conceptual schema for the process of producing ideas and judging the outcomes. In M. A. Runco (Ed.), *Critical creative processes* (pp. 115–127). Cresskill, NJ: Hampton Press.

Nęcka, E., & Brocławik, K. (1984). O możliwościach wykorzystania synektyki w procesie rozwiązywania zadań wynalazczych [On the possibility of using synectics in the process of solution of invention-type tasks]. In A. Góralski (Ed.), *Zadanie, metoda, rozwiązanie. Techniki twórczego myślenia. Zbiór 5* [Task, method, solution: Techniques of creative thinking] (Vol. 5, pp. 124–164]. Warszawa, Poland: Wydawnictwa Naukowo-Techniczne.

Nęcka, E., Gruszka, A., & Orzechowski, J. (1996). Selective attention in gifted children. *Polish Psychological Bulletin, 27,* 39–51.

Nęcka, E., & Kałwa, A. (2001). Criatividade, aprendizagem implícita e profundidade de processamento. [Creativity, incidental learning, and depth of processing]. *Psicologia: Teoria, Investigação e Prática, 6*(1), 135–147. [Journal's name: *Psychology: Theory, research, and practice*].

Nęcka, E., & Kubiak, M. (1989). The influence of training in metaphor understanding on creativity and level of dogmatism. *Polish Psychological Bulletin, 20,* 69–80.

Nęcka, E., & Kwaśniewska, J. (2005). *Climate for creativity in Polish companies: Does a new market economy need new ideas?* W. B. Jöstingmeier & H.-J.

Boeddrich (Eds.), *Cross-Cultural Innovation* (pp. 237–259). Wiesbaden: Deustcher Universitäts-Verlag.

Nicholls, J. G. (1972). Creativity in the person who will never produce anything original or useful. *American Psychologist, 44,* 717–727.

Pietrasiński, Z. (1969). *Myślenie twórcze* [Creative thinking]. Warszawa, Poland: Państwowe Zaktady Wydawnictw Szkolnych.

Perkins, D. N. (1981). *The mind's best work.* Cambridge, MA: Harvard University Press.

Popek, S. (1988). *Uzdolnienia plastyczne mżodziey. Analiza psychologiczna* [Artistic abilities in youth. Psychological analysis]. Lublin, Poland: Wydawnictwo UMCS.

Popek, S. (1998). *Z badań nad uzdolnieniami plastycznymi mżodziey.* [Research on artistic abilities in youth]. Lublin, Poland: Wydawnictwo UMCS.

Popek, S. (2000). *Kwestionariusz twórczego zachowania KANH* [Creative Behavior Questionnaire KANH]. Lublin, Poland: Wydawnictwo UMCS.

Popek, S. (2001). *Czżowiek jako jednostka twórcza* [Human being as a creative individual]. Lublin, Poland: Wydawnictwo UMCS.

Prince, G. M. (1970). *The practice of creativity.* New York: Harper & Row.

Pufal-Struzik, I. (1996). Demand for stimulation in young people with different levels of creativity. *High Ability Studies, 7,* 145–150.

Pufal-Struzik, I. (1998). Self-acceptance and behaviour control in creatively gifted young people. *High Ability Studies, 9,* 197–205.

Pufal-Struzik, I. (1999). Self-actualization and other personality dimensions as predictors of mental health of intellectually gifted students. *Roeper Review, 22,* 44–47.

Rawlings, D. (1985). Psychoticism, creativity and dichotic shadowing. *Personality and Individual Differences, 6,* 737–742.

Reber, A. S. (1992). An evolutionary context for the cognitive unconscious. *Philosophical Psychology, 5,* 33–51.

Renzulli, J. S. (1986). The three ring conception of giftedness. In R. J. Sternberg & J. Davidson (Eds.), *Conceptions of giftedness* (pp. 53–92). New York: Cambridge University Press.

Rosch, E. (1973). Natural categories. *Cognitive Psychology, 4,* 328–350.

Rudowicz, E., & Hui, A. (1997). The creative personality: Hong Kong perspective. *Journal of Social Behavior and Personality, 12,* 139–157.

Rudowicz, E., & Hui, A. (1998). Hong Kong Chinese people's view of creativity. *Gifted Education International, 13,* 159–174.

Rudowicz, E., & Yue, X. D. (2002). Compatibility of Chinese and creative personalities. *Creativity Research Journal, 14,* 387–394.

Runco, M. A., & Charles, R. (1997). Developmental trends in creative potential and creative performance. In M. A. Runco (Ed.), *Creativity research handbook* (Vol. 1, pp. 115–152). Cresskill, NJ: Hampton Press.

Słabosz, A. (2000). *Elementarne skżadniki procesu twórczego – aktywacja semantyczna i inhibicja poznawcza.* [Elemental components of creative process – semantic activation and cognitive inhibition]. Unpublished doctoral dissertation, Jagiellonian University, Kraków.

Słabosz, A., & Nęcka, E. (2005). *Creativity and processing of visual feature conjunctions: Serial or parallel?* Manuscript submitted for publication.

Smith, G. J. W. (1990). Creativity in old age. *Creativity Research Journal, 3,* 249–264.

Smith, G. J. W., & Meer, van der, G. (1994). Generative sources of creative functioning. In M. P. Shaw & M. A. Runco (Eds.), *Creativity and affect* (pp. 147–167). Norwood, NJ: Ablex.

Sołowiej, J. (2000). Badania nad efektywnościąburzy mózgów [Research on effectiveness of brainstorming]. *Annales Universitatis Mariae Curie-Skżodowska. Sectio J* (Vol. XIV). Lublin, Poland: Wydawnictwo UMCS.

Staabs, von, G. (1991). *The scenotest.* Bern: Hogrefe & Huber. (Original work published 1964)

Stavridou, A., & Furnham, A. (1996). The relationship between psychoticism, trait-creativity and the attentional mechanism of cognitive inhibition. *Personality and Individual Differences, 21,* 143–153.

Stein, M. I. (1953). Creativity and culture. *Journal of Psychology, 36,* 311–322.

Strelau, J., Angleitner, A., & Ruch, W. (1990). Strelau Temperament Inventory (STI): General review and studies based on German samples. In J. N. Butcher, & C. D. Spielberger (Eds.), *Advances in personality assessment* (Vol. 8, pp. 187–241). Hillsdale, NJ: Erlbaum.

Stróżewski, W. (1983). *Dialektyka twórczości* [Dialectics of creativity]. Kraków Poland: Państwowe Wydawnictwo Muzyczne.

Strzałecki, A. (1969). *Wybrane zagadnienia psychologii twórczości* [Selected problems in psychology of creativity]. Warszawa Poland: Państwowe Wydawnictwo Naukowe.

Strzałecki, A. (1989). *Twórczość a style rozwiązywania problemów praktycznych* [Creativity and real-life problem-solving styles]. Wrocław, Poland: Ossolineum.

Strzałecki, A. (1998). Creativity as a style. General model and its verification. In A. Lewicka-Strzażecka & O. Loukola (Eds.), *Science and society. Science, policy and ethics* (pp. 119–160). Warszawa Poland: IFiS Publishers.

Strzałecki, A. (2001). Twórcza przedsiębiorczośń. Próba analizy psychologicznej [Creative entrepreneurship. Psychological analysis]. *Prakseologia, 141,* 417–440.

Strzałecki, A., & Kot, D. (2000). Osobowościowe wymiary twórczej przedsiebiorczosci [Personality dimensions of creative entrepreneurship]. *Przeglad Psychologiczny, 3,* 351–360.

Strzałecki, A., & Kusal, A. (2002). Temperamentalne i osobowosciowe mechanizmy sprawnego zarządzania [Temperament and personality as mechanisms underlying efficient management]. *Studia Psychologica, 3,* 5–20.

Szmidt, K. J. (1995). *Porządek i przygoda – Lekcje twórczości. Przewodnik metodyczny dla nauczycieli* [The order and adventure – Creativity Classes. The handbook for teachers]. Warszawa, Poland: Wydawnictwa Szkolne i Pedagogiczne. (2nd and 3rd eds. published 1996 and 1997, respectively).

Szmidt, K. J. (1998). *Program kursu psychopedagogiki twórczości dla realizatorów programu edukacyjnego: Porządek i przygoda – lekcje twórczości* [The psychopedagogical program for teaching creativity: Order and adventure – lessons of creativity]. Warszawa, Poland: Wydawnictwa Szkolne i Pedagogiczne.

Szmidt, K. J. (2003). Współczesne koncepcje wychowania do kreatywności i nauczania twórczości: Przegląd stanowisk polskich [Contemprorary theories of nurturing and teaching creativity: A review of Polish conceptions]. In K. J. Szmidt (Ed.), *Dydaktyka twórczości. Koncepcje, problemy, rozwiązania.* [Creative education. Conceptions, problems, solutions]. Kraków, Poland: Impuls Publishers.

Szmidt, K. J., & Bonar, J. (1998). *Program edukacyjny "Żywioły. Lekcje twórczości w nauczaniu zintegrowanym"* [Educational program "Elements. Creativity classes in primary grade education"]. Warszawa, Poland: Wydawnictwa Szkolne i Pedagogiczne.

Szuman, S. (1927). *Sztuka dziecka. Psychologia twórczości rysunkowej* [Child's art: The psychology of creativity in drawing]. Warszawa, Poland: Ksiąnica – Atlas.

Tatarkiewicz, W. (1976). *Dzieje sześciu pojęć* [History of six notions]. Warszawa, Poland: Państwowe Wydawnictwo Naukowe.

Thagard, P. (1997). Coherent and creative conceptual combinations. In T. B. Ward, S. M. Smith, & J. Vaid (Eds.), *Creative thought. An investigation of conceptual structures and processes* (pp. 129–144). Washington, DC: American Psychological Association.

Tokarz, A. (1985). *Rola motywacji poznawczej w aktywności twórczej.* [The role of cognitive motivation in creative activity]. Wrocżaw, Poland: Ossolineum.

Tokarz, A. (1989a). O wzbudzaniu ciekawości. Część I: Charakterystyka zjawiska [Eliciting curiosity. Part I: Characteristics of the Phenomenon]. *Przegląd Psychologiczny, 32*(3), 729–747.

Tokarz, A. (1989b). O wzbudzaniu ciekawości. Część II: Stymulatory ciekawości i motywacji poznawczej [Eliciting curiosity. Part II: Stimulators and inhibitors of curiosity and cognitive motivation]. *Przegląd Psychologiczny, 32*(4), 899–921.

Tokarz, A. (1996). Wstępna korekta modelu autonomicznej motywacji poznawczej [The revision of the cognitive, autonomic motivation model]. In A. Grochowska, A. Jakubik, I. M. Marcysiak, S. Siek, A. Strzażecki, & J. Terelak (Eds.), *Studia z psychologii* [Studies in psychology] (Vol. VII, pp. 205–228). Warszawa, Poland: Wydawnictwo ATK.

Tokarz, A. (1998). Motywacja hubrystyczna i poznawcza jako dominanty systemu motywacji do pracy naukowej [Hubristic and cognitive motivation as determinants of motivational system in academic career]. *Przegląd Psychologiczny, 4,* 121–134.

Tokarz, A., Beauvale, A., żyła K., & Rudowicz, E. (2004, June 3–6). *Cechy poądane dla Polaków w opinii polskich studentów: Czy jest w nich miejsce dla twórczości* [Desired traits for Poles, according to Polish students. Is there creativity among them]? Paper presented at the Eighth National Conference of Polish Developmental Psychology, Augustów, Poland.

Tokarz, A., & Groborz, M. (2001). Recent advances in creativity research and applied projects in Poland. In M. I. Stein (Ed.), *Creativity's global correspondents 2001.* New York: Winslow Press.

Tokarz, A., & Sżabosz, A. (2001a). Cechy uczniów preferowane przez nauczycieli jako wymiar aktywności twórczej w szkole. Cz. I. Style Twórczego zachowania badanych nauczycieli [Teachers' perception of students' traits as a dimension of creative activity in school. Part I. Teachers' styles of creative behavior]. *Edukacja. Studia. Badania. Innowacje, 2,* 68–75.

Tokarz, A., & Słabosz A. (2001b). Cechy uczniów preferowane przez nauczycieli jako wymiar aktywności twórczej w szkole. Cz. II. Uczeń idealny i twórczy w preferencjach badanych nauczycieli [Teachers' perception of students' traits as a dimension of creative activity in school. Part II. An ideal and creative student as perceived by teachers]. *Edukacja. Studia. Badania. Innowacje, 3,* 36–48.

Tokarz, A., & Słabosz, A. (2002). Report on the creativity activities in Poland in the year 2002. In M. I. Stein (Ed.), *Creativity's global correspondents 2002.* New York: Winslow Press.

Tokarz, A., Żyła, K., Beauvale, A., & Rudowicz, E. (in press). Twórczość jako element wiedzy potocznej – dane z badań polskich i chińskich [Creativity as a component of implicit knowledge. Comparative analysis of nominations of the most creative Poles and Chinese]. *Psychologia Rozwojowa.*

Tokarz, A., Żyła, K., Ganczarek, J., Kudyba, K., & Latocha, A. (in press). Twórczość jako element wiedzy potocznej. Rezultaty analizy jakościowej nominacji na najbardziej twórczych Polaków i Chińczyków. [Creativity as a component of implicit knowledge. Qualitative analysis of nominations of the most creative Poles and Chinese] *Psychologia Rozwojowa.*

Trzebiński, J. (1978). *Z badań nad uwarunkowaniami oryginalności myślenia* [Research on the determinants of originality of thinking]. Wrocżaw: Ossolineum.

Trzebiński, J. (1981). *Twórczośń a struktura pojęć* [Creativity and the structure of concepts]. Warszawa: Państwowe Wydawnictwo Naukowe.

Ward, T. B. (1994). Structured imagination: The role of category structure in exemplar generation. *Cognitive Psychology, 24,* 1–40.

Weisberg, R. W. (1986). *Creativity. Genius and other myths.* New York: Freeman.

Weisberg, R. W. (1999). Creativity and knowledge: A challenge to theories. In R. J. Sternberg (Ed.), *Handbook of creativity* (pp. 226–250). Cambridge, U.K.: Cambridge University Press.

Yue, X. D., & Rudowicz, E. (2002). Perception of the most creative Chinese by undergraduates in Beijing, Guangzhou, Hong Kong and Taipei. *Journal of Creative Behavior, 36,* 88–104.

11

Research on Creativity in Israel

A Chronicle of Theoretical and Empirical Development

Roberta M. Milgram and Nava L. Livne

Israel is a small country in which the academic and creative abilities of people are considered a major natural resource (Milgram, 2000). The identification and education of gifted and talented children and adolescents have been the focus of considerable interest in Israel for many years. The rationale underlying this interest is that a small country, bereft of natural resources, must place high priority on its human resources, that is, on the abilities and talents of its people. This chapter is divided into four sections. In the first section, we present a summary of research in Israel on topics of creativity. In the second section, we present a theoretical model of the structure of giftedness and creativity (Milgram, 1989, 1991) that has generated the bulk of theory-driven empirical research on creativity in Israel. In the third section we report on international research on learning style and creativity that included Israel, and in the fourth section we discuss new directions in research on creativity in Israel.

CREATIVITY RESEARCH IN ISRAEL

In an effort to include in this chapter as much of the research done in Israel on creativity as possible, we conducted a computerized search by using several electronic databases, including FirstSearch (ERIC and MEDLINE) and EBSCO (PsychINFO). We searched these databases for the years from 1970 to 2004, using *creativity* and *Israel* as the two leading keywords and combinations of *creativity* and *Israel* with other keywords. This search yielded fourteen studies that we considered appropriate to report in the current section. We were also acquainted with the work of four Israeli researchers (Ziv, Landau, Kreitler, and Kreitler) and included it in this section. The work of Milgram and her associates is presented in subsequent sections.

Ziv

Ziv has been active for many years in the field of gifted education in Israel (Ziv, 1976a, 1977, 1990, 1998). He has also focused on the psychology of humor (1979, 1981, 1984, 1994), investigated the relationship of humor and creativity, and found that humor can enhance both learning and creativity. In an experimental study, Ziv (1976b) found that adolescents who listened to humor performed significantly better on creative thinking, as measured by the Torrance Tests of Creative Thinking (Torrance, 1966), than those who did not. In a related study (Ziv, 1983), adolescents who viewed humorous film clips and were asked to write captions for the cartoons scored higher on the Torrance tests than adolescents who were not exposed to this condition. Ziv concluded that a humorous atmosphere enhances creativity. In a third study (Ziv & Gadish, 1990), high-IQ gifted adolescents who received high scores on a sociometric test of humor were found to be more creative, more extroverted, and lower in need for social approval than gifted adolescents who scored lower on the humor test. The researchers suggested that humor helps gifted adolescents become more sociable. Finally, Ziv (1988) described two Israeli projects designed to foster creativity in adolescents, in which he encouraged teachers to use humor in their classroom instruction in order to enhance creativity. Overall, Ziv's work made an important contribution to our understanding of the influence of humor on creative thinking.

Landau

In most of her work, Landau focused on high-IQ academically gifted children (Landau, 1979, 1981, 1990; Landau & Wiessler, 1993; Landau, Wiessler, & Golod, 2001). In this section, only her research on creativity is reported.

Landau (1973)

Landau explored the role of creativity in the psychotherapeutic process. First, she conducted lengthy discussions with artists and scientists on what creativity meant to them. On the basis of these discussions, Landau proposed that psychotherapy might be a creative process, whereby new connections and relationships are created that result in new experiences and a new outlook on life. She then conducted guided psychotherapeutic sessions with three patients, during which the patients received directions and encouragement to become open to the environment in spite of their anxiety, to consider unfamiliar elements and pieces of information, and to fit them into new combinations. Landau reported that this therapeutic process led her patients to produce nonstandard, creative ways to develop more successful social contacts. On the basis of this case material, she concluded that the psychotherapeutic process itself could be a creative process that helps patients change maladaptive behavioral patterns and develop new and more constructive ones.

Landau and Maoz (1978)

The investigators examined the relationship of creativity and self-actualization to one's adjustment to aging and attitude toward death. Twenty-five new residents (ages sixty-five to seventy-three) in two Israeli homes for the elderly were interviewed about their new lifestyle in the home. Creativity was defined as an ability to break habits in order to initiate new behavioral patterns. The creativity measure in this study was a three-item Torrance-type scale scored for fluency, flexibility, and originality. The self-actualization measure, based on Maslow's hierarchy of needs (Maslow, 1943, 1954), consisted of a three-item scale scored for self-preservation, perceived respect from one's social group, and personal actualization of love and independence. Adaptation to aging was measured with reference to general adjustment to the home for the elderly and adaptation to illness and limited physical activity. Those elderly residents who received high scores on creativity and self-actualization were better adjusted to their life circumstances and had a more positive attitude toward death.

Landau (1981)

Landau examined the relationship between intelligence and personality traits associated with creativity in high-IQ gifted and nongifted high school students. She found no relationship between intelligence and personality traits associated with creativity. She suggested that a more complex research design including a psychometric measure of intelligence and creative thinking would clarify the relationships of personality characteristics to these measures. The next study was designed to examine this possibility.

Landau and Wiessler (1998)

Landau and Wiessler researchers explored the relationship of emotional maturity to creativity and intelligence in high-IQ gifted and nongifted children. Intelligence was measured with the Milta Intelligence Scale (Ortar, 1973) and Raven's Progressive Matrices tests (Raven, 1947). Creativity was measured with Torrance's Circles (Torrance, 1972) subtest, scored for fluency and flexibility. Emotional maturity was measured by summing scores of items selected from five measures of self-concept (Feldhusen, 1986; Gruber, 1982; Pearson & Beer, 1990), stress and anxiety (Beer, 1991; Landau, 1979; Lovecky, 1992), independence (Albert & Runco, 1986; Baumrind, 1971), peer group relationships (Kline & Short, 1991; Whitmore, 1986), and family interactions (Kline & Short, 1991; McGuffog, Feiring, & Lewis, 1987). Landau and Wiessler found that gifted children scored higher on both fluency and flexibility scores than nongifted children, and that emotionally mature gifted children scored higher on the fluency measure than less emotionally mature gifted children. On the basis of these findings, the researchers concluded that the interaction of intelligence and emotional maturity facilitates creative thinking.

Kreitler and Kreitler

Kreitler and Kreitler, highly respected Israeli researchers, investigated an aspect of creativity not investigated by other researchers in Israel. Most of the empirical research discussed in this chapter deals with the cognitive processes involved in creative behavior and the personality and sociocultural influences that affect the realization of creative ability. Kreitler and Kreitler are unique in their approach to creativity. In their widely acclaimed book, *Psychology of the Arts* (Kreitler & Kreitler, 1972), they focus on the *creative person* and the *process* through which that person experiences and understands real-world aesthetic products. In an effort to understand what art is, how it is created, and how it affects people, Kreitler and Kreitler conducted in-depth discussions of these issues with researchers, teachers, and students.

On the basis of these discussions, they concluded that there are two types of creative people, those who create art and those who view the works of artists. Creators experience art actively, and this process results in the creation of a new product. Spectators consume art passively and decide whether an artistic product is creative (Kreitler & Kreitler, 1972, p. 5). The processes of the artist's creativity and the motivation to generate innovative art creations at different levels of artistic expression are complex, unique, and difficult to understand. The psychological processes involved in the spectator's experience of art have both unique and non-unique characteristics, and they are simpler and easier to analyze. Spectators greatly outnumber creators of art and are much easier to identify. Kreitler and Kreitler (1972) focused on spectators of art. According to the Kreitlers, "it is the spectators who judge what is aesthetically creative and enjoyable, and from whom we can get a deeper insight into the beauty of art and its impact on human beings" (p. 6).

They cited two phases of the experience of art by the spectator: the perceptual-cognitive and the motivational. In the perceptual-cognitive phase, the work of art is a stimulus that elicits a response. In the motivational phase, the experience of art is motivated by psychological tensions that existed prior to the specific art experience within the personality of the spectator. These existing psychological tensions trigger the production of new tensions in response to the work of art (Kreitler & Kreitler, 1972, p. 6). These creative psychological processes allow the spectator to give meaning to the work of art and impose no restrictions on the development of meaning as the different aspects of the work of art gradually unfold for the spectator.

Kreitler and Kreitler operationally defined the acquisition of meaning or understanding of an art product by the spectator as a utilization of attributes or different combinations of attributes that result in the creative process of experiencing art (Kreitler & Kreitler, 1968, 1971). For example, in painting, color and form are the basic aspects of art. However, by combining color with movement rather than with form, a new and different meaning can be given by the spectator to the art product, which extends the range of depth of the effects produced by color to those produced by movement (Kreitler & Kreitler, 1972). In music, rhythm is the main dimension in which different types of organization result in different meaning of the artwork. In dance, the formal features of the movement are the basic dimension. However, the particular and sometimes unique expression of the movement is another dimension that can lead to a more creative understanding of either a single dancer or group of dancers. Operational definitions of art creations in sculpture and literature are specified in the theory as well. Kreitler and Kreitler suggested that experiencing art can be used to help people, especially to those with mental and physical disabilities, to develop meaning for their existence and to achieve wellness (Kreitler & Kreitler 1972).

Overall, the Kreitlers' (1972) theory of experiencing art may be thought of as a map that reflects major landmarks in the creative process of experiencing art. The merit of the theory resides in its generality, in that it provides guidelines for experiencing art for different users. For researchers, the map provides a basis for a theoretical framework for examining creative works of art. For art teachers, it offers guidelines to enhance their attention, sensitivity, and awareness to different aspects reflected in the artwork of their students. For art critics, the map defines explicit criteria to evaluate works of art and their possible impact on the spectators of art. For the common spectator, the map provides a means to better understand why one enjoys a particular work of art, and not another, and how one can decrease the gap between daily life and the experience of art. To pay tribute to the high quality of their research, in 1998 the Israel Museum in Jerusalem hosted their most popular exhibit of all time, "The Joy of Color," which summarized the research of Hans and Shulamit Kreitler on the psychology of color (Spencer, 2000).

Koichu, Berman, and Moore (2003)

These researchers examined heuristic strategies in the process of mathematical problem solving in a two-phase study. In the first phase, the researchers investigated heuristic strategies among eight academically gifted, high-IQ students, five of whom were members of the Israeli team for the International Olympics in Mathematics. On the basis of previous studies (Gorodetsky & Klavir, 2003, Montague & Applegate, 1993; Smith, diSessa, & Roschelle, 1993; Verschaffel, 1999), Koichu, Berman, and Moore (2003) defined *heuristic strategies* as standard or nonstandard approaches used in problem solving (analysis, representation, and transformation) to better understand a problem or to make progress toward its solution. The eight research participants were given a set of five problems – two geometric, two algebraic, and one open question. As they solved the problems, they were asked to speak out loud and to explain the strategies they were using to solve the problems. This think-aloud process was tape recorded while the students were working. When the participants had finished solving the problems, they were interviewed individually and asked to explain the strategies they used to solve the problems in their own words.

In the second phase of the study, a six-month-long intervention program designed to teach heuristic strategies in solving mathematical problems was conducted in a regular school with twelve nongifted eighth graders as research participants. The program was conducted twice a week in regular mathematics classes. One of the researchers taught these learners how to use the heuristic strategies in mathematical problem solving used by the highly gifted "experts" who had participated in the first phase of the study.

The twelve research participants were given three sets of mathematical problems defined as creative in that each required more than one strategy for a correct solution. While the research participants were working on the problems, they followed the same think-aloud format used in the first phase.

When the participants had finished solving the problems, each student was interviewed and asked to explain the strategies used in his or her own words. On the basis of the tape-recorded think-aloud protocols and the results of the subsequent interviews, the investigators developed a scoring system for analyzing patterns of heuristic strategies used by students as they solve mathematical problems that require creative thinking. The use of heuristic strategies was measured three times, that is, at the beginning, in the middle, and at the end of the intervention. The results indicated that the number of heuristic strategies used at the end was significantly higher than the number used at the beginning of the intervention.

On the basis of the findings of the two aforementioned studies, Koichu and his associates suggested that the heuristic instructional training they developed could be used to enhance creative thinking in mathematics in both gifted and nongifted learners.

Klavir and Gorodetzky (2001)

Klavir and Gorodetzky compared the process of problem solving in mathematics in two modalities, one visual-humorous and one verbal, in gifted and nongifted middle-school-aged children. Cartoons were used as stimuli for the visual-humorous modality and word problems for the verbal modality. The cartoons were considered to be creative stimuli, in that they generated more nonstandard ideas for problem solving as compared with standard academic word problems (Clabby, 1980). The problems used in the two modalities were identical in degree of difficulty; they differed only in modality. The children were asked to solve two problems in one modality, were exposed to the solutions in that modality, and then asked to solve two analogous problems in the other modality. Half the children were first exposed to the visual-humorous modality and then the verbal, and the others, the opposite.

The findings indicated that the gifted students received higher scores on the verbal problems after practice with the visual-humorous problems than they received on the visual-humorous problems after practice with the verbal problems. The opposite was found with the nongifted children. They received higher scores on the visual-humorous problems after practice with verbal problems than they received on the verbal problems after practice with visual cartoon problems. Klavir and Gorodetzky (2001) concluded that tasks using analogical visual-humorous or verbal problems could provide a valid measure for differentiating between the mathematical problem-solving processes of gifted and nongifted students. An additional interesting finding was that both the gifted and nongifted students improved their mathematical problem-solving skills on problems in both modalities after being exposed to the solution of problems in the visual-humorous cartoons modality.

Gorodetzky and Klavir (2003)

In a follow-up of the earlier study with a new sample of gifted and nongifted middle-school-aged children, the investigators instituted a think-aloud, tape-recorded procedure and made variations in the number of problems presented. They found, as expected, that gifted students were more successful in solving the problems in both modalities than nongifted students (70 percent vs. 30 percent correct solutions); gifted and nongifted children alike received higher scores on verbal and visual-humorous problems after practice than before practice. An analysis of the think-aloud data indicated that the gifted children spontaneously employed similar subprocesses (e.g., extracting information from the given problem and combining this information with presolution knowledge both before and after practice). By contrast, the nongifted children used only their presolution knowledge when they were first exposed to the problems, but they combined prior knowledge with knowledge extracted from the problems after the practice exposure to the solutions to the problems.

Gorodetzky and Klavir concluded that the think-aloud technique provided a way to understand the solution process as a whole as well as to identify points of strength and weakness in gifted and nongifted students when they were solving mathematical problems in either modality.

Barak (2004a)

Barak compared the efficacy of two methods of teaching high school electronics students how to produce computer projects. Research participants were fifty high school seniors, randomly selected from six schools, working in teams of two on twenty-five projects with personal computers over a period of ten months. Half of the teams developed their projects working on their own, while half interacted in the course of their project by means of the Internet with other high school students of the same age. Barak (2004a) reported that the students in the Internet-interaction group used cognitive flexibility and freedom of action to examine new ideas spontaneously; made progress by trial and error; and created successful innovative electronic products. By contrast, students in the personal-computer-only group produced more conventional products. Barak concluded that Internet interaction provides an opportunity to enhance creative achievement in students studying engineering and scientific subjects.

Barak and Goffer (2002)

Another phase of Barak's research dealt with enhancing innovative design and creative problem solving in industry. Numerous investigators (Goldenberg & Mazursky, 1999, 2002; Goldenberg, Mazursky, & Solomon, 1999; Kanter, Kao, & Wiersema, 1997; Multifamilypro, 2001) claim that people learn efficient techniques for solving problems or developing new products by breaking problems down to basic components and systematically combining the various components in order to achieve a new result.

Barak and Goffer (2002) examined the influence of one method on finding inventive solutions to technological problems. The method they investigated was systematic inventive thinking (SIT; Horowitz, 2001; Horowitz & Miamon, 1997), an elaboration of TRIZ, the Russian acronym for the theory of inventive problem solving (Altshuller, 1986, 1996). Barak and Goffer conducted the research in a medium-sized plant in Israel that manufactures measuring instruments (e.g., measuring tapes, squares, and rulers for professional and domestic use). A series of SIT workshops was given for twenty staff members. Participation in the workshops led to the development of a range of new, original, and commercially successful products. Barak and Goffer suggested that educators and scholars in technology education could successfully foster systematic original thinking and problem solving in their students by using these industry-based methods.

Barak (2004b)

On the basis of the aforementioned findings, Barak (2004b) evaluated other methods presumed to promote creative thinking for innovative design and problem solving in industry. He reported on TRIZ (Altshuller, 1986, 1996); SIT (Horowitz, 2001; Horowitz & Miamon, 1997); the substitute, combine, adapt, modify, put to other purposes, eliminate, and rearrange or Reverse, or SCAMPER, method (Eberle, 1997); and the eight-dimensional method (EDM; Raviv, 2002). By studying these methods and by using the results of his earlier study (Barak & Goffer, 2002), Barak concluded that these techniques for inventive problem solving enhance the capability of engineers and designers to produce innovative and commercially successful products.

THE 4 × 4 STRUCTURE OF GIFTEDNESS–CREATIVITY: A HEURISTIC MODEL

This section deals with theory-driven programmatic research conducted by Milgram over a period of thirty years. One impetus for the heuristic model formulated by Milgram was the controversy about whether creativity is general across different domains or is specific within a domain. The issue came to the forefront in the literature in the 1980s. Kaufman and Baer (2005) recently presented a systematic and integrative summary of the knowledge that has accumulated on this important question. With reference to this issue, Milgram (1990) takes the position that (a) general creative thinking, defined as ideational fluency, is a critical component of creative talent in every domain, and (b) creative thinking specific to a given domain is also necessary for optimal creative performance in that domain. In an effort to define operationally and to confirm empirically a broad formulation of giftedness that clearly included both general and domain-specific creativity, Milgram (1989, 1991) developed a multidimensional 4 × 4 model (see Figure 11.1).

Giftedness in this model is postulated as a structure with four dimensions. The first dimension consists of four distinct types of ability, two

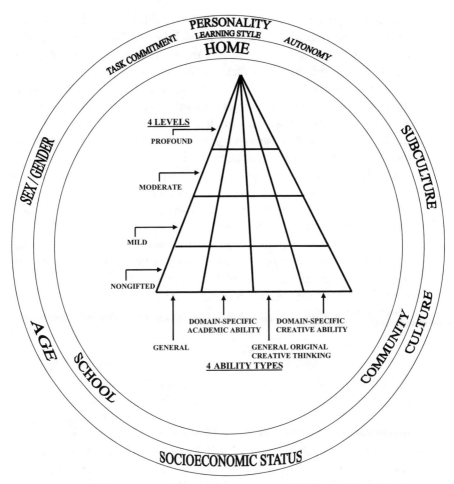

FIGURE 11.1. Milgram 4 × 4 giftedness–creativity model. (*Source*: From "Teaching Gifted and Talented Children in Regular Classrooms: An Impossible Dream or a Full-Time Solution for a Full-Time Problem?," by R. M. Milgram, Ed. *Teaching gifted and talented children learners in regular classrooms*, 1, p. 10. Copyright © 1989 by Charles C. Thomas.)

having to do with aspects of intelligence (general intellectual ability and domain-specific intellectual ability) and two having to do with aspects of creative thinking (general original or creative thinking and domain-specific creative talent). The second dimension of the structure of giftedness refers to four distinct levels of ability: one level of nongifted ability, and three levels of gifted (mild, moderate, and profound) abilities. The four ability levels represent different combinations of cognitive processes that are qualitatively differentiated by the complexity of the cognitive processes at each level. These distinct ability levels are depicted as a triangle, hierarchically ordered by their degree of difficulty, highlighting the fact that the higher the level, the fewer the number of people in society who achieve it. Each of the four types of ability may be obtained at each of the four levels. The model postulates relationships between general intellectual ability and domain-specific intellectual ability and between general original or creative thinking and domain-specific creative talent.

The third dimension of the 4 × 4 model refers to the influence of three interrelated learning environments (home, school, and community) on the actualization of these abilities in a given group or society. The fourth dimension refers to the effect on the actualization of potential abilities of individual differences: age, sex or gender, socioeconomic status, culture, subculture, and personality characteristics such as task commitment, motivation, persistence, and many others. The construct validity of the 4 × 4 structure of giftedness model (Milgram 1989, 1991) has been confirmed in studies using structural equation modeling to examine creativity in literature (Hong & Milgram, 1996) and in mathematics (Livne, 2002; Milgram & Livne, 2005).

To the best of our knowledge, this is the only multidimensional model of creativity that (a) specifically formulates the relationship between general and domain-specific creative abilities and (b) formulates four levels of each academic and creative ability category. Moreover, this theoretical model is unique in that specific psychometric measures of demonstrated reliability and validity operationally define each of the postulated components of the model. The three psychometric measures are the Tel Aviv Creativity Test (TACT; Milgram & Milgram, 1976), the Tel Aviv Activities and Accomplishments Inventory (TAAI; Milgram, 1983, 1987, 1990, 1998), and the Real-Life Problem-Solving measure (RLPS; Milgram, 2004).

The TACT

According to the 4 × 4 model, creative thinking is defined as a cognitive process of original problem solving by means of which original products of high quality are generated. A product may be a response of any kind, an idea, a solution to a problem, or an actual product in art, music, science, or mathematics. Original is defined as unusual, that is, statistically infrequent. High quality is defined as productive, valuable, or worthwhile. On the basis of the work of Guilford (1950, 1956, 1967), Torrance (1962), Mednick (1962), and Wallach and Kogan (1965), Milgram and Milgram (1976) developed the TACT. This test assesses an individual's ability to generate a large number of unusual, high-quality responses to a stimulus. Operationally, this ability is defined in terms of ideational fluency (as subsequently explained). The test has been translated into six languages and used over the years in Israel and other parts of the world (Milgram, Dunn, & Price, 1993), with research participants ranging in age from three years (Milgram et al., 1987) to young adult (Milgram, 2000).

Taken together, findings that have accumulated over the years provided considerable empirical support for the construct validity of the TACT. The TACT yields scores that are empirically distinct from intelligence test scores – even when group administered – in children, adolescents, and adults at the normal range of IQ and above (Milgram & Milgram, 1976). Consistent findings confirm the relationship between the quantitative measure of ideational fluency (the number of different responses to a given stimulus) and the qualitative measure of unusual, high-quality responses (Milgram, Milgram Rosenbloom, & Rabkin, 1978). The assumption is that the production of a large number of usual, low-quality responses is a necessary condition for the production of the relatively fewer, original, high-quality responses. This assumption is confirmed when one examines the sequence of usual and unusual responses in ideational fluency. Milgram found that popular or usual responses appear earlier in the response sequence than the unusual, high-quality creative responses (Milgram & Rabkin, 1980). Moreover, Milgram and others found the ability to generate many ideas on the TACT to predict the ability to generate many original solutions to laboratory problems in children at all age levels and in young adults (Milgram, 1983; Milgram & Arad, 1981; Milgram et al., 1987).

The TAAI

This instrument was developed to provide an operational definition and psychometric measure of the fourth type of ability postulated in the 4×4 model, that is, domain-specific creative talent. Creative thinking can be applied not only to the aesthetic domains of music, drama, dance, and art, but also to other domains that are equally important to society such as business and social, political, or religious leadership. These talents at the highest levels are evidenced in extraordinary accomplishments in their respective domains. The realization of potential talent requires time to incubate and develops as a result of life experiences. Such accomplishments are rare phenomena in adults and certainly even more so in children and adolescents. This observation does not preclude finding ways to identify and to nurture these potential talents in young people.

Creative talent may be evident long before adulthood. One way to identify specific creative talent in children before these abilities become fully realized in one's vocation is by examining leisure time, out-of-school activities. The activities in which gifted and talented children engage are often highly intellectual in nature, and they are done to satisfy their own curiosity and interests rather than to achieve high grades or to satisfy the needs of teachers and parents. The TAAI is a self-report measure of activities and accomplishments in eleven specific domains (Milgram, 1983, 1987, 1990, 1998). The inventory was developed to investigate the hypothesis that these out-of-school activities predict early evidence of creative ability in specific domains.

In developing the TAAI, Milgram distinguished between challenging and nonchallenging leisure activities. Challenging leisure activities (e.g., programming computers, conducting scientific experiments, composing music, writing poetry, or organizing peers to advocate social change) are pursued actively and enthusiastically, are intrinsically motivated, and generally require serious involvement and effort. They are more likely to be stimulating than relaxing. Challenging leisure activities lead to creative accomplishment, that is, to the generation of unusual and high-quality products in a specific domain. Nonchallenging leisure activities generally do not meet these criteria.

The TAAI (Milgram, 1983, 1987, 1990, 1998) has been translated from Hebrew into five other languages, including English, and has been used in different forms in research in many countries (Milgram, Dann, & Price, 1993). It has been used with children as young as three (Hong & Milgram, 1991), with adolescents who represent a wide range of intellectual abilities (Milgram & Hong, 1994), and with highly intellectually gifted young adults (Milgram, Hong, Shavit, & Peled, 1997). Over the years, these studies have provided moderate to strong evidence of the construct validity of the instrument (Hong & Milgram, 1996; Hong, Whiston, & Milgram, 1993).

Two longitudinal studies provided impressive evidence of the predictive validity of the TAAI (1973, 1983, 1990, 1998). One study was an eighteen-year follow-up of the students of an entire senior class characterized by a wide range of intellectual abilities (Hong et al.,

1993; Milgram & Hong, 1994); the second was a thirteen-year follow-up (Milgram et al., 1997) of highly intellectually gifted young people selected from the entire student population of Israel. Both studies demonstrated the efficacy of out-of-school activities and accomplishments as predictors of career choice and accomplishment. In both studies the results demonstrated that the performance of creative leisure activities in adolescence were better predictors of career choice and accomplishment later in life than intelligence or school grades (Hong et al., 1993; Milgram & Hong, 1994; Milgram et al., 1997). Furthermore, in both studies there was evidence of a match between the domain of adolescent leisure activities and the domain of adult occupational choice. This match was found in 35 percent of the high school students and in 45 percent of the young adults who participated in these longitudinal studies. In addition, in both studies, when activities and career choice domains were matched, career achievement was higher than when it was not.

The findings of the thirteen-year longitudinal study (Milgram & Hong, 1999; Milgram et al., 1997) indicated that (a) on the whole, the highly intelligent research participants reached high levels of accomplishment in their military service, academic studies, and subsequent careers; (b) many failed to attain these high levels of accomplishments; and (c) creative thinking and creative leisure time activities in late adolescence accounted in some measure for high levels of accomplishment in the former group, and lower levels in the latter group. On the basis of this research we concluded that, in order for an individual to attain outstanding achievements as adults, high IQ is not enough. The choice and commitment to challenging nonacademic activities in adolescence and the creative abilities, singleness of purpose, and persistence that these choices and commitment reflect are important factors in adult accomplishment.

Like others, the Israel Defense Force has also maintained an interest in creativity measures over the years. More recently, the force's Unit of Behavioral Sciences adopted tests of academic and creative thinking in mathematics (Livne & Livne, 1999a, 1999b) and challenging leisure activities in mathematics (Livne & Milgram, 1998) in the selection of military problem solvers.

Concurrent Validity: Psychometric Assessment – Authentic Evaluation
In a recent study, Milgram (2003) investigated the concurrent validity of the TAAI (1983, 1987, 1990, 1998) as a predictor of authentic talent in art, drama, social leadership, and dance. Four separate studies were done

with a total of 222 high school students in Grades 9–12. First, young
people completed the TAAI. Next, two expert judges in each of the four
domains assessed a behavioral sample of real-world performance in
that domain for each participant. Each judge made his or her assessment independent of the assessment of the other. In art, the judges were
experts who evaluated the end-of-year projects submitted by the students. In drama, professional actors or directors served as judges of the
performance of students in a drama workshop. In social leadership, the
judges were two professional workers, the director and the supervisor
of the Youth Council of which the students were members. In dance,
a thirty-minute dance class session was recorded on videotape and
judged by professional dancers. Predictor–criterion correlations were
.36, $p < .001$; .42, $p < .001$; .62, $p < .001$; and .57, $p < .001$ for art, drama,
social leadership, and dance, respectively. These correlations provided
impressive concurrent validity for the TAAI in predicting scores on an
authentic measure of accomplishment.

In summary, these findings demonstrate the construct, predictive,
and concurrent validity of the TAAI (Milgram, 1983, 1987, 1990, 1998).
The data on the role of leisure activities in predicting creative accomplishment that have accumulated over the years in Israeli research
represent an important addition to the literature of creativity. The contribution of intelligence, scholastic achievement, and personality characteristics to vocational choice and success is well recognized and frequently used in vocational guidance. The use of challenging leisure
activities as a tool in career counseling has, however, been largely
ignored. The findings reported herein indicate that leisure activities
inventories such as the TAAI are an important tool for counselors to
use in career counseling with students fo high school age.

The Relation of General Creative Ability to Real-Life Creative Problem Solving

Many investigators whose views are summarized in Kaufman and Baer
(2005) seriously questioned the contribution of general ideational fluency to creative problem solving in a specific domain. Our position is
that ideational fluency is a critical component of creative talent in every
domain (Milgram, 1990; Milgram & Livne, 2005). In order to provide evidence of the validity of this approach, a series of studies were conducted
at the College of Judea and Samaria, Ariel, Israel. In these studies the
TACT (Milgram & Milgram, 1976) served as the predictor, and real-life

TABLE 11.1. *Five Studies of General Creative Thinking and Specific Real-Life Problem Solving*

Research Participants	Predictor	Criterion Real-Life Problem Solving	Correlation
Jewish-Israeli preschool children ($n = 30$)	Creative thinking	Social leadership	$r = .35, p < .05$
Arab-Israeli children, Grades 1–6 ($n = 60$)	Creative thinking	Peer social interactions	$r = .50, p < .001$
College students ($n = 40$)	Creative thinking	Academic and personal problems	$r = .77, p < .001$
Young mothers ($n = 50$)	Creative thinking	Family interactions	$r = .63, p < .001$
Young salesmen ($n = 30$)	Creative thinking	Salesmanship	$r = .57, p < .001$

problem solving in a wide variety of domains served as the criterion measure. In Table 11.1, we present the findings of five studies. We are engaged in a meta-analysis of these data (Hong & Milgram, 2004a) and are planning to conduct studies with similar designs in other domains.

These findings document the important contribution of general ideational fluency ability to creative problem solving in real-life situations. They also indicated that creative thinking ability accounted for only a portion of the explained variance. Many other general cognitive abilities certainly contribute to the creative process. Curiosity, fantasy, imagery, problem finding, metaphoric production, and selective attention deployment have been cited as components of general creative thinking. Undoubtedly, there are many others as well.

Research in Israel on Creativity in Mathematics Based on the 4 × 4 Structure of Giftedness–Creativity Model: Livne (2002)

In a particularly important line of research in Israel, Livne and her associates developed two instruments for use in a large-scale study designed to identify creative ability in mathematics (Livne, 2002). One was the Multiscale Academic and Creative Abilities in Mathematics, or MACAM, instrument (Livne & Livne, 1999a, 1999b), used to measure academic and creative abilities in solving mathematical problems. Creative ability in mathematics was defined as solving problems that offered the possibility of generating more than one solution path or correct answer at varying levels of quality of solution to a given mathematics problem. The second was the Tel Aviv Activities and Accomplishments Inventory: Mathematics, or TAAI:M, instrument (Livne & Milgram, 1998), used to assess extracurricular activities and accomplishments in mathematics.

Two mapping sentences, one for each test, were used to define the specific conceptual components of the concepts to be assessed and to create the basis for the development of the test items for each instrument (Livne, Livne, & Milgram, 1999; Livne & Milgram, 2000). In a pilot study designed to develop a scoring guide, Livne (2002) administered the MACAM to 487 students in the tenth and eleventh grades, who represented a wide range of intellectual abilities. She interviewed a sample of these students about the processes they utilized in solving the MACAM problems. She and two professional mathematicians analyzed these think-aloud interviews and developed a detailed guide to score all items, both for assignment to one of the four postulated levels of difficulty and for cognitive complexity within each of these levels (Livne, Livne, & Milgram, 2005).

Livne (2002) administered the MACAM, the TAAI:M, the TACT, and other psychometric instruments to more than 1,000 high school students. She conducted a unified analysis of the interrelationships postulated by the 4×4 model (Milgram, 1989, 1991) among the conceptual components of general creative thinking and domain-specific creative ability in mathematics by using the structural equation modeling technique (Bollen & Long, 1993).

Livne found significant relationships between general creative thinking ability and both the ability to generate creative solutions to mathematical problems and the performance of domain-specific creative out-of-school activities ($r = .57$ and $r = .22$, $p < .001$, respectively). The findings provided strong support for the 4×4 model and indicate that general creative thinking is a necessary, but not a sufficient, condition for the emergence of creative ability in a specific domain – in this case, mathematics (Milgram & Livne, 2005).

Livne also found a significant but weak relationship between the MACAM and the TAAI:M ($r = .25$). This finding suggests that generating creative solutions to actual mathematical problems and the performance of extracurricular activities in mathematics might represent two distinct cognitive components of specific creative ability in mathematics. Previous studies indicated that some specific domains that appear closely related, such as writing short stories or poetry, involve underlying cognitive processes that are quite different from one another (Baer, 1993, 1998; Kaufman, 2002). It is reasonable, therefore, to conclude that solving mathematics problems creatively and engaging in extracurricular activities in mathematics are tapping two different substructures, the former associated with cognitive ability and the latter with motivated and persistent interest.

Milgram, Davidovich, Livne, Livne, & Lieberman (2004)

The research on creativity in mathematics just presented led to financial support by the Israel Ministry of Education and the College of Judea and Samaria in Ariel, Israel to conduct a new study. We investigated the efficacy of individualized computerized units in teaching high-school-level academic and creative mathematical concepts. Computerized units designed to teach academic and creative mathematical concepts at four levels (Livne, 2002; Livne et al., 1999) were constructed and applied to units of the high school curriculum in mathematics used by the Israeli school system. Each of eighty-four research participant college students spent ten hours over three laboratory sessions learning twelve academic and twelve creative individualized computerized units. There were three major findings. First, a very high proportion of the college students (87 percent) reached correct solutions of the problems presented to them in the individualized computerized units. This finding indicates that the students were able to attain mastery of the academic concepts by means of the computerized units. Second, participants who had studied higher levels of mathematics in high school and in precollege preparatory work learned to solve more problems by means of the individualized computerized units than those who had studied at lower levels. Students who had studied at the two increasingly higher levels of mathematics, designated in Israel as four and five units, learned to solve 91 percent and 92 percent, respectively, of the correct solutions to the problems presented to them in the individualized computerized units. Third, male and female students did equally well on these individualized computerized units. Unfortunately, no results on the efficacy of using individualized computerized units to teach creative concepts in math were obtained. We attribute this finding to the failure of the computerized units as constructed to distinguish empirically between the creative and academic concepts as postulated. The development of such units is a challenge for future research.

These initial findings represent a contribution to education of the gifted and the talented far beyond their importance for mathematics education. The use of individualized computerized units will contribute to teaching large classes of students with different levels of ability and interest in any academic domain. Moreover, the findings clearly demonstrate that girls and boys are equally capable of learning mathematics when the cognitive processes of mathematics are carefully defined, instruction is individualized and computerized, and the classroom circumstances that prevent girls from learning mathematics to the best of their abilities are neutralized. The promising approach of identifying mathematical talent theoretically and operationally described here might well be applied to the other talent domains.

INTERNATIONAL RESEARCH ON CREATIVITY AND LEARNING STYLES

The relationship between creativity and learning style in gifted and talented students was investigated in an international research project (Milgram et al., 1993). The Learning Style Inventory (Dunn, Dunn, & Price, 1987), originally in English, was translated into eight other languages and administered to approximately 6,000 adolescents in Grades 7 to 12 in nine countries (Brazil, Canada, Egypt, Greece, Israel, Korea, Guatemala, Philippines, and the United States). In seven of the nine countries, the TAAI, originally in Hebrew, was translated into six other languages and used to define the research participants as creatively gifted or nongifted in a specific domain according to the Milgram 4 × 4 model. The findings of this large-scale international study were reported in detail by Milgram et al. (1993). However, two important findings warrant inclusion in this chapter. First, adolescents who were characterized by specific creativity in one domain differed in learning style from those whose creative ability was focused in another domain (Milgram & Price, 1993). For example, adolescents talented in science reported a different profile of learning style preferences than those talented in mathematics, dance, or sports. Second, adolescents who were talented in the same domain were found to share the same learning style preferences even though they lived in different countries and were reared in very different cultures (Price & Milgram, 1993). These findings demonstrate (a) the value of international collaboration in research and in sharing knowledge in the field of gifted and talented education, and (b) that findings about gifted and talented learners in one country have implications for gifted and talented in other countries.

A new direction in research on learning style was initiated in further cooperative research between the United States and Israel (Hong & Milgram, 2000; Hong, Milgram, & Rowell, 2004). Earlier work had focused on learning style in the classroom. The new direction focused on individual differences in learning style in doing homework assignments. Hong and Milgram (2000) proposed an original conceptualization of the complex pattern of motivational, perceptual, and personal–social characteristics that are associated with homework, and they constructed an instrument to measure homework style – The Homework Motivation and Preference Questionnaire (Hong & Milgram, 1998). The new instrument was administered to 126 Israeli fifth graders along with TAAI scales of science, leadership, and dance. Findings were consistent with the hypothesis that certain homework preferences characterize students whose academic abilities are more closely associated with disciplined and systematic efforts, and other homework preferences characterize students whose talents are more creative and divergent.

Ohayon (1999) investigated the implications for homework achievement in cases of a disparity between one's preferred learning style at home and the actual learning style in the home. Disparities were found between preferred and actual homework style in children with low creative thinking. Interestingly, these disparities were easily resolved if parents were willing to make simple accommodations: to provide more light, to permit their children to move around while doing homework, and to allow them to shift from one place to another in the home as they did their homework. That a corresponding disparity was not found in children of high creative thinking ability suggests that they were able to persuade their parents to accede to their preferences or found other ways to have their preferences met. Since children high in creative thinking are able, by definition, to generate unusual and high-quality solutions to a variety of problems in their lives, it is not surprising that they were able to find ways to do their homework the way they preferred.

We recognize that teachers of large classes find it difficult to individualize instruction in terms of the learning style preferences of individual students. However, parents are able to accommodate the homework style preferences of their children, and in so doing create the conditions for optimal learning. The individualization of learning, both at home and at school, would greatly increase the degree of actualization of potential creative abilities in children and adolescents and reduce talent loss.

NEW DIRECTIONS IN RESEARCH ON CREATIVITY IN ISRAEL:
UPDATE OF THE 4 × 4 MODEL

Milgram and her long-time collaborator are engaged in preparing a book entitled *Preventing Talent Loss: Theory into Practice* that promises to make a major contribution to the field (Hong & Milgram, 2004b). The proposed book will present a major revision of the 4 × 4 model of giftedness–creativity that guided the research program reported in the current chapter, and it will indicate ways in which this model can contribute to preventing talent loss.

Many books on giftedness and creativity have appeared in the past few decades. Some focus on theories of giftedness, others on theories of creativity, and still others on school programs for gifted and talented children and youth. The Hong and Milgram book will summarize past and current theories on giftedness and creativity, their relationships, and empirical support for these theories. A perennial issue in the field has been the relationship between giftedness and creativity. This book will meet the challenge of defining this relationship systematically, examining the theoretical and empirical background of the issue, and offering a postulation that integrates creativity and giftedness.

Although some implications for talent loss have been drawn in prior books, none of the books have focused specifically on preventing talent loss. Studies have indicated that the majority of gifted children spend most of their time in regular classrooms, and the majority of these children do not receive proper education to help them realize their potential giftedness (Milgram, 1989; Tannenbaum, 1983). The Hong and Milgram book will propose some solutions to this problem. Although there are many elements associated with preventing talent loss (e.g., theoretical foundation, identification, assessment, programs), we will give a high priority to theories of giftedness because the manner in which giftedness is conceptualized necessarily influences the identification of gifted abilities and the special educational programs that will be offered to facilitate their development.

Individualized Computerized Units in Teaching Gifted and Talented Learners in Regular Classrooms

Milgram has insisted over the years that gifted and talented children of the different kinds and levels should be educated in regular classrooms (Milgram 1989, 1991) and that that instruction be individualized in terms of the abilities, learning styles, and interests of each child. The difficulty in teaching gifted and talented children in the regular classroom is reflected in the title of the opening chapter in the book in which the 4 × 4 model was first presented: "Teaching Gifted and Talented Children in Regular Classrooms: An Impossible Dream or a Full-Time Solution for a Full-Time Problem" (Milgram, 1989). Computerized instruction offers the possibility to meet the challenge of individualization of instruction and differentiation of curriculum.

The aforementioned research on individualized computerized units in Israel is a modest beginning. Development of computerized units will be a valuable tool to teachers seeking to individualize instruction and to differentiate curricula for gifted and talented learners in regular classrooms. Much research must be done before computerized instruction becomes an effective tool in the arsenal of approaches that teachers can use to help gifted and talented students learn more effectively.

Continued Theoretical and Empirical Development of the Real-Life Problem-Solving Approach

The relationship of creative thinking ability to real-world problem solving in a wide variety of situations is a major future direction for creativity research in Israel. This research will be applied not only to the performance of children and youth and their teachers, but also to the effectiveness of instruction in higher education. Davidovich and Milgram plan to administer a series of instruments to college lecturers. The predictor measures will include the TACT and the Activities & Accomplishments in Teaching Inventory (Milgram & Davidovich, 2004a). The criterion measures of effective teaching will include the Real-Life Problem Solving in Teaching (Milgram & Davidovich, 2004b), evaluations by students of their instructors' teaching, and measures of effectiveness in academic work (quantity and quality of research, service to the college, and service to the national or international community). The latter measures of teacher effectiveness in higher education will be incorporated in a new instrument, the Ariel Index of Teacher Effectiveness (Davidovich & Milgram, 2004).

CONCLUDING REMARKS

Modern conceptualizations of giftedness are broader than earlier ones and clearly specify a wide variety of real-world abilities or talents

(Gagné, 1995; Gardner, 1983; Milgram, 1989, 1991, 1993; Renzulli, 1986; Sternberg, 1988; Sternberg & Davidson, 1986; Tannenbaum, 1983). Leaders in the field assert that gifted education is undergoing a rapid shift in emphasis from seeking to identify and enhance the abilities of a highly select intellectual elite to a discipline devoted to identifying and developing a wide array of talents in the general population of young people (Feldhusen, 1994, 1995; Milgram, 2000; Renzulli, 1994; Treffinger & Feldhusen, 1996). The purpose of the programmatic research studies conducted in Israel has been to contribute theoretically and empirically to this worthy goal.

References

Albert, R. S., & Runco, M. A. (1986). The achievement eminence: A model of a longitudinal study of exceptionally gifted boys and their families. In R. J. Sternberg & J. E. Davidson (Eds.), *Conceptions of giftedness* (pp. 332–357). Cambridge, U.K.: Cambridge University Press.

Altshuller, G. (1986). To find an idea: Introduction to the theory of inventive problem solving. Novosibirsk, Russia: Nauka.

Altshuller, G. (1996). *The theory of inventive problem solving* (TRIZ), (2nd ed.). Worcester, MA: Technical Innovation Center.

Baer, J. (1993). Why you shouldn't trust creativity tests. *Educational Leadership, 1*, 80–83.

Baer, J. (1998). The case for domain specificity in creativity. *Creativity Research Journal, 11*, 173–177.

Barak, M. (2004a, June 22–26). *Implications of computer-based projects in electronics on fostering independent learning, creativity, and teamwork.* Paper presented at the International Conference on the Learning Sciences, Santa Monica, CA.

Barak, M. (2004b). Systematic approaches for inventive thinking and problem solving: Implications for engineering education. *International Journal of Engineering Education, 20*, 612–618.

Barak, M., & Goffer, N. (2002). Fostering systematic innovative thinking and problem solving: Lessons education can learn from industry. *International Journal of Technology and Design Education, 12*, 227–247.

Baumrind, D. (1971). Current practices of parental authority. *Developmental Psychology Monograph, 4*(4), 1–103.

Beer, J. (1991). Depression, general anxiety, test anxiety, and rigidity of junior high and high school children. *Psychological Reports, 69*, 1128–1130.

Bollen, K. A., & Long, J. S. (1993). *Testing structural equation models.* Newbury Park, CA: Sage.

Clabby, J. F. (1980). The wit: A personality analysis. *Journal of Assessment, 44*, 307–310.

Davidovich, N., & Milgram, R. M. (2004). *Ariel Index of Teacher Effectiveness (AITE).* [in Hebrew]. Ariel, Israel: College of Judea & Samaria, Department of Behavioral Sciences.

Dunn, R., Dunn, K., and Price, G. E. (1975, 1979, 1981, 1984, 1989). Learning style inventory. Lawrence, KS: Price Systems.

Eberle, B. F. (1997). *SCAMPER*. Buffalo, New York: D.O.K. Publishers.

Feldhusen, J. E. (1986). A conception of giftedness. In R. J. Sternberg & J. E. Davidson (Eds.), *Conceptions of giftedness* (pp. 112–127). Cambridge, U.K.: Cambridge University Press.

Feldhusen, J. F. (1994). *Professional development module: Talent identification and development*. Sarasota, FL: Center for Creative Learning.

Feldhusen, J. F. (Guest Ed.). (1995). Talent development [special issue]. *Roeper Review: A Journal on Gifted Education, 18*(2).

Gagné, F. (1995). From giftedness to talent: A developmental model and its impact on the language of the field. *Roeper Review: A Journal on Gifted Education, 18*, 103–111.

Gardner, H. (1983). *Frames of mind: The theory of multiple intelligence*. New York: Basic Books.

Gorodetzky, M., & Klavir, R. (2003). What can we learn from how gifted/average pupils describe their processes of problem-solving. *Learning and Instruction, 13*, 305–325.

Goldenberg, J., & Mazursky, D. (1999). The voice of the product: Templates of new product emergence. *Creativity and Innovation Management 8*(3), 157–164.

Goldenberg, J., & Mazursky, D. (2002). *Creativity in product innovation*. Cambridge, U.K.: Cambridge University Press.

Goldenberg, J., Mazursky, D., & Solomon, S. (1999). Creative sparks. *Science, 255*(5433), 1495–1496.

Gruber, H. (1982). *Frames of mind*. New York: Basic Books.

Guilford, J. P. (1950). Creativity. *American Psychologist, 5*, 444–454.

Guilford, J. P. (1956). The structure of intellect. *Psychological Bulletin, 53*, 267–293.

Guilford, J. P. (1967). *The nature of human intelligence*. New York: McGraw-Hill.

Hong, E., & Milgram, R. M. (1991). Original thinking in preschool children: A validation of ideational fluency measures. *Creativity Research Journal, 4*, 253–260.

Hong, E., & Milgram, R. M. (1996). The structure of giftedness: The domain of literature as an exemplar. *Gifted Child Quarterly, 40*, 31–40.

Hong, E., & Milgram, R. M. (1998). *Homework Motivation and Preference Questionnaire*. Las Vegas: University of Nevada, College of Education; Israel: Tel Aviv University, School of Education.

Hong, E., & Milgram, R. M. (2000). *Homework: Motivation and learning preference*. Westport, CT: Bergin and Garvey.

Hong, E., & Milgram, R. M. (2004a). *Creative thinking as a predictor of real-life problem solving in children, adolescents, and adults: A meta-analysis designed to validate ideational fluency measures*. Manuscript in preparation.

Hong, E., & Milgram, R. M. (2004b). *Preventing talent loss: Theory into practice*. Manuscript in preparation.

Hong, E., Milgram, R. M., & Rowell, L. L. (2004). Homework motivation and preference: A learner-centered homework approach. In H. C. Cooper & J. C.

Valentine (Guest Eds.), *Theory into practice. A special issue: Homework* (Vol. 43, pp. 197–204). Columbus: Ohio State University.

Hong, E., Milgram, R. M., & Whiston, S. C. (1993). Leisure activities in adolescence as a predictor of occupational choice in young adults: A longitudinal study. *Journal of Career Development, 19*, 221–229.

Hong, E., Whiston, S. C., & Milgram, R. M. (1993). Leisure activities in career guidance for gifted and talented adolescents: A validation study of the Tel-Aviv Activities Inventory. *Gifted Child Quarterly, 37*, 65–68.

Horowitz, (2001). Advanced Systematic Inventive Thinking (ASIT)'s five thinking tools with examples. *TRIZ Journal*. Retrieved June 15, 2005, from www.triz-journal.com/archives/2001/08/cl

Horowitz, R., & Miamon, O. (1997). Creative design methodology and the SIT method. *In Proceedings of DETC97, ASME Design Engineering Technical Conference* (pp. 1–10). Amsterdam, Netherlands: Elsevier Science.

Kaufman, J. C. (2002). Dissecting the golden goose: Components of studying creative writers. *Creativity Research Journal, 14*, 27–40.

Kaufman, J. C., & Baer, J. (Eds.). (2005). *Creativity across domains: Faces of the muse.* Mahwah, NJ: Erlbaum.

Kanter, R. M., Kao, J., & Wiersema, F. (1997). *Innovation: Breakthrough thinking at 3M, DuPont, GE, Pfizer and Rubbermaid.* New York: Harper Business Press.

Klavir, R., & Gorodetzky, M. (2001). The processing of analogous problems in the verbal and visual-humorous (cartoons) modalities by gifted/average children. *Gifted Child Quarterly, 45*, 205–215.

Kline, B. E., & Short, E. B. (1991). Changes in emotional resilience: Gifted adolescent boys. *Roeper Review, 13*, 184–187.

Koichu, B., Berman, A., & Moore, M. (2003). *The effect of heuristic training in a regular classroom on mathematical reasoning ability of middle school students.* Manuscript submitted for publication.

Kreitler, S., & Kreitler, H. (1968). Dimensions of meaning and their measurement. *Psychological Review, 23*, 1307–1329.

Kreitler, S., & Kreitler, H. (1971). Symbol and sign. In W. Arnold, H. J. Eysenck, & R. Meili (Eds.), *Lexikon der psychologie* (Vol. 3). Freiburg: Herder.

Kreitler, S., & Kreitler, H. (1972). *Psychology of the arts.* Durham, NC: Duke University Press.

Landau, E. (1973). The creative approach to psychotherapy. *American Journal of Psychotherapy, 27*, 566–578.

Landau, E. (1979). The young persons' institute for the promotion of art and science. In J. Gallagher (Ed.), *Gifted children: Reaching their potential* (pp. 146–147). Jerusalem: Kolleck.

Landau, E. (1981). The profile of the gifted child. In A. L. Kramer (Ed.), *Gifted children: Challenging their potential, new perspectives, and alternatives* (pp. 21–32). New York: Trillium Press.

Landau, E. (1990). *The courage to be gifted.* New York: Trillium Press.

Landau, E., & Maoz, B. (1978). Creativity and self-actualizing in the aging personality. *American Journal of Psychotherapy, 32*, 117–127.

Landau, E., & Wiessler, K. (1993). Parental environment in families with gifted and nongifted children. *The Journal of Psychology: Interdisciplinary and Applied, 127*, 100–105.

Landau, E., & Wiessler, K. (1998). The relationship between emotional maturity, intelligence, and creativity in gifted children. *Gifted Education International, 13*, 100–105.

Landau, E., & Wiessler, K., & Golod, G. (2001). Impact on enrichment program on intelligence, by sex, among low SES population in Israel. *Gifted Educational International, 15*, 207–213.

Livne, N. L. (2002). Giftedness in mathematics as a bi-dimensional phenomenon: Theoretical definition and psychometric assessment of levels of academic ability and levels of creative ability in mathematics. *Dissertation Abstracts International*, x, Telavis Retrieved July 28 2005, from www.tau.ac.il/education/toar3/archive/etakzir2003-5.htm

Livne, N. L., & Livne, O. E. (1999a). *Multiscale Academic and Creative Abilities in Mathematics (MACAM)* [in Hebrew]. Ramat Aviv, Israel: Tel Aviv University, School of Education.

Livne, N. L., & Livne, O. E. (1999b). *A scoring guide for the Multiscale Academic and Creative Abilities in Mathematics (MACAM)* [in Hebrew]. Ramat Aviv, Israel: Tel Aviv University, School of Education.

Livne, N. L., Livne, O. E., & Milgram, R. M. (1999). Assessing academic and creative abilities in mathematics at four levels of understanding. *International Journal of Mathematical Education in Science and Technology, 30*, 227–242.

Livne, N. L., Livne, O. E., & Milgram, R. M. (2004). *Assessing cognitive complexity within levels of academic and creative abilities in mathematics using open-ended problems*. Manuscript in preparation.

Livne, N. L., & Milgram, R. M. (1998). *Tel-Aviv Activities and Accomplishments Inventory: Mathematics* [in Hebrew]. Ramat Aviv, Israel: Tel Aviv University, School of Education.

Livne, N. L., & Milgram, R. M. (2000). Assessing four levels of creative mathematical ability in Israeli adolescents utilizing out-of-school activities: A circular three-stage technique. *Roeper Review, 22*, 111–116.

Lovecky, D. V. (1992). Exploring social and emotional aspects of giftedness in children. *Roeper Review, 15*, 18–20.

Maslow, A. (1943). A theory of human motivation. *Psychological Review, 50*, 370–396.

Maslow, A. (1954). *Motivation and personality*. New York: Harper.

McGhee, P. E. (1979). *Humor: Its origins and development*. San Francisco: Freeman.

McGuffog C., Feiring, C., & Lewis, M. (1987). The diverse profile of the extremely gifted child. *Roeper Review, 10*, 82–89.

Mednick, S. A. (1962). The associative basis of the creative process. *Psychological Review, 69*, 220–232.

Milgram, R. M. (1983, 1987, 1990, 1998). *Tel-Aviv Activities and Accomplishments Inventory (TAAI): Adolescent form* [in Hebrew]. Ramat Aviv, Israel: Tel Aviv University, School of Education.

Milgram, R. M. (1983). A validation of ideational fluency measures of original thinking in children. *Journal of Educational Psychology, 75,* 619–624.

Milgram, R. M. (1989). (Ed.). *Teaching gifted and talented learners in regular classrooms.* Springfield, IL: Thomas.

Milgram, R. M. (1990). Creativity: An idea whose time has come and gone? In M. A. Runco & R. S. Albert (Eds.), *Theories of creativity* (pp. 215–233). Newbury Park, CA: Sage.

Milgram, R. M. (1991). (Ed.). *Counseling gifted and talented children: A guide for teachers, counselors, and parents.* Norwood, NJ: Ablex.

Milgram, R. M. (2000). Identifying and enhancing talent in Israel: A high national priority. *Roeper Review, 22,* 108–110.

Milgram, R. M. (2003). Challenging out-of-school activities as predictor of creative accomplishments in art, drama, dance, and social leadership. *Scandinavian Journal of Educational Research, 47,* 305–315.

Milgram, R. M. (2004). *Real-Life Problem-Solving* [in Hebrew]. Ariel, Israel: College of Judea & Samaria, Department of Behavioral Sciences. Manuscript in preparation.

Milgram, R. M., & Arad, R. (1981). Ideational fluency as a predictor of original problem-solving. *Journal of Educational Psychology, 73,* 568–572.

Milgram, R. M., & Davidovich, N. (2004a). *Activities & Accomplishments in Teaching Inventory (AATI)* [in Hebrew]. Ariel, Israel: College of Judea & Samaria, Department of Behavioral Sciences.

Milgram, R. M., & Davidovich, N. (2004b). *Real-Life Problem-Solving in Teaching.* Ariel, Israel: College of Judea & Samaria, Department of Behavioral Sciences.

Milgram, R. M., Davidovich, N., Livne, N. L., Livne, O. E., & Lieberman, N. (2004). *Using individualized computerized units to advance the achievement of high school students in mathematics* (Final technical research report). Jerusalem: Israel Ministry of Education.

Milgram, R. M., Dunn, R., & Price, G. E. (1993). (Eds.). Teaching and counseling gifted and talented adolescents: An international learning style perspective. New York: Praeger.

Milgram, R. M., & Hong, E. (1994). Creative thinking and creative performance in adolescents as predictors of creative attainments in adults: A follow-up study after 18 years. In R. F. Subotnik & K. D. Arnold (Eds.), *Beyond Terman: Contemporary longitudinal studies of giftedness and talent* (pp. 212–228). Norwood, NJ: Ablex.

Milgram, R. M., Hong, E. (1999). Creative out-of-school activities in intellectually gifted adolescents as predictors of their life accomplishments as young adults: A longitudinal study. *Creativity Research Journal, 12,* 77–87.

Milgram, R. M., Hong, E., Shavit, Y. W., & Peled, R. (1997). Out-of-school activities in gifted adolescents as a predictor of vocational choice and work accomplishment in young adults. *Journal of Secondary Gifted Education, 8,* 111–120.

Milgram, R. M., & Livne, N. L. (2005). Creativity as a general and a domain-specific ability: The domain of mathematics as an exemplar. In J. C. Kaufman & J. Baer. (Eds.), *Creativity across domains: Faces of the muse.* Mahwah, NJ: Erlbaum.

Milgram, R. M., & Milgram, N. A. (1976). Group versus individual administration in the measurement of creative thinking in gifted and non-gifted children. *Child Development, 47*, 563–565.

Milgram, R. M., Milgram, N. A., Rosenbloom, G., & Rabkin, L. (1978). Quantity and quality of creative thinking in children and adolescents. *Child Development, 49*, 385–388.

Milgram, R. M., Moran, J. D. III, Sawyers, J. K., & Fu, V. (1987). Original thinking in Israeli preschool children. *School Psychology International, 8*, 54–58.

Milgram, R. M., & Price, G. E. (1993). The learning styles of gifted adolescents in Israel. In R. M. Milgram, R. Dunn, & G. E. Price (Eds.), *Teaching gifted and talented learners for learning style: An international perspective* (pp. 137–148). New York: Praeger.

Milgram, R. M., & Rabkin, L. (1980). A developmental test of Mednick's associative hierarchies of original thinking. *Developmental Psychology, 16*, 157–158.

Montague, M., & Applegate, B. (1993). Middle school students' mathematical problem solving: An analysis of think-aloud protocols. *Learning Disability Quarterly, 16*(1), 19–32.

Multifamilypro. (2001). *Bringing creativity to your company.* Palm Harbar, FL: The Sales & Marketing Magic Companies. Retrieved September, 2005, from http://www.smmonline.com/

Ohayon, Y. (1999). *Preferred and actual homework motivation and preference in high and low creative thinking children.* Unpublished master's thesis, Tel Aviv University, Israel.

Ortar, G. (1973). *Milta Intelligence Scale.* Jerusalem: The Hebrew University School of Education and Israel Ministry of Education.

Pearson, M., & Beer, J. (1990). Self consciousness, self esteem, and depression of gifted school children. *Psychological Reports, 66*, 960–962.

Price, G. E., & Milgram, R. M. (1993). The learning styles of gifted adolescents around the world: Differences and similarities. In R. M. Milgram, R. Dunn, & G. E. Price (Eds.), *Teaching gifted and talented learners for learning style: An international perspective* (pp. 229–247). New York: Praeger.

Raven, J. (1947). *Progressive matrices.* New York: Psychological Corporation.

Raviv, D. (2002, June, 18–21). Eight-dimension methodology for innovative thinking. Paper presented at the Annual National Conference and Exposition of the *American Society for Engineering Education (ASEE).* Montreal, Canada.

Renzulli, J. S. (1994). *Schools are places for talent development.* Mansfield Center, CT: Creative Learning Press.

Renzulli, J. S. (1986). The three-ring conception of giftedness: A developmental model for creative productivity. In R. J. Sternberg & J. E. Davidson (Eds.), *Conceptions of giftedness* (pp. 53–92). Cambridge, U.K.: Cambridge University Press.

Smith, J. P., diSessa, A. A., & Roschelle, J. (1993). Misconceptions reconceived: A constructivist analysis of knowledge in transition. *Journal of Learning Science, 3*(2), 115–163.

Spencer, M. J. (2000). *Live arts experiences: Their impact on health and wellness* (3rd ed.). New York: Hospital Audiences. Retrieved September 2, 2004, from http://www.hospitalaudiences.org/hai/pubs/monograph.pdf

Sternberg, R. J. (1988). *The nature of creativity.* New York: Cambridge University Press.

Sternberg, R. J., & Davidson, J. E. (Eds.). (1986). *Conceptions of giftedness.* Cambridge, U.K.: Cambridge University Press.

Tannenbaum, A. J. (1983). *Gifted children: Psychological and educational perspectives.* New York: Macmillan.

Torrance, E. P. (1962). *Guiding creative talent.* Englewood Cliffs, NJ: Prentice-Hall.

Treffinger, D. J., & Feldhusen, J. F. (1996). Talent recognition and development: Successor to gifted education. *Journal for the Education of the Gifted, 19,* 181–193.

Torrance, E. P. (1966). *The Torrance Tests of Creative Thinking: Norms-technical manual research edition – Verbal tests, forms A and B – Figural tests, forms A and B.* Princeton, NJ: Personnel Press.

Torrance, E. P. (1972). *Torrance Tests of Creative Thinking: Figural Test.* Lexington, MA: Personnel Press.

Verschaffel, L. (1999). *Realistic mathematical modeling and problem solving.* In J. Hamers, J. Van Luit, & B. Csapo (Eds.), *Teaching and learning thinking skills* (215–239). Lisse: Swets & Zeitlinger.

Wallach, M. A., & Kogan, N. (1965). *Modes of thinking in young children: A study of the creativity-intelligence distinction.* New York: Holt, Rinehart & Winston.

Whitmore, J. R. (1986). Preventing severe underachievement and developing achievement motivation. *Journal of Children in Contemporary Society, 18,* 119–133.

Ziv, A. (1976a). Guidance for the gifted. *Journal: School Guidance Worker, 32*(1), 45–47.

Ziv, A. (1976b). Facilitating effects of humor on creativity. *Journal of Educational Psychology, 68,* 318–322.

Ziv, A. (1977). *Counseling the intellectually gifted child.* Toronto: Toronto University Press.

Ziv, A. (1979). Sociometry of humor: Objectifying the subjective. *Perceptual and Motor Skills, 49,* 97–98.

Ziv, A. (1981). *The psychology of humor* [in Hebrew]. Tel Aviv: Yahdav.

Ziv, A. (1983). The influence of humorous atmosphere on divergent thinking. *Contemporary Educational Psychology, 8,* 68–75.

Ziv, A. (1984). *Humor and personality* [in Hebrew]. Tel Aviv: Papyrus.

Ziv, A. (1988). Using humor to develop creative thinking. *Journal of Children in Contemporary Society, 20,* 99–116.

Ziv, A. (1990). *Giftedness* [in Hebrew]. Jerusalem: Keter.

Ziv, A. (1994). *Personality and sense of humor.* New York: Springer.

Ziv, A. (1998). *Gifted and talented* [in Hebrew]. Tel Aviv: The Open University.

Ziv, A., & Gadish, O. (1990). Humor and giftedness. *Journal for the Education of the Gifted, 13*(4), 332–345.

12

Creativity in Turkey
and Turkish-Speaking Countries

Günseli Oral

Creativity in Turkey and Turkish-speaking countries in the Balkans and Turkish Republic is very colorful. In the Anatolia peninsula, hundreds of ethnicities and subcultures have mingled with each other, each protecting its own identity, for thousands of years. Turkey is surrounded by Russia (which at present includes Turkish republics such as Azerbaijan, Kyrgyzstan, Kazakhstan, and Uzbekistan), Iraq, Iran, and Syria to the east and south, and Bulgaria and Greece to the west.

Most of the Balkan countries include Turkish minorities and Muslims, such as those who live in Bosnia and Herzegovina, Croatia, Kosovo, Albania, Montenegro, and some parts of Greece and Bulgaria. Within this mosaic, the concept of creativity reflects a deep synthesis of Western and Eastern values.

It is useful to examine how fantasy is perceived in Turkish culture. The Turkish synonym for fantasy, *hayal*, originates from the Arabic word *heyl*. Interestingly, *heyl* means horse in Arabic. Thus in Turkish culture, fantasy could be described as a horse that takes its rider far away beyond the boundaries of the universe.

Today, there seem to exist two main approaches to the importance and function of fantasy within the creative process. One approach was developed by Ahmet İnam, a Turkish philosophy professor at Middle East Technical University, in Ankara. İnam (1996, p. 14) claims that fantasy is the main source of thought.

According to İnam, fantasy is the power that polishes and nourishes ideas. Because fantasy is the source of creative thinking, it can be changed into thought, action, or a product. One should keep in mind that fantasy without responsibility may be harmful, and it may take the individual in a direction that he or she is not prepared to go. İnam suggested that because fantasy is a limitless source of ideas, it has to be controlled by a strong sense of ethics. It is culture that controls and shapes the way fantasy can be used in creativity.

The second use of fantasy in the creative process was outlined by M. Yavuz Dedegil, a Turkish professor of mechanical engineering at Karlsruhe Technical University, in Germany. Dedegil described fantasy as being capable of ignoring the limits set by laws of nature. Unlike İnam, Dedegil (2004a, 2004b) suggested that, for creativity to occur, one needs to be totally unlimited in idea generation. According to Dedegil, fantasy makes one enter a new world, in which one can define space, time, and matter in entirely different perspectives, regardless of contradictions in the concepts familiar to him or her. Things that have never been seen or incidents that have never occurred can be produced and combined, modified, described, and transmitted to others. Dedegil claims that creative products may differ in appearance, but they come from the same source. Religion and superstition can be considered as the products of fantasies. Much of our thought consists of fantasy.

At this point, one can ask whether such a crazy, unreal world could be creative for one's real life and in particular for science. Could it lead to ignorance? Dedegil claims that this question could be answered by a good definition of the word *reality*. According to him, the concept of reality – and fantasy – continually changes according to the present knowledge of the facts; such a change is vital for cognitive progress. Even in modern science, fantasy products play an important role, but in these cases they are called *hypotheses* or *models*.

In this section, an interesting distinction seems to appear in the views of people from two different areas: philosophy and engineering. Whereas philosophers perceive fantasy as a tool that must be controlled by societal background and cultural needs, engineers and technologists perceive fantasy as an important item for the development of humankind, and thus they encourage nourishment of our fantasy (or idea) generation abilities.

ARTISTIC CREATIVITY IN TURKISH CULTURE

Talat Halman, a poet, scholar, and former Turkish Minister of Culture, claims that the Turkish cultural compass points in all directions. Mustafa Kemal Atatürk, founder of the Turkish Republic in 1923 and its president until his death in 1938, often said that culture is the foundation of the republic. At an age when many world leaders were propagating simplistic totalitarian ideologies, Atatürk placed his faith in the dynamics of a unique synthesis of the cultures alive in Turkey, and in the norms and values adapted from abroad (Halman, 2000).

Creativity and Aesthetics: A Proof for the Collective Unconscious

Although academic artists in Turkey accept and apply universal values and criteria in artistic creativity, Turkish folk art is anonymous. The major difference between Western and Eastern perspectives on art is that, in Western culture, art and science progress vertically (toward specialization in one specific area in depth). From an Eastern perspective, art takes place on the horizontal medium, which allows several domains to mingle with each other and synthesize into a new being. Subcultural changes in a society influence the quality of art. Artistic creativity depends on individuals and spontaneity; thus, creativity increases when individuals find ways to express themselves freely.

In Turkey, especially for women, there is little spare time in rural life. Fatma Meral Horne, a Turkish sociologist who has been investigating Turkish folk art for years, described a village woman's life like the flow of a river, perpetually striving to make life and the environment more beautiful. A Turkish village woman labors in the fields to produce food, cooks tasty meals, tends to animals, keeps her house and garden, and makes colorful and flowery outfits for all her family, for all seasons and for all cultural occasions. She also knits vests and socks, embroiders spreads and cushions, and crochets curtains. She weaves cloth and *kilim* designs filled with personal messages from her life and environment with a symbolism based on her cultural mystique and search for beauty. In Turkish folk art, topics of pain and sorrow take place only in songs, whereas in handcrafts and embroideries, the joy of life, happiness, and beauty exist. Negative feelings, such as anger or sorrow, are themed in beauty, a harmonic composition of figure and ground. Because of these attitudes and qualities in the arts, Horne (2003) claimed that the Turkish woman can be considered an idealist rather than a realist in traditional Turkish art.

From a cognitive developmental perspective, Turkish embroideries and the use of color and style in Turkish folk clothing are of significant value, especially the needle lace that is carried on the traditional head covers of most Anatolian village women. This lace is embroidered not only for aesthetic purposes but also for communication. Artistic expression and creativity are found in the motifs of the laces; interpersonal communication is done in the embroideries. For example, flowers and plants reflect love for nature and other people, whereas needle lace in the shape of red pepper reflects the woman's extreme anger toward her husband. A lace in the shape of green grass is the expression of the new bride's desire for friendship with her mother-in-law. Roses in two different colors represent a husband's mistress. Such examples indicate that Anatolian women may have a deeply organized way of communicating with others, from intimate communications to more mundane ones.

The folk art of Turkish women brings up two interesting points. One is that the quality of cognitive development and sources for formal operational thinking (Piaget, 1972) should be investigated not only in terms of academic skills but also in terms of cultural and creative context. Women in Anatolian villages are not educated in Western ways of schooling, which develop skills for inquiry, experimentation, and scientific observation. Rather, they usually receive training from their families on domestic work and caring for the household and do not receive education at school, and they are taught to accept family values and their role as women without question. Where their art is considered, they seem to possess a great potential with a high level of aesthetics and balance. Fashion, in terms of arts and clothing, is a concept that should be considered and evaluated within the cultural messages the products convey. Styles of outfits are highly appreciated when they are created by world-renowned masters of fashion. The criteria for their products to be qualified as creative must be well defined. Media are very important to establishing the aesthetic values of the modern world. Local art (although not well known) may also have enormous potential to contribute to universal concepts of creativity and aesthetics.

Artistic creativity in Anatolia seems to be an interesting field not only for anthropologists or sociologists but also for researchers interested in cognitive and cultural investigation of creativity and aesthetics.

The second interesting point with regard to Anatolian women's artistic creativity is related to the universal aspects of the arts. Regardless of the type or nationality of an artistic work, its color and form may share common features. Similar associations are found in the shape and color between needle lace and other types of embroideries of the trousseaux of teenage girls of Western and Central Anatolia, and the fine artworks of the Western masters.

Artistic Creativity in the Balkans: The Case of Two Bosnian Painters

Although the roots of creativity are common for people in different cultures, the effects of environmental and cultural factors may lead to different self-expressions and thus may result in great variations in art. Special interviews were conducted for this chapter with two famous Muslim Bosnian painters: Seid Hasanefendić Trabzon, a seventy-five-year-old graphic artist, painter, and professor at the Fine Arts Academy in Sarajevo, who uses Muslim tombstones as symbols of freedom and existence in his paintings; and Fuad Kasumović, a fifty-four-year-old academic painter and scholar who is famous for his studies of female faces and figures. During interviews, the men were asked to identify the factors that initiated their interest in painting, specific occasions and events that triggered their calling, and the effects of their personality characteristics on their career choices.

The responses of both artists were classified into two categories: variables related to childhood and family, and variables related to personality.

Variables Related to Childhood and Family
Seid Hasanefendić Trabzon and Fuad Kasumović both reported that, when they were at a young age, they were deeply influenced by one or both parents, who had artistic orientations and talents in visual aesthetics. Hasanefendić Trabzon's father was an *imam* (Muslim prayer leader) who was very talented at drawing. Hasanefendić Trabzon reported that one of the most vivid memories of his childhood was taking drawing lessons from his father when he was four years old. He added that drawing and painting were sins in Islam, as they were thought to represent human forms, which is God's business. Seventy years ago, obedience to Islamic rules was without question, and, in clear violation of his own religious values, Hasanefendić's father taught him, in secret, the principles of perspective, color spectrum, and other concepts to enhance his drawing ability. Fuad Kasumović, who is much younger than Hasanefendić Trabzon, did not have similar pressure. Rather, his mother was a fashion designer and tailor whose aesthetic dominance was famous.

His mother was the one who facilitated his artistic ability, by playing with light and colors.

Variables Related to Personality
Although both artists were born and raised in Bosnia, they witnessed different periods of history and were influenced by different variables in the changing culture. Hasanefendić Trabzon lost his parents as a teenager and had to struggle through life with his siblings. He said that difficult conditions and poverty forced him to work at an early age, but they also created self-confidence and a sense of independence. He refused to attend regular school and decided to go to an arts school, which many people thought to be of no value. Although Seid Hasanefendić Trabzon is a Muslim artist, he does not have a rigid attitude about Islam. As already mentioned, he uses Muslim tombstones as symbols of life and freedom for Muslim minorities in the Balkans.

Creative Writing in Turkey

Creative Writing Throughout Turkish History
The history of creative writing in Istanbul is rich. Ercan (2002) collected poems written on the theme of Istanbul in his book *Istanbul Poems from Byzantine To Our Day*. He examined the change and development of the poets in Istanbul over hundreds of years. The most interesting thing in his book is that the first known poet from Istanbul is Moiro (300 BC), mother of Homeros, the tragedy writer, and wife of Andromakhos, the philologist.

Writers in later years have been influenced by various developmental stages in Turkey, from the Ottoman Empire to the modern republic. Oral, Kaufman, and Sexton (2004) investigated 948 eminent Turkish writers. They analyzed gender, era, type of writing, education level, profession, and awards. The type of writing (fiction, poetry, plays, or nonfiction) and the era in which the writing was produced were both predictive of whether an author won a literary award. These two variables were interesting because they offered important clues about the cultural progress in Turkish society. Before 1920, fiction writers received more awards than poets. The authors had three hypotheses to explain this finding.

One hypothesis was that, during the Ottoman Empire, the native language was Turkish – however, the Arabic alphabet was used. This written alphabet was inconsistent with the sounds of the spoken language and created problems with rhyme and the linguistic properties of these poems, which led to many practical problems in poetic structure and design. These linguistic problems may have hurt the poets' success during this time. The second possibility was the attitudes of Ottoman sultans toward writers. The lack of a systematic and stable reward system in any area of writing during the Ottoman period meant that the messages – and, therefore, the related success of the writers – were dependent on the sultan's personal tolerance and viewpoints. The third speculation included the influence of the Koran, the holy book of Islam, on poets and poetry. The Koran was written in Arabic; therefore, it did not have the same disparity between the letters and sounds that existed in Turkish writings. Because of this harmony and strong quality of rhyme, the Koran was considered the "perfect" poem. The fluency of the messages in the Koran was considered to be highly musical and phonetic, and the prayers in the Koran were read by Islamic authorities as lyrics rather than as written texts. The Koran was not only perceived as a religious book but also as a book of poetry. This link between the Koran and poetry may have increased the association between mysticism and the arts. If poetry is thought of as a mystical art, then the individual poets may have received less credit for a brilliant creation.

Atatürk established the modern Turkish Republic in 1920, which ensured a democratic and secular political structure. Early on in the republic, all the arts were strongly encouraged. This encouragement led to a significant increase in playwriting. Oral et al. (2004) argued that before 1920 (because of Islamic guidelines), women were not allowed to participate in social and artistic venues. Dramatic plays, therefore, were performed with no Muslim women; either a non-Muslim actress performed or men performed as women. Although European plays of this time appealed to all levels of society, Turkish plays were considered a low-level form of entertainment. Playwrights may have been able to make a living but were not highly respected (p. 230).

Oral et al. (2004) showed that some measure of educational success, such as having a college degree, positively influenced a writer's success, whereas too much educational success, such as having a doctorate degree, seemed to inhibit success in writing. Too much specialization in an area may lead to scholastic thinking that is not creative; thinking within the boundaries of a particular field of interest may lead one to become too convergent. These findings are consistent with research on creativity and intelligence, in which intelligence is found to help creative performance up to a point (usually around an IQ of 120), after which point the relationship is either not significant or is slightly negative (Getzels & Jackson, 1962; Simonton, 1994).

Creative Writing and Gender Stereotypes: Being a Female Writer in Turkey

Unlike traditional and local art, writing has noteworthy complexities in the Turkish culture in terms of gender stereotypes. Females have talent in this area as well as in the other branches of the arts, but gender roles seem to create obstacles not only for writing professionally but also for the writers' self-perceptions. Erendiz Atasü, a contemporary Turkish writer, shares her thoughts about being a female writer in Turkish culture in her book, *My Writings* (2000):

> Throughout silent ages, the creativeness of womanhood remained submerged in the communal expressions of folk art. . . . The wave of Turkish women writers, which began rising during the 1960s, flowed forward from those social layers that absorbed the Kemalist movement. They were no longer daughters of the elite, but those of ordinary middle class families of towns or townships. (p. 2)

Creative Writers in the Balkan Countries: Some Samples from Turkish Minorities

Ömer Turan, a professor of history at the Middle East Technical University, examined the Turkish minority in Bulgaria from the historical perspective in his book, *The Turkish Minority in Bulgaria between 1878–1908*. In his book, the situation of Turkish minorities in Balkan countries is explained by political and cultural developments throughout history. Turan found that Turkish raids started in the thirteenth century from Anatolia to the Balkans. During the fourteenth century, the occupation of the Balkan Peninsula by Ottoman Turks was facilitated by political and social unrest in the region. The lack of unity among the Christian princes made the task of the conquerors easier. The Christian nobility of the Balkan states became allies with the Muslim forces (Ottoman Archives, 1994). The Turkish settlement in Bulgaria started in the fourteenth century and continued until the sixteenth century. Islam provided a cultural and linguistic link between the various groups of Turkish tribes and blurred the various ethnic and tribal identities and loyalties. Shortly after their arrival in Roumelia, the Ottomans started to build mosques, bridges, baths, foundations, and other public buildings in order to cultivate Bulgaria like any other area (Keskioğlu & Özaydin,

1983). Temples, mosques, free kitchens for the poor, baths, hostels, hospitals, schools, libraries, and institutions for economic, social, or cultural improvement were built to thoroughly cultivate the conquered land. Consequently, the area obtained a new face. The Turks brought their Anatolian culture with specific Seljuk and later Ottoman architecture to the Balkans (Goodwin, 1976).

Ottoman subjects were divided into two groups, as Muslims and non-Muslims. Each religious group was organized into a self-contained and autonomous community called *millet*. Each community was allowed to maintain its own traditions. All the non-Muslim subjects were granted total freedom of language, education, traditional marriage, and regulation of civil status.

The Ottoman State was spread over three continents and held more than thirty nations under its rule. It was the superpower of the time; its domination lasted about 500 years. Ottomans did not carry an assimilation policy, and they did not destroy any temples or signs of Christianity (Shaw, 1985).

In the nineteenth century, the central authority of the Ottoman Empire was no longer powerful. At the same time, the Bulgarian nationalist movement began (Dentu, 1869).

More recently, the communist regime in Bulgaria during the 1980s did not accept a Turkish presence in Bulgaria. Speaking Turkish and dressing in a Turkish way were prohibited. Religious practice was forbidden and mosques were closed and destroyed. Turkish names were replaced by Bulgarian ones, and the people who resisted were imprisoned in special camps, and even killed (Turan, 1998, p. 1). In particular, Turkish intellectuals were selected as victims, and they were forced to leave Bulgaria. Thus the intellectual part of the Turkish minority either left the country and migrated to Turkey and other Balkan countries nearby, or they had to conform to the new regime. Today, the population of Bulgaria is approximately 9 million, and the Turkish-Islamic minority is approximately 2 million. However, there is no regular newspaper or magazine for the Turkish minority. This demonstrates the decrease in the intellectual power in the minorities. As a result, there is no creative production in the area of science or arts.

Istemihan Talay, the Turkish Minister of Culture, once stated that the Balkans were one of the most important regions of the Ottoman Empire (2001). As a result, the Balkans became one of the most dominant platforms for the reflection of Turkish culture and creativity. Political developments in the nineteenth century led to the removal of the Balkans from

Turkish control; however, Turkish minorities were still part of Balkan culture. Unfortunately, because of different political views, strong relations failed to be established between Turkey and the Balkans. Some Turkish writers who are minority citizens in the Balkans prefer to publish their work in Turkey, as they feel themselves belonging to Turkey, and they expect that their work will be appreciated more in Turkey. The Turkish Ministry of Culture supports these publications and therefore contributes to the reunification of both cultures.

Depending on the assimilation policies of some Balkan countries, Turkish writers living in those countries cannot receive adequate education on Turkish language and culture. This situation leads to a difference in the shape and form of the writing, although the underlying viewpoints are similar to Turkish writers in Turkey. Poetry, for example, shares similar characteristics with the Turkish culture in Anatolia, but it also reflects the effects of European culture. Prizren, the second largest city in Kosovo, includes interesting samples of poetry in Turkish minorities. Findings show that music has been a dominant force in the culture in Prizren Turks. Recepoğlu (1991) found documents about the presence of an orchestra in Prizren in 1490. Moreover, female singers in Prizren were well known and appreciated by Prizren Turks. Prizren music included anonymous poems, written about a particular event in local history. In that sense, they could be considered auditory records of history. Today, civil organizations and volunteers give great support for the development of music in children and youth by offering educational opportunities to talented children.

Recepoğlu (1987) suggested that, in addition to the importance of politicians' messages to each other, messages conveyed in the poems of young poets are of significant importance in understanding how youth in Balkan countries perceive life. Many cultures and countries inhabit the Balkans, and the language of each country is given equal rights. The Balkans include Bosnia-Herzegovina, Montenegro, Croatia, Slovenia, Macedonia, Kosovo, and Serbia. Moreover, other Balkan countries such as Bulgaria, Hungary, Romania, Czech Republic, Italy, and Greece contribute to the cultural structure. Recepoğlu (1987) examined the messages conveyed in poems written by young Yugoslavian poets in the past five years, and he classified them into three groups, as a reflection of the social status of the poets: (a) youth living in poverty and with no hope for the future; (b) youth living in poverty who are nevertheless ambitious; and (c) occupied and satisfied youth, who no longer consider themselves as youth.

No matter which philosophy a poet espouses, the Yugoslavian poems tend to focus on the peace and beauty of life, similar to Anatolian folk art. Because Yugoslavia and other Balkan countries have had overwhelming experiences of war, it is understandable that young poets convey peaceful messages in their poems. Their poems may be also considered as a call to the world to end war and to initiate love and peace (Recepoğlu, 1991). This may be a defense mechanism for painful memories, and it may be reflected in the themes of beauty and energy for life.

SCIENTIFIC CREATIVITY IN TURKEY

The history of mankind is full of examples about how fantasy saved civilizations. In the Middle Ages, few people could read and write. Their "knowledge" consisted of information about nature and religious fantasies. The small governing class consisted of aristocrats and clergy. The upper-class people were believed to be wiser and more knowledgeable. This knowledge gradient was one of the basics of power the upper class held over the lower class.

In 1374, when plague broke out in Sienna and many people died, the priests were called to explain the epidemic and procure relief. The priests, who were well trained in the production and presentation of fantasies, first explained that the deceased were "sinners" and therefore had to die. However, after babies, young children, and priests themselves began to succumb to the disease, this explanation failed. Once the plague was present in a house, family members often died; it was then argued that the disease was transmitted from the deceased soul to the healthy soul. Therefore, plague-filled houses should be left alone. Many of the wealthy left their houses to escape the plague. These houses were plundered by the poor, who then contracted the plague through contact with clothing and other utensils without ever seeing a contaminated person. The explanation was then extended to utensils having a soul and being able to transmit the disease.

These mechanisms of disease transmission were a superstition that saved thousands of lives. In this case, superstition took the function of convincing proof, whereby the convincing force originates from the superstition. The disease transmission through direct or indirect contact with the patient could be proven by the analyses of the known cases and also recognized without mathematical interpretation. The scientific gap in proof of what caused the disease and how it was transmitted could not be closed because of the nonexistence of the microscope, electron

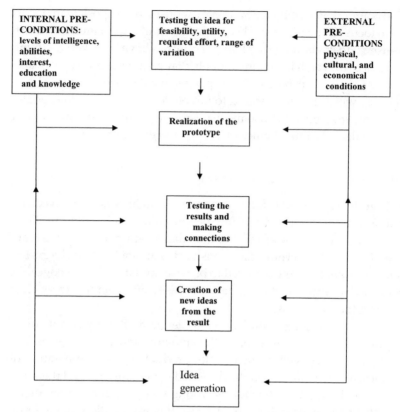

FIGURE 12.1. Dedegil's five-step model of creativity in modern science.

microscope, or any other methods for detecting microbes, viruses, and bacteria. The bridge of superstition lasted until Leeuwenhoek (1632–1723) invented the microscope and first discovered bacteria.

Dedegil (2004b) describes creative work in modern science as a five-step process model, as demonstrated in Figure 12.1. In Dedegil's model, the process of scientific creativity is nourished by internal (an individual's intelligence, education, and knowledge) and external (physical, cultural, and economical conditions) preliminary conditions. Dedegil claims that, because of such feedback, the creative process in modern science is a never-ending process. Dedegil has emphasized the importance of knowledge as the base of creative scientific progress.

It is therefore important, Dedegil argues, to have an advisor who has no emotional connections with the topic to help analyze the topic objectively and come to a logical decision. Just as bitter medicine is covered with a sweet coating, logical decisions would be accepted better when sweetened with a suitable emotion. Logical decisions have to be disguised in such a way that they pass the limbic system without resistance and come to execution. The behavior and conversations of many people reveal which disguise is suited for them.

Scientific creativity can also be examined in relation to the scope of the research in which a discovery takes place. S. Kocabas (1992b), professor at İstanbul Technical University, Department of Space Engineering, introduced a classification of scientific discovery: (1) logicomathematical discovery, (2) formal discovery, (3) theoretical discovery, and (4) empirical discovery. This classification is based on Kocabas' own categorization of descriptive knowledge (1992a), and it reflects the types of knowledge used in scientific research and the type of knowledge discovered. All four types of discovery have been studied by computational models in artificial intelligence.

According to this classification, logicomathematical discovery takes place, as the name suggests, in the abstract domain of logic and mathematics. Some of the earliest artificial intelligence systems such as Logic Theorist were logicomathematical discovery models designed to prove theorems in logic. Among several computational models, AM (Lenat, 1979) appears as a successful example for mathematical discovery. The distinguishing characteristic of logicomathematical discovery is that, in principle, it does not require experimentation or observation. It does not require the knowledge of a physical domain per se, except for analogical transference in some cases.

Formal discovery takes place in a formal domain involving abstract entities, their classes, and properties. Formal discovery requires logicomathematical knowledge as background knowledge for deductive inference on formal knowledge. Lenat's (1983) EURISKO, in its applications to naval fleet design, evolution, and three-dimensional circuit design, is a good example of formal discovery systems.

Empirical discovery is an extensively studied area, and a number of computational models have been designed to investigate its various aspects. Empirical discovery requires experimental and observational data, as well as logicomathematical and formal knowledge. Theoretical knowledge was not a prerequisite in the early empirical discoveries in the history of science (e.g., in seventeenth- and eighteenth-century chemistry), but in modern empirical research such as in oxide superconductivity and cold fusion experiments, extensive theoretical domain knowledge is necessary.

Kocabas (2004) claimed that scientific creativity has to be investigated within its natural environment, namely, within the processes of scientific research and discovery. Conventional philosophy of science, probably because of the limitations of its scope, has ignored a number of important issues. Scientific creativity displays itself in the form of scientific discovery, which, in turn, is the product of a series of complex tasks called scientific research. Therefore, a comprehensive study of science and scientific discovery requires a sufficiently rich set of concepts for a detailed and systematic investigation. Recent developments in the computational study of science provide some of these concepts. On the basis of these concepts, Kocabas introduced a more detailed definition of scientific creativity, classified scientific discovery, and creativity, and he examined the role of background knowledge in discovery within the wider dimensions of scientific research. A systematic investigation of scientific creativity cannot be conducted without considering the multiplicity of research tasks that have to be carried out by scientists during their activities.

Some practical suggestions to improve scientific thinking and scientific creativity can be derived from the views of Dedegil and Kocabas:

1. Impart the broadest possible knowledge of nature and social sciences and technology, without early specialization.
2. Impart the abilities to absorb knowledge and to express thoughts.
3. Advocate observation and experimental delight.
4. Advocate free thinking, without narrow-minded religious or moral barriers.
5. Teach the critical checking of creative ideas and one's own thoughts.
6. Teach the handling of criticism and scrutinizing questions.

Turkish Patents: Development and Problems

The number of patents in a country is a strong indicator of that country's level of scientific productivity and creative development. The quality of the products gives more information about the country's orientation and position in the creative process relative to other countries.

Although many discussions and developments take place in Turkey regarding the definition of creativity as a concept, practical implications of creativity are not considered equally. According to the National Innovation System report prepared by data obtained from the Ankara

Chamber of Commerce, the Turkish Patent Institute, the Inventors Association, and the World Intellectual Property Organization (WIPO), there have been more than 22,000 patent proposals in Turkey over the past decade. This number is reached in approximately 15 days in Japan and 20 days in the United States. In the WIPO report (2000), a patent is described as "the system which gives exclusion for a particular time period to the owner for producing, trading and using the subject of invention" (p. 217). The report states that Turkish inventors somehow cannot benefit from the rights and priorities given to the inventors in this description, and that almost 96 percent of Turkish patents are obtained by foreign inventors. There were 22,000 applications and 12,025 patents awarded in Turkey between 1993 and 2003. However, 11,545 of these patents were given to foreign nationals, whereas only 480 were Turkish. In 2001, 90 percent of 121,742 patents in Japan, 48 percent of 48,207 patents in Germany, and 83 percent of 16,292 patents in Russia were granted to natives of those countries.

Rate of Brand Creation

The number of applications for new brands in several countries is as follows (based on 2002 WIPO information): the United States had 212,971; Japan had 116,913; France had 71,944; Germany had 66,636; and Turkey had 35,818.

Turkey's rate of brand application rose to 38,219 in 2003. Of these, 30,188 were native brands, whereas 2,119 belonged to foreign brands and 5,912 belonged to international brands. According to the WIPO report, Turkey's rate is expected to eventually rise to 45,000 per year.

According to 2003 statistics, İstanbul had the highest rate of brand applications (5,518 new brands) among Turkish cities. Ankara – the capital city – followed İstanbul with 655 brands. Izmir was next with 581, and then Bursa with 512.

Applications for "useful models" of small inventions to be implemented in technology gives production and marketing rights to the new product for ten years. The rate of these applications is very low in Turkey, because inventors have to pay the Turkish government in order to guarantee their rights for their products for twenty years, even if no income is obtained from that product.

In 2004, a patent application cost approximately 5 billion Turkish lira (approximately $3,200). Thus, a patent starting from one-year protection to twenty-year protection costs more than 9 billion Turkish lira ($6,000), including taxes and other bureaucratic expenditures. These expenses are rather high for inventors who are not financially supported by the public or private sector, and it leads to the danger of decline in Turkish patents or brands on the Turkish market.

The low number of patent applications originates from lack of financial resources for scientific and technological research, limited opportunities for technology use at schools and universities, lack of reward for inventions, and "brain drain." According to the WIPO report, approximately 59 percent of Turkish researchers leave the country to seek a brighter future elsewhere. Another striking bit of information in the report is about the number of researchers in Turkey. While Turkey aimed to produce 15 researchers for every 10,000 people in the year 2003, the real number is limited to 10. Greece, in contrast, has 45 researchers for 10,000 people.

Development and Obstacles in Scientific Creativity

From a historical perspective, science has not been given enough attention in Turkey. Within the framework of scientific productivity and attitudes toward science during the Ottoman period and in the modern Turkish Republic, the government has generally ignored science, especially neglecting the contributions that universities can make to state politics (Heper, 1985, 2000). This situation has had a destructive influence on the politics of the state. Since the 1940s, politicization of universities has led to a dead end in state–university relations. This conflict led academicians to divide into two groups as supporting and opposing the regime, which has been a great obstacle for academic productivity. The negative factor has been the university structure, which discourages productivity in international standards. All these factors destroyed university prestige, which was already low in the eyes of the society and political decision makers. Media, which are influential on state policies and decisions based on these policies, have been controlled by "important" but noncreative (nonproductive) academicians; thus, academicians who are productive in international platforms were not included in decision-making procedures (Heper, 2000) in Turkish government.

Scientific creativity in Turkey has been a focus of both universities and the Turkish Science Academy for a long time. Öztürk (2002) claimed that the major obstacle in scientific creativity and related progress is inhibition of curiosity and intuition. Baysal (1999) argued that one problem is the inadequacy of scientific publications by university professors. İnönü

(1999) categorized Turkish scientific development into four stages; he explained the general characteristics of each stage as follows.

Stage 1 is the period from 1923 to 1933. These dates include the foundation of the Turkish Republic. During the early years of the Republic, institutionalization and attitudes reflecting the Ottoman Empire were prevalent. There was no noteworthy attempt at scientific research.

Stage 2 is the period from 1933 to the mid-1950s. The first scientific research attempts began with the establishment of İstanbul University Reform and the Ankara Higher Agricultural Institute in 1933. It was in these institutions, İstanbul Technical University and Ankara University, that first-generation research began and lasted until the mid-1950s.

Stage 3 is the period from the mid-1950s to the mid-1980s. The Atomic Energy Program started in 1955 and lasted until the 1980–1985 recession. During this period, the second generation of scientists emerged. At the same time, the Atomic Energy Commission was institutionalized, and the Turkish Scientific Technical Research Association (TÜBİTAK) and new universities modified their background structures and established research institutes.

Stage 4 is the period from the mid-1980s to 1998. Reconstruction of TÜBİTAK and emergence of the third generation of scientists initiated more innovative and wider progress, compared with previous stages.

Baysal claimed that, in 1998, the total number of Turkish scientific publications in the Science Citation Index was 5,150, which is equivalent to only 0.5 percent of the publications all around the world. Considering that the population of Turkey constitutes almost 1 percent of the world population, the annual number of publications from Turkey should number approximately 10,000. The major reason for this dearth of dissemination was lack of support for scientists and researchers in Turkish universities. During the past decade, a significant increase in the number of scientific publications has been observed in Turkey. These increases were caused by higher requirements brought by the Higher Educational Council for overall university promotions in Turkey, increased financial support TÜBİTAK and Turkish Science Academy, and increased support by university research foundations. However, this increase is still not adequate for Turkish scientists to have a leading role in science.

According to Baysal (1999), because the country has been ruled by dogma in its colorful and long history, some misbeliefs and prejudices preventing scientific progress became dominant. Scientific research had become a practicable profession only in the twentieth century, and it did not spread in society until after World War II. In Turkey, there is an expectation for great scientists who will lead to great progress. This seems to discourage scientists from pursuing smaller contributions, which may often lead to a big leap in the short or long term. Turkey may end up waiting for these "heroes of science" instead of supporting a larger number of active scientists. Baysal also claimed that creativity and progress in the arts and science are not the same. According to him, the world would have been the same if Einstein had not been born, because Einstein's equations implicitly existed in Lorenz's equations. In contrast, if Van Gogh or Sinan the Architect were not born, the world would not be in the way it is now. Art possesses creativity, whereas science progresses step by step.

A recent problem in Turkey is the view that scientific research could be better supported by the private sector. Baysal suggested that governmental support is necessary because there is no direct relationship between the research and financial profit. In other words, basic scientific research must be done under the support of the government. Only then might problems such as inadequacy of scientific research, difficulties in the establishment of scientific programs, and ethical problems in scientific publications in Turkish universities disappear.

Turkey's Place in the International Arena for Scientific Productivity

One indicator assessing Turkey's place among international citations is the Institute for Scientific Information rank. In 1990, Turkey was forty-first on the ISI list, and it has since increased its position to twenty-seventh, with 4,410 publications. There exists a great difference between Turkey and countries at the top of the rank (e.g., Denmark is twenty-second with 8,166 publications, Japan is third with 73,841 publications, England is second with 79,345 publications, and the United States is first with 303,308 publications). These numbers demonstrate a huge difference between Turkey and many other countries. Is there a relationship between the academic productivity and economic power of countries? The answer is no: When national income and number of publications are compared, one can see that they do not overlap. Although the research productivity of developed countries is higher, there are also differences originating from cultural diversity as well. For example, in Turkey, there were only twenty-two publications that received support for $1 billion in 1997. In 1997, there were twenty-two scientific publications in Turkey, fifty-one publications in Holland, thirty-nine in the United States, and sixty-five in England for the same amount of financial resources.

Besides these results in research productivity and publication, İnönü (1999), a physics professor and former prime minister of Turkey, claimed that the proportion of publications in Turkey did not change between 1960 and 1990; it remained at 0.004 percent. This finding demonstrates that the Turkish culture is not scientifically research oriented. According to İnönü, one way to shift focus toward science is to inform the media about recent scientific studies, objectively and continuously. International science awards are important factors that prove a country's advancement in science; however, no matter how brilliant Turkish scientists are, they are often faced with subjectivity and prejudices against research in developing countries. A scientist in a developing country has to spend extra effort to convince reviewers that his research was in fact done in that country, with its own resources. Because knowledge is perceived as power in Western cultures, scientific authorities that are well known in international platforms do not want to lose their power; thus, they do not welcome those who try to enter this platform. Resisting scientific prejudice is essential for Turkish scientists to progress. Although it seems quite discouraging at first glance, insisting on publishing research articles in international platforms is the only hope for Turkish scientists.

Heper (2000) claimed that Turkish universities must become centers in which most professors are internationally well known, productive academicians. Such centers must also actively participate in policy making. In order to create high-quality universities, it is necessary to train academicians who discover the "unknown" in the world and publish new knowledge in internationally prestigious journals. In 1993, the Higher Council of Science and Technology in Ankara initiated a program to encourage and support international scientific publications by Turkish scientists (Pak, 2000). The program has been quite successful in encouraging high-quality publications. After a year, 2,000 scientists were rewarded according to program objectives. The number increases each year.

Turkey's place in the international platform of scientific productivity, including research and development studies, is not in the top tier; however, it has demonstrated a stable increase over time (Pak, 2000). An interesting observation is the decline in the number of researchers in spite of the increase in financial support. One reason for that may be the relative insufficiency of income for a scientist. Although the financial support for scientific research has increased, the salary paid to the scientist may not be adequate to satisfy minimum living needs. Brilliant researchers who are capable of doing creative work in science are offered higher salaries by the private sector.

Suggestions for the Future

According to Bermek (2001), president of the Turkish Science Association, in addition to the relative position of research and development in different countries, there are important facts and actions to note. One of these actions includes increasing support for research and development in the private sector. For stable progress and development of a country, the proportion of research and development within the private sector must be over 50 percent. This factor is also vital for the progress of universities. In order to reach such a level, all scientific activities must be handled as elements of production. In 2001, research and development activities in Turkey were distributed as 65 percent by universities; 25 percent by the private sector; and 10 percent by the public sector. In 1991, research activities in the private sector amounted to only 10 percent; thus, there has been significant progress. However, the development is not sufficient and must be increased to at least 50 percent; the structure of research and development in Turkey at the moment is far from ideal.

The second action Bermek suggested includes the selection of practical ideas and realistic projects that are easier to complete. Focusing on utopias and spending efforts in hard-to-achieve projects are too luxurious for Turkey's current resources. In other words, local content must be given priority in research and development projects. One example here may include the development of software for education, because of the great population of children and youth, the existence of extreme competition, and the resources of the Ministry of National Education.

The third action consists of making innovations in university structure and the concept of what a university is. Universities in Turkey are organized to fulfill both research and tutoring functions with limited resources. Each function requires different and independent structures and financial sources. The separation of research and teaching in university organizations may create a balanced utilization of resources that includes money and human resources for each of these functions, and this will lead to higher-quality products.

Bermek (2001) claimed that scientific and educational projects planned by the European commission, including such projects as titled "SOCRATES", "EUREKA", and "TUENA", must be initiated on a realistic and local basis. Joint projects with other European countries are especially important for Turkey to strengthen its position in international evaluations, and they may be considered as stepping stones for thes enhancement of scientific creativity.

Related to Bermek's ideas, Baysal (1999) suggested the following actions for Turkey and other developing countries:

1. Adapt technology to local conditions and choose the right technology instead of producing new technology.
2. Integrate science into education.
3. Take an active role in formal and governmental decisions.

Similarly, İnönü (1999) suggested that science should be perceived within the cultural developmental process, not as a separate entity in Turkish culture. Turkish culture has been directed more toward the application and analysis of knowledge than toward research and synthesis. For scientists to go beyond the present limitations in Turkey, greater support from the media, the government, and the private sector is vital.

In 1990, TÜBİTAK established the National Innovation System and developed new policies including financial support for research and development activities through the Technology Follow-Up and Evaluation Council and the Turkey Technology Development Foundation (Taymaz, 2001). Such policies are thought to be helpful for the establishment of a system on which all technological innovative policies are based (Turkish Industry and Business Association) (TÜSIAD, 2003).

The Turkish Science Academy (TÜBA) organized the first meeting of science with the cooperation of Azerbaijan, Kazakhstan, and Kyrgyzstan in 2000. The major aim of the meeting was to create opportunities for science academies to better acquaint themselves and to search for future joint research areas by sharing research experiences, scientific values, and problems. The presidents, vice presidents, and other members of Azerbaijani, Kazakhstan, Kyrgyzstan, and Turkish Academies of Science endorsed the following common points of view (TÜBA, 2000):

1. As bearers of a common culture, science is the most important means of sharing close relationships with neighbors.
2. Scientific cooperation is an indispensable means for the resolution of technical, economic, social, and environmental problems.
3. It is necessary to make use of science and scientists with new models of cooperation in the resolution of their common problems by sharing their knowledge with each other.

4. It is a necessity to establish the council of the aforementioned Azerbaijani, Kazakhstan, Kyrgyzstan, and Turkish Academies of Science.
5. Those countries invited to this meeting but unable to attend may join the Council.

These items summarize the contents of the first meeting. The major focus of the meeting was to identify the differences in the organizational structure of science academies in different Turkish republics and to establish a common basis on which all these countries could rely to develop scientific progress, as well as to exchange ideas and experiences.

(Er, 2002a, 2002b, 2002c) claimed that industrial design is the transition of human intellect, creativity, and fantasy into a concrete product. Thus, industrial design is profession that reflects scientific creativity in Turkey. The existence of such a discipline and profession is relatively new in Turkey. The presence and even the necessity of industrial design has only been seriously discussed in the past decade. In spite of the presence of industry and designers, industrial design did not take root in Turkey. One primary reason was the absence of competitive market conditions, which induces creative activities such as industrial design. According to Er (2002c), competition is the reason for the existence of industrial design, and it is the basic element that mingles design and industry. Since the beginning of 2000, liberalization of the market, increased exports, and stronger connections to Europe have given unprecedented attention to this area. This new trend seems to be the beginning of a long process of cultural transition, which will probably be nourished by dynamic fields other than industrial design. Er (2002a) claimed that Turkey has a rich cultural potential, which is important for the potential power of design. Lack of experience and clear objectives about how to use this potential is a critical point. Industrial design education in Turkey has used technology at an optimal level for the past six years. The new generation of designers has been well developed technically and intellectually. University requirements have higher standards than before, and prospective designers are trained according to global standards. Er (2002b) highlighted the worldwide success of Turkish designers Ayşe Birsel, Murat Günak, and Defne Koz, and he mentioned that they show us how human resources, with more creative training and higher motivation, become the source of optimistic scenarios about the future of industrial design in Turkey.

Scientific creativity in Turkey seems to be influenced by higher-level strategies and policies. Rational and clever policies with realistic goals and the means to increase the motivation of researchers will certainly lead to innovations or even reforms in scientific creativity and techno-logical development in Turkey.

CREATIVITY AND EDUCATION

A study of Turkish history illuminates the country's many fluctuations in educational policies and decisions. Changes in policy and critical deci-sions in the arena of education have led to many problems in practice. Ismail Hakki Tonguc initiated educational reform in villages by curric-ula that enhance creative thinking and problem solving skills of young village people (Tonguc, 1997a, 1997b, Kurtuluş, 2001). His efforts took place in an early republican age, but in later years changing ideals and political views led to a conformist education. Village institutes created by Tonguc's ideal were to train creative teachers who would enlighten Turkish youth. However his approach was not considered with later govermental parties, and the educational system changed into a con-servative one. In recent years, scientific views have become dominant, leading the Ministry of National Education to become more sensitive to new philosophies and to create policy innovations. Since 2002, the Turkish elementary and secondary education systems have been work-ing to restructure according to the basics of the constructivist approach. This change is rather critical, as it is the first movement that draws a framework for more creative education in Turkey.

The first prospective academician to study and introduce the concept of creativity was İnci San, a psychology professor at Ankara University (the site of one of her big works). Her studies focused on the devel-opment of artistic creativity in children. Most of her research aimed to investigate the underlying sources of creative dramatics and the intro-duction of Western literature to Turkish educators and workshops in creative dramatics. Through these workshops, many Turkish educators and academicians gained a strong interest in creativity. San wrote books on artistic creativity and creativity in children (1990), theories of arts education (2003), and arts and creativity (2004).

Emrehan Halici, (2001) president of the Turkish Intelligence Founda-tion, claimed in the Workshop in Intelligence and Creative Education that creative will is a search for the better, correct, and beautiful, and it should be induced during the educational process. Most of the greatest developments and creations in science, technology, and arts are the results of this search. At the workshop, Ilhan and Okvuran (2001) asked the participants about the factors that inhibit creativity, and they identified four factors and concepts.

The first item is family pressure. This includes not allowing the youngster to go out after a particular time; inhibiting the youngster's choice of career; inhibiting his or her education; lacking respect for the child; inhibiting the child's development of self-confidence; and overloading a child with responsibilities.

The second item is social pressure. This includes lack of freedom, participation, tolerance, and conflict resolution; jealousy; egoism; employing freedom for destructive purposes; rejecting change and innovation; refusing responsibility; being teased; and social alienation.

The third item is the economy. This includes an insufficiency of physical facilities; poor teacher quality; teachers who have to have second jobs; the failure of families to satisfy primary needs; a lack of family planning; and problems concerning unemployment.

The fourth item concerns traditions. This includes a low-level education in the society; religious beliefs; and stereotypic attitudes.

At the workshop, alternatives for enhancing creativity in the Turkish educational system were generated. Among many suggestions, the most interesting ones are presented here:

1. Teachers should know themselves as individuals.
2. More time should be devoted to development of individuality.
3. Children's responsibilities must be reduced.
4. Learning environments, in terms of facilities and new concepts, must be developed.
5. In-service training programs that help teachers and administrators gain new view points and social skills must be developed.
6. There is no "creative job" – every type of career can be creative, depending on the potential of the individual.

Empirical research done in Turkey demonstrates findings that support the universal aspects of creativity. Research also shows the influence of cultural variables on the development of creative thinking. One question focuses on the distribution of creative individuals within a particular culture and the characteristics of creative individuals within that culture. In a study of the relationship between intelligence and creativity, Yontar (1992b) compared creative individuals with less creative ones in terms of intelligence and academic achievement, and she found no superiority of creative individuals in these competencies. Her findings of a low positive correlation between IQ and creativity supported the findings of other researchers (Urban, 1991; Vernon, 1989; Yontar, 1992b). When supportive findings are considered, one can notice that most creative characteristics are in fact related to an individual's affective characteristics – especially his or her level of motivation. Findings about the relationships between cognitive capabilities and creativity are relatively few.

A pioneering study about the effects of teaching methods on creativity and logical thinking was done by Aksu (1985). She investigated the effects of different types of teaching methods (laboratory oriented vs. lecture oriented) and gender on science achievement, logical thinking ability, and creativity of 131 fifth-grade students. Aksu found that the laboratory-oriented method of teaching science teaching was significantly beneficial for concrete operational reasoning, but not for creativity.

Günçer and Oral (1993) investigated the relationship between creativity and nonconformity to school discipline as perceived by teachers of 190 third and fourth graders. The researchers administered the Torrance Tests of Creative Thinking (TTCT) to the participants and administered to classroom teachers an observation scale that measured student conformity to school discipline. They found that students who have higher scores on creativity dimensions were perceived as nonconformists by their classroom teachers. This finding supported the view that creative children are perceived as nonconformists in terms of obeying the rules of school discipline, according to their teachers. The researchers suggested that creativity should be further studied by Turkish teachers. Creative children seem to exhibit more independence from norms in thought and action; they have high curiosity; they question more; and they are more persistent in what interests them. Such characteristics may be perceived as frustrating or even annoying by teachers who are unfamiliar with the concept of creativity in the educational process.

In a longitudinal study, Yontar (1992a) administered the TTCT to fifth graders. The test was readministered to the subjects in Grades 8 and 11 (attrition reduced the sample size to twenty-three subjects by the end of the study). Using nonparametric statistics, Yontar investigated the developmental period of figural fluency, flexibility, originality, and elaboration. Yontar's findings demonstrated that the score distribution of students for fluency and flexibility significantly changed when they reached the age of fifteen, while ranks of originality and elaboration remained similar during the seven-year range of the study. The eleventh-grade subjects (age seventeen) had significantly lower scores in fluency and flexibility. In spite of its limited sample size, Yontar's findings demonstrated an irregular developmental line for Turkish subjects – unlike Torrance's findings in a study with American subjects (Torrance, 1974).

Concerning creative development in different cultures, Torrance claimed that each culture has its own developmental process of creativity, because each culture has its own unique attitude toward the needs for creativity and curiosity (Sungur, 1992). Yontar's findings supported Torrance's ideas about the influence of culture on creativity. Yontar suggests that more developmental research is needed on creative development in Turkish culture. Such studies should be conducted with standardized measures for Turkish culture and in larger samples.

At different stages of the Turkish educational system, creative curricula for various age levels were developed by researchers to foster creative thinking skills. Oral (1997) developed an activity-based spiral curriculum for enhancement of creativity in five-year-olds. There were three classrooms for the five-year-olds, in the kindergarten. All three groups were taken as intact groups in the Middle East Technical University kindergarten, and they were randomly assigned as an experimental and two control groups. The TTCT–Figural Form A was administered as a pretest and post test measurement. The two control groups followed the existing curriculum, which was developed by the administrator and the teachers of the kindergarten, whereas the experimental group was given the activity-based curriculum. The program used by the kindergarten focused on teaching social rules and keeping children under control and safe. The activity-based curriculum, in contrast, other hand, aimed to develop children's creativity and divergent thinking skills through a systematic order and presentation of the topics, giving opportunities for observing, testing, and discussing, and generating alternative ideas on questions and problems.

Oral found significantly higher creativity scores on the posttest in the experimental group, whereas the two control groups had lower posttest scores. She suggested that programs specifically designed to improve creativity are beneficial at the preschool level, where logical frameworks for straightforward thinking are not yet established. She also discussed the influence of the teacher as a role model and instructor who leads children in their thought processes. Oral's findings indicated that creativity can be developed with specific training, and teachers who are well informed about creative development can be instrumental during implementation.

Ardaç and Muğaloğlu (2000) developed two instructional programs aimed at improving divergent and convergent thinking skills of sixth and seventh graders in economically disadvantaged regions of İstanbul; both programs were designed around the topic of "relationships between two variables" in science. Program 1 was designed to improve thinking skills on the relationship between two variables by observing relationships. Program 2 used similar content and activities, but with the additional goal of showing that science could be fun. The emphasis of Program 2 was to make the activities as enjoyable as possible. The researchers implemented both programs for six weeks. Results indicated that the treatment significantly influenced the performance on convergent thinking skills of students in Program 1, whereas no significant effect of Program 2 on divergent thinking skills was observed. In Program 2, the students showed very low performance levels and there were no differences in their pretest and posttest scores and mean performance gains. A close scrutiny of individual items indicated that the most students could produce was a duplication of the ideas presented or discussed. The researchers suggested that one possible explanation could be that the generation of ideas was rarely expected from these students, if at all. The students found it very hard to work on open-ended questions (which was evident even during implementation). In addition, the activities directed to foster divergent thinking took place at the end of each session. The time seemed to be insufficient and thus the activities were completed in a hurry or, in some cases, hardly completed at all. Finally, the generation of possible relationships rested on a sound understanding regarding the relationship between variables. Generating examples of related phenomena seems to be at higher levels of the learning hierarchy. Therefore, it might have been easier for the students to deal with items on convergent thinking than for those on divergent thinking.

Ardaç and Muğaloğlu (2000) found that improving thinking skills is possible, especially when these skills are specifically designed and explicitly stated during the instructional sequence. The researchers claimed that, although the content, conditions, and related variables are different, the thinking process used remains the same when different events are examined. The programs developed in this study develop convergent thinking abilities but not divergent thinking skills. The researchers claimed that it would be more useful to start with activities on convergent thinking and proceed to activities on divergent thinking, only after providing a satisfactory basis of the process skill.

In another study, the relationship between creativity and learning styles of university students was investigated (Oral, 1996). The TTCT–Figural Form and the Learning Styles Questionnaire (LSQ) developed by Oral were given to the students from the departments of Industrial Design (ID) and Physical Education and Sports (PES) at Middle East Technical University. The LSQ contained fourteen items including analytical and global learning styles. The analytical learning style referred to learning with a step-by-step presentation of information in a systematic manner. The global learning style, in contrast, referred to learning through the short and anecdotal presentation of information, including a mixture of different subjects, pictorial cues, and humorous illustrations. Results revealed higher mean scores of ID students on global learning style and the subdimensions of the TTCT. PES students, in contrast, had lower mean scores on the TTCT and higher mean scores on the analytical learning style. The results were as expected. The PES and ID departments required different learning styles. The PES department, on one hand, required coaches and teachers who could follow the rules of sports and games and apply the techniques analytically. The ID department, on the other hand, required designers who could create new designs for already existing materials by using their imaginations. Oral (1996) demonstrated that the two departments selected students correctly according to their requirements and instructed them in accordance with their objectives. The study was limited to two departments only, and more studies should be conducted to investigate the situation in different departments of different universities.

An important issue about creativity in Turkish education is how creative abilities can be integrated in higher education. In recent years, Turkish educators have criticized the system at all levels as ignoring students' abilities, interests, and creativity. New projects such as Support to Basic Education, which is financed by the European Council, have been implemented. The scope of the Support to Basic Education Project is the transformation of the basic philosophy of Turkish elementary education. In the project, the emphasis is directed from the previous didactic, knowledge-based education to a constructivist approach in education. The constructivist approach focuses on developing pupils' skills in cognitive, affective, and psychomotor domains, by considering their learning needs, intelligences, motivation, interests, and abilities, as well as their social and physical surroundings. The project, which includes first through fifth grades, is preparing textbooks to develop inquiry and creative problem solving in students, improving school–community relations, and building stronger bonds between universities and the Ministry of Education. These are positive empirical developments in elementary education; however, higher education is still being neglected in terms of using creative potential in different labor forces.

Oral (2004) investigated the effects of creativity on the University Entrance Examination (OSS) in Turkey. In the study, students at Akdeniz University School of Education were administered the TTCT–Figural Form A, and their scores on fluency, flexibility, originality, and elaboration were compared with their OSS scores. Interestingly, the fluency and flexibility scores of students aged seventeen to twenty seemed to have influenced their OSS scores both in verbal and numerical tests, while the fluency and flexibility scores of students aged twenty-one to twenty-five had no such no influence. This situation might reflect the changing content of the OSS in recent years. Research demonstrates that the Turkish OSS has high reliability and validity with knowledge structure (Köksal, 2002); (Sezen, 1998); (Ösym, 2004). The study by Oral demonstrated that, in recent years, creativity also has been included in the selection process of Turkish students for university. Taş (2002) claimed that the basic reasons for lack of creativity in Turkish education were (a) neglect of critical thinking; (b) overemphasis on knowledge presentation but not discovery; (c) lack of educational revisions in goals and methods; (d) lack of creative orientation and motivation in teachers; and (e) economic crisis.

According to Turkish literature on the enhancement of creativity, innovations are necessary at the elementary and secondary education level (Taş, 2002; Demircan, 1990) as well at the university level. Innovations for elementary and secondary education include having a new scope in teacher training (preservice and in-service teacher training) to bring critical thinking and creative staff in the area, redesigning textbooks that develop inquiry and critical thinking, and employing new curricula and teaching strategies in the learning process (Başar, 1999; Erdoğan, 2000; İlgar, 2000; Mill: Eğitim Bakanlığı, 2001).

Within the past decade, innovations in the Turkish educational system have started to be realized. Although these innovations are slow and limited to pilot studies, they are the pioneers of academic work produced by theoretical views and practical experiences in the field of creativity in Turkish culture. Our universities started courses and seminars such as creative writing, thinking education, and theories of creativity (Akdeniz

University, 2004) for various degrees, including education, mass media, fine arts, economics, and administration. The number of scholars who discover the importance of creative development in science and social science increases each year.

Civil Organizations to Promote Creativity in Turkish Education

In addition to academic research on creativity in the Turkish educational system, some volunteer work has focused on creative development. The Education Volunteers Foundation of Turkey (TEGV), established in 1995, is one of Turkey's most successful civil organizations and is known for its creativity, integrity, and vision in supporting public education. Today, TEGV reaches over 300,000 children and young people ages seven to sixteen, engages more than 8,000 volunteers, and is supported by nearly 100,000 individual and institutional donors. Its mission is to provide and develop after-school educational and training programs that encourage children to become rational, self-confident, creative, respectful, and tolerant individuals.

TEGV emphasizes interactive learning and individual intellectual and emotional development, making use of the latest technology and advanced concepts for learning. Programs capitalize on the active involvement of parents, neighbors, and community leaders in strengthening local civil society. Volunteer work at TEGV is focused on four main projects in education.

One project concerns peer-to-peer education. With the help of the IYF/Nokia *Make A Connection* initiative, this program aims to strengthen academic and life skills and promote active participation among 39,000 children and adolescents through a series of arts-related workshops.

Another project concerns education parks and learning centers. TEGV runs more than ninety educational facilities, providing children and their parents with an active, easily accessible learning environment and offering programs ranging from formal literacy training to entrepreneurship.

The *I am a Person, an Individual, a Citizen* program introduces children to the universal concepts of human rights, freedom, and citizenship. It encourages them to develop their own projects.

The *Young Achievements* course introduces young people to the concept of market economy and business enterprise. It gives them the opportunity to learn about business administration by creating and running their own firms.

Assessment of Creativity: A Model for Turkey

An important study on the assessment of creativity in Turkey was conducted by Ali Baykal (2000), professor of educational testing and measurement at Boğaziçi University, İstanbul. Baykal developed an assessment scale for communicative skills and vocational orientation behaviors for professionals who are to be employed in media and advertising sectors. Depending on the criteria of the Foundation of Turkish Advertisers, Baykal developed a scale to measure communication skills and vocational orientation behaviors. Validity studies of the scale demonstrated two main factors as creativity and disposition for managerial position.

Another assessment of creativity is the Toğrol adaptation of the Test for Creative Thinking–Drawing Production (TCT–DP; see Jellen & Urban, 1986) to Turkish norms. On a sample of 1,154 students ranging from preschool to college, Toğrol obtained a correlation coefficient of 0.98 for test–retest reliability and 0.97 for interrater reliability.

Research in Physiology and Creativity

Some research, although scarce, has been done on the negative effects of neurological problems on creative ability in Turkey. Creative thinking abilities of patients with multiple sclerosis (MS) were investigated and compared with the abilities of individuals without MS (Toğrol et al., 1998). The sample consisted of 35 MS patients and 129 non-MS patients. The researchers classified the MS patients according to the level and type of the illness. The TCT–DP (Jellen & Urban, 1986) and a screening instrument for testing creative skills that has already been adapted to the Turkish language (Toğrol, 1998), were administered to all subjects. Imaging and evoked potential studies were also done in 22 of the MS patients. Cognitive assessment was conducted before the test. None of the subjects had gross cognitive pathologies, although 12 patients had mild mood disturbances (mostly mild anxiety). Although the mean differences of the total creativity scores of the groups in the sample were not statistically significant, the patients with probable MS tended to get higher scores than those with clinically definite MS. In addition, the patients with longer duration of disease tended to score lower, with the lowest score (10) obtained by the patient with the longest duration of disease (twenty-five years). A correlation coefficient was calculated between the total creativity scores and duration of the disease for the patient group ($n = 35$). A moderate negative correlation coefficient was found between the variables ($r = -.4385$, $p < .01$). Results indicated that, as duration of the disease increases, the total score of creativity decreases.

In another study, Toğrol, Toğrol, and Can (2002) investigated creative thinking in epilepsy patients. In the study, the Torrance Test of Figural Creativity was used to measure creativity. The researchers compared the creativity of thirty epilepsy patients between twenty and twenty-eight years of age with thirty-six age-matched controls. They found that the creativity of the control group was significantly higher than that of the epilepsy group. The researchers attributed the difference to the effects of demographic conditions of the patients, the drugs used for the treatment of epilepsy, and the destructive effect of the disease on creative thinking ability.

CONCLUSION

This chapter introduces creativity in Turkey and Turkish minorities in terms of theoretical background and practical implications. Creativity in Turkey has common universal values with those mentioned in Western literature. A deep investigation demonstrates that Turkish creativity possesses universal values in the culture. Islamic authorities and the monarchic regime were two main obstacles for the enhancement of scientific creativity and production in Turkey for hundreds of years. However, after the foundation of the democratic and secular Turkish Republic by Atatürk in 1920, science and technology began to be influenced by the West. Although problems such as economic crises and the failure to implement consistent policies concerning scientific creativity in Turkey have hindered scientific progress, there is a gradual increase in scientific productivity. Because of the effects of Islam and the monarchic structure previously mentioned, the structure of artistic creativity has developed anonymously, in association with shape and color and verbal forms such as embroideries, miniature art, folk songs, and calligraphy. When investigated, we can easily observe that Anatolian folk art includes the structures of formal operational thought, higher-level aesthetic values, and sophisticated means of communication. Art in Anatolia was not exhibited as in Western society for hundreds of years, as arts were part of a natural flow of life. Anatolian people wear and use the masterpieces they make, but they do not think about exhibiting them in public. Anatolian folk art has an extreme functional value – even an ordinary family home is a museum in itself. For example, some regions such as Safranbolu in Turkey are famous for their houses, which are protected in their original styles and used as museums today. After the foundation of the modern Turkish Republic, Western influence brought academic perception to art, as well as new concepts of museums and art galleries. This is an enormous development, although being too heavily influenced by the West may lead to an ignorance of our cultural origins in arts and a loss of our own identity in artistic creativity.

Turkey has great potential for culture and creativity, even if it is not currently at the same level as other developed countries. To benefit from creativity in different cultures, the world should be aware of the variety of knowledge and creativity in Turkey. Only then will global development be less limited to technological and practical innovations, and more open to humanistic values.

References

Aksu, A. (1985). *The effects of method and sex on science achievement, logical thinking ability and creative thinking ability of 5th grade students.* Unpublished master's thesis, Middle East Technical University. Ankara.

Ardaç, D., & Muğaloğlu, E. (2000). Divergent production as an integral part of a program designed to improve basic science process skills. In S. Dingli (Ed.), *Creative thinking: An indispensable asset for a successful future.* Malta: Publishers Enterprises.

Atasü, E. (2000). *Benim yazarlarim* [My writers]. İstanbul: Bilgi Yayınları.

Başar, H. (1999). *Sınıf yönetimi* [Classroom management]. İstanbul: M.E.B. Yayınları.

Baykal, A. (2000). *A proposal for measuring creativity and communication skills.* (Advertisement Foundation 1999–2000 work schedule report). İstanbul: Advertisement Foundation.

Baysal, B. (1999). *Cumhuriyet döneminde Türkiye'de bilim* [Science in Turkey in the Republic era] (pp. 1–15). Türkiye Cumhuriyeti'nin 75. Yılında TÜBA Konferansları 1. Ankara: TÜBİTAK Matbaası. (TÜBA Conferences at the 75th Anniversary of Turkish Republic 1). Ankara: TÜBİTAK Press.

Bermek, E. (2001). *Türk bilim politikasında yeni arayışlar ve atılımlar* [New research and innovations in Turkish science policy]. New Research and Innovations in Turkish Science Policy. Ankara: TÜBİTAK press. TÜBİTAK.

Dedegil, M. Y. (2004a). *An analytical consideration of creativity.* (Technical Report No. 1). Karlsruhe, Germany: Karlsruhe Technical Institute.

Dedegil, M. Y. (2004b). *Creativity and superstition in life and science.* (Technical Report No. 1). Karlsruhe, Germany: Karlsruhe Technical Institute.

Demircan, Ö. (1990). *Yabancı dil Öğretim Yöntemleri* [Methods of foreign language teaching]. İstanbul: Ekin Eğitim Yayınları.

Dentu, E. (1869). *Les Turcs en Bulgarie.* Paris.

Er, H. A. (2002a). 1990'lı yıllarda Türkiye'de Endüstriyel Tasarım [Industrial design in Turkey at the end of the 1990s]. *Maison Française, 85,* 170–171.

Er, H. A. (2002b, March 18) *An introduction to the history of industrial design education in Turkey.* Paper presented at ITU Industrial Design Meetings IV: ICSID's Approach in Industrial Design Education, İstanbul.

Er, H. A. (2002c). *Tasarım ve Türk Ofis Mobilyasi Sektörünün Gelişimi: Bir Kader Birliği mi* [Design and development of Turkish office furniture sector: A joint destiny]? İstanbul: Ofis İletişim.

Ercan, E. (2002). *Bizans'tan Günümüze İstanbul Şiirleri* [İstanbul poems from Byzantine To Our Day]. İstanbul: Alfa Yayınları.

Erdoğan, İ. (2000) *Okul Yönetimi ve Öğretim Liderliği* [School management and teaching leadership]. İstanbul: Sistem Yayıncılık.

Getzels, J. W., & Jackson, P. W. (1962). *Creativity and intelligence.* New York: Wiley.

Goodwin, G. (1976). Ottoman architecture in the Balkans. *Art and Archeology Papers, April,* 55–57.

Günçer, B., & Oral, G. (1993). Relationship between creativity and nonconformity to school discipline as perceived by the teachers of Turkish elementary school children, by controlling for their grade and sex. *Journal of Instructional Psychology, 20 ,* 208–214.

Halıcı, E. (2001, November 13–15). *Intelligence and creative thinking.* Paper presented at the Workshop in Intelligence and Creative Education, Turkish Intelligence Foundation, Ankara.

Halman, T. S. (2000). *A many splendored culture.* Report presented to *The Washington Times* Advertising Department.

Heper, M. (1985). *The state tradition in Turkey.* Walkington, England: Eothen Press.

Heper, M. (2000). 2000'li yılların eşiğinde Türkiye'de devlet ve üniversite [State and university at the corner of the 2000s). In *Dünyada ve Türkiye'de bilim, etik ve üniversite* [Science, ethics and university in the world and Turkey] (pp. 13–21). Ankara : TÜBA Bilimsel Toplantı Serileri 1. Tubitak Yayinlari.

Horne, F. M. (2003, Spring). *Hand in hand with people's art: Projects in color.* Antalya, Turkey: Author.

İlgar, L. (2000). *Eğitim Yönetimi, Okul Yönetimi, Sınıf Yönetimi* [Education management, school management, classroom management]. (2nd ed.). İstanbul: Beta Basım Yayım Dağıtım A.Ş.

Ilhan, Ç., & Okvuran, A. (2001, November 13–15). *"Individual" in the process of intelligence and creative education.* Paper presented at the Workshop in Intelligence and Creative Education, Turkish Intelligence Foundation, Ankara.

İnam, A. (1996). *Düşten Düşünceye* [From fantasy to thought]. Ankara: İmge Yayınevı.

İnönü, E. (1999). *Cumhuriyet Döneminde Bilime Toplu Bir Bakiş ve Gelecek Hakkında Beklentiler* [A general outlook to science in the Republic era and expectations about the future]. (pp. 15–59). Türkiye Cumhuriyeti'nin 75. Yilinda TÜBA Konferansları 1. Ankara: TÜBİTAK Matbaası.

Jellen, H., & Urban, K. (1986). The TCT–DP (Test for Creative Thinking – Drawing Production): An instrument that can be applied to most age and ability groups. *The Creative Child and Adult Quarterly, 3,* 138–151.

Keskioğlu, O., & Özaydin, A. T. (1983). Bulgaristan'da Türk-İslam Eserleri [Turkish-Islam Masterpieces in Bulgaria]. *Vakıflar Dergisi* [Journal of Foundations] *17*, 112.

Kocabas, S. (1992a, March 25–27). *Functional categorization of knowledge.* Paper presented at the AAAI-SSS 92 Symposium Propositional knowledge Representation 25–27 March. Stanford.

Kocabas, S. (1992b). Evaluation of discovery systems. In *Proceedings of the ML92 Workshop on Machine Discovery* (pp. 168–171). İstanbul: İstanbul Technical University.

Kocabas, Ş. (2004). *AI and scientific creativity.* Unpublished manuscript İstanbul Technical University, İstanbul.

Köksal, E. A. (2002). *The assessment of the biology items in the 1998–2001 secondary school institutions student selection and placement tests.* Unpublished master's thesis, Middle East Technical University, Ankara.

Kurtuluş, Y. (2001). *Köy enstitülerinde sanat eğitimi ve Tonguç* [Art education in the village institutes and Tonguç]. Ankara: Güldikeni Yayınları.

Lenat, D. B. (1979). On automated scientific theory formation: A case study using the AM program. *Machine Intelligence, 9,* 251–283.

Lenat, D. B. (1983). EURISKO: A program that learns new heuristics and domain concepts. *Artificial Intelligence 21,* 61–98.

Lindley, L. D., & Borgen, F. H. (2000). Personal style scales of the Strong Interest Inventory: Linking personality and interests. *Journal of Vocational Behavior , 57,* 22–41.

Milli Eğitim Bakanlığı. (2001). 2001 Yılı Başında Milli Eğitim [National education in early 2001]. Retrieved October 18, 2001, from http://www.meb.gov.tr/Stats/ist2001/Bolum1s1.htm

Myers, D. G. (1995). *Psychology.* New York: Worth.

Oral, G. (1996). The relationship between creativity and learning styles of students. In *Proceedings of the Second International Conference on Creative Thinking.* Malta: Malta University.

Oral, G. (1997). *The effect of the activity-based, spiral curriculum on five-year-old children's creativity and behavior as perceived by their parents and teachers.* Unpublished doctoral dissertation, Middle East Technical University, Ankara.

Oral, G. (2004). Creativity and university entrance exams. Unpublished study. Antalya: Akdeniz University.

Oral, G., Kaufman, J. C., & Sexton, J. D. (2004). From empire to democracy: Effects of social progress on Turkish writers. *The Journal of Psychology, 138,* 223–232.

Ögrenci Seçme Yerleştirme Sınav Merkezi. (2004). *Student selection exam.* Retrieved July 20, 2004, from http://www.osym.gov.tr/altyapi/dosyagoster.asp.

Öztürk, O. (2002). *Sorma-Bilme Dürtüsü ve Girişim Duygusu Nasil Yok Ediliyor* [How curiousity and enterpreneuship are destroyed]. Türkiye Bilimler Akademisi Akademi Forumu. Ankara: TÜBİTAK Matbaası.

Pak, N. K. (2000). Universitede bilimsel performans değerlendirmesi [Evaluation of scientific performance at university]. In *Dünyada ve Türkiye'de bilim, etik ve üniversite* [Science, ethics and university in the world and Turkey] (pp. 93–111). Ankara: TÜBA Bilimsel Toplanti Serileri 1. Tubitak Yayınları.

Piaget, J. (1972). Intellectual evolution from adolescence to adulthood. *Human Development, 15,* 1–12.

The Ottomon Documents in Bulgaria (1994). Turkish Republic State Activites General Directory-Center of Ottoman Archives xxiii, 230p. Vol 17. Ankara.

Recepoğlu, A. S. (1987, October 26–28). *Yugoslavya genç şairlerinin iletisi* [The message of Yugoslavian young poets]. Paper presented at the First International Youth Congress, Selçuk University, Konya, Turkey.

Recepoğlu, A. S. (1991). *Prizren'de şairlik geleneği* [Poetry ritual in Prizren]. Üsküp: Birlik Publishers.

San, İ. (1990). *Sanatsal yaratma: Çocukta yaratıcılık* [Artistic creativity: Creativity in children]. Ankara: İş Bankası Yayınları.

San, İ. (2003). *Sanat eğitiminin kuramları* [Theories of arts education]. Ankara: Toplumsal Dönüşüm Yayınları.

San, İ. (2004). *Sanat ve eğitim* [Art and education]. Ankara: Ütopya Yayınevi.

Sezen, E. (1998). *ÖSS sayısal bölüm matematik alt-testinin sayısal muhakeme yeteneğini ne derecede ölçtüğü üzerine bir çalışma* [An investigation of the ÖSS mathematical subtest's ability to measure numerical rationalization]. Unpublished master's thesis, Hacettepe University, Ankara.

Shaw, S. J. (1985). Osmanlı İmparatorluğu'nda azınlıklar sorunu. *Tanzimat'tan Cumhuriyet'e Türkiye Ansiklopedisi. [Minority problems in Ottoman Empire. Encyclopedia of Turkey from the Tanzimat to the Republic] 5,* 1002–1006.

Simonton, D. K. (1994). *Greatness.* New York: Guilford Press.

Sungur, N. (1992). *Yaratıcı Düşünme* [Creative thinking]. İstanbul: Özgür Yayın Dağitim.

Talay, M. İ. (2001). Introduction. In A. S. Recepoğlu (Ed.), *Kosova'da Türk kültürü veya Türkçe düşünmek* [Turkish culture and thinking in Turkish in Kosova]. Ankara: Kültür Bakanlığı.

Teis, S. (2002). Creativity in Foreign Language Teaching in Turkey. – retrieved from www.inglish.com/ned5.htm on 21.06.2005.

Taymaz, E. (2001). *Ulusal yenilik sistemi: Türkiye imalat sektöründe teknolojik değişim ve yenilik sistemleri* [National innovation system: Technological change and innovation systems in Turkish production sector]. Ankara: TÜBİTAK/TTGV/DIE.

Toğrol, A. (1999). Yaratıcı Düşünme Testi – Çizim Ürünü'nün Türk örneklemlerinde uygulanması. [Implementation of the Test of Creative Thinking–Drawing Production (TCT–DP)]. *Eğitim ve Bilim Dergisi,* 23(112), 45–51.

Toğrol, A. Y., Toğrol, E., Saraçoğlu, M., Tanrıdağ, O., & Akyatan, N. (1998). Creativity in multiple sclerosis. *International Journal of Psychophysiology, 30,* 139.

Toğrol, E., Toğrol, A. Y., & Can, S. (2002, March). *Creative thinking in epilepsy.* Paper presented at the Twelfth Meeting of the European Neurological Society, Berlin.

Toğrol, A. Y. (1998, September 6–8). *Yaratıcı Düşünme Testi – Çizim Ürünü' nün Türkiye'de uygulanması* [Application of TTCT – Figural form in Turkey]. Paper presented at the Seventh National Psychology Congress, Ankara.

Tonguç, İ. H. (1997a). *Kitaplaşmamış yazıları* [Unpublished manuscripts], Volume 1. *The Turkish minority in Bulgaria between 1878–1908.* Ankara: Türk Tarih Kurumu Press.

Tonguç, İ. H. (1997b). *Köyde eğitim* [Education in the village]. Ankara: Köy Enstitüleri ve Çağdaş Eğitim Vakfi Yayınları.

Torrance, E. P. (1974). *Torrance Tests of Creative Thinking. Norms-technical manual.* Princeton, NJ: Personnel Press

TÜBA (2000). Joint Meeting of Science Academies in Turkey, Azerbaijan, Kazakhstan, and Kyrgyzstan. Ankara: TUBA Press.

Turan, O. (1998). *The Turkish Minority in Bulgaria (1878–1908).* Ankara: Turkish History Foundation.

TÜSİAD. (2003). *Ulusal inovasyon sistemi: kavramsal çerçeve, Türkiye incelemesi ve ülke örnekleri* [National innovation system: Conceptual framework, Turkey investigation and country samples] (Report no. 1). İstanbul: TÜSİAD Press.

Urban, K. (1991). On the development of creativity in children. *Creativity Research Journal, 4*(2), 177–191.

Vernon, P. E. (1989). The nature–nurture problem in creativity. In R. J. Sternberg (Ed.), *Handbook of creativity.* New York: Plenum.

World Intellectual Property Organization Report (WIPO) (2000). *WIPO periodical report on participation of Turkey to EC.* Retrieved November 30, 2004, from http://www.belgenet.com/arsiv/ab/ab_raporoo_4.html

Yontar, A. (1992a, October 11–14). *A follow-up study about creative thinking abilities of students.* Paper presented at the Third European Conference on High Ability, Munich.

Yontar, A. (1992b). *Yaratıcı Düşünce Testi- Çizim Ürünü ile ilgili araştırma raporu* [Research report on TTCT – Figural form]. Unpublished manuscript, Boğaziçi Üniversitesi, İstanbul.

13

Development of Creativity Research in Chinese Societies

A Comparison of Mainland China, Taiwan, Hong Kong, and Singapore

Weihua Niu

Creativity, as a continuing research area, has only a little over fifty years of history. The most acceptable catalyst for creativity research was Guilford's presidential address to the American Psychological Association in 1950, in which he spelled out the importance of studying creativity (Guilford, 1950, 1967; Sternberg, 1988). Since then, the field of creativity has attracted scholars in various subfields of psychology around the world. This chapter focuses on the development of creativity research in four different regions of Chinese culture, namely, Mainland China, Taiwan, Hong Kong, and Singapore. It starts with an examination of each region's history of creativity research, its research focus, and approaches adopted by researchers in the region. The chapter then concludes with a comparison of creativity research in the four representative regions of Chinese culture.

MAINLAND CHINA

Creativity research in Mainland China started in the late 1970s. In 1978, Zixiu Zhi (查子秀), a developmental psychologist from the Institute of Psychology of the Chinese Academy of Science (IPCAS), along with four educational psychologists from other institutes across the nation, formed a research group called the National Cooperative Research Group for the Study of Supernormal Gifted Children in China (NCRGSCC; See Shi & Qu, in press; Shi & Xu, 1998, 1999, 2004; Shi & Zha, 2000; Zha, 1983, 1993a, 1993b). Even though the primary goal of this research group was to study intelligence and giftedness, research in creative thinking was also included. It was deemed the "prodigal

374

stepbrother to research on intelligence," as noted by Sternberg (1988, p. vii). In a sense, creativity was studied as a by-product of intelligence and giftedness. In fact, creative thinking has been viewed as an important aspect of giftedness by Chinese scholars (Shi & Qu, in press; Shi & Xu, 1998; Zha, 1983, 1993a). Nevertheless, the formation of the NCRGSCC and its research symbolized the beginning of creativity research in Mainland China. Since then, creativity research in China has gone through two major stages. Research in the first stage primarily focused on studying the relationship between intelligence and creativity; in the second stage, more research was conducted to investigate the nature of creativity, using various approaches.

Stage I (1970s to mid-1990s)

The primary focus of this first stage of creativity research was to study the relationship between intelligence and creativity. Two different approaches were undertaken in this stage. The first approach, primarily adopted by scholars in the NCRGSCC, was to study children with high intelligence, also called supernormal children, as opposed to intellectually more typical children (Shi & Qu, in press; Shi, Zha & Zhou, 1995; Zhou, Zha & Shi, 1998). The second approach was to study the process of solving ill-defined problems, such as insightful problem solving, as opposed to solving well-defined problems, such as conventional reasoning and mathematical problems.

Study of Giftedness

Beginning in the late 1970s, the NCRGSCC team conducted a series of investigations focused on comparing various cognitive and noncognitive attributes between intellectually gifted and nongifted children. Creative thinking was perceived as one attribute that differentiated gifted children from other children. To identify gifted children, Zha and her colleagues developed a measure called the Cognitive Ability Test for Identifying Supernormal Children, or CATISC (Zha, 1983). One component of the test was to measure creative thinking, which included measures of insightful problem solving (e.g., the matchstick task – to rearrange matchsticks to solve a mathematical equation problem), divergent thinking (e.g., the unusual usage task – to list as many uses as possible of a common object), and creative thinking (e.g., to complete a story; See Zha, 1983, 1993a). The research conducted by the NCRGSCC was very important, and most publications (primarily books) related to creativity at this stage came from this group. The creativity component of the CATISC is also regarded as the first creativity measure used in psychological research in Mainland China.

In addition to the aforementioned national collaborative project, in 1988, Zha and her colleagues at IPCAS also started a collaborative project with psychologists from the University of Munich. This was a cross-cultural study on intellectually gifted and normal children in China and Germany (then West Germany). This collaboration, funded by the Volkswagen Foundation in Germany, has a very important status in the history of creativity research in China, for it was the first cross-cultural and longitudinal research undertaken. With the hard work of researchers from both China and Germany, it also started and preserved the earliest and longest longitudinal research data set that was suitable for future research (Shi & Qu, in press).

Study of Ill-Defined Problem Solving
Beginning in the mid-1980s, some researchers outside the NCRGSCC adopted a different approach to studying creativity, although at that time the word *creativity* was not explicitly used in these studies. Their approach was to study the processes of solving different types of problems, including both well-defined and ill-defined problems. Such an approach actually reflected a popular trend in the field of psychology and was part of mainstream research in Mainland China at the time. Chinese psychology underwent a serious crisis during the Cultural Revolution (1966–1976), and all psychology departments and research institutions were closed. After the Cultural Revolution, Chinese psychologists adopted many of the Western theories and frameworks of psychological research and rebuilt the field of psychology. The introduction of cognitive psychology in the late 1970s and the visit of Dr. Herbert A. Simon to China in the early 1980s made research on cognitive psychology a mainstream field. The study of problem solving attracted many new-era psychologists. In addition to studying the cognitive processes of well-defined problems, such as chess problems and mathematical problems, some scholars started to focus on ill-defined problems such as insightful problems. For example, Qinglin Zhang (张庆林) and his colleagues from Southwest Normal University studied the cognitive processes of insightful problem solving in the mid-1980s. In the mid-1990s, they expanded their research to include other types of creative problem solving, such as creative imagination, using the cognitive approach. This approach is introduced in the next section (e.g., Zhang, 1989, Zhang & Xiao, 1996).

Stage II (mid-1990s to 2004)

Since the mid-1990s, creativity research in China has steadily grown. The work from three institutions is introduced here and represents many of the studies on creativity from this period.

At IPCAS, under the leadership of Zha and, later, Jiannong Shi (施建农), research on giftedness continued. In addition to studying creativity as a by-product of giftedness, researchers at IPCAS also directly focused on investigating the nature and definition of creativity from a Chinese perspective (Qu & Shi, 2003; Shi, 1995; Shi & Xu, 1997). Moreover, they also studied the contemporary Chinese view of creativity (Cai, Fu, Sang, & Xu, 2001), the relationship among motivation, intelligence, and creativity (Shi, 1995, Shi & Xu, 1999; Zhou & Shi, 1996), cognitive styles and creativity (Zhou, Zhi, & Wu, 2004), the teaching of creativity by using cognitive models (Zhang & Chen, 1996), and the cognitive and neurocognitive basis of creative problem solving (Mai, Luo, & Wu, 2003).

At Beijing Normal University, Shenghua Jin (金盛华) introduced the Torrance Tests of Creative Thinking in the mid-1990s as a measure of creativity (Jin, 1996). Recently, Jin and his colleagues, using interview methods, started a project to study factors that influenced achievements of highly creative individuals in science. Also at Beijing Normal University, Qi Dong (董奇) and his colleagues, in collaboration with Chuansheng Chen and his colleagues from the University of California at Irvine, studied children's artistic abilities by using product-oriented measures (Chen et al., 2002). They have continued their research in investigating the cognitive mechanism of creative thinking.

At Southwest Normal University, following the tradition of the cognitive approach to studying insightful problem solving, Qinglin Zhang (张庆林) and his colleagues studied creative imagination and novel concept combinations (Xu, 2000; Zhang, Shi, & Wang, 2001). They also adopted other approaches to studying creativity, such as studying the relationship among personalities, motivation, thinking styles, and creative products as well as studying the social contexts that influence creativity in Chinese society.

In addition to the work from the aforementioned three institutes, some research on creativity using Mainland Chinese participants was conducted by scholars outside Mainland China and by research teams that comprised researchers from both Mainland China and other regions of the world. For example, Weihua Niu (牛卫华), originally from China and now studying and working in the United States, has collaborated with researchers from both China and overseas to study the cultural influence of creativity in various domains such as art (Niu, Antognazza, Liu, 2004; Niu & Sternberg, 2001) and language and literature (Niu, 2003a; Niu & Kaufman, 2005; Niu, Zhang, & Yang, 2004, in press). These studies have shown that the influence of culture on creativity can be manifested from different channels, such as people's view of what constitutes creativity (Niu, 2003b, Niu & Sternberg, 2002), educational systems and academic tracking (Niu & Sternberg, 2003), and social value and reward systems (Niu, 2003a).

Similarly, Chen and his colleagues from the University of California at Irvine also studied the influence of culture on creativity by comparing American and Chinese students' drawings of geometric shapes and evaluating the process of judges from the two cultures (Chen et al., 2002). They found that people from the two cultures used similar criteria in judging the quality of the drawings; these results were similar to those from the study by Niu and Sternberg (2001). These two studies together seem to suggest that the product-oriented measure can be used in future cross-cultural research as a valid measure of creativity.

Database Analysis of Creativity Research in Mainland China

For the two-stage claim to be verified further in terms of the developmental trend of creativity research in Mainland China, an analysis of academic publications (i.e., peer-reviewed journal articles) in Mainland China was conducted, using a search engine called China National Knowledge Infrastructure, or CNKI. Results of this analysis were presented at the Thirty-Fifth International Congress of Psychology in Beijing (Niu, Shi, & Liu, 2004).

CNKI, the largest Chinese-language academic search engine, is a collection of databases with more than 10 million articles from Chinese periodicals, most written after 1994. Two databases were chosen for this project: One was journal articles published before 1993 (including 1993) in social sciences and humanities, and the other was journal articles published after 1994 (including 1994) in social sciences and humanities. Therefore, the two databases included academic publications in major social science and humanities journals from the late 1970s to 2003.

Using title search, the Chinese word for creativity (创造力) was entered. After duplicates and seemingly nonacademic papers were removed, the results revealed 175 entries from the two databases.

TABLE 13.1. *Yearly Breakdown of Number of Publications in Chinese Periodicals in Mainland China*

Year	No. of Publications	No. of Psychological Studies	No. of Empirical Studies
1983	1	1	0
1984	1	0	0
1985	7	1	0
1986	2	0	0
1987	7	0	0
1988	7	0	0
1989	3	0	0
1990	5	1	0
1991	2	0	0
1992	2	1	0
1993	5	1	0
1994	9	3	0
1995	4	1	0
1996	11	5	4
1997	7	3	1
1998	17	3	1
1999	15	2	0
2000	20	5	0
2001	14	5	2
2002	20	6	4
2003	16	2	0
TOTAL	175	40	12

Judging from the titles and abstracts, each article was coded along two dimensions: (a) field, such as psychology, education, business, and political sciences, and (b) type of article, such as empirical research, introduction and translation of research or theories from other countries, or literature review. Table 13.1 shows a yearly breakdown analysis on these two dimensions.

Table 13.1 shows that the first peer-reviewed journal article on creativity appeared in 1983. The number of publications remained in the single digits until 1995, and none of these publications was empirical. After 1996, annual publications increased to two-digit numbers, and more and more publications were empirical papers from psychologists. These figures suggest that creativity research in China can be roughly divided into two stages. In the first stage, between 1983 and 1995, a

TABLE 13.2. *Trend of Creativity Research in Mainland China*

Period	No. of Publications	No. of Articles in Psychology	No. of Empirical Studies
I (1983–1995)	55	9	0
II (1996–2003)	120	31	12[a]
TOTAL	175	40	12

[a] Among the twelve publications, four were from cognitive psychology, four were from developmental psychology, two were from educational psychology, and two used a psychometrics approach.

total of 55 articles were published and only nine were in the field of psychology. In stage II, after 1996, there was a significant increase in the number of publications, resulting in a total of 120 articles, 31 of which were from the field of psychology. Table 13.2 summarizes the numbers of publications in these two stages.

In summary, creativity research in Mainland China began in the late 1970s, grew steadily, and has moved on to a new stage. However, even though there have been many studies conducted on the mainland in recent years, the number of research publications is still not very impressive, compared with those in other regions of Chinese culture, such as in Taiwan. Another search in the C-ERIC (Chinese Educational Resources Information Center) database[1] showed only eight entries when the key-words *China* and *creativity* (in Chinese) were used. Given the fact that Mainland China has set a goal to promote creativity in its citizens and in society, a flood of creativity research in Mainland China is yet to come (Niu, Shi, & Liu, 2004).

TAIWAN

Creativity research in Taiwan has also gone through several stages, from a focus on introducing Western theories and measurements of creativity

[1] C-ERIC is a database developed by the faculty of education and the Hong Kong Institute of Educational Research of the Chinese University of Hong Kong. It collects English and Chinese articles published in eighteen leading psychological and educational journals in Hong Kong, Mainland China, and Taiwan. It contains approximately 8,000 entries (including author, title, and date) on the Internet. More than 2,700 of these entries are accompanied by article abstracts. It has been chosen as a selection for the Scout Report for Social Sciences since 1998. The official Web site of the database is http://www.fed.cuhk.edu.hk/ceric

into Taiwan to the development of an indigenous psychology. At the turn of the millennium, research on creativity began to boom. The number of graduate theses grew almost tenfold compared with the previous decade. The entire region is trying to make creativity its regional icon. Educational programs targeted toward advancing creativity have never been more numerous, and grants to support creativity research are bountiful. Even at the governmental level, promoting creativity is supported with great enthusiasm. In 2002, the Taiwanese Ministry of Education initiated a series of projects aimed at making Taiwan a Republic of Creativity, or ROC, which is the same acronym used for the Republic of China. According to the *White Paper of Creative Education* promoted by the Advisory Office of Ministry of Education (2003), the hope of ROC is to make Taiwan a place where creativity is "indispensable to everyone's life and in which the preservation of creative capital will be maintained through knowledge management" (p. 17).

Nowhere else have such great efforts at such profound levels (policy, research, enterprise, and individual) been invested in such a short time. As much as creativity research flourishes in Taiwan today, most publications are written in Chinese, and therefore the impact on the rest of the world is limited. Aside from the language barrier, most creativity research in Taiwan is published in local academic journals or presented at local conferences. Access to creativity research is difficult from the outside. The following analysis is primarily based on a review of online resources of several major research teams and projects on creativity in Taiwan, and of a graduate thesis database called the Dissertation and Thesis Abstracts System in Taiwan (DTBST), with a total of 269,410 entries dated from 1956 to 2003.

A useful approach to studying the history of research in a given area is to analyze its graduate theses across different time periods. A careful examination of the DTBST database, using *creativity* (創造力) as the keyword, revealed that creativity research in Taiwan has gone through three major periods. The first period, the early period, includes the late 1960s and the 1970s, when many first-generation Taiwanese scholars pursued their degrees outside Taiwan. Within the territory of Taiwan, a total of only two relevant masters' theses completed between 1956 and 1979 were found in the database. The second period runs from the early 1980s to the mid-1990s, which I call the developing period. This is the period when scholars of the first generation returned to Taiwan and started to develop their own research and to train the second generation of researchers in Taiwan. A total of forty-seven theses (of which only one

TABLE 13.3. *Trend of Graduate Research (Master's Theses and Doctoral Dissertations) on Creativity in Taiwan*

Period I (1956–1979)		Period II (1980–1996)		Period III (1997–2003)	
Year	No. of Theses	Year	No. of Theses	Year	No. of Theses
1956–1979	2	1980	4	1997	16
		1981	1	1998	15
		1982	4	1999	15
		1983	1	2000	15
		1984	3	2001	40
		1985	7	2002	51
		1986	5	2003	16
		1987	0		
		1988	1		
		1989	3		
		1990	1		
		1991	3		
		1992	2		
		1993	3		
		1994	4		
		1995	1		
		1996	4		
SUBTOTAL	2		47		168

was a dissertation) were found between 1980 and 1996, with no more than ten completed each year. The last period can be called the flourishing period, and it refers to the years between 1997 and 2003 (with no record yet for 2004): Here the number of graduate theses rose to a two-digit figure per year (see Table 13.3). It is also a period when numerous educational programs were developed, and special government policies were formulated to promote creativity at the societal level. Also in this period, a large-scale collaboration (The Consortium for Research on Creativity and Innovation, to be introduced later in this chapter) with more than thirty accomplished scholars around Taiwan, was formed in 1998 to study creativity.

The Early Period (Late 1960s to 1970s)

Many first-generation creativity researchers had the experience of studying abroad, some of whom later had significant impact on the development of creativity research and education in Taiwan. The researchers in this period focused on introducing Western creativity theories and assessments into Taiwan. You-Yuh Kuo (郭有遹), for example, studied creativity at the University of Maryland in the 1960s. Although he continued his career in the United States at Bell State University, Kuo wrote the book *The Psychology of Creativity* (1973) in Chinese, which for the first time systematically introduced Western creativity theories and research to Chinese audiences. The influence of this book has been far reaching. Even thirty years later, it is still widely circulated in Chinese society, including both Taiwan and Mainland China, and it is regarded as a classic in the field of creativity.

During this same period, two other Taiwanese scholars, Jing-jyi Wu (吳靜吉) from the University of Minnesota (doctorate in 1967) and Wu-Tien Wu (吳武典) from the University of Kentucky (doctorate in 1975), returned to Taiwan to establish their research teams and educate young psychologists. They both became essential figures in the field of creativity and eminent leaders in many large-scale collaborations in Taiwan.

The two masters' theses completed in Taiwan this period are worth mentioning. The first study was conducted by Hsu (許健夫) from the National Cheng-Chi University (1972). In this study, Hsu introduced and revised two creativity measures, the Adjective Checklist Inventory (the subscale of creativity; see Gough & Heilbrun, 1965) and the Purdue Creativity Test (Lawshe & Harris, 1957). Using a Taiwanese sample, Hsu tested the reliabilities and validities of the two measures. The other master's thesis was completed by Wen-Hsiung Chen (陳文雄) from National Taiwan Normal University (1974). Chen's research focused on theories of creative personality, which later had an impact on the field of creativity through the personality and social approaches.

Developing Period (1980s to mid-1990s)

Compared with the earlier period, graduate research on creativity in the 1980s and early to mid-1990s grew steadily, with an average of 2.6 theses per year. A total of forty-four graduate theses on creativity were completed within seventeen years (1980–1996). Among these, nine theses studied factors attributable to the development of creative thinking (developmental approach), thirteen reported educational programs that promote student creativity (educational approach), ten investigated creativity in business organizations (organizational psychology approach), three studied creative personality (personality approach), and two were devoted to the development of creativity measurement (psychometric approach). Moreover, there were six theses on creativity from fields outside of psychology, including language, philosophy, music, and architecture. When these six theses are excluded, of the remaining thirty-eight theses, twenty-three (60.5 percent) studied creativity from a pragmatic approach, either designing educational programs to promote children's creativity (thirteen theses) or stimulating creativity in business organizations (ten theses). Therefore, an applied focus seems to characterize the research in this period.

Flourishing Period (Late 1990s to the Present)

Table 13.3 showed a significant increase in graduate theses devoted to creativity. The number of graduate theses in Stage III is 168, almost four times as many as in Stage II. The average annual number of theses produced in Stage III is 23.5, almost ten times more than were produced in Stage II (2.6 theses per year). However, the significant increase in graduate research is not the only indicator of the prosperity of creativity research in this period. There are at least three other features that further demonstrate that it is truly a flourishing period for creativity research in Taiwan.

The first feature regards research collaborations among institutions. Several large-scale research collaborations developed quickly in this period, among which is the Consortium for Research on Creativity and Innovation, or CROCI. CROCI was founded in 1998 under the leadership of Dr. Jing-jyi Wu (吳靜吉), a first-generation creativity researcher. According to its official Web site, CROCI is composed of more than thirty professors from nine different universities, all with doctorates from Taiwan or abroad, with extensive research records in psychology or related fields. An important goal of this collaboration is to seek large grants from both government and private sponsors. The professors have worked collaboratively as well as independently to complete two comprehensive research projects with multiple components, both funded by the Taiwan National Science Foundation. For example, the first project, called the Study of the Nature of Technological Creativity and Its Development (1998–2001), comprised nine components or subprojects, from studying eminent Chinese scientists, to the effects of organizational environment on creativity, to measures to assess technological creativity.

TABLE 13.4. *Content Analysis for Graduate Theses in Taiwan Between 1956 and 2003*

Approach	Stage I (1956–1979)	Stage II (1980–1996)	Stage III (1997–2003)
Developmental		9	25
Educational		13	50
Social and personality	1	3	20
Organization		10	35
Psychometric	1	2	8
Cognitive		1	10
Others		6	20
SUBTOTAL	2	44	168

Similarly, the second comprehensive project, the Study of the Creative Practice (1998–2004), includes fifteen components or subprojects. More individuals from more institutions have been involved in this project, using diverse approaches.

The second feature of this stage regards methodologies. Researchers in this period have adopted a wide range of approaches to studying creativity, including historiometric, psychometric, cognitive, social-personality, and organizational approaches.

A meta-analysis of graduate theses of this period also showed that more and more studies took nonpragmatic approaches. For example, among the 168 graduate theses, 10 (5.9 percent) used a cognitive approach; this is a significant increase from Stage II, in which only 1 graduate thesis (less than 1 percent) adopted a cognitive approach. Another significant increase is in the number of graduate works using the social and personality approach, from a total of 3 theses (6.1 percent) in Stage II to 20 (11.9 percent) in Stage III, suggesting an increase of theoretical approaches to studying creativity (see Table 13.4).

The last characteristic of this stage concerns increased support from the government. As mentioned earlier, promoting creativity has been a stated goal of the Taiwanese government, particularly in the Ministry of Education. Laws and reform policies have been formed to advocate the inclusion of creativity in Taiwanese educational curricula. With the endorsement of the government, creativity in Taiwan is not only an important research topic but also a lifelong learning goal and an asset for success in Taiwan.

HONG KONG

Creativity research in Hong Kong started with cross-cultural research comparing Hong Kong Chinese divergent thinking with that of Western societies. In the early 1980s, Jaquish and Ripple (1984a, 1984b) conducted a series of studies to examine creative thinking across different cultures (including American and Hong Kong Chinese) and different age groups (from elementary-school age to middle age), using the Torrance Tests of Creative Thinking (TTCT). Their results showed that, across all age groups, Chinese participants in Hong Kong performed less well than their American counterparts on the TTCT. The authors attributed this difference to the differences in the societal values of each culture. Studying cultural values, Ho (1996) concluded that Hong Kong had a tradition of emphasizing obedience, proper conduct, moral training, and the acceptance of social obligations and deemphasizing independence, assertiveness, and creativity. The results seemed to suggest that the Chinese culture was less supportive of creative development than the American culture.

Most creativity research in Hong Kong has been conducted in the past ten years. For example, continuing the line of research on cross-cultural comparison on creativity, Rudowicz, Lok, and Kitto (1995) found a cultural difference in favor of Hong Kong Chinese students over American students. They attributed this new result as the outcome of a prolonged effect of Hong Kong education with regard to promoting creativity.

Besides studying cultural difference in creativity, researchers have also been interested in examining the Chinese perspective of creativity and how to promote creativity in Hong Kong (e.g. Cheung et al. 2003, Rudowicz & Hui, 1997; Yue & Rudowicz, 2002).

For example, Rudowicz and her colleagues conducted a series of studies to investigate the contemporary Chinese view of creativity, first in Hong Kong (Rudowicz & Hui, 1997), and then in Mainland China, Hong Kong, and Taiwan (Rudowicz & Yue, 2000, 2002 Yue & Rudowicz, 2002). They found that Chinese individuals across all regions held a somewhat different view of creativity than Westerners (for a review, see Niu & Sternberg, 2002). For example, although Chinese and Westerners share many core features in terms of what constitutes creativity, when judging important aspects of creativity, Westerners tend to focus more on the individual characteristics of creative persons, such as sense of humor and aesthetic taste; Chinese people, in contrast, tend to focus more on the social influence of creative individuals, such as being inspirational, and contributing to the progress of society.

At the turn of the millennium, creativity research in Hong Kong began to increase rapidly and to attract researchers from different fields. For example, in social psychology, Wan and Chiu (2002) studied the effects of training in novel conceptual combination on subsequent performance in tests of creativity, and they found that solving novel conceptual combination problems enhanced creativity, which provided evidence for the notion of teaching creativity. Chan et al. (2001) studied gender difference in ideational fluency among primary-school students, using both verbal and figural forms of divergent-thinking measurements. The results revealed significant gender differences in the verbal task but not in the figural task. In the field of education, the study of giftedness and multiple intelligences attracts both researchers and schoolteachers in Hong Kong alike. To examine the validity of a self-report measurement of multiple intelligences in identifying different aspects of giftedness among Hong Kong secondary-school students, Chan (2001) gave participants two types of intelligent measures. One was the conventional IQ test and the other was a self-estimation by students of their intelligence along the seven multiple intelligences (linguistic, logic-mathematical, spatial, music, body-kinesthetic, intrapersonal, and interpersonal). A lower correlation between the two measures was found, which seemed to suggest that the two measures should both be used, complementary to one another, in identifying giftedness.

SINGAPORE

Singapore gained independence from the Federation of Malaya in 1968. The first article on creativity using Singaporean participants appeared in 1970 (Torrance et al., 1970). From that point until the late 1990s, the academic literature on creativity in Singapore was silent.

Ai-Girl Tan from Singapore Nanyang Technological University recently published a review article to introduce creativity research in Singapore (Tan, 2000). According to Tan, although promoting creativity is central to Singaporean education, and many innovative programs existed to foster creativity in school and business organizations in the 1980s and even more so in the 1990s, psychological research on creativity was sparse. Only six unpublished seminar presentation papers and one master's thesis were dedicated to studying creativity in the 1980s. Even in the 1990s, graduate theses (three doctoral projects and four masters' theses) and empirical articles (five journal articles, one book chapter, and six proceedings) on creativity were limited. The amount of research on creativity was marginal (less than 1 percent) compared with that of other research areas (e.g., 5 percent of research was devoted to suicide and mental health) in Singapore. Tan concluded that, at least by the end of the twentieth century, creativity had yet to become a significant research theme in Singapore.

To examine the recent development of creativity research in Singapore, I conducted a PsycINFO search using *Singapore* and *creativity* as keywords. I found a total of twelve entries. Eight articles were published after Tan's 2000 review article, compared with two articles published in the 1990s and only one article before that, which was published in 1970. Among the eight articles that published in the twenty-first century, five of them focused on promoting creativity in schools, such as studying teachers' perception of activities useful for fostering creativity and designing educational programs promoting student creativity in elementary schools. Results from these studies seemed to suggest that Singapore schoolteachers became more and more receptive to trying out new educational initiatives to promote student creativity. There were also another two articles addressing issues of creative personalities. For example, using the Big Five personality factors and the measure of adapter and innovator, Kwang and Rodrigues (2002) studied 164 teachers from both primary and secondary schools, and their results confirmed what had been found in other studies using Western participants; that is, innovators were strongly associated with certain personality traits such as extraversion and openness to experience. In sum, with a significant emphasis in school settings, creativity research in Singapore in the twenty-first century has grown at a promising pace, and we can expect a rapid growth in this area over the next ten years.

SUMMARY

Following this examination of creativity research in four different regions of Chinese society, it seems that the four regions followed different developmental trajectories, had different focuses, and adopted different approaches to studying creativity. In terms of research history, research in Taiwan started earlier and has enjoyed a longer history than that in the other regions (see Figure 13.1). It has also come into its

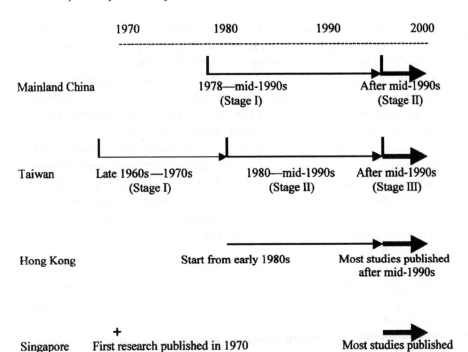

FIGURE 13.1. Comparison of the history of creativity research in Mainland China, Taiwan, Hong Kong, and Singapore.

mature stage, where both theoretical research and educational programs are given attention by researchers, funding agencies, and policy makers alike. Nowhere else in Chinese societies has creativity research attracted so much attention from both the field of psychology and the public as it does in Taiwan. In contrast, creativity research in the other three regions does not enjoy the same status. However, given the fact that there is demand for more creativity research and educational programs in each of the three regions, the study of creativity has the potential to become a rising star in both academia and practical fields (such as education and business) in these three regions.

In terms of the research focuses in the different regions, creativity research started as a by-product of giftedness in Mainland China. In this tradition, intelligence and creativity are inseparable constructs and a major theme in Mainland China's creativity research, even though more researchers are involved in creativity research and study other aspects of creativity. Mainland China also seems to have a stronger interest than the other regions in studying theoretical issues of the topic, such as cognitive and neurocognitive mechanisms of creativity. Creativity research in Taiwan, in contrast, seems to be driven by practical goals: to make its people and its society more creative. The majority of research in Taiwan focuses on how to stimulate creativity in school or business organizations rather than investigating the nature of creativity or people's views of creativity. Revising and redesigning creativity measurements has been another important research theme in Taiwan.

Different from Mainland China and Taiwan, Hong Kong and Singapore seem to share many similarities: They both started with cross-cultural research and then moved on to study creative personality and people's implicit views of creativity. Even though researchers have adopted other research methods, research on creative personality and implicit theories still accounts for significant proportions of publications in Hong Kong and Singapore.

Approaches have always been related to the research contents. Although all regions use a wide range of approaches to study creativity, they have different preferences in practicing each approach. Taiwan seems to have adopted, from the beginning, a pragmatic approach, such as educational and organizational approaches, or promoting products from a psychometric approach, whereas Mainland China from early on tried more theoretical approaches, such as cognitive, social, developmental, and neurocognitive approaches. Hong Kong and Singapore seem to have adopted more social approaches than the other regions.

Although differences in history, content focus, and research approach are many, the four regions – Mainland China, Taiwan, Hong Kong, and Singapore – share the same cultural tradition and the same fate in terms of nurturing the creativity of their people; that is, creativity is no longer devalued in the Chinese societies. With the rapid growth in global economy and cultural exchange, Chinese societies cannot afford not to promote creativity. Research on creativity has begun to draw more and more attention in both the academic and social domains in Chinese societies.

References

Advisory Office of Ministry of Education. (2003). *White paper of creative education*. Retrieved October 6, 2004, from the official Web site of the Republic of Creativity, http://www.creativity.edu.tw/modules/wfsection/article.php?articleid=195

Cai, H., Fu, Q., Sang, B., & Xu, J. (2001). Survey (I) of the public view of creativity – about the traits of the highly creative [in Chinese]. *Psychological Science, 24,* 46–49, 105.

Chan, D. W. (2001). Assessing giftedness of Chinese secondary students in Hong Kong: A multiple intelligences perspective. *High Ability Studies, 12*(2), 215–234.

Chan, D. W., Cheung, P., Lau, S., Wu, W., Kwong, J. M. L., & Li, W. (2001). Assessing ideational fluency in primary students in Hong Kong. *Creativity Research Journal, 13*(3–4), 359–365.

Chen, C., Kasof, J., Himsel, A. J., Greenberger, E., Dong, Q., & Xue, G. (2002). Creativity in drawing of geometric shapes: A cross-cultural examination with the consensual assessment technique. *Journal of Cross-Cultural Psychology, 33*, 171–187.

Chen, W. (1974). A study of creativity and creative personality (In Chinese). Unpublished master's thesis. Taipei: Taiwan.

Cheung, C., Rudowicz, E., Yue, X., & Kwan, A. S. F. (2003). Creativity of university students: What is the impact of field and year of study? *Journal of Creative Behavior, 37*, 42–63.

Gough, H. G., & Heilbrun, A. B. (1965). *The Adjective Check List manual.* Palo Alto, CA: Consulting Psychologists Press.

Guilford, J. P. (1950). Creativity. *American Psychologist, 5*, 444–454.

Guilford, J. P. (1967). *The nature of human intelligence.* New York: McGraw-Hill.

Ho, D. Y. F. (1996). Filial piety and its psychological consequences. In M. H. Bond (Ed.), *Handbook of Chinese psychology* (pp. 155–165). Hong Kong: Oxford University Press.

Hsu, J. (1972). A Study of Creativity measurements (In Chinese). Unpublished master's thesis, National Cheng-Chi University, Taipei: Taiwan.

Jaquish, J. W., & Ripple, R. (1984a). Adolescent divergent thinking: A cross-cultural perspective. *Journal of Cross-Cultural Psychology, 15*, 95–104.

Jaquish, J. W., & Ripple, R. (1984b). A cross cultural study of the life span development of divergent thinking. *International Journal of Aging and Human Development, 120*(1), 1–22.

Jin, S. (1996). On nature and measurement of creativity [in Chinese]. *Journal of Beijing Normal University (Social Science), 1*, 68.

Kuo, Y. Y. (1973). *The psychology of creativity* [in Chinese]. Taipei: Zhengzhong Publishing .

Kwang, N. A., & Rodrigues, D. (2002). A Big-Five personality profile of the adapter and innovator. *Journal of Creative Behaviour 36* (4), 254–268

Lawshe, C. H., & Harris, D. H. (1957). *Purdue Creativity Test.* West Lafayette, IN: Purdue University.

Mai, X., Luo, J., & Wu, J. (2003, June, 18th to 20th). "Aha!" effects in guessing riddle task: An ERP study. Poster session presented at the Ninth Annual Conference of the Organization for Human Brain Mapping, Beijing, China.

Niu, W. (2003a). Individual and environmental influences on Chinese student creativity. *Dissertation Abstracts International, 64* (3–B), 1517.

Niu, W. (2003b). Ancient Chinese view of creativity. *Inquiry, 22*(3), 29–36.

Niu, W., Antognazza, D., & Liu, D. (2004, August 8th to 15th). Parental rearing and children's artistic creativity: A cross-cultural comparison. Paper presented at the Thirty-Fifth International Congress of Psychology, Beijing, China.

Niu, W., & Kaufman, J. (2005). Creativity in troubled times. Individual differences in prominent Chinese writers, *Journal of Creative Behavior*, 39(1), 57–67.

Niu, W., Shi, J., & Liu, Z. (2004, August, 8th to 13th). Development of creativity research in Mainland China. Paper presented at the Thirty-Fifth International Congress of Psychology, Beijing, China.

Niu, W., & Sternberg, R. J. (2001). Cultural influences on artistic creativity and its evaluation. *International Journal of Psychology, 36*, 225–241.

Niu, W., & Sternberg, R. J. (2002). Contemporary studies on the concept of creativity: The East and the West. *Journal of Creative Behavior, 36*, 269–288.

Niu, W., & Sternberg, R. J. (2003). Societal and school influence on students' creativity. *Psychology in the Schools, 40*, 103–114.

Niu, W., Zhang, J. X., & Yang, Y. (2004, July 30th to August 5th). Does cultural always matter? Creativity yes! Deductive reasoning, no! Paper presented at the 112th Annual Conference of the American Psychological Association, Honolulu, Hawaii.

Niu, W., Zhang, J. X., & Yang, Y. (in press). Cross-cultural studies on reasoning and creativity. In J. Kaufman & J. Bare (Eds.), *Reason and creativity in cognitive development*. New York: Cambridge University Press.

Qu, X., & Shi, J. (2003, August 8th to 13th). Improving students' creativity in senior high school. Paper presented at the Fourteenth World Conference of the WCGTC, Adelaide, Australia.

Rudowicz, E., Lok, D., & Kitto, J. (1995). Use of the Torrance Tests of Creative thinking in an exploratory study of creativity in Hong Kong primary school children: A cross-cultural comparison. *International Journal of Psychology, 30*, 417–430.

Rudowicz, E., & Hui, A. (1997). The creative personality: Hong Kong perspective. *Journal of Social Behavior & Personality*, 12(1) 139–157.

Rudowicz, E., & Yue, X. (2000). Concepts of creativity: Similarities and differences among Mainland, Hong Kong, and Taiwan Chinese. *Journal of Creative Behavior, 34*, 175–192.

Rudowicz, E., & Yue, X. (2002). Compatibility of Chinese and creative personalities. *Creativity Research Journal*, 14(3–4), 387–394.

Shi, J. (1995). A systematic model of creativity [in Chinese]. *Developments in Psychology, 3*, 1–5.

Shi, J. (2000, August 8th to 13th). A natural perspective on giftedness, creativity, and education. Keynote speech at the Sixth Asia–Pacific Federation Conference for Gifted and Talented Children, Beijing, China.

Shi, J., & Qu, X. (in press). Psychological study on creativity in China in the last 25 years. *Annual Educational Psychological Review*.

Shi, J., & Xu, F. (1997). Supernormal children's creativity and its relation to intelligence [in Chinese]. *Psychological Science, 20*, 468, 477.

Shi, J., & Xu, F. (1998). Progress and problems of studies on supernormal children in China in the last 20 years [in Chinese]. *Acta Psychologica Sinica, 30*(3), 298–305.

Shi, J., & Xu, F. (1999). Intelligence, motivation, and creative thinking of supernormal and normal children, *Australasian Journal of Gifted Education, 8*(2), 11–15.

Shi, J., & Xu, F. (2004). *Developmental psychology of supernormal children* [in Chinese]. Hefei: Anhui Education Press.

Shi, J., & Zha, Z. (2000). Psychological research on and education of gifted and talented children in China. In K. Heller, F. Moenks, R. Sternberg, & R. Subotnik (Eds.), *International handbook of research and development of giftedness and talent (2nd ed.)* (pp. 757–764). Amsterdam: Elsevier Science .

Shi, J., Zha, Z., & Zhou, L. (1995). A comparative study on technical creative thinking in supernormal and normal students [in Chinese]. *Development in Psychology, 1*, 51–56.

Shi, J., Zha, Z., & Zhou, L. (1998). A cross-cultural study on the development of numerical creativity of supernormal and normal children between China and Germany. In Z. Zha (Ed.), *The mystery of the development of supernormal children – The collection of research on psychological development and education of supernormal children in China in the last 20 years* (pp. 69–76). Chong Qing: Chong Qing Publishing.

Sternberg, R. J. (1988). Preface. In R. J. Sternberg (Ed.), *The nature of creativity* (pp. vii–viii). New York: Cambridge University Press.

Tan, A. (2000). A review on the study of creativity in Singapore. *Journal of Creative Behavior, 34*, 259–284.

Torrance, E. P., Gowan, J. C., Wu, J., & Aliotti, N. C. (1970). Creative functioning of monolingual and bilingual children in Singapore. *Journal of Educational Psychology, 61*(1), 72–75.

Wan, W., & Chiu, C. Y. (2002). Effects of novel conceptual combination on creativity. *Journal of Creative Behavior, 36*, 227–240.

Xu, Z. (2000). *Construction of dimensions in Creative Intelligence Test*, Unpublished master's thesis, Southwest Normal University, Chong Qing.

Yue, X. (2001). Understanding creativity and creative people in Chinese society: A comparative study among university students in Beijing, Guangzhou, Hong Kong, and Taipei [in Chinese]. *Acta Psychologica Sinica, 33*(2), 148–154.

Yue, X., & Rudowicz, E. (2002). Perception of the most creative Chinese by undergraduates in Beijing, Guangzhou, Hong Kong, and Taipei. *Journal of Creative Behavior, 36*, 88–104.

Zha, Z. (1983). A three-year longitudinal study of supernormal children [in Chinese]. In *CRGSCCL: Monograph of study on supernormal children* (pp. 1–22). Xining: Qinhai Publishing .

Zha, Z. (1993a). *Psychology of supernormal children*. Beijing: People's Education Press.

Zha, Z. (1993b). Programs and practices for identifying and nurturing giftedness and talent in the People's Republic of China. In K. A. Heller, F. J. Moenks, & A. H. Passow (Eds.), *International handbook of research and development of giftedness and talent* (pp. 809–814). Oxford: Pergamon Press.

Zhang, J., & Chen, Z. (1996). A study on the experiment of creativity teaching for children [in Chinese]. *Acta Psychologica Sinica, 28*(3), 277–283.

Zhang, Q. (1989). An experimental analysis of the mechanism of solving insight problems [in Chinese]. *Journal of Psychology, 4*, 23–28.

Zhang, Q., Si, J., & Wang, W. (2001). The development of hypothesis-testing strategies [in Chinese]. *Acta Psychologica Sinica, 33*(5), 431–436.

Zhang, Q., & Xiao, C. (1996). Insight problem solving and representation change, [in Chinese]. *Acta Psychologica Sinica*, 28(1), 30–37.

Zhou, L., & Shi, J. (1996). *Manuscript of the Creative Ability Test*. Beijing: Chinese Academy of Sciences, Institute of Psychology.

Zhou, L., Zha, Z., and Shi, J. (1998). A cross-cultural study on the technical comprehension of supernormal and normal children between China and Germany. In Z. Zha (Ed.), *The mystery of the development of supernormal children – The collection of research on psychological development and education of supernormal children in China in the last 20 years* (pp. 52–58). Chong Qing: Chong Qing Publishing.

Zhou, Y., Zhi, F., & Wu. D. (2004). Cognitive styles and creativity among high school students in Chinese rural area [in Chinese]. *Journal of Quizhou Normal University (Natural Science)*, 22(1), 80–84.

14

Creativity – A Sudden Rising Star in Korea

In-Soo Choe

Over the past two decades, the Korean economy has grown an average of 8.6 percent annually; it became the eleventh largest economy in the world at the end of 1996. Korea also joined the Organization for Economic Cooperation and Development in late 1996. Despite this, Korea suffered an economic crisis in 1997 that lasted three years, resulting in an emergency bailout from the International Monetary Fund. Faced with this crisis, the Korean government assigned an investigation to a joint task force consisting of the Korea Development Institute and an authoritative international consulting firm. After thorough analysis, they posited five main reasons for the crisis (Booz, Allen, & Hamilton, 1997). One of the reported reasons pertinent to this chapter's main focus was the inadequate ability to create knowledge and the poor conditions for nurturing it. The investigation concluded by suggesting educational reforms to stimulate entrepreneurialism, as well as creativity.

Sparked by the report and expert advice, the Korean government has become seriously concerned about how to enhance the creative potential of the Korean people. One of the steps it took was the establishment of a national education reform committee for the task in 1996 (Korea Education Reform Committee [KERF], 1996). Creativity has become a main topic in education, business, and almost every sector recently, and the demand for finding ways of maximizing creative potential has never been higher. However, supply from the academic community has left much to be desired. Furthermore, academic research on creativity in Korea has been mainly based on a Western definition and methodology, and the amount of research exploring the role of the Korean culture is very sparse. Scholars in this field have started to examine creativity

395

within the Korean cultural context. This chapter is on the continuum of this new academic trend.

Is there Korean creativity?

Is Korean creativity a viable concept? In order to answer this question, one needs to examine the definition of creativity. To date, the widely accepted definition of creativity has been focused on the characteristics of a product as the distinguishing signs of it. The products have to be both novel and appropriate (Barron, 1988; Lubart, 1994).

If creativity is considered at the personal level, as many contemporary theorists do, it becomes hard to propose the notion of Korean creativity. This is because the psychological process is considered beyond cultural specifics. If novelty and appropriateness are considered the salient characteristics of creative products, then there should be an evaluation process deciding which product is more novel and more appropriate. In that evaluation process, the value system of each culture and society should be relevant. The previous definition of creativity, therefore, has the logical connotation of relativism. On the basis of this argument, scholars in this field argue that we also need to consider sociocultural variables that determine the manifestation of creativity (Csikszentmihalyi, 1988, 1996; Gardner, 1993; Simonton, 1999).

So far, creativity research in Korea has mainly been based on the results of Western countries, especially America (Jeon, 2000a). Foreign creativity research results that are relatively culture free, such as those of cognitive or biological studies, can be applied with equal applicability to Korean people. Idea-generation techniques and creative problem solving models have been popularly used and recognized in many areas in Korea. What about research that is particularly sensitive to cultural differences? Could that research be applied here? For example, could values that are considered to be conducive to creative achievement in foreign counties be also relevant here? Could environmental factors that facilitate Western creativity also facilitate Korean creativity? These are questions that one can answer only by considering Korean sociocultural factors.

This chapter consists of three main parts. The first part explores how Koreans view creativity. Implicit knowledge is a useful index for developing a more concrete and elaborated definition (Sternberg, 1985) and can allow cross-cultural comparisons (Niu & Sternberg, 2002). The second part reviews the trends and topics of creativity research in Korea. Topics are categorized and their corresponding frequencies are summarized to see which topics are the focus of creativity research in Korea. Finally, for a qualitative inquiry, the third part analyzes creative individuals' interviews to discover factors related to creative achievement in Korea based on the systems model of creativity (Csikszentmihalyi, 1996, 1999).

KOREAN PEOPLE'S IMPLICIT KNOWLEDGE OF CREATIVITY

Implicit Knowledge of Creativity

Implicit knowledge is the psychological constructions that are present in people before they have been taught (Sternberg, 1985). This knowledge can guide us to develop a more explicit knowledge of the construct. Exploring people's implicit knowledge also helps us to understand cross-cultural differences, as sociocultural influences are projected into implicit knowledge (Ruzgis & Grigorenko, 1994). So far, most research on this issue has been conducted in Western countries (Runco, 1990). Even though recent studies have begun to explore implicit theories in non-Western societies, the numbers are few (Chan & Chan, 1999; Lim & Plucker, 2001; Pektus, 1994; Rudowicz & Hui, 1997). There are some studies on Korean implicit theories on creativity, but most of them were written in Korean and published here (Jeong, 2002; Lee, 2001; Park & Choe, 2004), except the research by Lim and Plucker (2001), which was written in English.

Korean Adults' Implicit Theories of Creativity

There has been little agreement on the concept of creativity in Korea, although the importance of creativity is emphasized. The first step, then, should be to explore Koreans' implicit knowledge of creativity to see how they conceptualize this subtle construct.

Lim and Plucker (2001) examined Korean adults' conceptions of creativity and compared them with those of Americans. They found four interpretable factors in creativity among Korean lay people. Even though the identified factors are similar to those of Western societies (Barron, 1969; Runco, 1990), one major cross-cultural difference is that social behaviors that carry only negative connotations within the Korean culture are included in the factor of independence and deviance. Lim and Plucker also found that Korean participants regarded the creative person, or creator, as a lone person, with little of the social responsibility cherished in Korean culture. The negative conceptions of creativity are also found in Chinese culture (Chan & Chan, 1999; Rudowicz & Hui, 1997). The research of Chan and Chan showed that Chinese teachers nominated socially undesirable traits as characteristics of creative students.

On the basis of their findings, Lim and Plucker argued that Korean people's image of the creator as a loner may inhibit creative activity.

These previous results on the negative connotations of creativity led me to set about the following research.

Young Korean Students' Implicit Theories of Creativity

Given the results of implicit theories of Korean adults, I thought that investigating how Korean children think about the concept might be helpful. First of all, children are less focused on the product-oriented concept of creativity. Therefore, they would have a more free and imaginative approach to the concept of creativity because their thoughts do not have the constraint that their creative ideas should be novel and appropriate in a sociocultural context. Second, adult Koreans value Confucian tradition, which encourages individuals to obey collective social norms. It has been reported that the younger generation shares the traditional Confucian attitude much less and is characterized as more independent, self-oriented, and expressive (Kwon, 2001). Because these characteristics of young children are known to be conducive to creativity, it would be interesting to see how they perceive the behavioral characteristics of creative people. Unfortunately, studies on implicit knowledge of creativity are sparse, and those investigating young students' conceptions of it even more rare, so I conducted new research for this chapter.

Method

I used Sternberg's (1985) method to explore Korean students' implicit knowledge of creativity. I performed a preliminary study to collect behavioral checklists of creative individuals. Out of the possible domains, I selected science, because the qualitative research of this chapter is related to a domain of science – information technology (IT) – which I discuss later.

A brief questionnaire was filled out by twenty science professors (e.g., physics, biology, chemistry, and mathematics) at several leading Korean universities. They were asked to list the behavioral characteristics of

TABLE 14.1. *Characteristics of Creative People as Perceived by Korean Students*

Rank Order	Creative People are Most Likely to (be)	Rank Order	Creative People are Least Likely to (be)
1	Have original ideas	1	Selfish
2	Interested in new ideas	2	Stay alone
3	Have strong curiosity	3	Self-complacent
4	Imaginative	4	Not get along well
5	Enjoy challenge	5	Simple minded
6	Have broad interests	6	Appealing
7	Have multiple perspectives	7	Want to be only the best
8	Peculiar	8	Appreciate the beauty of nature
9	Adventurous	9	Smart
10	Open to new experiences	10	Tolerant
11	Committed	11	Plan ahead
12	Put ideas into practice	12	Do only what they want
13	Persistent	13	Calm
14	Observant	14	Behave rationally
15	Sensitive	15	Stubborn

creative leaders. I designed the main questionnaire measuring children's implicit knowledge of creativity on the basis of the frequency of mentioned items in the list. The cutoff frequency was three and, finally, I selected 57 out of 120 items.

I asked around 700 students in three different age groups (160 elementary, 265 junior high, and 277 high school students) to rate the questionnaire on the basis of how close the description is to the characters of creative people.

Results

I analyzed results by using an item-response theory, the Rasch model (Wright & Linacre, 1995); they are summarized in the tables that follow. Table 14.1 shows the comparison of the fifteen most and least likely characteristics of creative people as perceived by Korean students. In other words, for Korean students, having original ideas, being interested in new ideas, and having strong curiosity were judged as the most likely characteristics of the creative person, while being selfish, staying alone, and being self-complacent were the least likely traits.

Discussion

The results can be discussed from several points of view.

First, the behavioral characteristics of creative people found and explicitly elaborated by Western creativity researchers were also perceived as important by young Korean students. It is especially interesting that Korean students share the fairly stable set of core personality characteristics of creative people reviewed by scholars in this field such as Barron and Harrington (1981) and Davis (1998). Most of these characteristics can be found in Table 14.1.

Second, while one side of the coin reveals positive personality traits for creative individuals, the other side of the coin seems to show negative habits and dispositions that might disturb close human relations. Torrance (1981) and Domino (1970) found a list of negative traits, such as being egotistical, impulsive, and childish. As I pointed out earlier, Korean adults view the social behaviors of the creator as negative and deviant within Korean culture, which might reflect the aforementioned perceived negative traits. The young Korean students did not share this perspective. It turned out that Korean students perceive the creator as a successful leader, just as Westerners do (Niu & Sternberg, 2002). It seems that there is no deviant loner myth about creative people that is believed by Korean students.

Is it possible that two such different versions of the implicit knowledge of creative individuals exist between Korean adults and young students? This will be considered in the final discussion.

Third, although most personality characteristics needed for creative achievement were seen in the Korean sample's preliminary list of 120 items, two major traits were not apparent: ethical traits and tolerance of ambiguity. Tolerance of ambiguity is one of the five attributes (Sternberg & Lubart, 1991) and one of the sixteen traits (Davis, 1998) appearing across numerous studies of the personality attributes for creativity. Ethical attributes have also been emphasized in the behavior of creative people (Davis, 1998; Csikszentmihalyi, 1996).

TRENDS AND TOPICS OF RESEARCH ON CREATIVITY IN KOREA

Creative Research Trends and Topics in Korea Since 1980

In order to find the academic trend of current research in creativity in Korea, I searched exhaustive list of master's theses, doctoral dissertations, and published articles in major Korean journals on creativity

TABLE 14.2. *Content Analysis of Korean Creative Research Since 1980: Percentages of the Main Topics*

Creativity Research Focused on	No. of Master's Theses and Doctoral Dissertations (%)	No. of Published Articles (%)
1. Education and development	222 (42.4)	120 (43.5)
Educational methods and media program	67 (12.8)	23 (8.3)
Environment and culture	27 (5.2)	11 (4.0)
Role of teachers	39 (7.5)	8 (2.9)
Role of family	73 (14.0)	9 (3.3)
SUBTOTAL	428 (81.9)	171 (61.9)
2. Personal traits	79 (15.1)	35 (12.7)
3. Definitions and theories	6 (1.1)	46 (16.7)
4. Measurement and evaluation	10 (1.9)	12 (4.4)
5. Others		12 (4.4)
TOTAL	523 (100)	276 (100)

within the past twenty years; I categorized them by topic. For the search of published articles, I used the two largest databases in Korea: the National Assembly Library and KERIS (which stands for Korea Education & Research Information Service).[1] For the data on theses, I used results from a recent paper (Kim & Kim, in press). In Table 14.2, more than 80 percent of theses and 60 percent of published articles are focused on creativity education and its development. Without comparable data in other countries, I cannot assert that this is a salient phenomenon in Korea. It can be argued that this fact reflects the current educational situation in Korea. College examinations have become a serious social issue in Korea. This used to be called "examination fervor," but now it may well be called "examination warfare," as a Korean newspaper reported ("Staggering Korean Family," 1996). This is because, first, one's performance on the entrance examinations held during the fall semester of the senior year of high school determines college enrollment in Korea; and, second, there is a huge discrepancy between the limited number of spaces at prestigious colleges and the enormous number of applicants.

A heavy focus on the research of creativity education in Table 14.2 seems to reflect the responses of academia to the recent boom in

---

[1] The web site is http://www.keris.or.kr/

creativity and gifted education from the public. To the Korean public, the goal of creative and gifted education has been somewhat misleading; such education has been perceived as that which will help Korean children to be smart and enhance academic aptitude to guarantee good scores on the college entrance examination. The real problem is that college admission is the most salient motivation, even among the most talented Korean students (Choe, 1995). Intrinsic rewards are the third most important motivation, after material rewards for future social prestige and job and financial security, to talented and creative Korean students. However, as I will show later, eminent creative persons in Korea emphasize intrinsic rewards as a foremost motivator in creative achievement. I discuss the implications of this phenomenon in the final section of the chapter.

Change Over Ten Years of the Number of Publications in Main Topics

As explained in the introduction, there is an upsurge of national concern for the development of creativity. This interest has also been reflected in the academic domain.

Compared with the total number of publications on creativity in the 1980s, that in the 1990s has increased over 500 percent. Percentage increases in main topics during the corresponding interval were (a) 669 percent in education, (b) 300 percent in personal traits, (c) 600 percent in theories, and (d) 133 percent in measurement. The number of papers after the year 2000 is calculated only for three years, but it has already come close to the total of the 1990s. If this trend continues, projections for the first decade of the twenty-first century may increase exponentially.

Discussion

An academic focus on creativity education and development issues should not be considered a negative trend. What matters is the need for balanced research in divergent issues. In spite of the current research trend of creativity, which emphasizes the role of culture as well, creativity research in Korea has borrowed much from Western definitions and methodology (Choe, 1998). Considering the fact that there has been little effort to develop indigenous Korean creativity theories, I hope that this piece of work draws scholars' attention to that issue.

Research that focuses on theory and evaluation also has to be supplemented. To date, divergent tests such as the Torrance Tests of Creative Thinking (Torrance, 1966) have been used more than 50 percent of the time for measuring creative potential over the past twenty years in Korea (Kim & Kim, in press). Divergent–thinking tests have been challenged by two criticisms: first, divergent-thinking test scores have low prediction validity in real life, and second, there may be covariates in these test scores, such as general intelligence (Barron & Harrington, 1981). Furthermore, given that there is convincing evidence that Asians have different perspectives on creativity than do Westerners (Niu & Sternberg, 2002), the validity of using the same divergent-thinking tests for Korean samples should be reexamined.

Recently, two standardized tests – the Creative Inventory for Young Students (CIS, Choe & Lee, 2004) and the Korean Comprehensive Creativity Test for Young Children (K-CCTYC; Jeon, 2000b) – have been published. The CIS is considered the first standardized Korean creativity test to use a large sample size ($n = 7,250$). It is based on confluent theories of creativity, which emphasize that cognitive, personality, motivational, and environmental components must co-occur for creativity to exist (Csikszentmihalyi, 1996; Gruber, 1981; Lubart & Sternberg, 1995). The CIS is a pencil-and-paper test and has three main components: personality, cognition and motivation, and twelve subfactors. However, the CIS and K-CCTYC only cover kindergarten to elementary-school-aged students. More tests for measuring various aspects of creativity and covering different age spans have to be developed.

Second, another indirect suggestion based on the current research trends is that Korean parents' misconception of creative and gifted education has to be reoriented. While utilitarian definitions of creativity, focused on generating novel and appropriate ideas and products, have been welcomed mainly as a result of the need for economic survival, the aspect of creativity related to self-actualization should not be underemphasized. If creativity is part of self-actualization as Maslow (1968) and Rogers (1961) stressed, parents' main interest in instrumental benefits has to be complemented to make the education equally focused on nurturing their children's potential and helping them actualize their true selves.

Third, education policy change is also suggested. The Ministry of Education should take steps to alleviate the concern of gifted students by easing the enrollment requirements for advanced academic institutions.

This will allow the gifted students to continuously pursue their talents without diverting their precious attention from their areas of talent.

QUALITATIVE ANALYSIS OF KOREAN CREATIVITY

In the first two parts of this chapter I explored creativity in Korea on the basis of quantitative data. In order to add a more elaborate depiction of Korean creativity, here I add qualitative data from the interviews of creative leaders.

For the interviews, I selected creative leaders in the domain of IT, because (a) Korea is regarded as one of the most developed countries in the world in IT; (b) the achievement was made quickly, which enables us to view the overall dynamics of it; and (c) the innovative leaders are still alive and available for interviews. I analyzed transcribed interviews to find factors contributed to personal and national creative achievement in IT.

Creative Achievement in Korea: IT

As of the end of 2003, 11.18 million households – more than 73 percent of the total number of households – subscribed to broadband Internet access, and 66 percent of the total population had access to the Internet. According to the International Telecommunication Union 2003 Internet Report, Korea ranks first in the world in terms of broadband Internet penetration rate, has the third largest population of Internet users, and has the fourth highest personal computer penetration rate in the world. These statistics indicate Korea's firm standing as a leading IT country (National Computerization Agency, 2004). In comparison with Korea, slightly more than 20 percent of homes in the United States have broadband connections (Lewis, 2004). Evaluation of the Korean IT industry as a world leader has been reported in many world-renowned sources such as the *New York Times* (2001, 10), the *Financial Times* (2002, 5), the Organization for Economic Cooperation and Development (2001, 11) and the United Nations (2002, 6; all recited from the Korean MIC, 2003).

Korea was also a pioneer in putting the Code Division Multiple Access CDMA mobile phone system into use designed by Qualcomm. CDMA, used in many countries and expected to have more than 165 million users by the end of 2004, was once believed to be impractical for commercial use because of its technical complexity. However, Korea, in collaboration with the government and private sectors, has succeeded in using the CDMA system in commercial business since 1996 (International Cooperation Agency for Korea IT, 2003). On the basis of this technology, Korean CDMA mobile phones hold 44 percent of the U.S. market. The fact that pioneering mobile phone company Motorola has launched its mobile phone R & D center in Korea might be evidence of Korea's technical edge in the IT domain.

Method

Interview
For the research, I conducted a semistructured interview,[2] based on Csikszentmihalyi's research (1996), with participants in their offices or homes. The interview was typically two hours in length, addressing aspects of the individual's life, career, significant relations, working habits, present interests, and so on. I transcribed and analyzed the interviews.

Respondents
At the starting stage, I contacted individuals who had made significant contributions in creative achievement in the IT domain and told them the purpose of the interview. Only those who consented were interviewed. After the interview, I asked the respondents to nominate two or three candidates who they regarded as creative leaders in IT. My selection was based on the list of nominations thereafter. There were a total of eighteen participants. All the individuals are in their second half of life. The list of names and the abbreviation letters used for their identification are listed in Appendix A.[3]

Coding and Taxonomy of Factors Based on the Systems Model of Creativity
Coding for finding factors was conducted by two researchers who were aware of the systems model of creativity and its coding categories developed by Nakamura and Choe (1996). The taxonomy faithfully reflects the systems perspective (Csikszentmihalyi, 1988, 1999). First, factors

---

[2] The methods I used here are primarily based on the creativity in later life research at the University of Chicago led by Csikszentmilahyi.
[3] For the essential biographical data of the creative Korean leaders, send requests to me (flow@skku.ac.kr).

related to the "individual" system include personal qualities that affect the incidence of creativity, such as talents, motivation, cognitive styles, work habits, and personal traits. Second, factors associated with a "field" are related to its function, that is, the role of gatekeepers who have the right to evaluate and select the creative ideas and products of individuals and add them to a relevant domain. Social correlates that influence the function of gatekeepers are also included in the so-called field such as resources, opportunities, expectations, rewards, and human interactions. Finally, factors that enable a domain to preserve and transmit creative ideas developed by individuals and selected by the field are the ones with epistemological relevance, such as learning, teaching, clarity, and accessibility of knowledge.

Results

Factors needed for creative achievement in Korean IT are summarized in Table 14.3. The total number of coded factors mentioned by at least three respondents was 75, but the 14 factors that were most frequently mentioned are described in detail. Table 14.3 has information on (a) to what systems – individual, field, or domain – each factor belongs, (b) how many creative individuals mentioned the value (transformed in percentile), and (c) the rank of the percentile. Note that there are factors mentioned by the same number of respondents, resulting in the same rank.

Intrinsic Motivation

Intrinsic motivation can be considered as the single most powerful force in creative achievement. Not surprisingly, this factor turned out to be the most frequently mentioned (fifteen out of eighteen persons). There are two ways that intrinsic motivation works for the Korean creative individual. First, it gives psychological elements related to "flow" (Csikszentmihalyi, 1990) such as enjoyment, full absorption, and passion. Researchers often heard that "I've never worked in my life" in the interviews of Western creative individuals (Csikszentmihalyi, 1996). Once motivated, these people don't perceive their work as duty or investment, but play time. The conventional work–play dichotomy does not apply to them.

Second, intrinsic motivation enables people to engage in challenging tasks. CK described his preference for intellectual exercise: "I like to solve problems, which keeps me ever trying to find difficult problems.

TABLE 14.3. *Factors Related to Creative Achievement in Korea*

No.	Factor	System[a]	%[b]	Rank
1	Intrinsic motivation	I	83	1
2	Quality–excellence	I/D	83	1
3	Concentration–commitment	I	77	2
4	Learning–reading	D	72	3
5	Strong government support	F	72	3
6	Social concerns–responsibility	F/D	66	4
7	Human relations–network	I/F/D	66	4
8	Problem solving ability	I	66	4
9	Broad interests–experiences	I/F/D	66	4
10	Openness	I/D	66	4
11	Diligence	I	66	4
12	Luck	I/F	66	4
13	Sociocultural influences–zeitgeist	F/D	66	4
14	Risktaking–courage	I	61	5

[a] This is the system to which each factor belongs: I (individual), F (field), or D (domain).
[b] This is the number of respondents who mentioned the factor divided by the total number of respondents ($n = 18$).

Whenever I find a solution of a once seemingly impossible task, I fly into rapture."

Quality–Excellence

More than seventy percent of the creative adults mentioned the importance of high quality or excellence in their work. The goals of quality here are grouped into three categories: (a) thorough self-discipline and self-reflection, (b) best quality and excellence in their work and knowledge, and (c) setting clear and concrete goals and principles. All three categories are needed for perfecting the individual self, but the last two categories are related to enhancing the quality of knowledge for maintaining the status of the domain; therefore, *quality* is assigned to two systems: individual and domain.

For pursuing perfection in work, KY describes, "my interest in design will never be diverted away . . . there is always better."

Concentration–Commitment

The meaning of concentration here implies (a) focusing full attention to a task and (b) having personal commitment to one's work. Creative work requires fully functioning attention for some duration of time. CH comments that "a creative idea is just a spark of fire, you need to fuel it. That fuel is concentration." Full absorption in a task enables a person's cognition to function optimally (Csikszentmihalyi, 1990).

CK, a recipient of the World Technology Award in 2003 who succeeded in connecting the Internet from Korea to the United States, states that commitment to a challenging mission for a long duration was the key in his achievement.

Learning–Reading

Knowledge acquisition and transmission is the essential function of the domain. Participants placed strong emphasis on these processes of knowledge. Creative individuals very often emphasize the importance of reading the classics. I can't overemphasize the value of reading classic books, but it seems to apply especially to creativity.

What is salient in the interviews with Korean creative respondents is that more than 70 percent of them have read books voraciously, including the classics, since they were young. LO stressed, "my creativity comes from both reading and deviation. Books are just a verbal expression of deviation."

Most respondents also emphasized the role of passing their knowledge or practices to the following generation.

Strong Government Support and its Policy

This factor mostly describes the roles of the field succinctly.

A majority of respondents agreed that the government was also crucial to IT development in Korea. According to their reflections, government influenced its development in several ways.

First, based on the advice of the senior presidential secretaries and experts such as SJ and YS, past presidents of Korea with strong leadership in the 1980s provided enormous resources to IT.

Second, the human capital was backed up. In the 1970s, the Korean government invited Korean talent in science working outside of the country to set up laboratories in Korea and be rewarded.

Third, immunity was guaranteed. There was great support from the government to compensate for losses coming from trial and error caused by pioneering IT technology.

Fourth, government policy has encouraged competition among rival companies.

However, respondents also mentioned the negative side of the policy. For example, policies formulated at early stages of development that contributed to laying down a solid foundation for IT were unable to catch up to the rapid advancement of IT.

Social Concerns–Responsibility

Here respondents have had a strong sense of responsibility for (a) society, (b) having their work, and (c) the transmission of knowledge and skills.

Confucian tradition has valued obedience to collective social and familial norms and encouraged sacrifice of individuality to the benefit of the group (Choe, 1995; Yoon, 1977). Therefore, Koreans are expected to value social responsibility and be very patriotic. Almost all respondents are concerned about the prosperity of the nation, partly because they experienced difficult times during the colonial period of Japan and during the Korean Civil War (1950–1953). LY responded, "the only thing I've committed [to] was to help this nation to become a developed country."

Human Relations–Network

Managing good human relations has always been a universal virtue. However, in societies in which their members' autonomy and individuation have been subordinated to collective regulations, and forms of interdependent and emotional symbiosis are allowed (Doi, 1981; Triandis, 1989), the importance of human interactions cannot be overemphasized.

To Korean creative leaders, human relations are cherished as (a) an ultimate principle of behaving in everyday life, (b) having an instrumental value for outsourcing talented human resources (LSK), and (c) a source of learning and enjoyment. Human relations can be shown as a smaller subset of a larger network: diplomatic relations. Diplomatic relations were also emphasized for the development of the IT domain by PS.

A maxim of Meng-tzu (1999) was cited by LW to illustrate the importance of human relations here: "a heaven-sent opportunity is not as good as a geographical advantage, and the latter is not as good as harmony in human relations."

Learning and enjoyment are other important rewards from interacting with colleagues (SJ and CK).

Problem Finding–Solving Ability

Even though the publication by Getzels and Csikszentmihalyi (1976) of an empirical study of problem finding aroused considerable academic interest, parameters related to this were not clearly examined. However, as Einstein mentioned, "the formulation of a problem is often more essential than its solution" (Einstein & Infeld, 1938). The importance of problem identification is acknowledged among Korean creative leaders. RS and LS emphasize that "the most important thing to creative leadership is to find the true nature of a problem." CK explains, "for creative achievement, you need two essential elements. First, you must find and define the problem you want to tackle by yourself, and then stick to it. This applies to science as well as arts."

Broad Interests–Experience

Creativity may be seen as a result of a forced connection between seemingly unrelated objects (Mednick, 1962). Respondents have been involved in different domains besides their own expert areas. What is important, though, is that they are not amateurs in other areas. They have profound knowledge in those areas as well; therefore, they are in a good position to connect remote ideas: ones with a flat associative hierarchy, in Mednick's terminology. Initial involvement in different domains might have started for many reasons, but pure curiosity has helped these individuals to keep widening their knowledge. For example, CC, who majored in computer science, is now studying biology and tries to bridge genetic codes and computer programming.

The importance of broad experiences is also emphasized. LH stated that "creative leadership comes out of diverse experiences, as political power grows out of the barrel of a gun, as Mao Zedong, the late Chinese leader, believed."

Openness

Here openness first implies a receptiveness to others' criticism and different opinions; second, it implies a flexibility in the decision-making process; finally, it implies a willingness to unlearn everything that can inhibit creativity.

Emphasizing the importance of receptiveness, LW argues, "it is very important not to learn from the wrong model. You should accept diversity which can guide you to see both the forest and the trees."

In the decision-making process, balance and flexibility are also stressed. KS says, "sometimes you use intuition, but there are other times you should use all your reason. It is very important to have a balanced perspective."

For creativity, many creative individuals here put an emphasis on unlearning. RS urges, "you should forget what you experienced in the analog era, because changes are too fast in the digital age."

Diligence

Respondents stressed the value of diligence and hard work for creative achievement. JC made this observation: "Creative products are just the outcome of earnest and concentrated efforts in what one loves to do." WT added, "I would say that diligence is more important than skills in computer science." Many respondents chose the words *devotion, commitment,* and *integrity* to describe the most important virtues for young students who want to pursue IT.

Luck

An interesting finding is that many creative individuals ascribed their success to good luck. Luck is a very subtle and abstract concept to define. However, if we delve into the context of related mentions of it, we could categorize how they thought of the notion into a few understandable sets.

First, luck was mentioned in the context of human relations. LH interprets it this way: "Luck refers to relations or reciprocal communication. Once you have a relation, it triggers a chain reaction resulting in a complex human network – if a situation is linked to the network, then something happens. Caesar's Rome is just the case."

Second, being located at the right place at the right time was another factor in luck. CK commented that he happened to be at the University of California–Los Angeles, where Internet technology was developed, and that was the reason why he decided to devote his life to it.

Third, luck was mentioned as implying serendipity. WT is using the method of the so-called epoche; after a long period of deliberation, "an idea incidentally hit upon [him] within a week."

Sociocultural Influences–Zeitgeist

The naming of this factor looks vague, because it implies innumerable elements. However, the manifestations of creativity are contingent on massive and impersonal influences from Zeitgeist such as cultural, societal, and economic factors (Simonton, 1984). It is possible to find a few salient common social and cultural denominators contributed to the creative achievement in IT here.

First, there has been a social atmosphere conducive to creativity here. LO emphasizes that creativity is possible only when there is a balance between order and chaos in a society. Even though Korea's chaotic social and political order has been substantially stabilized since the Korean Civil War (1950–1953), to a Westerner, Korean society is still seen as outrageously dynamic (Bergeson, 2002). Nevertheless, there have been ordered and intense aspirations and efforts toward economic revival from all social sectors.

Second, necessity has been the mother of invention. As a result of rapid economic development, the need for efficient communications has been increased. Unfortunately, the infrastructure for it was insufficient. PS testified, "the price of a phone was the same as that of a house in the middle of the 1970s." The Korean government's strong drive for IT development was an inevitable and urgent measure.

Third, opportunities were perceived by business. The beeper business was a huge success; statistically, every person carried more than one beeper in the early 1990s. HJ explained, "after having witnessed this success, almost all the venture capital resources were put into IT."

Fourth, a totally new culture of human interaction has emerged and boomed in Korea – cyber culture (Hwang & Han, 1999) – which is due to Internet service and the new culture that keeps IT developing further. A synergistic circle is working.

Courage–Risk Taking

Are creative individuals innate risk takers? There is a motivation-related trait called sensation seeking, which includes traits of adventurousness and risk taking (Zuckerman, 1979). Davis and his colleagues reported that personality tests measuring sensation seeking would be a better predictor of creative tendencies than some creativity tests (Davis, Peterson, & Farley, 1973). There were respondents who seemed to love thrill seeking. The lists of hobbies for CK and HJ include skydiving, rock climbing, wind surfing, and running marathons. The trait may not be a prerequisite, but it seems to help in creative achievement.

In terms of personality, pride seems to be an important reason for taking risks. PS and LSJ mentioned that they decided to plunge into CDMA development because competing countries played down the Korean technology in IT.

Cross-Cultural Comparison of the Factors

For cross-cultural comparison, Korean factors were compared with those found in the sample of Western creative leaders (Nakamura

& Choe, 1996). After reviewing the interviews of the research led by Csikszentmihalyi (1996), Nakamura and Choe developed coding categories based on the systems model of creativity and found values conducive to creative achievement among Western creators.

The result shows that intrinsic motivation and social concerns are primary elements in both sets of research. A number of factors also appeared in the two nations' lists at the same time.

The difference is that there are factors in Korean research related to field and domain such as strong government support and sociocultural influences, which do not appear in the Western study. The role of the field and domain in IT development in Korea could be likened to that of the booming of nuclear physics after World War II (Csikszentmihalyi, 1996).

It is also interesting to find that the family item positioned second on the Western list was not listed in Korean research, where filial piety and harmony among family members are cherished (Yoon, 1977). One big reason is that the Korean respondents did not willingly want to mention their families' history, interacting styles, and influences on them. Koreans are reported to have a lower self-disclosure scale compared with Westerners (Lee, 1977), and they consider asking about detailed family matters to be impolite. However, it is presumed that the role of parental and marital support is essential to Korean creative leaders.

FINAL DISCUSSION AND CONCLUSION

On Implicit Knowledge of Creativity

There have been two major perspectives on creativity. First, creativity is viewed from the utilitarian perspective. From this perspective, creativity is defined as a personal capability to create novel and appropriate solutions, as explained before.

The other view sees creativity from a psychological growth perspective. This view characterizes a creative person as a fully functioning and integrated, ever-growing, mentally healthy human being, that is, as a self-actualized person. In educational settings, creativity and self-actualization have become almost synonymous (Moyer & Wallace, 1995). This view is still gaining momentum with the general public. Until recently, lay people held myths about creativity that have negative connotations; for example, creative individuals are mysterious, mystical, or even "mad." It is not difficult to cite examples from biographies of creative individuals that contributed to these myths. On the basis of dramatically bizarre episodes, lay people would easily imagine that a Renaissance man should pay some cost for his versatility. The personal traits of creative individuals would have a more panoramic range than people generally have, and their implicit theories might mainly reflect the negative end of the continuum. Having made a thorough review of the literature, Gardner (1993) argued that the "creating minds" such as those of Picasso, Stravinsky, and Freud actually had a "Faustian deal" to extend their potential.

In the research in Korea and other Asian countries, the negative conceptions of creative individuals have been reported. However, the research results of the present chapter from young Korean students' implicit knowledge provide evidence counter to the previous research. Korean students' view was also supported by the interviews of creative leaders here. Korean creators are concerned about social responsibility and ethics, which is consistent with Csikszentmihalyi's research (1996), providing evidence of a positive and optimistic picture of Western creative individuals.

Why are the implicit theories of creativity different between young students and adult lay people in Korea?

Two answers are possible.

First, a generation gap is the usual suspect. Because it is a general tendency of the younger generation to have an independent, rebellious, and even hostile attitude toward existing social norms, conceptions of creativity implying these elements, cherished by the younger generation, would be welcomed.

Second, the difference between the two generations may reflect an actual change of implicit knowledge caused by the massive influences of a Zeitgeist (Simonton, 1999) in Korea. Recently, mass media here, in line with the policy of the government, has come to treat the adjective *creative* as being synonymous with *achieved* or *succeeded*; they intensively spotlight successful creative leaders because they believe that the economic payoff to Korea is potentially huge. A recent example is that the featured article of the major press, *The Korea Times*, was that the presidential office would take the unusual step of launching a pan-government task force to financially support a scientist, Woo-Suk Hwang, who pioneered the successful cloning of a human embryo for the first time in the world, and who is expected to receive the Nobel Prize in the near future (Yoo, 2004). Slogans encouraging creative development can be seen everywhere in education as well as in business. It seems that creativity has risen to stardom, as the title of the chapter suggests. Students' implicit conceptions of creativity might be ascribed to these social phenomena.

How can we know the true cause of the difference? Is it just a generation gap, or is it a reflection of actual change? This would be an interesting avenue for future research. There is a need to compare the implicit theories of creativity between younger and older generations among Asian countries where the levels of social emphasis on creativity differ. If the results of the countries where the emphasis is lower still show a gap in implicit theories of creativity between the two generations, the answer will be clear.

Regardless of whether a person is being individually creative or historically creative, if a person is motivated intrinsically and striving for fulfilling his or her life theme, and, therefore, gets one step closer to his or her true self, why should the person necessarily become a deviant and socially irresponsible loner?

On Intrinsic Motivation

Intrinsic motivation turned out to be the most mentioned factor in the Korean sample, and third in the sample of Western creators.

This is an interesting result because, while the Western expressions attribute personally meaningful and intrinsic motives as the cause for their success, Koreans seem to prefer attributing social or instrumental motives to success, rather than intrinsic motives. One pertinent example comes from research that compared the talented and gifted students' self-reports on their academic motivational orientations between Korea and America (Choe et al., 2003). Here, regardless of their areas of talent, American students put intrinsic rewards as the primary reasons for their engagement in domains of talent. Social reasons were the least important motivators to them. In contrast, to talented Korean students, intrinsic reasons were the third most important motivators after social and material rewards.

Does weak endorsement by Koreans of intrinsic reasons reflect that they are less motivated by the reasons than Americans are, or that they just follow the contemporary rhetoric of Asian culture?

Contemporary rhetorical differences seem to be partially responsible for it. One good example is how the players express their feelings at an all-star game interview. You probably hear "I just want to have fun" from American players, while you expect from Korean counterparts that "I will try my best to win it to pay back all the debts to the family, fans, and coaching staff." Another cause of the differences may be attributed to the characteristics of an interdependent society, such as filial piety and conformity. As Hamilton et al. (1989) discovered, Japanese students, when they are studying, feel as positively about social rewards, such as meeting parental wishes, as they do about intrinsic rewards.

The results of the chapter suggest that it would be wrong to over-look the importance of intrinsic reasons as a motivating drive and its influence on the actual achievement of Korean creative individuals.

It has been researched that properties of intrinsic motivation, such as enjoyment, interest, curiosity, and challenge, are the essential determinants of talent development and creative achievement (Csikszentmihalyi, 1996; DeCharms, 1968; Deci, 1981). Consistent with the previous research, intrinsic motivational orientation has been correlated with achievement better than other motivational orientations in both nations for talented students (Choe et al., 2003).

Though East Asian contemporary rhetoric may downplay the elements of intrinsic motivation such as enjoyment, interest, and preference for challenge, the importance of them was recognized even back in the fifth century B.C. by Confucius (2004):

> Those who know a thing are not equal to those who like it.
> Those who like a thing are not equal to those who enjoy it.

Final Comments

Creativity as a catalyst for changing human conditions has to be cherished as it is. The dichotomous perspectives on creativity, whether overly optimistic or overly psychosocially deviant, are too restrictive and may hide a true understanding of the broad spectrum of creativity. It seems that implicit theories of creativity in Korea have been undergoing changes, even though we cannot affirm this until further research is conducted. The spirit of the times in Korea surely has exercised an influence on people's minds; as a result, creativity has suddenly risen to stardom here. What's missing here is a notion of creativity that arises from a natural human tendency toward growth and self-actualization. The self-actualizing creators show love for their work and become fully engaged in what they love. It is not a coincidence that Korean creative leaders ascribed their achievement to the love and enjoyment of their work. It seems that the relationship between creativity and self-actualization is in evidence in Korea, too.

I mentioned before that tolerance of ambiguity and ethical traits, which are explicitly emphasized for creativity in Western literature, were missed in the preliminary list of creative behavioral characteristics based on the implicit conceptions of Korean people. Once again, though, the importance of ethics in creative achievement was mentioned explicitly by Korean creators.

It would be interesting to see whether those missing pieces of the puzzle for Korean implicit theories of creativity will be supplemented in the near future.

Finally, I hope that more attention is paid to formulating indigenous theories of creativity based on Korea's 5,000-year-old cultural tradition.

This chapter was prepared in part with support from Brain Korea 21 project.

I thank the creative Korean leaders for contributing their time to the interviews, and I thank Jung-ha Kang for her valuable assistance with data analysis.

APPENDIX A.   LIST OF THE CREATIVE KOREAN LEADERS
INTERVIEWED, WITH ABBREVIATION LETTERS IN PARENTHESES

Cho, Hyun Jung (CH)
Chong, Chul (CC)
Kim, Young Se (KY)
Lee, Hun Jai (LH)
Lee, Sang Chul (LS)
Lee, Sung Kyu (LSK)
Lee, Yong Tae (LY)
Rhee, Shang Hi (RS)
Wui, Teri (WT)

Chon, Kil Nam (CK)
Hur, Jin Ho (HJ)
Kyong, Sang Hyon (KS)
Lee, O Young (LO)
Lee, Seung Jae (LSJ)
Lee, Won Ung (LW)
Park, Sung Deuk (PS)
Seo, Jung Uck (SJ)
Yang, Seung Taik (YS)

References

Barron, F. (1969). *Creative person and creative process.* New York: Holt.

Barron, F. (1988). Putting creativity to work. In R. J. Sternberg (Ed.), *The nature of creativity* (pp. 70–98). New York: Cambridge University Press.

Barron, F., & Harrington, D. M. (1981). Creativity, intelligence, and personality. *Annual Review of Psychology, 32,* 349–376.

Bergeson, J. S. (2002). *Outrageous Korea* [in Korean]. Seoul, Korea: Eclio.

Booz, E., Allen, J., Hamilton, C. (1997). *Revitalizing the Korean economy toward the 21st century.* Seoul, Korea: Korea Development Institute (KDI).

Chan, D. W., & Chan, L. (1999). Implicit theories of creativity: Teachers' perception of student characteristics in Hong Kong. *Creativity Research Journal, 12,* 185–195.

Choe, I. S. (1995). *Motivation, subjective experience, family and academic achievement in talented Korean high school students.* Unpublished doctoral dissertation, University of Chicago.

Choe, I. S. (1998). 5W and 1H questions for understanding creativity [in Korean]. *Korean Journal of Psychology: General, 17(1)*, 25–47.

Choe, I. S., Choi, K. S., Lee, S., & Kim, H. C. (2003, July 29). *Academic motivational orientations and achievement in talented and Korean high school students.* Paper presented at the Fifth Biennial Conference of the Asian Association of Social Psychology. Manila, The Philippines.

Choe, I. S., & Lee, J. K. (2004). *Creativity inventory for young students* [in Korean]. Seoul, Korea: Korea Guidance Press.

Confucius. (2004). *The Analects (Book VI)* [in Korean] [Translated with notes by J. K. Yoon]. Seoul, Korea: DongHak.

Csikszentmihalyi, M. (1988). Society, culture, and person: A systems view of creativity. In R. J. Sternberg (Ed.), *The nature of creativity* (pp. 325–339). New York: Cambridge University Press.

Csikszentmihalyi, M. (1990). *Flow: The psychology of optimal experience.* New York: HarperCollins.

Csikszentmihalyi, M. (1996). *Creativity: Flow and the psychology of discovery and invention.* New York: HarperCollins.

Csikszentmihalyi, M. (1999). Implications of a system's perspective for the study of creativity. In R. J. Sternberg (Ed.), *Handbook of creativity* (pp. 313–338). Cambridge, U.K.: Cambridge University Press.

Davis, G. A. (1998). *Creativity is forever.* Dubuque, IA: Kendall/Hunt.

Davis, G. A., Peterson, J. M., & Farley, F. H. (1973). Attitudes, motivation, sensation seeking, and belief in ESP as predictors of real creative behavior. *Journal of Creative Behavior, 7*, 31–39.

DeCharms, R. (1968). *Personal causation.* New York: Academic Press.

Deci, E. L. (1981). *The psychology of self-determination.* Lexington, MA: Health.

Doi, T. (1981). *The anatomy of dependence* (2nd ed.). New York: Harper & Row.

Domino, G. (1970). Identification of potentially creative persons from the Adjective Check List. *Journal of Consulting and Clinical Psychology, 35*, 48–51.

Einstein, A., & Infeld, L. (1938). *The evolution of physics.* New York: Simon & Schuster.

Gardner, H. (1993). *Creating minds.* New York: Basic Books.

Getzels, J. V., & Csikszentmilahyi, M. (1976). *The creative vision: A longitudinal study of problem finding in art.* New York: Wiley.

Gruber, H. E. (1981). *Darwin on man: A psychological study of scientific creativity* (2nd ed.). Chicago: University of Chicago Press. (Original work published 1974)

Hamilton, V. L., Blumenfeld, P. C., Akoh, H., & Miura, K. (1989). Japanese and American children's reasons for the things they do in school. *American Educational Research Journal, 26*, 545–571.

Hwang, S. M., & Han, K. S. (1999). *Korea – cyber culture* [in Korean]. Seoul, Korea: Pakyoungsa.

International Cooperation Agency for Korea IT. (2003, October) Factors related to CDMA success [in Korean]. *IT Export, 10*, 119–126.

International Telecomunications Union. (2003). *ITU Internet reports 2003: Birth of broadband* (5th ed). Geneva, Switzerland: Author.

Jeong, E. I. (2002). Implicit theory of everyday creativity and eminent creativity. *Korean Journal of Educational Psychology* [in Korean], *16(4)*, 147–167.

Jeon, K. W. (2000a). *Creatology* [in Korean]. Seoul, Korea: Hakmun.

Jeon, K. W. (2000b). *Korean comprehensive creativity test for young children* [in Korean]. Seoul, Korea: Hakjisa.

Korea Education Reform Committee. (1996). *Report on new policy for Korean educational reform* [in Korean]. Seoul, Korea: MOE.

Kim, K. E., & Kim, R. J. (in press). The literature review of research concerning Korean children's creativity [in Korean]. *The Korean Journal of Human Development*.

Korean MIC. (2003). *Annual report of telecommunication in 2003* [in Korean]. Seoul, Korea: Author.

Kwon, O. M. (2001.) *Understanding digital culture* [in Korean]. Seoul, Korea: Saemi.

Lee, J. E. (2001). *Development of creativity measurement based on implicit knowledge* [in Korean]. Unpublished master's thesis, Sungkyunkwan University, Seoul, Korea.

Lee, K. T. (1977). *Who are Koreans* [in Korean]? Seoul, Korea: Moonleesa.

Lewis, P. (2004, September 20). Broadband communication systems. *Fortune: Broadband wonderland, 150*(6), 191.

Lim, W., & Plucker, J. A. (2001). Creativity through a lens of social responsibility: Implicit theories of creativity with Korean samples. *Journal of Creative Behavior, 35*, 115–130.

Lubart, T. I. (1994). Creativity. In R. J. Sternberg (Ed.), *Thinking and problem solving* (pp. 290–332). San Diego: Academic Press.

Lubart, T. I., & Sternberg, R. J. (1995). An investment approach to creativity: Theory and data. In S. M. Smith, T. B. Ward, & R. A. Finke (Eds.), *Creative cognition approach*. Cambridge, MA: MIT Press.

Maslow, A. (1968). *Toward the psychology of being* (2nd ed.). Princeton, NJ: Van Nostrand.

Mednick, S. A. (1962). The associative basis of the creative process. *Psychological Review, 69*, 220–232.

Meng-tzu. (1999). *Meng-tzu* [in Korean] (Translated with notes by K. W. Park). Seoul, Korea: Hong Ik.

Moyer, I., & Wallace, D. (1995). Issues in education: Nurturing the creative majority of our schools – A response. *Childhood Education, 72*(1), 34–35.

Nakamura, J., & Choe, I. S. (1996). *The values of creative individuals*. Unpublished manuscript, University of Chicago.

National Computerization Agency. (2004). *White paper Internet Korea 2004*. Seoul, Korea: Author.

Niu, W., & Sternberg, R. J. (2002). Contemporary studies on the concept of creativity: The east and the west. *Journal of Creative Behavior, 36*, 269–288.

Park, S. A., & Choe, I. S. (2004). A comparison of parents' implicit knowledge on young children's creative trait [in Korean]. *Human Life Science, 7*(1), 207–222.

Pektus, E. (1994). Ninja secrets of creativity. *Journal of Creative Behavior, 28*, 133–140.

Rogers, C. (1961). *On becoming a person*. Boston: Houghton Mifflin.

Rudowicz, E., & Hui, A. (1997). The creative personality: Hong Kong perspective. *Journal of Social Behavior and Personality, 12*, 139–148.

Runco, M. A. (1990). Implicit theories and ideational creativity. In M. A. Runco & R. S. Albert (Eds.), *Theories of creativity* (pp. 234–252). Newbury Park, CA: Sage.

Ruzgis, P., & Grigorenko, E. L. (1994). Cultural meaning systems, intelligence, and personality. In R. J. Sternberg & P. Ruzgis (Eds.), *Personality and intelligence* (pp. 248–270). New York: Cambridge University Press.

Simonton, D. K. (1984). Generational time-series analysis: A paradigm for studying sociocultural influences. In K. Gergen & M. Gergen (Eds.), *Historical social psychology* (pp. 141–155). Hillsdale, NJ: Erlbaum.

Simonton, D. K. (1994). *Greatness: Who makes history and why.* New York: Guilford Press.

Simonton, D. K. (1999). Creativity from a historiometric perspective. In R. J. Sternberg (Ed.), *Handbook of creativity* (pp. 116–136). Cambridge, U.K.: Cambridge University Press.

Staggering Korean family due to "examination warfare." (1996, January 29). *The Korea Central Daily,* p. 1.

Sternberg, R. J. (1985). Implicit theories of intelligence, creativity, and wisdom. *Journal of Personality and Social Psychology, 49,* 607–627.

Sternberg, R. J., & Lubart, T. I. (1991). An investment theory of creativity and its development. *Human Development, 34,* 1–31.

Torrance, E. P. (1966). *Tests of Creative Thinking.* Lexington, MA: Personnel Press.

Torrance, E. P. (1981). Non-test ways of identifying the creatively gifted. In J. C. Gowan, J. Khatena, & E. P. Torrance (Eds.), *Creativity: Its Educational Implications* (2nd ed., pp. 165–170). Dubuque, IA: Kendall/Hunt.

Triandis, H. C. (1989). The self and social behavior in different cultural contexts. *Psychological Review, 96,* 506–520.

Yoo, D. H. (2004, October 8). Support due for stem cell pioneer [in Korean]. *The Korea Times.* Retrieved October 8, 2004, from http://times.hankooki.com/lpage/nation/200408/kt2004 081017022811970.htm

Yoon, T. L. (1977). *The characteristics of Korean people* [in Korean]. Seoul, Korea: Hyun-am.

Wright, B. D., & Linacre, J. M. (1995). *Bigsteps: Rasch analysis for all two-facet models.* Chicago: MESA Press.

Zuckerman, M. (1979). *Sensation seeking.* Hillsdale, NJ: Erlbaum.

15

Culture and Facets of Creativity

The Indian Experience

Girishwar Misra, Ashok K. Srivastava,
and Indiwar Misra

Sa vai naiva reme, tasmādekākī na ramate.
Sa dwitiyamaichata.

[He did not enjoy himself alone.
He desired – I am alone, let me have a second one.]

– Brhadāranyaka Upanishad, 4.3

Apāre kāvyasamāre kavirekah prajāpatih
Yathāsmai rochate viswam tathetadparivartate

[In the endless world of poetry the poet is the only Creator and he shapes
this world, as he likes.]

– Anandvardhan (1975; Dhvanyaloka Commentary on 3.42)

INTRODUCTION

It is often believed that creativity is demonstrated when we indulge
in contributing something original or novel and useful to the domains
of objects and ideas. Thus any creation, irrespective of its domain, is
deemed "creative" to the extent that it is different from earlier creations
and has functional value (Runco, 2004; Sternberg & Lubart, 1996). In this
way, creativity challenges tradition, questions the status quo, and brings
in change and innovation. At the same time, the flexibility introduced
by creativity empowers people to act more effectively in relation to self
as well as environment.

We acknowledge the support of the Indian Council of Social Science Research, New
Delhi. Correspondence concerning this article should be addressed to Girishwar Misra,
Department of Psychology, University of Delhi, Delhi-110007, India. Email: misragirish-
war@hotmail.com

421

Since creativity involves originality and novelty, it is sometimes considered to be a gift of God, but discoveries and inventions clearly imply the role of human effort. In fact, creativity is paradoxical in many respects and defies any simple characterization. Creativity is often conceptualized as a general human ability, but its apparent recognition in different areas suggests the need to accommodate diverse creative talents. Similarly, while it is related to intelligence, highly intelligent people are not necessarily highly creative. Formal schooling, which is considered to nurture knowledge, is also not very strongly related to creativity. Creativity is often considered as an outcome of sudden insight, but most people tend to agree with the view that endurance too is important. Poets, artists, scientists, and other thinkers generally agree that seeing, thinking, and acting in novel ways requires hard work, motivation, and concentration. Drawing attention to asynchronies, Gardner (1993) made a pertinent observation: "What seems defining in the creative individual is the capacity to exploit, or profit from, an apparent misfit or lack of smooth connections within the triangle of community consisting of individual, domain and field" (p. 381). Interestingly, the most asynchronous case in Gardner's sample happened to be an Indian – Gandhi – who "had to cultivate, to embody, a being who was at once synchronous with the rest of the society and humanity and distinctly marginal, someone positioned to bring about radical social change" (p. 383).

Until recently, the scientific analysis of creativity has largely been appropriated by a strong compulsion to depend on discrete, objective, quantitative, and abstract analysis, with little care for the context. This positivistic analysis has been preoccupied with creative product or the creative person. The systemic and multilevel view offered by Csikszentmihalyi (1996) recognizes that creativity results from the interaction of a system composed of three elements – a *culture* that contains symbolic rules, a *person* who brings novelty into the symbolic domain, and a *field* of experts who recognize and validate the innovation. All three are necessary for a creative idea, product, or discovery to take place. In this context, Gardner's (2001) remark is pertinent: "the question is no longer what creativity is? Instead we must ask where creativity is. And creativity inheres in the dialectic or the dialogue among the field, the domain, and the individual" (p. 130).

Creativity is undoubtedly universally valued, but diverse cultures do appear to selectively nurture specific domains of creativity. As a consequence, the conceptualization, manifestation, and societal organization of creativity vary across cultures. It seems reasonable to assert that different forms and domains of creativity flourish in different cultures, which, in turn, shape the culture. We need to respect multiple visions, pluralism, and diversity of thought, reflecting what Raina (1996) termed the *Torrance phenomenon*. Recently, Raina (2004) proposed that the metaphor of *garland making* is more promising and practicable in addressing cultural variety in the human creative potential. He argued that the complexity and complexion of creativity can be understood in terms of a garland made out of flowers of different colors, fragrance, and shape. A garland is structure that respects diversity. Against this backdrop, in this chapter we endeavor to expand the scope of discourse on creativity by presenting an overview of the conceptual and empirical developments in the field of creativity in the Indian context. First, we delineate an indigenous perspective on conceptualizing creativity. To this end, we discuss Indian thought systems, creation myths, and Indian views on intuitive creativity. We then present the diverse trends in creativity research in India.

CREATIVITY: A CULTURALLY POSITIONED PROCESS

Bhawuk (2003) proposed that cultures moderate the channeling of individual abilities toward certain creative behaviors. Since creativity is a sociocultural behavior, it is applied to solve social or ecological problems. Culture provides the Zeitgeist for creative behaviors, and it influences the area of creative behavior. Geniuses also go on to shape the Zeitgeist, and culture in the long term, in a significant way. Thus culture, Zeitgeist, and genius are reciprocally related in shaping creative behavior. Gardner (2001) has also hinted at this point by saying that, while the Western idea of creativity is *revolutionary*, the Asian cultures favor an *evolutionary* view. Western cultures have recognized creativity most in the service of human needs, largely in a materialistic sense. This has led to an emphasis on a product-oriented approach (Lubart, 1999). It is, therefore, not surprising to find the qualities of novelty and functionality as critical to the identification of creativity. This, however, cannot do justice to the idea of creativity in other cultural traditions (see Misra, 1996; Pandeya, 1981; Raina, 1993). As Nisbett et al. (2001) argued, cognitive processes are embedded in different naïve metaphysical systems and tacit epistemologies, which in turn are rooted in divergent social systems. They have marshaled evidence, based on philosophic-historical analysis as well as experimental work, to argue that the Asians, particularly the Chinese, are *holistic*. They attend to the entire field and assign causality to it, make limited use of formal logic, and rely on dialectical reasoning. In contrast, Westerners are more *analytic* and pay attention to objects and categories to which things belong and use formal logic to understand behavior.

Creativity as a value has received considerable attention since antiquity from thinkers of various pursuits in India. Creation is considered as a natural desire of human beings involving self-extension. The Indian worldview has strong commitments to the idea of renewability and transformation. The doctrine of *karma* (deeds) and reincarnation bring into the center the interplay of continuity and change in one's existence. Life is a part of a cycle of birth and death controlled by one's own actions (*karmas*). The *karmas* shape creative potential (Chapple, 1986). Destruction as well as construction both are given due importance in this cyclical perspective. Realizations of life goals (*purushartha*) require the pursuit of enduring meditative effort (*sādhana*). At the macro level, a divine trinity of Brahma, Vishnu, and Mahesh are posited to regulate the processes of creating, maintaining, and destroying the world.

It may, however, be noted that the contemporary Indian mentality has been informed by many sources that make Indian culture pluralistic. The Indian way of thinking has been characterized as context sensitive (Gergen et al., 1996; Misra, 1999; Misra, Suvasini, & Srivastava, 2000; Nakamura, 1964; Ramanujan, 1990) and operates with abstract generalization and universal categories. This tradition is continuously represented in the Indian mind. It is this quality that distinguishes Gandhi from other creators in the study by Gardner (1993). He noted that, alone among the creators he studied,

[Gandhi used] to speak directly to other human beings, not as members of a group or domain but by dint of their humanness. He sought to create a story, a conception, and a way of being that could make sense to every other individual irrespective of his or her particular history or craft. Difficult as it is to change a domain, it is far more challenging to create a new narrative and to render it convincingly to other individuals. (Gardner, 1993, p. 356)

India, more than any other cultural region, offers a pluralistic vision of knowledge. Even a casual analysis of systems of thought such as Vedic, Samkhya, Yoga, Vedant, Buddhist, Jain, and the like makes it clear that there is diversity in viewing reality. The vast amount of indigenous literature deals with almost all areas, including philosophy, medicine, mathematics, polity, and literary theory. They are empirical, oral, language informed, and full of a multidisciplinary orientation. The remarkable openness to different views is because the Indian mind accepts the possibility of more than one path to truth. Following Misra and Gergen (1993), the Indian perspective on reality and human functioning is characterized by the following features:

- a holistic–organic worldview;
- a coherence and natural order across all life forms;
- a socially constituted–embedded and relational concept of person;
- nonlinear growth in life;
- continuity across various life forms;
- social individualism;
- the temporal and atemporal existence of human beings;
- a contextualized relationship depending on time, person, and place;
- an emphasis on self-discipline;
- a shared and relational notion of control;
- knowledge as moral and sacred;
- a functional belief in multiple worlds (material-transitory and spiritual-eternal); and
- a moral code centered on *Dharma* (duty).

Sinha (2002) identified Western influence, ancient Indian wisdom, and folkways as important components of contemporary Indian tradition. He noted that Vedant tradition provides an integrated and comprehensive psychospiritual worldview that is ingrained in the minds of Indians. It has three main facets, namely, *cosmic collectivism, hierarchical order*, and *spiritual orientation* (Roland, 1988, p. 294). Cosmic collectivism posits that the universe consists of forms and elements. They are compatible as well as conflicting, but are blended, balanced, or held together by an underlying sense of unity derived from being parts of the same ultimate reality. Hierarchical order signifies that the whole cosmos and everything within it are arranged in a hierarchical order of being superior to some and inferior to others. Spirituality implies that, although human beings are by nature restless, unstable, greedy, selfish, impulsive, and so on, they have an inbuilt disposition toward self-transformation through the acquiring of finer and subtler qualities of spiritual nature, which they can realize by cultivating an "observer (drashtā) in their mind. The observer enables them to integrate various activities and emotions, expand consciousness, acquire purity in thought and action, and transcend (rather than suppress) impulses, to become fully liberated of all those concerns which constrain self-transformation" (Roland, 1988, pp. 444–445).

In the Hindi language, the terms *srijanātmakatā* and *sisrksā* are used for creativity. They indicate the desire or purpose to create (Apte, 1973, p. 604; Williams, 1974, p. 1218). *Sisrksā* means intending to eject and emit, wishing to create and produce, and wishing to create. Thus a creator is someone desirous, or wishing, to flow and emit. The root *sri* from which it is derived means to produce, to create, procreate, let go, let loose, and release. These words refer to the creative action or activity of a person. This world is called *srsti* (creation) because it is created. The creator is like a person in search of liberation. "Creation" implies immediately the feeling of a need to create some product or other. The need for creation is located in the need for people's adjustment to their environment, as required by the struggle for survival. The need for perfect adjustment or harmony involves transcendence on the part of artists' minds from the world of change of which they themselves are a part. Shastri (1997) argued that creativity engages inspiration and imagination that helps one to think beyond the given and bring in the elements of novelty in our world of experience.

CONCERNS FOR CREATIVITY: INDIAN CREATION MYTHS

Conceptions of creativity often derive from a culture's creation myths. These myths are narratives of prototypical forms of creativity and articulate expectations for its inheritors. With this in mind, our quest for Indian perspectives on creativity may begin with an examination of some of the creation myths.

Interestingly enough, the early Indian texts, namely, Vedic and Upanishadic ones, do not share the idea of a central creator god. The following verses from *Rig Veda*, one of the earliest texts, present an abstract idea of creation and being. It wonders whether the origin was out of Being or nonbeing. It was asserted in the Upanishads that being could come out of being only, so in the beginning there was being. When this Being is identified with the absolute reality (Brahman), can we treat the Brahman as a person? The Indian thinkers gave both affirmative and negative answers.

> First, there was neither Absence of Being nor Being,
> Nor the spacious sprawl of the void overhead.
> What kept everything hid? What shut everything in?
> Was it the deep and dark waters without an end?
> . . .

Desire it was that lifted out at the start –
That very first seed, thrusting the spirit up,
And Desire that thinkers found as the bridge that led back
From Being to Absence of Being, when they sounded their hearts.
. . .
Surely He knows this secret for He has contrived it.
He controls it from Heaven: He, the first thrust
Of creation, who parted Being and Absence of Being –
Or Maybe He doesn't know what He's done, or how.

> – *Rig Veda*, Nasadiya Sukta, X.129 (translation by Misra,
> Nathan, & Vatsyayan, 1983, pp. 51–52)

In *Praśnopanisad* (another ancient Indian text), the sage Pippalada responds to the inquiry about how creatures were created by saying that Prajapātii (the creator God) did penance and through it created couples (polar opposites), which in turn created the world. The couples were *Rayi* (material, stuff) and *Prān* (the life principle). The life principle is the cosmic person. The *Taittirīpanisad* indicates that the reason for creation is the intense experience of aloneness and the purpose is self-extension.

The *Brhadāranyaka Upanisad* states that, in the beginning, there was the *Ātman* (Being). It did not know anything else and asserted, "I am," and became the "I." Then it felt lonely and was afraid, but it wondered why it was afraid. One is afraid of some other, but there was no other. Then it became the two, man and woman. Humans were born of them. The state of love and embrace, which is unmanifest, becomes the manifest world. In many narratives the primordial man desires, or in order to actualize himself, emanates, emits, releases, or lets flow out of himself a part of his substance. This self-substance progressively evolves into the world and its creatures, including the human body and mind; finally the emanator may "enter" his world or its constituent parts as himself (ātman).

Maharshi Mahesh Yogi (1970) put the essence of this thinking in the following manner (see Aron & Aron, 1982; Bonshek, 2001):

When an artist expresses himself, he tells the whole story of creation. The Upanishads describe this aspect of the Creator in a very beautiful expression. They say, "Having created, he enters into creation." The expression of a piece of art is the expression of the life of the artist. Just this phenomenon is described in terms of the Creator entering his creation, and when the Creator enters his creation, the creation becomes lively. When the artist expresses himself in a piece of art, which is an automatic phenomenon, spontaneously the creation contains its creator. This phenomenon of the piece of art containing the expression of the heart and mind of the artist is itself the promotion of life. The artist promotes life on a lifeless piece of paper or stone. (Maharshi Mahesh Yogi, 1970, p. v)

AN EVOLUTIONARY VIEW OF CREATIVITY: SRI AUROBINDO'S VISION

Contrary to deviance, the change and discontinuity emphasized in the West, the Eastern view emphasizes self-fulfillment or self-realization and the development of creative purpose. Thus while innovative products are not disregarded, creativity is often treated as a state of fulfillment or the expression of inner essence. As Raina (2002) articulated, the essence of human existence in the Indian tradition is to "affirm themselves in the universe" and "to evolve and finally to exceed themselves" (p. 168). The aim of human life is "to grow by an inner and outer experience till he could live in God, realize his spirit, and become divine in knowledge, in will, in the joy of being. This is the deeper intention, the dominant motive in all creative strivings in India" (Raina, 2002, p. 168).

In the Indian tradition there are many approaches to self-transformation or evolution. However, for want of space, we refer to the views of Sri Aurobindo that integrate many of the earlier perspectives and explicitly use an evolutionary framework. From this perspective, creativity involves self-transformation and discovery of the inner self, as "we are not only what we know of ourselves but an immense more which we do not know; our momentary personality is only a bubble on the ocean of our existence" (Dalal, 2001, p. 337). Sri Aurobindo referred to the levels and evolution of consciousness:

Consciousness appears in what seems to be inconscient, and once having appeared is self impelled to grow higher and higher and at the same time to enlarge and to develop towards a greater and greater perfection. Life is the first step of this release of consciousness; mind is the second; but the evolution does not finish with mind, it awaits a release into something greater, a consciousness which is spiritual and supramental. (Dalal, 2001, p. 338)

While thinking about being, people usually think of the individual being, just as when we consider consciousness, we generally take it at the level of the individual. However, seen from the perspective of spiritual consciousness, both the individual and the universe are simultaneous and interrelated expressions of the same transcendent Being: "Universe is a diffusion of the Divine All in infinite Space and Time, the individual its concentration within limits of Space and Time" (Dalal, 2001, p. 348).

Sri Aurobindo (1985) distinguished two systems simultaneously active in the organization of the being and its parts. One system is concentric, like a series of rings or sheaths; the other is vertical, like a flight of steps. The concentric system consists of the outer or surface being, the inner being, and, supporting both of these, the inmost being or the psyche. The outer being and the inner being have three corresponding parts – mental, vital, and physical. Thus, it might be said there are two beings in us. One is on the surface, that is, our ordinary exterior mind, life, and body consciousness; the other is behind the veil, that is, an inner mind, an inner life, an inner physical consciousness – constituting another or inner self. The vertical system consists of various levels or gradations of consciousness below and above mental consciousness – the level with which we are most familiar as human beings. The misperception is the contribution of ego, which creates a wall and a sense of separation between the individual being and the universal being. This is why a reconditioning of ego has been recommended. Yoga, through its various stages, leads to self-realization.

Here, it is also important to note that a similar process is described in creativity in the material world. The artist's concentration on the object of his or her creativity is an analogue of the yogic meditation. The practice of visualization, as Coomarswamy (1957) remarked, is "identical in worship and in art" (p. 27). He identifies seven stages of an artist's meditation:

1. The artist ceremonially purifies himself or herself.
2. He or she will withdraw to a solitary place.
3. There the artist he offers daily acts of worship to the deities and the deity.
4. He or she must realize in thought the four intimate moods of friendliness, compassion, sympathy, and impartiality.
5. Then the artist must meditate on the vast emptiness. It destroys the ego consciousness (*ahamkāra*).
6. Then he or she could invoke the desired divinity of the desired utterance of the appropriate *bīja* or the mystical letter forming the essential part of the mantra of a deity.
7. Finally, on pronouncing the *dhyāna* mantra (description of the personal attributes of the deity), the divinity appears visibly, "like a reflection" or "as a dream."

The artist in stone or in words then realizes this image. The artist is in the role of a pious artisan, a worshiper or a practitioner of meditation (*sādhaka*). The artist is not a creator – he or she is a revealer of the inherent *tattva* (element) or *bhāva* (affect). The Indian tradition treats *kumbhakār*, the potter, as the paradigm artist, who merely fashions forms (*rupa*) out of preexisting substance (*dravya* or clay) by shaping. With his or her hands, this artist is in communion with the clay; in that state, the "form" in the mind flows through the hands to the clay and the form comes alive. The forms are inherent in the substance – the artist reveals them and makes it possible for the senses to recognize them (see Kapoor, 1998, pp. 82–83 for details).

THE PARADIGM OF *PRATIBHĀ* (INTUITIVE CREATIVE FACULTY)

The word *pratibhā* refers to a flash of light, a revelation; it is usually found in the literature in the sense of wisdom, characterized by its immediacy and freshness. It may be called the supersensuous and suprarational appreciation, grasping truth directly, both as a faculty and as an act in Indian philosophy, as intuition has in some of the Western systems (Kaviraj, 1966). It is this human faculty that is distinct from intellect, in which originates all human creativity. Thus, the insights into the human condition that we owe to the great poets, novelists, and storytellers have their origin in that mysterious faculty of pratibhā.

Within the Indian poetic discourse, the concept of pratibhā or creative power has received detailed attention. It leads to a realization of new meanings (*Navanavonmesasālinī pratibhā*) and a creation of something new that had no prior existence (*Apūrvastunirmanksamā prajna*). It enlightens the artist inwardly and helps in visualizing unseen and remote things. In some ways a poet is considered as a creator, and in some sense he or she is more powerful than the god. One of the Indian mythological narratives holds that the god Prajapati is the creator of the world. While engaging in any creation, he needs some material from which a thing is to be created and also an instrument for creating the intended object. In contrast, a poet requires nothing other than his or her own capacity or pratibhā to create the poetic world. The poet's unique creative power manifests in a world on the substratum of his or her own will. The poet uses his or her mind and creates something original (*apurva*). Abhinavagupta maintains that a poet is like a Prajapati (creator god), is capable of creating a new meaning. A poet is capable of creating things without any cause–effect boundaries (*apurvam yadvastu prathayati vinā kāranākalām*).

The notion of pratibhā, however, is not necessary only for the poet to produce a poetic work, but equally for the aesthete to grasp the suggested meaning of the literary work. It is possible only for a person gifted with pratibhā to visualize the suggested meaning. Such an appreciation is not simply a matter of inference but direct experience. "It involves the subjective experience of overcoming one's individuality, and entering into what is presented by the creator or poet. . . . The aesthete does it by getting merged into it through identification with the focus on situation. Hence the experience of the power of poetic production is secured by the aesthete not by inference, but by experiencing in him what is directly presented" (Deshpande, 1989, p. 124). The functioning of pratibhā has its start in the blissful state of the poet's mind (*rasāvesa*) and realizes its completion in filling the reader's heart with the same kind of bliss (*rasāswād*). Thus the creative faculty and an appreciative taste both are important. According to Rajshekhar (1924), pratibhā is of two types: creative (*kārayitrī*) and critical (*bhāvayitrī*). Karayitri pratibha or creative talent is the ability to put or represent one's felt experience in words and other devices of communication. It is the faculty of the poet to create. Bhāvayitrī pratibhā is the ability to feel and understand the experience put in the composition or the ability to appreciate and understand life's experiences. A person who is endowed with an experiencer's sensibility can feel the suffering of the other, as his or her own is called *sahrdaya* (a person having a heart that shares with others). The person has comprehension of the general nature of a bhava (emotion), from particular instances independent of specific objects and events. Such a person shows communion with the aesthetic experience.

The creative talent (kārayitrī pratibhā) is rooted in three sources. It may be innate or genetic (*Sahajā*), developed by knowledge (Āhāryā), and instructed or acquired by training (Aupdeshik). The creative artist is made through the processes of practice (abhyāsa), concentration leading to heightened consciousness (samādhi), erudition (vyutpatti), and pratibhā. The primacy and weighting of these factors in the composition of creativity has been an issue of debate. There are three positions. Some say that pratibhā is the source of composition. It is a kind of intellect that keeps getting new insights and ideas. Some argue that vyutpatti and abhyāsa constitute the source of poetry. Some others hold the view that pratibhā, vyutpatti and abhyāsa, all three, are the sources of composition. Pratibhā is considered as an innate faculty – a predisposition. It may be impressions and memories from previous births (*samskārās*), or it may be produced here and now by the example and guidance of others or by a study of theoretical texts and poetry (*sāstras* and *kāvyas*). According to Suroor (1992), the creative imagination constructs a new combination of ideas and images from its inner resources and thus gives to "airy nothing, a local habitation, and a name."

CREATIVITY IN THE INDIAN TRADITION: SOME INDIGENOUS FEATURES

The creative works in the Indian tradition show a number of features that distinguish them from other traditions. For instance, creative people often remain anonymous. The result is that the work belongs to the community. This tradition attaches little significance to the individual (author) in the creative process. In no other country can one find such a rich folk tradition, breath-taking architectural and sculptural works, monumental epics, and the meticulously elaborated texts in law, literature, and science that do not carry with them any signs of their creators. One reason for this is that creativity is attributed to spirit or divinity. While referring to creativity in music, Sharma (1996) considered that creation can be understood as self-extension. The search for the relationship between the inner world and the outer existence is a central inspiration to creativity. It is present in the life and work of modern artists too. For instance, in a study of artistic creativity, Maduro (1976) noted that "the creative artist is one who contacts the psychic reality within the depths of himself... strive(s) to make it manifest, to become one with it, integrating it through differentiation. In the very real sense, the artist is enjoined to recreate, or reactivate, what is already latent in his unconscious" (p. 135).

The second feature that draws attention is that creativity is rooted in the surroundings. It is continuous with the environment and seeks relationship. It is not incidental that the Sanskrit term for literature, *sahitya*, has an inherent meaning of companionship. As Misra (1992) put it, "creation is an act of intervention in the void and is impelled by a compulsion to come out of one's shell at the risk of one's partial or total annihilation. Therefore, every creative writer or for that matter every artist is deeply concerned with how to interact with his or her environment, natural, cultural and socio-political" (p. 1). In addition to the external environment, the internal environment that we carry within ourselves also has to be explored. Indian seers and sages have sought refuge in this vast internal environment and have sometimes, even deliberately, been oblivious of external phenomenon.

The absence of a clear dichotomy between self and nonself brings in the third feature: A human and the environment share a symbiotic relationship in which the human is not the conqueror of the environment, but is one among all living matter. Creativity, therefore, is conceived as inherently positive. It is in this context that the goal of literature was considered to be removal of evil (*shivetatraksataye*).

Celebration of variety and diversity is the next aspect of creativity. The genre of *nrtya* (dance) clearly demonstrates this quality. Even the gods dance, and the dance of each god has a different connotation. For example, the dance of Lord Ganesh was considered a dance of creation and well-being. It shows the way true creativity can shape the whole universe. Maha Kali danced to address the evils. Sri Krishna's dance with Radha represents the yearning of the individual soul to merge with the divine universal soul. The lord of dance is Shiva (Nataraj). When a dancer dances to the beat of the mridangam (a drumlike musical instrument), to the note of the flute, with the movement of limbs, gestures, bhava or expression, rhythm of feet and the song of the musicians, one could not help but experience the divine. Bharat Natyam, Odissi, and Kuchipudi all are vibrant and dynamic Indian dance forms that share these features (for details, see Vatsyayan, 1968).

Creativity in various domains involves experiments and innovations, which excel in organization, interpretation, and presentation of traditions in newer ways. They are evolutionary and extend or elaborate the tradition. It is interesting to note the peculiar style of aphorism or brief statements (*sūtra*) that are easy to memorize and have elaborate interpretations (*bhäsya*). We find a great variety of interpretive texts like *tīkā* (commentary) on various sutra texts in almost all areas of scholarship.

CONTEMPORARY TRENDS IN CREATIVITY RESEARCH

Scientific Creativity

Psychologists have tried to answer this question: What enables scientists to make notable contributions to their disciplines? In the recent past, many Indian scientists tried to reflect and analyze the notion of creativity. For instance, Majumdar (1996) noted that the creator's intuitive feeling for the form or beauty of the thing being created is central to scientific creativity. It guides the creator in his or her endeavor. Here beauty is considered as the proper conformity of parts to one another and to the whole. A creative scientist can also see the correct pattern from the mass of data. This is termed the *musicality of scientists*. As an organized social institution, science distinguishes itself from artistic creativity, which is primarily an individualistic and spontaneous effort. There is beauty in functional things, and scientists are driven by the desire to capture that beauty in the things they create. Mukunda (1996) considered art and science to be are two complementary domains of human creativity. Both are dedicated to communication, it is just that their spheres are different: One deals more with the inner or subjective world, while the other deals with the outer objective or public world.

Bhargava and Chakrabarty (1996) examined the interplay of creativity and beauty. They proposed and tried to substantiate the interesting thesis that "when man creates, he is essentially generating beauty. His success depends on the extent to which what he has created is analogous to what is found in Nature and is in consonance with certain natural laws. Consequently, in man's eternal search for beauty, he is also – sometimes consciously and sometimes unconsciously – seeking similes with Nature" (pp. 67–68). Creativity and beauty are related in all areas of human endeavor, including science. The prime motivation for all creative activity is an awareness of the surrounding environment, and the recognition of the fact that there are unanswered questions. It is only when one transcends personal interest that a person becomes creative.

Tripathi (1993) reported on a study that was based on interviews of outstanding scientists working in the physical and biological sciences, about various aspects of creativity. The findings showed that there are multiple pathways to scientific creativity. For instance, the scientists enumerated a number of conditions favoring creative thinking, including a quiet place, music, discussion with students, and walking. Asked about the process of creativity, the scientists mentioned, "formation of a new combination out of elements which were previously not associated together." One of the scientists reported that, in order to make original contributions, we have to start the work *ab initio*. This is important to becoming original. Another scientist indicated the value of "novelty of problem formulation." Some of the scientists said that "insight comes in small steps," while others described experiences in which "the whole problem got solved in one moment." Some of them drew attention to "concentration" and "intuition" in creative ventures. Dreams, fantasy, and imaginary companions were also mentioned as relevant to creativity by some of the scientists. These trends are suggestive of a quasi-random combinatorial process (see Simonton, 2003).

An important study was undertaken by Nandy (1995), which he called "a journey in the cultural psychology of scientific creativity." He tried to examine the personal contexts of scientific creativity outside the normal habitat of modern science. The first case is of Jagdis Chandra Bose (1858–1937), who was an influential plant physiologist. Bose is famous for a more humane concept of science and an integrated view of the organic and inorganic worlds. Nandy traces Bose's science to his early socialization, the distinctive concept of science in his society, and the needs of modern science in his time. The changes in the scientific creativity of Bose are explained on the basis of the interactive demands of his subject society, his personality, and the culture of world science dominated by societies. As Nandy observed, "what compromised Bose's creativity was the combination of his personality and private theory of science, the colonial situation and the culture of the Bose Institute. Creativity involves not merely the ability to use one's personal fantasies and the myths of one's culture; it is the ability to do so without being rigidly defensive and retaining a creative cognition and emotional flexibility" (p. 84).

Srinivasa Ramanujan (1887–1920) was considered to be a natural genius in mathematics. As Nandy argued, Ramanujan showed a "prototypical style of reconciling the relatively universal and rational structure of outer science and the extra logical, culturally and psychologically bound inner science of India. This style, apparently non-rational and anti-science, is close to the core of the objective, secular, and universal body of the outer science but – this is its strength – without disturbing the authenticity of either" (p. 89). His is the story of a conservative but integrated scientist for whom ancient meanings and modern knowledge were one.

Today scientific creativity is institutionalized and requires a large workforce and a lot of financial and technological support. The story of the development of science is quite instructive in this sense. Wali (1987) did the biographical study of S. Chandrashekhar, who won the Nobel Prize in 1983. The life and work of M. N. Saha, who established the Indian School of Physics, was analyzed by Sen (1954). P. C. Ray presented his own autobiography (Ray, 1958). All these studies portray the personal struggles and contextual influences on the growth and development of science in India.

Creativity in Literary People

Appreciating literary creativity is quite challenging. Researchers have used several approaches. Avasthi (1984) interviewed twenty authors and poets of the Hindi language. The analysis of responses pointed out that creativity is an emotion-centered mental process. The emotions emanate from internal or external struggles or conflicts and want expression. At the source of creativity lie freedom, liberation, self-extension, revolution against *jadatā* (inertness), escape from the self, and the wish to have a parallel free life. Creativity is not purposeless. It is rooted in either self-developed values or healthy social desirability. Creativity requires genius, imagination, and the ability to express. The chief characteristic of creativity is novelty or originality. It involves pleasure as well as pain. Dwivedi (1970) reflected on the autonomy and freedom of the writer or poet and noted that there is no difference between the creation of God's poetry (*Devasya kāvyam*) and a person's poetry. A noted Indian poet, Ajñeya (1975), maintained that it is the partly explainable desire that leads to literary creation. Sadarangani (1978) noted that a poet creates because he or she feels lonely in the midst of crowds: "He finds himself surrounded by strange contrasts which he cannot accept, and yet they are so vivid that he cannot even shut his eyes to them – there is abject poverty in the midst of affluence" (Sadarangani, 1978, p. 48).

In a study of creative complexity, Raina (1997) mapped the networks of enterprise. Rabindra Nath Tagore (1861–1941), a Nobel laureate in 1913, exemplified a unique and rare form of literary creativity. He grew up in a lonely and somewhat isolated family in which literature, music, and painting were prized. His career and creative enterprises were conditioned by many influences and traditions. He was master of several literary forms and showed diversity in works. The extensive range of Tagore's complexity and impact was phenomenal. According to Raina,

He was one of the greatest forces in the renaissance of his own native language. He had a long creative spell, starting early and continuing steadily through a long life. The continuous experimentation that one finds in his creative life flowed side by side with his other activities. He experimented with many forms of art and sought an outlet first in music then in opera, and ballet, and toward the end of his life, in painting, which makes his contributions to this domain of great significance in the history of modern art in India. (p. 157)

The complexity and extraordinariness was not of one kind, and he did not satisfy the demand for continuous development. His growth was not linear. Raina adopted historical, developmental, and contextual approaches to analyze Tagore's creativity. The network of Tagore's enterprise provides the basis for uniqueness, along with the density, longevity, cyclicity, and branching. Raina noted that Tagore's highly complex network of enterprises was characterized by an overwhelming variety (*vaicitrya*), abundance (*prāchurya*), and dynamism (*gatimayatā*). The diverse, multiple, continuous, and simultaneous literary enterprises of Tagore were very challenging. His network was dense, highly complex, and included simultaneity of works (doing many things in the same period, such as poetry, drama, music, novel, short story, essays, textbooks, and extensive travels). Cyclicity was another feature: "Reaching after new experiences and new expressions almost to the last days of his life, Tagore had to impose restraints on some genres at certain times, and he liberated them at other times. These up-and-down cycles are evident not only in dominant enterprises but also in terms of content and approach within the specific enterprise itself" (Raina, 1997, p. 165).

In a study of those who have received the Jnanpith award, which is the highest literary award in India, Raina, Srivastava, and Misra (2001) analyzed various aspects of the lives of winners ($N = 38$). The authors' content analyzed the details available from a variety of sources, including speeches, biographies, autobiographical works, and interviews. They found that a number of awardees were prodigies. One of them, Mahadevi Verma, composed a short verse at the age of six. Many others also showed early signs of writing. A majority of the laureates came from rural areas where they had to undergo a lot of frustrations and suffering, including attending school with an empty stomach. Sivaram Karanth, a recipient of the Jnanpith award, argued that failure and hardships provide fresh opportunities to work. The knowledge of the world that failure brings is also a kind of pleasure. The failure, and the pain associated with failure, accelerates the process of formation of a live and artistic creation. Interestingly, most of the creative figures were born in remote villages. More of the awardees were from the southern than the northern part of India. Surprisingly, the same was true in the case of a study of laureates of the Shanti Swaroop Bhatnagar (an award for science and technology achievement). Raina et al. speculated that "Perhaps a sophisticated intellectual tradition, an emphasis on indigenous values in life, exposure to modern scholarship, social mobility, and the capability to express in modern ways, all contributed to this effect" (p. 152). A sizable number (about 30 percent) had less than a graduate level of education. They pursued various odd jobs for survival. However, it did help them to come into contact with a variety of people at different places, thus providing enriched experiences for their creations. In regard to marital status, there was no consistent trend. The majority in this group were married; some of those married led unhappy lives or had to separate themselves. Nonconformism and defiance of accepted traditional patterns of life emerged to be a common feature of the lives of these awardees. A large majority of these laureates were influenced by the struggle of a toiling mass of people under a foreign yoke during the period before independence. The crisis arising out of social injustice, inequality, cruelty in social life, and the plight of the simple and exploited poor people had great impact on the creative work of these awardees. Nature has been a strong source of inspiration for many poets.

Raina et al. (2001) also analyzed the network of enterprises for poets. These networks have been quite varied; many awardees have been poets, and poets, in addition to writing poems, have also written essays, stories, novels, and criticisms. In contrast, only two novelists and writers were poets. Plays have been written by an equal number of poets and novelists. Both poets and novelists have written autobiographies. The creative writers were not confined to one genre but attempted many tasks simultaneously. An analysis of the longevity and durability of enterprises was noted. One poet took six years to complete his poetry, another took ten years to complete his poetry, and another one completed his story in fifty-nine years. This reflects the importance of perseverance in creative work.

CREATIVITY IN THE SPIRITUAL DOMAIN

Bhawuk (2003) argued that people strive to excel in areas that are valued in a culture (see Simonton, 1996), and geniuses appear in a local configuration as a result of the social situation. Spirituality is a cultural phenomenon for India. Bhawuk argued that innovation in spirituality is valued even today in India, and this continues to produce eminent spiritual *gurus* (teachers). After presenting a list of 100 spiritual gurus from the past 2,000 years, Bhawuk presented detailed case studies of three gurus. The first was of Ramkrishna Paramhans (1836–1886), who integrated religions and pointed out that all religions lead to the same end. The second case study was of Maharshi Mahesh Yogi (1917–present), who championed the technique of transcendental meditation. The third case was of Osho Rajneesh (1931–1990). He gave the theory of from sex to superconsciousness, which shook the Indian culture but also found many followers both locally and globally. Following the lead of Simonton (1996), Bhawuk argued that both domain-specific and systematic, i.e., cross-domain, configurations determine how a genius or eminent achiever would be placed historically, and that these configurations operate independently and may have different loci of influence.

Implicit Creativity

Kapur, Subramaniyam, and Shah, (1997) examined the Indian scientists' view of creativity. According to them, "newness" is the chief characteristic of creativity. They considered that family and educational institutions play important roles in fostering creativity. Padhi (1998) examined the notion of creativity as an aspect of personality held by primary- and secondary-school teachers. He noted that "curiosity" and "preoccupation with tasks" were the most salient qualities.

In a more systematic analysis, Yadava (2003) used a checklist to understand the notion of implicit creativity. Using a young adult sample ($N = 205$), he found four attributes, namely, sociability, leadership, unconventional personality orientation, and task persistence. They explained 36.65 percent of the variance. There were certain gender-related differences in the pattern of responses. In men, the attributes were sociability and social responsibility, unconventional personality orientation, manipulation, and independence. In women, the attributes consisted of leadership, sociability, openness, and perceptiveness. The attributes seem to reflect the predominantly collectivist culture of India.

Sen and Sharma (2004) analyzed the changes in teachers' conceptions of creativity across a time span of four decades. Their focus was on what creativity-relevant traits should be nurtured among children. The data during the 1970s and 1980s emphasized obedience, courteousness, affection, remembering well, doing work on time, being considerate of others, and being altruistic. They imply that Indian teachers place greater emphasis on the receptive nature of humans as compared with the self-acting nature of humans. Sen and Sharma found that, in 2002, a teachers' list of the most important factors included being courageous in convictions, curious, independent in thinking, and persistent. It may be noted that some of the least-valued traits of Torrance's experts were most valued by Indian teachers. They were traits of being courteous, neat and orderly, socially well adjusted, and timely in doing work.

CORRELATES OF CREATIVITY: A GLIMPSE OF INDIAN RESEARCH

Creativity as a field of inquiry occupies an important place in the agenda of psychological and educational research in India. However, research in the field of creativity began quite late. Manas Raychaudhari was the first to complete the doctoral dissertation in creativity in 1962 at the University of Calcutta. Since then there has been significant growth in the quantity of research in this area. It may be noted that research on creativity in India has been conducted both in university departments of psychology and in departments of education, though the share of the departments of education in creativity research has been larger than the share of the departments of psychology (Raina, 1991).

About 3 percent of the total research in psychology and education has been related to the theme of creativity. In a review of research literature in educational research for the period from 1980 to 1995, Raina and Srivastava (1997) found that, out of 1,090 studies related to educational psychology, 32 (about 3 percent) were related to creativity. The doctoral studies in education conducted during 1961–1993 (Passi, 1997) showed that, out of a total of 6,531 doctoral studies, 214 (3.3 percent) were related to creativity. However, Tripathi (1988) and Buch (1991) observed conceptual and methodological problems that have made the results indefinite and inconclusive.

Creativity has predominantly been studied from the psychometric point of view. As a consequence, a number of instruments have been constructed to study the relationship of creativity with intelligence, achievement, and a host of other psychological variables. Tools modeled after Guilford, Getzels, and Torrance have been developed, adopted, and adapted to map these relationships. Raina (1991) analyzed 136 doctoral researches related to creativity conducted during 1968–1987. Of these, about 50 percent of the studies examined the personality correlates of creativity, which were followed by studies related to sociocultural factors in creativity (about 17 percent), nurturance of creativity (about 12 percent), identification and measurement of creativity (about 11 percent), and the theoretical or philosophical nature of creativity (about 1 percent). Some of the major trends that emerge from these studies are given in the paragraphs that follow.

Age: A sizeable number of studies (e.g. Badrinath & Satyanarayana, 1979; Gakhar, 1974; Joshi, 1974; Khire, 1971; Lalithamma, 1979) have reported that creativity as assessed through psychometric measures increases with a person's advancing age up to thirteen to fifteen years. However, a few studies have also reported a negative or no relationship (e.g., Passi, 1972a; Shukla, 1980; Vohra, 1975).

Gender: The studies examining the relationship between gender and creativity have shown different patterns. On one hand, there are a few studies (e.g., Behera, 1993; Kapoor, 1996; Verma, 1993) that do not report any difference in the creativity of boys and girls. On the other hand, many Indian studies (e.g., those of Acharyulu, 1984; Gupta, 1981;

Talesara, 1992) have reported a higher level of creativity among boys than girls. Agarwal and Agarwal (1999) reported that boys are more creative than girls. Hussain and Sinha (1995) found that boys outperform girls on verbal measures. On nonverbal measures, boys perform better than girls in respect to originality only. Rajyalakshmi's (1996) findings contradict the results of earlier studies. She found that boys scored higher on flexibility but not on fluency and originality. Sudhir (2002) found that female participants were better in the creative process and the creativity in visual thinking. It seems that the nature of relationship between gender and creativity is contingent on a number of related contextual factors. As Passi (1997) observed, "gender seems to play a wedging role. The presence of socio-cultural stimulation, differential incentives for growth and development in the home, school or college environment, availability of resources for creative output and such other factors need to be considered while interpreting the diverse results" (p. 179).

Birth order: The findings about the relationship between birth order and creativity are inconclusive. While some studies (Sharma, 1986) have indicated that first-born children are superior to later-born children with respect to different components of verbal creativity, no such differences are observed in other studies (Badrinath & Satyanarayan, 1979). It seems that birth order in itself is not as important as the sociocultural and physical environment of the home. Passi (1997) has noted that there is a need to examine these findings with respect to the nature of the in-home environment. Thus child-rearing practices, size and type of family, nature of sibling relations, isolation, overprotectiveness, and recognition of autonomy have to be investigated to map the impact of the home environment.

Socioeconomic background: Several studies have examined social class differences in creativity. Gupta (1995) reported that urban, upper-caste boys were more creative. Studies (e.g., Chaurasia, 1993; Kaur & Kharb, 1993) have documented positive correlations between creativity and high socioeconomic status (SES). In addition, SES is positively related to originality and elaboration among students studying in the eighth grade (Pandey & Kharkwal, 1993). However, Kaile and Punia (1994) did not find any effect of SES. A relationship between family climate and creative personality has also been reported (Verma, 1997). James (2001) found that, in Kerala, among ninth-grade students, children belonging to scheduled castes (families showing extreme social, education, and economic backwardness arising out of the traditional

practice of untouchability) were low on creativity. Kumar and Singh
(1999) found that scheduled caste students belonging to urban locality
were superior to their rural counterparts on all dimensions of verbal
and figural creativity. In a review of studies on poverty and deprivation, Misra and Tripathi (2004) have observed that high SES and low
deprivation are positively related to creativity, particularly on verbal
measures. The low caste status and residential disadvantage were negatively related to creativity. The low- and middle-SES children scored
significantly lower than the high-SES children. However, the disadvantaged students could benefit from the creativity development program.

Personal dispositions: Efforts have been made to relate creativity with
personality variables, such as intelligence, adjustment, self-confidence,
locus of control, security–insecurity, and fatalism. Early work showed
that high-creative students had greater degrees of achievement, autonomy, dominance, change, and endurance than low-creative students.
Mehdi (1970, 1973) noted that, in real-life situations, the people who
make creative contributions are not necessarily high achievers. He noted
a slight negative relationship with intelligence in the urban sample.

The studies suggest that intelligence is positively related to creativity
(Agarwal & Agarwal, 1999). Pradhan, Akhani, and Janbandhu (1997)
found a positive effect of intelligence on verbal fluency in girls studying in sixth to eighth grades. After examining secondary-school students in Kerala, Raj (1994) reported that flexibility was related to verbal
and nonverbal intelligence. Sudhir and Khiangte (1997) noted that high-
creative girls from urban areas turned out to be more intelligent, emotionally stable, conscientious, and apprehensive than the high-creative
girls from rural background. The rural high-creative boys were outgoing, conscientious, tender minded, and self-sufficient as against their
reserved, group-dependent, and expedient urban counterparts. Raju
(1996) reported a low positive correlation between creativity in science and social adjustment among ninth grade students. The students
with high self-confidence were high on scientific creativity (Sansanwal
& Sharma, 1993). Creativity was positively correlated with security–
insecurity (Ahmed, 1992), and negatively with locus of control (Sohi,
1994) and fatalism (Ahmed, 1992). It has also been reported that high
academic achievers in schools are not as creative in comparison with the
medium achievers (Mondol, 1999).

Mattoo (1994) found that the high-creative tenth-grade students had
greater interest in fine arts, and in literary, scientific, technical, and
household areas. They were socially maladjusted, emotionally unstable,

and academically bright. Rajagopalan (1998) observed that, in ninth grade, students' creative talent was related to both convergent and divergent thinking. However, divergent thinking had greater weight for aesthetic and scientific creativity. In students with a high IQ (above 120), achievement was related to convergent and divergent thinking. Bhawalkar (1992) studied scientific creativity among high school students. Factors such as self-confidence, tolerance of ambiguity, risk taking, low dependence, intelligence, scientific attitude, academic motivation, and achievement in mathematics and science predicted creativity. The highly creative are more warm hearted, intelligent, emotionally stable, excitable, enthusiastic, and self-controlled (Chaturvedi, 1997). Studies also reveal that the high-creative students are less anxious and more extroverted (Kumar, 1981), and more secure and mentally healthy (Verma & Sinha, 1981), than their low-creative counterparts. Bhatnagar and Gulati (1998) found that high-creative girls exhibited higher career aspirations, were self-guided in choosing their career choices, and were vocationally more mature.

Scholastic achievement: Studies of the relationship between creativity and scholastic achievement (generally measured in terms of annual examination scores) show a positive and significant relationship (see, e.g., Brar, 1986; Desai, 1987; Srivastava & Srilatha, 1992). The aspects of creativity such as fluency, flexibility, and originality have been positively correlated with scholastic achievement. Rao (1995) reported that teacher effectiveness is positively related to creativity and interpersonal relationships.

FOSTERING CREATIVITY

Attempts have been made to foster creativity among samples of students. A group of researchers (e.g., Amin, 1988; Nandanpawar, 1986; Patel, 1988) tried creative thinking programs, creative methods, divergent-thinking programs, and teaching programs for developing fluency, flexibility, originality, language proficiency, and mathematical creativity. Jarial (1981) developed instructional material to enhance fluency, flexibility, and originality as measured by the Torrance Tests of Creative Thinking (nonverbal) among ninth-grade students. The effect of brainstorming and morphological analysis as experimental treatment techniques for enhancing creativity and divergent thinking has been demonstrated (Miyan, 1982; Patel, 1987; Venkataraman, 1993). Sharma (1995) developed instructional materials to enhance creativity among fifth-grade students. The instructional material designed with flexible time was more suited to the highly intelligent group. Bapat (1991) described the efforts made at Jnana Prabodhini institute at Pune for training at the school meant for the talented and gifted students. The studies showed that intelligence is not necessarily correlated with creativity. A program designed for enhancing cognition, divergent production, and evaluation and application was successful in enhancing creativity.

Gulati (1995) developed a training program that successfully enhanced flexibility and originality in fifth-grade students. A similar effort has been made to enhance creativity among school children (Katiyar & Jarial, 1985). It has been reported that exposure to computers facilitates creativity (Bansal & Agarwal, 1997). The facilitative effect of role-play methods and the use of audio–video materials has also been demonstrated. Joman (1996) has shown a positive effect of a creative learning environment on learning and performance, responsibility taking, and school attendance. Imagery exercises have a positive effect on creativity. These exercises allow the expression of latent thoughts, imaginations, and emotions.

Rao (1996) noted that teaching through drama activity increased pupils' imagination, creativity, cooperative activity, concentration, self-expression, communication, knowledge of organization, and disciplined behavior. Pupils' capacity improved in listening attentively, fluency and precision of speech, developing a new kind of teacher–pupil relationship, gaining confidence in editing, and their eagerness to learn more. This method of teaching helped students to make their concepts clearer.

Sharma and Misra (2004) reported the results of a longitudinal intervention based on creative drama in primary school children, namely eighty children six years of age or older in third grade in a primary school in Delhi. The two-year-long intervention showed marked improvement in elaboration, originality, and flexibility. The baseline assessment was done in July 1999, and the endline assessment was in January 2002. The intervention group performed at a higher level than the control group. The intervention also had a positive impact on the scholastic achievement of children.

The positive effect of meditation in enhancing creativity has also been demonstrated. Travis (1979) used the Torrance Tests of Creative Thinking to measure figural and verbal creativity in a control group and in a group that subsequently learned the transcendental meditation technique. On the posttest five months later, the transcendental meditation group scored significantly higher on figural originality and flexibility and on verbal fluency.

ASSESSMENT OF CREATIVITY

Attempts have been made to assess creative functioning through testing and nontesting techniques. Among the most popular general creativity tests used in Indian studies are Torrance's (1974) Tests of Creative Thinking, Mehdi's (1970, 1973) Tests of Creativity (a battery), and Passi's (1972b) Tests of Creativity (verbal and nonverbal). Some verbal tests have been developed in regional languages such as Oriya (Tripathi, 1987), Telugu (Rao, 1982), Marathi (Joshi, 1981; Kundley 1977) and Gujarati (Gilitwala 1978). Tests have been developed for different age groups, including young children (Singh 1993), primary- and middle-school students (Mehdi, 1970), high school students (Gilitwala, 1978; Kaul, 1974; Singh 1978), and university students (Bal, 1989). Sudhir and Khiangte (1991) developed a test battery for the assessment of creativity among the Mizo tribal group. Khire (1993) developed a measure of creative behavioral intelligence that captures divergent and convergent thinking in nonverbal sensitivity, interpersonal perceptions of others' behavior, and interpersonal perception. It is rooted in Guilford's structure of intellect model (Guilford, 1977).

Some researchers have also been interested in developing domain-specific tests of creativity, such as literary creativity (Kundley 1977; Rao, 1982), creativity in second-language learning (Ponnuswamy, 1980), mathematical creativity (Singh, 1988), scientific creativity (Raina, 1986), and creativity in the physical sciences (Gupta, 1980). Like researchers in other fields in psychology, creativity researchers in India have borrowed items or patterned the items after some tests developed in the West. According to Raina (1991, p. 474), "The tests developed here lack a conceptual framework and carry no theoretical support, except for the fact that they are poor imitations of American tests." There has been a lack of sustained research and development related to the measurement of creativity in India. As a result, tests without sound psychometric properties are available and are in use in a majority of the research.

EPILOGUE

This review shows that creativity is a multifaceted or syndrome-like process having multiple pathways, which not only respond to the adaptive contingencies in a strictly reactive sense but also operate proactively or as an effort toward self-realization or self-expression. In psychological studies, the journey of creativity has largely been outbound, where product is at the center and the person is a constituent component contributing to it. The limited work on literary creativity tends to suggest that a process orientation with a scope for encompassing transformation of self as well as environment (product) would prove more useful. Similarly, the work on spiritual creativity draws attention to an important innovation that expands the discourse, filling an important gap by addressing the evolutionary dimension of creativity that can contribute to the domain of health and personal growth (Sorenson, 2004). The analysis of the spiritual domain, where divinity is central, need not necessarily be looked at as an alternative mode of analysis and understanding. It is complementary to the ongoing efforts to understand creativity. A move in this direction would help researchers to appreciate the subjective and evolutionary changes that a person undergoes. Research endeavors of this kind are rare. They require imagination, sensitivity, and intuition.

The Indian thought system recognizes the multiple determination of creativity and emphasizes the search and refinement of self. Since life is considered to be a station in the pathway to liberation or enlightenment and not a destination in itself, a human being has a dual purpose: progress in worldly life (*abhyudaya*) as well as spiritual upliftment (*nihsreyas*). The inspiration for creativity may be directed to one of them or to both, depending on a particular person's stage of development. There is a need to balance these concerns with due regard to cultural diversity.

The majority of Indian research, however, has been inspired by the psychometric tradition. This is not surprising since the disciplinary training has been primarily organized around the Euro-American paradigm. The colonial legacy has been quite strong, and it has been quite difficult, if not impossible, to grow out of the alien framework. As a consequence, the studies have employed samples from formal school systems. The creativity of out-of-school persons has largely gone unnoticed. Creativity has been measured either by general tests of creativity (verbal and nonverbal) or domain-specific tests referring to science, mathematics, physical science, and language. The responses to these tests are popularly scored for the components of fluency, flexibility, originality, and elaboration. The recent studies of implicit creativity do suggest a need to go beyond the limited view of creativity and include culturally specific qualities. Culture-specific studies shall enrich our understanding of creativity in important ways.

It is becoming increasingly clear that creativity is not a single or unitary ability. It is, rather, a cluster of abilities. Some of the important abilities include flexibility in responding to a situation in a variety of ways, such as fluency, speed of responding, originality, understanding contradictions, elaboration, recognition of future possibilities, and divergent thinking. A creative person can respond in many ways. A creative person integrates and reorganizes the cognitive structures and is able to effectively apply the available cognitive structures. Creativity is also looked on as the process of problem solving. It is found not only in complex academic settings but also in everyday life.

It was mentioned earlier that creativity is a general characteristic found in every normal human being. This, however, does not mean that everybody is creative or that creativity is expressed in everyone's behavior. The expression of creativity takes place in a sociocultural environment that may help or hinder an individual. Barriers often thwart creative activities. In order to grow and actualize one's creative potential, it is important that one has to cope with barriers. The programming of developmental ecology can play an important role in fostering creativity.

People do get opportunities to express creativity, and they are appreciated. The mystery of creativity lies in an individual's will power, commitment, and effort. Keeping an open mind, remaining sensitive to the environment, and viewing possibilities in an imaginative way are the foundations for creativity. The journey, which starts from thought and imagination, can open doors of possibilities. The world scenario is changing very fast, and we need to respond to local as well as global demands simultaneously. As a result, cultural diversity is increasingly becoming an important aspect of the emerging social reality across the globe. This necessitates a greater degree of cultural sensibility. Future studies in creativity have to expand the scope of within-culture as well multicultural collaborations across various domains.

References

Acharyulu, S. T. V. G. (1984). The effect of nutritional status, age and sex on creativity of Indian children. *Journal of Creative Behavior, 18,* 273.

Agarwal, S., & Agarwal, S. (1999). Creativity and intelligence: Exploration with sex differences. *Psycholingua, 29,* 127–132.

Ahmed, M. I. (1992). *A study of the influence of parental value orientations, teacher leader behaviour and students' mental health on the creativity of 9 standard students of the same SES.* Unpublished doctoral dissertation, Bangalore University, Bangalore.

Ajyeya, S. H. V. (1975). Antara [in Hindi]. Delhi: Rajpal & Sons.

Amin, M. J. (1988). *To study the effectiveness of creative thinking programmes on the creativity level of the school-children in relation to the programme coordinates.* Unpublished doctoral dissertation, Sardar Patel University, Vallabha Vidyanagar.

Anandvardhan. (1975). *Dhvanyaloka* (Edited with introduction by K., Krisnamoorthy). Dharwar: Karnatak University.

Apte, V. S. (1973). *The students' Sanskrit English dictionary.* Delhi: Motilal Banarasidas.

Aron, E. N., & Aron, A. (1982). An introduction to Maharishi's theory of creativity: Its empirical base and description of the creative process. *Journal of Creative Behavior, 16,* 29–49.

Avasthi, O. (1984). *Sirajana aur sirjanhar* [in Hindi]. Delhi: Rashtrabhasha Sansthan.

Badrinath, S., & Satyanarana, S. B. (1979). Correlates of creative thinking of high school students. *Creativity Newsletter, 7–8,* 1–2.

Bal, S. (1989). Alpha II biological inventory as a predictor of creative personality of university students. *Indian Educational Review, 24,* 1–13.

Bansal, I., & Agarwal, S. (1997). Role of computers in the enhancement of creativity among young children. *Psycholingua, 273,* 111–114.

Bapat, G. S. (1991, July 29 to August 2). *Evolving teaching programmes for the gifted: Review of a twenty-year experiment.* Paper presented at the Ninth World Conference on Gifted and Talented Children, Hague, Netherlands.

Behera, A. P. (1993). Sex differences in creativity: A study in Navodaya Vidyalayas. *Journal of Indian Education, 19,* 46–48.

Bhargava, P. M., & Chakrabarty, C. (1996). Interplay of science, creativity, beauty, nature and evolution. In K. C. Gupta (Ed.), *Aesthetics and motivations in arts and science* (pp. 66–84). New Delhi: Indira Gandhi National Centre for Arts.

Bhatnagar, A., & Gulati, S. (1998). *Career development of creative girls.* New Delhi: Vikas Publications.

Bhawalkar, S. (1992). *Prediction of scientific creativity through cognitive and affective variables among high school students.* Unpublished doctoral dissertation, Devi Ahilya Vishwavidyalaya, Indore.

Bhawuk, D. P. S. (2003). Culture's influence on creativity: The case of Indian spirituality. *International Journal of Intercultural Relations, 27,* 1–22.

Bonshek, A. (2001). *Mirror of consciousness: Art, creativity and Veda.* Delhi: Motilal Banarasidas.

Brar, S. S. (1986). *A comparative study of the performance in Bachelor of Education examination and high creative and low creative boys and girls at different levels of general intelligence and socio-economic status.* Unpublished doctoral dissertation, Kurukshetra University, Kurukshetra.

Buch, M. B. (Ed.) (1991). *Fourth survey of research in education.* New Delhi: NCERT.

Chapple, C. (1986). *Karma and creativity*. Albany: State University of New York.

Chaturvedi, A. (1997). *Creativity as related to personality traits and scholastic achievement of tribal students*. Unpublished doctoral dissertation, Rani Durgavati Vishwavidyalaya, Jabalpur.

Chaurasia, O. (1993). Family functioning and creative abilities. *Perspectives in Psychological Researches, 16*, 61–63.

Coomarswamy, A. K. (1957). *The dance of Shiva*. New York: The Noonday Press.

Csikszentmihalyi, M. (1996). *Creativity, flow and the psychology of discovery and invention*. New York: HarperCollins.

Dalal, A. S. (2001). *A greater psychology: An introduction to the psychological thought of Sri Aurobindo*. New York: Tarcher/Putnam.

Desai, N. N. (1987). *An investigation into the creative thinking ability of higher secondary of Gujarat state in the context of some psycho-social factors*. Unpublished doctoral dissertation, Sardar Patel University, Vallabha Vidyanagar.

Deshpande, G. T. (1989). *Abhinavagupta*. New Delhi: Sahitya Academy.

Dwivedi, H. P. (1970). *Kalidas ki lalitya yojna* [Aesthetic plan of Kalidas]. Delhi: Rajkamal Prakashan.

Gakhar, S. (1974). Creativity in relation to age and sex. *Journal of Education and Psychology, 32*, 13–16.

Gardner, H. (1993). *Creating minds: An anatomy of creativity seen through the lives of Freud, Einstein, Picasso, Stravinsky, Eliot, Graham, and Gandhi*. New York: Basic Books.

Gardner, H. (2001). Creators: Multiple intelligences. In K. H. Pfenninger and V. R. Shubik (Eds.), *The origins of creativity* (pp. 117–143). New York: Oxford University Press.

Gergen, K. J., Gulerce, A., Lock, A., & Misra, G. (1996). Psychological science in cultural context. *American Psychologist, 51*, 496–503.

Gilitwala, P. J. (1978). *Standardisation of a test of creativity for the high school students of South Gujarat*. Unpublished doctoral dissertation, South Gujarat University, Siurat.

Guilford, J. P. (1977). *Way beyond IQ*. Buffalo, New York: Creative Education Foundation.

Gulati, S. (1995). Instructional materials to promote children's creativity in the classroom: Studying the effectiveness of materials fostering creativity. *Indian Educational Review, 30*, 59–72.

Gupta, A. K. (1981). Sex differences in creativity: Some fresh evidence. *Journal of Creative Behavior, 15*, 269.

Gupta, S. M. (1980). *Standardisation of a test of creativity in physical sciences*. Unpublished doctoral dissertation, Kurukshetra University, Kurukshetra.

Gupta, S. M. (1995). Effect of social class status on creative ability of students. *Bharatiya Shiksha Shodha Patrika, 14*, 121–128.

Hussain, S., & Sinha, R. (1995). A comparative study of creativity among male and female students of industrial and non-industrial belts of Bihar. *Praachi Journal of Psychocultural Dimensions, 11*, 1–8.

James, A. (2001). Socio-cultural differences in creative thinking: A discriminant function analysis. *Perspectives in Education, 17*, 94–104.

Jarial, G. S. (1981). An experiment in the training of nonverbal creativity. *Journal of Creative Behavior, 15,* 72.

Joman, M. G. (1996). Towards creative learning – A shift in paradigm. In *Studies on classroom processes and school effectiveness at primary stage: International Perspective.* New Delhi: National Council of Educational Research and Training.

Joshi, D. C. (1974). *A study of creativity and some personality traits of the intellectually gifted high school students.* Unpublished doctoral dissertation, M.S. University, Baroda.

Joshi, S. P. (1981). *A study of verbal creativity in Marathi language in relation to achievement in Marathi and environmental factors of the students as well as teaching.* Unpublished doctoral dissertation, University of Bombay, Mumbai.

Kaile, H. S., & Punia, T. K. (1994). Relationship between creativity and SES. *Experiments in Education, 22,* 35–39.

Kapoor, K. (1996). A study of creative thinking ability of high school pupils of Arunachal Pradesh in relation to their sex and academic achievement. *Progress of Education, 30,* 172–175.

Kapoor, K. (1998). *Literary theory: Indian conceptual framework.* New Delhi: Affiliated East-West Press.

Kapur, R. L., Subramaniyam, S., & Shah, A. (1997). Creativity in Indian science. *Psychology and Developing Societies, 9,* 161–187.

Katiyar, P. C., & Jarial, G. S. (1985). Training programs for developing creativity among school children. *Journal of Creative Behavior, 19,* 219.

Kaul, B. (1974). *Construction and standardization of a verbal test to identify creative children in the age range of 14 to 16 years.* Unpublished doctoral dissertation, M.S. University, Baroda.

Kaur, P., & Kharb, D. (1993). Creativity in children: The impact of school and home environment. *Journal of Indian Education, 18,* 46–49.

Kaviraj, M. G. (1966). *Aspects of Indian thought.* Burdwan: The University of Burdwan.

Khire, U.S. (1971). *Creativity in relation to intelligence and personality factors.* Unpublished doctoral dissertation, University of Poona, Pune.

Khire, U. (1993). Guilford's SOI model and behavioral intelligence with special reference to creative behavioral abilities. In S. G. Isaken, M. C. Murdock, R. L. Firestein & D. J. Treffinger (Eds.), *Understanding and recognizing creativity: The emergence of a discipline* (pp. 369–399). Norwood, NJ: Ablex.

Kumar, A. (1981). Personality identification of high and low creatives. *Journal of Creative Behavior, 15,* 73.

Kumar, G., & Singh, S. (1999). A study of different dimensions of creativity in relation to locality of scheduled castes and non-scheduled caste students. *Journal of Psychological Researches, 24,* 43–48.

Kundley, M. B. (1977). *A test of literary creativity in Marathi.* Unpublished doctoral dissertation, Nagpur University, Nagpur.

Lalithamma (1979). *Self-concept and creativity of over, normal and under-achievers amongst X grade students of Baroda city.* Unpublished doctoral dissertation, M.S. University, Baroda.

Lubart, T. L. (1999). Creativity across cultures. In R. J. Sternberg (Ed.), *Handbook of creativity* (pp. 339–350). New York: Cambridge University Press.

Maduro, R. (1976). Artistic creativity in a Brahmin painter community. *Research Monographs, 14*, 222.

Majumdar, C. K. (1996). Creativity in science. In K. C. Gupta (Ed.), *Aesthetics and motivations in arts and science* (pp. 27–34). New Delhi: Indira Gandhi National Centre for Arts.

Maharshi Mahesh Yogi. (1970). Art and the artist. In M. Cain (Ed.), *Art and the science of creative intelligence: Interdependence of part and whole* (p. V). IA: Fairfield.

Mattoo, M. I. (1994). Vocational interests, adjustment problems and scholastic achievement of high and low creative students. *Indian Educational Review, 29*, 86–88.

Mehdi, B. (1970). *Development of a battery of tests for identifying creative talent at the primary and middle school stages*. Unpublished doctoral dissertation, Aligarh Muslim University, Aligarh.

Mehdi, B. (1973). *Nonverbal test of creative thinking*. Aligarh: Quamar Fatima.

Misra, G. (1999). Towards indigenous psychology of cognition: Knowing in the Indian tradition. *Journal of Indian Psychology, 17*, 1–22.

Misra, G., & Gergen, K. J. (1993). On the place of culture in psychological science. *International Journal of Psychology, 28*, 225–245.

Misra, G., & Tripathi, K. N. (2004). Psychological dimensions of poverty and deprivation. In J. Pandey (Ed.), *Psychology in India revisited – Developments in the discipline. Vol. 3. Applied social and organizational psychology* (pp. 118–215). New Delhi: Sage.

Misra, G., Suvasini, C., & Srivastava, A. K. (2000). Psychology of wisdom: Western and eastern perspectives. *Journal of Indian Psychology, 18*, 1–32.

Misra, V. N. (1992). Foreword. In V. N. Misra (Ed.), *Creativity and environment* (pp. 1–4). New Delhi: Sahitya Akademi.

Misra, V. N. (1996). *The Indian creative mind*. Agra: Y. K. Publishers.

Misra, V. N., Nathan, L., & Vatsyayan, S. H. (1995). *The Indian poetic tradition*. Agra: Y. K. Publishers.

Miyan, M. (1982). *A study to examine the effectiveness of methods of teaching mathematics in developing mathematical creativity*. Unpublished doctoral dissertation, Jamia Millia Islamia, New Delhi.

Mondol, K. C. (1999). Are high achievers creative learners? *Journal of Centre for Pedagogical Studies In Mathematics, 2*, 14–18.

Mukunda, N. (1996). Beauty and creativity in art and science -comparisons and reflections. In K. C. Gupta (Ed.), *Aesthetics and motivations in arts and science* (pp. 53–62). New Delhi: Indira Gandhi National Centre for Arts.

Nakamura, H. (1964). *Ways of thinking of eastern people: India, China, Tibet and Japan*. Honolulu: The University Press of Hawaii.

Nandanpawar, B. S. (1986). *Development of linguistic creativity among the students: An experimental study*. Unpublished doctoral dissertation, Nagpur University, Nagpur.

Nandy, A. (1995). *Alternative sciences: Creativity and authenticity in two Indian scientists*. New Delhi: Oxford University Press.

Nisbett, R. E., Peng, K., Choi, I., & Norenzayan, A. (2001). Culture and systems of thought: Holistic versus analytic cognition. *Psychological Review, 108,* 291–310.

Padhi, J. S. (1998). Creative students. *The Primary Teacher, 23,* 12–15.

Pandeya, A. N. (1981). Endogenous intellectual creativity; reflections on some etic and emic paradigms. In Abel Malek (Ed.), *Intellectual creativity in endogenous cultures* (pp. 0–0). Tokyo: The United Nations University.

Pandey, R. C., & Kharkwal, M. K. (1993). Creativity and socioeconomic status. *Perspectives in Psychological Researches, 16,* 27–29.

Passi, B. K. (1972a). *An exploratory study of creativity and its relationship with intelligence and achievement in school subjects at higher secondary stage.* Unpublished doctoral dissertation, Panjab University, Chandigarh.

Passi, B. K. (1972b). *Passi tests of creativity: Verbal and non-verbal.* Agra: National Psychological Corporation.

Passi, B. K. (1997). Creativity and innovations. In *Fifth survey of educational research* (pp. 170–215). New Delhi: National Council of Educational Research and Training.

Patel, J. Z. (1987). *An investigation into the effectiveness of Purdue Creative Thinking Programme on the creative abilities of elementary school children.* Unpublished doctoral dissertation, Sardar Patel University, Vallabh Vidyanagar.

Patel, R. P. (1988). *Development of brainstorming technique programme and to study its effects on creativity of the secondary school children.* Unpublished doctoral dissertation, Sardar Patel University, Vallabh Vidyanagar.

Ponnuswamy, S. (1980). *A study of programmed instruction and creativity in second language learning.* Unpublished doctoral dissertation, University of Delhi, Delhi.

Pradhan, D., Akhani, P., & Janbandhu, D. S. (1997). Effect of SES and intelligence on verbal fluency. *Psycholingua, 27,* 81–88.

Raina, K. (1986). *Psycho-social correlates of scientific creativity among high school students.* Unpublished doctoral dissertation, Kurukshetra University, Kurukshetra.

Raina, M. K. (1991). Research in creative functioning: A trend report. In M. B. Buch (Ed.), *Fourth survey of research in education* (pp. 467–522). New Delhi: National Council of Educational Research and Training.

Raina, M. K. (1993). Ethnocentric confines in creativity research. In S. G. Isaken, M. C. Murdock, R. L. Firestein, & D. J. Treffinger (Eds.), *Understanding and recognizing creativity: The emergence of a discipline* (pp. 435–453). Norwood NJ: Ablex.

Raina, M. K. (1996). The Torrance phenomenon: Extended creative search for Lord Visvakarma. *Creativity and Innovation Management, 5,* 151–168.

Raina, M. K. (1997). "Most dear to all the muses": Mapping Tagorean networks of enterprise – A study in creative complexity. *Creativity Research Journal, 10,* 153–173.

Raina, M. K. (2002). Guru–Shishya relationship in Indian culture: The possibility of a creative resilient framework. *Psychology and Developing Societies, 14,* 166–196.

Raina, M. K. (2004). I shall be many; the garland making perspective on creativity and cultural diversity. In M. Fryer (Ed.), *Creativity and cultural diversity* (pp. 25–44). Shipley, West Yorkshire: The Creativity Center Educational Trust.

Raina, M. K., & Srivastava, A. K. (1997). Educational psychology in India: Its present status and future concerns. *International Journal of Group Tensions, 27,* 309–340.

Raina, M. K., Srivastava, A. K., & Misra, G. (2001). Explorations in literary creativity: Some preliminary observations. *Psychological Studies, 46,* 148–160.

Raj, H. S. S. (1994). Fluency, flexibility, and originality as correlates of intelligence. *The Creative Psychologist, 6,* 25–30.

Rajagopalan, M. (1998). Creative talent in relation to convergent and divergent thinking. *Perspectives in Education, 14,* 105–112.

Rajshekhar (1924). *Kavya mimansa* [Enquiry in poetry]. Baroda: Gaikwar Oriental Series.

Raju, S. (1996). Creativity in science in relation to social adjustment. *Experiments in Education, 24,* 60–65.

Rajyalakshmi, T. (1996). Creativity and cognitive preference styles in biology. *Journal of Indian Education, 22,* 47–51.

Ramanujan, A. K. (1990). Is there an Indian way of thinking? An informal essay. In M. Marriott (Ed.), *India through Hindu categories* (pp. 41–58). New Delhi: Sage.

Rao, G. K. (1995). *A study of teacher effectiveness in relation to creativity and interpersonal relationships.* Unpublished doctoral dissertation, Andhra University, Visakhapatnam.

Rao, U. (1996). Drama activity – A tool in teaching–learning process. *Education in Asia, 16,* 126–130.

Rao, V. R. (1982). *Standardization of a test of literary creativity in Telugu for the students of secondary schools.* Unpublished doctoral dissertation, Osmania University, Hyderabad.

Ray, P. (1958). *Autobiography of a Bengali chemist.* Calcutta: Orient Book Company.

Roland, A. (1988). *In search of self in India and Japan.* Princeton, NJ: Princeton University Press.

Runco, M. A. (2004). Creativity. *Annual Review of Psychology, 55,* 657–687.

Sadarangani, H. I. (1978). The making of a poem. *Indian Horizons, 27,* 47–52.

Sansanwal, D. N., & Sharma, D. (1993). Scientific creativity as a function of intelligence, self-confidence, sex and standard. *Indian Journal of Psychometry and Education, 24,* 37–44.

Sen, S. N. (1954). *Professor Meghnad Saha: His work and philosophy.* Calcutta: M. N. Saha 60th Birthday Committee.

Sen, R. S., & Sharma, N. (2004). Teachers' conception of creativity and its nurture in children: An Indian perspective. In M. Fryer (Ed.), *Creativity and cultural diversity* (pp. 25–44). Shipley, West Yorkshire: The Creativity Center Educational Trust.

Sharma, P. L. (1996). Musical creativity: Motivations and aesthetics – a comparison with sciences. In K. C. Gupta (Ed.), *Aesthetics and motivations in arts and science* (pp. 109–114). New Delhi: Indira Gandhi National Centre for Arts.

Sharma, C., & Misra, G. (July 2–8, 2004). *Creative drama for humane education: An Indian experience.* Paper presented at IDEA 2004, Fifth World Congress, University of Ottawa, Ottawa, Canada.

Sharma, H. L. (1986). *A comparative study of engineers and civil services personnel belonging to different socio-economic status in relation to their interests and creativity.* Unpublished doctoral dissertation, Kurukshetra University, Kurukshetra.

Sharma, R. D. (1995). Influence of recent life experience on mental health of school teachers. *Indian Educational Review, 30,* 102–109.

Shastri, J. I. (1997). *Khyal: Creativity within north India's classical music tradition.* New Delhi: Motilal Banarasidas.

Shukla, J. P. (1980). *Conservation and scientific creativity through cultures during the period of formal operations.* Unpublished doctoral dissertation, Ravi Shankar University, Raipur.

Simonton, D. K. (1996). Creative expertise: A life-span developmental perspective. In K. A. Ericsson (Ed.), *The road to expert performance: Empirical evidence from the arts and sciences, sports and games* (pp. 227–253). Mahwah, NJ: Erlbaum.

Simonton, D. K. (2003). Scientific creativity as constrained stochastic behaviour: The integration of product, person, and process perspectives. *Psychological Bulletin, 129,* 475–494.

Singh, B. (1988). Relationship between mathematical creativity and some biological factors. *Indian Educational Review, 23,* 157–161.

Singh, B. (1993). *Measurement of creativity in young children.* Ambala Cantt: The Associated Publishers.

Singh, C. (1978). *Scientific creativity test for high school students.* Unpublished doctoral dissertation, Ranchi University, Ranchi.

Sinha, J. B P. (2002). Towards indigenization of psychology in India. In G. Misra & A. K. Mohanty (Eds.), *Perspectives on indigenous psychology* (p. 440–457). New Delhi: Concept.

Sohi, B. S. (1994). *A study of locus of control, self-concept and rigidity in relation to creativity among tenth graders.* Unpublished doctoral dissertation, Punjabi University, Patiala.

Sorenson, R. L. (2004). *Minding spirituality.* London: The Analytic Press.

Srivastava, S., & Srilatha, R. (1992). *Impact of enrichment programme to foster creativity among academically gifted elementary school children.* Madras: JBAS Women's College.

Sri Aurobindo. (1985). *The upanishads.* Pondichery: Sri Aurobindo Ashram.

Sternberg, R. J., & Lubart, T. I. (1996). Investing in creativity. *American Psychologist, 51,* 677–688.

Sudhir, M. A., & Khiangte, V. (1991). Testing creativity in India. *Journal of Creative Behavior, 25,* 27–33.

Sudhir, M. A., & Khiangte, V. (1997). Personality and creativity among secondary school students: A study in talent development. *Indian Educational Review, 32,* 115–125.

Sudhir, P. (2002). *Creativity in visual arts in relation to selected non-cognitive variables among pupil teachers.* Unpublished doctoral dissertation, University of Delhi, Delhi.

Suroor, A. A. (1992). How to meet the challenge. In V. N. Misra (Ed.), *Creativity and environment* (pp. 97–100). New Delhi: Sahitya Akademi.

Talesara, S. (1992). *Literary creativity among adolescents*. New Delhi: Uppal Publications.

Torrance, E. P. (1974). *Torrance tests of creative thinking*. Lexington, MA: Personnel Press.

Travis, F. (1979). The TM technique and creativity: A longitudinal study of Cornell University undergraduates. *Journal of Creative Behavior, 13*, 169–180.

Tripathi, L. B. (1988). Higher mental processes. In J. Pandey (Ed.), *Psychology in India: The state of the art* (Vol. 1, pp. 289–328). New Delhi: Sage.

Tripathi, S. (1987). *Construction and standardization of a test of creativity in Oriya.* Unpublished doctoral dissertation, Kurukshetra University, Kurukshetra.

Tripathi, S. N. (1993). Indian scientists and creativity: A study. *Indian Educational Review, 28*, 57–64.

Vatsyayan, K. (1968). *Classical Indian dance in literature and the arts*. New Delhi: Sangeet Natak Academi.

Venkataraman, D. (1993). *The effect of synectics training on creativity and hemisphericity of higher secondary students.* Unpublished doctoral dissertation, University of Madras, Madras.

Verma, B. P. (1993). Creativity styles of university women students. *Psycholingua, 23*, 105–113.

Verma, B. P. (1997). The family climate and creative personality. *Journal of Educational Research and Extension, 34*, 25–33.

Vohra, I. N. (1975). *A study of non-verbal creativity in relation to socio-economic status, age, sex, medium of instruction, and personality characteristics amongst the pupils of English and Gujarati medium of 'Bazm-E-Hidayat' primary school from Baroda city.* Unpublished doctoral dissertation, M.S. University, Baroda.

Verma, L. K., & Sinha, R. (1981). Mental health and creativity. *Journal of Creative Behavior, 15*, 271.

Wali, K. C. (1987). *Chandra: A biography of S. Chandrashekhar*. Calcutta: Penguin Books India.

Williams, M. (1974). *A Sanskrit English dictionary*. Delhi: Motilal Banarasidas.

Yadava, R. K. (2003). *Notion of implicit creativity among Indian students: A social psychological study of graduate and postgraduate students in Allahabad.* Unpublished master of philosophy dissertation, School of Social Science, Jawaharlal Nehru University, New Delhi.

16

African Perspectives on Creativity

Elias Mpofu, Kathleen Myambo, Andrew A. Mogaji,
Teresa-Anne Mashego, and Omar H. Khaleefa

The fact that Africa has a rich heritage of creative endeavors is hardly contested. For instance, the African continent has some of the world's major historical architectural artifacts, such as the Great Pyramids of Egypt and the Great Zimbabwe National Monument (Zimbabwe). Archeological discoveries have revealed evidence that several ancient African societies were as technologically advanced as any of their time. For example, the Ugbo-Uku works of art in metal, which date back to between the ninth and tenth centuries, were the subjects of acclaimed exhibitions in the United States and Europe in the first half of the 1980s (Oshodi, 2004; Oyowe, 1996). These works and similar others radically changed the international perception of African civilization during these periods. African art and sculpture adorn museums all over the world, and millions of citizens of African countries make a living from artistic productions of many types (Silver, 1981). African creative expressiveness in music, dance, and in the design and use of clothing, ornaments, and human habitats is widely acknowledged (Olaniyan, 2004). Evidence also abounds on the innovativeness of African communities in meeting the demands of living in ecologically rich and highly competitive geocultural environments. For instance, many African communities have distinguished themselves in adapting cultural artifacts

Address correspondence to Elias Mpofu, PhD, Department of Counselor Education, Counseling Psychology and Rehabilitation Services, The Pennsylvania State University, University Park, PA 16802, E-mail: exm31@psu.edu

We extend our acknowledgment to Mr. Tinga Nhabomba Felisberto (Mozambique), Dr. Almon Shumba (South Africa), and Professors Peter Baguma, Munhuweyi Peresuh, and Krishin Mohan (Uganda), who helped with the data collection.

and practices from the global community to local needs (Mogaji, 2004a).

Recognition of the importance of creativity by federal or state governments and professional associations varies across the continent. The Nigerian government is a leader in celebrating the significance of creativity to national development. For instance, on January 23, 1995, the federal government of Nigeria declared September 14 to be the National Day of Creativity. The declaration was in line with the signing of the Bern Convention for Protection of Literary and Artistic Works and intended to draw attention to the contribution of creativity to national development. Observance of the National Day of Creativity involves showcasing the immense national talents in the arts, sciences, and technology. The National Creativity Award (NCA) was instituted by the Obasanjo administration in 1999. The award is aimed at acknowledging artists and other creative talents of distinction and encouraging creative expression. The first recipient of the NCA was Professor Chinua Achebe, author of the highly acclaimed *Things Fall Apart*, and father of modern African literature. The coveted NCA carries a cash prize of 1 million naira (approximately $10,000 U.S.).

The South African Creativity Foundation (SACF; http://www.kobusneethling.com) and Global Creativity Network (GCN; http://global-creativity.net/book.html) provide a forum for researchers and practitioners of creativity from Africa and the international community to share perspectives on the development of creativity as a resource for human and national development. The SACF was founded by Dr. Kobus Neethling in 1986, and it hosted the Tenth Annual International Creativity Conference in October 2004. The SACF offers training in creativity to all sectors of the South African society, and it is one of the longest functioning creativity associations in the world (Kobus Neethling, President and Founder of the SACF, personal communication, October 24, 2004). The GCN is a worldwide association of individuals and groups committed to the promotion of creativity as a universal human ability. It is currently developing an African creativity promotion initiative for the advancement of creative expression by African communities (Efiong Etuk, President and Founder of the GCN, personal communication, October 24, 2004). However, we could not identify special interest groups within national professional psychology associations in Africa for the promotion of theory and research in creativity.

Despite the recognition of creativity as a resource for human and national development by some African jurisdictions, there is scarcely

any published research on the creativity of native Africans, associated theories, and practices (Groenewald, 1970; Mpofu, Myambo,
& Mashego, 2004; Myambo & Mpofu, 2004; Otmane Ait-Ouarasse,
Morocco, personal communication, September 25, 2003). In this chapter
we discuss conceptions of creativity in Arab and sub-Saharan Africa.
We (a) present an ecocultural–developmental model for understanding
conceptions and practices in creativity in Africa; (b) characterize the
evolution of the study of creativity on the African continent; (c) review
current theory and research on creativity in Africa; (d) present the findings of a survey on conceptions and practices in creativity in Arab Africa
and sub-Saharan Africa; (e) discuss how the theories on and practices
in creativity on the African continent compare with those in the international community; and (f) present some views on promoting theory
and research on creativity in the African region.

In this chapter we draw from the few studies and works on creativity
in Africa that we could identify, and especially from a survey of African
creativity that we conducted for this chapter. From the literature survey,
we sought to explore the extent and nature of research on creativity
in Africa, and historical–cultural factors that influence conceptions and
practices in creativity on the continent. Our goals for the survey were to
supplement the gaps in the literature on African creativity and to clarify
conceptions of creativity in Africa. We used also the survey to explore
regional variations in conceptions of creativity (e.g., between Arab and
aBantu Africa) that would be helpful to future studies on creativity in
Africa.

THE ECOCULTURAL AND DEVELOPMENTAL CONTEXTS OF
CREATIVITY IN ARAB AND SUB-SAHARAN AFRICA

Arab Africa consists of Algeria, Egypt, Libya, Mauritania, Morocco,
Tunisia, and the Sudan. Sub-Saharan Africa comprises all countries
south of the Sahara desert. Arab and sub-Saharan Africa are overlapping
geocultural regions, particularly on the southern fringes of the Sahara,
and northwestern and eastern Africa. The two regions are substantially
different in culture, particularly with regard to religion. Over 70 percent
of people in Arab Africa are Muslims, and they have more in common
with people in the Arab-Islamic states of the Middle East than with
those in sub-Saharan Africa. The Sudan is an exception. In the Sudan,
15 million people are Muslim and 17–18 million people are Christians or
animists. However, the government of the Sudan has historically been
predominantly Islamic.

The vast majority of people in sub-Saharan Africa are aBantu and follow traditional indigenous religions or the Christian faith (although Islam has a significant following in northwestern and eastern sub-Saharan Africa). Both Islam and Christianity are religions that people in sub-Saharan Africa inherited from centuries of interaction with the Arab-Islamic and the Western Judeo-Christian religions (Mazrui, 1978; Nsamenang, 1998, 2002). Communities in Arab Africa and sub-Saharan Africa also use a diverse range of languages. Hundreds of languages and dialects are spoken in sub-Saharan Africa, although less than fifty of these languages exist in written form, and even fewer are official languages within nation states. Arab Africa uses a range of dialects of the Arabic language. While there are colloquial differences in the spoken Arabic language throughout the Middle East and northern Africa, the written language is classic Arabic, which is the language of the Islamic sacred writings, the Koran.

Islam represents a religion, a culture, and a daily lifestyle. It is also the basis of the legal system and influences government policies. Most countries in sub-Saharan Africa have secular governments with varying degrees of democratic rule. The state of democratization of governments in Africa and the respect for freedom of expression influence opportunities for creative practices on the continent (Khaleefa, Erdos, & Ashria, 1996a; Mpofu et al., 2004). For example, Khaleefa et al. (1996a) observed that rigid Islamic traditions metaphorically castrate creative expression in sculpture related to the human body.

Africa is also a geographically diverse continent, and with tremendous differences in economic opportunity from farming, modern commerce, and industry. Some of the world's worst recurrent droughts occur in Africa (as do some of the world's longest civil conflicts). African creative practices are, in part, a product of their individual and collective expressive selves resulting from the challenges of diversity, as well as from religion, modernization, language, geography, and political systems.

Figure 16.1 presents a descriptive model of creative expression in societies in transition, such as in Africa. Constructions of creativity by citizens of African communities emerge from multilayered socioecological contexts, which are in turn transformed by creative expressions and outcomes. Modern Africa comprises a significant minority of communities in Arab, and sub-Saharan Africa with direct participation in the global economy. Modern economies in Africa are relatively successful, in spite of operating without the infrastructure that is taken for granted in developed countries. The development of modern economies

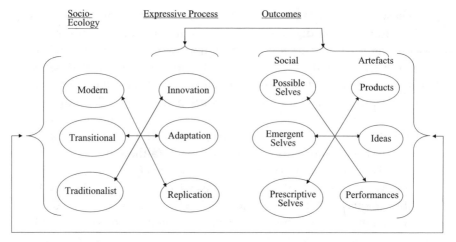

FIGURE 16.1. Creative expression in societies in transition: Contexts, processes, and outcomes.

on the African continent attests to the creative abilities of African citizens. Both Arab and sub-Saharan Africa have colonial heritages from previous conquest and occupation by Western countries, which provided the initial impetus for modernization. However, modernity in African communities is also from the need to meet the evolving development needs of the individual countries within regional or global economies.

As a result of modernization (which in many instances is accompanied by Western- style urbanization), many of the communities in Arab and sub-Saharan Africa are in transition from traditionalist to modern beliefs and practices (i.e., transitional Africa). For example, an ever-growing number of Africans are migrating to the cities, seeking opportunities to participate in the modern industrial sector, particularly in retail and marketing. Successful participation in transitional society requires creative innovation and adaptation. The vast majority of Africans live in rural areas and practice subsistence farming for a livelihood (i.e., traditionalist Africa). They also interact with the modern cash economy at some level, and most of them have relations in the cities. Africans in the cities also tend to remain socioeconomically involved with family in the rural areas (Bourdillon, 1987; Mpofu, 1999, 2003a). For the most part, Africans in rural areas may be involved in creative activities that value replication and modification of established practices rather than their transformation (Khaleefa et al., 1996a). However, people from traditionalist societies are capable of significant creative expression within the value system of their communities (Mar'i, 1976; Vanderweide & D'hondt, 1983). Creative expression in traditionalist Africa is influenced by gender in that there is a cultural expectation for male and female individuals to be creative in different domains. For instance, among the Kung San of Namibia–Botswana, men can be creative in healing, and women in embroidery (Shostak, 1993). The expectation that male and female individuals should be creative in different domains is not necessarily an expectation in transitional and modern Africa, where people are experimenting with new, nontraditional roles.

Influences from modern, transitional, and traditionalist Africa, in interaction with a globalizing world economy or the challenges of (in) hospitable geopolitical systems, call for innovation, adaptation, and replication of successful sociocultural practices as resources for meeting national or local development needs. Thus, across socioecologies (modern, transitional, and traditionalist), some level of innovation, adaptation, and replication by citizens of African communities is necessary.

Innovation, adaptation, and replication for successful participation within an ecocultural setting (i.e., modern, transitional, and traditionalist) calls for redefinition of the self at both the individual and the collective (e.g., clan or community) level (Bekker, 2001; Franchi & Swart, 2003). For instance, modern Africa and demands from collateral values such as egalitarianism challenge Africans to redefine their subjective sense of self toward what they could be (possible selves) from the opportunities in a modernizing economy (Kasfir, 1983; Mpofu, 1999). Citizens of African communities may also experience themselves in evolving roles (or emergent selves), which may be different from their traditionalist or prescriptive selves. The new or emergent roles that Africans achieve from participating in modernizing economies are the product of innovations and adaptations necessary for effective functioning in their changing communities. Evolving individual and community identities in interaction with the demands of ecocultural diversity provide the impetus for further innovation and adaptation, including emergent selves (as previously defined), products, ideas, and performances. The artifacts resulting from creative participation in changing communities could be products (goods and services), ideas (ways of knowing or doing) and performances (as in dance, music, or ritual). The processes and outcomes of creative expression in Africans can be presumed to be mutually reinforcing. For example, a possible self could be realized through adoption of a product, idea, or performance that makes it possible to achieve a newly aspired role, whereas an achieved role through self-definition could create opportunities to experience new products, ideas, and performances. The outcomes of creative expression are realized within ecocultural contexts (modern, transitional, and traditionalist), which are transformed by the outcomes, thus potentiating further replication, adaptation, and innovation.

In the sections that follow, we present perspectives of creativity that are indigenous to a cross section of African communities and are interpretable from the developmental model of creativity that we proposed (i.e., Figure 16.1). We also adopt a primarily implicit theory perspective while also applying descriptive constructs from explicit theories of creativity as appropriate.

Implicit theories have been defined as "constructions by people... that reside in the minds of these individuals" and "are discovered rather than invented because they already exist... in people's minds" (Sternberg, 1985, p. 608). These implicit theories are captured in the peoples' communications (e.g., language) pertaining to their notions about specific phenomena (Irvine, 1988; Sternberg, 1985). Implicit theories of native African communities have been documented by researchers in the areas of human intelligence (e.g., Irvine, 1988; Mpofu, 2004; Serpell, 1993; Sternberg et al., 2001) and disability and disease (Burch, 1989; Devlieger, 1998; Mpofu, 2002a, 2002b, 2003a). The implicit theories that individuals and communities hold serve as guides to behavior, including practices in creativity. Explicit theories are those that are developed, documented, and shared by the research community (Sternberg, 1985, 2003a). By considering African perspectives of creativity from both implicit and explicit theoretical approaches, we hope to (a) add to an understanding of the etics (cross cultural) and emics (monocultural) of creativity as a resource for development; and (b) provide preliminary evidence for a developmental model for understanding creativity in Africa.

DEFINING CREATIVITY IN AFRICAN SETTINGS

We envisaged that several definitions or meanings of creativity are possible across modern, transitional, and traditionalist Africa, and also within the Arab and aBantu cultures. To explore conceptualizations of creativity among contemporary African communities, we surveyed inhabitants of African countries. Specifically, we sought to establish native language terms for creativity, define creativity from an African personal and culture-of-origin perspective, and describe creative activities in

African settings from the viewpoint of native Africans. Creativity is defined from the perspectives of the participants, perhaps more than by objective criteria (Groenewald, 1970; Puccio & Chimento, 2001; Smuts, 1992).

Participants and Settings

The participants were 211 citizens (71 men and 140 women) of Arab Africa $n = 82$ and sub-Saharan Africa $n = 129$. They were from two Arab African countries (Egypt and The Sudan) and six aBantu African countries (Kenya, Mozambique, Nigeria, South Africa, Uganda, and Zimbabwe). The participants comprised about twenty-eight linguistic–cultural groups, including the following (and by country): Arabic (Egypt–Sudan); Luo–Iango, Kikuyu, and Kisovo (Kenya); Shangaani and Ronga (Mozambique); aLege, Yoruba, Ogbu, Oyo, and Tarok (Nigeria); Afrikaans, Ndebele, Northern Sotho, sePedi, seTswana, Tsonga, and siZulu (South Africa); Acholi, aTeso, Kiga, Luganda, Lusoga, Rukinga, Runyanko, and aTeso (Uganda); and Korekore, Shona, and kiTonga (Zimbabwe). The participants ranged in age from eighteen to sixty-two years, with a median age of thirty-three years. There were 154 participants who were college students at national universities and represented fifteen majors. There were 47 participants who were workers in nineteen professions, including the priesthood, farming, teaching, and administration; 57 of the participants reported their area of residence as rural and 154 as urban. All participants were at least bilingual (i.e., native African language or Arabic, and English).

Instrument

Participants completed the Regional Survey on Creativity (Mpofu, 2003b). The survey consisted of semistructured and open-ended questions. As previously stated, the major areas of investigation were the personal and culture-of-origin (or community) definition of creativity, experience with creativity, indigenous words for creativity, and implicit theories of creativity. A number of previous studies on indigenous constructions of psychosocial phenomena by Africans have reported that participants are able to reliably present their personal views and also those of their communities of origin (e.g., Devlieger, 1995; Irvine, 1972, Mpofu, 1994; Ngwarai, 1995). For example, Irvine (1972) observed that educated Africans functioned with a dual frame of reference: modern and traditionalist. According to Irvine, the juxtapositioning of "two systems of causation" in the Africans made it possible for them to reliably represent experiences from their cultures of origin, even though these may differ from their current, personal beliefs. We expected that participants would provide multilayered conceptions of creativity from their knowledge of and participation in diverse cultures.

Procedure

We analyzed the participants' responses thematically by using panning approaches (Tesch, 1990; van Manen, 1997) to reveal major themes. With the use of panning, preliminary themes are identified and tentative frameworks for thematic clusters created. Themes are clarified and revised as new ones emerge. In other words, the generation of themes and the analysis of the data occur concurrently. We established credibility of the themes by means of the consensus of the research team, by member checks, and by other data-triangulation techniques. We used back-translation methods to establish equivalence of meaning between the English- and native-language terms for creativity. We analyzed responses for the total sample of participants, and we also differentiated them by region (Arab Africa; sub-Saharan Africa) where appropriate.

To elicit personal and culture-of-origin definitions of creativity, we had participants respond to three complementary questions. First, we asked participants to list the words from their local languages (or mother tongue) that "mean the same as *creativity* or are closest in meaning to *creativity.*" They also provided an English translation for each of the terms listed. Back translations were provided by other bilingual persons from the same linguistic cultural background to check the credibility or reliability of the translations. In addition, similarity of translations of a comparable native-language word by several participants provided a reliability check for the translations. Our expectation was that native-language terms would add to a culture-of-origin view of creativity. Second, an introduction to the survey stated that "People understand creativity in different ways, and . . . there is no 'correct' definition of creativity." We then asked participants to provide their "personal definition of creativity." Third, we asked participants how often they and people of their culture of origin were creative. They could choose one of four responses, from very rarely, rarely, often, to very often. Fourth, we asked participants to describe creative things that they and people from their community of origin did in the past twelve months, and to indicate in which ways those activities were creative. These questions probed the salience of creativity to the participants and also provided concrete examples of creativity from the participant's own perspectives.

Terms for Creativity

Our content analysis of the list of native-language words that directly translated to creativity revealed that only the Arabic language had a word for creativity (i.e., *ibda*). Khaleefa, Erdos, and Ashria (1996b, 1997) regarded the Arabic word *ibda* to mean the same as creativity. They also reviewed works by Islamic scholars who distinguish among expressions of and contexts for creativity. For example, the word *bid'a* refers to innovation, which among the Muslims is regarded as an aspect of creativity. Muslims distinguish between innovation and bid'a in religious and secular contexts. Innovation in religious matters is bid'a and refers to the introduction of unconventional religious ideas. Such innovation is considered an ill behavior or sin (*dalala* or *fitnah*). Two forms of the word *bid'a* are recognized for secular (or "donya") affairs: *bida't hoda,* or good innovation, and *bida't dalal,* or bad innovation. Thus abstract art such as calligraphy is bida't hoda, whereas representational art involving animate things is bida't dalal. Poetry and drumming are bida't hoda. Criticism of core Islamic teachings is bida't dalal.

None of the other twenty-seven languages of Africa that we sampled had a word equivalent in meaning to creativity with back translation. Within the twenty-seven linguistic–cultural groups of sub-Saharan Africa that we surveyed, the word *creativity* was synonymous with being (a) resourceful (e.g., *kujingirisa*, chiShona, Zimbabwe–Mozambique; *kurendzeveta*, Ronga, Mozambique; *okuyiiya*, Banyanko, Uganda; and *obukujukuju*, Luganda, Uganda), (b) intelligent (e.g., *n'tlhari*, Shangaani, Mozambique; *botlhale*, seTswana, South Africa–Botswana; *imo*, Yoruba, Nigeria; and *adiru*, Luo, Kenya), (c) wise (e.g., *atinuda*, Ogbu, Nigeria; *ojogbou*, Yoruba, Nigeria; and *umunyabwenge*, Kisovo, Uganda), motivated (e.g., *akankanyu*, Yuruba, Nigeria; and *mahatus*, Baluhya, Uganda), (d) talented (e.g., *dimpa*, *mpho*, seTswana, South Africa–Botswana), and (e) artistic (e.g. *kunstig*, Afrikaans, South Africa; and *fanan* or *fundi*, Arabic). Other indigenous terms for creativity that were identified less frequently translated to *ability, cleanliness, creating, innovation, inventiveness, inspiration, knowledge, patience,* and *originality*.

Definitions of Creativity

The question requesting a personal definition of creativity yielded responses that could be clustered under the following themes: innovative, adaptive, personal agency, integrative, incremental, social impact oriented (or community oriented), domain specific, mystical, and imitative. Sample elaborations of these themes are as follows: "process that aims to transform existing reality" (innovation), "effective solution to a problem or situation" (adaptive), "carrying out an activity without being pressured" (personal agency), "able to produce something using existing resources" (integrative), "adding value to what already exists" (incremental), "to produce something of value to the self and others" (having social impact), "it is to do with beauty; anything beautiful is creative" (domain specific), "it is a gift from God and we make it better by care" (mystical), and "able to imitate new things" (imitative). Over 95 percent of the statements could be unambiguously categorized under each of these themes. We scored complex statements or those that combined several themes for each of the relevant themes. For example, we multiply scored "to use many things in one, to integrate parts and facilitate problems" for the themes "integrative" and "adaptive."

Across regions (and by percentage), participants defined creativity to include being innovative (37.9 percent), social impact oriented (28 percent), personal–agentic (17.1 percent), incremental (6.6 percent), and domain specific (2.8 percent). Within Arab Africa, participants defined creativity as primarily concerned with being innovative (40.2 percent), personal–agentic (20.7 percent), social impact oriented (14.6 percent), domain specific (7.3 percent), and incremental or integrative (3.7 percent). Participants from aBantu Africa regarded creativity to include being innovative (35.4 percent), social impact oriented (36.4 percent), personal–agentic (14.7 percent), incremental (8.5 percent), and mystical (2.3 percent).

Creative Activities

About 72 percent of the participants regarded themselves as being frequently engaged in creative activities. Within the Arab African sample, 68.5 percent of the participants perceived themselves as performing creative activities often. About 73 percent of participants from sub-Saharan Africa considered themselves as being frequently engaged in creative activities. Responses to the question on the specific activities that the participants did in the previous twelve months that they deemed creative were scored thematically under four categories: innovative (e.g., "I sculpted an Egyptian woman"; "I traveled to Lebanon"), adaptative (e.g., "I setup a family farm"; "I trained in sign language"), social impact oriented (e.g., "I created a journalist network against AIDS"; "I reconciled two families that had lived in enmity for over three years"), and artistic (e.g., "I composed a poem"; "I decorated my house"). For the combined group of participants, 36.1 percent participants regarded themselves as creative because they engaged in adaptive behaviors. About 27 percent perceived themselves as having enacted some innovations, 19 percent as having involvement in an activity with wider social impact, and 11 percent as participating in artistic activities. Within Arab Africa, participants perceived their participation as creative in artistic production (49.3 percent), innovation (19.1 percent), social impact (13.2 percent), and adaptation (12.3 percent). Participants from aBantu Africa regarded personal creativity involving innovation (33.6 percent), social impact (28.3 percent), artistic (23.8 percent), and adaptation (17.6 percent).

With regard to specific creative behaviors performed by people from their cultures of origin, participants from Arab Africa considered the activities innovative (52 percent), social impact oriented (30 percent), artistic (16 percent), and adaptive (4 percent). Examples of community level innovations from Arab Africa included "there have been several competitions encouraging creativity in drawing and writing" and "trying to solve the Palestinian–Israel dispute." Examples of creative practices under social impact were "the honoring of a politician who helped in the march for peace" and "building a new hypermarket." Examples of creative artistic productions by community members included "a friend made a video with his friends showing different faces and voices expressing important issues," and "paintings." Some adaptive behaviors by community members in Arab Africa were "built a greenhouse as a nursery for flowers" and "they dug deep near a spring and made a well where people fetched water."

Participants from aBantu Africa perceived people from their communities to be engaged in creative activities involving adaptation (48.5 percent), innovation (23.8 percent), social impact (16.1 percent), and artistic expression (10.4 percent). Examples of identified innovations included "they used an old wheelbarrow to make a wheelchair" and "designed a logo for traditional healers." Social-impact-oriented activities by members of the community included "women participated in nontraditional roles" and "immunizing all children in the community." Examples of creative arts were "traditional dance, which involved the making of costumes" and "modeling pots." Creative adaptations by community members included "they formed the arrow group to fight Kony (a tribal group) rebels" and "collected used polythene papers for recycling."

HISTORICAL AND CULTURAL INFLUENCES ON THE STUDY OF CREATIVITY IN AFRICA

The study of psychological constructs in any setting is influenced by both internal factors (e.g., the needs of consumers) and external factors (related developments in other settings). Ideally, the needs of consumers should take priority in how the construct is defined, operationalized, and practiced (Mpofu, 2002b; 2004; Mpofu et al., 2005). The needs of the consumers may be historical, transitional, or emergent, and for which research and practices involving a construct are a solution. In a previous section, we presented a model on the ecocultural factors influencing the expression of creativity in African communities. In this section we add to the previous discussion by exploring how colonialism and religion as historical–cultural factors have influenced the study of creativity in Africa.

The formal study of creativity in Africa is of relatively recent origin and is associated with the history of the establishment of the arts or humanities and social science departments at institutions of higher learning in the respective countries. Studies of creativity from the arts and humanities (e.g., performance arts, sculpture, music, and drama) predate psychological studies (or those that focus on conceptions of creativity), for several reasons. First, the arts or humanities departments were established at many African universities before the psychology departments (Oshodi, 2004; Nsamenang, 1995). Hence, researchers from the arts or humanities had a longer period of preparation and exposure to creative expressions in African communities than those from psychology. Second, the curricula for the arts or humanities programs at African universities also produced and used local creative productions (e.g., short stories, novels, and graphic arts) earlier and to a greater extent than that for psychological studies. Art and (oral) literature have long traditions on the African continent and are readily adopted in arts education rather than psychological studies curricula. In addition, most African communities have ongoing collective artistic creations and exhibitions, the documentation and appreciation of which has been the basis for scholarship in creativity in the arts or humanities.

With few exceptions, psychological research on the African continent has historically tended to address the issues and needs of Western audiences rather than those of African communities (Abou-Hatab, 1997; Badri 1979, Mpofu, 2002b; Serpell, 1993). This is explained by the fact that the development of psychology as a discipline on the African continent is in the translational and modeling stage, which is characterized by an uncritical adoption of Western psychological concepts and technologies (Mpofu et al., 1997). For example, Abou-Hatab (1997) noted that the overreliance on Western conceptions of psychology by psychologists in Arab Africa inhibited creativity in the field of psychology and in psychological research. Mpofu (2002b) and Serpell (1993) observed that the uncritical adoption of Western psychological constructs and associated practices by psychologists in Africa would retard the indigenization of psychology on the African continent. National psychology associations on the continent tend to have a Western bias in their practices and developmental agendas (e.g., WebPsySoft Arab Company, 2003).

The specific ways in which the arts have influenced the study of creativity on the African continent differ by region. For example, creative expression in Arab Africa is circumscribed by Islamic teachings. Islam influences creative expression in certain areas of art, especially in painting and sculpture, in that it prohibits the visual representation of man and any living being. By Islamic tradition, art is used as a decoration and not as a representation. In the decorative arts, Arab artists developed their skills in the plant motif, the Arabic script motif, and the geometric motif. The medium is typically metal, stone, tile, or wood. The plant motif represents the original *Arabesque* but some artists use the term to designate Islamic decorative motifs in general (Patai, 2002). The general visual presentation of art is to repeat small elements with minor variations or unchanged in form. Arab music is similarly based on small elements that are repeated over and over, and the same repetition appears in literature as well as in the spoken form of the language.

In Islamic tradition, creativity is not the creation of something new but simply an extension of the past. The introduction of Western traditions, with an emphasis on art as a representation, including representation of the human form and other living beings, or art as an original creation, introduces new values to the Arab-Islamic artist. For instance, sculpture is a medium that does not exist in traditional art in Arab countries. While art schools that use the Western medium have existed in Egypt since the early twentieth century, Western styles of art are still not widely accepted. Indeed, art and architecture professor Mira Cantor, who taught in Egypt in 1994, found that art students were limited in their creativity, imagination, and the exploration of new ideas, as they feared being rejected by the closely knit extended-family system typically found in Egypt and most Middle Eastern countries (Irons, 1999). Badri (1979) observed that many Muslim psychologists cannot reconcile Western psychological concepts, which are based on Judeo-Christian values and sometimes atheism, with Islam. Some psychologists in Arab Africa are restricted in their research by political and social systems that discourage creativity (Abou-Hatab, 1997; Khaleefa et al., 1996a).

Creative expression in aBantu Africa has long traditions in secular interests. For instance, the traditional African religions impose no restraints on producing replicas of living beings. In aBantu Africa, potent medical remedies, magic, and charms are stored in elaborately carved and scripted ornaments from wood, stone, or animal products. Utensils, walking sticks, and other paraphernalia for religious rites are crafted by renowned artists in the villages. Cave paintings found in sub-Saharan Africa date back thousands of years and show paintings of human figures along with animal figures (Phillips, 1996; Wassing, 1988). Sculptures in both wood and stone depicting living creatures were prevalent. Ashanti wood sculptors have a positive view of each other's works and consider each piece a potential celebrity (Silver, 1981). Houses in sub-Saharan Africa were traditionally decorated with geometric designs, and literature in the form of stories existed in the oral tradition. With the advent of colonialism, Europeans brought Christianity into these geographic areas. The Christian religion did not pose any limitations on most forms of the creative arts, although African dance forms were less appreciated, particularly by Protestant missionaries. Europeans also introduced an educational system based on the curriculum of their home countries, and the Western model of art was included in the curriculum. Many citizens of communities in aBantu Africa make a living from selling works of art, including those that depict animals and humans.

Theories of Creativity in African Settings

Many of the propositions by researchers on creativity on the African continent would be consistent with implicit theories of creativity in that they do not present well-articulated explicit theories. For instance, Khaleefa et al. (1996a) regarded innovation to be a characteristic of social groups rather than individuals. From that perspective, innovative works or products are those that are regarded by a social collective to be meriting distinction. According to Khaleefa et al., the social aspects of the recognition and designation of innovation suggest that only social groups rather than individuals can be innovative. Khaleefa et al. regarded creativity as a characteristic of individuals rather than collectives. However, these authors do make a convincing case for ascribing innovation only to social groups and creativity only to individuals.

Oyowe (1996) and Mogaji (2004a) were of the view that creativity in African settings has a social-group basis. Mogaji referred, by example, to the fact that some African communities are relatively more dynamic, enterprising, and creative than others (e.g., the Ibos in Nigeria and the Bamilekes in Cameroon). Creativity in these sociocultural groups seemed to be a collective rather than individual characteristic. Amali (1984, 1998) considered creativity to be both an instrument and product of the collective culture. Paulus (2000), while acknowledging the fact that groups could inhibit creativity, was of the view that the interaction in groups and teamwork can be an important source of creative ideas and innovations. Akarakiri (1998) observed that innovation cannot be divorced from creativity; the quality of innovation results from the originality of the creative minds of one or a few individuals. Akarakiri (1998) maintained that the rate of economic and technological development is low in developing countries because the utilization of creativity and innovation in new product development still remains in its infancy in those countries. He identified seven areas of power attained by developed countries through the creation and innovation of new products, and he considered them as challenges to developing countries.

The view that creativity is a resource for nation building (e.g., Gourly, 2000; Maas, 1999; Mashego, 2004; Needling, 2000) is consistent with a theory of creativity as mediated by groups to achieve objectives desired by a collective. Mashego (2004) referred to an innovative artistic creation at the Grahamstowm Art Festival of 1997. A performance group, the amaBokoboko, presented Mozart's well-known opera "The Magic Flute." The opera was placed within an African context and sung in English with Zulu exclamation in between. The troupe reviewer introduced the opera as follows: "Auf Wiedersehen Wolfgang. Woza Ama Deus!" As is well known, Mozart's first names were Wolfgang Amadeus. By saying *Auf Wiedersehen* (goodbye in German) to Wolfgang and welcoming the South African production through *Woza* (Zulu for come), and then cleverly utilizing the *ama* part of Mozart's name, the reviewer then slips into the pattern stated by the amaBokoboko, that is, using the *ama* prefixes and then duplicating the *Deus* part. The performance was perceived as contributing to nation building in a democratic South Africa by helping breakdown prior barriers between South African linguistic-cultural communities from the apartheid era (Mashego, 2004; Needling, 2000).

Creativity in African settings has also been explained from the perspective of constructs from explicit theories of personality. For example, Abdel-Ghaffar (cited in Osman, 1998) and Habib (1990b) noted that creative individuals showed the following personality traits: emotional sensitivity, emotional stability, self-control, and liberal attitudes. Soueif (cited in Abdel-Khalek, 1998), who also studied the psychology of creativity in literature, hypothesized that the Egyptian personality consisted of four basic types: the depressive or helpless, the egocentric, the parasitic, and the cynical. However, neither he nor any other Arab psychologists expanded the model.

To further explore implicit theories of creativity, we asked the participants from eight African countries whom we surveyed for definitions of creativity (as already described) to list the characteristics that they expect of a creative person of their culture of origin. We also asked the participants to provide personal views on what makes a person creative.

The question on culture-of-origin characteristics of individuals with creativity yielded responses represented by the following themes: artistic, imaginative, responsible, motivated, flexible, analytical, educated, and cooperative. Statements indicative of these themes were judged by peer review to include the following qualities: artistic (aesthetic, romantic, beautiful, unique, talented, and clean), imaginative (visionary, original, innovative, productive, and inventive), responsible (resourceful, planful, timewise, diligent, independent, poised, calm, and a leader), motivated (proactive, risk taker, spontaneous, ambitious, participatory, and hard worker), flexible (adaptive, sensitive, confident, dynamic, communicative, patient, optimistic, sociable, and open minded), analytical (intelligent, clever, investigative, observant, perceptive, inquisitive, and wise), educated (literate, achiever, and cultured), cooperative (team player, networked, and collectivistic), and egocentric (lazy, serious, humorless, and self-centered). Statements combining several qualities were multiply scored. About 55 percent of statements could be reliably scored in only one category.

The top five characteristics expected of a creative person by the participants were as follows: imaginative (28 percent), flexible (22.3 percent), analytical (20.4 percent), responsible (14.2 percent), and motivated (8.1 percent). Participants from Arab Africa considered the following characteristics to define a creative person: analytical (25.6 percent), flexible (25.6 percent), imaginative (23.2 percent), responsible (13.4 percent) and motivated (6.1 percent). Those from aBantu Africa characterized a person with creativity similarly, and as follows: imaginative (31 percent), flexible (20.2 percent), analytical (17.1 percent), responsible (14.7 percent) and motivated (9.3 percent).

In response to the question on personal theories of creativity, participants regarded it to result from social influence (58 percent; e.g., "creativity emanates from the way a person is brought up and educated"; "how others evaluate and encourage being creative, and how they perceive being creative"), personal agency or motivation (23.7 percent; e.g., "someone who risks anything and learns from mistakes"; "an eagerness to be different"), natural endowment (9 percent; e.g., "DNA determines whether you are creative or not"; "I think people are born with it"), personal intelligence (6.2 percent; e.g., "It results from high intelligence"; "If intelligent, a person finds a suitable environment to be creative"), and a mystical source (4.3 percent e.g., "It is a gift from God"; "Sometimes it is a talent from God"). There were no apparent regional differences in both the magnitude and rank ordering of the factors perceived by the participants to explain creativity in persons.

African Research on Creativity

The very limited research on creativity from Africa has tended to be in four traditions: psychometric, literature, calligraphy, and performance arts (Myambo, 2004; Otmane Ait-Ouarasse, personal communication, September 25, 2003). Many of the studies are anecdotal in nature. We could not identify any psychological studies of creativity out of Africa that used an ethnographic approach. A limitation in our efforts to identify studies on creativity from Arab Africa is that most of the research out of Egypt, for example, has been published in Arabic and only a few summaries of the research have been written in English (see Ahmed & Gielen, 1998).

Psychometric Studies

These studies used pencil-and-paper tests to examine the development of creative potential in African students in a variety of environments. They typically used Western constructs and measures of creativity. For example, Khaleefa et al. (1996b, 1997) investigated differences in creativity between urban and rural school students in the Sudan. They measured creative ability by using three Western tests: the Consequences

Test (CT; Guilford & Guilford, 1980), the Alternative Uses Test (AUT; Guilford et al., 1978), the Creative Personality Test (CPT; Gough & Heilbrun, 1980; as adapted by Habib, 1990a) and one locally developed measure, the Creative Activities List (CAL; Habib, 1990b). The CT is a measure of ideational fluency (i.e., number of ideas in response to a scenario), the AUT, is a measure of divergent thinking (i.e., unusual use of common items), the CPT is a measure of creative personality traits, and the CAL measures verbal creativity. Students from urban schools scored significantly higher on the CT than their rural peers. There were no significant differences between the rural and urban students in performance on the AUT, and the CPT. However, students from the rural areas scored higher on the CAL. The authors interpreted the findings to mean that urbanization had a positive effect on ideational fluency (hence the higher scores on the CT by students from urban areas), and traditional, Islamic education emphasized verbal skills (hence the higher scores on verbal creativity by the rural students). Thus, creative expression in Sudanese students was mediated by both environment (i.e., modern vs. traditional) and task characteristics (e.g., ideational fluency; verbal creativity). The superior effects of modernization on creativity in students relative to traditionalism was also reported by Khaleefa et al. (1996b) in an earlier study with college students. In that study, a sample of Sudanese college students who differed in the number of completed years in college (a proxy measure for modernization) took the AUT. Students with more college education scored higher than those with less college education. The use of decontextualized tasks to measure creative ability in a non-Western society may have resulted in an underestimation of creative potential in the Sudanese students. There is research evidence to suggest that students from African environments perform better on ability tasks that are ecologically meaningful (e.g., Serpell, 1993; Sternberg et al., 2001).

Akinboye et al. (1989) reported the results of a Nigerian study in which the relationship between creativity, school learning, and retention was investigated. They observed that highly creative students were above average in academic performance, but not necessarily the best achievers in their classes. Akinboye et al. interpreted the finding to suggest that highly creative students may prefer to learn only those things of interest to them. They further speculated that highly creative students had complex cognitive systems and an attitude of constructive discontent. As a result, the students may be uncomfortable with the status quo, prone to querying events, and seek unusual solutions to learning problems. According to Akinboye, regular classroom teachers may not consider highly creative learners capable or fail to give the learners the educational support they need to excel in their interests. Hannourah and Sami (cited in Osman, 1998) conducted a study in the area of the psychosocial context of creativity. They studied the effect on creativity of exposure of six- to twelve-year-old Arab African children to the mass media. They found that the children with higher exposure to mass media scored higher on tests of creativity.

Mogaji (1999) administered the Adjective Check List (Gough & Heilbrun, 1980) to measure creativity in 230 Nigerian workers. The sample included 150 subjects (75 men and 75 women) from the public sector organization and 80 subjects (40 men and 40 women) from the private sector organization. He observed a significant sex and sector difference. Female participants had higher mean creativity scores than their male counterparts in both private and public sectors. The author concluded that the female Nigerian workers were more creative, and this conclusion was also supported by self-observational reports.

Psychology of Creativity in Literature and Calligraphy

Research on creativity in Arab Africa has largely focused on the psychology of literature and art. According to Otmane Ait-Ouarasse (personal communication, September 25, 2004), the research on creativity from Arab Africa pertains mostly to the development of appropriate criteria for judging the quality of literary works that could be considered creative. The psychology of creativity in literature was studied by M. I. Soueif at the University of Cairo. Soueif was influenced by Gestalt psychology, and he mainly studied the creative process in poetry. His methods consisted of interviews, questionnaires, and content analysis. In his 1970 study (cited in Abdel-Hamid, 1998), he characterized adaptive flexibility, creative leaps, creative anticipation, and closure.

Several of Soueif's students expanded on his work beyond poetry to other written forms, and applied psychometric methods. Hannourah, in 1979 (cited by Abdel-Hamid, 1998), studied the creative process in the novel and found that novelists created the whole before they produced the "parts." In 1980, Hannourah (cited in Abdel-Hamid, 1998) replicated the study in the field of creative drama. He concluded that authors who write creative plays are supported by a psychological base that consists of social, emotional, aesthetic, and cognitive dimensions. Finally, it should be noted that, in 1979, both Soueif and Hannourah (cited in Abdel-Hamid, 1998) indicated the crucial role of society, as well as the Arabic language, in producing constraints on creativity. In 1980, Abdel-Hamid, a student of Soueif, studied the creative processes in the short story. He used a principal component factor, analysis and oblique rotation to reveal three factors: a social factor, a concentration factor, and a creative ordering of percepts factor.

Osman (1998) wrote an article in English that summarized much of the research done in Arabic on psychological creativity in the field of art. While interest in this topic began in the 1950s, most studies were carried out between 1967 and 1991; unfortunately, most studies were not published. Osman placed the studies of art as a creative act into three categories: studies on creativity as a process, studies on the processes underlying creativity, and the psychosocial context of creativity. Osman did not elaborate on the research studies done on creativity as a process, except to mention that assessment criteria were established to study creativity as a process. In 1973, Abel-Ghaffar (cited in Osman, 1998) studied the processes underlying creativity. He found that there was no relationship between excellence in the plastic arts (i.e., enamel or porcelain based) and mental health. A cross-cultural study done by Hannourah and Eissa in 1984 (cited in Osman, 1998) found that Egyptian university students were superior in originality while their Kuwaiti counterparts were superior in ideational fluency.

Research on Creativity in the Performance Arts
Studies in the performance arts tradition are characteristically historical–anthropological and attempt to capture or describe the creative shifts or adaptations that transform a traditional performance into a multilayered modern choreography. In a previous section, we reported a review of a creative performance by the amaBokoboko of South Africa, which has been an inspiration for numerous performance arts groups in that country. Precursors to multilingual and instrumentation innovation to the amaBokoboko include the performances by Savuka/Juluka beginning in the 1980s (Clegg, 2004), and the world renowned Lady Smith Black Mambazo (Shabalala, 1999). Studies of Fuji music (e.g., Mogaji, 2004a, Olaniyan, 2004) exemplify systematic research on African creativity in the performance arts. According to Mogaji, Fuji music originated from the Yorubaland of Nigeria. This type of music evolved from the use of African traditional musical instruments of Nigerian variety to a mixture of both African and Western musical instruments in making music. This technique of creativity started with the idea of the use of simple musical instruments that could enable the musicians to move around

as dictated by the events, which necessitated their performance, and also to enable them to move around with the celebrants. The troupe's creativity manifests in their psychomotor performance. Olaniyan (2004) observed that changes have occurred in both the instrumentation and the vocal style of the Fuji musicians. He studied the recordings of prominent Fuji artists such as Ayinde Barrister, Ayinla Kollington, and Ayinde Wasiu. Olaniyan also interviewed those prominent musical artists and concluded that the basic technique of creating Fuji music includes the use of unaccompanied vocal declamation, solo, chorus response, and text (mostly in Yoruba and occasionally mixed with Arabic and English languages). The use of simple duple time, praise texts and texts based on current affairs, throaty vocal techniques, and unison singing were notable creative musical adaptations, as was innovative performances with the talking drums, drum sets, conga, bell, and rattles.

Creative adaptations also included drumming accompaniment with textually based background, rhythmic pattern for dance gestures, and drumming interludes with truncation. Influences on musical creativity from modernization include the use of digital keyboards and Western wind instruments. Thus, the opportunities from modern trends in the development of electronics and computer systems have affected the creativity of Fuji music tremendously. The music has passed through several stages of evolution such that its original features of identification have changed with time. Fuji music as a creative product is considered a core element in advancing a Nigerian national identity.

Anecdotal Reports

Anecdotal reports are an important source of information on sociocultural practices that are under researched, or from settings that are underrepresented in the literature. Mogaji (2004b) observed that Nigerian mechanics, welders, and panel beaters are creative and innovative in their repair works. The engineers, who worked on his defunct car over a two-week period, demonstrated impressive creativity in the ways they improvised parts of the vehicle engine from so-called junk materials, which became functional. Garth Walker, a graphic designer, was inspired by the street of Durban teenagers with colors to create *I-Jusi*, an impressive eight-page irregularly published magazine that debuted at the end of 1995. The magazine achieved international distribution and was awarded the coveted Art Directors Club Silver Cube at New York (Todd, 1998). Hartfield (2003) reported on a creative director and a playwright of the TBWA/Hunt Lascaris Company of South Africa, who sold his first advertisement from the back of a car in a recession, set up the first internationally renowned South African advertising agency, and assisted post-Apartheid democracy by handling Nelson Mandela's presidential campaign. Gaobepe (2003) reported on an encounter in an interview with a creative and talented South African musician, Selaelo Maredi, who graduated with a music degree. Salaelo was born and raised in a poor family, was a street vendor, and worked the South African mines before his great success in the music industry. According to Gaobepe, Salaelo was inspired by a stringent work ethic that he acquired in childhood. Needling (2000) observed that mainly Afrikaan (South Africa) sport journalists have been quite creative and innovative in creating new "pet names" for national or representative sides. The general public has subsequently adopted the names for sport teams suggested by the journalists. The examples suggest possible areas for organized research in creativity in African settings.

COMPARISON WITH CREATIVITY THEORY AND RESEARCH IN OTHER JURISDICTIONS

A number of strands in conceptions of creativity from an African perspective are similar to those from the international community. For instance, the observations from the review of the literature and a survey of participants from African countries suggest that Africans consider creativity to derive from at least five components: thinking styles, personality, motivation, environment, and the confluence of the aforesaid attributes. For instance, according to the studies reviewed in this chapter, Africans consider people who are creative to be innovative or adaptive in their thinking. Creative people are also perceived to have a personality orientation characterized by imaginativeness, unconventionality and openness to new experiences. They also have a high sense of personal agency or motivation and a willingness to take risks. From the viewpoint of the research from Africa, being creative stems from decisions to express values important to individuals or their communities. Africans also consider the environment critical to the development, display, and recognition of creativity in persons. A majority of the respondents to our survey on conceptions of creativity believed that creativity is learned through social influence or education in a supportive environment. These components of creativity are similar to those proposed in the investment theory of creativity (Sternberg, 2003b) and the systems theories of creativity (Csikszentmihalyi, 1996, 2000; Lubart,

1999; Simonton, 1999). In brief, the investment theory of creativity proposes that people decide to exploit performance-relevant attributes in themselves and the environment to engage activities that would result in high-value outcomes. Systems theories of creativity explain its occurrence in terms of goal-oriented or meaning interactions with enabling environments.

The research on African conceptions of creativity also identified creative expression to encompass a range of behaviors, including replication, integration, adaptation, and innovation, elements which, in part, are consistent with the propulsion theory of creativity (Sternberg, 2003c) and creativity as a style of thinking (Kirton, 1989, 1994). The basic premise of the propulsion theory of creativity includes a range of different types of creativity, from acceptance of the status quo (as in replication) to those that radically transform existing practices way beyond the best expectation for a historical period (as in reinitiation). From the viewpoint of creativity as a style of thinking, adaptors and innovators are regarded as being creative in different ways. Adaptors have a reactive creativity style whose goal is to solve existing problems. By contrast, innovators have a proactive creativity style or one that is oriented toward problem finding for solutions. People may use both adaptive and innovative approaches, depending on salience or appropriateness to settings.

Africans conceptualize creativity as an everyday activity for most people, and in all settings. The notion of everyday creativity was proposed by Runco and colleagues (Runco & Richards, 1997; Runco, 2001; 2004), and Etuk (2004). For instance, Runco and Richards considered creativity to be a widely distributed or universal human experience and possible even with children. Creativity in everyday domains does not require high levels of achievement or maximal solutions to problems. It involves original interpretations and actions from the individual's personal perspective, and achievements of personally satisfying outcomes. Creativity as an everyday phenomenon is regarded as directly beneficial to participants, who apply it to their present or prospective needs (Etuk, 2004).

Unlike some of the research and theorizing from Western countries, Africans seem to consider creativity an attribute of collectives, perhaps more than of individuals. For example, some ethnic groups in Africa are perceived to be more enterprising than others, which suggests reliable between-group variations in creativity. Creativity in African societies may be held to a standard that places a higher value on community welfare (e.g., living in harmony or good neighborliness) than the achievement of personal ends. The bias toward collectively shared creativity may be a consequence of the fact that a majority of African communities are traditionalist–subsistence rather than modern–egalitarian. Within a traditionalist–subsistence sociocultural milieu, human participation requires the symbiotic participation of members of the collective in all life major activities. For that reason, the conception and execution of creative practices is based on the presumption of the participation and endorsement of the collective. However, in transitional and modern Africa, individualistic conceptions of creativity may prevail as creative practices in those contexts are often from emergent selves in rapidly evolving socioecologies.

On the basis of the findings from our survey, it appears that Africans do not make a distinction between creativity and related constructs such as knowledge, domain–specific ability, intelligence, or wisdom. This is unlike traditions in Western countries, where the research has identified creativity as a distinct psychological construct and different from other human abilities (Albert & Runco, 1999; Sternberg, 2003a). The lack of differentiation of creativity as a unique ability in African native languages may reflect the fact that creative expression in African settings is largely of the everyday or functional type and not readily separable from related abilities. With increasing modernization and consequent cultural shifts toward emergent selves, it is likely that creativity will be recognized more as sharing an overlap with other human abilities, although different from them.

Psychometric studies on creativity in Africa have tended to be modeled after those from Western countries in a variety of ways. For instance, they have adopted Western concepts and measures of creativity and applied them to investigate creativity in Africans (e.g., Habib, 1990a, 1990b; Khaleefa et al., 1997; Mogaji, 1999). As previously noted, the overreliance on Western models is explained, in part, by the lack of explicit indigenous psychological theories of creativity to guide research. It is also a consequence of the underdevelopment of psychology on the African continent from a lack of a critical mass of researchers in creativity and also the uncritical adoption of Western concepts and measures. The more creative psychometric studies on creativity from an African perspective are exemplified by the use of factor analytic approaches to study creativity from literary works (see Abdel-Hamid, 1998).

Unlike the research from Western countries, much of the research on creativity in Africa appears to be in literature, calligraphy, and the performance arts. The majority of studies have tended to be of anthropological rather than psychological in nature. Such studies have documented the evolution of practices in the arts rather than the psychological processes behind the observed performances, or their psychological appreciation by audiences. A number of researchers from Western countries have proposed constructs for psychological studies of the performance arts (e.g., Csikszentmihalyi, 1997; Sawyer, 1998) that have potential for cross-cultural adaptation.

VIEWS ON THE DEVELOPMENT OF THEORY AND RESEARCH ON CREATIVITY WITHIN THE AREA

The development of theory and research on creativity on the African continent is likely to be enhanced over the next decade. Influences on the development of theory and research on creativity on the African continent include the greater availability of formal education to the general population, increasing modernization and democratization of African communities, indigenization of psychology, and opportunities from interdisciplinary research on creativity. An increase in levels of general education in the population makes it possible for participants to think in less traditional or routinized ways. It also adds to the corpus of psychology researchers on the African continent, some of whom may have an interest in research in creativity. Nearly all the major African national universities have psychology departments, making it more likely that studies on creativity would attain significance. The survey of practices in creativity and anecdotal reports reviewed previously suggest that Africans consider creativity to be an important human ability, which makes it likely that greater attention will be paid to that resource by African scholars and governments through supportive programs (e.g., educational and awards programs).

In this chapter, we presented a model for the development of creative expression in developing societies, differentiating three formative influences: modern, transitional, and traditionalist. We believe that, as more Africans are engaged in modern economies, creativity and studies based on it will be at the forefront of national efforts toward economic and sociocultural competitiveness in the global village (Khaleefa, 1999a, 1999b). The opportunities or challenges from participating in a global economy can reasonably be expected to have ripple effects reaching the most remote of African villages. Villagers will be challenged to consider possible selves from the opportunities filtering to them from the national, globally oriented culture. Our model suggests that significant innovation is possible within traditionalist communities and within their actual and aspired values. Increasing modernization and general education can reasonably be expected to enable Africans in traditionalist settings to be more assertive about their values, including need for freedom of expression, good governance, and democracy. They may need to be creative in laying their claims to freedom to creative expression. On the one hand, millions of Africans have to creatively negotiate self-expression with some of the conservative or traditionalist political systems that are oppressive of the development of creative talent. On the other hand, they also risk being manipulated and exploited by neocolonial interests who may have exploitative agendas.

A greater number of African and international scholars are increasingly recognizing the cultural situatedness of psychology as a discipline, and the need to develop indigenous psychological theories and practices. For example, both Abou-Hatab (1997), who wrote about psychology in Egypt, and Khaleefa (1999a, 1999b), who wrote about creativity research in the Arab world, have emphasized that further psychological studies should be based on indigenous psychologies and not on Western methods and theories. Abou-Hatab hoped that indigenous psychology in Egypt would soon become a respected field of inquiry. However, Khaleefa noted that, in the Arab world, there was little interest in studying indigenous psychology. He further observed that there were prevalent negative attitudes toward the study of creativity, especially in Western forms of art such as sculpture, as this form of art is viewed as forbidden by God or *Allah*. Nonetheless, Khaleefa was also of the view that, even with the constraints of religion and tradition in certain African jurisdictions, indigenous forms of creativity, such as poetry, calligraphy, and Arabesque should be studied in more detail, because these forms of creativity are culturally acceptable and represent an indigenous psychology.

The trend toward studies to indigenize psychology could benefit from the selective adoption of successful experiences from other jurisdictions (Mpofu, 2002b, Nsamenang, 1998). For example, African researchers on creativity could learn from experiences in the development of creativity theory and research in Western countries to put into a larger time perspective their own research agendas, while at the same time being respectful of local traditions. Our previous discussion suggested many areas of overlap in conceptualizations of creativity by contemporary

Africans as compared with current trends in conceptualizations of creativity in Western countries. The previous review also suggested that there is evidence of interest in studies on the creative aspects of the performance arts in some African jurisdictions (e.g., Olaniyan, 2004). The study of the psychological aspects of the arts in Africa could be enhanced through interdisciplinary approaches combining expertise from the humanities, social sciences, and medicine. The psychological studies in Africa are largely new to scientific interaction with indigenous constructions, as compared with studies in the humanities and anthropology. Theory and research on creativity in Africa could grow from strategic partnerships between scientific disciplines with a more established track record and African thought and philosophies. Expertise in ethnographic methodology, through collaboration with researchers, from the humanities and anthropology, would complement the efforts of African psychological researchers, who tend to be trained in quantitative methods. Active participation in regional and international scholarship in creativity by African researchers and national professional associations would also be assets for the development of creativity research on the continent. As we previously mentioned, the SACF and GCN are two associations with a commitment to developing creative expression in African communities. We presented a model for the development of creative expression in developing societies that has potential for development from research by scholars on creativity in Africa.

SUMMARY AND CONCLUSIONS

The rich tapestry of cultural, ethnic, geographical, linguistic, political, and religious diversity in Africa influences constructions of and practices in creativity within the individual and collective communities of Africa. The findings from our survey to define creativity from the perspective of citizens of African communities suggest that it serves replicative, adaptive, and innovative functions involving everyday activities. The practice of creativity in African communities is better understood from the sociocultural benefits for the individual or community. Individuals may strive for creative practices that are personally meaningful, even though they may not have wider social impact. Arab Africans consider innovation to define creativity, perhaps more than people from aBantu Africa. It would seem that innovation as creativity in Arab Africans is "explained" by personal artistic or social expressions that challenge customary Islamic expressive practices. Adaptation as creativity in sub-Saharan Africa may be explained by practices in coping with the environmental presses from a geocultural environment, including the needs of subsistence economies, nascent modernization, and political instability. Art is also recognized as a major creative expression in sub-Saharan Africa, but for aesthetic, ritualistic, or commercial purposes as opposed to a social statement for transforming a way of life rooted in religion. Increasing formal education in the general population and participation in global economies by the national governments is likely to result in an extension of areas of creative expression by African communities.

Research on creativity in Africa is still in its infancy, particularly from the perspective of psychological studies instead of historical–anthropological studies. There is potential to advance the research in creativity on the continent through the indigenization of psychology within the African jurisdictions while maintaining an openness to learning from experiences from other jurisdictions. National and regional psychology associations have the potential to provide for the development and research on locally relevant inquiry into creativity. An ecocultural model for understanding creativity in societies in transition was proposed in this chapter and is in need of empirical study. Interdisciplinary studies hold promise for the efficient study of creativity in Africa, in all its complexity.

References

Abdel-Khalek, A. M. (1998). Personality. In R. A. Ahmed & U. P. Gielen (Eds.), *Psychology in the Arab countries* (pp. 267–287). Menoufia, Egypt: Menoufia University Press.

Abdel-Hamid, S. (1998). Psychology and literature. In R. A. Ahmed & U. P. Gielen (Eds.), *Psychology in the Arab countries* (pp. 225–235). Menoufia, Egypt: Menoufia University Press.

Abou-Hatab, F. A. L. H. (1997). Psychology from Egyptian, Arab and Islamic perspectives: Unfulfilled hopes and hopeful fulfillment. *European Psychologist*, 2, 356–365.

Ahmed, R. A., and Gielen, U. P. (1998). Psychology in the Arab world. In R. A. Ahmed & U. P. Gielen (Eds.), *Psychology in the Arab countries* (pp. 225–235). Menoufia, Egypt: Menoufia University Press.

Akarakiri, J. B. (1998). Utilization of creativity and innovation by the practice of new product planning in developing countries. *Ife Psychologia: An International Journal*, 6(2), 64–80.

Akinboye, J. O., Fagbami, D., Majekodunmi, S. O., Okafor, C. N., & Esezobor, S. O. (1989). *Psychological foundations of education*. Ibadan, Nigeria: Heinemann Educational Books.

Albert, R., & Runco, M. A. (1999). A history of research on creativity. In R. J. Sternberg (Ed.), *Handbook of creativity* (pp. 16–31). New York: Cambridge University Press.

Amali, S. O. (1984). *"Creative Writing." Our Pride*. Lagos, Nigeria: Plateau State Council for Arts and Culture.

Amali, S. O. (1998, September 12). *The Amalian two theories on cultural creativity and change*. The Seventh Inaugural Lecture, Department of Theatre Arts, University of Jos, Nigeria.

Badri, M. B. (1979). *The dilemma of Muslim psychologists*. London: MWH London.

Bekker, S. (2001). Identity and ethnicity. In S. Bekker, M. Dodds, & M. Khosa (Eds.), *Shifting African identities* (Vol. 2, pp. 1–6). Pretoria: HSRC.

Bourdillon, M. F. C. (1987). *The Shona peoples: An ethnography of the contemporary Shona*. Gweru, Zimbabwe: Mambo Press.

Burch, D. J. (1989). *Kuoma rupandi (The parts are dry): Ideas and practices about disability in a Shona ward* (Research Report 36). Leinden: African Studies Center.

Clegg, J. (2004). *Johnny Clegg with Savuka and Juluka: Live* [DVD]. Available from www.eaglerocket.com.

Csikszentmihalyi, M. (1996). *Creativity: Flow and the psychology of discovery and invention*. New York: HarperCollins.

Csikszentmihalyi, M. (1997). Musical improvisation: A systems approach. In R. K. Sawyer (Ed.), *Creativity in performance* (pp. 43–66). Greenwich, CT: Ablex.

Csikszentmihalyi, M. (2000). *Beyond boredom and anxiety*. San Francisco: Jossey-Bass.

Devlieger, P. (1995). Why disabled? The cultural understanding of physical disability in an African society. In B. Ingstad & S. R. Whyte (Eds.), *Disability and culture* (pp. 94–106). Berkeley: University of California Press.

Devlieger, P. J. (1998). Physical "dsability" in Bantu languages: Understanding the relativity of classification and meaning. *International Journal of Rehabilitation Research, 21*, 63–70.

Etuk, E. (2004). Great insights on human creativity: Transforming the way we live, work, educate, lead and relate. Retrieved October 24, 2004, from http://www.trafford.com/robots/02-0830.html.

Farag, S. (2000). Egypt and the Arab states. In *Encyclopedia of psychology* Vol. 1, (pp. 224–228). Washington, DC: American Psychological Association.

Franchi, V. E., & Swart, T. M. (2003). Identity dynamic and the politics of self-definition. In K. Ratele & N. Duncan (Eds.), *Social psychology: Identities and relationships* (pp. 148–176). Cape Town, South Africa: UCT Press.

Guilford, J., Christensen, R., Merriefiled, P., & Wilson, R. (1978). *Alternative uses manual*. Orange, NJ: Sheridan Psychological Services.

Guilford, J., & Guilford, J. (1980). *Consequences manual*. Orange, NJ: Sheridan Psychological Services.

Habib, M. (1990a). *The Creative Activities List*. Cairo, Egypt: Dar al-Nahdah al-Masriyah.

Habib, M. (1990b). *The Creative Personality Test*. Cairo, Egypt: Dar al-Nahdah al-Masriyah.

Irvine, S. H. (1972). The African contribution to new thinking about intelligence. In S. H. Irvine & J. T. Sanders (Eds.), *Cultural adaptation within modern Africa* (pp. 97–102). New York: Teacher's College Press.

Irons, M. E. (1999, January 26). Inspirational journey: Prof's travels to Egypt prompt her to return to the canvas. *The Northeastern Voice*. Retrieved November 25, 2003, from http://www.voice.neu.edu/PAPER/990126/research.html

Gaobepe, T. (2003, July 13). Soul-ful brother! *Sunday Sun*, p 10.

Gough, H. G., & Heilbrun, A. B. (1980). *The Adjective Checklist manual*. Palo Alto, CA: Consulting Psychology Press.

Gourly, B. (2000). In praise of the write stuff. *Times Higher Eduction Supplement*, *1432*(2),9.

Groenewald, F. P. (1970). *'n Deurskouing van enkele aspekte van die kreatiwiteitsverskynsel*. Unpublished masters's thesis, University of South Africa, Pretoria.

Hartfied, S. (2003). Continental drift. *Creativity*, *11*(3), 2–7.

Hunsankea, S. (1992). Toward an ethnographic perspective on creativity research. *Journal of Creative Behavior*, *26*, 235–242.

Irvine, S. H. (1988). Constructing the intellect of the Shona: A taxonomic approach. In J. W. Berry, S. H. Irvine, & E. B. Hunt (Eds.), *Indigenous cognition functioning in a cultural context* (pp. 156–176). Dordrecht, Netherlands: Martinus Nijhoff.

Kasfir, N. (1983). Relating state to class in Africa. *Journal of Commonwealth and Compatative Politics*, *21*, 1–8.

Katz, A. N. (2003). Pragmatic psycholinguistics as a framework for the evaluation of creativity. In M. A. Runco (Ed.), *Critical creative processes* (pp. 225–251). Cresskill, NJ: Hampton Press.

Khaleefa, O. (1999a). Research on creativity, intelligence and giftedness: The case of the Arab World. *Gifted and Talented International*, *14*, 21–29.

Khaleefa, O. H. (1999b). Who's who in the Sudan: A biographical study. *Gifted and Talented International*, *14*, 100–111.

Khaleefa, O. H., Erdos, G., & Ashria, I. H. (1996a). Creativity, culture and education. *High Ability Studies*, *7*, 157–167.

Khaleefa, O. H., Erdos, G., & Asharia, I. H. (1996b). Creativity in an indigenous Afro-Arab Islamic culture: The case of the Sudan. *The Journal of Creative Behavior*, *30*, 268–283.

Khaleefa, O. H., Erdos, G., & Ashria, I. H. (1997). Traditional education and creativity in an Afro-Arab Islamic culture: The case of the Sudan. *Journal of Creative Behavior*, *31*, 201–211.

Kirton, M. A. (1989). *Adaptors and innovators: Styles of creativity and problem solving* London: Routledge.

Kirton, M. J. (1994). *Have adaptors and innovators equal levels of creativity and problem solving?* London: Routledge.

Lubart, T. I. (1999). Creativity across cultures. In R. J. Sternberg (Ed.), *Handbook of creativity* (pp. 339–350). New York: Cambridge University Press.

Maas, G. J. P. (1999). Identifying indicators that can play a meaningful role in promoting creativity in SME – A South African Study. *South African Journal of Business Management, 30*(2), 9–39.

Mar'i, S. (1976). Towards a cross-cultural theory of creativity. *Journal of Creative Behavior, 10,* 108–116.

Mar'i, S. (1983). Creativity in Arab culture: Two decades of research. *Journal of Creative Behavior, 16,* 227–238.

Mashego, T. (2004). *Review of creativity in South Africa.* Unpublished manuscript, University of the North, Sovenga, South Africa.

Mazrui, A. (1978). *Political values and the educated class in Africa.* London: Heinemann.

Mogaji, A. A. (1999). *Measuring the creative personality.* Unpublished manuscript, University of Lagos, Department of Psychology, Nigeria.

Mogaji, A. (2004a). *Review of creativity in Nigeria.* Unpublished manuscript, University of Lagos, Nigeria.

Mogaji, A. A. (2004b). *Creativity and innovation of some Nigerian mechanics, welders and panel beaters.* Unpublished manuscript, University of Lagos, Department of Psychology, Nigeria.

Mpofu, E. (1994). Exploring the self-concept in an African culture. *Journal of Genetic Psychology, 155,* 341–354.

Mpofu, E. (1999). Modernity and subjective well-being in Zimbabwean college students. *South African Journal of Psychology, 29,* 191–200.

Mpofu, E. (2002a). Types and theories of aggression in an African setting: A Zimbabwean perspective. *International Society for the Study of Behavioral Development Newsletter, 2*(42), 10–12.

Mpofu, E. (2002b). Psychology in Africa: Challenges and prospects. *International Journal of Psychology, 37,* 179–186.

Mpofu, E. (2003a). Conduct disorder: Presentation, treatment options and cultural efficacy in an African setting. *International Journal of Disability, Community and Rehabilitation, 2,* 1. Retrieved July 24, 2004, from http://www.ijdcr.ca/VOL02_01_CAN/articles/mpofu.shtml

Mpofu, E. (2003b). *Regional Survey on Creativity.* Unpublished manuscript.

Mpofu, E. (2004). Being intelligent with Zimbabweans: A historical and contemporary view. In R. J. Sternberg (Ed.), *International handbook of intelligence* (pp. 364–390). New York: Cambridge University Press.

Mpofu, E., Myambo, K., & Mashego, T. (2004, August 8–13). Creativity in African settings. Paper presented at the Twenty-Eighth International Congress of Psychology, Beijing, China.

Mpofu, E., Peltzer, K., Shumba, A., Serpell, R. & Mogaji, A. (2005). School psychology in sub-Saharan Africa: Results and implications of a six country survey. In C. R. Reynolds & C. Frisby (Eds.), *Comprehensive handbook of multicultural school psychology* (pp. 1128–1151). New York: Wiley.

Mpofu, E., Zindi, F., Oakland, T., & Peresuh, M. H. (1997). School psychology practices in East and Southern Africa: Special educators' perspective. *Journal of Special Education, 31,* 387–402.

Myambo, K. (2004). *Creativity research in Egypt.* Unpublished manuscript, American University at Cairo, Egypt.

Myambo, K., & Mpofu, E. (2004). Implicit theories of creativity in Africa. In *Proceedings of the Eleventh AUC Research Conference, Quality Education for Egypt: Achievements and Challenges* (pp. 41–49). Cairo, Egypt: The American University in Cairo.

Needling, S. J. (2000). An Anosmatic renaissance: African names to the fore. *South African Journal of Languages, 20*(3), 10–20.

Ngwarai, R. (1995). *Down Syndrome: Etiological perspectives and help-seeking of parents of children with Down Syndrome in Zimbabwe.* Unpublished Bachelor of Education Special Education dissertation, University of Zimbabwe, Educational Foundations Department, Harare.

Nsamenang, A. B. (1995). Factors influencing the development of psychology in sub-Saharan Africa. *International Journal of Psychology, 30,* 729–739.

Nsamenang, A. B. (1998). Developmental psychology as political psychology in sub-Saharan Africa: The challenge of Africanization. *Applied Psychology: An International Perspective, 47,* 73–87.

Nsamenang, A. B. (2002). Adolescence in sub-Saharan Africa: An image constructed from Africa's triple inheritance. In B. B. Brown, R. W. Larson, & T. S. Saraswathi (Eds.), *The world's youth: Adolescence in eight regions of the globe.* (pp. 61–104). New York: Cambridge University Press.

Olaniyan, O. (2004). *The evolution of the technique of the creativity of Fuji – A Nigerian popular music genre.* Monograph Series, Obafemi Awolowo University, Department of Music, Ile-Ife.

Oshodi, J. E. (2004). *Back then and right now in the history of psychology: A history of human psychology in African perspectives for the new millennium.* Bloomington, IN: Author House.

Osman, A. H. (1998). Psychology of art. In R. A. Ahmed & U. P. Gielen (Eds.), *Psychology in the Arab countries* (pp. 225–235). Menoufia, Egypt: Menoufia University Press.

Oyowe, A. (1996). Are Africans culturally hindered in enterprise and commercial creativity?. *The Courier ACP-EU, 157,* 62–64.

Patai, R. (2002). *The Arab mind* (rev. ed.). New York: Hatherleigh Press.

Paulus, P. B. (2000). Groups, teams, and creativity: The creative potential of idea-generating groups. *Applied Psychology, 49,* 1–23.

Phillips, T. (1996). *Africa: The art of a continent.* New York: Guggenheim Publications.

Puccio, G., & Chimento, M. D. (2001). Implicit theories of creativity: Laypersons' perceptions of the creativity of adaptors and innovators. *Perceptual and Motor Skills, 92,* 675–681.

Runco, M. A. (2001). Creativity as optimal human functioning. In M. Bloom, & T. P. Gullotta (Eds.), *Promoting creativity across the lifespan* (pp. 17–44). Washington, DC: CWLA Press.

Runco, M. A. (2004). Creativity. *Annual Review of Psychology, 55,* 657–687.

Runco, M. A., & Richards, R., (Eds.), (1997). *Eminent creativity, everyday creativity, and health.* Norwood, NJ: Ablex.

Sawyer, R. K. (1998). The interdisciplinary study of creativity in performance. *Creativity Research Journal, 11,* 11–19.

Serpell, R. (1993). Wanzelu Ndiyani? A Chewa perspective on child development and intelligence. In *The significance of schooling: Life journeys in an African society* (pp. 24–71). Cambridge, U.K.: Cambridge University Press.

Shostak, M. (1993). The creative individual in the world of the Kung San. In S. Lavie, K. Nayaran, & R. Rosaldo (Eds.), *Creativity/Anthropology* (pp. 54–69). Ithaca, NY: Cornell University Press.

Shabalala, J. (1999). *The Mambazo Foundation for South African music and culture.* Retrieved October 24, 2004, from http://www.mambazo.com/foundation.html

Silver, H. R. (1981). Calculating risks: The socioeconomic foundations of aesthetic innovation in an Ashanti carving community. *Ethnology, 20,* 101–114.

Simonton, D. K. (1999). Talent and its development: An emergenic and epigenetic mode. *Psychological Review, 106,* 435–457.

Smuts, H. E. (1992). An interactional approach to creativity. *South African Journal of Psychology,.* 22(2), 44–51.

Sternberg, R. J. (1985). Implicit theories of intelligence, creativity, and wisdom. *Journal of Personality and Social Psychology, 49,* 607–627.

Sternberg, R. J. (2003a). Background work on creativity. In *Wisdom, intelligence and creativity crystallized* (pp. 89–105). New York: Cambridge University Press.

Sternberg, R. J. (2003b). The investment theory of creativity as a decision. In *Wisdom, intelligence and creativity crystallized* (pp. 106–123). New York: Cambridge University Press.

Sternberg, R. J. (2003c). The propulsion theory of creative contributions. In *Wisdom, intelligence and creativity crystallized* (pp. 124–147). New York: Cambridge University Press.

Sternberg, R. J., Nokes, C., Geissler, P. W., Prince, R., Okatcha, F., Bundy, D. A., & Grigorenko, E. L. (2001). The relationship between academic and practical intelligence: A case study in Kenya. *Intelligence, 29,* 163–169.

Tesch, R. (1990). *Qualitative research analysis types and software tools.* New York: Palmer Press.

Todd, P. (1998). Durban renewal. *Advertising Age's Creativity, 6*(8), 2–11.

Vanderweide, M., & D'hondt, W. (1983). How do conformist Senegalese adolescents consider themselves to be? *Journal of Adolescence, 6,* 87–92.

van Manen, M. (1997). *Researching lived experience: Human science for an action sensitive pedagogy* (2nd ed). London, Ontario: Althouse Press.

Wassing, R. S. (1988). *African art: Its background and traditions.* New York: Portland House.

WebPsySoft Arab Company. (2003). Web site accessed November 25, 2003, at http://www.arabpsynet.com [in Arabic, French, and English]

17

Creativity Around the World in 80 Ways ... but with One Destination

Dean Keith Simonton

To a very large degree, creativity made the world we live in. Remove everything about us that was not the product of the creative mind, and we would find ourselves naked in some primeval forest. Moreover, each culture and civilization on this planet is defined by the accumulation of creative products generated by the humans that have occupied this globe. Indeed, each society is distinguished from all others by the unique nature of its accumulation. For example, if we want to describe how Chinese civilization differs from all others, we have no other recourse but to make some reference to the philosophers, poets, painters, artisans, and other creators who left their unique mark on its cultural, aesthetic, and intellectual legacy. Given the universality of human creativity, it should come as no surprise that creativity attracts universal interest. Moreover, in nations having strong scientific traditions, this interest almost invariably inspires research on creativity as a phenomenon. That consequence is reflected in the preceding chapters of this book. At the same time, because each national tradition is a distinct cultural creation, this research is by no means homogeneous. On the contrary, the research carried out in each part of the world to some extent reflects the special needs, values, and concerns of a given heritage. This is also apparent in the earlier chapters. To some degree, there are as many ways of studying creativity as there are cultural traditions, perhaps as many as there are independent nations.

Nonetheless, my assignment in this concluding chapter is to integrate rather than differentiate. Accordingly, here my emphasis is on the core themes that permeate the diverse research traditions.

CORE THEMES

In the paragraphs that follow, I examine the central topics, theories, and techniques that are most conspicuous in world research on creativity. Specifically, each topic, theory, or technique has played a major role in two or more research traditions.

Topics

Worldwide research on creativity can be differentiated along two substantive dimensions: applied and basic.

Applied Research

I believe it safe to say that the bulk of the research is applied in nature. That is, investigations are directed at solving practical issues, or at least at resolving questions of potential practical application. The two most prominent areas of interest concern creativity in education and industry, with the former topic being by far the most prevalent (see Choe, Chapter 14, this volume; Niu, Chapter 13, this volume). The educational research concentrates on such issues as the optimal teaching methods for nurturing creative development and the best methods for identifying creatively gifted children (Choe, this volume; also see Baer & Kaufman, Chapter 2, this volume; Genovard et al., Chapter 4, this volume; Neçka, Grohman, & Słabosz, Chapter 10, this volume; Niu, this volume; Oral, Chapter 12, this volume; Preiser, Chapter 7, this volume; Stepanossova & Grigorenko, Chapter 9, this volume). With respect to industrial psychology, the primary focus is on identifying and enhancing creativity in the workplace (Genovard et al., this volume; Smith & Carlsson, Chapter 8, this volume). Perhaps the specific topic that has attracted the most attention is the circumstances that favor creative problem solving. A case in point is the work on brainstorming and similar forms of group creativity (Preiser, this volume). These research endeavors seem to be especially conspicuous in highly industrialized countries, where innovations are essential to maintaining a competitive edge in the world economy.

Basic Research

Far more diverse are the inquiries that address more fundamental questions about creativity. Some of this research deals with the very basic question of the very nature of creativity (Choe, this volume; Neçka et al., this volume: Smith & Carlsson, this volume). How is creativity to be defined? What qualities must a person or product possess to earn the ascription "creative"? Going beyond this central issue is abundant research on other aspects of creative phenomena. This research can be broken down into the following four categories.

The first category is cognitive psychology. These inquiries concentrate on the mental operations that underlie the creative process (Baer & Kaufman, this volume; Genovard et al., this volume; Neçka et al., this volume; Niu, this volume; Smith & Carlsson, this volume). These may include remote association, defocused attention, intuition, incubation, imagination, insight, heuristic thinking, divergent thinking, logic, and a host of other processes (Genovard et al., this volume; Mouchiroud & Lubart, Chapter 5, this volume; Milgram & Livne, Chapter 11, this volume; Preiser, this volume; Stepanossova & Grigorenko, this volume). Although most investigators assume that a small number of cognitive operations underlie creativity in a diversity of domains, others have raised two alternative possibilities: (a) there are no processes unique to creativity but rather creativity involves the same processes found in other forms of thinking, and (b) no process is general to all forms of creativity but rather the processes are all domain specific (Baer & Kaufman, this volume).

The second category is developmental psychology. Much of the applied work in educational psychology overlaps that of developmental psychologists who want to divulge the family circumstances and educational experiences in childhood and adolescence that contribute to creative growth (Choe, this volume; Neçka et al., this volume; Smith & Carlsson, this volume). However, developmental research can extend well beyond this temporal interval. At one extreme are those inquiries that focus on the consequences of the moment of conception, namely the genetic endowment bestowed on each individual human being – the primary province of behavior genetics. At the other extreme are those investigations into adulthood development, including the final years of life (Smith & Carlsson, this volume).

The third category is differential psychology. It is likely that most pure research is devoted to understanding individual variation in the capacity for creativity (Mouchiroud & Lubart, this volume; Mpofu et al., Chapter 16, this volume). Many of these inquiries have concentrated on individual differences in performance on creativity tests, as well as the correlation between such performance and scores on more conventional intelligence tests (Baer & Kaufman, this volume; Niu, this volume; Stepanossova & Grigorenko, this volume). Other investigations have examined the role of personality variables, including the impact of motivational traits (Baer & Kaufman, this volume; Genovard et al., this volume; Milgram & Livne, this volume; Neçka et al., this volume; Stepanossova & Grigorenko, this volume). Of special interest in this literature is the research on a classic issue: the association between creativity and psychopathology (Antonietti & Carnoldi, Chapter 6, this volume; Milgram & Livne, this volume; Mouchiroud & Lubart, this volume; Smith & Carlsson, this volume). Finally, in this category can be placed the investigations into gender and ethnic differences in creativity and creative expression (Baer & Kaufman, this volume; Smith & Carlsson, this volume).

The fourth category is social psychology. Creativity clearly takes place in a social context, and yet this aspect of the phenomenon has received somewhat less attention than it probably merits. Besides the applied research in industrial psychology, studies on this topic have looked at the general sociocultural environments or conditions that most favor creative activity or that shape the nature of that creative activity (Choe, this volume; Mpofu et al., this volume; Neçka et al., this volume; Niu, this volume; Smith & Carlsson, this volume; Stepanossova & Grigorenko, this volume). A somewhat more rare subject matter concerns the factors involved in aesthetic communication or experience (Milgram & Livne, this volume).

It is worth noting that worldwide research has largely concentrated on small-c rather than big-C creativity (Mouchiroud & Lubart, this volume). Whereas the former concerns everyday manifestations of the phenomenon, the latter concerns genius-grade creativity. The emphasis on ordinary forms of creativity likely reflects the applied nature of most research. Studies of creative geniuses are more often driven by theoretical rather than practical questions.

Theories

Because of the predominance of applied research, theory has played a relatively minor role in most empirical inquiries. Nevertheless, certain classical theoretical positions have informed research in several nations across the globe. These include psychoanalytic, Gestalt, associationist, combinatorial, Piagetian, and Marxist theories (Baer & Kaufman, this volume; Mouchiroud & Lubart, this volume; Preiser, this volume; Preiss & Strasser, Chapter 3, this volume; Smith & Carlsson, this volume;

Stepanossova & Grigorenko, this volume). Although these theoretical perspectives transcend national boundaries, many research traditions have developed unique positions as well (Milgram & Livne, this volume; Oral, this volume; Smith & Carlsson, this volume). Needless to say, the field of creativity theory has a long way to go before it can boast a unified theoretical orientation.

Techniques

Given the diversity of topics and theories, it should come as no surprise that worldwide research on creativity has adopted a variety of methodological approaches. The leading technique is psychometric. In particular, a vast amount of research involves the application of some test of creativity or divergent thinking, with the Torrance and Guilford instruments attaining the status of outstanding favorites (Genovard et al., this volume; Mpofu et al., this volume; Niu, this volume; Preiser, this volume). Even so, psychometricians in some nations have developed their own unique psychometric measures (Choe, this volume; Genovard et al., this volume; Milgram & Livne, this volume; Neçka et al., this volume; Smith & Carlsson, this volume). Somewhat less conspicuous are laboratory experiments on various features of creative problem solving, psychoanalytic case studies, surveys and questionnaires, and various archival methods, such a psychobiography, historiometry, and comparative methods (Choe, this volume; Mouchiroud & Lubart, this volume; Niu, this volume; Smith & Carlsson, this volume). Psychometric methods likely figure so prominently not so much because those methods are inherently superior to alternative approaches but because psychometric instruments are best suited to applied research. In fact, the proportion of studies using experimental methods tends to be more substantial in theory-driven empirical research, especially in cognitive psychology.

UNITY IN DIVERSITY

Although I have emphasized the commonalities in the worldwide literature, it is also clear that the diverse research traditions cannot be considered equivalent. Each nation is clearly distinct with respect to cultural heritage, economic resources, and scientific history – differences that are necessarily reflected in the nature of the work that is done on creativity. In particular, distinct national traditions vary along the following five dimensions.

The first is the strength and duration of their general scientific infrastructure, with some nations having a strong base that goes back centuries while others having a more tenuous and perhaps sporadic scientific foundation (Mpofu et al., this volume; Preiss & Strasser, this volume).

The second is the depth and breadth of specific scientific interest in creativity, with some nations having a fascination with the phenomenon that enjoys deep philosophical roots (Antonietti & Cornoldi, this volume; Mouchiroud & Lubart, this volume; Neçka et al., this volume; Preiser, this volume).

The third is the degree to which there exists external governmental, institutional, or legislative support for creativity research, with some countries having set a much higher level of public support for encouraging creativity in the schools or the workplace (Genovard et al., this volume; Mouchiroud & Lubart, this volume; Preiser, this volume; Preiss & Strasser, this volume).

The fourth is the extent to which the nation's research is heavily dependent on the pioneering research of U.S. investigators, especially the classic work of Guilford, Torrance, and others in the 1960s and 1970s (Genovard et al., this volume; Mouchiroud & Lubart, this volume; Neçka et al., this volume; Niu, this volume).

The fifth is the relative status of basic and applied research, the former having higher status in Europe (Antonietti & Cornoldi, this volume; Mouchiroud & Lubart, this volume; Neçka et al., this volume; Preiser, this volume; Stepanossova & Grigorenko, this volume) and the latter having a somewhat more prominent place in the developing world (Choe, this volume; Preiss & Strasser, this volume).

Besides the contrasts enumerated here, there are perhaps less conspicuous differences. For example, distinct linguistic heritages underlie the separate research traditions. Thus, the words used to denote "creativity" in various languages do not always have the same connotations (Neçka et al., this volume; Oral, this volume), and some languages do not even possess an explicit word for the concept (Mpofu et al., this volume). According to the classic Whorf-Sapir conjecture, these linguistic differences could exert a subtle influence on the nature of creativity research in a particular nation. Whether this influence actually materializes remains to be seen.

Despite all of these contrasts, I believe that creativity research across the globe is headed in the same direction. Creativity is, after all, a universal phenomenon. Moreover, as is evident in the chapters written for this volume, scientific curiosity about creativity has expanded throughout

Author Index

Abdel, H., 475, 480
Abdel-Khalek, A., 472
Abou-Hatab, F., 469, 470, 482
Acharyulu, S., 440
Agarwal, S., 441, 442, 444
Agrell, A., 206, 210
Ahmed, M., 442
Ahmed, R., 473
Ajyeya, S., 436
Akarakiri, J., 471
Akhani, P., 442
Akinboye, J., 474
Akoh, H., 415
Aksu, A., 361
Akyatan, N., 367
Albert, R., 12, 124, 310, 480
Aldila, R., 45, 46, 47, 48, 56, 62
Aldrich, H., 19
Alencar, E., 49, 50, 51, 53, 54
Alencar, Martinez, Gravie & Fleith, 54
Aliotti, N., 387
Alonso, M., 77
Altshuller, G., 293, 315, 316
Aluni, R., 49
Amabile, T., 15, 18, 20, 22, 250, 286, 297
Amadori, A., 157
Amali, S., 471
Ambrosi, L., 132

Amietta, P., 157
Amin, M., 443
Amner, G., 218
Anargyros-Klinger, A., 116
Anderson, H., 133
Anderson, K., 208
Anderson, N., 210
Andersson, A., 204, 217, 218
Andersson, G., 216, 225
Andreani, O., 134
Angleitner, A., 288
Antognazza, D., 378
Antonietti, A., 133, 134, 138, 139, 142, 144, 145, 148, 149, 156
Antonietti & Roveda, 145
Anzieu, D., 116
Apel, H., 181
Applegate, B., 312
Apte, V., 426
Arad, R., 319
Archer, T., 217, 228
Ardac, D., 363
Argulewitz, Elliot & Hall, 25
Argulewitz, Kush, 25
Arieti, S., 133
Armellin, M., 148
Armesto, M., 55
Aron, A., 61, 427
Aron, E., 427
Arvonen, J., 210, 211

Ash, M., 171
Ashria, I., 459, 460, 465, 470, 473, 474, 480
Asturias, M., 61
Atasu, E., 344
Ataturk (1920)?, 368
Aurobindo, S., 428
Avasthi, Om, 435
Ayala, F., 47
Aznar, G., 78, 118

Babayeva, Y., 245, 246, 247, 250
Baddeley, A., 135, 136, 140
Badri, M., 469, 470
Badrinath, S., 440, 441
Baer, J., 13, 14, 16, 17, 18, 19, 20, 22, 23, 24, 25, 322, 325
Bakhtin, M., 240
Bal, S., 445
Balas, R., 285, 286
Baldwin, 26
Banissoni, F., 129, 143
Bansal, I., 444
Bapat, G., 444
Barahona, E., 49, 50
Barak, M., 315, 316
Barolo, E., 139, 142
Barron, F., 13, 22, 68, 133, 396, 397, 400, 403
Basadur, M., 17, 55
Basar, H., 365
Baughman, W., 280–281, 289, 296
Baumrind, D., 310
Baykal, A., 367
Baysal, B., 352, 353, 357
Beaudot, A., 114, 133
Beauducel, A., 191
Beauvale, A., 288, 290
Becchi, E., 148
Becker, M., 12, 16
Beer, J., 310
Behera, A., 440
Bekker, S., 461
Belcher, T., 16
Bellu, R., 131
Beltran, Martinez, 69, 71, 83
Bem, D., 18

Bem, S., 217
Benedan, S., 145
Bengtsson, M., 218
Berezanskaya, N., 245, 246, 247
Bergeson, J., 412
Bergson, H., 104, 105
Berman, A., 312
Bermejo, M., 78, 79, 85, 86
Bermek, E., 356
Bertone, V., 157
Besancon, M., 117
Besdine, M., 116
Bhargava, P., 434
Bhatnager, A., 443
Bhawalker, S., 443
Bhawuk, D., 423, 438
Biasi, V., 134
Biasutti, M., 134
Bibler, V., 241
Bindoni, A., 131
Binet, A., 109, 111
Biondi, A., 17
Biuso, C., 131
Bloom, H., 58
Blumenfeld, P., 415
Bocci, F., 148
Boden, M., 203, 276
Boetto, C., 41
Boger-Huang, X., 190
Bogoyavlenskaya, D., 251, 253, 254
Bollen, K., 324
Bonaiuto, P., 134
Bonar, J., 295
Bonnardel, N., 118
Bonshek, A., 427
Bosio, A., 133, 144
Bourdillon, M., 460
Bovio, G., 126
Brackfield, S., 250
Bradshaw, G., 20
Brandimonte, M., 138
Brar, S., 443
Braunstein, J., 98, 99, 100
Brinck, I., 204
Brissoni, A., 134
Broclawik, K., 294
Brognoligo, G., 128

Brooks, L., 135
Bruno-Faria, M., 53, 54
Brushlinsky, A., 237, 238
Buch, M., 440
Buchholz, N., 167
Bugdahl, V., 185
Bundy, D., 462, 474
Burch, D., 462

Cai, H., 377
Cajide, J., 76, 77
Calvi, G., 133, 134, 136, 143, 144
Camara, W., 27
Campbell, D., 12, 107
Can, S., 368
Carlier, M., 114
Carlsson, I., 207, 208, 212, 213, 214,
    215, 216, 217, 218, 221, 222, 224, 225,
    226, 227
Carraher, D., 61
Carrington, D., 25
Carroy, J., 100, 109, 110
Casillas, M., 52
Castaneda, A., 25
Castejon, J., 86
Castello, A., 72
Castillo, L., 16
Cattell, R., 274
Caude, R., 118
Cecchini, I., 139
Cerioli, L., 134, 144, 145, 149,
    156
Cesa-Bianchi, M., 133, 134
Chakrabarty, C., 434
Chan, D., 387, 397, 398
Chan, L., 397, 398
Chapple, C., 424
Charles, R., 270, 274
Chasseguet-Smirgel, J., 133
Chassell, L., 192
Chaturvedi, A., 443
Chaurasia, O., 441
Chen, C., 377, 378
Chen, W., 383
Chen, Z., 377
Childs, C., 41, 56
Chimento, M., 463

Chiu, C., 387
Choe, I., 397, 402, 403, 405, 409, 412,
    415, 416, 423
Choi, K., 415
Christensen, B., 203
Christensen, P., 17
Christensen, R., 474
Churbanova, S., 237, 239
Ciani, M., 128
Clabby, J., 313
Clandfield, D., 111, 113
Claparede, E., 100, 102, 110
Clark (1988)?, 26
Clegg, J., 476
Clements, D., 16
Cocco, G., 157
Coley, R., 27
Colozza, G., 132
Confucius, 416
Coomarswamy, A., 429
Corne, S., 61
Cornoldi, C., 134, 135, 136, 137, 138,
    139, 140, 141, 142
Cox, C., 13, 15
Cristante, F., 134
Cropley, A., 133, 184, 185
Csikszentmihalyi, M., 20, 168, 202,
    252, 396, 397, 400, 403, 405, 406, 408,
    409, 413, 414, 416, 422, 478, 481
Czarnocki, M., 289

da Costa, L., 46, 47
Dackert, Brenner, & Johnsson,
    210
Dackert, I., 205, 210
Dackert, Loov, Martensson, 211
Dalal, A., 428
D'Alessio, M., 143
Daniels, R., 16
Davidovich, N., 325, 328, 329
Davidson, J., 85, 86, 330
Davidson, L., 222
Davis, G., 16, 400, 412
Davis, S., 19, 20
De Beni, R., 138
De Bono, E., 80, 113–114, 157
De Groot, A., 246

De la Torre, 70, 72, 80, 81, 85, 87
de-Leon-de-Bernaedi, B., 46
De Masi, D., 157
De Prado (1987, 1991a)?, 76, 80, 82
De Ribaupierre, A., 111
De Sanctis, S., 128, 129
De Stefanis, P., 129
DeCharms, R., 18, 416
Deci, E., 416
Dedegil, M., 338, 348
Del Greco, F., 128, 132
DeMers, S., 22
Demory, B., 157
DeMoss, K., 22
Denes-Raj, V., 242
Dentu, E., 345
Dernbach, D., 181
Desai, N., 443
Deshpande, G., 431
Devlieger, P., 462, 463
Dhillon, P., 22
D'hondt, W., 461
Diakidoy, I., 145
Diehl, M., 179
Diriwaechter, R., 23
diSessa, A., 312
Doi, T., 409
Dominguez, L., 52
Domino, 26
Domino, G., 400
Dong, Q., 377, 378
Donoso, J., 59
Dorner, D., 176
Druzhinin, V., 250, 256, 261, 262
Dudek, S., 22, 23
Duncker, F., 13
Duncker, K., 171, 236, 237
Dunn, Dunn, & Price, 326
Dunn, R., 319, 320, 326
D'Urso, 134
Dwivedi, H., 436

Eberle, B., 16, 316
Einstein, A., 410
Ekvall, G., 205, 206, 208, 209, 210, 215, 218, 219, 223

Elovainio, M., 210
Enns, K., 16
Epstein, S., 242
Er, H., 358
Ercan, E., 342
Ercilla y Zuniga, A., 42
Ercolani, A., 143
Erdogan, I., 365
Erdos, G., 459, 460, 465, 470, 473, 474, 480
Erixon, A., 217
Esezobor, S., 474
Etienne, S., 46
Etuk, E., 479
Eysenck, H., 215

Facaoaru, C., 176
Fagbami, D., 474
Faldt, E., 217
Fan, X., 22
Farley, F., 412
Fasko, D., 17
Fattori, M., 144
Faucheux, C., 114
Faure et al., 89
Feiring, C., 310
Feldhusen, J., 310, 330
Fernandez Huerta, J., 71
Fernandez Pozar, F., 83
Ferrandiz, C., 78
Ferreiro, E., 58
Fiedler & Windheuser, 186
Figari, P., 58
Figueiredo, E., 54
Finke, R., 19, 138, 139, 279, 284, 285, 286
Firsova, L., 250
Fleith, D., 47, 49, 51, 52, 53, 54
Flournoy, T., 100, 110
Fontcuberta, 71
Fontenot, N., 17
Franchi, V., 461
Frank, P., 57
Frankenhaeuser, M., 210
Freire, P., 61
Freud, S., 13, 105
Frigotto, D., 142

Fritz, R., 16
Fryer, M., 290
Fu, Q., 377
Fu, V., 319
Funke, J., 177
Furnham, A., 26, 282
Fustier, M., 293

Gadish, O., 308
Gaedike, A., 251
Gagne, F., 330
Gakhar, S., 440
Galli, P., 133
Galperin, P., 239
Ganczarek, J., 290
Gaobepe, T., 478
Garcia-Canclini, N., 43
Garcia, J., 25
Garcia, M., 50
Gardner, H., 20, 133, 223, 330, 396,
    414, 422, 423, 424
Gebert, D., 189
Gedo, J., 218
Geissler, P., 462, 474
Genovard, C., 72
Gentile, C., 16, 22, 24, 25
Georgsdottir, A., 117
Gergen, K., 424, 425
Geschka, H., 194
Getz, I., 102, 117, 118
Getzels, J., 68, 134, 344, 409
Giacchetti, C., 131
Giannattasio, E., 143
Giannini, A., 134
Gielen, U., 473
Giese, F., 192
Giesler, M., 190
Gilford, J., 374
Gilitwala, P., 445
Gilligan, Lyon, & Hammer, 23
Gissi, J., 40, 43, 44, 59, 61
Glover, J., 16, 24
Godoy, H., 59
Goffer, N., 315, 316
Gold, D., 22
Goldberg, A., 218
Goldenberg, J., 315

Goldfarb, P., 250
Golod, G., 308, 310
Gonzalez, C., 50
Goodwin, G., 345
Goralski, A., 271, 292, 293
Gordon, W., 113–114, 278, 292, 294
Gorodetzky, M., 312, 313, 314
Goryunova, N., 256
Gough, H., 383, 475
Gourly, H., 471
Gowan, J., 387
Graen, C., 17
Green, M., 282
Green, S., 17
Greenberger, E., 377, 378
Greene, D., 18
Greenfield, P., 41, 56
Greenstreet, R., 225
Greiffenhagen, M., 169
Griffin & McDermott, 26
Grigorenko, E., 236, 240, 397, 462, 474
Grinberg-de-Ekboir, J., 46
Griswold, B., 280–281, 282
Groborz, M., 280, 284, 285
Groenewald, F., 463
Gruber, H., 19, 20, 310, 403
Gruszka, A., 283, 285
Guignard, J., 117
Guilford, J., 12, 13, 14, 17, 68, 87, 101,
    113, 133, 135, 141, 172, 190–191, 192,
    221, 227, 236, 247, 249, 271, 319, 445,
    474
Guillaumin, J., 116
Gulati, S., 443, 444
Gulerce, A., 424
Guncer, B., 361
Guntern, G., 193
Gupta, A., 440
Gupta, S., 441, 445
Gustafson, R., 206, 210

Habib, M., 472, 474, 480
Hadamard, J., 19, 107, 108, 109, 110
Halman, T., 339
Hamilton, V., 415
Hammond, K., 242
Han, K., 412

Hany, E., 185
Harding, H., 133
Hargreaves, D., 22
Harrington, D., 22
Harris, D., 383
Hartfield, S., 477
Hartmann, H., 207
Harty, Adkins, & Sherwood, 24
Heath (1983)?, 25
Heath, R., 16
Hedges, L., 27
Heier, H., 242
Heikkila, A., 210
Heilbrun, A., 383, 475
Heinelt, G.,
Heinrich, W., 177
Heister, M., 178
Heller-Heinzelmann, R., 131
Heller, K., 184, 251
Henri, V., 111
Heper, M., 352, 355
Himsel, A., 377, 378
Ho, D., 386
Hoff, E., 217, 221, 222
Hogan, J., 24
Hogarth, R., 242
Hong, E., 318, 320, 321, 323, 327, 328
Honigsztejn, H., 46
Horn, J., 274
Horne, F., 339
Horowitz, R., 315, 316
Horstman, V., 225
Houtman, S., 16
Hsu, 383
Huertas, Fernandez, 69
Huhn, G., 193
Hui, A., 290, 386, 397, 398
Hussain, S., 441
Huteau, M., 100, 109, 110, 111
Hwang, S., 412

Idvall, I., 224, 225
Ilgar, L.,
Ilhan, C., 360
Inam, A., 337, 338
Infeld, L., 410

Inonu, E., 352, 355, 357
Irons, M., 470
Irvine, S., 462, 463
Isaksen, S., 209
Iscoe, I., 24

Jackson, P., 68, 134
Jager, A., 191, 192
James, A., 441
Janbandhu, D., 442
Jaoui, H., 157
Jaques, E., 116
Jaquish, J., 386
Jarial, G., 443, 444
Jaspers, K., 133
Jaworowska, A., 297
Jellen, H., 184, 191, 367
Jeon, K., 396, 403
Jeong, E., 397
Jevons, W., 12
Jin, S., 377
Johnson-Laird, 19, 20
Johnson-Laird, P., 133
Joly, H., 100
Joman, M., 444
Jones, R., 20
Jonsson, P., 217
Jordan, V., 41
Joshi, D., 440
Joshi, S., 445
Jungk, R., 181

Kahneman, 242
Kaile, H., 441
Kalliomaki-Levanto, T., 210
Kaltsounis (1974)?, 24
Kalwa, A., 285
Kanevskaya, M., 250
Kanizsa, G., 134
Kanter, R., 315
Kao, J., 315
Kapoor, K., 430, 440
Kapur, R., 439
Kasfir, 461
Kasof, J., 282, 377, 378
Katiyar, P., 444
Kauffman, G., 138

Kaufman, J., 15, 16, 18, 21, 22, 24, 25, 322, 325, 342, 343, 378
Kaufmann, Fustier & Drevet, 294
Kaufmann, G., 203, 211, 212
Kaul, B., 445
Kaur, P., 441
Kaviraj, M., 430
Kay, S., 16
Kelly, H., 18
Kenworthy, A., 19
Kerala, Raj, 442
Keskioglu, O., 344
Kessler, C., 25
Khaiangte, V., 442, 445
Khaleefa, O., 459, 460, 465, 470, 473, 474, 480, 481, 482
Kharb, D., 441
Khazratova, N., 261
Khire, U., 440, 445
Kholodnaya, M., 245, 255, 263
Kim, H., 415
Kim, K., 401, 403
Kim, R., 401, 403
King, McGee, Broyles, 26
Kirkland, D., 55
Kirton, M., 479
Kivimaki, M., 210
Kjellgren, A., 228
Klavir, R., 312, 313, 314
Klebert, K., 179
Klein, M., 218
Kline, B., 310
Knox & Glover, 24
Kocabas, S., 349
Kocowski, T., 273, 276, 288
Kodelpeter, T., 181
Kogan, N., 15, 22, 114, 143, 191, 319
Kohler, W., 171
Kohut, H., 218
Koichu, B., 312
Kolanczyk, A., 283
Kosslyn, S., 140
Kot, D., 289
Kotik, N., 239
Kozielecki, J., 276, 290
Kragh, U., 212, 218

Krampen, G., 191
Krapp, A., 184
Krause, D., 189
Kreitler, H., 310, 311, 312
Kreitler, S., 310, 311, 312
Kreuzig, H., 176
Kris, E., 207
Krogius, N., 246
Kubiak, M., 286, 296
Kubicka, D., 291
Kudyba, K., 290
Kuk, G., 210
Kumar, A., 443
Kumar, G., 442
Kundley, M., 445
Kuo, Y., 383
Kurth, W., 169
Kusal, A., 289
Kwang & Rodrigues, 388
Kwasniewska, J., 298
Kwon, O., 398

Lalithamma, 440
Landau, E., 173, 308, 309, 310
Lanfranchi, S., 138
Lange-Eichbaum, W., 168, 169
Langley, P., 20
Larocca, 148
Larsson, U., 206
Latocha, A., 290
Lauer, K., 209
Lautrey, J., 111, 115
Lawshe, C., 383
Lee, J., 397, 403, 413
Lee, S., 415
Leif, G., 225
Lenat, D., 349
Leontiev, A., 237, 238, 239
Lepper, M., 18
Lewis, D., 17
Lewis, M., 310
Lewis, P., 404
Lezak, M., 227
Li, 375
Lieberman, N., 325
Lieberson & Mikelson, 26
Ligeza, W., 296

Lilja, A., 223, 224, 225, 226
Lim, W., 397
Limont, W., 292
Lin, H., 15, 17
Lin, L., 22
Lindholm, E., 282
Lindstrom, L., 222
Liu, D., 378, 380
Livne, N., 318, 321, 322, 323, 324, 325
Livne, O., 321, 323, 324, 325
Lock, A., 424
Loehlin, J., 26
Logie, R., 138
Lombroso, C., 109, 126, 127, 129
Long, J., 324
Lopez, O., 78
Lopez, Ricardo, 52
Lovecky, D., 310
Lubart, T., 21, 22, 86, 102, 105, 117,
    118, 191, 237, 290, 396, 400, 403, 421,
    423, 478
Luchins, A., 172
Ludwig, A., 169
Luo, J., 377
Lupi, G., 138
Luther, M., 169
Lyons, W., 98, 99
Lytton, H., 133

Maas, G., 471
Maciejczyk-Clapham, M., 16
Maduro, R., 432
Maharshi Mahesh Yogi, 427, 438
Mai, X., 377
Maier, N., 172
Mainberger, U., 191
Majekodunmi, S., 474
Majumdar, C., 433
Malmstrom, P., 224, 225
Maneckshana, B., 27
Manly (1998)?, 25
Mannetti, L., 143
Maoz, B., 309
Mari, S., 16
Mar'i, S., 461
Marin, R., 70, 71, 72, 73, 74, 79, 80,
    84

Marmeche, E., 118
Martin-Baro, I., 61
Martindale, C., 208, 282, 283, 285
Martinez Beltran, J., 83
Martinez Zaragoza, F., 77
Martini, E., 138
Martorell Pons, A., 71
Mashego, T., 458, 459, 471, 472
Masini, R., 142
Maslow, A., 133, 309, 403
Masten, Plata, Wenglar, & Thedford
    (1999)?, 25
Masters, M., 27
Matczak, A., 297
Mathieu, M., 116
Mattoo, M., 442
Matyushkin, A., 259
Maury, L., 112, 113
Maynard, A., 41, 56
Mazrui, A., 459
Mazurski, D., 315
McCormack, A., 16
McCrae, 26
McDougall, J., 46
McGuffog, C., 310
Meador, K., 16
MEB, 365
Mednick, S., 127, 247, 261, 282, 319,
    410
Mehdi, B., 442, 445
Mehlhorn, G., 174, 177, 178
Mehlhorn, H., 174, 177, 178
Mehra, D., 22
Meibner, W.?, 188
Meirieu, P., 112
Melear & Alcock, 26
Melucci, A., 157
Mena, I., 48
Mencarelli, M., 148
Menchan, F., 75, 76
Mendelsohn, G., 280–281, 282
Meng-tzu, 409
Merkelbach, V., 186
Merriefiled, P., 474
Metelli Di Lallo, C., 148
Metzger, W., 173
Miamon, O., 315, 316

Micklus, C., 16
Milgram, N., 318, 319, 322
Milgram, R., 307, 316, 318, 319, 320,
    321, 322, 323, 324, 325, 326, 327, 328,
    329, 330
Milich, R., 22
Miller, M., 43, 57, 58
Mingazzini, G., 128
Misra, G., 424, 425, 437, 438, 440, 442,
    444
Misra, V., 423, 427, 432
Mistral, G., 60
Mitchell (1988)?, 25
Mitjans, A., 52
Miura, K., 415
Miyake, A., 135
Miyan, M., 443
Mogaji, A., 457, 468, 471, 475, 476,
    477, 480
Moger, S., 194
Moles, A., 118
Mondol, K., 442
Montague, M., 312
Monticelli, M., 135
Mooney, R., 167
Moore, K., 208
Moore, M., 312
Moran, J., 319
Morande, P., 44
Moreau de Tours, J., 109
Moreno, J., 24, 177
Morgan, R., 27
Mosconi, G., 134
Moscovici, S., 114
Mouchiroud, C., 117, 118
Mouchroud, C., 117
Moyer, I., 413
Mpofu, E., 458, 459, 460, 461, 462, 463,
    468, 469, 482
Mugaloglu, E., 363
Muhle, G., 173, 182
Mukunda, N., 434
Mullert, N., 181
Multifamilypro, 315
Mumford, M., 202, 280–281, 289, 296
Munari, B., 148
Murphy, F., 60

Myambo, K., 458, 459, 473
Myers & McCaulley, 26
Myers, 26

Nakamura, H., 424
Nakamura, J., 405, 412
Nandanpawar, B., 443
Nandy, A., 434
Nathan, L., 427
Navon, D., 285
Necka, E., 274, 275, 277, 278, 281, 283,
    285, 286, 294, 295, 296, 298
Needling, S., 471, 472, 478
Neisser, U., 203
Nencini, R., 143
Neruda, P., 59
Neumann, E., 133
Ngwarai, R., 463
Nicholls, J., 273
Nickerson, R., 17
Nicolas, S., 99, 100
Nijstad, B., 179
Nisbett, R., 10, 18, 423
Niu, W., 378, 380, 386, 396, 400, 403
Nobre, M., 49
Nokes, C., 462, 474
Noller, R., 16, 17
Norenzayan, A., 423
Norlander, T., 217, 227, 228
Norquay, G., 105
Nowell, A., 27
Nsamenang, A., 459, 468, 482
Nunes, T., 61

Oakland, T., 469
Obukhova, L., 237, 239
Ohayon, Y., 327
Okafor, C., 474
Okatcha, F., 462, 474
Okvuran, A., 360
Olaniyan, O., 456, 476, 483
Olmetti Peja, D., 134
Oral, G., 342, 343, 361, 362, 364, 365
Orio, S., 134
Ortar, G., 310
Orth, I., 178
Orzechowski, J., 285

Osborn, A., 17, 68, 82, 113–114
Oshodi, J., 456, 468
Osman, A., 472, 475, 476
Ouvinen-Birgerstam, P., 221
Oyowe, A., 456, 471
Ozaydin, A., 344
Ozhiganova, G., 262
Ozturk, O., 352

Pacini, R., 242
Padhi, J., 439
Padovan, A., 129
Pagnin, A., 133
Pak, N., 355
Pandey, R., 441
Pandeya, A., 423
Park, S., 397
Parnes, S., 16, 17, 133
Parr, D., 210
Passi, B., 440, 441, 445
Patai, R., 469
Patel, J., 443
Patel, R., 443
Patrizi, M., 128
Paulhan, F., 101
Paulus, P., 471
Paz, O., 44, 59
Pazzaglia, F., 141
Pearson, D., 138
Pearson, M., 310
Pedrabissi, L., 148
Peeke, Steward, & Ruddock, 26
Pektus, E., 397
Peled, R., 320, 321
Peltzer, K., 468
Penagos, J., 49, 52
Peng, K., 423
Peresuh, M., 469
Perkins, D., 203, 279
Perleth, C., 184
Peterson, J., 412
Petter, G., 134
Pettersson, P., 210
Petukhov, V., 236
Petzold, H., 178
Pewzner, E., 98, 99, 100
Phillips, T., 470

Piaget, J., 113, 115, 340
Piepoli, N., 157
Pierce-Jones, J., 24
Pierce-Williams & Ramirez, 25
Pieron, H., 106, 111
Pietrasinski, Z., 271
Piirto, J., 18
Pinheiro, P., 42
Plucker, J., 20, 397
Poincare, H., 13, 107, 108
Ponnuswamy, S., 445
Ponomarev, I., 241, 242, 243, 244,
    245
Pool, 23
Popek, S., 297
Poveda, D., 70
Pradhan, D., 442
Preiser, S., 167, 168, 173, 180, 181, 183,
    190
Presbury, J., 13, 15
Pretz, J., 15, 18, 21
Price, G., 319, 320, 326
Price-Williams, D., 24
Prieto, M., 78
Prince, G., 278, 293, 294
Prince, R., 462, 474
Pringle, P., 55
Puccio, G., 463
Pufal-Struzik, I., 289
Punia, T., 441

Qu, X., 374, 375, 376
Quadrio, A., 134
Quinn, M., 25

Rabkin, L., 319
Raidl, M., 117
Raina, K., 423, 445
Raina, M., 423, 428, 436, 437, 438, 440,
    445
Rajagopalan, M., 443
Rajshekhar, 431
Raju, S., 442
Rajyalakshmi, T., 441
Ramanujan, A., 424
Ramirez, M., 24, 25
Rank, O., 13

Rao, G., 443
Rao, U., 444
Rao, V., 445
Rapagna, S., 22
Raven, J., 310
Ravizza, C., 131, 132
Rawlings, D., 282
Ray, P., 435
Reber, A., 244, 285
Recepoglu, A., 346, 347
Reisberg, D., 138
Reiss-Schimmel,?, 116
Reither, F., 176
Rejskind, F., 22
Renzulli, J., 16, 49, 86, 296, 297, 330
Ribot, T., 12, 100, 101, 106
Richards, R., 479
Richardson, A., 22
Richardson, J., 141
Rickards, T., 194
Rieben, L., 114, 115, 116
Ripple & Jacquish, 24
Ripple, R., 386
Risberg, J., 215, 227
Rivas, F., 84
Robinson, A., 118
Rodari, G., 148
Roe, A., 13
Roff Carballo, J., 71
Rogers, C., 133, 403
Rohrbach, B., 180
Roland, A., 425, 426
Romagnoli, A., 143
Rosas, R., 41, 50
Rosati, L., 157
Rosch, E., 279
Roschelle, J., 312
Rose, L., 15, 17
Rosenbloom, G., 319
Rossetto, A., 148
Rossi, S., 133
Rowell, L., 327
Roweton, W., 16
Rubini, V., 133, 134, 135, 136
Ruch, W., 288
Rudowicz, E., 290, 386, 397, 398
Rump, E., 16

Runco, M., 12, 22, 124, 174, 202, 270, 274, 310, 397, 421, 479, 480
Ruyra (1938)?, 71
Ruzgis, P., 236, 397
Ryabova, T., 248
Ryhammar, L., 215, 217, 219

Sadarangani, H., 436
Saeki, N., 22
Sager, C., 280–281, 289, 296
Sahlin, N., 204, 205, 206
Salazar, J., 45, 46, 47, 48, 56
Salford, L., 223, 224, 225, 226
Sampascual, G., 75
Sanchez Sosa, J., 45, 46, 48, 50, 56
Sanders, B., 27
Sandstrom, S., 223
Sang, B., 377
Sansanwal, D., 442
Saracoglu, M., 367
Sartre, J., 106
Satyanarana, S., 440, 441
Sawyer, R., 481
Sawyers, J., 319
Scandura, T., 17
Scheblanova, G., 250
Schell, C., 173, 182
Scherbo, N., 250
Schliemann, A., 61
Schmidt, A., 27
Schmidt, J., 168
Schoon, I., 215
Schoppe, K., 190–191
Schrader, E., 179
Schuster, D., 16
Segure, T., 52
Sen, R., 439
Sen, S., 435
Sergi, G., 128, 129
Serpell, R., 462, 468, 469, 474
Serve, J., 170, 182
Sexton, J., 342, 343
Sezen, E., 365
Shabalala, J., 476
Shade, 25
Shah, A., 439
Shah, P., 135

Sharma, C., 444
Sharma, D., 442
Sharma, H., 441
Sharma, N., 439
Sharma, P., 432
Sharma, R., 443
Shastri, J., 426
Shavit, Y., 320, 321
Shaw, S., 345
Shcheblanova, E., 251, 260
Shi, J., 374, 375, 376, 377, 378, 380
Shimabukuro, L., 49
Shirley, D., 244
Short, E., 310
Shostak, M., 461
Shukla, J., 440
Shumakova, N., 250, 260
Shumba, A., 468
Si, J., 377
Siekierzynski, W., 289
Silver, H., 456, 470
Simon, H., 20, 246
Simon, T.,
Simonton, D., 12, 15, 107, 344, 396, 411, 414, 434, 438, 478
Singer & Singer, 26
Singer, D., 133
Singer, J., 133
Singh, B., 445
Singh, J., 425
Singh, S., 442
Sinha, R., 441, 443
Sisto, F., 54
Sivell, J., 111, 113
Slabosz, A., 280, 282, 285, 290, 294
Slayton, K., 138, 285
Smith, G., 204, 207, 208, 212, 213, 214, 215, 216, 217, 218, 223, 224, 225, 226, 286
Smith, J., 312
Smith, Johnson, & Almren, 216
Smith, S., 19, 174, 279, 284, 286
Smuts, H., 463
Soh (2000)?, 49
Sohi, B., 442
Solar, M., 52

Soloman, S., 315
Solowiej, J., 296
Sorenson, R., 446
Souriau, P., 101
Spanoudis, G., 145
Spear-Swerling, L., 133
Spearman, C., 13
Spencer, M., 312
Spira, M., 133
Srilatha, R., 443
Srivastava, A., 424, 437, 438, 440
Srivastava, S., 443
Stanczak, J., 297
Stanish, B., 16
Staudel, T., 176
Stavridou, A., 282
Stein, M., 271, 273
Sternberg, R., 15, 18, 21, 27, 79, 85, 86, 133, 141, 151, 174, 191, 236, 330, 374, 375, 378, 386, 396, 397, 398, 400, 403, 421, 462, 474, 478, 479, 480
Stocker, T., 170
Stramba-Badiale, P., 139, 148
Straub, W., 179
Strelau, J., 288
Stricker, Rock, & Bennett (2001)?, 24
Strobel, M., 22
Stroebe, W., 179
Strom & Johnson, 26
Strom, Johnson, Strom, & Strom, 26
Strough, J., 23
Strozewski, W., 271, 272
Strzalecki, A., 271, 288, 289
Sub, H.?, 191
Subramaniyam, S., 439
Sudhir, M., 442, 445
Sudhir, P., 441
Sudres, J., 116
Suler, J., 207, 215
Sullwold, F., 176, 192
Sully, J., 100
Sungur, N., 362
Suroor, A., 431
Suvasini, C., 424
Swart, T., 461

Szmidt, K., 295
Szuman, S., 270

Taber, T., 16
Taine, H., 100
Talay, M., 345
Talesara, S., 440
Tan, A., 387, 388
Tannenbaum, A., 328, 330
Tanridag, O., 367
Tas (2002)?, 365
Tatarkiewicz, W., 270
Taylor, C., 68
Taymaz, E., 357
Tebaldi, A., 128
Teberovsky, A., 58
Tesch, R., 464
Thagard, P., 286
Thomas, C., 225
Thomson, L., 210
Thorne & Gough, 26
Thurstone, L., 141
Thurstone, T., 141
Tikhomirov, O., 245, 246, 247
Todd, P., 477
Togrol, A., 367, 368
Togrol, E., 367, 368
Togrol, Y., 367
Tokarz, A., 280, 286, 287, 288, 289, 290, 294
Tordjman, S., 117
Torrance, E., 13, 15, 17, 23, 68, 69, 86, 114, 135, 143, 190–191, 192, 236, 247, 308, 310, 319, 362, 387, 400, 403, 445
Toulouse, E., 110, 111
Travis, F., 444
Treffinger, D., 17, 260, 330
Triandis, H., 409
Tripathi, K., 442
Tripathi, L., 434, 440
Tripathi, S., 445
Trombetta, C., 133, 148
Trouillot, N., 44
Trzebinski, J., 279, 280, 297
Turan, O., 344, 345
Tversky,?, 242
Tversky & Kahneman, 242

Ulmann, G., 173
Urban, K., 167, 184, 188, 191, 361, 367
Urton, G., 42
Ushakov, D., 243, 245, 246

Vaid, J., 174
Valderrama-Iturbe, P., 45, 46, 48, 56
van der Meer, G., 223, 286
Van Dusen, L., 22
van Manen, M., 464
Vanderweide, M., 461
Vanni, F., 133
Vaschide, N., 111
Vasilyev, I., 245, 246, 247
Vatsyayan, S., 427, 433
Vecchi, T., 135, 136, 137, 139, 140, 141, 142
Venkataraman, D., 443
Verga, T., 145
Vergara, P., 49
Vergine, S., 133
Verma, B., 440, 441
Verma, L., 443
Vernon, P., 361
Verreault, R., 23
Verschaffel, L., 312
Vetrani, G., 128
Vianello, R., 138
Vicari, S., 157
Vivante, L., 130
Vivas, D., 47, 50, 51
Vizcarra, R., 48
Vohra, I., 440
von Staabs, 291
Vosburg, S., 211
Vygotsky, L, 42, 257
Vygotsky, Leu, 42

Wainrib, S., 116
Wali, K., 435
Wallace, D., 20, 413
Wallach, M., 114, 191, 319
Wallach, N., 143
Wallas, G., 13, 102, 103, 242
Wallner, M., 174, 177, 178
Wan, W., 387

Wang, H., 22
Wang, W., 377
Ward, T., 19, 174, 279, 280, 284, 286
Warren, T., 16
Wartegg, E., 191
Wassing, R., 470
Wearing, A., 176
Wechsler, S., 54
Weidenmann, B., 184
Weinbrenner, P., 181
Weinert, F., 184
Weinlader, H., 251
Weisberg, R., 19, 20, 133, 279
Weissmann (1992)?, 46
Wendt, P., 215, 227
Wermke, J., 186
Wertheimer, M., 13, 171, 172, 177, 186, 236, 237
West, A., 208
West, M., 203, 210
Westberg, K., 49
Westby, L., 222
Westmeyer, H., 168
Whiston, S., 320, 321
Whitmore, J., 310
Widenberg, L., 219
Wiersema, F., 315
Wiessler, K., 308, 310
Wikstrom, B., 223
Williams, F., 143
Williams, L., 282
Williams, M., 426
Wilmes, L., 191
Wilson, R., 17, 474
Winn, 43, 44
Witthaus, U., 180
Wittwer, W., 180
Wohlgemuth, R., 185

Wolff, C., 98
Wolfradt & Pretz, 26
Wollschlager, G., 182
Wright, B., 399
Wu, D., 377
Wu, J., 377, 387

Xiao, C., 376
Xu, B., 22
Xu, F., 374, 375, 377
Xu, J., 377
Xu, Z., 377
Xue, G., 377, 378
Xypas, C., 112

Yadava, R., 439
Yang, Y., 378
Yaroshevsky, M., 240
Yontar, A., 361
Yoo, D., 414
Yoon, T., 409, 413
Yue, X., 290, 386
Yurkevich, V., 257, 258

Zenasni, F., 117
Zha, Z., 374, 375
Zhang, J., 22, 377, 378
Zhang, Q., 376, 377
Zhi, F., 377
Zhiyan & Singer, 26
Zhou, L., 377
Zhou, Y., 377
Zindi, F., 469
Zingales, M., 157
Ziv, A., 308
Zuckerman, M., 412
Zwicky, F., 176
Zyla, K., 285, 290
Zytkow, J., 20

Subject Index

AATI. *See* Activities & Accomplishments in Teaching Inventory

ACI. *See* Adjective Checklist Inventory

active-forming method, 261

Activities & Accomplishments in Teaching Inventory (AATI), 329

actualism, 130

adaptive behaviors, 467, 478, 479

Adjective Checklist Inventory (ACI), 383, 475

adolescents, 220–221, 308, 320, 326, 492. *See also* education; *specific topics*

aesthetic theory, 100, 311, 339, 431, 434, 493. *See* arts

Africa, 7
  aBantu cultures, 462, 467, 470
  anecdotal data, 477
  Arabic groups, 458, 469, 483–484
  Brazil and, 57–58
  cultural influences, 468
  defining creativity, 462
  historical perspective, 468
  Regional Survey, 463–464
  research in, 456

African Americans, 23–24, 25–27, 40

age, 24, 134, 223, 291, 309. *See also* education; *specific groups*

aggression, 23, 224

agriculture, 56

AITE. *See* Ariel Index of Teacher Effectiveness

alcohol, 227

Alencar studies, 51

alertness strategy, 278

altered states, 134

Alternative Uses Test (AUT), 473–474

Amabile three-factor model, 20

Amado, J., 57

ambiguity, 117, 134, 400, 416

Amerindian cultures, 42–43

analogies, 102, 274, 286, 294, 295

analysis/synthesis, 238, 249

analytic approach, 423–424

analytical learning style, 364

anecdotal reports, 477

angles of attack, 79

Anthropophagite Manifesto (de Andrade), 57

antinomy, 293

Antonietti-Cerioli test, 144

anxiety, 227, 367

applied research, 491

Appropriation for Creativity Test (TAC), 49

aptitude tests. *See* intelligence; *specific instruments*
Aptitudes Research Project (ARP), 14
Aquinas, Thomas, 124–125
Arabic cultures, 469, 482
　in Africa, 458, 469, 483–484
　Islamic tradition, 343, 345, 459, 465, 482
　language in, 7, 465, 469
archival methods, 494
Argentina, 57–58
Ariel Index of Teacher Effectiveness (AITE), 329
Aristotle, 79–80, 128
ARP. *See* Aptitudes Research Project
Arrau, C., 58
arts, 87, 310, 339, 434, 469
　aesthetics, 100, 311, 339, 434, 465, 493
　Art Education Movement, 170
　art therapy, 116
　artists, 87, 310, 426, 429, 430, 432
　creative talent, 319
　critical theory, 312
　drawing production, 191
　experience of, 311
　humanities and, 39, 57, 468
　imagination and, 97
　language and, 465
　literature. *See* literature
　meditation and, 429–430
　psychoanalysis and, 116
　psychology and, 39
　talent in, 319
　traditional, 339, 340, 432, 469
　See also specific types, artists
Art Education Movement, 170
Artificial Grammar Learning Task, 285
Arvonen questionnaire, 211
association, 76, 78–79, 84, 247, 250, 261, 286
associationism, 99, 106, 132, 171, 493–494
Asturias, Miguel, 61
asynchronies, 422
Atatürk, M. K., 338–339, 343

atheism, 470
attentiveness, 77, 281, 283, 284
Aurobindo, Sri, 428–429
AUT. *See* Alternative Uses Test
autonomic motivation, 286, 287

Baddeley group studies, 136
Bakhtin, M., 240
Balkan countries, 337
Batelle-Institut, 194
Baysal study, 352–353, 354
beauty, 434
behaviorism, 18, 46, 172–173
Beltrán creativity tests, 82
Benton Visual Retention Test, 75
Bergson, H., 104, 105, 106, 110
Berlin Intelligence Test, 50
bilingual students, 25
Binet scale, 5, 109, 111
BIP Center (Leipzig), 188
birth order, 441
Bloom, Harold, 58, 74
Boden theory, 276
Bohr, Niels, 207
Bolivia, 60
Bonnet, C., 98
Borges, J-L., 58
Bose, J. C., 435
Bosnia, 341, 342
bottom-up processes, 285
Brahman, 426
brain activity, 49, 227, 283
brainstorming, 17, 76, 79, 82, 149, 173, 179, 296, 491
brainwalking, 180
brainwriting, 180
brand creation, 351
Brazil, 42, 43, 52–53, 54, 57–58
Bruno, Giordano, 125
Bulgaria, 345
Byron, Lord, 128

CAD processes, 183–184
calligraphy, 465, 475
cancer, 223–224, 225
cane, 226
Cantor, M., 469

Caribbean region, 39, 41
  arts of, 57
  humanities and, 57
  Latin America and, 41, 42, 57
  research in, 45, 57
  scientific productivity in, 46
cartoons, 313
categorical relationships, 140–141
CATISC. *See* Cognitive Ability Test
  for Identifying Supernormal
  Children
Cattell 16PF questionnaire, 87
causal relations, 83
cave paintings, 470
CCQ. *See* Creative Climate
  Questionnaire
CDMA. *See* Code Division Multiple
  Access System
C-ERIC. *See* Chinese Educational
  Resources Information Center
CFT. *See* Creative Functioning Test
chance, 101, 411, 434
Chandrashekhar, S., 435
chess, 245, 247, 252–253
children, 134, 143, 146–147, 320
  childhood, 221, 492
  drawings of, 270–271
  education. *See* education
  family. *See* family
  gifted. *See* giftedness
  interdisciplinary curriculum, 263
  motivation of, 251
  play, 185, 270–271
  pre-school, 144
  subjective influences, 221–222
  talented, 320. *See also* giftedness
  testing of. *See specific instruments,*
    programs
  values of, 250
Chile, 52, 58, 59
China National Knowledge
  Infrastructure (CNKI) database,
  378
China, 1, 4, 374, 378, 386, 397–398. *See*
  specific topics
Christensen model, 203, 228
Christianity, 459, 470

CIS. *See* Creativity Inventory for
  Young Students
civil society, 366
CNKI. *See* China National Knowledge
  Infrastructure database
Code Division Multiple Access
  System (CDMA), 404
Cognitive Ability Test for Identifying
  Supernormal Children
  (CATISC), 375
cognitive theory, 13, 74, 281, 492
  algorithmic behavior, 297
  cognitive determinants, 255
  cognitive deficits, 256
  cognitive resource model, 256
  communication and, 114
  critique of, 204
  cross-cultural studies, 56
  developmental theory, 114
  differential psychology and, 77
  flexibility and, 25
  insight and, 376
  intuition and, 242
  mathematics and, 326
  neuropsychology and, 140
  social systems and, 423–424
  three dimensions of, 13
collective unconscious, 339
collectivism, 425
colonialism, 470
color, 145, 147, 311, 312, 339–340
combinatorial process, 434, 493–494
commerce, 103, 316
communication, 114
comparative methods, 494
competition, 358
complexity, 204, 239
componential frameworks, 20
computational psychology, 204
computer software, 49, 315, 326, 328,
  329
Comte, A., 98–99
concentration, 407–408, 475–476
conceptual core, 279, 280
confluence models, 20
conformity, 297, 361
Confucian tradition, 398, 409, 416

consciousness, evolution of, 428
consensual assessment technique, 15–16
Consequences Test, 473–474
Consortium for Research on Creativity and Innovation (CROCI), 382, 384
construct validity, 320
constructivist theory, 151
context, in testing, 145
continuity models, 135, 137, 140, 182
contradictions, 293
convergent thinking, 71, 75, 175
Corsi span, 141
Cortazar, J., 58
counseling models, 76
CPCC. *See* Creativity-Fostering Instructional Priorities Questionnaire
CPS model. *See* Creative Problem-Solving model
CPT. *See* Creative Personality Test
Craik-Lockhart theory, 286
Creando Foundation, 193
creation myths, 426
Creative Activities List, 473–474
Creative Assessment Scale (EEC), 77
Creative Climate Questionnaire (CCQ), 208
Creative Education Foundation, 68, 75
creative evolution, 104
Creative Functioning Test (CFT), 213, 218–220, 223–224, 226
Creative Innovation (journal), 73
Creative Personality Test (CPT), 473–474
Creative Problem Solving (CPS), 17
Creative Process Questionnaire, 87
Creative Self-Assessment Inventory (IAC), 77
Creatividad Plura (De la Torre), 70
creativity, 2, 57, 68
    age and. *See* education; *specific groups*
    arts and. *See* arts
    barriers to, 50
    as cognitive style, 77

cognitive theory of. *See* cognitive theory
continuum of, 101
creator as loner, 398
cultural relativity and, 1, 4, 271
definitions of, 12, 71, 72, 73, 78, 80, 104, 167–168, 203, 271, 309, 466, 491–492
development of, 2
didactic view of, 72
duty and, 272
economic crisis and, 395
education and. *See* education
exceptional behavior and, 77
fear of, 251
first publications on, 71
five themes of, 12
flexibility and. *See* flexibility
four factors in, 83
four types of, 275
general, 145
gifted and. *See* giftedness
government programs, 2, 408, 495. *See specific programs, countries*
groups and. *See* group methods
history of research, 11, 12, 71
humanities and, 39, 57. *See also* arts
innovation and, 79, 188, 465, 470, 479
intelligence and. *See* intelligence
investment theory and, 21
journals for, 27
logical process and, 78
management and, 55
models of. *See specific models, theories*
negative conceptions of, 397–398
novelty and, 73, 203. *See* novelty
paradoxical, 422
perception of, 75
pluralist context, 71–72
psychopathology and, 116
redefinition, 21
relativity of, 4–5
research on, 2, 3, 11, 12, 45, 49, 71. *See specific programs, instruments*
science and. *See* scientific creativity

self-esteem and, 55. *See*
    self-confidence
sensitivity and, 73
as social construct, 167–168, 192
sociogeographics and, 76
synthesis and, 73
testing of. *See specific instruments*
thought and, 55–56, 71, 252
training courses, 16, 55–56, 76, 292.
    See specific methods, programs
as transformation, 78
universal aspects of, 360–361
uses of, 12
writing and, 23, 186. *See* literature
See also specific countries, programs
Creativity and Innovation
    Conference, 194
Creativity Assessment Packet, 143
Creativity-Fostering Instructional
    Practices Questionnaire (CPCC),
    49
Creativity Inventory for Young
    Students (CIS), 403
Creativity Research Journal, 11, 18, 27
Creativity Test for Preschool and
    School-Age Children (KVS),
    191
CROCI. *See* Consortium for Research
    on Creativity and Innovation
cross-cultural studies, 44, 56, 175, 412
cross-domain configurations, 438
crystallization, 6–7, 274–284
cultures, 395–396
    creation myths, 426
    culture-of-origin definitions, 464,
        472
    hybridization, 44
    influences in, 362, 378
    psychology and, 175. *See* social
        psychology
    symbols and, 422
    zeitgeist and, 423
    See specific cultures, countries
curiosity, 8, 76, 260

dance, 279, 311, 319, 433
Darmstadt Circle, 194
Darwinian theory, 20, 107

De Bono, E., 51, 80, 113–114
De Prado program, 82
death, 309
decorative arts, 469
Dedegil model, 7, 338
deductive thinking, 296. *See* logical
    thinking
defense mechanisms, 218, 227
defocused attention, 492
democracy, 1, 481
Descartes, R., 292–293
determinism, social, 236–237, 240
developing nations, 480, 482. *See also*
    specific countries, organizations
developmental psychology, 114, 219,
    257, 291, 492
Dewey, J., 112
dialogical activity, 240
differential psychology, 74–75, 97, 492
diligence, 411
dimensions, of creativity, 145
discovery, 97
discriminatory intent, 129
disposition, 286
distancing strategy, 278
distracter tests, 283
divergent thinking, 16–17, 71, 75, 133,
    175, 176, 492
diversity, 433
divine,- 271, 422, 432, 473
dogmatism, 296
domain-specific skills, 2, 20, 319, 406,
    438, 492
drama, 319, 343, 444
dreams, 105, 434
Druzhinin model, 256
DSA. *See* Dynamic Selective Attention
dual task studies, 141, 282
duck-rabbit image, 138, 141
Dunker insight problems, 237
duty, of creators, 272
Dynamic Selective Attention (DSA),
    284–285

Eastern cultures, 4, 290, 339, 374, 378,
    386, 397–398, 403, 423. *See specific*
    topics, countries
EBSCO database, 307

ecological psychology, 172
Ecuador, 60
education, 48, 49, 51, 68, 111, 117–118, 491
  academic disciplines, 76
  achievement tests. *See specific instruments*
art education, 182. *See* arts
  bilingual students, 25
  children, 439
  civil society and, 366
  elementary, 25, 49, 148, 258, 361, 364–365, 388, 398–399
  environment, 49, 53–54, 73, 182, 366, 474
  foreign tests,
  gifted. *See* giftedness
  high school, 309, 324, 325, 361, 398–399, 442–443
  homework assignments, 327
  instruments. *See specific instruments*
  interdisciplinary curriculum, 263
  kindergarten, 154, 190, 362
  mathematics, 312–313. *See* mathematics
  mental age, 111
  middle school, 23, 51, 312–313, 314, 365, 387, 442–443
  pedagogical systems, 112. *See specific systems*
  play projects, 185, 270–271
  preschool, 219
  reform education, 170
  rural areas, 77
  science, 398–399. *See* scientific creativity
  teachers and. *See* teachers
  university. *See* university studies
  urban areas, 77
  See also specific countries, programs
Education Act of 1970, 8, 69–70
EEC. *See* Creative Assessment Scale
egalitarian communities, 480
ego, 219–220, 429
Egypt, 472
elaboration, 83, 87
elderly, 134, 223, 309

embroideries, 339–340
eminent creativity, 6–7
emotions, 102, 105
  affect, 102, 286
  connections of, 348
  regulation of, 245
empirical methods, 109, 349
encoding, selective, 78, 85–86, 102
Encyclopaedia (Diderot/d'Alembert), 97
engineers, 316
English-speaking countries, 10
  assessment of creativity in, 14
  cognitive approaches, 19
  confluence models, 20
  creativity research, 12
  ethnic differences, 23
  gender differences, 22
  motivation and, 17
  organizational creativity, 17
  personality studies, 17
  social psychology and, 17
  Western creativity and, 10
  See also specific authors, programs
environmental conditions, 188, 236, 249, 261, 262, 290
epilepsy, 368
Espressioni test, 143
ethical traits, 400
ethnic cleansing, 43
ethnic differences, 12, 23, 43, 493. *See also specific groups*
European Americans, 24–26
everyday tasks, 145, 149–150, 181, 479
evolutionary theory, 5, 20, 107, 428
excellence, in work, 407
experimental conditions, 156
explicit theories, 472
extensive attention, 284
external determination, 259

factor analysis, 13–14, 133, 288, 296–297, 405–406, 480
family
  birth order, 441
  childhood and, 341
  familial norms, 409

genetics and, 110
home, 327, 441
influence of, 117–118, 263, 415, 492
parents and, 403
fantasy, 7, 76, 131, 192, 337, 434
Faustian deal, 414
feedback, 18
Ferreiro, E., 62–63
Festinger, L., 173
field factors, 405–406
FirstSearch database, 307
flexibility, 73, 83, 84, 103, 117, 441
flotation tank, 227–228
Flournoy-Claparède questionnaire,
110
fluency, 251–252, 255, 316, 322–323,
387, 441, 476
fluid intelligence, 83, 274–284
folk arts, 339, 340, 432, 480, 482. See
specific groups, countries
forecasting, 238
forward thinking, 21
four-stage model, 242
France, 96
French-speaking countries, 5
history of research in, 97
introspection, 98
multivariate/differential approach,
117
positivism and, 98
phrenology and, 98
psychology in, 46
Freinet, C., 111–112, 113
Freire, P., 61
Freud, S., 105, 168–169
functional analysis, 293
functionalist psychology, 132
Fustier technique, 293
Future Conference method, 180, 181

Gall, F., 98
Galperin, P., 239
Galton, F., 68, 111
game events, 261
Gandhi, M., 422, 424
garland metaphor, 344, 423
GCN. See Global Creativity Network

gender differences, 493
Africa and, 461, 475
creativity and, 18
ethnic group differences, 12
ideational fluency, 387
socio-cultural factors, 440, 441
U.S. and, 22
Geneplore model, 19
general creativity, 145
generalization, 260
generation gap, 414
genetics, 431, 473, 492
genius, 6, 19, 127, 128–129, 131
Genius, Insanity and Fame
(Lange-Eichbaum), 168–169
Gentile, G., 130
Geography of Thought, The (Nisbett), 10
geometric figures, 142, 176, 243, 285,
469, 470
German-speaking countries, 5, 167
creativity diagnostics, 190
Gestalt theory. See Gestalt
psychology
organizational research, 178
research in, 174
socio-cultural backgrounds, 168
therapeutic context, 177
Gestalt psychology, 475
associationism and, 171
fantasy and, 132
Italy and, 134
Marxism and, 6–7, 235–236
problem-solving and, 172
theory of, 168, 171, 493–494
Getzels-Jackson study, 133–134
giftedness, 16, 260, 328–329
Center of Creative Giftedness, 250
Chinese studies, 374–375, 377,
387
cognitive theory and, 285
computerized units, 328
conceptualizations of, 329–330
creativity and, 75, 78, 85, 258, 259
four dimensions of, 316–317
German studies, 184
GIFT questionnaire, 78, 83, 86–87
Gifted Child program, 260–261

giftedness (*cont.*)
  International Congress on the
    Highly Gifted, 70
  Korean studies, 415
  measures of, 23–24
  personality and, 251
  schools and, 86. *See* education
  self-concept and, 310
  structural model, 318
  supernormal children, 375
Global Creativity Network (GCN),
  457
global learning style, 364
GMAT exams, 27
goal-seeking, 274–278, 284. *See also*
  problem solving
Góralski theory, 293
Gordon synectics, 292
government programs, 2, 408, 495. *See*
  specific nations, programs
Graduate Record Exam (GRE), 27
graphic tests, 84
Group Inventory for Finding Creative
  Talent (GIFT) Creativity
  Questionnaire, 78, 83, 86–87
group methods, 180, 294, 296,
  297–298, 471, 491
Gruber model, 20
guess, 236
Guilford model, 4–5, 12, 68, 75, 101,
  113–114, 191, 236, 440, 445
Guntern, G., 193

H/P model, 276
Hadamard, J., 107, 108
Haiti, 58
Hands On program, 145
Harvard intelligence project, 81
Heider, F., 173
heredity, 12
heuristics, 240, 252, 253–254, 292–293,
  295, 297, 312, 316, 492
Hindi language, 9, 426
historiometry, 494
holistic approaches, 260, 423–424, 425
Homework Motivation and
  Preference Questionnaire, 327

homework style, 327
Hong Kong, 4, 386
hubris, 276, 288
Huidobro, V., 58
human relations, 409
humanistic psychology, 18, 133
humanities, 39, 57
humor, 308, 313, 314, 386
Hwan, W., 414
hypnagogic state, 139

IAC. *See* Creative Self-Assessment
  Inventory
iconic memory, 256
idealism, 126
ideograms, 80
images, 139, 243
imagination, 97, 492
  art and, 97. *See also* arts
  cognitive approach, 376, 377, 492
  constructive, 132
  diffuse, 103
  fantasy and, 131
  imaginary companions, 221
  IOE model, 75–76
  IR method, 76, 82
  prospective, 192
  Ribot on, 101
  study of, 102
  typology of, 102
Imaginative Relaxation (IR) method,
  76, 82
implicit creativity, 439
implicit learning, 244
implicit theories, 397, 462
Inam theory, 337
incubation, 103, 227, 284, 285, 492
independent thinking, 190, 260
India, 9, 421
  contemporary trends, 433
  correlates of creativity research,
    439
  creation myths, 426
  cultural influences, 423
  indigenous features, 432
  pratibha and, 430
  spiritual domain, 438

indigenous psychology, 482
individual differences approach, 135
individuals, vs. groups, 470
inductive thinking, 296
industrial design, 358, 364
industrial psychology, 118, 315, 491, 493
industrialized countries, 491
information, 284–285
   Craik-Lockhart theory, 286
   information feeding, 278–279
   relevant, 278, 282
   selection of, 285
information technology (IT), 398–399, 404
ingenuity, 168
innatist view, 129
innovation, 79, 188, 465, 470, 479
Inquiries into Human Faculty (Galton), 68
insight, 236, 247, 422, 492
   cognitive processes and, 376
   defined, 237
   Dunker problems, 237
   incubation and, 285
   intuition and, 244, 285
   processes of, 85
   Sternberg and, 78
   tasks, 86
institutional creativity, 297–298, 495
integrative programs, 186, 479
intelligence, 13–14, 69
   creativity and, 15, 77, 203, 249, 375, 442
   genius and. *See* genius
   intellectual dimension, 102
   giftedness and, 258. *See* giftedness
   IQ. *See* IQ tests
   mental age, 111
   organization of, 241, 244–245, 255
   tests of, 15, 26–27, 49, 258, 493. *See specific instruments*
interaction, in groups, 278–279, 471
interdisciplinary research, 263, 481, 483
International Congress on Creativity, 70, 73

International Congress on the Highly Gifted, 70
Internet, 315, 404
intrinsic motivation, 286, 287, 406, 415
introspection, 98
intuition, 168, 247, 492
   cognitive theory and, 242
   German studies, 177
   Hadamard on, 109
   implicit learning and, 244
   incubation and, 284
   insight and, 244, 285
   logic and, 7, 241, 242
   Mendelevich test, 248
   pratibha and, 430
   Sergi on, 129
   stimulation of, 76
inventics system, 294
invention, 97, 350–351, 412
   antinomy and, 293
   Bergson and, 104, 106
   brand creation, 351
   chance and, 101
   contradictions and, 293
   inventiveness and, 74, 351
   TRIZ method, 315
Inventive Problem Solving Theory (TRIZ), 315
investment theory, 21
IQ tests, 15, 75, 86, 309, 319, 321, 360–361, 387, 443
IR method. *See* Imaginative Relaxation method
ISCI rank, 354
Islamic tradition, 343, 345, 459, 465, 469
Israel, 5–6, 307, 318, 326. *See specific programs, persons*
Italy, 6, 124
   assessment in, 143
   empirical research, 132
   historical antecedents, 126
   theoretical perspectives, 132
   training creativity, 148
   See also specific programs, persons
item-response theory, 399

Jnanpith award, 437
Journal of Creative Behavior, 11, 18, 27
journals, scientific, 354. *See specific publications*
Judeo-Christian values, 470. *See also religion*

Kant, I., 168
karma, doctrine of, 424
Kepler, J., 106–107
Kholodnaya model, 255
kindergarten, 143, 263, 362
Kingdom of This World, The (Carpentier), 58
Kocowski, T., 273, 294
Kognitive Faehigkeits tests, 251, 260
Kolanczyk model, 283
Koran, 343. *See also* Islamic tradition
Korea, 395
  implicit knowledge, 397
  qualitative analysis for, 404
  research in, 400
  See also specific programs
Korean Comprehensive Creativity Test for Young Children (K-CCTYC), 403
Kozielecki theory, 276
Kreitler model, 310, 311
KVS. *See* Creativity Test For Pre-School and School-Age Children

labyrinth problem, 243
laces, motifs of, 340
Landau study, 308, 309
Latin America, 8, 39, 40
  arts in, 57, 60
  Caribbean and, 41, 42, 57
  creativity research, 45, 53, 56, 57
  mestizaje and, 43, 44
  psychology in, 45–46
  scientific work in, 46
  See specific nations, programs
Latinos, 24–25, 26–27
leader, creator as, 400
leadership, 210, 439
learning styles, 326, 364

leisure activities, 320, 321
Lem, S., 272
Leontiev, A., 238
Leopardi, G., 128
Lewin theory, 172
Likert-type questionnaires, 87
literature, 116, 311, 318, 432, 435, 475. *See also specific types, authors*
logical thinking, 227–228, 242, 361
  creativity and, 78
  intuitive and, 241, 242
  mathematics and, 349. *See* mathematics
  rules of, 7, 492
Lombroso, C., 6, 126, 127–128, 129
Loti, P., 110
luck, 411
Luther, M., 168, 169

MACAM. *See* Multiscale Academic and Creative Abilities in Mathematics
macroscopic theories, 276
Maharshi Mahesh Yogi, 427, 438
Mainberger creativity test, 191
management, 55, 183–184, 211
Maredi, S., 478
Marín model, 73, 74, 84
Marxist theory, 6–7, 170, 235–236, 493–494
Maslow hierarchy, 5–6, 309
mass media, 414, 475
mathematics, 62–63, 107, 110, 312, 323, 349, 375, 445
Matta, Roberto, 58
mature creativity, 275
Matyushkin theory, 259
Mayan studies, 56
mechanistic models, 103, 236
medicine, 71
meditation, 429–430, 444–445
Mednick tests, 84, 247, 262
Mehdi tests, 445
memory, 77, 97, 131, 134–135, 142–143, 182, 256, 298
Menchen model, 75
Meng-tzu, 409

mental age, 111
mental health, 116, 133–134, 168–169, 476, 493
mentors, 54
Meta-Contrast Technique (MCT), 216, 219, 220, 226
metacognition, 151, 154
metaphorical thinking, 255, 286, 292, 294, 296
metaphysical systems, 423–424
Metaplan method, 179
Metzger, W., 172, 173
Mexico, 52, 56
Michigan State University symposium, 133
microscopic theories, 277
Milgram model, 5–6
Mill, J. S., 99–100
Milta test, 310
moderation method, 179
modernization, 460, 481, 482
Montessori system, 112
mood, 211, 367
moral creativity, 105
morphological theory, 176
Mosconi model, 134
mothers, 54
motivation, 17, 287
    creativity and, 253
    as determinant, 249, 250, 257
    disposition and, 286
    intrinsic, 406
    paratelic,
    personality and, 473
    role of, 251
    traits and, 493
Mozart, W. A., 471
multi-dimensional constructs, 145
multi-level view, 422
multi-stage models, 17
multiple intelligences, 387
Multiscale Academic and Creative Abilities in Mathematics (MACAM), 323–324
multivariate approach, 117–118
Muratori, Antonio, 125

music, 97, 103, 143, 253, 292, 319, 346, 432, 433–434, 476, 477
Muslims, 343, 345, 459, 465, 469, 470
Myers-Briggs tests, 26
mystical imagination, 103
myths, 103

naive creativity, 116, 257, 258
Nakamura-Choe categories, 405–406
Napoleon, 128
native languages, 465. See specific groups
natural endowment, 473
Necka model, 6, 294–295
negative priming effect, 282
neocolonial interests, 482
nephropathical temperament, 109
Neruda, P., 59
neuropsychology, 140, 226, 227
new school movement, 112
Nigeria, 457
Nisbett, R., 10
Nobel prizes, 61, 206, 414, 435
non-conformism, 437–438
non-rational methods, 435
non-specific processes, 139
nonverbal process, 245, 249
novelty, 79, 203, 237, 270, 387, 426, 434, 436, 439

Open Space method, 180
openness, 410
opposition, 240
order, hierarchical, 425
organizational psychology, 17, 18–19, 188
originality, 73, 83, 84, 131, 238, 255, 318–319, 434, 436, 441, 476. See also novelty
Osborn, Alex, 17, 68
Osborn-Parnes (CPS) model, 17
Ottoman Empire, 342–343, 344–345
Outward Bound Movement, 170
overjustification research, 18

P-creativity, 276
Padovan model, 129, 130

painting, 97, 311, 341
panning approaches, 464
paradigm-shifting, 19
paradox, 256
paratelic motivation, 284
parents, 403. *See* family
Passi tests, 445
Pasteur Institute, 207
Pasteur, L., 102
patent proposals, 350–351
Paz, Octavio, 59
perceptual process, 207, 212, 228,
     475–476
perfection, 407
performance arts, 466, 476
Perls, Fritz, 177–178
persistence, 439
personality, 17, 87, 133, 173, 177, 190,
     250, 405–406, 439, 442, 472, 473,
     493. *See also* self-concept;
     self-confidence
personification, 102
Peru, 60
philosophical tradition, 6, 495
phrenology, 98
physiology, 367
Piaget, Jean, 5, 58, 113, 114, 219–220,
     493–494
plant motif, 469
plastic imagination, 103
Plato, 79–80
play, 185, 270–271
poetry, 97, 343, 346, 430, 431, 435–436,
     438, 465, 475
Poincaré, H., 107, 110
Poland, 6, 270
     assessment in, 296
     definitions of creativity, 271
     research in, 6, 290
     traditions in, 275
     training in creativity, 292
     university system, 288
political systems, 61, 471
Polya, G., 292–293
Ponomarev model, 7, 241–242, 244
Popek Creative Behavior
     Questionnaire (CBQ), 296–297

popularization, 3
positivism, 98, 126, 129
potential creativity, 270–271, 273, 274
poverty, 61
pratibha model, 430
pre-consciousness, 223
preschool see kindergarden, 219
principal component analysis,
     475–476
problem solving, 491
     creativity and, 19, 50, 239
     forecasting and, 238
     Gestalt theory and, 172
     ill-defined, 376
     problem definition, 376, 409
     processes of, 175
     real-life, 329
     Ribot on, 103
     TRIZ method, 315
     See brainstorming; *specific methods*
productive thinking, 236, 252, 423
PROPEL program, 223
propulsion theory, 479
prospective imagination, 192
prototype, concept of, 279
PSCI training program, 150, 151, 152,
     154, 155, 156
psychoanalysis, 46, 116, 308, 493–494
psychobiography, 494
psychodynamic approach, 116
psychological theory, 39, 45–46, 127.
     See specific types, concepts
Psychology of Creativity, The (Kuo),
     383
Psychology of the Arts, The (Kreitler &
     Kreitler), 310
psychometrics, 68, 327, 440, 473, 494.
     See specific instruments
psychopathology, 116, 133–134,
     168–169, 493
psychosomatics, 223
psychotechnics, 48
psychotherapeutic process, 308
Purdue Creativity Test, 383

qipus system, 42–44
quality, 407

questioning, 79–80
Quispe, Diego, 60

racism, 42–43, 44
Ramanujan, Srinivasa, 435
random words test, 78–79
Rare Association Test, 84
Rasch model, 399
RAT. *See* Remote Associates Test
Rath, Louis, 50
Raven Progressive Matrices test, 75, 310
reactivity threshold, 289
reading, 408
real-life situations, 323
reason, 97
relating, art of, 79
relativism, 396
relaxation, 6, 227
religion, 44, 271, 338, 422, 432, 473, 482
Remote Associates Test (RAT), 84, 247, 250, 261
remote association, 492
replication, 21, 479
responsbility, 409
reversal, of images, 138
reward systems, 18
Ribot model, 100, 102
risk-taking, 18–19, 251, 253–254, 412
Rivera, D., 60
Rockefeller, N., 60
Rodin, A., 110
role-play methods, 444
Rorschach test, 191
Rousseau, J-J., 112
Rubinstein, S., 237
rural areas, 460–461
Russel Adjective Check List, 211
Ryhammar study, 219

SACF. *See* South African Creativity Foundation
Sampascual study, 75
Sanskrit terms, 427
SAT. *See* Scholastic Assessment Test

Scales for Rating the Behavioral Characteristics of Superior Students (SRBCSS), 25
Scandinavia, 4, 202
  empirical studies, 208
  gender differences, 216
  Nobel Prize, 206
  organizational studies, 210
  percept-genetic theory, 212
  system perspective, 205
  See also specific programs
SCB. *See* Strzalecki SCB scale
scenario technique, 180
scenotest, 291
Scholastic Assessment Test (SAT), 27, 218, 219
scientific creativity, 288, 361, 434, 442–443
  adolescents and, 326
  classification of, 106, 349
  humanistic psychology and, 18
  imagination and, 103, 350, 352, 433
  music and, 433–434
  process model, 348
  scientific productivity, 354
  See specific persons, disciplines
screening, 282
sculpture, 311
second language learning, 445
selective attention, 282
selective interference paradigm, 135
self, 432–433
self-actualization, 5–6, 288, 289, 309, 403, 413
self-assertion, 225
self-concept, 310
self-confidence, 55, 190, 212, 225, 442–443
self-fulfillment, 428
self-image inventory, 221
self-realization, 289, 428, 429
self-regulation, 172–173
self-solving task, 293
self-transformation, 428
semantic network, 283
sensation seeking, 412
sensivity, 73

separation anxiety, 116
sex. *See* gender differences
shapes, 191, 243
Singapore, 4, 387
single-factor theories, 13–14
SIT. *See* systematic inventive thinking
    method
situational influences, 290
Situational Outlook Questionnaire
    (SOQ), 209
skirting process, 78
slave trade, 43, 44
small people technique, 293
sociability, 439
social psychology, 17, 493
    cognitive theory and, 423–424
    context in, 181, 309
    determination and, 240
    environment in, 76, 181, 493
    gender and, 441
    grosups and, 470
    individuals and, 470
    responsibility and, 409
    social concerns, 409
    social factors, 475–476
    social impact, 467
    socialization and, 435
    sociocognitive model, 81
    sociocultural factors, 396, 397, 411,
        423, 471, 473
    socio-economic status, 441
    socio-historical theory, 240
    sociogeographics, 76
sociology, 99
Socrates, 79–80, 292–293
Soh Index of Creative Fostering
    Behavior, 49
SOQ. *See* Situational Outlook
    Questionnaire
Soueif, M.I., 475
South African Creativity Foundation
    (SACF), 457
South Korea, 7–8
Soviet/Russian psychology, 6–7, 235
    Guilford/Torrance theories in, 237
    internal and external determinants,
        249

psychology of creativity in, 236
    socio-historical determination, 240
    Western psychology and, 245
    See specific programs, persons
Spain, 8, 69
    education in, 72
    first publications on creativity, 71
    history of creativity in, 68
spatial relationships, 140–142,
    475–476
spiral aftereffect technique, 218
spirituality, 425, 438
SRBCSS. *See* Scales for Rating the
    Behavioral Characteristics of
    Superior Students
Sri Aurobindo, 428
Sternberg, R. J., 51
    implicit theory and, 398
    insight processes, 78
    propulsion model, 21
    three-factor model, 20–21
Stevenson, R.L., 105
stimulation, 252, 292
Strelau Inventory, 288
stress, 289
Stroop task, 285
Strózewski model, 271
structural equation models, 318, 324
structural factors, 134
structure-of-intellect model, 14, 176
structured imagination theory, 280
Strzalecki SCB scale, 288, 289, 296–297
subconscious, 102
suicides, 129
supernormal children, 375
superstition, 338, 347
Support to Basic Education Project,
    364–365
susceptibility, 255
Switzerland, 96
symbolic play, 291
syncretism
synectics, 173, 294, 295
synthesis, 73, 74, 79–80, 138
systematic inventive thinking (SIT)
    method, 315
systems theory, 172, 276–277, 405

Szent-György, A., 206–207
Szilard, L., 206–207
Szmidt program, 295

TAAI. *See* Tel Aviv Activities and
    Accomplishments Inventory
TAC. *See* Appropriation for Creativity
    Test
tachistoscope, 213, 214–216
TACT. *See* Tel Aviv Creativity Test
Tagore, R. N., 436
Taine, H., 100
Taiwan, 4, 380
talent, 127. *See* giftedness
Tasso, T., 128
Tatarkiewicz, W., 270
Taylor, C. W., 68
TCI. *See* Team Climate Inventory; Test
    di Creativa Infantile
teachers, 439
    curriculum and, 54, 76
    idea of creativity, 439
    influence of, 54
    students and, 48, 153, 398, 444, 474
    training of, 8, 68, 76, 148, 185. *See
        also specific programs*
    See also education
Team Climate Inventory (TCI), 210,
    211
technology, 315, 384, 471
Tel Aviv Activities and
    Accomplishments Inventory
    (TAAI), 318, 320, 324, 326
Tel Aviv Creativity Test (TACT), 318,
    319, 322–323
telic motivation, 283–284
tentative structures model, 277, 278
Test di Creativita Infantile (TCI), 144
think-aloud technique, 309, 312, 313,
    314–315
thought, vs. fantasy, 338
three-mountain test, 219–220
threshold hypothesis, 289
Thurstone PMA test, 75
Tikhomirov, Oleg, 245, 246
Tokarz model, 287
top-down processes, 285

Torrance, E. P., 5, 15, 440
Torrance Tests of Creative Thinking
    (TTCT), 49, 75, 310, 361, 386
    awards and, 54
    creativity variables, 78, 86–87, 308
    critique of, 423
    deveopment of, 5, 15, 69
    elementary level, 24
    environmental effects, 262
    gender and, 23
    influence of, 15
    objectives of, 69
    pluralism and, 423
    translations of, 143, 250, 444–445
Torre, S. de la, 71–72
Toulouse scale, 109, 111
traditional communities, 480, 482
training courses, 148, 174, 183–184,
    185, 292. *See also specific courses*
transcendence, 426
transformation, 102, 286
transgression theory, 276
tree structure technique, 81
TRoP system, 295
Trzebinski theory, 279
TTCT. *See* Torrance Tests of Creative
    Thinking
Turkey, 7–8, 337
    artistic creativity in, 338
    assessment of creativity, 367
    creative writing in, 342
    education system, 359
    Intelligence Foundation, 359
    scientific creativity, 347
Turkish Intelligence Foundation, 359
two-stage model, 19

unconscious, 102, 241, 248, 339
United States, 495. *See*
    English-speaking countries
university studies, 49, 362, 398–399,
    402, 481
    career and, 288
    creativity in, 218, 364, 384, 398–399,
    400
    entrance exams, 365, 402. *See also
        specific instruments*

university studies (*cont.*)
  innovation in, 356, 365
  learning style and, 364
  teachers, 54, 329
Unusual Uses Test, 221
Upanishads, 426, 427
Urban-Jellen Test, 297
urbanization, 460
Ushakov, Dmitrii, 245
utilitarianism, 403, 413
utopian assumptions test, 192
utopian imagination, 103–104

validation, 422
values, 250
variety, 433
Vedanta tradition, 425
Venezuela, 51
Verbal Creativity Test, 191
verbal tests, 84, 135, 314
Verma, M., 437
visual puzzle tasks, 141, 142
visualization, 429
visuospatial tasks, 138, 139–140,
  142
Vivante, L., 130
Vygotsky, L., 257

Waldorf School, 170
Wallach-Kogan test, 143

Wartegg Drawing Test, 191
Wertheimer, M., 172
Weschler scale, 114
Western cultures, 10
  African cultures and, 469, 480
  Eastern views and, 386, 395–396,
    397–398, 403
  intelligence studies, 245. *See also*
    intelligence; *specific tests*
  intuition in, 242. *See also* intuition
  self-concept in, 290
  *See also specific countries, programs,
    persons*
Whorf-Sapir hypothesis, 495
WISO-net database, 178
Witkiewicz, S., 270–271
Wollschläger plan, 182
women, 339–340. *See also* gender
working memory model, 135, 137,
  139, 141, 182
workplace, 53, 491
writing, creative, 23
Wundt, W., 98–99, 168, 175

Yaroshevsky model, 240
yoga, 429
Yurkevich model, 257

Ziv, A., 308
Zola, E., 109